Beginning Windows 10

Do More with Your PC

Mike Halsey

D1340138

Apress®

Beginning Windows 10: Do More with Your PC

ISBN-13 (pbk): 978-1-4842-1086-4

ISBN-13 (electronic): 978-1-4842-1085-7

Managing Director: Welmoed Spahr
Lead Editor: Gwenan Spearing
Technical Reviewer: Zeshan Sattar
Editorial Board: Steve Anglin, Mark Beckner, Gary Cornell, Louise Corrigan, Jim DeWolf, Jonathan Gennick, Robert Hutchinson, Michelle Lowman, James Markham, Susan McDermott, Matthew Moodie, Jeffrey Pepper, Douglas Pundick, Ben Renow-Clarke, Gwenan Spearing, Matt Wade, Steve Weiss
Coordinating Editor: Melissa Maldonado
Copy Editor: Kimberly Burton
Compositor: SPi Global
Indexer: SPi Global
Artist: SPi Global

Distributed to the book trade worldwide by Springer Science+Business Media New York, 233 Spring Street, 6th Floor, New York, NY 10013. Phone 1-800-SPRINGER, fax (201) 348-4505, e-mail orders-ny@springer-sbm.com, or visit www.springer.com. Apress Media, LLC is a California LLC and the sole member (owner) is Springer Science + Business Media Finance Inc (SSBM Finance Inc). SSBM Finance Inc is a Delaware corporation.

For information on translations, please e-mail rights@apress.com, or visit www.apress.com.

Apress and friends of ED books may be purchased in bulk for academic, corporate, or promotional use. eBook versions and licenses are also available for most titles. For more information, reference our Special Bulk Sales–eBook Licensing web page at www.apress.com/bulk-sales.

Any source code or other supplementary material referenced by the author in this text is available to readers at www.apress.com/. For detailed information about how to locate your book's source code, go to www.apress.com/source-code/.

With thanks to my colleagues and peers within the MVP community, many of whom helped make this book the comprehensive resource that has made me so proud.

Contents at a Glance

Contents

About the Author

Mike Halsey is the author of more than a dozen books on Microsoft Windows, including many *Troubleshooting* books such as *Windows Registry Troubleshooting* and *Windows File System Troubleshooting* (Apress, 2015). He was first named a Microsoft Most Valuable Professional (MVP) in 2011.

Based in Sheffield (UK) Mike gives many talks on how to get the very best from Microsoft Windows. He makes help, how-to, and support videos under the brands *PC Support.tv* and *Windows.do*. You can follow Mike on Facebook, Twitter, and YouTube by searching for *PCSupportTV*.

About the Technical Reviewer

 **Zeshan Sattar** is head of curriculum development at Agilisys Arch – an apprenticeships training provider in the United Kingdom. He is responsible for devising the training and certification curriculum for apprentices aged between 16 and 24. This includes a diverse range of topics from across infrastructure and development. He has delivered training to audiences across the world both in person and via online platforms. Zeshan has also worked and spoken at a number of Microsoft events including Microsoft Ignite and TechEd.

Introduction

Shortly after the release of Windows 10, it became clear that this was going to be a hugely popular operating system. The reintroduction of the Start menu was welcomed by many. Popularity alone, though, doesn't change the fact that Windows 10 is still a hugely complex and often confusing operating system to use. There are so many features, time-savers, productivity enhancements, and utilities that a non-expert PC user might never find them all.

That's where this book comes in. Showing people how to use feature X or Y is one thing, but in *Beginning Windows 10*, you'll learn not just how to get the very best from each feature to aid in your productivity and enjoyment of using your PC, but also why you'd want to be doing so. After all, we all need to get stuff done, and nobody wants the very tool they use to achieve that productivity to also stand as a barrier to it.

Whether you use your PC at work, at college, or at home for enjoyment, and whether you work in a large multinational corporation, a small business, or on your own at home (as I do), there's something here for you. Everything from making the most of your photo and video collections, to streaming games from your Xbox One console, to juggling multiple apps, windows, and desktops, or to building a robust and resilient OS that'll keep working and keep you productive—everything is covered.

Need a little extra help using Windows 10? In this book you'll find a whole chapter dedicated entirely to making Windows 10 easier to use. Whether color blindness, poor eyesight, a motor skills disorder, or another disability—I'll help you make the most out of your PC.

Want to take things a little further? Well, there's no need to buy an extra book, because tweaking and customizing the OS is included here—even some fun and handy registry tweaks that you can try as your skills develop.

All of this for desktop PCs, laptops, convertibles, tablets, and smartphones, and for users of any (or even no) ability, I've got it all covered. I wanted to make *Beginning Windows 10* the most comprehensive, useful, and easy to understand book there's ever going to be on Windows 10. I hope you enjoy reading it as much as I've enjoyed writing it.

CHAPTER 1

■ ■ ■

Introducing Windows 10

To begin describing Windows 10 is to take a step back and look holistically at practically every device in our lives. Long gone are the days when Microsoft would release an operating system for just the PC on our desk. The aim with Windows 10 is to create a connected operating system (OS) that will simplify and synchronize our lives across *every* device that we use. Whether it is your smartphone, Xbox console, Raspberry Pi programming and development board, HoloLens augmented reality headset, or the computer in your refrigerator, the entertainment and navigation system in your car, or the ATM from which you withdraw cash for a night out, everything will be running Windows 10.

It's for this reason that Microsoft announced that Windows 10 is the last "major" version of Windows, but what does this actually mean? For the first thirty years of the Windows operating system, Microsoft released a new major version roughly every three years. You'll probably be familiar with names such as Windows 95, Windows XP, and Windows 7. Each version was distinctly different from its predecessor. There were user interface (UI) changes, new features, and major updates to the core system files, known as the *kernel*.

As our PCs and their operating systems have evolved, however, a few things have become clear. First and probably foremost is that no matter how popular touch devices such as smartphones and tablets become, if you want to get real work done, no interface has ever emerged to challenge the keyboard, mouse, and multiple desktop windows. We've also reached a point with technology that just about every interface style the human body can accommodate—from the gesture-based approach of Microsoft's Kinect sensor, to facial recognition and speech—has been implemented and already refined in some form. Add to this that our PCs are now so powerful that we're keeping them for many more years than we used to, and a clear picture emerges.

Handwriting recognition has not changed much on PCs since the advent of Windows XP, and touch was fully embraced with Windows 8. Cameras and other sensors have been in general use since Windows 7, and biometric devices, such as fingerprint scanners, have existed for many years longer. When coupled with a clear understanding of how people like to both create and consume content on their devices, be that desktop PCs, smartphones, tablets, TVs, or laptops, it's fairly obvious that for the next twenty years at least, operating system interfaces won't be changing very much from what we currently have.

And so this brings us back to the reason why Windows 10 is the last major version of Microsoft's operating system. There simply isn't the need to change and evolve it that existed before. Couple this with the fact that we all live connected lifestyles, and want all of our devices to be able to do the same things, provide us with the same information, and help us to organize our lives; and releasing and maintaining a new operating system every three years for all of these devices would be economically unfeasible.

With Windows 10, Microsoft is giving us a core interface experience that will not change dramatically over time. All of the elements of how we work and play are being ported from Windows 7, Windows 8.1, and Windows Phone, where they have proven hugely successful, with new and improved features being added over time.

For you, the PC user, this means a more fluid and consistent experience, as there'll be no need to relearn how to use Microsoft Windows every few years, and no concern over whether to skip a version because your PC doesn't yet need replacing. New features and improvements will filter down, over the years, via Windows Update alongside security and stability fixes; and for the most part, you're unlikely to even notice.

That isn't to say that Windows 10 doesn't bring some major new features and productivity enhancements to the table, and in this book I'll detail everything you need to know to get the very best from whatever Windows 10 device you use. We'll begin, though, by looking at some of the questions and technical aspects of Windows 10 that you might encounter when moving to Windows 10 for the first time.

There's an SKU for You

On the face of things, Windows 10 comes in three main variants, known as Stock Keeping Units (SKUs): Windows 10 Home, Windows 10 Pro, and Windows 10 Enterprise. In truth, however, there are many more variants than this, and it's important to know that you get the right one if you're purchasing a new copy of Windows 10.

If you've upgraded to Windows 10 from Windows 7 or Windows 8.1, then the version you're using matches the version that existed before (see Table 1-1). The upgrade paths from Windows Phone 8 and Windows 7 and 8.1 Enterprise are simpler and clearer, with the first upgrading to Windows 10 Mobile and the latter to Windows 10 Enterprise.

Table 1-1. *Windows 10 Upgrade Paths*

Upgrade from ...	Upgrade to ...
Windows 7 Starter	
Windows 7 Home Basic	
Windows 7 Home Premium	Windows 10 Home
Windows 8.1	
Windows 8.1 with Bing	
Windows 7 Professional	
Windows 7 Ultimate	Windows 10 Pro
Windows 8.1 Pro	

Some additional SKUs exist, however, and if you are a student, you might be asked if you want to upgrade your own Windows 10 laptop or pro tablet to Windows 10 Education. This version enables college IT administrators to more easily provide you with apps and services related to your time on campus. Additionally, businesses that subscribe to Microsoft's Volume Licensing service can upgrade smartphones to Windows 10 Mobile Enterprise, which, again, includes additional management and integration services not available in the core Windows 10 Mobile version.

The Encryption Question

It's most likely that you'll use Windows 10 Home or Windows 10 Pro. So what are the differences? There are a few features of Windows 10 that only exist in the Pro and Enterprise editions. Largely, these apply to connecting PCs to company networks, such as domain connections, and enterprise-level features, such as Workplace Join and Group Policy. If you want to use virtual machines in Windows (effectively running a different PC inside a window on your desktop), you need Windows 10 Pro. One important difference that might make you want to choose Windows 10 Pro over Windows 10 Home, however, is Microsoft's BitLocker drive encryption system.

I'll show you how to use it in depth in Chapter 11, but to summarize, BitLocker is a technology that allows you to fully encrypt the hard disk(s) on your PC, laptop, and tablet. If the device comes with a necessary chip called a Trusted Platform Module (TPM) on the hardware, you can use BitLocker. (You can check your PC's specifications to see if it does, but all Windows 8.1 and Windows 10 laptops and tablets with screens larger than 10 inches almost definitely include a TPM because it's part of Microsoft's reference specification for those devices).

Being able to silently and securely encrypt the hard disk in your PC means that, while your files will always be visible and available to you, the moment you sign in to the device, anybody who might steal your beloved laptop or tablet from a coffee shop or a train station won't be able to see your files at all, not even if they remove the hard disk and plug it into a different PC.

Given that we often carry our PCs with us—complete with sensitive files containing account details and automatic logins to banking and shopping web sites, it's important to ensure that information is safe and secure from thieves. BitLocker allows you to have this peace of mind. I believe that if your PC includes a TPM, it's well worth paying the upgrade price from Windows 10 Home to Windows 10 Pro.

If you're already using Windows 10 Home, you can upgrade the OS "in place" without having to reinstall Windows or your apps. To do this, open the Settings app and navigate to **Update & Security** and then **Activation**, which allows you to purchase an upgrade to Windows 10 Pro by clicking either the **Change product key** button (if you already have a Windows 10 Pro key) or **Go to Store** where you will be able to purchase one (see Figure 1-1).

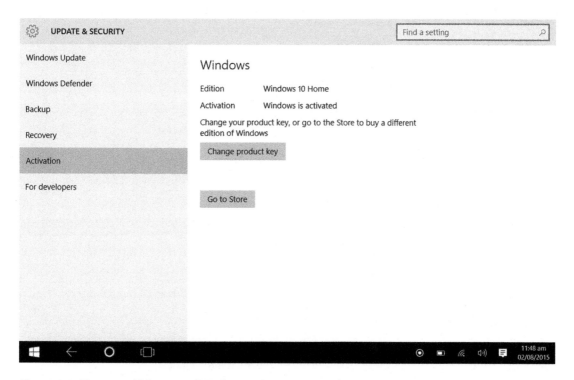

Figure 1-1. *You can add features to Windows 10 Home to upgrade it*

32-Bit (x86) and 64-bit (x64) Windows

That last major consideration when purchasing or upgrading to a copy of Windows 10 is whether to use the 32-bit or 64-bit version of the OS. In layman's terms, the difference between the two is that 64-bit operating systems can see and use much more memory in a PC. This can make the operating system and your apps run faster and enable you to do much more simultaneously, such as running many apps on the desktop. 64-bit operating systems are also considered more stable than 32-bit operating systems, though with Windows 10 the difference is very minor.

You can find out which version your PC has installed by looking in the Settings app. Navigate to **System** and then **About** to see details about your PC and the installed copy of Windows. The **System type** information will tell you if you are using a 32-bit or 64-bit edition of the operating system (see Figure 1-2).

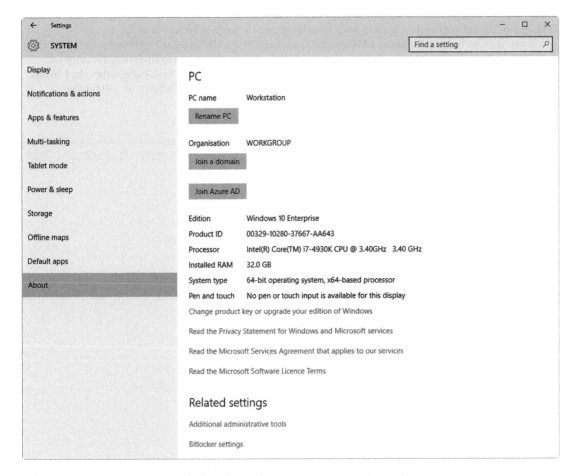

Figure 1-2. *Windows can tell you which version of the OS you are using*

If your PC supports 64-bit operating systems, it can be well worth upgrading, but there are some important caveats. The first of these is that the version of Windows 10 you have, either on DVD or as a digital download, might be locked to 32-bit only. Also, you cannot carry out an in-place upgrade from a 32-bit version of Windows to a 64-bit version. If you are currently using the 32-bit version, you need to perform a "clean install" and then also reinstall your apps. I will show you how to do this in Chapter 15.

Will My PC Run Windows 10?

As with any new version of Windows, to begin with, you are always asked if your PC can actually run it. Microsoft Windows has become leaner over the years, even as more features were added, allowing it to run on PCs that might have struggled with upgrades in the past. In theory, this means that any PC currently running Windows 7 or Windows 8.1 can run Windows 10 just fine. In practice, it's a little more complex.

The following are the minimum specifications for a PC running Windows 10:

- **Processor:** 1GHz or faster

- **Memory (RAM):** 1 gigabyte (1GB) for the 32-bit version and 2GB for the 64-bit version

- **Hard disk space:** 16GB for the 32-bit OS and 20GB for the 64-bit OS

- **Graphics card:** DirectX9 or later with WDDM 1.0 driver

- **Display:** 800 × 600 pixels or greater

If you are not sure what hardware your PC has, you can check with the manufacturer or the specification documentation that came with the machine. Even cheap Windows 8.1 tablets meet this specification, and any PC that came with Windows 7 preinstalled should not have a problem.

There are some features of Windows 10 that require specific hardware, however, and if you wish to use these features, you'll need to check your PC's specification to see if they will run.

Windows Hello is a new feature that allows you to sign in to your PC and even some Windows and web services by simply sitting in front of it. This requires a compatible infrared camera, and only a tiny number of Windows 8.1 tablets and laptops would ship with this. For desktop PCs, you are able to purchase a USB webcam that includes the correct functionality.

Device Guard is a new security feature that acts as a barrier to malware infection on your PC. This requires a newer PC with a UEFI secure boot system, a TPM 2.0 chip, and virtualization support. It's unlikely that the typical PC user will know what any of this is, let alone whether or not their PC hardware supports it. The information can be obtained from your PC manufacturer or the specification documentation that came with the machine.

If you want to use Microsoft's Hyper-V virtualization software to run virtual machines on your desktop, then your processor will need virtualization support. If you've already been using Hyper-V in Windows 8.1, however, you will be fine.

Some other features of Windows won't be available to you without the correct hardware. A TPM chip is required for BitLocker drive encryption, and other features—such as Miracast wireless display connections, Wi-Fi Direct printing, Secure Boot to help prevent malware rootkits from infecting your PC, Instant Go to enable your PC to resume from sleep in just 1 second, and touch-features—require specific hardware.

This means that as you're reading about Windows features in this book, you might find that something isn't available to you, but I will highlight where this might be the case.

New Features in Windows 10

As with all new versions of Windows, Windows 10 brings a whole host of new and improved features. There are two different ways to look at this, however, because many people upgrading from Windows 7 will skip the features that Windows 8.1 introduced. It seems sensible, then, to begin with the features that have been around for a while, but will still be new to many Windows 10 users.

Reset

It was Windows 8 in which we first saw the new Reset feature, called Reset and Refresh at the time. This feature brings two important benefits for PC users. If Windows 10 begins to misbehave and needs to be reinstalled, this feature can reinstall the OS through an easy-to-understand-and-use interface without affecting your apps, files, and accounts. Alternatively, it can also be used to return the PC to a "factory fresh" state, deleting all your accounts and files if you wish to sell your PC or give it to a friend or family member. Reset can be sound in the Settings app (see Figure 1-3); in Chapter 12 we'll look at how it works in more detail.

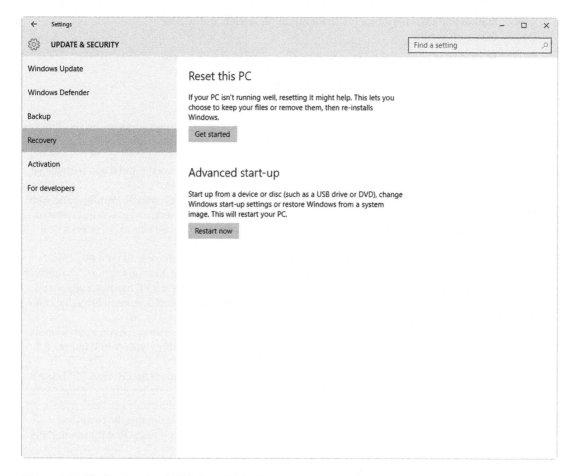

Figure 1-3. *The Reset option in Windows 10 Settings*

Settings

Called PC Settings in Windows 8 and refined further in Windows 10, the new Settings app (see Figure 1-3) contains all the configuration and management options you need to use Windows day to day, in an easy-to-use, easy-to-navigate app. From adding and managing user accounts, to changing personalization options, making Windows 10 easier to use and managing Windows Updates, these actions can all be performed in Settings. We'll look in depth at the Settings app in Chapters 9 and 13. And the Windows Control Panel also still exists for those who want to use it.

The Windows Store

Probably the most talked-about feature in Windows 8 was the inclusion of an app store for the first time. The Windows Store (see Figure 1-4) was a central location to go to for the new-style Windows universal apps. With Windows 10, the store has been expended to include desktop software (sometimes referred to as Win32 software), music, video, and more.

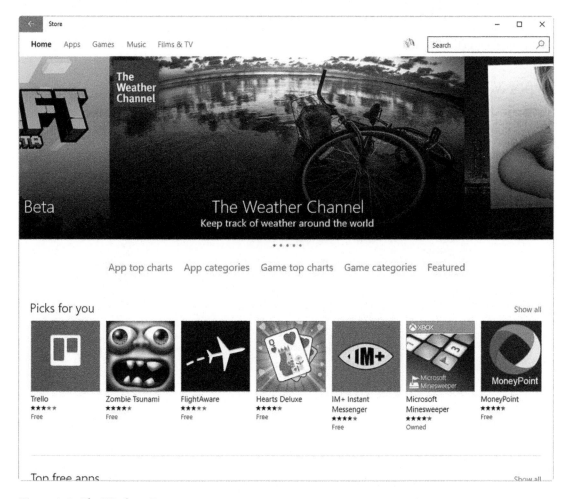

Figure 1-4. *The Windows Store*

The Windows Store is useful in some important ways. While it's true that not all the software you wish to use will be featured in the Store, because software developers, including Adobe and Sony, won't want to part with 30% of their revenue in store fees, all apps in the store have been tested for security and stability as part of the submission process. The upshot is that you're extremely unlikely to get a malware-infected or unstable app when you install through the store itself. Installation of apps also becomes much simpler than it has been in the past. We'll look more at the Store in Chapter 2.

Windows To Go

Windows To Go allows you to create a bootable USB flash drive containing your copy of Windows 10 with its software and settings. Not all USB flash drives are compatible with Windows To Go; those that are state this in the product description.

Windows To Go sounds like a takeaway option for a very good reason. No longer will people have to worry about finding mobile versions of apps or using cloud services. With Windows To Go, you really can carry around your entire Windows installation, safely and securely.

Windows To Go is an Enterprise-only feature in Windows 10, however, so it isn't included in the Home and Pro editions of the OS.

Hyper-V

First released in 2008 as part of the Windows Server 2008 OS, Hyper-V is a virtualization tool that allows other OSs—including earlier versions of Windows and GNU/Linux—to be run inside the main installed host OS, this being Windows 10 (see Figure 1-5).

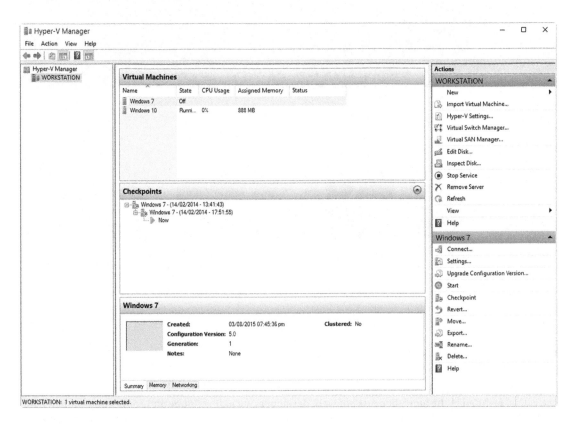

Figure 1-5. *Hyper-V in Windows 10*

Each virtualized OS runs effectively in a self-contained ISO disk image file. You can run multiple OSs side by side on a single Windows desktop.

Hyper-V is a Type-1 hypervisor, which means that it can communicate directly with your computer's hardware and take full advantage of it. One advantage of this type of hypervisor is that it can be programmed to take full control of a specific processor core in a multicore chip. This maximizes processing efficiency and ensures that there is no latency while each running OS waits for processing resources to become available.

By contrast, older Type-2 hypervisors used the host OS to *simulate* the hardware of a computer, not allowing access to the actual PC's hardware. This type included the now-defunct Microsoft Virtual PC.

Storage Spaces

Storage Spaces is a feature that allows you to aggregate multiple hard disks into a single large storage location. For example, if you have a 750GB HDD and a 2TB HDD, you can pool them into a single 2.75TB drive. You can also use USB-attached disks with the feature.

Windows 10 manages the data distribution and can also create built-in resiliency with mirroring or striping of data across the various physical hard disks to prevent data loss.

OneDrive and OneDrive for Business Integration

Microsoft's cloud backup and storage services—OneDrive and OneDrive for Business—are baked into Windows 10, with the OS automatically able to make a backup copy of your Documents, Music, Pictures, and Videos libraries; Internet Favorites; and their Windows settings—and sync those files and settings across your different Windows 10 devices. This can be incredibly helpful, but the total amount of free storage you get with your Microsoft account is 15GB; it's much larger with OneDrive for business, with 1TB of storage. With large files such as digital photographs, it is easy to completely fill this space on a PC. You can buy additional storage with OneDrive, if necessary, or you can turn off this backup feature in part or in full. I will show you how to do this in Chapter 12.

Miracast

If you've ever had to give a presentation at a remote office or training center, you'll be familiar with the mess and tangle of cables that you need to carry, and know that your laptop will be resolutely static in one place throughout your presentation. Miracast (previously referred to as Wi-Di) allows a laptop or tablet with compatible hardware to connect wirelessly to a compatible projector or display. This hands-free approach means you can present while carrying a tablet, such as a Microsoft Surface, and at the very least remove one lead from your bag.

You might have guessed that Miracast requires your PC and the projector/display you'll be using to be compatible. You can check the manufacturer's documentation that came with your device to see if Miracast is supported.

Wi-Fi Direct and NFC Printing

Again requiring compatible hardware both on your PC and the printer, Wi-Fi Direct and NFC printing can be used to quickly pair a laptop or tablet with a printer without having to (in the case of a business environment) know the network or IP address of the printer, or without having to plug it in directly by USB.

The benefit this brings is that when people are visiting your home or workplace, or when you are out and about, it is possible to print quickly and simply by either pairing the laptop or tablet with the printer directly via Wi-Fi, or by tapping the two NFC-equipped devices together to pair them.

Mobile Tethering

If your laptop or tablet includes a cellular SIM card for mobile data use away from Wi-Fi or a wired network, this mobile data connection can be shared with up to 10 other Windows 8.1 and Windows 10 PCs. While mobile data can be useful, this can be useful if, for example, the Internet connection in your workplace temporarily fails and you want to help people to keep working.

Workplace Join and Work Folders

A feature of the Pro and Enterprise editions of Windows 10, Workplace Join provides an easy-to-use interface whereby people can use their own laptops and tablets with the company domain and network. You can get access to files and resources shared on the network, as well as business-specific apps. Work Folders allows you to synchronize to your PC the work files you need access to, all stored in a safe and encrypted container. For the business, Workplace Join and Work Folders provide a quick and straightforward way to support bring-your-own-device (BYOD) hardware, while having control over the maintenance and the updates for the device, and being able to remotely wipe company files at any time. We will look more at these features in Chapter 8.

Secure Boot

One of the more controversial features of Windows 8.1 is Secure Boot, a feature that prevents any Unified Extensible Firmware Interface (UEFI)–equipped motherboard from booting an OS that is not signed with a security certificate. This feature, sometimes called Trusted Boot, is most commonly found on the computers you buy from manufacturers such as Samsung, HP, Dell, and so forth, in which it is enabled by default.

The reason behind Secure Boot is to stop unauthorized firmware, OSs, or UEFI drivers from loading at boot time. This is to prevent the spread of malware and viruses that can attack the computer at boot time.

■ **Note**   Secure Boot can be disabled, but UEFI systems vary across manufacturers. To disable it, you need to refer to the documentation for the system used on your computer.

Cortana and Improved Search

Our first Windows 10–only feature is a big one. Cortana was first introduced in Windows Phone 8, but has at last made her way to the desktop. Cortana (see Figure 1-6) is a personal assistant for Windows, able to do everything from assist you with searching your files and the Internet, to setting reminders (based on both time and location), track parcels and flights, identify that music track playing in the background, set alarms to keep you on time, and remind you of events in your calendar— like that all-important wedding anniversary.

Figure 1-6. *Cortana!*

We'll look in depth at Cortana in Chapters 5 and 8, including all the things she can do to assist you in your home or work life.

Action Center

Popping out from the right side of your desktop screen, or from the top of your screen on a smartphone, is the new Action Center (see Figure 1-7). This new feature brings several improvements to Windows 10. First, you see quick access buttons to useful features, such as Settings, Airplane mode, Wireless displays, Tablet mode, and more. These buttons can be configured to suit your own preferences; we'll look at how to do this in Chapter 9.

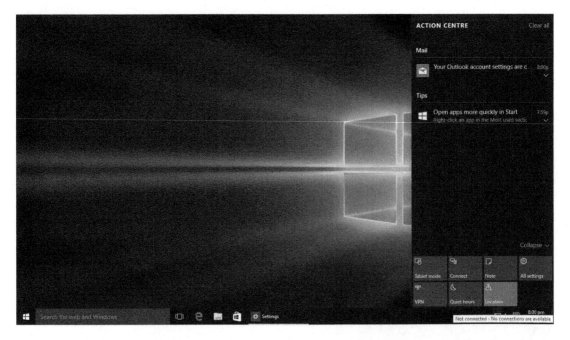

Figure 1-7. *The Windows 10 desktop Action Center*

Additionally, and as the name suggests, this is the central hub for all notifications on your PC. You'll likely already have been using Windows versions that pop up an alert (called a *toast* because of their pop-up nature) that only appear for a few seconds before disappearing again, never to be found.

The Action Center aggregates all these alerts and allows you to interact with them individually or in a group. Useful features include being able to interact with some notifications directly in the Action Center, such as replying to SMS text messages or emails without having to open your messaging app. Notifications carry across devices too, meaning that you'll never miss a reminder on your desktop just because you set it on your phone, and that you won't have to see a notification on other devices once you've dismissed it once. We'll look more at this feature in Chapter 2.

Continuum

Convertible tablets are becoming more and more popular. The idea of having a device with a keyboard that snaps off, like the Microsoft Surface, or that can be folded out of the way, such as the Lenovo Yoga, to turn the device into a tablet is appealing to many people. Microsoft has included a new Windows 10 feature called Continuum to aid with this.

In short, Continuum can change—automatically or at a user prompt—the mode in which your PC operates. When you switch to Tablet mode, your Start menu and apps run full screen; window furniture such as buttons become larger; and a universal back button appears on the taskbar. When you reconnect your keyboard, everything returns to "desktop" mode—ready for use with a mouse or trackpad.

Continuum has another, fairly major trick up its sleeve though. On a compatible Windows 10 smartphone, you can connect a keyboard, mouse, and monitor, and run the full Windows 10 experience, complete with desktop and windowed apps as though your smartphone was a full PC. We'll look at both of these features in Chapter 8.

Microsoft Edge

Internet Explorer (IE) is dead (sort of, anyway), and the new kid on the block is called Edge. This is Microsoft's next generation web browser that allows you to load web pages faster and more compatibly than you could in Windows 7 or Windows 8.1. It doesn't end there, however, because Edge allows you to annotate and share web pages using a mouse or a pen, or with touch.

For everybody needing compatibility with older web sites and company Intranet sites, however, Internet Explorer is still present, but only in Windows 10 Pro and Enterprise. It remains unchanged from the version of IE in Windows 8.1 and will continue to be supported. We'll look at Edge in more depth in Chapter 2.

Multiple Desktop Support

Having multiple workspaces is something that many PC users have been requesting for years, and Windows 10 finally brings the feature to the desktop. This allows you to create multiple desktop workspaces, each with its own running apps and layout. You can, for example, have Microsoft Word and an accountancy package open on one desktop, while Adobe Creative Cloud and Microsoft Visual Studio exist on another (or your work apps on one desktop and Amazon and Solitaire on another).

This feature allows you to rationalize the complex mess of open windows by separating apps into different workspaces—to help keep you focused on the task at hand. We'll look more at multiple desktops in Chapter 8.

Four-Way Snap

I have always loved the Windows snap feature, first introduced in Windows 7. This allowed you to quite literally snap two Windows to the left and right of your desktop screen so that you can perform actions such as working on or comparing two documents side by side, without having to spend time resizing windows and lining everything up.

Windows 10 improves on this in three ways. First, by permitting four apps to be snapped in the four corner quarters of the display, but also by suggesting apps that can fill the remaining space by providing thumbnail images of what's running.

Snapped apps don't have to remain as fixed sizes either (see Figure 1-8). They can be resized when snapped with other windows, automatically resizing to fill the remaining space. Even if you resize snapped Windows, when you unsnap them, they automatically return to the size they were before, eliminating window resizing frustration. We'll look at snap more in Chapter 8.

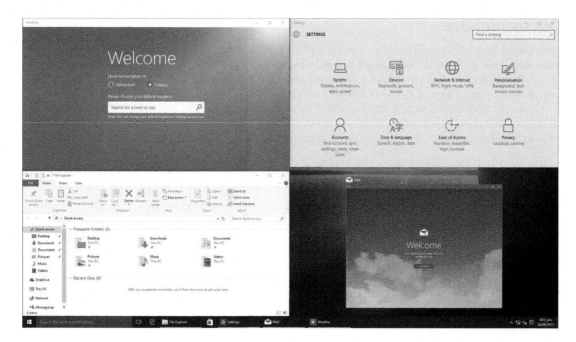

Figure 1-8. *Windows 10 includes four-way desktop snap*

Single Sign-on

A new feature both for consumers and businesses, Single Sign-on allows your Windows 10 PC or smartphone to automatically sign you into web services, such as those owned by Microsoft or Google, or those used in business, such as Office 365 or Azure Active Directory, if you are already signed into another. This can reduce the need to sign in to multiple services separately, which can boost your productivity time.

Xbox Streaming

If you have an Xbox One console in your home, then the good news is that it will also be running Windows 10. This permits more integration than has yet been possible, such as being able to stream your gameplay from the console to a Windows 10 PC or tablet so you can play it on that device instead.

End-to-End Encryption and Other Security Features

Security has been a major focus for Microsoft with Windows 10, and new features such as the automatic encryption of traffic over the Internet between your PC and web services such as Windows Server systems, Office 365, and Azure Active Directory provide a valuable extra layer of security.

Identity Protection and Access Control use virtualization technology to store enterprise access details where they can't be intercepted or hacked, and two-factor authentication that now includes support for other Windows 10 devices. This means that you can use your Windows 10 phone as a pairing device with your PC, automatically securing the PC when the smartphone goes in and out of range.

Peer-to-Peer Updates and Better Update Management

I've definitely saved the best new feature for last, however. If you are in the workplace where Internet bandwidth is at a premium, or in a rural environment where fast Internet connections are uncommon, Windows 10 is able to distribute and obtain Windows updates via a peer-to-peer network.

This means that only *one* PC on your network will need to have downloaded all of a patch or update and the other PCs can then get the update directly from that PC, rather than having to use valuable Internet bandwidth to download their own copies.

Windows 10 also improves update management, giving businesses two tracks from which they can choose. The first track contains all the new Windows feature improvements, updates, and patches, while the second track contains only the updates and patches needed to secure and stabilize a PC. We'll look at Windows Update in depth in Chapter 12.

Signing in to Windows 10

When you start your Windows 10 PC, the first thing you'll see is the lock screen, which can display useful information about messages, emails, and events, as well as highlight Windows 10 features that you may not have used. You can unlock your PC by clicking anywhere on it with your mouse or pressing any key on your keyboard.

■ **Tip** On a desktop PC or laptop, you can quickly open the logon screen without having to swipe upward with your mouse. Just press any key on your keyboard—and the logon screen opens.

When you open the lock screen, you're presented with the sign-in screen. If you have more than one person with an account on the PC, such as a friend or family member, then their names and thumbnail image (if they are using a Microsoft Account or have previously set a sign-on image) appear. You can click your account to sign in.

If you have set a password (which is always a good idea), or a PIN, on your PC, you are asked for it (see Figure 1-9). Here you have different options. The standard way to sign in to your PC is to use the password associated with either the PC or your Microsoft Account (depending on whether you signed up for a Microsoft or Local account when you first installed Windows on the PC).

Figure 1-9. *The sign-in screen has multiple options available*

Other options are available, however, and if you have set up another access method, such as a PIN or Windows Hello (more on how to do this shortly), you can click the **Sign-in options** link below the password input box to choose how you want to sign in to your PC. Let's have a look at the other options.

- **Switch User**: This option is in the bottom-left corner of your screen, and is displayed if there is more than one user account on the PC. It allows you to step back to the screen, where you can choose which person is to sign in to the PC.

- **Network Connection**: This icon may look different to the one shown in Figure 1-9, depending on whether your PC connects to the Internet via a wired network cable or via Wi-Fi. Clicking this allows you to connect to the Internet if your PC does not automatically make a connection, and it can be useful when signing in to a Microsoft account or a company domain account.

- **Ease of Access**: Clicking this icon displays a list of options that can make signing in to and using Windows 10 easier. These include turning on the narrator, high-contrast visibility mode, or sticky keys, which allows you to perform keyboard actions such as Shift + a letter by pressing each key in turn rather than together.

■ **Tip**   If you are signing in to a tablet or other touch screen device, and the onscreen keyboard does not automatically appear, you can click the Ease of Access icon to display an onscreen keyboard display control.

- **Power:** If you don't want to sign in to your PC, but would rather shut down or put it to sleep, you find **Shut Down**, **Sleep**, and **Restart** options available in the bottom right of the sign-in screen.

■ **Tip**   On a Windows 10 smartphone, the lock screen and sign-in screen do not display the options that I just listed. Instead, you are automatically presented with the sign-in option you chose in Settings (more on how to do this shortly).

Configuring the Windows 10 Lock Screen

As with all aspects of Windows 10, the lock screen is highly configurable, and you can change everything—from the picture that appears there to the information that it displays. To change the lock screen settings (Figure 1-10), press the Windows icon on the bottom left of the taskbar that runs along the bottom of your screen, or press the Windows icon key on your keyboard or tablet bezel to open the Start menu.

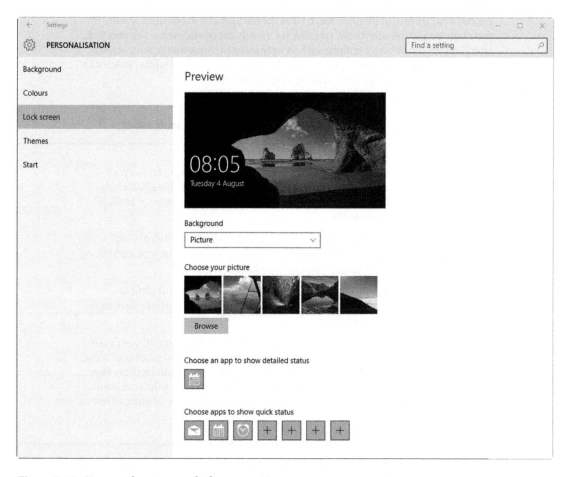

Figure 1-10. *You can change many lock screen settings*

With the Start menu open, you see a Settings icon and link in the bottom left corner of the Start menu. Click this. When the Settings app appears, click the **Personalization** icon, and then click the **Lock screen** link.

■ **Tip**   To access Settings on a Windows 10 smartphone, swipe downward from the top of your screen with your finger. If you do not see a Settings button, click the Expand link near the top right of the screen. Not all of the options described next are available on Windows 10 smartphones.

You are now presented with the lock screen settings (see Figure 1-10). The options you have here allow you to change the following.

- **Background**: There are different background image options available from a drop-down menu, and these might vary depending on who manufactured your PC. The first option is **Windows Spotlight**. This displays a standard picture on the lock screen most of the time, but might occasionally change to highlight a feature of Windows 10 you haven't used, such as the Cortana personal assistant.

  Other options include a static picture or a slideshow, where options allow you to choose what picture or pictures are used as the background for the lock screen. If you choose a picture slideshow, you also see an **Advanced slideshow settings** link, which allows you to select options such as only using pictures that fit your screen, and turning off the slideshow when the PC has been inactive for a while (which can be a good way to preserve battery life on a laptop or tablet).

■ **Tip**   Changing the lock screen settings changes the lock screen for *all* users of the PC.

- **Choose an app to show detailed status**: This allows you to choose one of your installed apps so that it can display detailed information. Useful apps to include might be Calendar, to show any forthcoming appointments you have, or Mail, to display any newly arrived emails.

- **Choose apps to show quick status**: Here you can choose up to seven of your installed apps to display a numeric counter signifying how many new or unread items, such as email or messages, you have received.

- **Screen timeout settings**: When you are using a laptop or tablet and want to maximize your battery life, you can use these options to set the period of inactivity, after which your PC will go to sleep.

- **Screen-saver settings**: If you are using a laptop, tablet, or a desktop PC with a flat screen, you should ignore these settings, because running a screen saver uses more electricity; on a laptop or tablet, it runs down your battery more quickly. For older PCs that that still have a cathode ray tube (CRT) monitor, you can select a screen saver animation to prevent image burn-in, which can occur when an image if left on the screen for some time.

■ **Tip**   PCs, laptops, and tablets with OLED screens, which admittedly are not very common, are also susceptible to image burn-in. Check the specifications for your PC or monitor to see if it has an OLED screen type. On these devices, it is advisable to have your display turn itself off after a maximum of one minute of inactivity.

Changing Your Password and Sign-in Options

In the Settings app, you can change your password or choose another method of signing in to your PC, such as a PIN or a picture password. To get to these options, click the **Accounts** icon and then the **Sign-in options** link.

The **Sign-in options** screen (see Figure 1-11) displays all the different ways you can sign in to your PC. At the top of the screen you'll see a **Require sign-in** box, which allows you to turn off the requirement to use a password for that PC. This can be okay for a PC in a secure home that's not used to store personal files, or for online shopping and banking, but it's always advisable to have a password for your PC. This is especially true for laptops and tablets that are used in places where they might be stolen, and for work PCs that may contain, or have access to, personal and customer data that's protected by data protection laws.

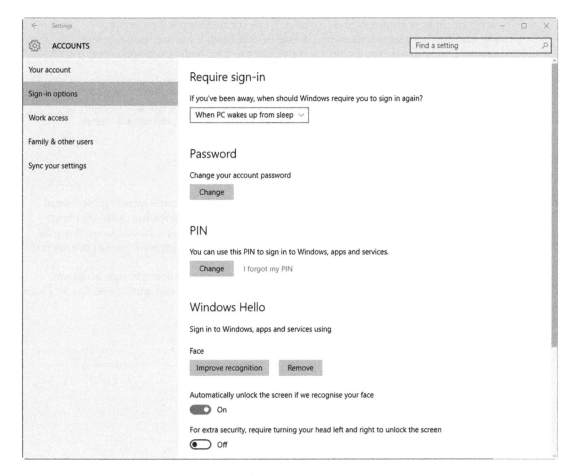

Figure 1-11. *You can change your password and choose different sign-in options*

- **Password**: This is the option to change the password you use to sign in to your PC, or to create one if you have a Local account and didn't create a password when you created your account.

- **PIN**: Here you specify a PIN code of your choice that can help you sign in to your PC more quickly than with a password. The PIN works similarly to that of your bank ATM card.

- **Windows Hello**: This requires a compatible webcam or camera and can recognize your face when your sit in front of the PC, to automatically unlock it for you. This option is only available if you have a Windows Hello–compatible camera installed.

- **Picture password**: This allows you to choose a photograph on which you can make three tap, circle, or swipe gestures to sign in. These can include poking a person's eyes and drawing a semicircle around the top of their head. If you are using a Picture password, try to avoid easy-to-guess gestures, like touching both of a person's eyes and swiping on their smile.

- **Fingerprint**: If you have a biometric fingerprint reader installed on your PC, you can choose this option to sign in to Windows 10 by swiping or scanning a finger. You will be guided through setting up your fingerprint, which involves swiping several fingers over the sensor five times so that Windows 10 gets accurate scans.

Windows Hello

Passwords can be a pain to remember, especially if you (sensibly) use very secure ones to protect your personal information and files. Windows 10 includes a new biometric sign-in feature called Windows Hello that can make signing in to your PC a breeze. Windows Hello requires specific hardware that your PC may already have or that you can purchase separately. This is either a fingerprint scanner or a special type of 3D webcam.

You'll know if you can use Windows Hello on your PC, because when you open the sign-in options, Windows Hello is available to you (see Figure 1-12). Click the **Set up** button to configure the feature for either your camera or your fingerprint scanner.

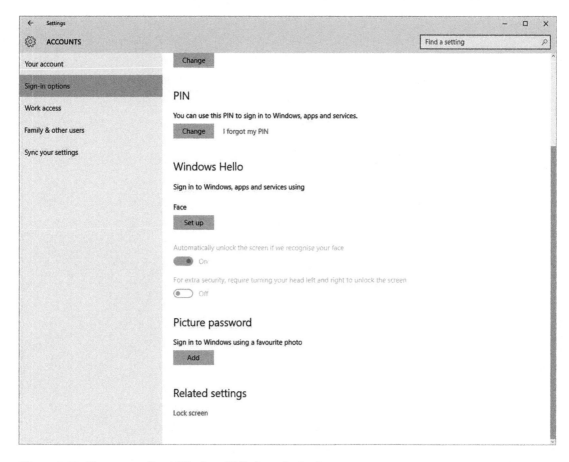

Figure 1-12. *You can configure Windows Hello from the Settings app*

If you are using a fingerprint scanner with your laptop or Ultrabook (they're uncommon on desktop PCs and tablets), you are asked to swipe your finger across the reader so that Windows can get five good swipe images. This can take some time, but Windows will tell you if you are swiping too quickly or too slowly.

If you are using a compatible 3D camera, then you are asked to sit still in front of it while Windows Hello scans your face; this literally takes just a couple of seconds. Once this is done, additional controls appear in the Settings app, such as turning on and off facial unlock for your PC, and boosting security by making you turn your head to the left and right to sign in (see Figure 1-13).

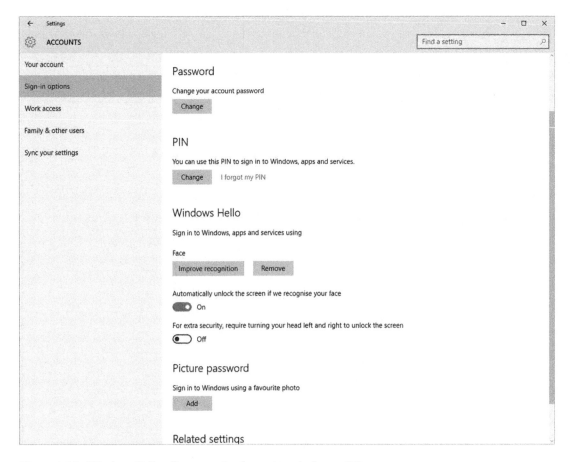

Figure 1-13. *Windows Hello offers a couple of ways to unlock your PC*

When Windows Hello is set up on your PC, at the sign-in screen you can either swipe your finger over your fingerprint scanner for auto-unlock of your account, or, and this is extremely cool, sit at the lock screen looking at your PC for just a second (it really is that fast) for the facial recognition system to unlock your PC. When Windows Hello is activated, at the top of the lock screen you'll see an animated eye and a message that Windows Hello is looking for you.

The reason a 3D camera is used—which includes infrared and color sensors, as well as a depth-sensor—is to guarantee that somebody can't just print a high-resolution photograph of your face and use it to sign in to the PC. It's an extremely secure method to sign in to a PC, and unquestionably makes signing in an absolute breeze.

Creating Strong Passwords

When you are using passwords with your PC or with any online web site or service, it's essential to have strong and secure passwords. Here are my top tips for creating secure passwords. You can also watch my *Creating Secure (and Memorable) Passwords* online video at `http://pcs.tv/1B1NOja`.

- Use a long password with a minimum of 12 characters. Using a phrase, such as a saying or a line from a book, is a good idea.

- Use a mixture of uppercase and lowercase letters. Do not just capitalize the first letter of each word. Try capitalizing the second letter of the first word, the third letter of the second word, and so on.

- You can substitute some numbers for letters to make your password more secure, such as 1 instead of i or L, 3 instead of e, 5 instead of s, 7 instead of L, 8 instead of B, and 0 (zero) instead of O.

- You can use some symbols to make your password even more secure, such as ! instead of i or L, $ instead of s, & instead of a, () instead of O, ^ instead of v or y, # instead of H, and / instead of j or 7.

- You can add a few letters representing the web site or service a password is for, and randomizing this too, such as capitalizing the first alphabetic letter. This would give you Ama (Amazon), ebA (eBay), or miC (Microsoft) to add to the beginning or end of your password. This not only makes it more secure, but unique to that web site or service—meaning that if their security is compromised, it's harder for your accounts elsewhere to also be compromised.

Mastering Touch in Windows 10

Touch is everywhere in our computing lives, and it's quite astonishing how quickly this transformation occurred. As you might expect, then, Windows 10 fully embraces touch and even has some clever features (such as Continuum, which I will talk more about in Chapter 8) that makes Windows 10 just as easy to use with touch as it is with a keyboard and mouse.

The touch interface is remarkably intuitive and operates in a way that you might expect it to work on any other tablet or touch OS. The following are the main gestures:

- **Tap** an item to open it (equivalent to a mouse click).

- **Double-tap** to open an item on the desktop (equivalent to a double mouse click).

- **Swipe** in from the right of the screen to open the Action Center.

- **Swipe** in from the left of the screen to open the Task View.

- **Drag** an item on screen by tapping and holding it, and then drag to move it.

- **Tap and hold** to highlight an item on the screen.

- **Pinch inward** to zoom out of a view.

- **Pinch outward** to zoom into a view.

When you are swiping in from the edges of the screen, try to start on the actual screen bezel, because doing so produces better results. For some screens, however, the bezel and screen might not be completely flush against each other. In this case, practice might be required to get the best results.

Using the Onscreen Keyboard in Windows 10

Windows 10 is very good at detecting when you have selected something with touch that requires keyboard entry and pops up the onscreen keyboard (see Figure 1-14). This happens if it detects a finger tap on an input field such as the password box.

Figure 1-14. *The onscreen keyboard in Windows 10*

■ **Tip**   Windows 10 includes predictive text and displays a selection of words along the top of the onscreen keyboard as you type. You can tap the word to insert it, whereupon it attempts to predict the word you want to use next. Sometimes whole sentences can be completed this way.

There are several different keyboards you can choose from in Windows 10. I want to describe each one for you, as follows:

- The **default keyboard** is a standard affair; you can see the QWERTY keyboard in Figure 1-12. The &123 key brings up numbers and symbols; and an Emoticon button brings up happy and sad faces for email, social networking, and instant messaging. On the bottom right of the keyboard is a key that allows you to change your input method to one of the next four options.

- **Split keyboard** splits the keys to the far left and right of the screen, making it much simpler to hold a tablet in both hands and type with your thumbs.

- **Written input** allows those with a tablet stylus to input text, numbers, and symbols using Windows 8.1's excellent handwriting recognition. This is useful for writing notes while carrying a tablet.

- **Full keyboard**'s full keyboard option gives you all the keys you expect to find on a PC keyboard, including a number row across the top of the keyboard and access to function keys. You can switch on the full onscreen keyboard in PC Settings by clicking **PCs & Devices**, and then **Typing** and activating the switch for **Add the standard keyboard layout as a touch keyboard**.

- **Undock keyboard** is the first of three icons at the top right of the onscreen keyboard. This allows you to move the keyboard to a different location on the screen.

- **Maximize the keyboard** is the next icon, which stretches the keyboard area so that it fills the whole width of your screen.

- **Close** is the final option; it allows you to close the onscreen keyboard until it is needed again.

■ **Tip** Tap and briefly hold a letter on the onscreen keyboard to display international variations for that letter, including accented letters.

The default onscreen keyboard doesn't show the full PC keyboard layout with number, row, and page control keys. You can activate a full onscreen keyboard by searching for **onscreen keyboard** in the Start menu (see Figure 1-15). This appears in a moveable and resizable window on your screen.

Figure 1-15. *The full onscreen keyboard*

■ **Tip** If you are using Windows 10 Mobile on a smartphone, you also see a small dot in the bottom-left corner of the onscreen keyboard. You can touch this and gesture up, down, left, and right to use it as a cursor control for editing and highlighting text.

Summary

Windows 10 is not merely an evolution of Windows, but rather a significant step forward. Features such as Continuum, Cortana, and the syncing of notifications, reminders, and settings between different Windows 10 PCs and phones will make life much easier and more straightforward for many people.

If you are coming to Windows 10 from Windows 7 (or an earlier version of Windows), the differences in what the OS can do for you "out-of-the-box" is even more pronounced. In the following chapters, rather than focusing on a button-by-button look at each feature, instead I'll present a guide to how to leverage every feature to its maximum potential—and get the very best from it and your Windows 10 device.

CHAPTER 2

■ ■ ■

Finding Your Way Around Windows 10

The main user interface for Windows has undergone some significant changes in recent years. Windows 7 introduced a cleaner look, with an uncluttered desktop, and Microsoft's acclaimed Ribbon interface for features such as File Explorer (called Windows Explorer at the time). Windows 8 brought the Start screen, filling your display with grouped live tiles—each of them an app capable of displaying live information right there, without having to be opened first. Many people didn't like the move away from the Start menu, which went away when Windows 8 was introduced, but live tiles offered many benefits, including being able to quickly view the news and your email and calendar without having to open the relevant app.

In Windows 10, Microsoft seeks to address all the criticisms and concerns people have with Windows 8, while keeping the best aspects of what that version of Windows brought. In this chapter, I'll show you how to find your way around Windows 10, but also how to get the very best from the experience you have with it.

The experience of using Windows 10 has been carefully designed to be uniform across whatever device you're using. For example, while there are a few understandable differences between the Start menu/Start screen on a Windows 10 Mobile smartphone, as opposed to a PC (due to the completely different way that we use phones), the overall experience of tiles, an All Apps list, the Settings app, and app menus and options are the same.

Inevitably, though, some user experience features that work brilliantly on one type of device won't work so well on another, and trying to overcome this problem has long been the Holy Grail of user-experience designers working on tablets. You'll be pleased to hear, though, that the experience of using Windows 10 on any type of device, and of any size, is extremely fluid and consistent.

If you're using Windows 10 on a desktop, it'll look and work just like Windows 7; if you're using Windows 10 on a tablet, it'll look and work just like Windows 8.1; and indeed Microsoft has brought together the best aspects of both previous versions of Windows.

Small Tablets with Screens Less Than 8 Inches

One of the best benefits of Windows 10 for home users is that for devices with screens of less than 8 inches, Microsoft doesn't charge PC makers for the operating system. This helps make these small, low-power devices incredibly cheap. There are trade-offs of having such a small screen, however; the most obvious being that working on the desktop with tiny icons and buttons could be extremely fiddly, even on a good day.

For this reason, there is no desktop on these small Windows 10 tablets. All the features of Windows are still there, and you can install all of your legacy win32 desktop software and Store apps, but everything appears in full screen. It's all there—all the features of a full version of Windows 10 Home as you get on a desktop PC; but running multiple apps on the screen at the same time isn't possible, except in a side-by-side snap view, which I'll detail in a minute.

■ **Tip**   Microsoft has made it easy to switch between running apps on tablets, just swipe from the left of the screen to reveal the Task View, where large thumbnails of your apps appear, and that you can tap to open. You can read more on Task View later in this chapter.

Using Two Apps, Side by Side, on Tablets

I talk about using more than one app on the desktop, and how you can snap them to the sides or the four corners of the screen, in Chapter 8. For small tablets, though, the situation is slightly different, and so it seems appropriate to discuss the changes here. By default, each app that runs on a small Windows 10 tablet—and by this I mean a tablet with a screen smaller than 8 inches—runs full screen, although it is possible to have two (but no more than two) apps running side by side. When you run more than a one app at a time, each app occupies 50% of the screen.

To pin an app to the left or right of the screen, when the app is running, drag it away from the top center of your screen with your finger, and it becomes a large thumbnail. Drag this thumbnail to the left or right side of the screen, and part of the screen darkens to signify that the app will be docked left or right. If you have a Bluetooth keyboard attached to your tablet, you can dock an app to the left or right of the screen with the key combination Windows key + left cursor or Windows key + right cursor.

■ **Tip**   To switch back to a single app on your screen, drag the vertical bar separating the two apps all the way to the left or right. This swipes the other app off the screen.

If you have any other apps running in the background, thumbnail images of them appear on the other half of the screen. Tap one to run it, snapped to that half of the screen. If no other apps are running, tap the Windows key, and the next app you open will fill the remaining half of the screen. This feature allows you to use a main app, perhaps your email, next to another app, such as social media (see Figure 2-1).

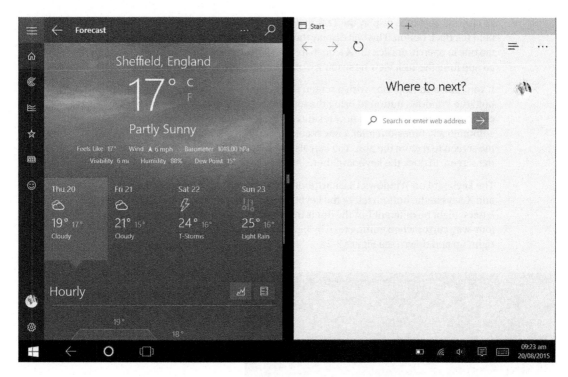

Figure 2-1. *The side-by-side app view*

■ **Tip** With a Bluetooth keyboard connected to your tablet, you can quickly close an app by pressing the Windows key + down cursor or by touching the app at the top center of your screen and dragging it off the bottom center of the screen.

Windows 10 Mobile Smartphones

Just in the way that small Windows 10 tablets have their own ways of working, so do Windows 10 smartphones. It's not possible to run more than one app onscreen at a time on a smartphone, but with a screen size of typically around 5 inches, it would be difficult anyway. There are some tips and tricks, however, that will make your experience of using a Windows 10 smartphone much easier and more enjoyable, so here are my top tips:

- If you have an all-screen smartphone with no physical Back, Windows, and Search buttons below the screen, you can swipe upward from the bottom of the screen to display or hide the virtual Back, Windows, and Search buttons.

- From the Start screen, swipe right to left to reveal the **All Apps** list. There is a search box at the top that you can type into, or you can tap any of the alphabetic header letters (A, B, C, etc.) to display a list of all letters, making it quicker to find the app you want.

- To close an app, or to display the Task View thumbnails of all running apps, tap and hold the **Back** button. This will display thumbnail images of all running apps. You can tap one to open it, or click the **X** icon in its top-right corner to close it. You can also close an app from the Task View by swiping it off the bottom of the screen with your finger.

- If you have a smartphone with a screen that is 5 inches or larger, you can tap and hold the Windows button to bring the top of the screen downward, making it easier to use the app, which now resides in just the bottom half of the screen. This automatically times-out after a few seconds, or if you tap anywhere in the top half of the screen to restore the app. You can also slide the space bar to the left and right of the screen, to dock the keyboard there, making it easier to type with one hand.

- The keyboard on Windows 10 smartphones includes a small dot underneath the Z and X keys in the bottom left of the keyboard (on some international keyboards, the letters might be different but the dot is in the same place). You can use this dot as a four-way cursor when editing text, by tapping and holding it and then dragging it left, right, up and down (see Figure 2-2).

Figure 2-2. *The Windows 10 Mobile keyboard has a cursor control in its bottom-left corner*

- When editing, you can select text by tapping it. If you tap a word, it highlights and you see draggable bars appear before and after the highlighted word (or letter). You can drag these bars around to highlight the text you want and a **Copy** icon will appear above the highlighted text.

- If you have any copied text, a **Paste** icon will appear in the top left of the onscreen keyboard. Click this to paste the copied text. A **Microphone** icon will also appear here in some, but not all, apps. You can tap this to dictate your text instead of typing it.

- If you are using a dual-SIM phone, you have two each of the Phone and SMS apps on your Start screen and in the All Apps view, enabling you to independently and effectively control your usage of each SIM.

All other functions on Windows 10 Mobile smartphones operate as they do on tablets, although I'll always discuss wherever there are minor differences in operation. For example, the Action Center opens by swiping from the right the screen on a tablet, but you swipe downward from the top of the screen on a smartphone. I'll cover the Action Center later in this chapter.

The Start Menu

The Start menu is your main place to find and launch apps, and to find Windows Settings and controls. The Start menu has different sections, not all of which are always visible, because the experience you get on a tablet is slightly different than if you are using a keyboard and mouse. Figure 2-3 shows the differences between how the Start menu appears on a desktop when used with a keyboard and mouse (left) and on a tablet (right).

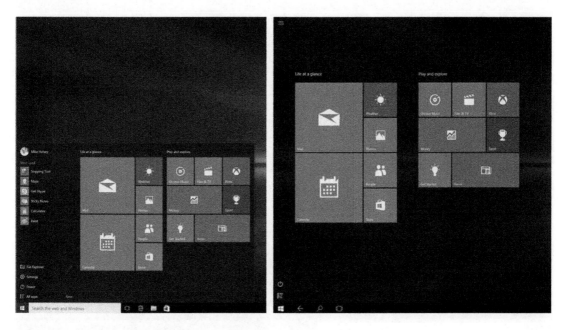

Figure 2-3. *The normal and full screen Start Menus*

There are different sections in the Windows 10 Start menu. At the top left is your user avatar. You can click this to access quick links to **Change [your] account settings**, **Lock** the PC, or **Sign out** of your account on the PC.

Below your avatar is a list of your **Most used** apps. This list updates dynamically and automatically to help you always access the apps you use most often. Below this are quick links for **File Explorer,** the **Settings** app, and the **Shut down**, **Restart**, and **Sleep** power controls, and to open the **All apps** list (more on these shortly). If you are using a tablet and the Start menu appears full screen, you notice that none of these are visible. To make them visible, tap the hamburger icon in the top-left corner of the screen.

■ **Tip**   If you are using Windows 10 on a tablet, you see that the taskbar is also different, showing more widely spaced buttons for Search and Task View, but also a universal Back button that you can tap at any time to move backward one stop in Windows or in an app.

If you open the All Apps list, all of your installed apps appear in an alphabetized list, just as they always have on Windows phones (see Figure 2-4). You can click one of the grouping letters to display a full alphabetical list, which makes it much quicker to get to the app you need.

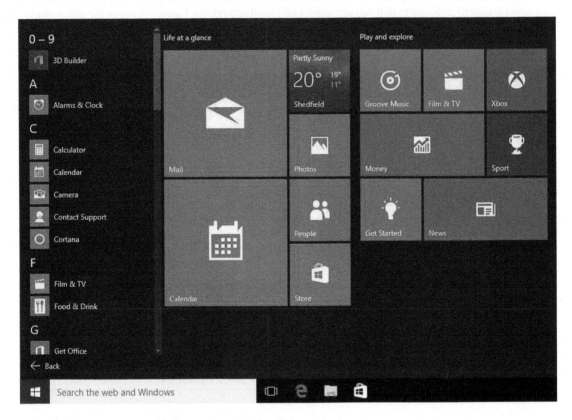

Figure 2-4. All of your installed apps appear in the All Apps view

---

■ **Tip**   If you are using Windows 10 on a tablet, you can open the All Apps view by clicking the icon in the bottom-left corner of the full screen Start menu, just above the Windows button.

The main area of the Start menu is reserved for live tiles. You can pin any app here by dragging it from the All Apps view or from the Most Used section, including non-store win32 apps (although these won't display a live tile). I'll show you how to resize and control tiles shortly.

Resizing and Customizing the Start Menu

The Start menu on Windows 10 desktops, laptops, and tablets (and to some extent, smartphones) can be fully customized and I'll show you the many ways you can customize your Windows 10 PC in Chapter 9. The default size of the Start menu though means that if you have a lot of tiles pinned to it you'll need to scroll up and down in the main part of the Start menu to find them all.

While there's always the option to invoke Tablet mode and run the Start menu full screen, which you can do without making all of your apps full screen automatically (I'll show you how to do this in Chapter 9 too), you can very easily resize the Start menu.

You can resize the Start menu by clicking and dragging its top and right edges. The top resizing works smoothly, so that the Start menu can be as tall or as short as you like. Resizing outward from the right operates in a series of jumps, which fit additional columns of tiles.

It's also possible to customize the Start menu in other ways too, such as adding buttons to the bottom left (see Figure 2-7) and removing the Most Used app section. Again, I'll show you how to do all of this in Chapter 9.

Locking the Computer and Signing Out

If you want to lock your PC, sign out so someone else can use the PC, or restart or shut down your PC, you do this from the Start menu. In the top left of the Start menu is your account image (known as an *avatar*). Click this and several options will appear (see Figure 2-5).

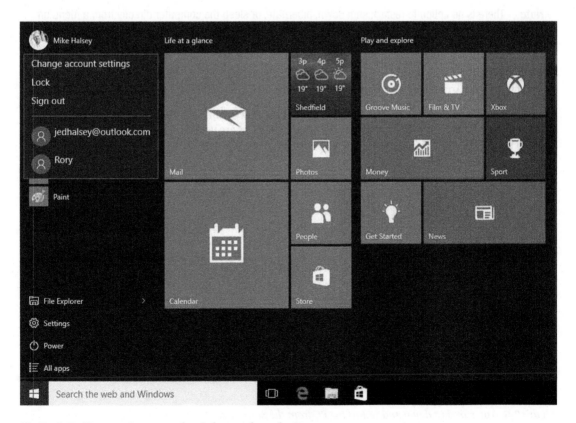

Figure 2-5. *You can sign out and switch users from the Start menu*

- **Change the account settings** takes you to the Settings app, where you can change your password, use a PIN, or set up the Windows Hello facial recognition feature to sign in to the PC.

- **Lock** is the option you choose to lock the computer without turning it off. It is useful if you are leaving your computer for a short break. You can also lock the computer the more traditional way by pressing Ctrl+Alt+Del on your keyboard and selecting Lock from the options; or you can press WinKey+L to lock the computer instantly.

■ **Tip**   Use WinKey+L to lock your computer quickly.

- **Sign out** is the option to use if you are finished with your computing session and want to let somebody else use the computer with his own user account. This option does not shut down the computer.

- With **Switch users**, other people who have accounts on this PC have their names listed here. You can click a person's name to switch to her account. This does not log you out, so any programs and apps you have running remain open until you are logged out or the PC is switched off.

■ **Note**   There is no option to restart, shut down, hibernate, or sleep the computer directly from a menu on the Start screen. To do this, you need to access the charms (more on this shortly) and select Settings.

Shutting Down and Restarting the PC, and Putting It to Sleep

To shut down or restart the PC, or to put it to sleep, click the **Power** button in the bottom-left corner of the Start menu (see Figure 2-6). This appears all the time, even if you are using the Start menu full screen on a tablet. It's really simple and straightforward to control the power options for your PC in Windows 10.

Figure 2-6. *You can shut down and restart the PC from the Start menu*

Pinning, Unpinning, and Resizing Live Tiles

I mentioned earlier in this chapter that you can pin live tiles in your Start menu. You do this by finding the app you want in the **All apps** list and right-clicking it (tap and hold with your finger). Several options appear in a context menu, including **Pin to Taskbar** (I'll show you how to use the taskbar later in this chapter). Click **Pin to Start** to pin the app to the Start menu.

You can pin anything to the Start menu as a tile, even older win32 desktop apps, although these aren't able to show live information and can only be resized a certain amount. To perform actions on live tiles in the Start menu, right-click (tap and hold) on the tile so that the various options will appear.

The actions you can perform on a tile vary depending on what you have selected.

- **Unpin from Start** allows you to remove a tile from the Start screen. It is still available in the All Apps view (more on this shortly) and it can be launched from there. It is useful for programs and apps that you use only occasionally.

- **Resize** allows you to resize compatible app tiles up to four sizes (depending on which sizes the app supports). For example, you may have a live tile in which you only see limited information about the current weather in a small square, but in a large square, you can see more information and the forecast for the next few days as well (see Figure 2-7). You may decide that you want to make some tiles smaller so that your organized groups on the Start screen take up less space or look more organized.

Figure 2-7. *The four live tile sizes*

- **Turn live tile off** deactivates the live component of a compatible tile. You may want a larger rectangular tile for email to make it easier to find and open, but not have the tile display the subjects and senders of your most recent emails.

- **Pin to Taskbar** pins the tile to the desktop taskbar as an icon, so that you can quickly open it without first having to open the Start menu.

- **Run as Administrator** is an option that only appears for desktop win32 apps. It allows you to run the program or feature with full admin privileges.

- **Open File Location** works only on installed win32 apps. It opens a File Explorer window and navigates directly to the folder on your hard disk in which the program or link you have selected is located. (I discuss File Explorer in Chapter 5.)

■ **Note**   Tiles for desktop programs can only be resized between small and medium squares.

Arranging Live Tiles into Groups and Naming the Groups

You can arrange your tiles on the Start menu into customizable groups and then rearrange them within those groups. This is something that can be used to bring your most commonly used programs to the beginning (left) of the Start menu and to group together related tiles, such as Internet links or development software.

You can rearrange tiles within a group or move one to a different group by dragging and dropping an app using touch or your mouse. Sometimes you see a horizontal bar appear as you drag tiles around the Start menu. If you drop a tile onto this highlighted bar, a new group is created.

The Start menu automatically gives names to groups when you first install Windows 10 (**Life at a glance** and **Play and explore**), but it is possible to rename these, and any other groups that you create. You might want to name your groups—*Work, Games, Internet,* and so on. To name or rename a group, move your mouse over the name or tap to the right of the name; an icon displaying two horizontal lines will appear, a bit like the hamburger icon, but where somebody has stolen the patty—damn them! (see Figure 2-8). If you click this icon, the group name becomes editable. Click or tap anywhere outside of the name, or press Enter, when you're done.

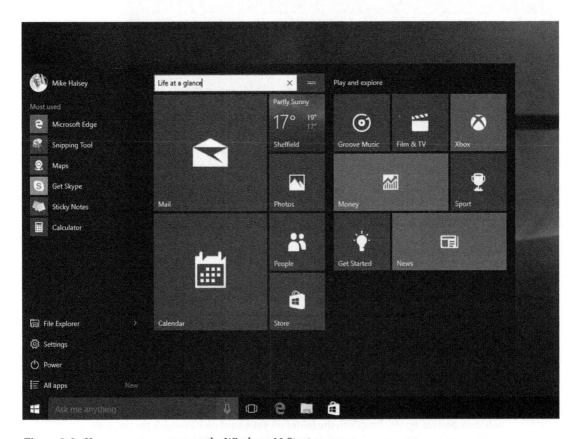

Figure 2-8. *You can name groups on the Windows 10 Start menu*

Using and Managing Apps

You open an app from the Start menu with a single click or tap. If you're using a tablet, the app opens full screen, or if you have a keyboard and mouse on your PC, it opens in a resizable window. In the top-right corner of all apps are three (sometimes four) controls (see Figure 2-9). Starting from the far right there is a **Close** button (the **X**) to exit the app. Next to this is a **Maximize** control (the square), which makes the app run full screen or to return a full-screen app to its previous size. The line represents a **Minimize** control, which hides the app down to the taskbar.

Figure 2-9. *There are three (sometimes four) controls in the top-right corner of windows*

In Store apps you may see a pair of diagonal arrows. This control invokes Tablet mode for the app, and it can also be used to restore the app to a window. It should be noted that on small Windows tablets, with screens less than eight inches, the Maximize control won't do anything because apps already run full screen and can't be run in smaller windows.

■ **Tip**   In Tablet mode, the Close button may not always be visible. Move your mouse to the top-right corner of the screen to make it appear.

Switching Between and Shutting Down Running Apps

There are two different ways to switch between apps in Windows 10. If you are on the desktop, the well-known Alt+Tab key combination displays small thumbnail images of all of your running apps. You can switch between them by continuing to press Alt+Tab until the one you want is highlighted, but you can't shut them down from here.

Windows 10 introduces a new way to switch between and close your running apps—the Windows key+Tab key combination. This displays large thumbnail images of all of your running apps, making it much easier to identify which app is which. From this "task view," which is also available by clicking the Task View icon next to the Cortana Search icon on the taskbar, you can click the app that you want to switch to (see Figure 2-10).

Figure 2-10. *Task View shows large thumbnail images of all of your running apps*

When hovering your mouse over a thumbnail, a close (X) icon appears in its top-right corner; these close icons are always visible on a tablet or laptop with a touchscreen. Just click or tap the icon to close the app. If instead you wish to bring one of the running apps to the foreground, all you need to do is click or tap its thumbnail image. Full details of how to switch between apps can be seen in Table 2-1.

Table 2-1. *Task View and App Switching Shortcuts*

Action	Keyboard	Mouse	Touch
Switch between running apps	Alt+Tab (for small thumbnails of running apps)	N/A	N/A
	Win+Tab (to invoke Task View)	Click the Task View icon on the taskbar and click the app thumbnail	Tap the Task View icon on the taskbar and click the app thumbnail
Close the currently running app	Alt+F4	Click the Close button in the top right of the app window	Tap the Close button in the top right of the app window

Using the Hamburger Menu in Apps

All apps in Windows are different, and some software developers and companies develop their own unique interfaces and ways of working, Microsoft's Ribbon interface is a great example of this. It means that apps you get from the Windows Store are all different and have their own ways of working. To help you get started, however, many Store apps use a standard hamburger menu in the very top-left corner of the window.

Clicking the hamburger icon (if it exists in your app), reveals a drop-down menu of options (see Figure 2-11). These options vary from one app to another but may include the following.

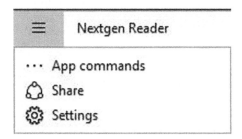

Figure 2-11. *The hamburger menu in Store apps*

- **App commands** opens a panel in the app that contains menu or other options for controlling the app.

- **Share** allows you to share text, images, and other items between apps, such as a photo with a social networking app to publish it there. You can use the Share option to email a photo to a friend or share a link on a social network. You can only share with other Windows Store apps; win32 desktop apps don't support the Share functionality.

- **Settings** displays a fly-out panel with settings for the app, such as its options and privacy controls.

■ **Tip**   Many win32 desktop apps have an icon in the top-left corner that you can click, just like the hamburger menu. It provides a drop-down menu of options for resizing and closing the app.

Using the Desktop in Windows 10

Using the desktop in Windows 10 is the same as with any previous version of the operating system (OS). You can pin apps to the taskbar, which offers a very quick and efficient way to open programs on the desktop without having to interact with or even see the Start menu.

All the usual desktop clicks—such as right-clicking with the mouse to bring up a context menu— work. On a touchscreen, you can tap and hold to simulate a right-click. This is the same way that touch has worked in Windows going back to Windows XP, and it's also consistent with other touch-based operating systems, including iOS and Android, which makes it intuitive and easy to use.

■ **Tip**   If you are using touch on the Windows 10 desktop, context menus are larger and their options are spaced farther apart when you right-click or tap and hold. This makes them more finger-friendly.

The Windows Button

The Windows button, often referred to as the *Start button*, sits at the very left of the taskbar; it's what you click to open the Start menu. It doesn't do much else, but it's central to the Windows experience, because it's from here that you can sign out, restart, and shut down your PC, as well as open the Settings app. The Windows button has a little trick up its sleeve, however, because right-clicking it (or tapping and holding it), opens the Administration menu (see upcoming section), which provides additional options.

The Taskbar

The Windows 10 taskbar is the same as it is in Windows 7 and Windows 8.1. You can pin programs on it that can be launched with a single click, or that on a click up-and-drag-upward motion (also on a right-click) opens a Jump List with additional options (see Figure 2-12). I talk more about Jump Lists shortly. To pin a program to the taskbar, right-click (touch and hold) its icon in the Start menu or in the All Apps list, and from the app bar click the **Pin to Taskbar** option. Icons on the taskbar (including non-pinned but running programs) can be dragged left and right to change their position. This can be very useful for grouping similar or commonly used programs together.

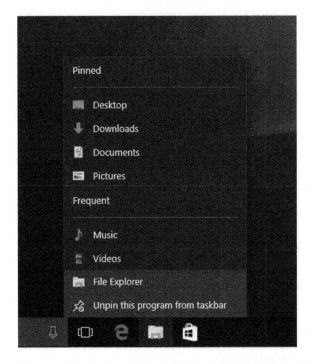

Figure 2-12. *The Windows 10 desktop and taskbar Jump Lists*

On the right side of the taskbar sits the system tray (see Figure 2-13), which is the area that you commonly see the time and date. The following list describes the other icons in the system tray.

Figure 2-13. *The system tray icons on the desktop taskbar*

- The **system tray** is represented by a small white up arrow. This is the bucket container for all the system tray icons that are hidden. I show you how to customize the system tray in Chapter 9.

- The **Battery icon** shows only when you are running Windows 10 on a computer that has a battery. This icon gives you a visual representation of the battery's charge level and overlays a Plug icon if your computer is currently connected to mains electricity.

- The **Network icon** changes depending on whether you are connected to your network and the Internet by a physical Ethernet cable, Wi-Fi, or a mobile Internet connection, such as 3G or LTE via a SIM card in your computer or via a dongle. This icon changes to an airplane if you have Airplane mode switched on.

- The **Volume icon** offers a quick way to control the computer's volume, or to mute it, and also to control your sound devices. If you click this icon, a volume control appears. I talk more about the additional functionality of this icon in Chapter 9.

- The **Action Center** is the central location for Windows and all your app messages, including those about anti-malware, backup, problems, and errors. When there is a notification for you, the icon changes to solid and filled-in. The Action Center is also where you can launch the Settings app and control features such as Airplane mode. I talk more about the Action Center shortly.

- The **Keyboard icon** brings up the onscreen keyboard. It appears by default when Windows 10 detects a touch-screen interface attached to your computer, but it can also be switched on by right-clicking in a blank space on the taskbar and clicking **Show Touch Keyboard** button from the options that appear.

- The **Date and Time** format can be changed. I talk about how to customize and configure the Date and Time settings in Chapter 9. If you click the time and date in the system tray, a dialog box shows the current month's calendar, the currently displayed clock(s), and any messages relating to Daylight Saving Time. I talk more about using this window shortly.

- The **Show Desktop button** was a visible button on the Windows 7 taskbar, but it is hidden in Windows 10. Clicking in the very bottom-right corner of your screen temporarily hides all open windows on the desktop. Clicking the button again restores all previously minimized windows.

Viewing Taskbar Thumbnails

When you hover your mouse over a button on the taskbar, a pop-up showing a live thumbnail image of the running program appears (see Figure 2-14). If that program is minimized, mousing over the thumbnail image temporarily brings that application to the foreground without having to restore it to the desktop.

This is an excellent way to get a quick peek at what is going on in a program. Because the thumbnails are completely live, you can see any progress bars or motion in the thumbnail that is occurring in the window at that time. This is useful for keeping an eye on programs that you only want running in the background while they complete tasks.

▪ **Tip**   When you move your mouse over a thumbnail, a Close button appears in its top-right corner. You can click it to quickly close the program.

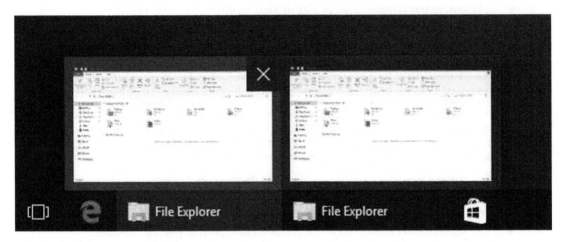

Figure 2-14. *Using live thumbnail previews on the taskbar*

Using Taskbar Jump Lists

I find Jump Lists to be one of the most useful features of Windows (see Figure 2-15). I use them all the time. They are pop-up menus that appear above program buttons on the taskbar. You display a Jump List by right-clicking a taskbar button, or by clicking it and dragging upward with your mouse or finger. Jump Lists make actions with desktop programs simple, such as providing quick access to your commonly or recently used files, or opening multiple instances of a program, or closing windows that are hidden deep in the background of a busy working desktop environment.

▪ **Tip**   You can open multiple instances of an open program by clicking the taskbar icon with the center button on your mouse, if you have one (sometimes pressing down on the mouse scroll wheel performs the same action).

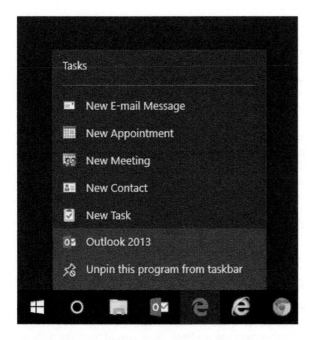

Figure 2-15. *A Windows 10 taskbar Jump List*

Jump Lists can contain any of the following elements:

- **Recently opened files** in a program for quick access. Some apps, such as Microsoft Edge, show a list of frequently visited web sites, and audio and video apps can display a list of recently played files.

- **Pinned files** that always display in the Jump Lists for quick file access.

- **Tasks** that can be performed with a program.

- The **Program Launch**, which is very useful if you want to start multiple instances of a program.

- The **Unpin** button unpins the program from the taskbar.

- The **Close Window** button closes the program.

■ **Tip**   You don't need to open a file to pin it to the Jump List for the associated program; just drag the file's icon onto the program's icon on the taskbar to pin the file there.

Jump Lists are programmable, not only by software packages but also by web sites. You can drag a web site's icon from the address bar in the desktop version of both Edge and Internet Explorer and pin it to the taskbar by dropping it there. Many web sites, such as Facebook and Outlook.com, are programmed to provide quick links to specific parts of the site or specific features.

Managing Windows on the Desktop

When you have a lot of windows open on your desktop, things can get very muddled. You can use the taskbar thumbnails to give you previews or quick views of windows. But what if you want to clean away all but the current working window or work on two windows together?

Both of these tasks are easy with the Windows shake and snap features. Shake allows you to grab and shake a window. This has the effect of automatically minimizing every window except the one you're shaking.

Sometimes you want to work on two documents, side by side, or maybe even three or four apps simultaneously, perhaps to move data from one to another, or to compare two web pages or documents. You can do this by dragging windows to the far left or right of the desktop, or into the four corners of the screen. When you do this, an outline appears, indicating that the window will fill exactly half the screen, or a quarter of the screen if you've dragged it into a corner. You can use this feature to snap up to four windows on your screen, which can be useful for comparing documents, working on multiple windows simultaneously, or moving or copying from one location to another. I show you how to get the best out of this functionality in Chapter 8.

Using the Action Center to Manage Notifications

The new Action Center (see Figure 2-16) is the central location in Windows for all important app notifications and system messages, and it pops out from the right side of your screen. You access it by clicking the notification icon in the far right of the taskbar system tray, or by swiping inward from the right side of your screen, or by pressing Windows key + A. This icon, which looks a bit like a speech bubble, highlights when there are notifications for you to read.

■ **Tip**　You can open the Action Center on a Windows 10 Mobile smartphone by swiping downward from the top of your screen with your finger.

The Notification Center shows all of your available notifications grouped by category; for example, it groups all unread emails together and all messages from Windows or an app, in different groups.

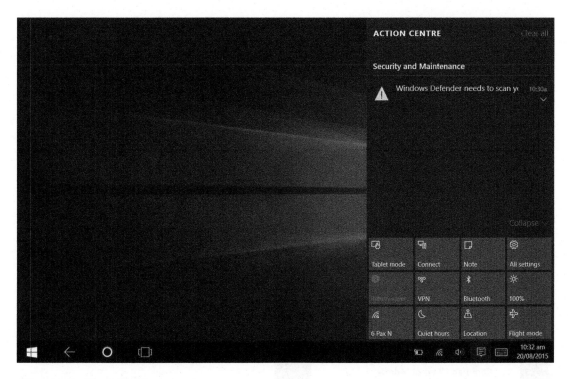

Figure 2-16. *The Action Center*

You can interact with notifications in several ways, including swiping them off the right side of your screen with your mouse or finger to dismiss them. Some notifications, depending on app support, show a downward (expand) arrow that can be used to display more information, such as the content of a message, and some apps even allow you to respond to messages or emails directly in the notification without having to open the app itself. Other notifications display selection buttons, allowing you to perform actions such as dismissing calendar reminders. Lastly, you can dismiss all notifications at once by clicking the **Clear all** link in the top right of your screen.

Right-clicking (touching and holding) a notification displays a context menu of options, including completely turning off all future notifications for that particular app. You can also click **Go to notification settings** to open the Settings app and choose which apps are allowed to notify you, or even turn off notifications completely. These buttons also have an **Expand** link that you can press to show (or hide) additional buttons.

■ **Tip** If you sign in to your Windows 10 PCs using a Microsoft account, any notifications dismissed on one device is also dismissed on all of your other devices, including PCs, tablets, and smartphones, so you don't need to see each notification more than once.

At the bottom of the Notification Center are quick access buttons to common and useful Windows features, such as Settings, Tablet mode, and Bluetooth and Wi-Fi connectivity. You can click any button to directly launch the feature or options for that feature. Some of these buttons can be customized in the Settings app; I'll show you how to do this in Chapter 9.

The Windows Administration Menu

Although the Start menu offers quick links to features such as the Settings app, if you want quick access to the full Control Panel, Command Prompt, and other features that you are familiar with in Windows, you can still access them easily with the Windows Administration menu. Right-clicking with your mouse on the Windows button, or tapping and holding it with your finger (it's also accessible by pressing the Windows key + X) brings up a menu of options, such as Run and Command Prompt. This menu offers a great many administration options and controls for your PC (see Figure 2-17).

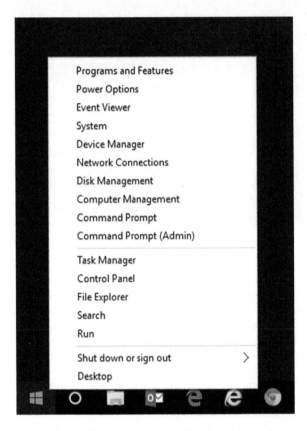

Figure 2-17. *The Win+X menu in Windows 10*

Using the Date and Time Dialog Box

The Date and Time dialog box, which is viewable by clicking the date and time on the taskbar, is very powerful, and one of its best features is the calendar. (I explain how to configure the settings in Chapter 9.) At the top of the calendar are up and down arrows that navigate to the previous or next month (see Figure 2-18).

Figure 2-18. *The date and time accessible from the taskbar*

Clicking the month name changes the display to show all the months in the current year. Clicking it again shows more years from which you can choose. This makes it an excellent tool for quickly locating dates. You can also add up to two additional clocks to this view, which display graphically when you click the time and date on the taskbar (see Figure 2-19), or that display as a pop-up when you hover your mouse over it. (Again, I show you how to configure this in Chapter 9.)

Figure 2-19. Using the calendar and additional clocks

Using the Microsoft Edge Web Browser

Edge is the new web browser in Windows 10, and as such it should be discussed first because it's the app you're most likely to use. Edge is a Store app in Windows 10, which means that it will be updated regularly with new features, but the core functionality of Edge won't change over time. Thus you might find that some things in your current version of Edge vary slightly from what I cover here.

When you open Edge, which is the blue "e" icon on the taskbar, similar to the Internet Explorer icon (this is deliberate to help you find it), you see that it has a very clean look (see Figure 2-20). Along the top are your tabs for web sites. Each tab has a close (X) button to its right and to the right of all the currently open tabs is a new tab (+) button.

Figure 2-20. *Microsoft Edge has a clean look to it*

Below the tabs are a series of buttons...

- **Back** to move back a page.

- **Forward** is used if you've moved back by one or several pages, and then want to return forward again.

- **Refresh** reloads the current page, which is useful if you're waiting for something on the page to update, such as financial or sports information.

- **Home** is an optional button that's disabled by default but that you can switch on (I'll show you how shortly) that takes you immediately to the home page you have set in Edge.

- Sitting between the Home button and the Reading mode button is the **address bar**. Here you type the address of web sites that you want to visit.

- **Reading mode** is not available for all web sites. If clicked, it switches the view to a special reading mode that better resembles a book or magazine, streamlining the text and images and removing extra content such as advertisements, menus, and buttons. Click the Reading View button again to return to normal mode.

- **Favorites** allows you to add the current web page to your Internet Favorites (if you're signed in to your PC using a Microsoft account, this is automatically synchronized across all your Windows 10 devices) or to a reading list. I'll show you how to work with favorites and reading lists shortly.

- The **Hub** is where you can access all your saved Internet Favorites, reading lists, browsing history, and downloads. To the right of this pop-out panel is a **pin** icon that you can click to permanently pin the Hub to the right edge of Edge.

- **Web notes** is a really cool feature that allows you to annotate and otherwise scrawl all over web pages, and then save or share them. I'll show you how to use this shortly.

- **Share** allows you to share the current web page with other Windows Store apps on your PC.

- The **Menu** is signified by three dots. I'll show you what's in the menu options and how to get the best from them shortly.

Using the Address Bar in Edge to Stay Safe Online

These days, every web browser changes the color of text in the address bar to alert you to safe, potentially unsafe, and known malware web sites. Edge (and Internet Explorer) displays text in green (safe), amber (potentially unsafe), or red (known unsafe) to inform you about web sites (see Figure 2-21).

Figure 2-21. *The address bar alerts you about safe and unsafe web sites*

If a web site shows the padlock icon, it means that there is a secure certificate for the web site and that all traffic is encrypted. This is important for everything from email to online banking. You can click the padlock icon to get more information about the security certificate, and if you have *any doubts at all* about the web site, you can use this to check that the company name on the security certificate matches the web site name.

Additionally, many spam and phishing emails try to disguise the links they want you to click, pretending that they're from a reputable company or bank, when actually they're not. Edge (and Internet Explorer) helps here too by highlighting in bold the *actual* web domain you're visiting.

Managing and Saving Internet Favorites in Edge

We all have a list of Favorites that we like to visit, and Edge is no different than any other browser in providing this. If you click the Hub icon, you are immediately presented with any Internet Favorites that you have saved (see Figure 2-22). There is also an **import favorites** link that will auto-detect any other web browsers you have installed, and allow you to easily import any save favorites you have in those browsers to Edge.

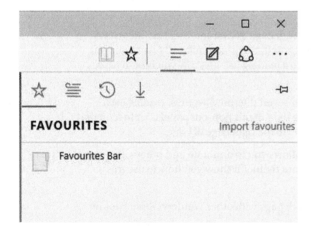

Figure 2-22. *You can easily access Internet Favorites in Edge*

To save a new Internet favorite, click the **Favorites** button to the right of the address bar. You will be asked what you want to call the favorite, and which Favorites folder you want to save it in, or if you want to create a new folder (see Figure 2-23). Folders are a great way to organize your favorites if you have many of them.

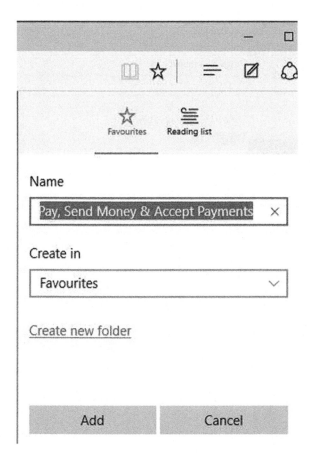

Figure 2-23. *You can save Favorites from the address bar icons*

You can show a Favorites bar below the address bar if you wish, on which you can pin quick links to the web sites that you visit most often. This can make accessing those favorites really quick and simple. To activate this feature, open the Edge menu (by clicking the three dots icon) and turn on the **Show the favorites bar** switch (see Figure 2-24). To save a favorite to the Favorites bar, save it to the **Favorites bar** folder. You can later drag and drop these favorites to arrange them how you like.

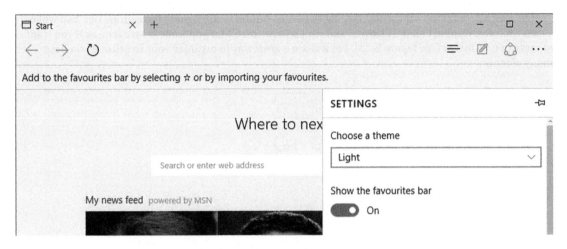

Figure 2-24. You can display Internet favorites in a bar below the address bar

Using the Reading List in Edge

Sometimes you want to be able to save something on a web site to read later, but you don't want to fill up your favorites with lots of articles that you'll read once and then discard. When you click the Favorites button, you are also given the option to save a web page to your reading list, as seen in Figure 2-23.

You can open your reading list by clicking the Hub icon and then clicking the Reading List icon. Each item in the reading list appears with an image (if available) and a short summary of the title (see Figure 2-25).

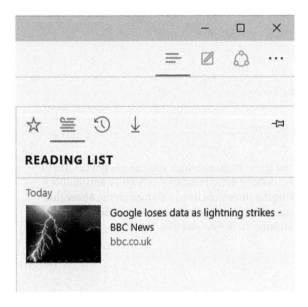

Figure 2-25. You can save web site to a reading list

You can click an item in the reading list to reopen that page, just as you would with an Internet favorite, and you can right-click (tap and hold) on the item to display a **Remove** option, useful for when you no longer want to keep the item.

Using Web Notes to Annotate and Share Web Pages

Probably the coolest feature of Edge is its ability to let you annotate and share whole web pages or just snippets of pages. Clicking the web notes button on the Edge toolbar opens the editing and annotation options (see Figure 2-26).

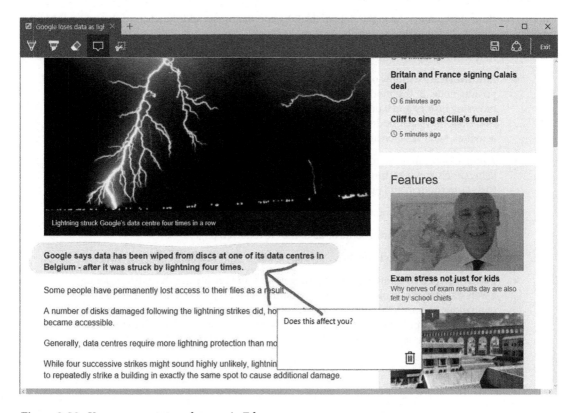

Figure 2-26. *You can annotate web pages in Edge*

The available options let you draw (with your mouse or finger) in different colors, highlight text in different colors and styles, clear what you've already done, add typed or handwritten notes, and cut out areas of a web page. When you cut an area of a web page, which you can do with your mouse or by drawing with your finger, the selected area is automatically copied to your PC's clipboard, ready to be pasted into a graphics app, an email, or any other app that supports pasting from the clipboard.

To the right of the annotation options is a button to **Save** the current page, either to your favorites or to your reading list, or you can send it to someone, perhaps via email. If you save the page to your favorites, anything that's been annotated is locked so that if the web page changes, those changes won't be reflected in your annotations.

Next to it is a **Share** button that allows you to share the annotated page on other Store apps, such as email and social networking. Last, an **Exit** button at the far right allows you to exit the annotation tool, perhaps when there's nobody else in a picture to draw a moustache on.

Edge Settings and Options

Clicking the three dots menu icon to the right of the Edge toolbar opens additional controls and access to the browser settings. Included in these controls are the following:

- **New window** opens a new Edge browser window on your desktop**.**

- **New InPrivate window** opens a new instance of the Edge browser in a special private mode. In this mode, Edge does not store any information about your browsing history and it does not allow tracking or other cookies to be stored from web sites. InPrivate mode is very useful when you want to disguise your online activities, such as when shopping for gifts.

- **Zoom** allows you to zoom into an out of a web page. With touch you can do this using pinch-zoom gestures with two fingers, and with a keyboard you can use Ctrl -/+ to zoom in and out.

- **Find on page** allows you to search a web page for specific text.

- **Print** enables you to print some or all of the current web page.

- **Pin to Start** pins a quick link to a web page on your Start menu.

- **F12 Developer Tools** are used by web developers and businesses that wish to debug a web site or make an older web site compatible with Edge. If you find that a web site or an older company Intranet site doesn't display properly, you can open these tools, and in the **Emulation** tab of the window that appears, you can select a different web browser that the site works in to help manage compatibility (see Figure 2-27).

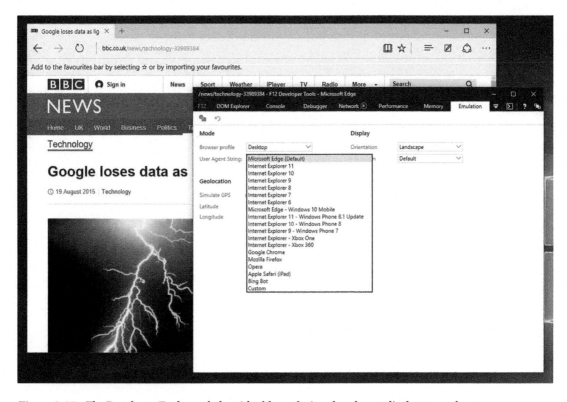

Figure 2-27. *The Developer Tools can help with older web sites that do not display properly*

- **Open with Internet Explorer** only appears in the Pro and Enterprise editions of Windows 10, because only these versions include the legacy Internet Explorer web browser.

- **Settings** allows you to open the settings for Edge (see Figure 2-28). The settings are straightforward and easy to understand; they include the options to choose a color scheme and your home (start) page, as well as what happens when you open a new tab and how Reading mode displays. Below these options is a button to access the advanced settings. I'll show you what's in there in Chapter 9.

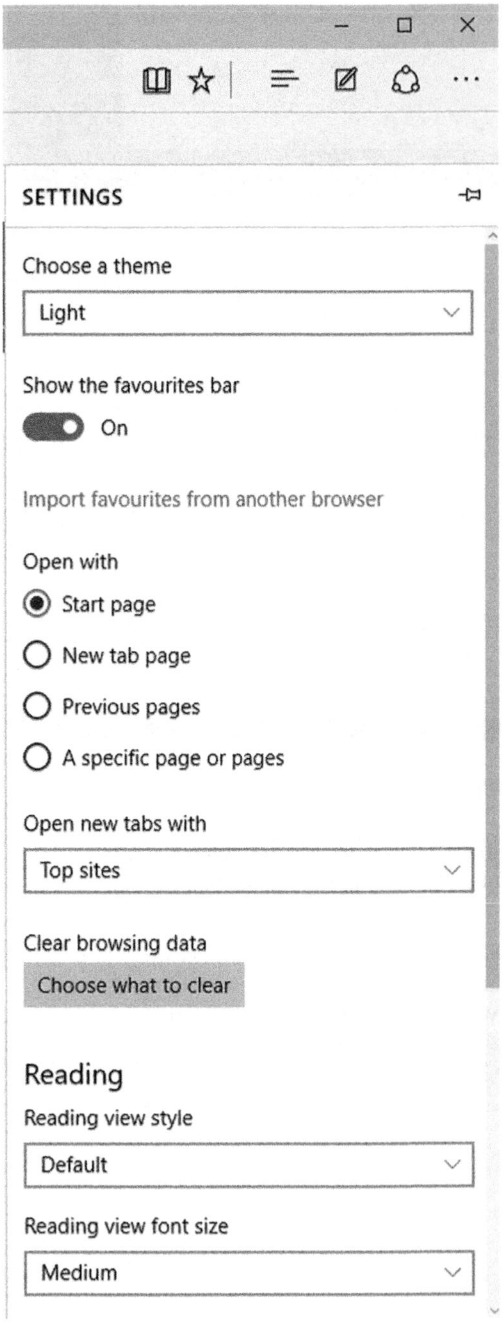

Figure 2-28. *The Settings in Edge are easy to understand*

Preinstalled Windows 10 Apps

There are a great many apps provided with Windows 10. Many are the standard apps that you now expect to find bundled with an OS or are there to showcase the capabilities of the system. I will discuss the apps with features that can genuinely aid productivity. I won't detail all the included apps with Windows 10, partly because they may vary depending on where you bought your PC, but also because they'll be updated on a regular basis and going into too much detail now will likely mean that by the time you read this, the apps will be a different color and have space thrusters on them.

■ **Note**   One of the biggest advantages of the default apps in Windows 10 is that they are more regularly updated than previously experienced with desktop programs.

Alarms and Clocks

This app is available on all Windows 10 devices, including smartphones, and it offers some great functionality. Not only can you set alarms to wake you in the morning or to notify you at an important time, but a countdown timer and a stopwatch are also available.

Perhaps the most useful feature in the Alarms and Clock app is the ability to view a world map, with the local time of anywhere you specify (see Figure 2-29). The map also very helpfully shows you which parts of the world are currently in daylight.

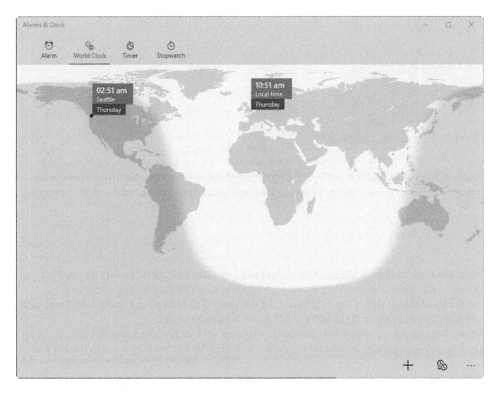

Figure 2-29. *You can view a world clock in the Alarms and Clock app*

Calculator

Also found in all Windows 10 devices, including smartphones, the Calculator app is very powerful indeed. It offers Standard, Scientific, and Programmer modes, as well as a calculation history view and unit conversions of everything from length and weight to data and pressure (see Figure 2-30).

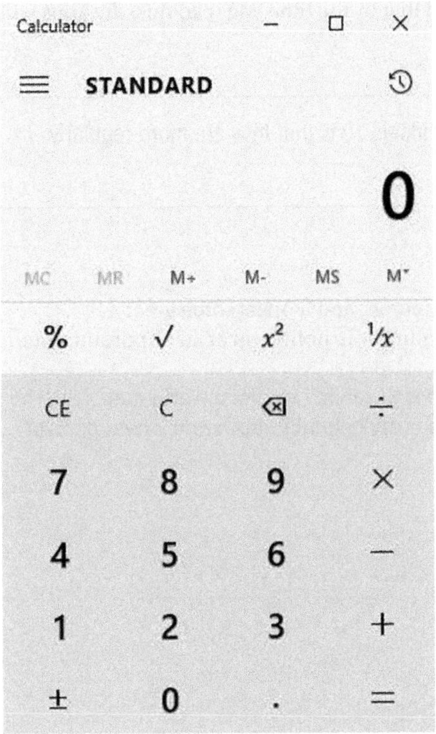

Figure 2-30. *The Calculator app in Windows 10*

You can choose different calculator types by clicking the hamburger icon. The clock icon near the top right of the app opens the history view, which on the desktop and tablet you can extend the size of the app sideways.

Calendar

When you log in to Windows 10 using a Microsoft account linked to a Hotmail, MSN, Live, or an Outlook. com account, Windows Calendar automatically syncs your appointments and shows any upcoming appointments on the lock screen. This is especially useful if you use a Windows phone and you manage your calendar there, or if you log in using an ID linked to a Microsoft Exchange server.

By default, the Calendar app shows several different calendars, such as birthdays and national holidays (see Figure 2-31). You can switch these individual calendars on and off by unchecking them in the left panel of the app.

Figure 2-31. Turning individual calendars on and off

Additional options, such as adding more calendars to the app, can be accessed by clicking the Settings (cog) icon in the bottom right of the vertical toolbar. This app can be found in all Windows 10 devices, including smartphones.

Character Map

The Character Map allows you to view all available text characters from the installed fonts on your computer. You can copy these characters, many of which are not available via a keyboard combination, and paste them into your documents.

■ **Tip** You can get quick access to common international characters with the onscreen keyboard by pressing and holding the associated root letter. International variants then appear around it; these can be individually selected.

Film & TV / Groove Music

These are Microsoft's new video and music apps, where you can purchase or stream video and music from the Microsoft Store. These apps are in all Windows 10 devices, including smartphones. I'll talk more about these apps in Chapter 7.

Mail

Windows 10's Mail app (see Figure 2-32) is a powerful and fully featured email client. It includes support for full-text formatting, the pasting of images into emails (for example, from the editing features in Edge), and the management of multiple email folders and email signatures. This app is in all Windows 10 devices, including smartphones.

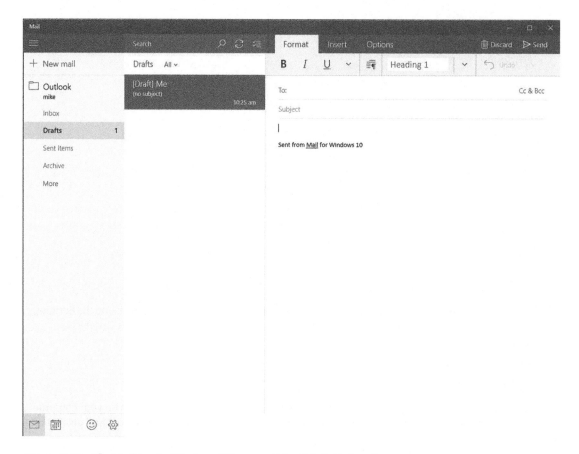

Figure 2-32. *The Mail app in Windows 10 is powerful and fully featured*

If you have signed in to your PC using a Microsoft account, the mail app is automatically set up for you, but you can click the Settings (cog) icon in the bottom right of the left panel to add more email accounts and to choose how much email you wish to download to your device; for example, from the past week, past month, or all of your email.

Maps

Maps is one of the most useful and powerful apps in Windows 10. It does everything you expect a standard mapping app to do, such as support both road and aerial views, but it also contains a quick and effective route planner with the ability to use an Internet connection to show traffic congestion; its built-in GPS (or location information obtained from your IP address) pinpoints your location. This app is in all Windows 10 devices, including smartphones.

Math Input Panel

If you have a stylus for your computer or tablet, Math Input is useful for turning scribbled equations and formulas into text that can be inserted into your documents. It is extremely good at recognizing handwriting, as you can see in Figure 2-33 (it's not easy writing on my laptop's screen, honest).

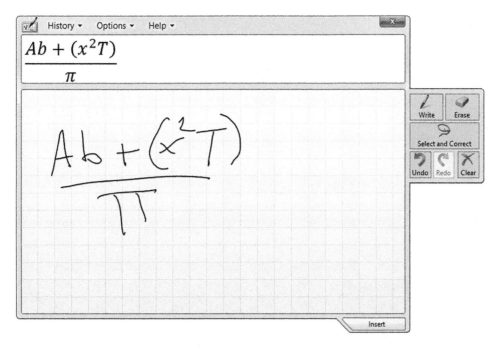

Figure 2-33. *The Math Input window*

Messaging / Phone / Video

For some years now, Skype has been the go-to app for video communication and conference calls. Skype is now a part of Windows in the Messaging, Phone, and Video apps, allowing you to make and receive both audio and video calls on whatever device you are using; you can also have text chats with friends and colleagues. The Messaging app integrates well with the Action Center, allowing you to continue messaging chats without needing to open the app itself. For those needing more control over the Skype experience, though, the full win32 desktop app is available to download from www.skype.com.

Office Mobile (Word / Excel / PowerPoint / OneNote)

If you have a Windows laptop, tablet, or smartphone with a screen smaller than 10 inches, it has come preinstalled with free copies of Microsoft's Office Mobile apps. These apps include Word, Excel (see Figure 2-34), PowerPoint, and OneNote. If your screen is larger than 10 inches, the apps are available to purchase from the Windows Store and also come with an Office 365 account.

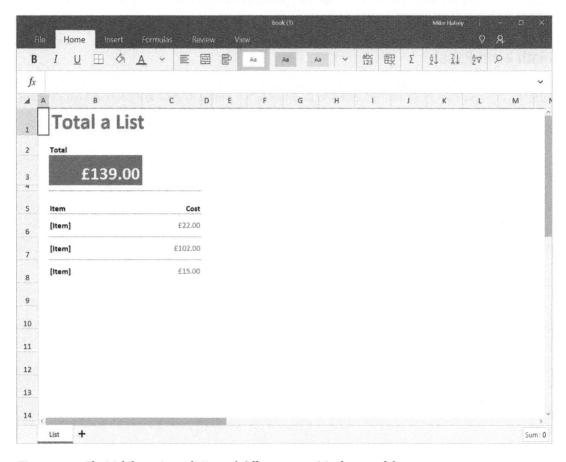

Figure 2-34. *The Mobile versions of Microsoft Office are surprisingly powerful*

These apps are surprisingly powerful, and they provide all the power and functionality most people will ever need. They've also been optimized for touch control too, so they work fine on tablets. I'll show you how to use these apps in Chapter 8.

People

The People app is where you can view and manage the information you store about the people in your contacts list, including their email addresses and phone numbers. Your work contacts are stored here if you sign in to Windows 10 using a work account. Contacts are drawn from your email account and from social networks that you connected to your Microsoft account (such as Facebook and LinkedIn). A useful feature is the chain-link icon located in the top right of the app when viewing a contact. It can be used to link contacts if you find that one person is appearing twice because his contact information is coming from different places.

Phone Companion

Getting smartphone connectivity on a PC can often be a difficult and fiddly process. In Windows 10, Microsoft has greatly simplified and streamlined the process with the Phone Companion app (see Figure 2-35). This app can connect to Microsoft Windows, Google Android, and Apple iPhone smartphones. It allows you to manage the music, video, and photos on the handset and helps you back up your precious memories. Fairly obviously, this app is not available on Windows 10 Mobile devices.

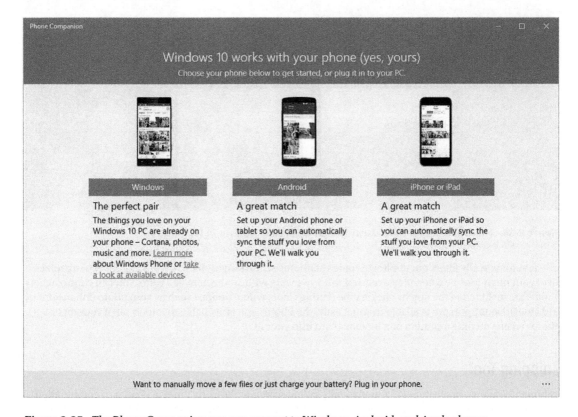

Figure 2-35. *The Phone Companion app can connect to Windows, Android, and Apple phones*

Photos

The Photos app in Windows 10 is extremely useful and powerful, and during the development of the OS, Microsoft put a lot of effort into telling testers and the media how good it is, which is unusual for an app. The Photos app pulls together all of your pictures from your different Windows 10 devices and services, including smartphones and your OneDrive storage, and sorts them into albums (see Figure 2-36).

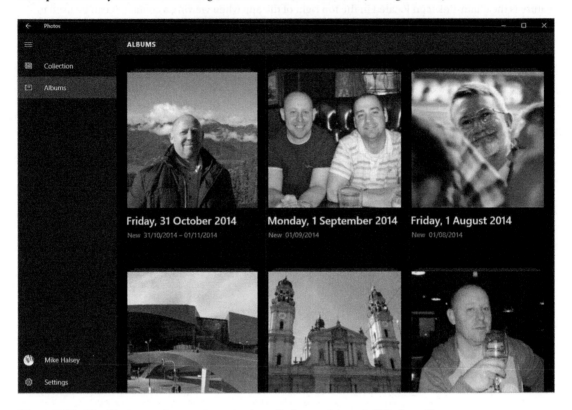

Figure 2-36. *The Photos app is a great way to view all of your pictures in Windows 10*

It automatically filters out duplicate copies of photos and arranges them in ways to help you organize all of your memories by when they occurred, who you were with, and where you were. You can control what photos are included in the app by clicking the Settings icon, where options such as auto photo enhancement and OneDrive support are available to you. Lastly, the Photos app is available to import all of your digital photos when you plug a camera or a memory card into your PC.

Snipping Tool

Although Windows 10's feature for automatically saving screen grabs using the Win+PrntScrn combination is welcome (Power key + Volume Up on a Windows 10 smartphone), sometimes you just want to capture a specific window or a part of the screen. This is where the Snipping Tool is useful. It can grab any part of your screen, in any shape, and save it as a file (see Figure 2-37). One useful feature of the Snipping Tool is the Delay feature, which allows you to delay the capture for up to 5 seconds, making it possible to capture open menu dialogs and other transitionary interface elements in Windows and apps. This app is not available on Windows 10 Mobile devices.

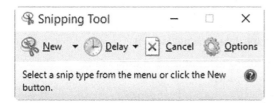

Figure 2-37. *The Snipping Tool*

Sticky Notes

Sticky Notes were formerly gadgets on the Windows Vista sidebar, but in Windows 7, they made their way into the Start menu as a full program. Sticky Notes still exist in Windows 10 as a useful way to put notes on your desktop without getting glue all over the screen (please don't try that at home!).

Xbox

This is a great app if you have an Xbox One games console, or if you like to play Xbox Live games on your PC. It allows you to view your gaming activity, achievements, and friends; you can also record games and interact with other people by using messaging. I'll talk more about the Xbox app in Chapter 7.

Other Windows 10 Apps

The following are other apps included with Windows 10:

- **3D Builder** is a way to design three-dimensional shapes that can be printed using a 3D printer (Windows 10 includes full support for 3D printers) or viewed using the Microsoft HoloLens augmented reality headset. This app is not available on Windows 10 Mobile devices.

- **Camera** is on all devices with a physical camera, including smartphones. You can take photos, record video, and perform basic editing functions.

- **Contact Support** provides an easy way to get help and support from Microsoft if you are experiencing problems with your PC copy of Windows 10. This app is not available on Windows 10 Mobile devices.

- **Food and Drink** contains recipes and useful information on diet and nutrition.

- **Get Office** is useful if you don't have a copy of Microsoft Office, or if you already subscribe to Office 365, because it helps you download and install the Office apps. By using this app, you can get a free month-long trial of Office 365. I talk more about Microsoft Office in Chapter 8.

- **Get Started** offers hints and tips on how to use and get the best from Windows 10... not that you'd need it. This app is not available on Windows 10 Mobile devices.

- **Health & Fitness** contains news and information about health, fitness, diet, and exercise.

- **Microsoft Wi-Fi** is a subscription service that can connect you to many paid-for public Wi-Fi networks worldwide. This can help keep you online when you are out and about, or traveling.

- **Money** is an app used to track stocks, shares, and currencies. You can select what you want to follow and then be automatically updated in a live tile. Bear in mind that there is a delay (usually around 30 minutes) in the data presented to you.

- **News** is a news and current affairs aggregator, pulling in headlines and stories from many different news agencies and web sites, worldwide.

- **Notepad** has been on Windows now for decades. It's a very basic text editor that's very popular with coders and programmers. This app is not available on Windows 10 Mobile devices.

- **Paint** is another app that's been in Windows for decades. It is a very basic painting, drawing, and image editing app. This app is not available on Windows 10 Mobile devices.

- **Scan** is a useful app that can be used with your home or office scanner to scan documents and photos to your PC. It works with USB and network scanners. This app is not available on Windows 10 Mobile devices.

- **Sport** is similar to the news app in that it aggregates sport headlines and stories from around the world.

- **Windows Fax and Scan** is a utility that can be used to scan documents and pictures from your scanner, just like the Scan app, but that can also be used to send faxes. Your PC needs a modem installed to use this feature. This app is not available on Windows 10 Mobile devices.

- **Windows Journal** is a note-taking app, which can be used to jot down reminders and lists, and to help you organize your thoughts and workflow. This app is not available on Windows 10 Mobile devices.

- **WordPad** is a slimmed-down word processor. It can be used for writing documents and letters that can be saved, emailed, or printed. This app is not available on Windows 10 Mobile devices.

- **Voice Recorder** can be used to record voice conversations or music for either short or long periods. You may want to use it to record a tune or perhaps a college lecture.

- **XPS Viewer** is an app that lets you view and read documents stored in the XPS file format, which is an alternative to PDF. This app is not available on Windows 10 Mobile devices.

Finding and Installing Apps from the Windows Store

The Windows Store is where you can find and download more apps for your PC. You need to sign in to the Store with a Microsoft account to use it. Downloading apps from the Windows Store (to find it, search for **Store** in the Start menu) has many advantages over the older-style win32 desktop apps, in that all submitted apps are rigorously tested for stability and to make sure they don't include malware.

The Store categorizes all apps appropriately, but it also gives you access to additional content, such as games, music, and video. In the top right of the Store app is a search box that allows you to quickly find the app or the type of app that you want. Next to this is your Microsoft account avatar. You can click this avatar to get access to controls for your Store account, such as the apps that you already purchased, your Store settings, and your payment options (see Figure 2-38).

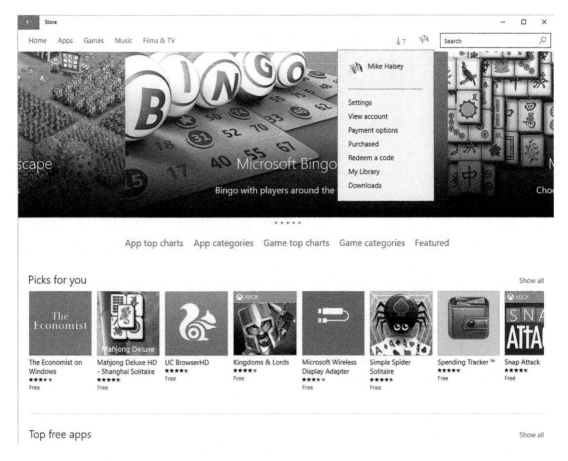

Figure 2-38. *You can get apps from the Windows Store*

Next to your account avatar is a downloads indicator that appears when any app downloads (and app updates) are currently in progress. By clicking it, you can pause and cancel downloads, as well as fix any problems that may occur with downloads, such as the Store informing you that you cannot download an app over a 4G/LTE connection and need to be first connected to Wi-Fi.

By default, all Windows Store apps are updates automatically when new versions are released. If you wish to, you can disable this feature in the Store settings. Also, if you have previously purchased apps and wish to download them to a different Windows 10 PC, click your avatar, followed by **My library**, where you can see all of your purchased apps. Any apps that are not installed on the current device have a download indicator to their right. Click this icon to download and install the app, whereupon it appears in the Start menu's All Apps list.

Uninstalling Store and win32 Apps

Each app in Windows 10 can be uninstalled by right-clicking (touching and holding) its icon in the Start menu or All Apps list, and selecting **Uninstall** from the options that appear. If the app came from the Windows Store, it is automatically and seamlessly uninstalled.

When you uninstall win32 desktop apps in Windows 10, you are taken to the **Programs and Features** options on the Control Panel. Here you find a list of all the win32 software installed on your computer. You can click the column headers (Name, Publisher, Installed On, etc.) to sort and arrange the software to make it easier to organize (see Figure 2-39). You may want to arrange your list by date, for example, to see the most recently installed software first; you can do this by clicking the column headers to sort your programs in ascending (one click) or descending (two clicks) order.

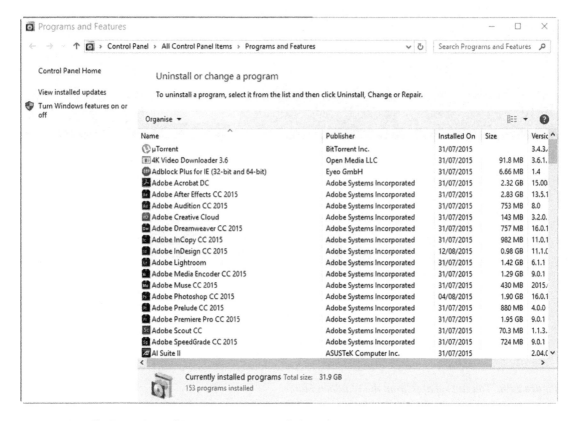

Figure 2-39. *The Programs and Features page in Windows 8*

To uninstall apps (and desktop software) from the Start screen, right-click (touch and hold) an app and select **Uninstall** from the app bar (see Figure 2-37).

Summary

Using apps in Windows 10 is easier than it's ever been, and the redesigned Start menu offers interesting and innovative ways to organize and arrange your apps. Live tiles can be incredibly useful, enabling you to see information as it arrives from your email, calendar, finances, news, and more. When it comes to using apps, there might be differences between small Windows 10 tablets and larger screens, and you might wonder why the Office Mobile apps are available on one of your devices but not others, but the experience across all Windows 10 devices is surprisingly fluid and consistent.

You've had a look around now and this is the part of the book where we'll start examining all of these components in much more detail, from how you connect to networks and the Internet, to how you can get the best from your apps, and how to customize both the Start menu and Windows itself. If you want to get the very best from your PC, you've certainly come to the right place!

■ ■ ■

CHAPTER 3

Connecting to Networks and the Internet

Windows 10 is the best-connected version of the Windows operating system (OS) yet. It includes support for new wireless standards such as 4G mobile broadband. It's also simpler to connect to networks than ever before, but with this flexibility and simplicity come new dangers to your personal security and that of your files.

In this chapter, I want to take a holistic look at safely and securely connecting to networks and the Internet. You don't want to worry about securely checking your email. Worse still, you don't want to worry about your business or personal data being open and available to hackers and coffee-shop Wi-Fi thieves.

I will give you the knowledge you need to use network and Internet connections safely and securely, whether you are at home, at work, or on the move. This is especially important as we keep more of our personal and business lives in digital files and in online cloud services. With all our precious photographs, music, documents, and business projects now stored digitally, we need to be certain that we're protected on any device, because everything is now interconnected in ways we've not previously experienced.

Getting Online with Windows 10

One of the very first things you do with a PC is to connect it to the Internet. So much of what you do these days is online; email and social networking are now part of the fabric of society. Long gone are the days when you might use an MSN or IRC chat client for a couple of hours on a weekend. Now it's constant access to chat via PCs and smartphones; social updates across multiple platforms; and access to email, even work email, 24 hours a day.

There really is no getting away from the Internet wherever you go. If you are a web enthusiast, a gamer, an IT pro, at work, or running a business, or even just on your daily commute looking for something to occupy your time, odds are that you'll be on a computer and that you'll be online. Tablets offer multiuser setups, and smartphones and other Windows 10 devices can automatically connect to both public and private Wi-Fi networks using sign-in data shared by your colleagues. Use of Windows 10 is more widespread than in the previous Windows editions that were used only on desktop PCs and laptops. You really do need to make sure that all of your data is safe and secure.

Understanding Public and Home and Work Networks

When you connect to a network for the first time, Windows 10 asks you this question: "Do you want your PC to be discoverable by other PCs and devices on this network?" (see Figure 3-1.) This question is asked because there are differences between home, public, and work networks that determine how the security on your PC should be set up. I want to spend a little time explaining these network differences.

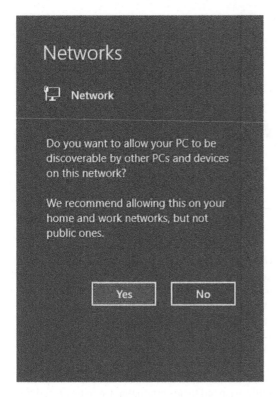

Figure 3-1. Setting network sharing and security on first connect

Home Networks

Home networks are the types where you simply trust everything. You are, after all, in complete control of the network and all the hardware attached to it, including other computers, smartphones, tablets, game consoles, and maybe even storage attached to your home Wi-Fi router. What could possibly go wrong with all this?

Well, for starters, many people are confused by or simply don't understand home network security. Why should they? As consumers, we're used to home electronics being like a television, a microwave, or a Blu-ray player. It's not true that all consumer electronics are simple to use. Take the new Internet-connected smart televisions, for example. Some of these TVs can take three-quarters of an hour to set up the first time you use them. They have a myriad of menus that control tuners, movie and TV downloads, plug-in services, and 3D and surround sound.

With home computer equipment, it can be even more complicated. The most common piece of hardware at fault is the router that connects your home to the Internet. While Internet service providers (ISPs) are much better than they used to be at programming individual Wi-Fi passcodes into devices, they still usually leave the administration password as the default *password* or *admin*.

When coupled with the fact that the name of your Wi-Fi network commonly includes the make and model of the router, it's simple for a neighbor or a drive-by hacker to casually access the router and gain access to your network and the devices and files on it.

While this type of drive-by hack is rare, it is commonly blamed in file-sharing legal cases in which unsuspecting people are accused by the authorities and big movie studios of downloading the latest blockbuster movie.

The first thing to do with your own home network is make sure that you have unique passwords on both your Wi-Fi access and your router's administration interface. How you do this depends on the make and model you have, but your ISP can talk you through it, and the router should come with a manual or help files.

You likely don't only connect to home networks in your own house; you may also connect to home networks at friends' and family members' houses. You have no control over their network or hardware, nor do you have any idea whether they have adequate anti-malware protection on their network-connected computers and devices.

When you connect to their Wi-Fi, however, you know whether they have a strong password or even no password at all (be very careful when connecting to networks in which you don't know whether any of the computers are infected with malware).

Home networks are really for use only in your own safe and secure environment, your little bubble in which you absolutely know the state of your security, and where you can implicitly trust the person who put it all together.

Work Networks

Workplace networks are inherently more trustworthy than home networks because they are managed by qualified personnel (mostly anyway). In a work network, the other computers attached to the network can't see the documents, pictures, music, or video you have shared in HomeGroup (more on this in Chapter 4), but well-written malware can still infect network-connected computers.

Work networks are really only useful only in managed server environments in which a company is running its own Windows Server and you have access to shared storage. If you are connecting to a work network that's run from a Windows Server system, for example, telling Windows that you want to be able to connect with other computers is essential to ensuring that all the relevant network systems in Windows 10 have permission to talk to the server and receive data back from it.

If you are in a workplace, however, in which you are using the network only for Internet access, and your computer is stand-alone or not connected to a server (for example, when you're visiting a client), I don't recommend turning on the sharing settings unless you really have to. The reason for this is that in your own company, you have to take it on trust that the IT department has set security appropriately on the network. You may even manage that network yourself. If it's somewhere else, though, and especially if it's a small business, you don't have any reliable knowledge about how security is set on the network and the router.

Public Networks

For everywhere else, and for your peace of mind, there are public networks. This is what you should *always* use if you are in a public place such as a coffee shop, library, or even connected via a mobile dongle or SIM card.

When you tell Windows you do *not* want to connect to other PCs and devices, the OS throws up its full defenses against other computers and network nasties, not allowing file sharing or other sharing unless you explicitly permit it, and thus preventing people on other computers from getting access to your own PC and its files.

If you are ever uncertain about the network you are connected to, or perhaps you only need to get on the Internet, I recommend you tell Windows 10 not to find other PCs. This is the best way to avoid problems and security concerns.

Connecting to Networks in Windows 10

To connect to networks and the Internet in Windows 10 Home or Pro, click the network connection icon in the system tray area of the taskbar. When you click it, you are shown the different networks that are available for you to connect to (see Figure 3-2). On Windows 10 Mobile devices, you automatically connect to a data network through your SIM card. You can connect to Wi-Fi networks by swiping downward from the top of your screen to open the Action Center, and then tap the Wi-Fi icon.

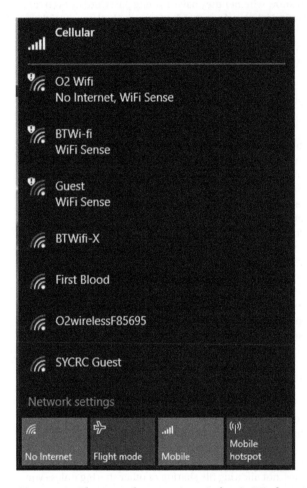

Figure 3-2. *The network connection window in Windows 10*

***

■ **Note** If your PC has an internal SIM card, you also see options for turning the cellular connection on and off, which can be useful to disable it, and for sharing your connection by creating a mobile hotspot. I show you how to do this later in this chapter.

***

CHAPTER 3 ■ CONNECTING TO NETWORKS AND THE INTERNET

If you are connected to a wired Ethernet or a mobile broadband connection, the details of the connection appear at the top of the network connections dialog. If you have Wi-Fi on your PC, below this is a list of currently available Wi-Fi networks that you can connect to, with indicators showing their signal strength. Any unsecured networks, such as a Wi-Fi network that doesn't require a password for you to access it, has a security alert symbol in the top left of the signal indicator. This alerts you that other people can use this network and they may be able to gain access to your PC and files.

At the bottom of the network connections dialog is a link to the Network Settings, which I discuss later in this chapter; if you are using a laptop or a tablet, the on/off controls for your Wi-Fi connection and for Flight mode are located here.

Flight mode (sometimes call *Airplane mode*) was first introduced on mobile phones because radio signals given off by the phones can cause interference with airplane computer systems during takeoff and landing. They can also interfere with other equipment, such as sensitive medical equipment in hospitals. You also find airplane mode settings on GPS-enabled equipment, such as digital cameras. The Airplane mode feature is present in Windows 10 because people now commonly use laptops and tablets with mobile broadband while traveling. Switching on Airplane mode in Windows 10 deactivates all communication signals, effectively cutting off all radio communication from being sent and received by the computer. You are reminded by signage onboard the aircraft or by the cabin crew when you need to activate airplane mode on your computer.

Mobile broadband networks are those you access through a SIM card in your laptop or tablet; through a USB mobile broadband dongle; or by sharing the data connection from your mobile phone, which is now the most common way. There are data usage concerns with mobile broadband because of Windows 10 needing to download updates and drivers over these connection that typically come with limited data allowances, but I show you how to manage this shortly.

Wi-Fi networks are standard home, workplace, or public networks. They have limited range and do not work when you move away from the router or base station.

When you choose a network to connect to, you are asked for the network password if there is one (see Figure 3-3). (Remember to be extremely wary about networks that don't because anybody with nefarious motives can connect and get access to any shared PCs.) There is a box that also allows you to share the network security key for this Wi-Fi network with people in your Windows 10 contacts list. This can make it simpler for you and others to connect to networks in bars, coffee shops, and workplaces, but you might *not* want to select this option for your own home network, where you need tight control over security.

Figure 3-3. *You are asked if you want to share this network connection with your contacts*

You are also asked if you want to always connect automatically to a particular network; this box is checked (selected) by default, but unless you want to connect to this network regularly, you should uncheck it. Just because you are fairly sure that a given network is safe, don't assume that it will always stay secure. All it takes is a single setting to be changed.

Managing Cellular Broadband

As I mentioned earlier, one of the problems with network connections in Windows is that they can be set (deliberately or accidentally) to connect automatically whenever you are in range. I will show you how to manage your network connections shortly, but with 3G or 4G/LTE mobile broadband, this can be a problem, especially if your laptop or tablet has a built-in SIM card.

Mobile data packages regularly cap usage and impose heavy charges for additional data use, so it's bad news if your PC connects to such a network when you don't specifically want it to. This can result in hefty data usage bills if you go over your allotted limit (or you may also find you can't get a connection when you need to because you used up your allotment).

While you can set your mobile broadband connection to *not* connect automatically, the only way to be completely safe and secure is to switch it off when you don't need it. Why do I recommend this? Simply because while we're all used to uncapped Wi-Fi usage at home and at work, mobile broadband is still very expensive. Personally, I am not prepared to risk running up huge bills on my laptop and Windows tablet (both of which have a SIM card slot), so I always have mobile broadband switched off in Windows when I'm not using it.

Mobile broadband connections work in two different ways, depending on if you are using a USB dongle with a SIM card inside or if your PC has an internal SIM card slot. For the former, plugging in your USB dongle treats the mobile broadband connection as a standard wired Ethernet connection. Windows 10 automatically makes a connection to your cellular operator, and this can only be disabled by unplugging the dongle.

If your tablet, laptop, or Ultrabook has 3G/4G LTE built-in, things are different, as obviously you can't easily remove your SIM card when you don't want the PC using cellular data. Instead, clicking the name of the cellular connection in the networks pop-up opens the Settings app and shows you controls such as automatic connections and roaming permission (see Figure 3-4). *Roaming* occurs when your cellular connection is used with mobile operators other than your own, such as when you are abroad. The data charges can be very steep. If your contract does not permit roaming, you are not able to select this item.

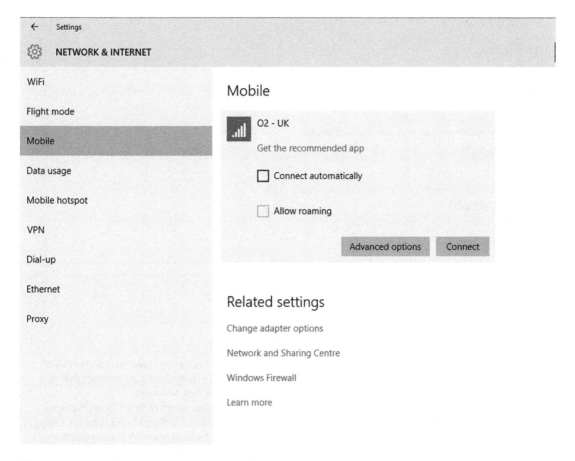

Figure 3-4. *Network & Internet connection options*

Clicking the **Advanced options** button offers you more control over your cellular connection (see Figure 3-5), such as setting it as a metered connection and obtaining optimal network settings over the Internet from the mobile operator, which might improve the connection stability and quality. If you need additional information at any time, such as the IMEI number to identify the SIM, this is also found in the Advanced options panel.

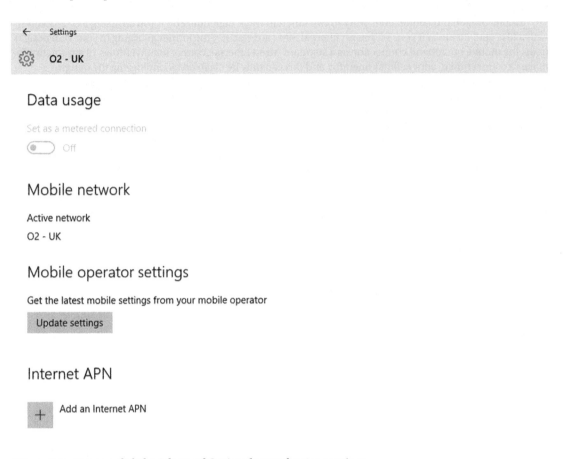

Figure 3-5. *You can click the Advanced Options button for more settings*

Connecting to Hidden Wi-Fi Networks

Wi-Fi networks that are hidden (usually to improve their security) don't appear or give their name in the general network connections panel; you have to enter their settings manually. These are settings that you need to have provided to you by the people responsible for maintaining that network.

Usually when hidden networks are available, you see the text **Hidden network** listed as available to connect to in the Network Connections pop-up on the taskbar. When you click the network, you are asked for the network name and the password. Occasionally, you might find that a hidden Wi-Fi network doesn't appear in the list, but it is still possible to connect to it by following these steps.

1. From the desktop, right-click (or touch and hold) the network icon on the far right of the taskbar. From the pop-up that appears, click **Open the Network and Sharing Center**. You can also search for the Network and Sharing Center from Cortana or the Start menu.

2. In the Network and Sharing Center, click the **Set up a New Connection or Network** link, located roughly in the middle of the page.

3. Click **Manually Connect to a Wireless Network** in the dialog that appears and then click **Next** (see Figure 3-6).

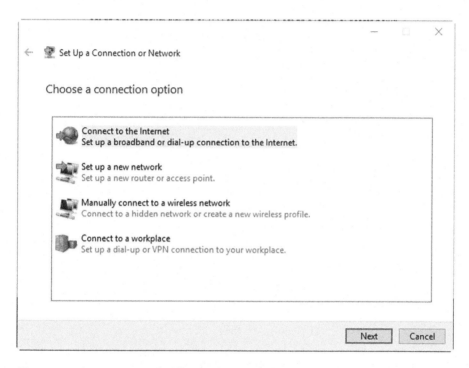

Figure 3-6. *Connecting to a hidden wireless network*

4. On the next page, you are required to enter information that has to be provided by the Wi-Fi network manager. This information includes the name of the network, its security key, and its security encryption type.

You may find it helpful to also check the **Start this Connection Automatically** box, which autoconnects your PC to the hidden Wi-Fi network whenever you are in range of it. This is a different default behavior than if you connect to a network using the network connections panel from the Settings charm.

Connecting to a Company or School Workplace

If you use your Windows 10 laptop or tablet at work, or you have been provided with a Windows 10 PC by your employer, you probably need to connect to the company or college network (often called a *domain*). Sometimes, however, you want to use your own PC, so for this purpose Microsoft introduced a new feature called **Work access**. This feature allows the IT department to grant certain network access permissions to computers and staff members who are not directly connected to the company domain.

1. To connect to a workplace, open the **Settings** app.

2. Click the **Accounts** icon.

3. Click **Work access** on the left of the screen (see Figure 3-7).

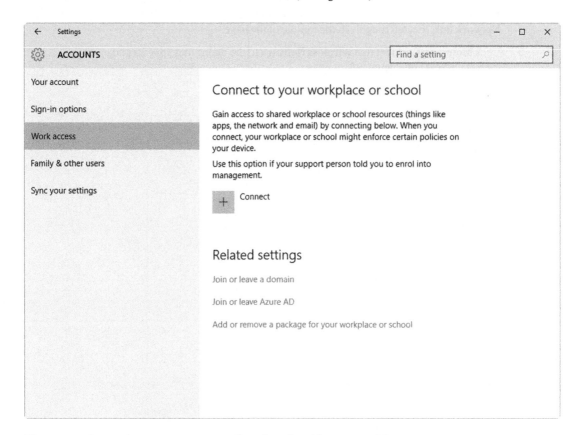

Figure 3-7. *Connecting to a company or college domain with your own PC*

4. Click the **Connect** button.

When you're in the Workplace settings, enter the email ID recognized by your company or college, and the **Continue** button becomes available to click. You may be asked for a password at this point.

Connecting in this way means that you are giving permission for your workplace or college to have some remote management control over your PC. This allows system administrators to remotely install apps and programs that are essential for your role in the workplace. This feature saves you from having to install them manually and helps the IT department ensure that the correct versions are installed and updated in the proper manner. You may be asked by your IT department to click the **Turn on** button to activate this feature.

Connecting to a Virtual Private Network (VPN)

If your company doesn't support the Workplace feature on your PC or if the PC is *only* used in the same workplace, you may need to manually join the company's virtual private network (see Figure 3-8). Doing so gives your computer access to the company's network and shared files and drives, and it also grants the IT department management control of your PC.

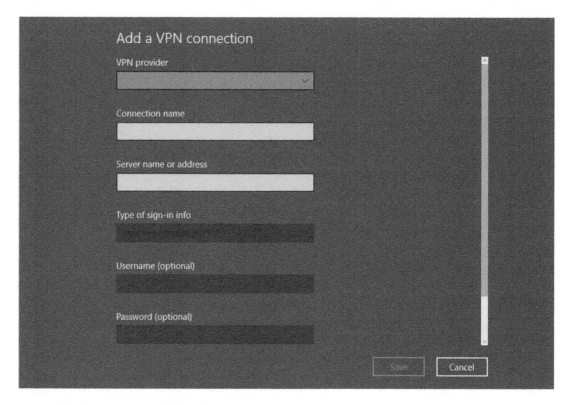

Figure 3-8. *Connecting to a VPN in Windows 10*

To connect to a company VPN, follow these instructions:

1. Open the **Settings** app (you can also get to the VPN connection settings by clicking the network icon on the taskbar and then clicking **Network Settings**).

2. In the Settings app, click **Network & Internet**.

3. Click the **VPN** option in the left panel.

4. Click the **Add a VPN connection** button.

5. You are prompted for information such as the VPN provider and connection name. You should check with your IT department for the correct information to enter here.

6. Click **Save** to make the connection. Optionally, you can ask Windows 10 to remember your sign-in information.

Connecting to a Company Domain or Azure Active Directory (AD)

If you just need to connect your PC to a company domain or Active Directory account, which is something available with an Office 365 business subscription, click **System** in the Settings app and then click the **About** option. You see buttons to join a domain or to join Azure AD. Clicking the former asks you for the name of the domain, which you can get from your IT administrator. Joining Azure AD (see Figure 3-9) asks for the username and password that you have been assigned for your sign-in.

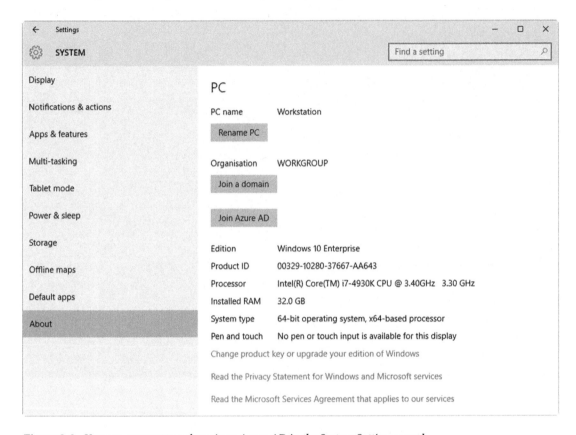

Figure 3-9. *You can connect to a domain or Azure AD in the System Settings panel*

Managing and Deleting Wireless Network Profiles

Windows 10 offers several ways to manage Wi-Fi Internet connections. I mentioned earlier in this chapter that you can share passwords and other access details with your contacts (should you want to). Clicking **Network & Internet** in the Settings app displays a list of available Wi-Fi connections along with an on/off switch for your PC's Wi-Fi. Below these are a couple of links: **Advanced options** and **Manage Wi-Fi Settings**. The first opens a management page for the currently active Wi-Fi connection (see Figure 3-10).

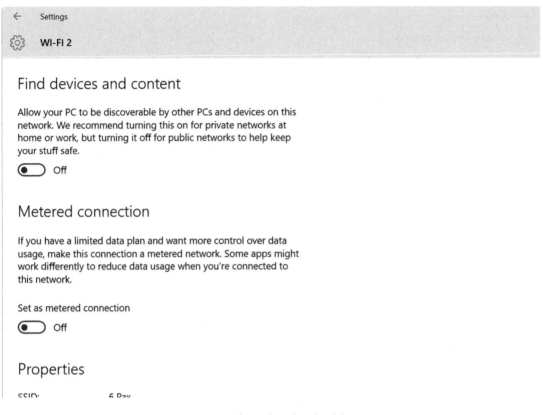

Figure 3-10. *You can set connections as Metered to reduce bandwidth consumption*

Here you can turn on or off the discovery of other PCs and devices on the network. You might want to do this if you have connected to a public network while accidentally allowing your own PC to be visible to other computers, or if you have accidentally specified that your home network should be public.

You can also specify that the current connection should be metered. Metered connections are commonly used when connecting via a cellular connection where there are strict caps on your data usage. Similar to a cellular connection, turning this on for a Wi-Fi connection limits what Windows will download in the background in regards to app and Windows updates.

Lastly there is information about your Wi-Fi connection that might be useful if you need support from an IT specialist. A **copy** button sits below this information, so you can easily copy and paste it into an email should you need to.

The **Manage Wi-Fi Settings** link takes you to a page where you can manage how Wi-Fi connection information is shared with your contacts (see Figure 3-11).

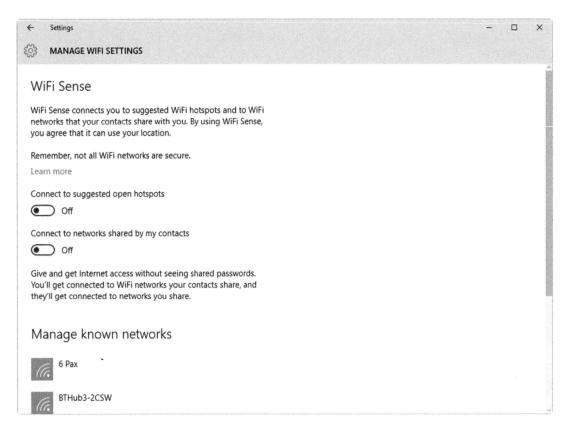

Figure 3-11. *You can manage Wi-Fi Settings from the Settings app*

You can tell Windows 10 to share passwords for Wi-Fi networks with your friends to make it easier for them to sign in to the networks. Similarly, your friends might share passwords with your PC(s) too. What's of real interest though is the **Connect to suggested open hotspots** switch. With this activated, Windows 10 uses information such as your name and email address to automatically sign you in to some open Wi-Fi hotspots, such as those in cafes and airports (note that not all hotspots are compatible with this).

There is a potential privacy issue here, however, and if you do not want Windows 10 giving out your name and email address to the companies managing these hotspots, you can disable the feature by unchecking the switch.

At the bottom of this panel is a list of all the Wi-Fi connections that are known to your PC. Next to each one is information on whether or not it is shared with your friends. Clicking a network name reveals options to share (or not share) the network information, and also to forget the network (see Figure 3-12).

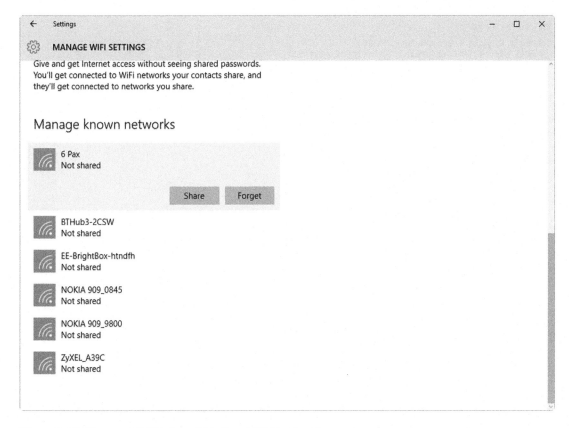

Figure 3-12. *You can tell Windows 10 to forget Wi-Fi networks*

Forgetting a Wi-Fi network can be useful if the settings become scrambled or corrupt, especially if the password changes. If you find that you cannot connect to a network that you previously connected to easily, then telling Windows to "forget" it deletes all the settings you have for that network. The next time you connect, you will be asked for the password again.

It is also possible to manage both Wi-Fi and cellular connections from the Command Prompt. This is more advanced, but I mention it because of the ability to manage cellular networks and tell Windows 10 to forget them. You can manage these connections from the Command Prompt by following these instructions.

1. Open the **Command Prompt** from the WinX menu (Press Win+X on your keyboard, right-click in the bottom left of your screen, or search for **Command Prompt** in the Search charm).

2. In the Command window, type **netsh wlan show profiles** and press **Enter**. A list of your stored Wi-Fi networks appears (see Figure 3-13).

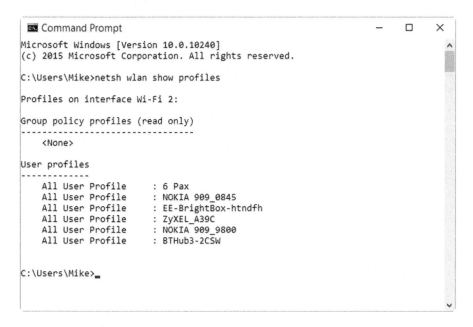

Figure 3-13. *Wireless networks appear in the Command window*

3. Choose the wireless network that you want to delete and type **netsh wlan delete profile name="ProfileName"**, where *ProfileName* matches the name of the network you want to delete as it appears in the list; then press **Enter**.

The wireless network profile is now deleted, and the next time you connect to that network, it will seem as if you never connected to it before on that PC.

■ **Tip**   You can manage saved mobile broadband profiles in the same way by substituting **wlan** in these commands with **mbn**.

It is also possible to recover the password for a wireless network if you forget it and need it to connect another PC. To do this, follow these instructions:

1. Make sure that your PC is already connected to the wireless network.

2. Open the **Network and Sharing Center** by right-clicking the network icon in the system tray (on the right of the taskbar) or by searching for it using the Search charm.

3. In the Network and Sharing Center, click the name of the wireless network in the **Connections** section (see Figure 3-14).

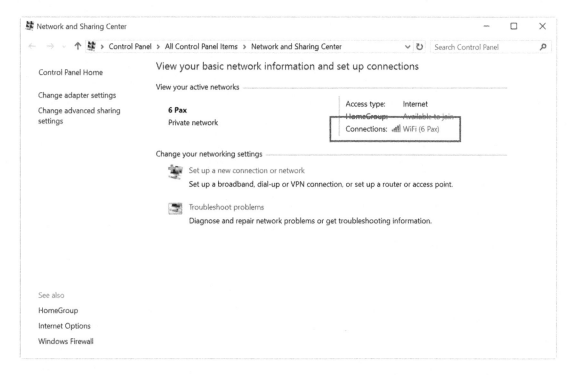

Figure 3-14. *You see the name of the currently connected network*

4. In the dialog that appears, click the **Wireless Properties** button. If you do not see this button, you are connected to an Ethernet or 3G/LTE network for which these properties do not apply.

5. In the next dialog, click the **Security** tab.

6. Now check the **Show characters** box (see Figure 3-15); the passphrase for the wireless network is revealed.

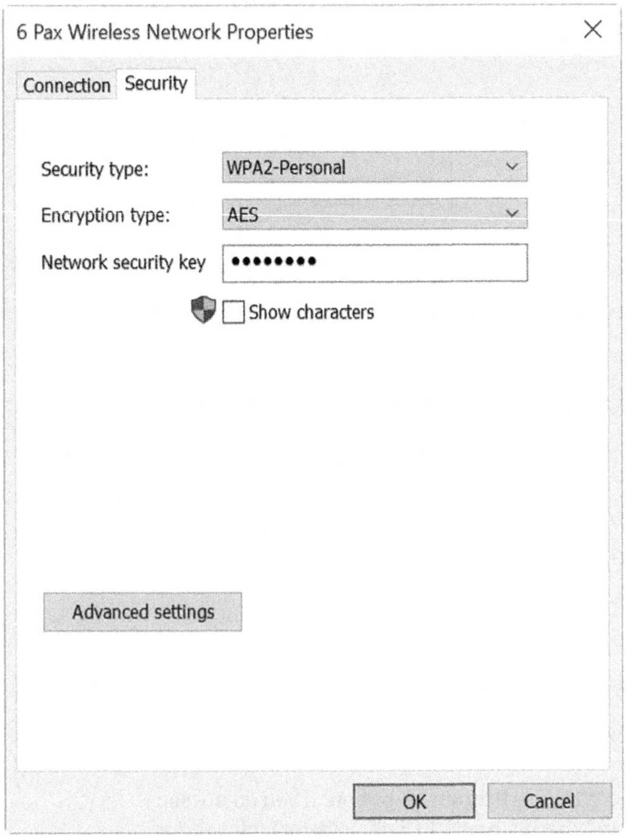

Figure 3-15. *You can display the passphrase for the current network*

Managing Network Connections

You also use the Network and Sharing Center for managing your main network connection hardware, whether Ethernet, Bluetooth, Wi-Fi, mobile broadband, or other connection types. You can access the Network and Sharing Center by either searching for it in the Start menu, or navigating to the desktop and right-clicking the **Network** button, in which there is an option to open it.

To see the network hardware you have installed on your computer, click **Change Adapter Settings** in the left pane. The window that opens contains all the network connections that you have on your PC (see Figure 3-16).

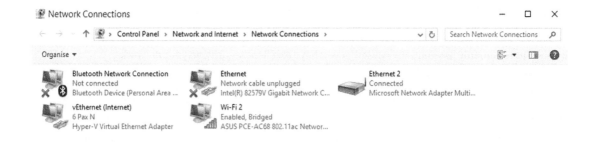

Figure 3-16. *Managing network connections in Windows 10*

You can right-click these connections to perform various actions, but the following actions are also available on the toolbar at the top of the window:

- **Disable** the connection so that you keep it in your network settings, but the network cannot be accessed.

- **Connect** or **Disconnect** from the network.

- Check the **Status** of the network, which is useful if you are having connection difficulties.

- **Diagnose** a problem or a fault with the connection. This runs an automated troubleshooter that resets the connection to its default state.

- Check the **Properties** of the connection. This is where you can change specific settings with the network adaptor. Use your computer to share this connection with other computers by turning your PC into a mobile hotspot, or turn on/off specific features that may be causing problems, such as IPv6.

- There is no direct option to delete a connection or change its autoconnect or stored password settings. To delete a connection, highlight it and press the **Delete (Del)** key on your keyboard.

■ **Note** Windows 10 only allows you to select the status of a connected network or Internet connection. Sometimes it is simpler to delete the connection and have Windows rebuild it on a restart.

Network Management Best Practice

If you manage a network at home or at work, you should take a holistic view of security and network management, including consideration for who will be using the network.

It is worth the money, especially in a small business environment, to buy a router that allows you to set up multiple main and guest SSIDs. The advantage of doing this is that you don't have to worry about visitors to your work environment having accidental access to your computers, the files stored on them, or any shared storage you have in the workplace.

Many mid- to high-end routers offer this functionality, and in the workplace I couldn't recommend it more. It can also be useful in the home, especially if you have shared network storage, such as an NAS drive or a USB hard disk attached to your router, on which you keep backups and private files.

You should always make sure that the router has two passwords on it: one for the administration interface and another for the Wi-Fi. These passwords should *always* be different. If you have a router that supports multiple SSIDs, each one should have its own unique password. This is the best way to guarantee—as much as is humanly possible, anyway—that you have excellent security on your network.

■ **Tip**   To create a secure password, make sure that it is *at least* 12 characters long and includes a mixture of uppercase and lowercase letters, numbers, and symbols. You can also use some numbers and symbols to represent letters, such as 5 instead of S, 1 instead of i or L, and & instead of A. Additionally, you can append some characters from the name of the service or web site the password is for to make it unique, and apply a code to them too; for example, you can capitalize the first alphabetical letter. With these strategies implemented, the *very insecure* eBay password *MikesPassword* then becomes *mlk3spAs5wordebA*. The second letter of each word has been capitalized and the fourth letter has been substituted with a number, making it easy to remember your code.

Securing Wi-Fi Networks

When you set up your Wi-Fi network, it can be difficult to decide which type of security to use on the password; after all, there are so many. Do you choose WEP, WPA-Personal, WPA2-Personal, WPA-Enterprise, or WPA2-Enterprise encryption? Because they are all combinations of letters and numbers, what does each one mean? There is a temptation to choose a basic encryption type, such as WEP, because it allows for the use of short passwords that are easy to remember. This makes it very insecure, however. The higher the level of encryption you add, the longer and more complex the default password requirement is.

Suffice it to say that WEP, WPA, and WPA2 can all be compromised, especially in the business space, by an experienced and determined drive-by hacker (a person sitting outside the building in a car or on a bench who hacks into a network from a laptop). So unless your router offers additional security options that can be used in conjunction with the key—such as AES encryption or a RADIUS authentication server—you are never completely protected.

Each type of secure encryption and authentication you add to a Wi-Fi network makes the password longer due to requirements that are more stringent. On the upside, it has to be entered on each computer only once; but on the downside, it still has to be entered.

I bring this up because it's a legitimate security concern, especially for business. On the other hand, you need to think about the likelihood of a drive-by hacker trying to crack your security.

What do you have on your network? How sensitive are your files and documents? Are you really a hacking target? Most enthusiasts and IT pros reading this have the same types of files on their networks as any consumer, but also have business files. Only if you store particularly sensitive data on your network—you work in the biochemical industry or for a government agency, for example—are you likely to be the target of drive-by hackers. And if the last few years have shown us anything, it is that data theft from governments is much more likely to come from within than from outside.

This isn't to say hacking will never happen to you, but I want to present a balanced argument. For home users, I recommend WPA2 encryption. The minimum password length might be a bit long to remember, but it is always recommended by security professionals to have long passwords. You should keep the password written in a safe location—a desk drawer in your home or workplace, for example, is good because it is unlikely that someone will physically break into the building to access your Wi-Fi network. If they did, they could just plug a physical network cable into your router and bypass the passphrase anyway. WEP and WPA simply don't offer enough security, so I recommend you avoid them.

Managing Internet Data Usage

If you use your computer on a mobile broadband connection (3G/4G LTE), you probably want to make sure that you don't go over your data usage limits.

Windows 10 can help you monitor your usage and limit the amount of data used by displaying the amount of data you use along with a breakdown of how much data your apps have used. To access this data, open the Settings app and click **Data usage**. Your usage from the last 30 days is displayed (see Figure 3-17). You can click the **Usage details** link to get a breakdown on how much data each installed app on your PC or smartphone has used. Both win32 and Store apps are listed here.

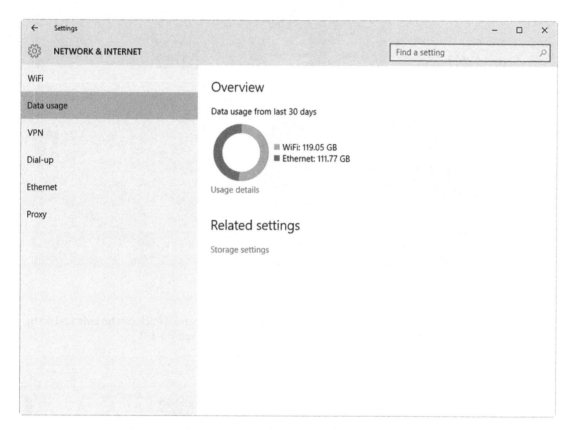

Figure 3-17. *Windows 10 helps you monitor your Internet usage*

Using Internet Explorer

In Chapter 2 I wrote about the Windows 10 Edge web browser. Edge is Microsoft's next-generation browser; it's designed to be highly compatible with modern web sites, fast, and powerful. In the business space, however, there might be compatibility issues with older intranet sites or essential browser plug-ins, which means that, for some purposes, Edge simply won't work for you.

If you're using Windows 10 Pro or Enterprise, however, the good news is that Internet Explorer (IE) 11 (the same version that shipped with Windows 8.1) is still present, and that it continues to be supported with security and stability patches.

Perhaps the better news is that because IE has essentially been decommissioned, it won't be changing in the future, ever. This means no new features, no updates that break site compatibility, and no removal of abilities. If Internet Explorer is working for your business, then it will always continue to work for your business.

Internet Explorer is a very powerful browser (see Figure 3-18) and highly configurable too, so I want to spend some time in this chapter showing you how to get the very best from it.

Figure 3-18. *Internet Explorer on the Windows 10 desktop*

One of the most useful features of the browser is in its toolbars and extras, which can be switched on by right-clicking anywhere in the blank space at the top of the window (see Figure 3-19).

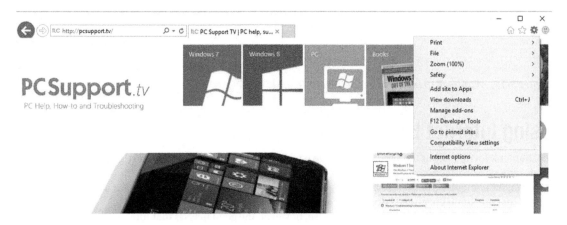

Figure 3-19. *Right-click the top of the Internet Explorer desktop browser to display additional options*

Internet Explorer toolbars and extras include the following features:

- The **menu bar** is the traditional drop-down menu with the typical Internet Explorer options displayed. There is really no need for this now because the options are all easy to get at and because almost nothing else in Windows 10 has drop-down menus. This is only a legacy feature.

- The **Favorites bar** is a quick way to launch commonly used links to web sites. It is a far quicker way to launch web sites than the Favorites menu.

- The **Command bar** contains tools now found in the Settings menu, including Print, Home, RSS, and Safety.

- The **Status bar** sits at the bottom of the browser and gives feedback on loading and other aspects of the page.

- The **address bar** offers extra display options. If you want a full-width address bar or if you want to place a toolbar next to the address bar, you can choose to **Show tabs on a separate row**, which moves the browser tabs below the address bar.

■ **Tip**   If you unpin Internet Explorer from the taskbar and then worry that you can't find it in the All Apps view to repin it, don't worry. Select the Internet Explorer app; a Pin to Taskbar option appears in the app bar.

- To the left of the address bar are the **Back** and **Forward buttons**. Inside the address bar are buttons for Search, Compatibility (for a web site that doesn't display properly in the browser, but worked in earlier versions of Internet Explorer), and Refresh (reloads the current page). To the far right of the tabs are buttons for Home, Favorites, and Settings.

■ **Tip**   You can pin a web site to the Windows taskbar by dragging its button (found to the left of the address bar) onto the taskbar. Some web sites contain their own custom Jump Lists, enabling you to quickly access different pages or features within the web site.

Managing Browser Tabs in Internet Explorer

Web browser tabs in Internet Explorer work in the same way as they have in previous versions of the browser and in other web browsers. Each tab, when you mouse over it, displays a Close button (represented by an X) on its right. You can also drag and drop browser tabs to rearrange them in any order you want.

■ **Tip**   You can drag a tab out of Internet Explorer to open it in its own window; you can also drag tabs from other Internet Explorer windows to amalgamate them into a single window with multiple tabs.

Internet Explorer Safety Features

Some features in the Settings menu may be familiar, but there are some that deserve special attention. The Safety options are chief among these because Internet safety is very important to us all (see Figure 3-20).

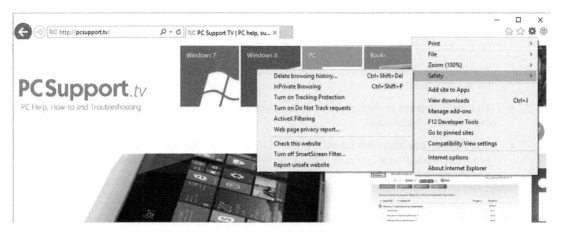

Figure 3-20. *The Safety option s in Internet Explorer*

Internet Explorer includes the following safety features:

- **Delete browsing history** deletes all records of the web sites that you have visited in Internet Explorer. You may not want anyone else seeing the web sites you have visited because they appear automatically in the address bar when a user clicks in it or searches in it.

- **InPrivate Browsing** is a special mode within Internet Explorer that doesn't keep any record of the web sites you visit and that doesn't allow those web sites to leave cookies or other tracking files on your computer. This mode is useful for gift shopping or if you need to sign in to multiple Microsoft, Google, or Office 365 accounts simultaneously.

- **Tracking protection**. Sometimes you visit web sites in which cookies are placed on your computer by third-party web sites, often through advertisements. Tracking protection is disabled in Internet Explorer by default, but you can turn it back on here if you want.

- **Turn off Do Not Track requests**. Internet Explorer requests (politely, of course) that web sites do not track your online activity. If you want to turn off this functionality, you can do so here.

- **ActiveX Filtering** is a feature that blocks small programs, sometimes used to play video, from running in your web browser. ActiveX controls can be programmed to run malicious code on your computer when activated.

- **Webpage privacy policy** displays the privacy policy, if available, of the web site that is currently displayed.

- **Check this website** is available for some (but not all) web sites. It enables you to check a web site against the Microsoft master list of known safe and unsafe sites to see whether there is a potential security risk. Fortunately, my own web site (shown in Figures 3-15 to 3-18) is known to be safe. ☺

- **Turn off SmartScreen Filter**. Microsoft SmartScreen, which I will talk about shortly, helps prevent malicious code from web sites from running on your PC. If you want to turn this feature off, perhaps because it interferes with a company intranet, you can do so here.

- **Report unsafe website** is where you can report a web site (to Microsoft and relevant authorities) that you know contains malware or that is being used for criminal purposes.

Using the SmartScreen Filter to Block Malicious Web Sites

The Windows 10 SmartScreen filter runs in Internet Explorer to help prevent malicious code on web sites from infecting your computer. Unless you turn it off in the Safety options, it automatically checks every web page you visit against a list of known malicious sites compiled in collaboration with other browser makers and security companies.

In the Safety menu, you can manually check a web site against the SmartScreen database. If you suspect a web site to be malicious, you can use this menu to manually report to Microsoft that the web site is potentially unsafe.

You can manually configure Windows SmartScreen in the Security and Maintenance Center (or by searching for **SmartScreen** from the Start menu). When in the Action Center, click the **Change Windows SmartScreen Settings** link in the top left of the window. There are three settings you can choose with SmartScreen, as shown in Figure 3-21.

Figure 3-21. *Changing Windows SmartScreen settings*

- The default setting is to **Get administrator approval before running an unrecognized app from the Internet**. Microsoft recommends this, and so do I. It offers the best level of protection while still giving you the choice of running a suspect app if you want to.

- **Warn before running an unrecognized app, but don't require administrator approval** allows Standard users on your PC to run suspect apps. This could pose a security risk to your PC and files, especially if the person running the app is inexperienced in such things, such as a child.

- **Don't do anything (turn off Windows SmartScreen)** isn't a setting I recommend at all. It should be set only if you use your PC for work, and SmartScreen is blocking essential features of your company intranet.

Managing Add-ons, Toolbars, and Search Providers

Toolbars and add-ons are incredibly useful in Internet Explorer, including Adobe Flash Player and Java (though Flash Player is now built into Internet Explorer). Occasionally, however, they can get in the way, slow down your browser, or even be malicious and hijack your search submissions.

You can manage and remove toolbars from Internet Explorer in the Settings menu by selecting Manage Add-ons. In the window that appears (see Figure 3-22), you can highlight an add-on or a toolbar; Enable and Disable buttons appear in the bottom-right corner of the window.

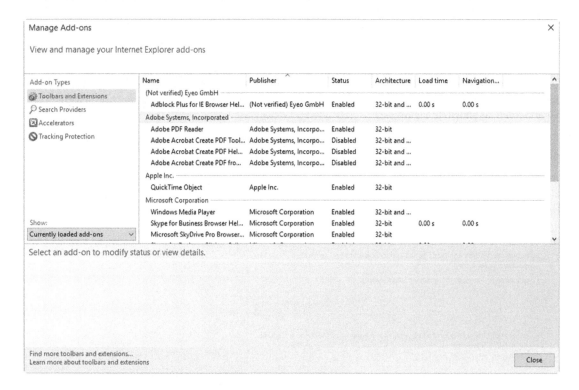

Figure 3-22. Managing add-ons and toolbars in Internet Explorer

■ **Note**   Disabling an IE add-on or toolbar is not the same as uninstalling it from your computer. You can uninstall add-ons and toolbars in Programs and Features in the Control Panel.

I mentioned at the beginning of this section that abusive toolbars can hijack your search providers. Having this happen can be as annoying as having a problem toolbar, and disabling the toolbar won't fix the problem, either. In the left column of the Manage Add-ons window, you can click **Search Providers**, which is where you can remove problem search providers, or even add new ones like Google or Yahoo!.

Internet Explorer Options and Configuration

The extensive Internet options in Internet Explorer (see Figure 3-22) also need a mention. I want to talk you through some of these settings. You access Internet Options from the Settings button to the far right of the browser tabs.

■ **Note** Windows 10 automatically syncs your browser tabs across different Windows 10 computers in the Internet Explorer app. It can't be controlled here, but it can be switched on and off in PC Settings. I show you how to do this in Chapter 9.

The first tab to appear in Internet Options is the General tab (see Figure 3-23). Under this tab, you can set a single or multiple (write each one on a different line) home pages for your web browser. You can also set IE to automatically reload all the pages from your last browsing session when you start it. Note that this is something the Internet Explorer app does automatically.

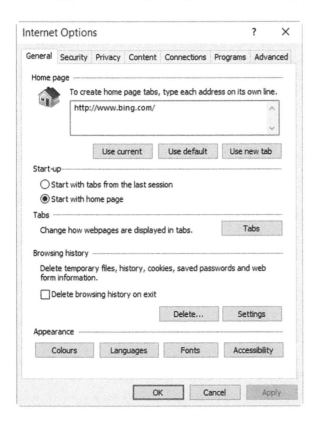

Figure 3-23. The General tab in Internet Options

The Tabs options are interesting. When you open a tab from another browser tab, IE color-codes them automatically. It also opens all new tabs next to the existing one. These are features that some people find irritating. It is here where they can be switched off.

You can also turn off tabbed browsing completely if you want, forcing each new web site to open in its own window.

■ **Tip**   You can completely delete your web browsing history in the Settings panel by clicking the Delete button. Optionally, you can force Windows to delete your browsing history every time you close your browser by selecting the **Delete browsing history on exit** check box.

Managing Safety and Privacy in Internet Explorer

These days, two things that greatly concern people (especially parents whose children use the Internet) are safety and privacy. Internet Explorer comes with built-in options to help with this. Click the Settings button near the top right of the window and select Internet Options from the menu.

The Safety options (which are also selected from the Settings button in Internet Explorer) block potentially unsafe web sites or allow web sites that Internet Explorer blocks by default. These settings can be further customized, but unless you have good reasons for changing this control, you will probably find that it proves more of a hindrance than a help because useful and perfectly legitimate web sites are blocked if you increase the safety settings.

The Security tab (see Figure 3-24) allows you to set general rules for your Internet security, such as whether to allow or block certain types of *cookies*, which are small tracking files placed on your computer by web sites to permit actions such as remembering login passwords.

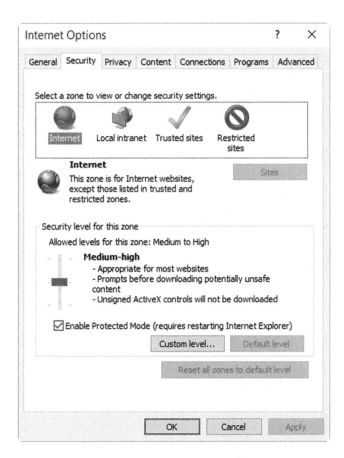

Figure 3-24. *The Security tab in Internet Options*

Of more interest are the Privacy options (see Figure 3-25), which allow you to block tracking and other cookies from web sites, depending on your own criteria. The feature also allows you to import whitelists and blacklists from third parties (perhaps parental or privacy groups).

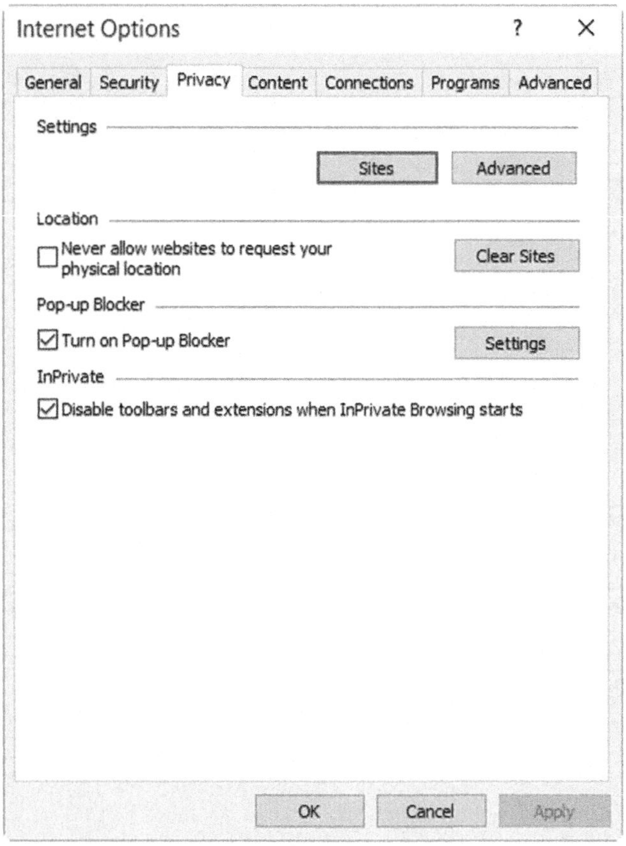

Figure 3-25. *The Privacy tab in Internet Options*

In the Location section of this tab, you can block web sites from being sent to your physical location. This is useful because computers now come fitted with GPS systems and because your location could be determined from your PC's IP address.

It is also on this tab that you can turn on or off Internet Explorer's built-in pop-up blocker. It is turned on by default, but if it interferes with your company's intranet, for example, you can deactivate it.

The Content tab (see Figure 3-26) is commonly of interest to parents. Windows 10's Family Safety can be accessed from here. It is also where you can manage the AutoComplete settings, whereby Internet Explorer remembers passwords, usernames, and more from your browsing history. Individual components in AutoComplete can be switched on and off here.

Figure 3-26. *The Content tab in Internet Options*

Recovering Lost Web Site Usernames and Passwords

While I'm on the subject of stored usernames and passwords, it is a good time to tell you that Windows 10 can show you your usernames and passwords for web sites, if you forget them. You can do this by searching for **credentials** and running the **Manage web credentials** settings.

The Web Credentials panel lists all the web sites that you have stored usernames and passwords for (see Figure 3-27). You expand the information on a web site by clicking the down arrow to the right of its name. Then information such as your username and whether the credentials are permitted to roam (i.e., if they are being synched between Windows 10 PCs) are displayed.

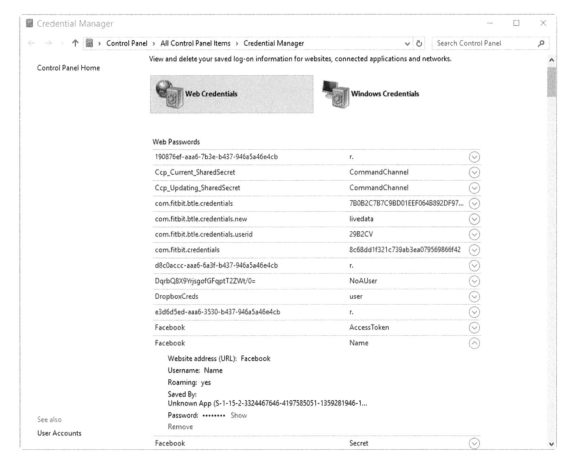

Figure 3-27. *Recovering usernames and passwords for web sites in the Credential Manager*

By default, the password is blanked out, but you can click the **Show** link next to a password to display it. If you have a password on your Windows 10 user account, you are asked to enter it here as authorization.

If you want to remove the credentials for a certain web site, you can click the **Remove** link; they are deleted from stored memory in the Credential Manager.

What Is InPrivate Mode?

I want to insert a quick note about InPrivate mode here because it is relevant to your privacy online. This mode, which can be easily activated in both Internet Explorer and Edge, as I have discussed earlier, is a special mode that prevents the web browser and web sites you visit from collecting any information about you.

This mode is useful for a wide range of activities, including shopping for secret birthday presents and for communication inside a country where Internet activity can be monitored. (Some regimes have mechanisms in place that track you anyway, and additional software such as a mobile browser or Tor, www.torproject.org, may be required for complete anonymity.) Generally speaking, and especially for present shopping, InPrivate Mode is a great way to hide what you've been doing from the people who use your PC and user account.

Staying Safe Online

Staying safe online is a challenge these days. Criminals are everywhere, ready to infect our computers with malware or to steal our credit card information or identities. So when we increasingly spend our time on online social networks and Internet shopping sites, how can we know that we are safe and secure?

I want to discuss online threats, how you can spot them, and how you can protect yourself, your friends, and your family against them.

Internet Threats Explained

There are several major types of Internet threats.

- **Malware** is malicious software that infects a computer to steal information, steal or encrypt files, or simply corrupt a machine and delete things. It can come from various sources, including *macros* (small programs than run inside files, usually word processor or spreadsheet files); *keyloggers* that record everything you type, including credit card information and bank logins; and browser plug-ins that pretend to be something that you need, such as a codec required to view a video online.

- **Phishing** emails try to trick you into revealing sensitive information, such as passwords, by pretending to be from a reputable bank or business institution.

- **Compromised web sites** may look perfectly legitimate, but they ask for sensitive information that can be used to hijack your account or that are programmed to download and run infected files to your computer.

■ **Tip**   No legitimate web site will *ever* email you asking you to confirm your security information. If you notice the web site that you regularly use has changed and is asking for additional login information, you should email abuse@*companyname*.*com* (where *companyname.com* is the web address of the company) to report it.

Identifying Safe and Unsafe Web Sites

Both Edge and Internet Explorer are great at telling you whether a web site is safe. Displaying a padlock in the address bar that indicates the site is a known, secure web site. Also, the address bar is green when the URL is a safe web site, amber if the browser and Microsoft are unsure about the web site, and red when it is known to be used by criminals (see Figure 3-28).

Figure 3-28. *Internet Explorer highlights safe web sites*

The web site safety reporting in both Edge and Internet Explorer, or any web browser for that matter, is not infallible and is only as good as its last update.

Setting Internet Explorer As Your Default Browser

When you install Windows 10, the default browser (the one all web links open in) is Edge. If you want to change this to the desktop version of Internet Explorer, it's easy to do:

1. Open Settings in Internet Explorer by clicking the **Settings** icon in the top right of the window.

2. In the options panel that appears, click the **Programs** tab.

3. In the **Choose how you open links** section at the top of the panel, change the drop-down option from **Let Internet Explorer Decide** to **Always in Internet Explorer on the desktop** (see Figure 3-29), and then click **OK** to confirm the change.

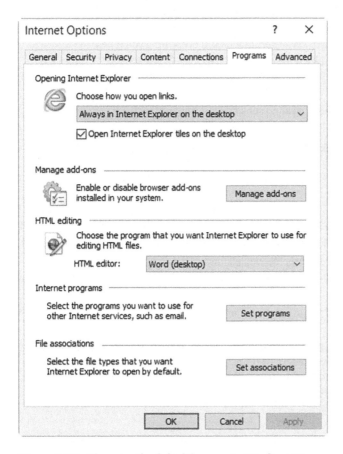

Figure 3-29. *Changing the default browser in Windows 10*

Summary

Windows 10 offers new ways to connect to the Internet, but these new ways also bring challenges (the worry that comes from being accidentally connected to your 3G or LTE network and using expensive data, for example).

There are also challenges with staying safe on the Internet. Internet Explorer does an excellent job of keeping you safe, but the weak link is always the user. Malware writers and criminals will prey on you, trying to trick you into entering sensitive information on the pretense that it's perfectly safe to do so.

On my web site (PCSupport.tv), I have tutorial videos about regularly maintaining your security and privacy online. You can always find more information there.

CHAPTER 4

■ ■ ■

Sharing with Family and Friends

Sharing is everywhere on our PCs and devices these days, from social media to instant messaging, cloud backup, and syncing to Office 365. Long gone are the days when we zipped up files and burned them to disc to stick in the mail. We can now share our photos, files, and even snippets of web pages with anyone online.

In Windows 10, store apps that send or receive information, such as pictures, don't need to be programmed to import and export files to and from other programs. Windows 10 handles it all. This opens new opportunities for sharing, but some of the traditional methods of sharing files, folders, and network hardware still exist. In this chapter, I'll show you how to share a wide variety of hardware, file types, and data libraries in Windows 10.

Working with User Accounts

One of the traditional strengths of Windows has been its support of multiple users. On the face of things, this may seem relatively minor, but if you have a tablet in the living room that's used by multiple people, when you work from home, do school work, or just want some privacy, the usefulness of this feature steps up to another level. Handling multiple user accounts on a tablet device is still something few non-Windows devices are capable of, straightforward as you might think it would be. This is a major feature of Windows 10, and you'll be pleased to hear that the operating system handles user accounts admirably.

Windows 10 practically begs people to sign in with a Microsoft account—the same ID you use to log on to a Live, Hotmail, Outlook.com, or MSN email account. When you do this, much of the system is automatically set up for you, including the Windows Store and the email and calendar apps. This can present issues for multiple user systems where only one user account is set up on the PC, because you might not want other people in your household or workplace reading your email.

There is also the matter of file security. We generally trust the people we live with, but accidents do happen. If somebody doesn't know the importance of a particular file or Internet favorite, it can be deleted all too easily.

The ability to set up Windows 10 so that each user has his or her own account is a benefit. It is also a task that's extremely simple to perform.

Setting Up New User Accounts

To set up new users on a PC, open the Settings app, click the **Accounts** link, and finally click **Family & other users**. Having a family member's account is new in Windows 10, and it serves two purposes. First, if you have children who wants to use the PC, but whom you wish to keep safe online, then you can set up their account in the Family accounts section. Additionally, because of the interconnected nature of Windows 10 PCs, tablets, and smartphones, Family accounts enable you to share information and photos easily with anyone in your family, safe in the knowledge that they won't be seen by other people.

Family accounts require everyone to have a Microsoft account, because this enables the sharing and integration features. The Family features in Windows 10 will largely be rolled-out over the coming years; when major updates to Windows 10 are released, you'll see these new features available to you on your Windows 10 devices.

Setting Up a Family Account

To create a Family account, follow these instructions:

1. Click the **Add a family member** button.

2. You are asked if the family member is a child or an adult. Select the appropriate option (see Figure 4-1).

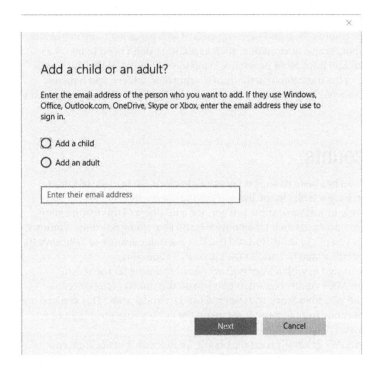

Figure 4-1. *Creating a new user account in the Settings app*

3. In the **Enter their email address** box type, enter the email address associated with the family member's Microsoft account. If this person doesn't have an email address, click the **The person who I want to add doesn't have an email address** link.

4. If the person does have an email address, you are asked to confirm that you want to add them to your PC. If they do not have a Microsoft account, you are prompted to set one up (see Figure 4-2).

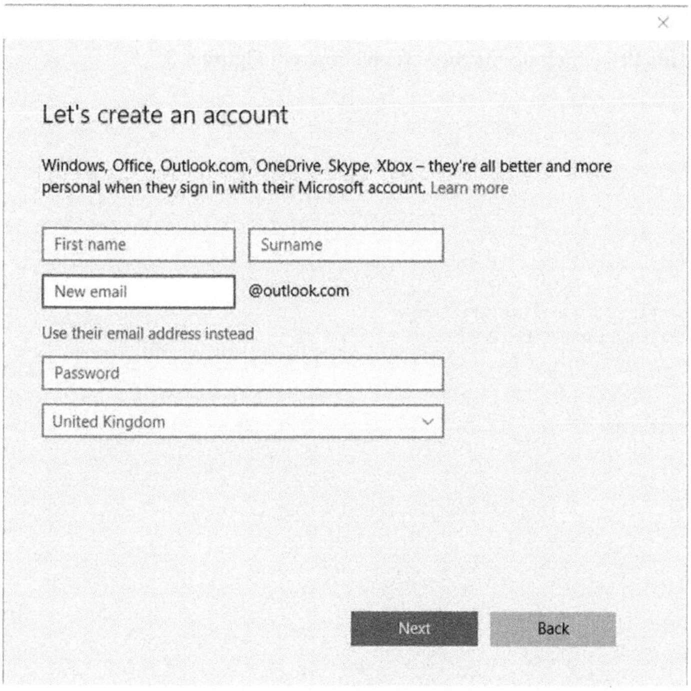

Figure 4-2. *You can create a new Microsoft account in the Settings app*

5. Enter the name of the person and choose a new @outlook.com email address for them (you'll be told if the email address you want isn't available). Then set a password for the person and click **Next**.

■ **Note** I will show you how to manage computer and Internet safety for children later in this chapter.

The **Other users** category is for people who use your PC who aren't in your immediate family, such as people who aren't children but that you need to keep safe online, or that you want to share photos and other private things with. If you live or work in a shared environment, for example, and want each person to have their own account on the PC, this is where you'd set it up.

■ **Tip** If you are creating an account for another person using a Microsoft account ID, she doesn't need to be present. Just enter her email address and you're done. The PC won't ask for the password until the first time that *she* logs in to the PC.

To create an **Other user** account, follow these instructions:

1. Click **Add someone else to this PC**, which opens the screen shown in Figure 4-3.

Figure 4-3. *Adding a new user*

2. To add someone who already has a Microsoft account, enter their email address (the one associated with the Microsoft account) and click **Next**.

3. If the person doesn't have a Microsoft account but would like to set one up, click the **The person who I want to add doesn't have an email address** link. You are then prompted to create an email address for them in the same way seen in Figure 4-2.

4. If this person doesn't have an email address, or doesn't want or need the Microsoft account sync facilities on your PC, then click the **Add a user with a Microsoft account** link. This will create a local account.

5. You are prompted for the name of the user, their password, and a password hint (which can't just be the password) (see Figure 4-4).

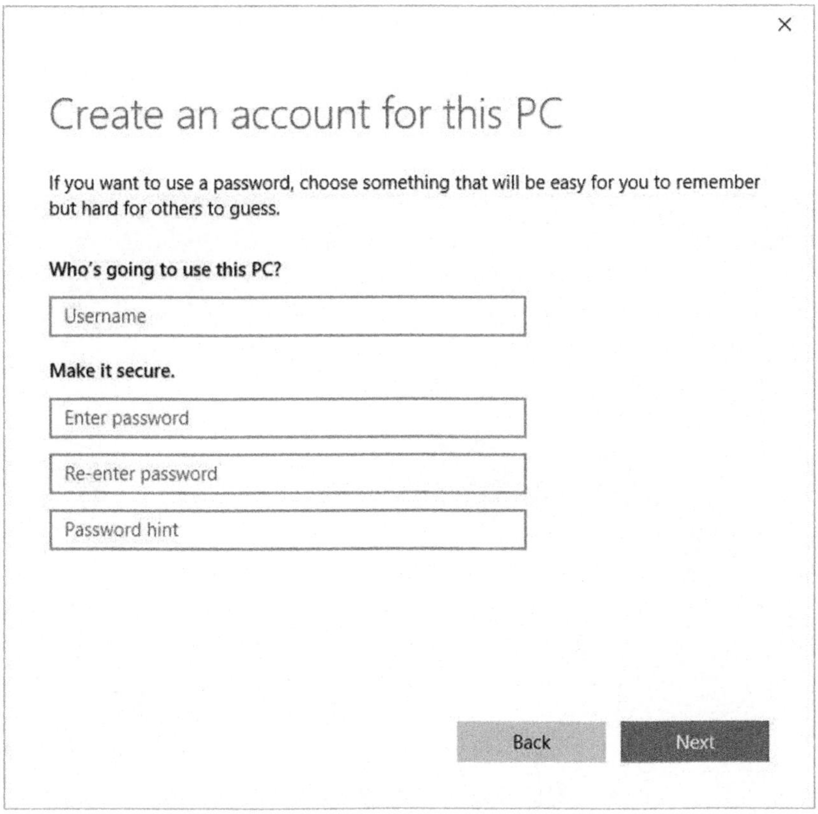

Figure 4-4. *You can add a local user without a Microsoft account*

▪ **Note** So what difference does it make whether you create a local account or a Microsoft account? A local account has advantages if you use only one PC in which everything is stored locally, so there's nothing in the cloud if you're concerned about privacy. However, you can't use the Windows Store to purchase apps and your Internet favorites, and other settings won't be synched to other Windows 10 PCs.

Creating a Password Reset Drive

If you use a Microsoft account and ever forget your password, you can visit http://account.microsoft.com and reset it. This is especially easy if you have set up two-factor authentication on your account to use a smartphone or an alternative email address. I recommend that you set this up; you can find it in the **Security & privacy** section of the web page.

If you have a local account on your PC, however, you can't reset your password online; instead, you can create a password reset drive to help you if you forget the password to the PC. To create a password reset drive, you need a blank USB flash drive (any size will do, so it's a good use for an old one) already plugged into the PC. Search for **password reset** from the Search charm and run **Create a password reset disk** from the options that appear.

This displays a wizard that quickly walks you through creating a password reset system on the USB flash drive.

If you forget your password at logon, just click the arrow to the right of the password entry box, insert your password reset flash drive into a USB port, and then click the **Reset password** link below the password input box (see Figure 4-5).

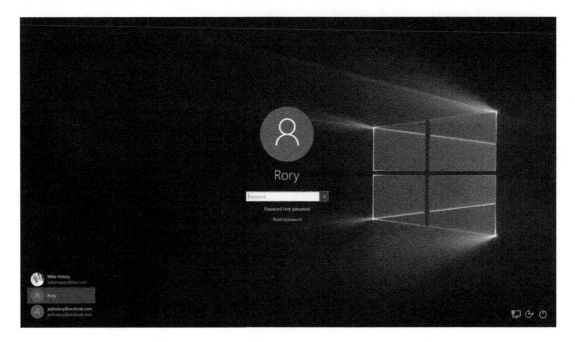

Figure 4-5. *You can reset your password using a password reset disk*

The password reset wizard asks which port or drive you have inserted your password reset disk into. It uses this to reset your password, enabling you to log in to the computer again.

Resetting Your Microsoft Account Password

If you log in to your PC using a Microsoft account, you don't have the option to create a password reset disk. Instead, you are pointed at the Microsoft account password reset web page at http://account.microsoft.com/password/reset (see Figure 4-6). You need to do this on a PC or account that you can log in to, or perhaps on a smartphone.

Figure 4-6. *You can reset a Microsoft account password online*

Here you are prompted to enter the email address associated with your Microsoft account and to confirm the security captcha code that displays. You are then asked if you want Microsoft to email you a temporary password (if you have set up a backup email address in your Microsoft account) or send you a text message by phone (assuming that you have a current mobile phone number registered to your Microsoft account).

If these are not suitable for you, you are asked to enter an alternative email address that somebody from Microsoft can contact you about. They typically contact you within 24 hours, which is a good incentive to set up an alternate email address or a mobile phone on your account! I show you how to manage your Microsoft account online later in this chapter.

■ **Tip**   You can change the password for any local account by signing in as an administrator and opening the Users controls in the full Control Panel. Click **Manage another account**, followed by the user you want to change the password for, and a **Change the password** link appears.

Managing User Accounts

There are two types of users in Windows 10: *administrators*, who have authority to make any changes they want to the operating system and the computer's files, and *standard users*, who can make only changes that affect their own user account. The first user account created when you start using Windows 10 will always be an administrator, (the account that was set up when Windows 10 was first installed or activated), and all accounts created after this are standard users. For general use, this is the most secure way to run the operating system (OS), but you might find that a second user needs to install software and needs the administrator password to do so. Under this circumstance, you may want to consider having more than one administrator account on the PC.

There are two ways to manage user accounts: one in which you can simply change the account type in PC Settings, and another with more controls in the full Control Panel. To do this, you first need to be logged in to the PC as an administrator. In the Settings app, click **Accounts**, and then click **Family & other users** (see Figure 4-7). Clicking the **Add a family member** or **Add someone else to this PC** button enables you to change the account type between administrator and standard user.

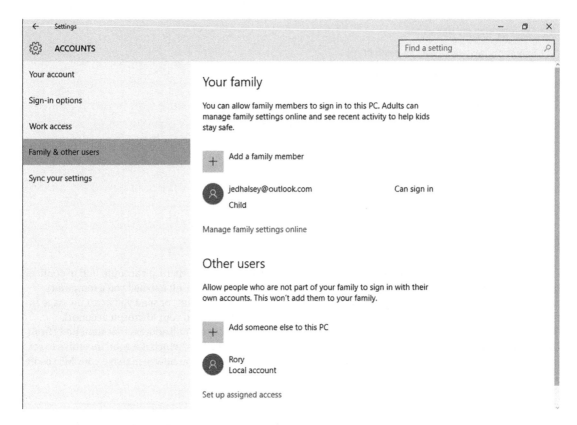

Figure 4-7. *You can change the account type in PC Settings*

■ **Tip**   You can also remove user accounts in the Other Accounts section of PC Settings.

When you need more control over user accounts, you need to open the full Windows 10 Control Panel, which you can do by searching for **control** at the Start screen. Managing user accounts is done from the User Accounts section of the Control Panel. When you load this panel, you are first shown your own user account (see Figure 4-8). Here you can perform various actions, as follows:

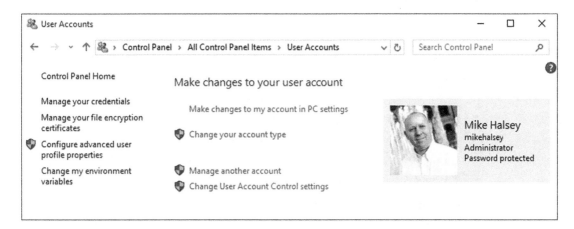

Figure 4-8. Managing user accounts in Windows 10

- **Change your account type**: You can change from standard user to administrator (or vice versa). This might be useful to upgrade a user to an administrator.

- **Manage your credentials**: You can view, edit, and delete the stored password for Windows, Windows software, and web sites that are associated with your account. This can be useful if something has become corrupt, and Windows or Internet Explorer gets confused when you change your password.

- **Create a Password Reset Disk** (not seen): This option appears only for local user accounts and allows you to create a USB flash drive that can be used to reset your password if you forget it.

- **Manage your file encryption certificates**: This option allows you to back up and restore any Encrypting File System (EFS) encryption keys associated with this account. For more on this, see Chapter 12.

- **Change advanced user profile properties**: This option is used if your user account has been created as part of a Windows Server domain.

- **Change my environment variables**: This option allows you to change certain aspects of your profile, such as where your user and temporary files are stored by default.

- **Manage your fingerprint data** (not seen): This option appears if your computer has a biometric fingerprint reader.

If you click **Manage another account**, you are shown a list of the other user accounts on your computer. Clicking an account allows you to change the settings for that user (see Figure 4-9).

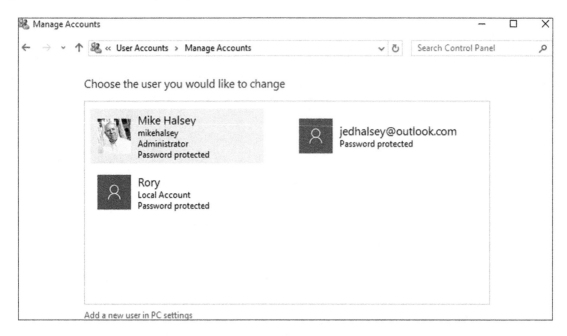

Figure 4-9. *Managing another user account*

The options found for managing other users include the following:

- **Change the account name**.

- **Create a password** for the account if it doesn't have one. If it does, you see options to change or remove the password.

- **Change the account type** from standard user to administrator (or vice versa). All secondary users are standard users by default.

- **Delete the account** gives an alert that the user has files on the computer and gives the opportunity to save these files to a desktop folder before the account is deleted.

■ **Tip**   If you log on to someone else's computer with your Microsoft account, but you don't use that computer very often, be aware that Windows 10 might have downloaded your Internet Favorites or other personal files to the computer. Obviously, you don't want them to remain on someone else's computer, so you can remove them by performing a few steps. When logged on as another user, open **Accounts** in the Settings app and click the name of the account you want to delete. Next, click **Remove**, and when prompted, click **Delete account and data**. This process removes the files, but you should make certain by checking the C:\Users folder. If a folder still exists for that user account, delete it manually.

Managing a Microsoft Account Online

The management tools for your Microsoft account can be found online at http://account.microsoft.com, as shown in Figure 4-10. Here you can control all aspects of your account: display name, date of birth, billing and credit card information for the Windows Store, and your alternate email address and mobile phone number if you forget your password or if for some reason (such as being hacked) you become locked out of your account.

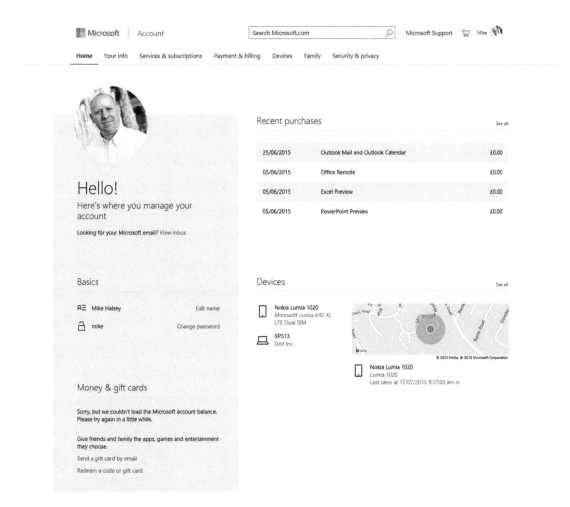

Figure 4-10. *You manage your Microsoft account at* http://account.microsoft.com

There are a great number of options to be found on this web site, and even if you have had your Microsoft account for some time, it can be well worth looking through the options here to ensure that everything is as it should be and that all the correct account permissions have been set.

Using Family Safety to Keep Your Children Safe Online

With children using the Internet at ever-younger ages, it's more important than ever before to shield them from inappropriate games, web sites, and images. Windows 10 comes with an excellent suite of tools that enables you to do this and more, including determining when children can use their PCs, and it all comes with a reporting tool with which parents can monitor children's Internet usage.

When you create a new family user account in Windows 10, you are asked if the user that you are adding is a child. Checking this option allows you to manage the Family Safety users for that account online. Click the **Manage family safety online** link to open the settings options in a web page.

You are taken to your Microsoft account page online, where you see the **Family** options displayed. The child account you set up should already be listed (see Figure 4-11).

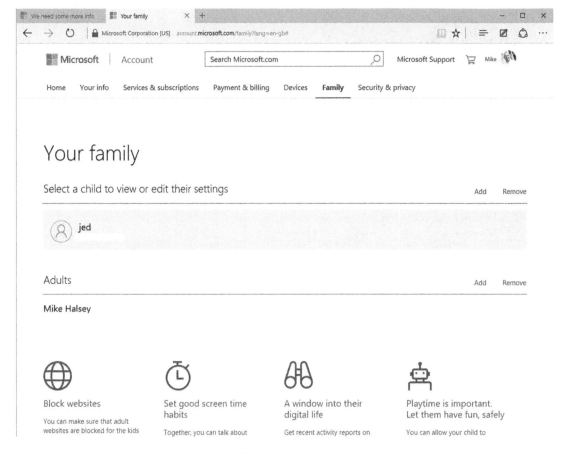

Figure 4-11. *You can manage family safety online*

Family Safety is very powerful and flexible in Windows 10. It includes web filtering for the first time. The activity report is a very helpful addition to these controls because they show you the types of activities that your child is participating in online and which web sites they visit.

You access the activity report by clicking the child's name at the online Family Safety page. This displays reports about their Internet, Games, and PC usage. It also has a switch for activity reporting, which you can choose to be emailed to you each week (see Figure 4-12). Your child cannot see these reports, they are visible only to administrators on the computer, but the child is informed when logging in to the PC that the account's activity is being monitored. This is a privacy and safety feature to prevent unwanted snooping.

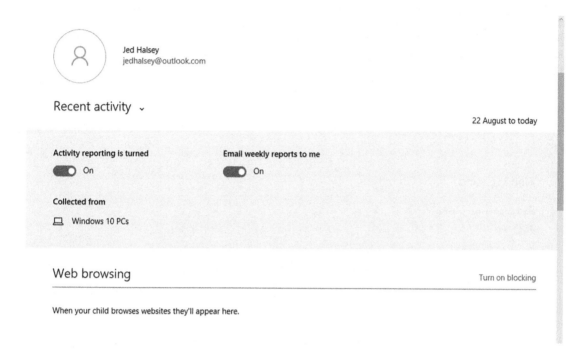

Figure 4-12. *The Family Safety page*

At the main Family Safety screen, select the user you want to set controls for, and then scroll down the page to see the options available to you (see Figure 4-13). These include web filtering, PC time usage, and which games they can play.

Block websites

You can make sure that adult websites are blocked for the kids in your family. You can also block specific sites – or choose which sites you want your kids to see.

Set good screen time habits

Together, you can talk about good habits and set limits on how much time they can spend with their screens.

A window into their digital life

Get recent activity reports on sites visited, apps used, games played and screen time. Or, check-in online at any time.

Playtime is important. Let them have fun, safely

You can allow your child to download apps and games appropriate for their age, and still make sure they don't get anything they're not ready for yet.

Figure 4-13. *The main Family Safety options*

I want to spend a little time discussing each of these settings in detail. Each category has a clear description of what it is, so you can feel certain that your children are seeing only appropriate web sites. You can also block Internet downloads, which helps protect your computer from malware.

Web Filtering

The web filtering options work from safe and unsafe sites lists that are maintained by Microsoft and third-party security and web-filtering companies. When you turn this feature on, it's not necessary to specify the age of your child, because the feature automatically applies the correct settings for the age you specified for the child when you set up their Microsoft account (see Figure 4-14).

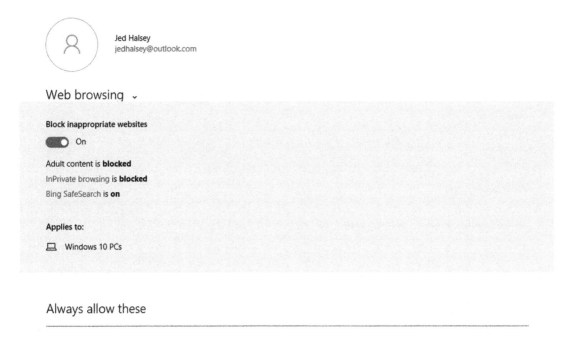

Figure 4-14. Choose the web sites that are suitable for your child

Below the main control are options to specifically block or allow certain web sites (see Figure 4-15). You might, for example, not want your child using certain social networking web sites, or some sites might be unsuitable on religious grounds. Alternatively, your child might come to you saying that site X or Y has been blocked, but that they need to use it for their school work, or that they feel it should be okay for them to use. You can use the Allow list to permit any web site, overriding the standard filtering controls.

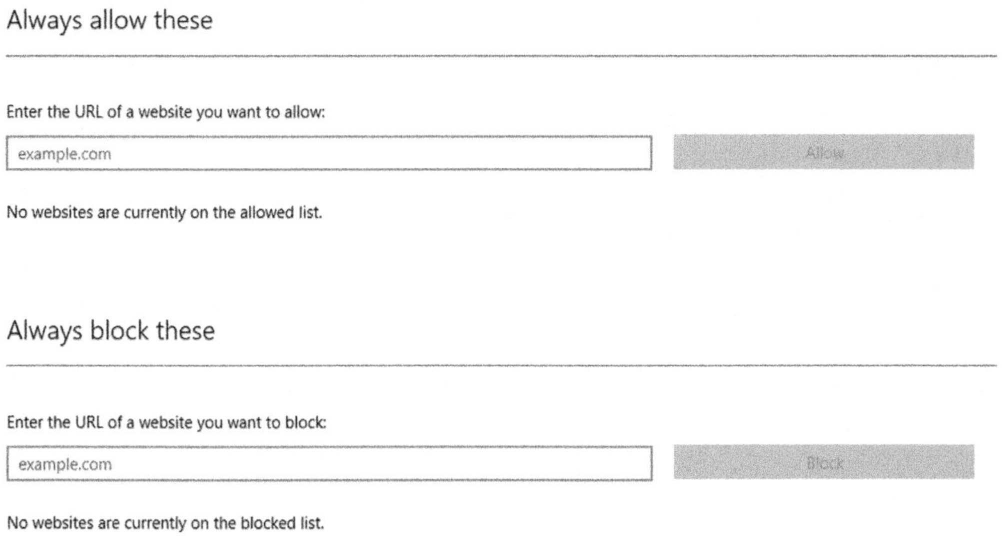

Always allow these

Enter the URL of a website you want to allow:

example.com

Allow

No websites are currently on the allowed list.

Always block these

Enter the URL of a website you want to block:

example.com

Block

No websites are currently on the blocked list.

Figure 4-15. *You can allow and block specific web sites in Family Safety*

Setting App and Game Permissions

You can prevent your children from using apps and from playing games that aren't suitable for them, although I would like to caveat this with a caution that it's not a silver bullet. Apps that don't come from the Windows Store aren't included. And whereas games that come through platforms such as Steam and Origin are compliant with game ratings systems, there's no guarantee that they'll all integrate with the Windows Family Safety feature.

That said, you can select the age of your child (from 3 right up to 20, or any age (no restrictions)), as shown in Figure 4-16. This is not managed in the same way as web filtering, because the age range recommendations for games vary considerably, and you might feel that your child is mature enough to play games in an age category that is slightly older than they are.

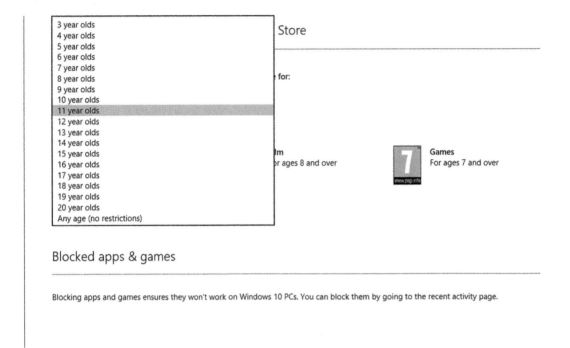

Figure 4-16. *You can block unsuitable games and apps*

If you find that there are particular games that you'd prefer your child not to play, you need to navigate to the **Recent activity page**, where you can see the games that they have played, and are able to block one or more individually.

Setting Permitted Screen Time

We've all seen it: some video of a very young child who is so accustomed to using a tablet that when presented with a magazine, the child is wondering why pinch and swipe gestures don't work on the pages. Perhaps this is just an indication of where we're going as a society, but it's been long established that sitting in front of a PC for too long can have harmful effects, such as damaging eyesight, causing posture and joint problems, and sometimes, though I gather this is incredibly rare, making children unwilling to do their chores or go outdoors and play with their friends. Oh, so it's not rare!? <Shudder> :/

Fortunately, the Family Safety feature allows you to set at which times the child can use their PC, and optionally, for how many of those hours they can actually use it (see Figure 4-17). You might, for example, say that the child should not be able to use the PC before 9 a.m. each weekday morning and not after 8 p.m. each night, so as to give them a healthy night's sleep every day. You might want to vary the rules a bit on weekends, allowing an extra hour on Friday and Saturday nights, for example, or saying they can't use the PC for more than three or four hours a day.

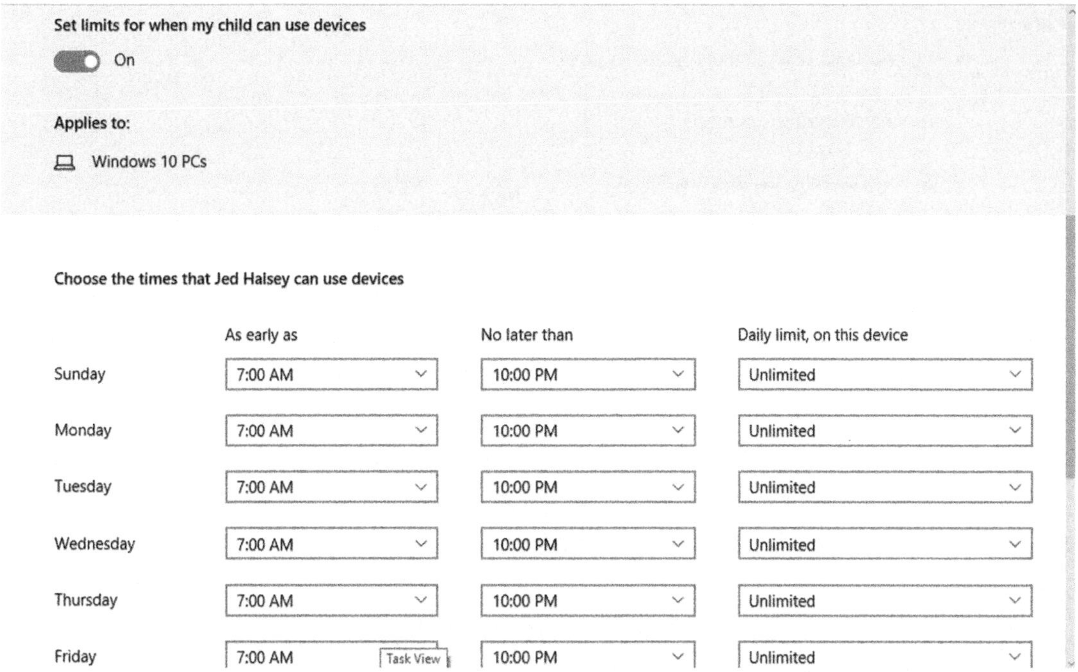

Set limits for when my child can use devices

⬤◯ On

Applies to:

🖳 Windows 10 PCs

Choose the times that Jed Halsey can use devices

	As early as	No later than	Daily limit, on this device
Sunday	7:00 AM ⌄	10:00 PM ⌄	Unlimited ⌄
Monday	7:00 AM ⌄	10:00 PM ⌄	Unlimited ⌄
Tuesday	7:00 AM ⌄	10:00 PM ⌄	Unlimited ⌄
Wednesday	7:00 AM ⌄	10:00 PM ⌄	Unlimited ⌄
Thursday	7:00 AM ⌄	10:00 PM ⌄	Unlimited ⌄
Friday	7:00 AM Task View	10:00 PM ⌄	Unlimited ⌄

Figure 4-17. *You can set time limits for PC use*

When a child is nearing the end of the usage time, normally 30 minutes before, they are alerted by a message on the desktop, and if more time should be allowed on that occasion, a parent can override it by authorizing extra time using their Microsoft account credentials.

Sharing Files and Folders with HomeGroup

HomeGroup was introduced in Windows 7 as a means of sharing documents, pictures, music, video, and printers across small, protected home networks. Think of a HomeGroup as a quick way to share files between your home computers. This is because Windows knows which environment you're sharing things in, and as a result, automatically sets all the correct permissions and parameters on the files, folders, and networking settings for you, minimizing your configuration.

HomeGroup still exists in Windows 10. It's easy and straightforward to set up and configure. HomeGroup is in the Control Panel (see Figure 4-18), which is available by pressing the Windows Key + X and clicking the **Control Panel** link. Once in PC Settings, click **Choose HomeGroup and Sharing Options**, or if you're looking at all the items in the Control Panel, click **HomeGroup**.

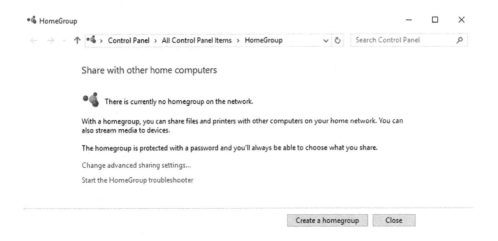

Figure 4-18. *The HomeGroup options in the Control Panel*

If a HomeGroup has already been set up on another computer, you are asked to enter the password. You may have a Windows 7 or 8.1 PC on which you have previously set up and configured a HomeGroup, for example.

If a HomeGroup does not exist, or if Windows 10 can't detect one on the network, you are asked if you want to set one up.

■ **Note**   HomeGroup works only over Wi-Fi for networks on which you have said you want to find other PCs and devices. It is automatically disabled and blocked on work and public networks to help maintain your file and PC security.

Once you are connected to a HomeGroup, the HomeGroup page in the Control Panel gives you options for sharing files and devices, including documents, pictures, music, videos, printers, and devices such as USB attached storage and external hard disks (see Figure 4-19).

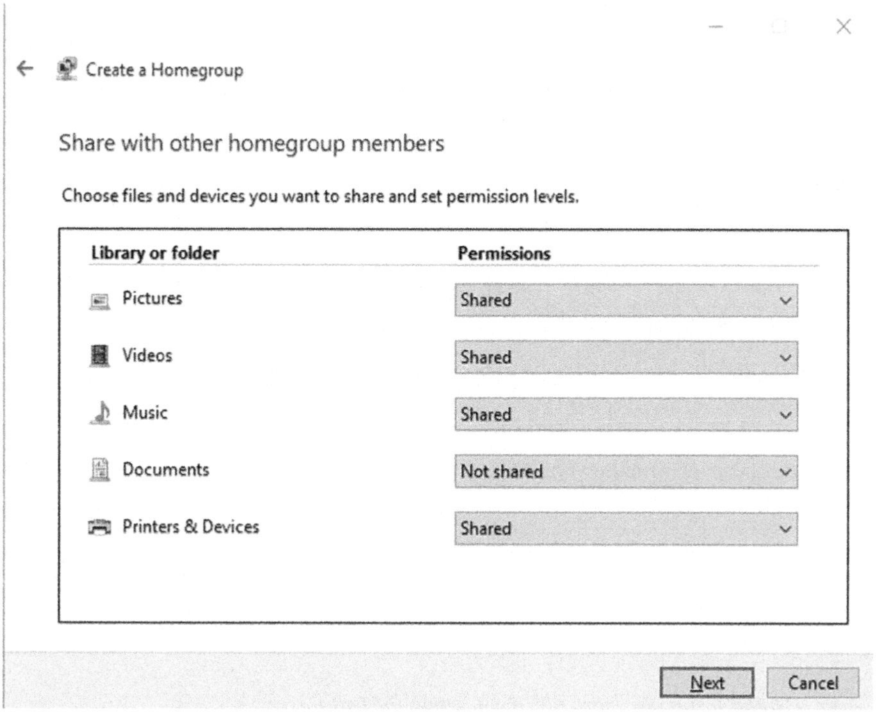

Figure 4-19. *The HomeGroup sharing settings*

When you have set up your HomeGroup, you are given a password that must be entered into any PC that wants to join the HomeGroup (see Figure 4-20).

Figure 4-20. *You are given a HomeGroup password when you set up the feature*

You are then returned to the main HomeGroup screen, from which you can control what is shared. You also see an option to **Allow all devices on this network such as TVs and game consoles to play my shared content** (see Figure 4-21). Selecting this permits compatible devices to stream audio and video from your PC.

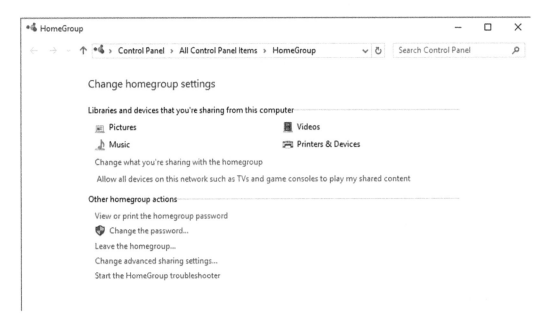

Figure 4-21. *You can manage the HomeGroup options*

Below this are options to view, print, and change the HomeGroup password. If a HomeGroup already exists on the home network, because it's been set up on another PC, Windows will find it automatically and prompt you to join it (see Figure 4-22). You will need the HomeGroup password.

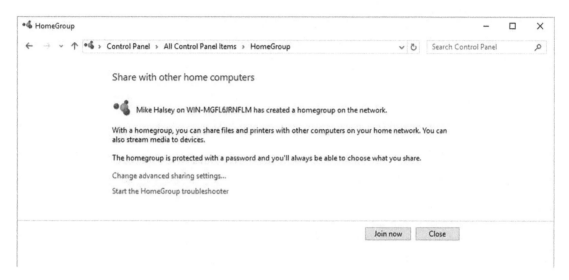

Figure 4-22. *If a HomeGroup already exists, you are prompted to join it*

There are security concerns to take into account with HomeGroups. With a HomeGroup, you have a secure password, which is also shown in the HomeGroup page in PC Settings; but when you share media via this setting, all that is required is access to your network. You need not worry about having to remember and enter a very secure password for your Wi-Fi router because media connectors and modern routers have a pairing button on them, usually called WPS, which connects secure devices without the need to enter complex passwords using awkward interfaces.

If you do not have a password on your Internet router, or if it has an insecure password, "admin" is common, you should create one right away. Unsecured routers can provide outsiders with access to your Internet connection and the shared files on your computers and devices.

Media shared on a HomeGroup cannot be deleted from your computer, and they don't include your documents. It is always wise to know who has access to what before you share it, however.

Sharing Files and Folders on a Network

There are several ways to share files and folders across a network in Windows 10. First, I want to discuss why you might want to share files and folders, and in what environments you should do it.

In the home environment, by far the simplest way to share files and folders is in a HomeGroup, as I have discussed already. HomeGroup gives you easy ways to share devices such as printers, which means you save money from not having to buy expensive new Wi-Fi printers.

You may have set up a HomeGroup and decided to share your pictures, music, and video, but not your documents. You may decide to keep your documents private, but want to share a folder or two's worth of documents with another person in the family.

HomeGroup can sometimes have connection difficulties, however, and you may want to share only a particular folder with another person or persons. Let's say, for example, that you are collaborating with another individual in a home office or at work, and you want to be able to share the resources and workflow documents.

In a Windows Server environment, all of this is managed by the System Center Configuration Manager, SharePoint, or a similar or alternative service, such as Microsoft Office 365; but many small businesses can't afford their own server system and don't have an Office 365 cloud-services subscription. This is where the built-in sharing in Windows 10 is very useful.

Again, in an office environment, you may want to set up one PC as a file store. I've done this myself, placing project documents and resources—in my case, teaching resources, lesson plans, schemes of work, and contractual paperwork—on a single machine (with a backup kept on another). I provided network access to the main PC with a desktop shortcut to the shared files to make it easy for everyone to access them.

Sharing with Individuals

Let's say that several people use the same computer in your home, and you want to be able to share files such as household documents, bills, legal documents, and perhaps homework assignments. File Explorer and Microsoft have made this type of sharing simpler than ever.

In File Explorer, navigate to and highlight the folder you want to share. Then, in the ribbon, click the **Share** tab; you see a section called Share With. Here, you highlight to share file(s) and/or folder(s) and click the name of the person(s) with whom you want to share. Windows 10 automatically and silently sets the sharing permissions.

If you want to choose a specific user, perhaps because he doesn't appear on the list, or if you want to choose the privileges for users, select **Specific People** to display a full list of the users on your computer (see Figure 4-23).

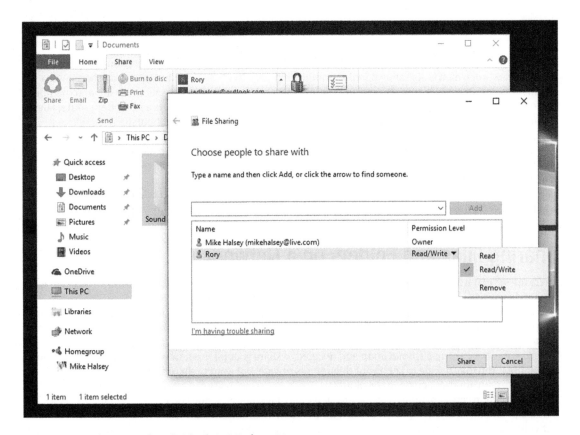

Figure 4-23. *Sharing with individuals in Windows 10*

This dialog comes in handy when you want to choose specific privileges for a user, such as Read Only, so that files can be accessed but not modified—and, crucially, not deleted!

■ **Caution**   Be careful giving others access to files and folders that you do not want changed or deleted.

For most sharing scenarios within a home with one PC, this is all you need; but many homes now have multiple PCs to share across. In a business environment, it is rare for several people to use the same PC, except in instances of small businesses in which people need only occasional access to a PC.

Sharing with Groups of People

If you have a multicomputer setup and don't want the risk that comes with sharing absolutely everything in your Documents folder, you want finer control over sharing. Windows 10 offers finer control in an easy-to-manage way.

It is managed by right-clicking a folder and selecting its properties. A Sharing tab contains all the controls (see Figure 4-24). There are only three, the first of which takes you to the settings dialog, similar to the one I talked about in the last section.

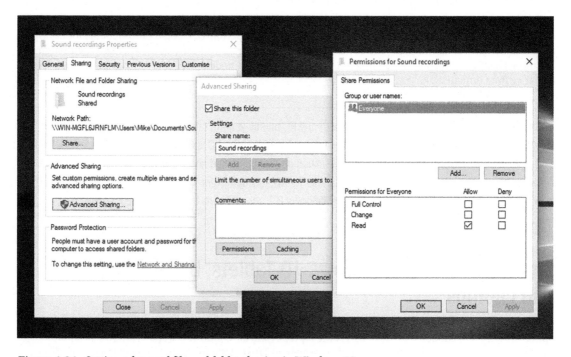

Figure 4-24. *Setting advanced file and folder sharing in Windows 10*

Click the Advanced Sharing button to get access to the settings for sharing a folder across a network. There is a simple check box to turn sharing on and off, making it simple to rescind sharing at a later stage, perhaps when a project has completed and you want to archive the folder. You can also give the shared folder a custom name. By default, sharing gives others permission to read files within the folder, but nothing else. This means that although others can access the files in a folder and read them, if they modify a file, they can't save it back to that folder. They also can't create or copy new files into the folder.

To change these settings, click the **Permissions** button. You are offered a variety of permissions options for separate user lists.

- **Full Control** enables you to create new files, and to copy files to and delete files from a folder. This is something you should be aware of when setting full control on any shared folder.

- **Change** allows people to make changes to files that already exist in the document; for example, opening, working on, and saving the updated copy of the file in the folder.

- **Read Only** grants permission to only open and read the contents of a folder.

■ **Note**   If you want to share folders from a computer running Windows 7 or Windows 8.1 with a Windows 10 computer, the sharing setup works the same way as described here.

Sharing with Non-Windows Computers

Setting the advanced sharing properties for folders is also useful if you want to share with non-Windows computers, such as an Apple Mac, PCs running GNU/Linux, or perhaps a Google Chromebook, for example, if someone in your household has one of these computers. Their network shares are accessible, although additional configuration may be required on the other computer to deal with minor incompatibilities that can arise from time to time.

■ **Caution**   Be cautious about sharing files with any PC unless you are certain that the anti-malware and firewall security on the other end is properly maintained, and that the PC is kept current with Windows Update. If any PC is running an older version of Windows, such as XP, you should not share with it because Windows XP no longer receives security support from Microsoft. Also, all support for Windows Vista ends in April 2017, Windows 7 support ends in January 2020, and Windows 8.1 support ends in January 2023.

Sharing Files with Windows 10 Tablets, Ultrabooks, and Laptops

You should never consider any mobile computer to be completely secure because they are so prone to opportunist theft or sudden loss. Although some laptops (and all Windows 8.1 and Windows 10 laptops and tablets with screens larger than 10 inches) come with Trusted Platform Module (TPM) security chips onboard to support full-disk encryption via BitLocker, older PCs do not, and if the PC is running Windows 10 Home or Windows 8.1 (Home edition), they can't use BitLocker anyway. TPM chips store encryption and keys for your hard disks in their firmware, and as such are very secure. I talk more about TPM chips and encrypting your files and computer in Chapter 12.

If you are carrying volumes of data around, it probably includes personal and sensitive information; and the simple fact remains that tablets, Ultrabooks, and laptops are highly desirable items for thieves.

The next consideration is what you can actually *do* with those files on these portable devices. Do you want Word, Excel, and PowerPoint documents? Do you want your entire photo or music library when you'll likely only ever access a small portion of it when you're on the move? One advantage is that Windows 10 is capable of synching mobile devices with your OneDrive account, and keeping a local copy of files once you've accessed them once. I show you how to use this effectively in Chapter 8.

I believe it is folly to assume that any portable device is completely secure, even when it is encrypted properly with a TPM chip and a technology such as BitLocker. There are just too many variables to justify carrying around your entire libraries of documents, photos, and more.

The final consideration is whether the computer is properly password protected. You may have a local account on your tablet (or other device) that doesn't require a password, which means that anyone picking up your device has complete access to the hard drive.

Alternatively, you may have a Microsoft account that you use to log on to your device. This could be a long, super-secure password at least 10 characters long and containing a mixture of uppercase and lowercase letters, numbers, and symbols. But there's a temptation to create a PIN or picture password for Windows 10 access because you don't want to have to enter such a long password every time you start your device.

A PIN code instantly reduces a secure multicharacter password to a simple, four-digit numeric code, which isn't anywhere near as secure; and although a picture password might be more secure if presented with a photo of three or more people, the temptation would be to poke the first three people on the nose or draw circles around their faces. Is this what you would do? Is this what you might consider for a picture password? Although web enthusiasts and IT pros are generally more security aware than consumers are, a great many people think that a "plonk, plonk, plonk" approach to picture passwords in a fun pattern is also secure. Believe me, it isn't any more secure than having the name of your dog as a password.

You can watch my video tutorial on how to create secure (and memorable) passwords online at `http://pcs.tv/1B1N0ja`.

Windows 10 and OneDrive File Sync / Backup

Microsoft's cloud backup and sync service, OneDrive, comes built into Windows 10, and the implementation can really help you gain access to your files and documents when you're using devices with small amounts of storage, such as tablets and Ultrabooks.

You can synchronize any files and folders on your PC with OneDrive. To set up OneDrive, search for it in the Start menu and click the OneDrive (cloud) icon in the taskbar system tray. You are prompted to sign in with your Microsoft account and then asked where you want your OneDrive files to be stored (see Figure 4-25).

Figure 4-25. You can access OneDrive apps in File Explorer or from within apps

---

■ **Tip**   You can also use an Office 365 OneDrive for business accounts with OneDrive in Windows 10.

You typically keep all of your files on a desktop PC, and from here you can synchronize them with your other Windows 10 devices and back them up to the cloud. If you are using a laptop, Ultrabook, or tablet that's short on storage space (tablets can come with as little as 16GB of space, and Ultrabooks and pro-tablets typically come with 64GB, 128GB, or 256GB of storage), you might not want to have many files synchronized down to the device.

■ **Tip**   Access your OneDrive files on your PC by clicking the OneDrive link in the left panel of File Explorer.

Thus, you might want to change where you store your OneDrive files, depending on what type of device you are using and how many files there are. For example, on my main desktop PC I have a second hard disk, but you can also split your hard disk into several partitions, with each appearing as their own disk (see Chapter 12 for how to do this). This enables you to store your files and documents separately to your Windows 10 installation.

Let's look for a moment at why you might want to do this. If something goes drastically wrong with your copy of Windows 10, you might have to reinstall the operating system from scratch. This might involve a complete wipe and format of the drive, perhaps because of the nature of the problem or because the hard disk is short on free space.

Should this happen, you'll lose all the files that are stored on it. If you don't have many files, perhaps just 5GB or so, then it's not too great a problem to sync them back down from the OneDrive backup you created previously. Some people have a huge amount of files, however; I've got 1.1TB (about 1,100GB) on my main PC, and syncing that back down from the cloud would take weeks on even the fastest broadband connection.

For this reason, I store my OneDrive (and all other files I choose to only keep locally) separately from Windows 10. If you want to do this, I'll show you how in Chapter 12. It's useful that you can tell OneDrive on your PC where you want your files stored (or where they're already stored).

On the other hand, if your PC has only limited amounts of storage (it's a low-cost laptop or a tablet), then you simply won't have space for all of your files, and you may only want to store a few of them. In this case, it's perfectly fine to leave the default C:\Users\YourName\OneDrive location, because they won't take long to synchronize back down to the PC should disaster strike.

Next, you're asked which files and folders you want to sync to the local PC. You are shown your main libraries (Documents, Pictures, Music, and Videos) along with any folders already stored on OneDrive (see Figure 4-26).

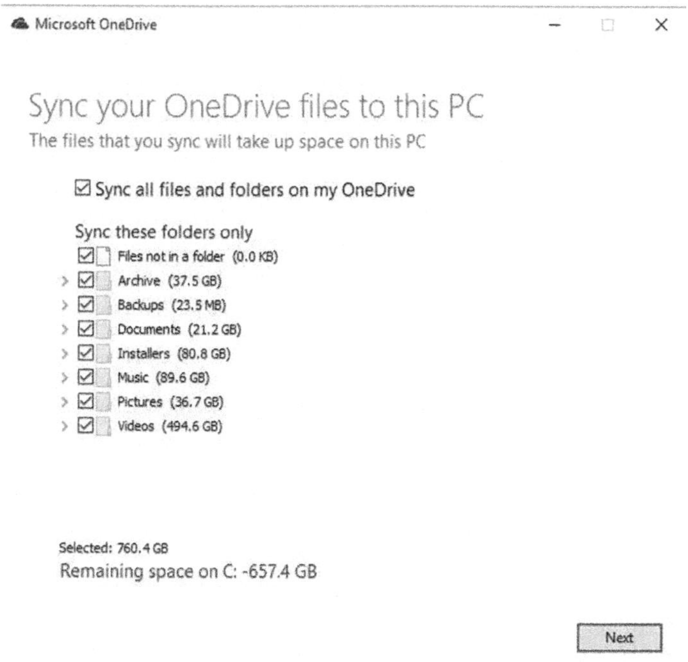

Figure 4-26. *You can choose which files to sync with OneDrive*

■ **Tip**   You can store any folder in OneDrive by simply moving it to the OneDrive store folder on your PC.

If there isn't enough space on your PC to store all the files you currently have stored in OneDrive (see Figure 4-26), you are alerted of this. Once you have selected the files and folders you wish to sync on that PC, any changes you make to files, or any new files that you create in those folders, or any files that you delete (this is important!) are replicated in your OneDrive cloud backup and also across all the other PCs that synchronize those folders.

Opening Files Stored Only in OneDrive

It's possible to access and open files you have stored in OneDrive without needing to first have them stored on your PC. While not a feature that shipped with Windows 10 when it launched, this was activated via an update a few months later, and by the time you read this, it's probably available.

If you used Windows 8.1, you may be familiar with OneDrive pointer files. These look like your actual files and documents, but when you click one to open it, the file is automatically downloaded from OneDrive first, so you don't first need to store it on the PC. The file remains on the PC until you perform a right-click it, and tell Windows to only store that file online.

This is a great way to be able to access all the files that you have stored in OneDrive on any device, no matter how little storage it might have. Indeed, from launch this is exactly how Windows 10 Mobile apps (such as OneDrive and Photos) on smartphones act.

You know that this feature is available on your PC if all of your OneDrive files and folders appear when you click the OneDrive link in the left panel of File Explorer. Although this feature hasn't been included at the time I write this, it's so incredibly useful that it's definitely worth mentioning.

Using Microsoft OneDrive to Share Files

You might want to share a file that you have stored in OneDrive. You can do this at the OneDrive.com web site. Right-click the file(s) or folder(s) you want to share with other people and click the **Share** link at the top of the screen. A dialog asks who you want to share the files with and what permissions you want give them (see Figure 4-27).

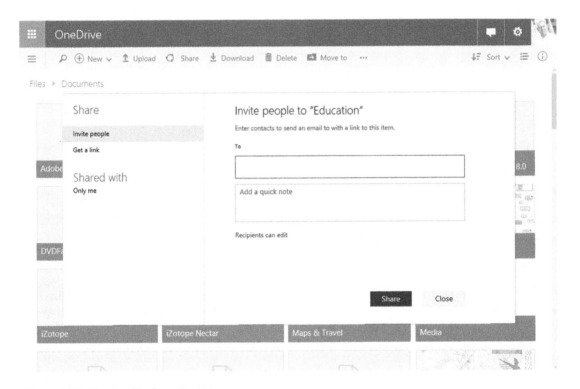

Figure 4-27. *Sharing files from OneDrive*

■ **Caution** You can also right-click a file in File Explorer and select **Share with** followed by **OneDrive** to open a OneDrive browser window.

Be careful what permissions you grant people when sharing your files. You might not want to give permission to delete file(s) because accidents can very easily happen.

Sharing Content Within Apps

One of the best new features in Windows 10 is the capability to share content directly from one store app to another. This is done without the apps having to know how it is done and without the developers having to add any code into the app other than support for the sharing service because the sharing mechanisms are part of Windows 10.

How this will actually be used over time remains to be seen, as industrious app developers will no doubt constantly find new and innovative ways to use the feature. At its most basic, however, it is a way to share photos vie email or with photo-sharing services such as Flickr, Facebook, and PhotoBucket, or to send documents to friends and colleagues from the Office 365 store apps.

You can also highlight text, perhaps on a web page, and share it between apps; you can share any type of content, really. This is where it will be fascinating to see how app developers use this feature. There's not really been anything quite like it in an operating system before, so anticipating how it will be used over time is impossible to guess right now.

You can share in Windows 10 by selecting or highlighting the item or items you want to share or just by being on a page in the app, and then clicking the hamburger menu in the top left of the app window (if you do not see this icon, which consists of three horizontal lines, sharing is either not supported in that app or the share button is located elsewhere). All compatible apps for that type of content appear in a flyout on the right side of your screen (see Figure 4-28). Click the app you want to share the content with, and the content is transferred to the other app for sharing without kicking you out of the app that you are currently using.

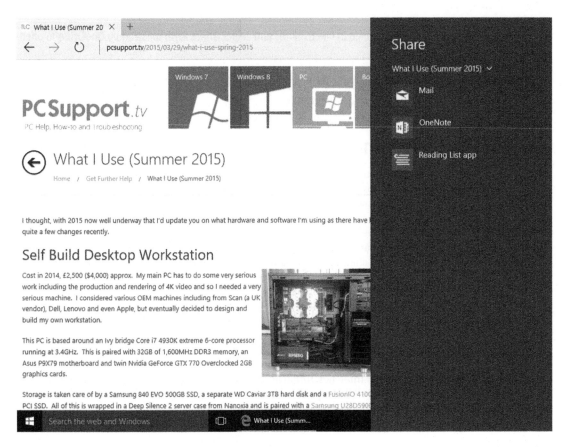

Figure 4-28. Sharing via Windows 10

Of course, this sharing feature comes with risks. The easier it is to share content with apps, web sites, and the like, the easier it becomes to accidentally put content where you didn't intend for it to go, or for it to go on web sites where your privacy settings mean that it is generally accessible to the whole world. I always recommend, strongly in fact, that you make sure that your privacy settings on web sites are set to automatically block all access to people you have not *deliberately* invited to view your stuff.

Sharing Optical Drives

One of the biggest challenges facing users of Windows tablets and Ultrabooks is the lack of an optical drive. Sure, you can install software (and even Windows 10) from a USB flash drive or the Internet, and Windows 10 allows you to mount ISO (CD and DVD disc image) files; but there will be occasions when you'll need an optical drive.

One solution is to buy a USB optical drive, but this isn't always a practical solution. Indeed, I bought one the other year for my Windows tablet and then promptly left it at a Microsoft Research event in Cambridge (UK), where it isn't doing me much good any more, although someone has hopefully found it useful.

A better solution is to share the optical drive on another computer. To do this in Windows 10 and both Windows 7 and Windows 8.1 (because the instructions are the same), do the following:

1. On the host computer (the one with the optical drive), open File Explorer (Windows Explorer in Windows 7) and click Computer in the left pane.

2. Right-click the optical drive you want to share. From the options, click Share with ➤Advanced sharing (see Figure 4-29).

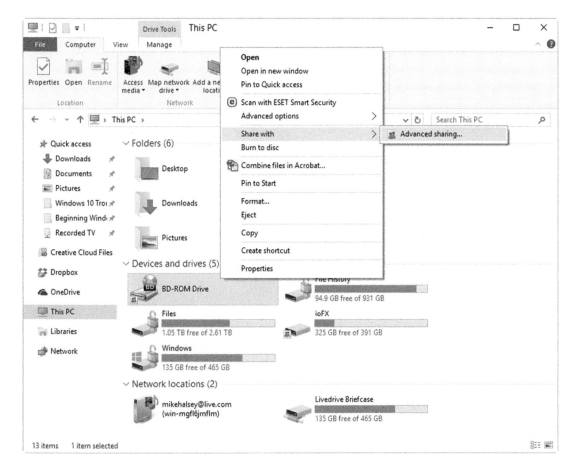

Figure 4-29. *Select an optical drive to share*

3. In the dialog, click the **Advanced Sharing** button (see Figure 4-30).

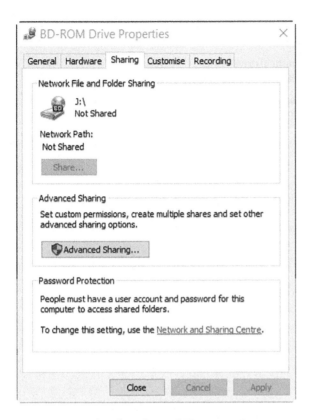

Figure 4-30. Select the Advanced Sharing settings

4. Select the **Share this folder** box and then give the share an appropriate name, such as **Blu-ray Drive** (see Figure 4-31).

Figure 4-31. Share the drive and give it a name

5.   Click **OK**. You are shown the full network name of the share, in this case \\WORKSTATION\Blu-ray Drive (see Figure 4-32). You also see a small share icon in the bottom left of the drive's icon in File Explorer to indicate that it has been shared.

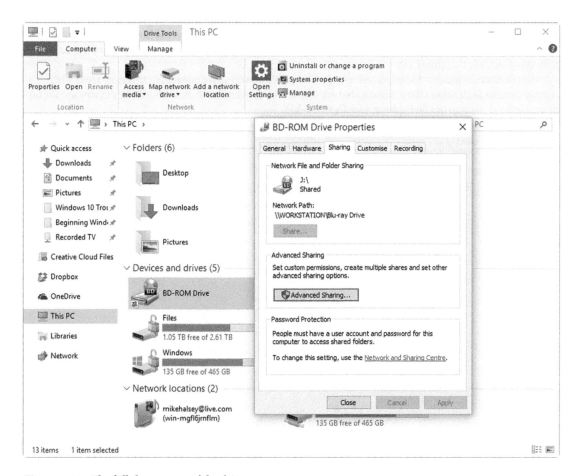

Figure 4-32. *The full share name of the drive*

■ **Note**   For the drive to be visible on other computers, you need to have File and Printer Sharing turned on in the Advanced Sharing Settings page of the Network and Sharing Center. Users of other computers may also need the username and password of the host computer to gain access to the shared drive.

This optical drive is now accessible to other computers (including Ultrabooks and tablets) when they are attached to the same network and the computer with the optical drive is switched on.

Streaming Music and Videos to Devices and Computers

At the beginning of the chapter, I showed you how to set up a HomeGroup to share your documents, music, pictures, and videos with other Windows 10 and Windows 7 computers. Among the HomeGroup settings was **Allow devices such as TVs and games consoles to play my shared content**. Activating this feature turns your computer (when it is switched on) into a Universal Plug and Play (UPnP) server. Many devices support this feature, including Internet radios, MP3-playing hi-fi systems, external network-attached storage (NAS) and USB hard disks, game consoles, and even devices you wouldn't normally expect to work happily with Windows, such as smart TVs.

Not only can Windows 10 (and previous versions of Windows) share content in this way, it can also stream content from other UPnP devices that are connected to your home network. UPnP devices are found in the Network section of File Explorer (see Figure 4-33).

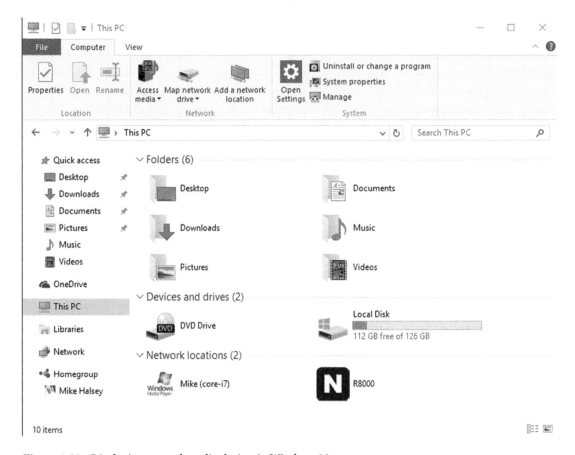

Figure 4-33. *Displaying network media devices in Windows 10*

Here you can check whether Windows 10 is sharing your content properly and (I think somewhat crucially) that nothing is being shared by accident.

Windows 10 shares only media files such as pictures, music, and video; you can be sure that your documents will not be shared with media devices. This comes in particularly handy if you have downloaded movies or TV shows onto your computer and you want to watch them on your TV, perhaps through your Xbox One console, or a smart TV media streaming app.

Changing the Advanced Sharing Settings in Windows 10

Sometimes you may have trouble with network sharing in Windows, which could be caused by something switched off in the Advanced Sharing Settings page. Alternatively, you may want to deliberately switch something off if you no longer want a certain type of sharing to take place from a specific computer.

You can access the Advanced Sharing Settings page from the Network and Sharing Center, itself accessible from either the ribbon in the Network view of File Explorer, or by right-clicking the Network icon on the desktop taskbar.

Once in the Network and Sharing Center, there is a link to Change Advanced Sharing Settings in the left pane.

There are a great many options in the Advanced Sharing Settings page (see Figure 4-34), and some are very important and significant.

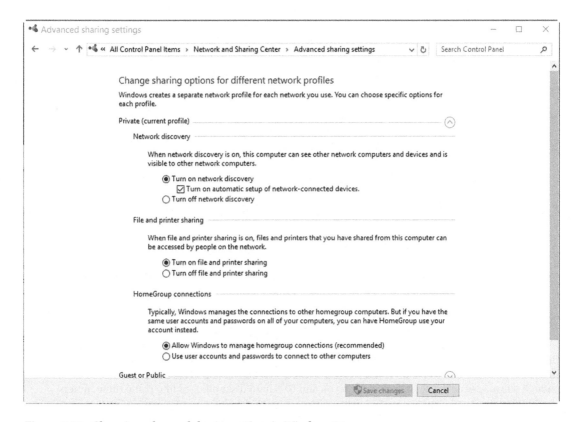

Figure 4-34. *Changing advanced sharing settings in Windows 10*

The network settings are separated into three groups: Private, Guest or Public, and All Networks. The sharing settings for Public networks are understandably different from those for Private networks. The following describes the main settings:

- **Network Discovery** is the setting to go to when your computer can't be found on a network or you can't see any other computers and devices. There is a switch here to automatically turn on setup for network connected devices. You may not want this on, however, if you are commonly in environments in which networked devices such as storage might be prone to malware infection and distribution.

- **File and Printer Sharing** is the main switch for sharing all of your files, documents, pictures, music, and videos on networks. Printer sharing affects only printers physically attached to the computer.

- **HomeGroup Connections** is a useful setting if you want to choose between Windows automatically managing user access from computers in HomeGroup and finer control with specific user accounts and passwords required.

- **Public Folder Sharing** isn't what you might first believe. It's not about sharing your files and folders with the public. Instead, it is about the public folders that Windows has always set up in user accounts to aid the sharing of files. These folders are not commonly used, however.

- **Media Streaming** controls the options for live broadcasting of pictures, audio, and video over a network to UPnP devices. Uncheck this if you do not want your music, videos, and pictures to show up on your network as shared media.

- **File Sharing Connections** is the setting for controlling the amount of encryption used on the network when sharing files. This should not ever be changed from the default unless you are requested to do so by a company IT administrator because making changes can potentially compromise your PC's security.

- **Password Protected File Sharing** is something that you shouldn't normally change; however, if you do not have a password on the computer from which you use to share files, you will find that you can't access those files from another computer unless you turn this setting off.

Connecting to Network Shared Storage

These days, most networked shared storage automatically appears in the Network section of File Explorer. This is the case whether you're on a home or a work network, and can include NAS boxes, file servers (though you may need to sign in to access these), and USB hard disks plugged into compatible routers.

In Windows 7, you could view a full network map through the Network and Sharing Center to locate devices. You can no longer do this in Windows 10 (mostly because it didn't always work reliably), but the operating system is much better at connecting to network resources than its predecessors.

Unfortunately, with the removal of the network map, the option to automatically log in to the network storage administration interface is also gone. In Windows 10, if you want to change a configuration option, you have to know the IP address of the device, which you can get through your router or through the Devices and Printers page.

■ **Note**   The default IP address of a router is normally 192.168.0.1 or 192.168.1.1. You can type this into your web browser address bar to gain access.

Why You Might Not See Network Storage on Your Computer

Sometimes network resources fail to appear. This is usually a problem caused by your router. A typical home router provided by your ISP can be unreliable at simultaneously managing multiple devices on the network.

In my own home, for example, I regularly have a desktop PC, a laptop (perhaps even a second laptop), a tablet, a smart TV, a Windows phone or two, and an NAS drive on at the same time—so six devices plus the router. Very occasionally, and back when I was using a cheap router provided by my ISP, I found that Windows started with a message that it had detected an IP address conflict. This happens when the router has incorrectly assigned the IP addresses of the PCs and devices on the network, and one device thinks it has a different IP address from the one the router has assigned it.

In practice, however, Windows is very good at sorting out these types of problems on its own. It is very rare that you are completely unable to see a networked device.

You can manually set the IP addresses for computers and devices on your router. This is also possible within the Network and Sharing Center. If you can see the device on another PC, right-click the device, select its properties, click **Internet Protocol Version 4 (TCP/IPv4)** (or the v6 option), and then click the **Properties** button to set a static IP address. If a device still fails to appear, then restarting that device (and the router) normally rectifies the problem.

Another thing that can prevent your computer from seeing network storage is a firewall with settings that are too aggressive. I have found that some security suites have this problem with the default configuration. The solution depends on your security suite and the way its configuration options work. It is always worth checking if you experience problems. You can best check by temporarily switching the firewall off. After you are successfully connected to your network storage, you can turn the firewall back on again without interrupting the connection in the future.

Viewing the Status of Network Drives

When you use the Network page in File Explorer, it's simple to view and access other hard disks and attached storage on your network. The ability to see the amount of remaining storage is more difficult. There's no point in performing a backup to a network drive, for example, if you don't know that you first need to clear some space.

You can do this by connecting your computer to a folder on the drive; any folder will do, but it's usually a good idea to create a root folder on the disk into which you put everything else. This way, when you open the shared drive, you can view and work with all of its content.

To see how much available storage is on your Network drives in File Explorer, follow these instructions:

1. Open File Explorer and click **Network** in the left pane.

2. Double-click the network drive you want to attach to your computer.

3. Right-click a folder within that drive. From the options, click **Map network drive** (see Figure 4-35).

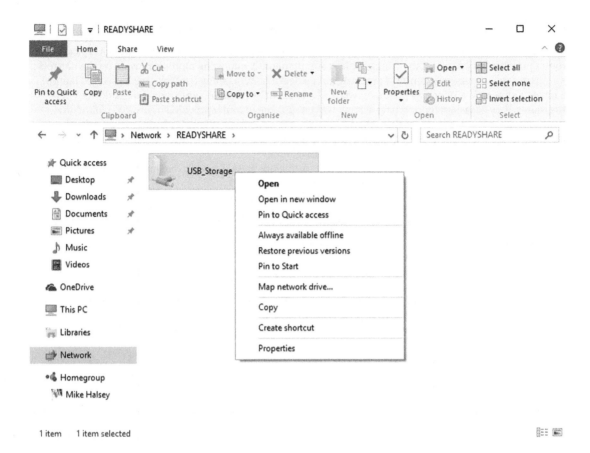

Figure 4-35. *Connecting a network drive*

4. In the dialog, choose any free drive. If you want Windows to automatically connect to this drive every time you start your computer, make sure that **Reconnect at Logon** is checked. If the mapped drive is on another computer, you may need to log in to it with different credentials; this is the username and password for the host PC (see Figure 4-36).

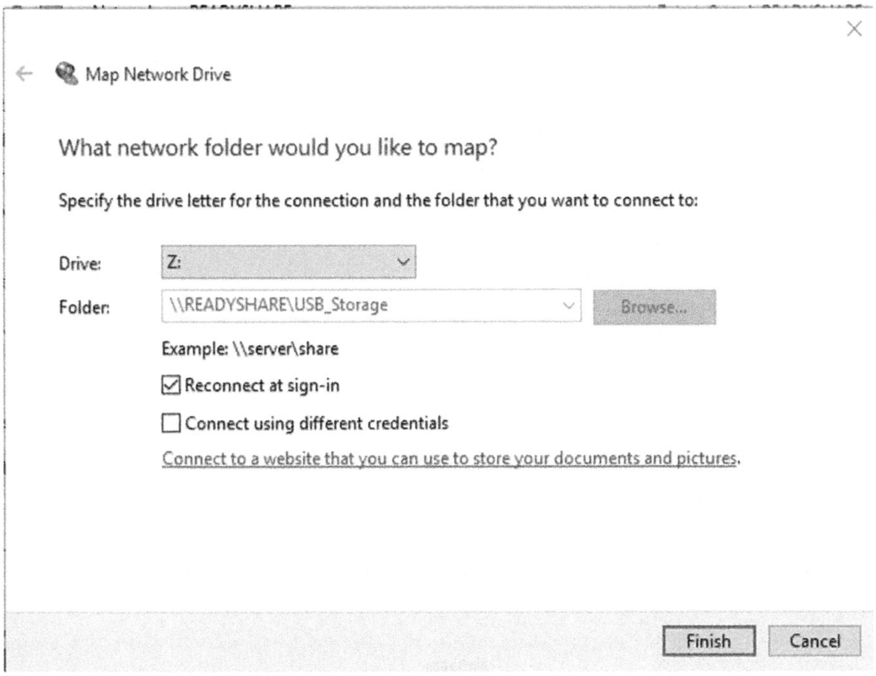

← ⊛ Map Network Drive

What network folder would you like to map?

Specify the drive letter for the connection and the folder that you want to connect to:

Drive: Z:

Folder: \\READYSHARE\USB_Storage   Browse...

Example: \\server\share

☑ Reconnect at sign-in

☐ Connect using different credentials

Connect to a website that you can use to store your documents and pictures.

Finish   Cancel

Figure 4-36. Map Network Drive options

5.   Click **Finish** when you are done.

The network drive now appears in File Explorer in the Network Location section of the This PC view. It displays the total size of the drive, along with the amount of available free space. As you can see in the screenshot shown in Figure 4-37, it's good that I checked, because the available space is beginning to run low.

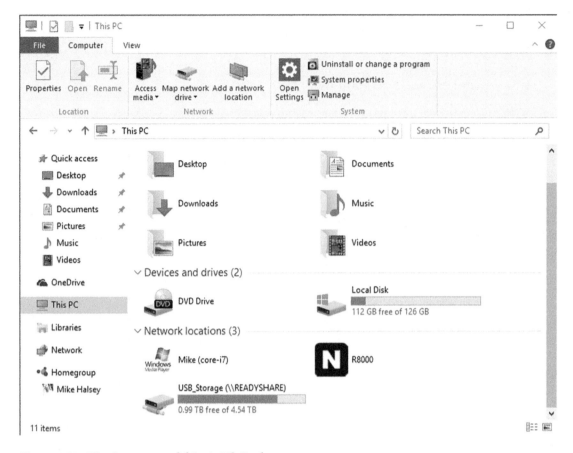

Figure 4-37. *Viewing a mapped drive in File Explorer*

■ **Tip** Sometimes your network drives don't show up in File Explorer, perhaps because they're on a subnetwork such as a powerline system in your home or office. You can manually connect to them in the address bar by typing \\ followed by the name of the network drive; for example, \\N3 to connect to the drive called N3.

Summary

There are more ways to share documents, media, and network resources in Windows 10 than ever before offered in a Windows operating system. The sharing integration with apps is something that I am personally excited to see developers use to push sharing in new directions.

Of course, there are security considerations. You should always make sure that you have up-to-date anti-malware protection, that you're getting all available Windows updates, and that you're not sharing anything with PCs that might be insecure.

The Devices and Printers page is far more powerful than it first appears to be. The networking settings for sharing are also very powerful. When it comes to sharing media files and printer access, Windows 10 is a great operating system to use, especially with its helpful wizards—something Microsoft has always been good at—walking you through each step.

Despite the removal of a couple of Windows 7 features that I personally found very useful, it is still very possible to robustly work with network resources.

CHAPTER 5

■ ■ ■

Organizing and Searching Your PC and the Internet

Our computing devices—be they desktop PCs, laptops, tablets, smartphones, or new Ultrabooks—are all about content. We either make it or consume it, but we all have ever-growing quantities of it. You may store it on a network share, in the cloud, on an external hard disk, or on the computer's hard disk or solid-state drive (SSD)—but there will probably be a lot of it wherever it is stored.

Of this content, you'll likely have an ever-ballooning collection of digital photographs, a big music library, and possibly a growing video collection. These files take a lot of space to store and can make finding exactly what you're looking for problematic, especially with photos.

At the other end of the file-size scale are all of your Microsoft Word, Excel, PDF, and other file types, which you have for personal, household, work, and school purposes. Although they may not take up large amounts of space, these files can be equally difficult to find and organize.

Traditionally, the way to organize files and documents was to use a folder structure. I remember using software such as XTree on the first IBM PCs to perform this task (see Figure 5-1).

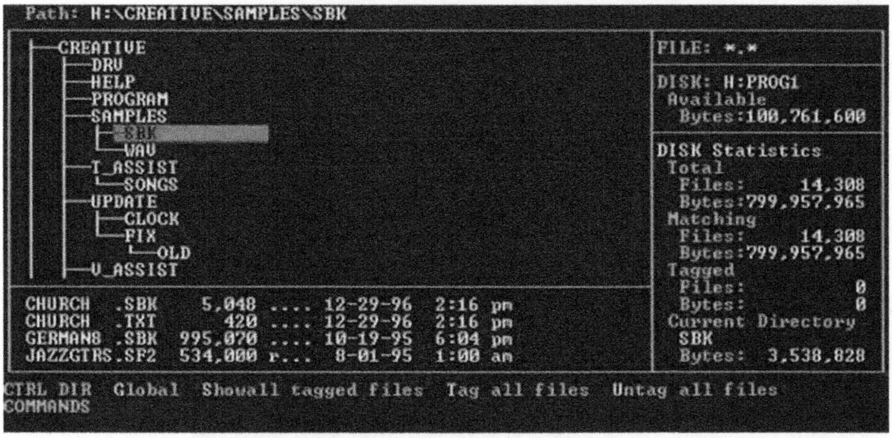

Figure 5-1. *XTree on the original IBM PC*

Folders aren't always a suitable way to organize our files and documents because some have crossovers between categories; and as the volume of files, music, pictures, and videos we collect expands, even the most organized folder structure can become unwieldy and difficult to navigate.

For many years now, Windows has tried to help us organize our files through user folders, My Documents, and so forth. They still exist, but there are much more powerful ways to help you organize. In this chapter, I'll show you how to optimize file organization and access.

With Windows 10, Microsoft is taking search to the next level with the introduction of the Cortana personal digital assistant. Cortana can help you find files and content online, but also can use the files, emails, and data that you have, or which is found on the Internet, to set smart reminders, track packages, and much more.

Cortana

We'll start with Cortana, as she's really the central hub for search and for organizing your PC (and quite possibly organizing large chunks of your life too). Cortana can be found on the taskbar, next to the Windows icon. You see the search box there when you first use Windows 10 (see Figure 5-2). Clicking in the search box and entering text lets you search for files, folders, Windows settings, and online content, but this is just Cortana at her most basic.

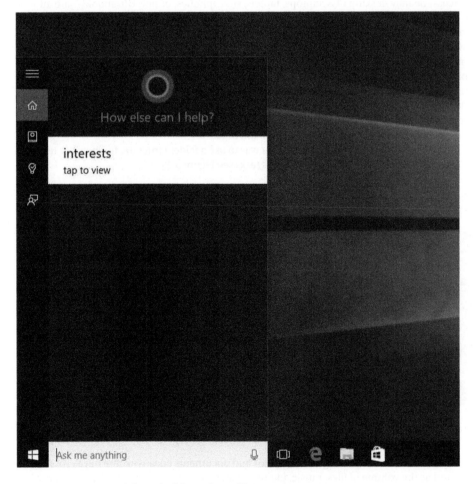

Figure 5-2. *Cortana is launched from the taskbar*

If you are using a Windows 10 Mobile smartphone, Cortana can be launched by pressing the search button at the bottom right of your screen.

___

■ **Note**   You can switch between the search box and the Cortana icon, and even hide Cortana completely, by right-clicking the taskbar and then clicking the Cortana option on the pop-up menu that appears.

___

When you first use Cortana, you're asked for permission to access personal information, such as your profile, location, and files. Don't worry if you give permission for something you later wish you hadn't, because Cortana takes your privacy extremely seriously (as would any good personal assistant). Managing your privacy settings is pretty straightforward; we'll look at this later in this section.

___

■ **Tip**   You can also open the Start menu to launch a Cortana search automatically.

___

When you type a search term into the **Ask me anything** box, Cortana displays a list of web search options, settings, and Store apps (see Figure 5-3). If you then click the **My stuff** button in the bottom left of the Cortana window, you can expand your search into content on your own PC.

Figure 5-3. *Cortana displays web, settings, and store search results by default*

When searching your PC, you first see a list of any apps, settings, documents, pictures, music, and videos that match your search term (see Figure 5-4). At the top of the search results window are two drop-down menus. The first allows you to switch between the **Most relevant** and **Most recent** search results. This can be useful when searching for documents you have recently been working on, or for photos you have just copied to your PC.

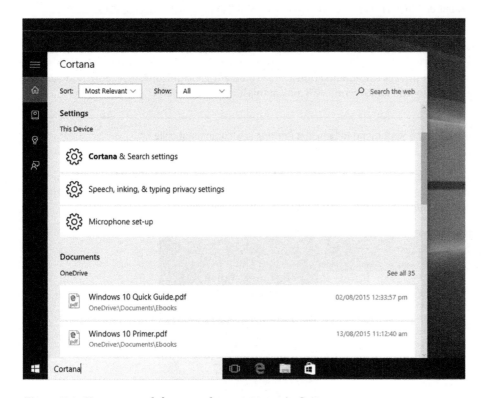

Figure 5-4. *You can search for many document types in Cortana*

The next drop-down menu allows you to specify that you want to search for documents, folders, apps, settings, photos, videos, or music. Additionally, at the top right of the window is a **Search the web** button, which opens your web browser and autosearches online for your search term.

Each search results category (documents, photos, etc.) has a **See all...** link to its right if the results include more than a handful of files, making it quick and easy for you to expand the results and find the file you're after.

Hey Cortana!

Cortana isn't just about typing search queries into your PC, though; she's way cooler than that. On the far right of the search box on the taskbar, or on the right of the search box when you click the Cortana icon, is a microphone icon. Click this and you can give Cortana instructions or request searches; she's remarkably good at understanding natural language.

■ **Note**   You might be asked to set up your microphone to work with Cortana the first time you use the speech option.

Better still, Cortana can be launched with voice (this needs to be activated in her settings; I'll show you how to do this shortly). All you need to do to launch Cortana is say "Hey Cortana," to your PC. She can even be told to only respond to your voice and not others, which is useful if a colleague thinks it's amusing to launch Cortana every time he walks past your desk.

If you have speakers on your PC, Cortana will respond to your voice by speaking back to you. Her language is surprisingly natural too.

So what can you do with Cortana when speaking or when typing? The natural language recognition works just as well with both. You can ask things such as "What is the weather doing tomorrow?" or command such things as "Tell me what appointments I have today." You can also search for files and documents, such as with a command like "Show me my recent photos." And saying "Search for documents about Windows 10," displays search results of document titles or contents that contain the text *Windows 10*.

Just a Reminder...

One of the main areas of focus Microsoft had with Windows 10 is productivity, and Cortana has her own cool tricks to help keep us organized. Reminders can be set based on criteria such as a specific date or time, a place you visit, or even a person you're with.

Saying or typing "Remind me to …" sets a reminder in which Cortana prompts you about when you should be reminded (see Figure 5-5). You can speak these instructions: "This afternoon at 4 p.m.," or "Next Wednesday morning." Additionally, you can specify a place or person. Giving the instruction "When I'm with Rory Webster," or "The next time I'm at Carrigan Court," or "When I get to Walmart," uses your calendar to see when you're due to be meeting a person, or if that person is also using Cortana, it alerts you when you are both in the vicinity of one another. If you set a location-based reminder, it uses your device's location services to determine the right place to alert you.

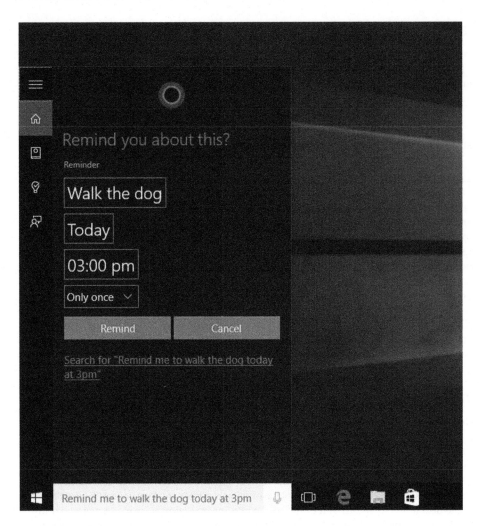

Figure 5-5. You can set reminders using Cortana

■ **Tip** If you click the Reminder icon on the left side of the Cortana window, and then click the three dots (…) icon in the bottom right of the window, an option displays your reminders history. This is useful if you want to quickly set up a repeat event.

Reminders follow you across your Windows 10 devices, so you don't need to worry about setting one on your PC, but being away from your desk at the time its due. If you have a Windows 10 tablet or smartphone, you are still reminded. Better still, once you snooze or dismiss a reminder on one device, it's automatically snoozed or dismissed on all of your other devices too.

Configuring Cortana

Cortana is controlled by the icons on the left side of her window. The top one, the hamburger menu (see Figure 5-6), so called because its three horizontal lines look a bit like a hamburger (no, me neither!) display the full names of the controls available to you. The first control, **Home**, can be used to cancel the current search and return to the main Cortana display, which might show you the weather or news and sports results.

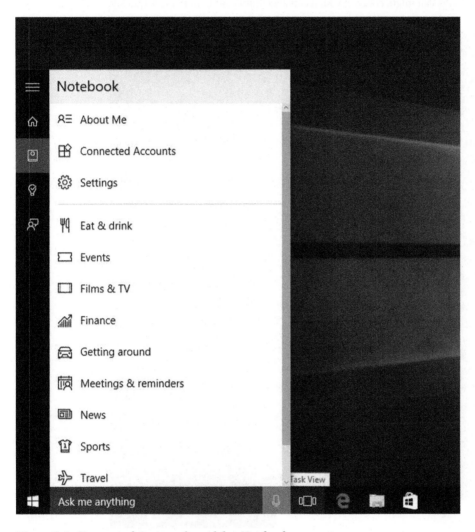

Figure 5-6. *You control Cortana through her Notebook*

Next up are the **Notebook** options, and it's here that you can fully control Cortana on your Windows 10 device. **Clicking About me** allows you to set the name Cortana calls you. I choose the name "Mike," although "fluffy bunnykins" or "big boy" also work perfectly well. Here you can also set your favorite places. These are searched for by using a combination of Internet search and location services and can include your home, office and perhaps the gym. Creating some favorite places can help with setting reminders, such as "Remind me to ask about the new membership fee when I get to the gym."

Connected Accounts lets you also connect Cortana to your Office 365, company or college domain, or Azure Active Directory account. This allows Cortana to additionally alert you to events, reminders, and notifications for those accounts, as well as the Microsoft account you use to sign in to Windows 10.

Then comes Cortana's Settings (see Figure 5-7). Cortana is highly configurable and is extremely respectful of your privacy. The first option allows you to switch off suggestions (more on these shortly), reminders, and alerts. You can also disable the Hey Cortana feature, as this constantly monitors your microphone, and aside from any privacy issues that might concern you, it can also drain your battery more quickly.

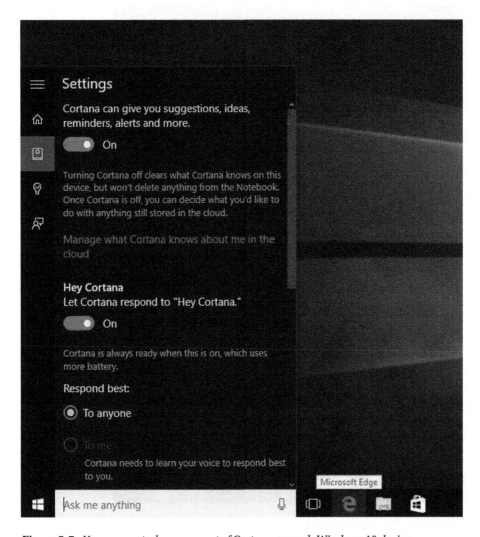

Figure 5-7. *You can control every aspect of Cortana on each Windows 10 device*

Cortana's settings are also where you can tell her to only respond to your voice and nobody else's, which is useful in a workplace where more than one person is using Windows 10. By far one of the coolest features in Cortana is her tracking ability, not to track you or even for hunting big game (because that would probably be illegal), but for identifying parcel and flight information in your email inbox, SMS, and other messages, and then automatically tracking those items for you. Cortana then displays alerts in your taskbar (or by toasts in Windows 10 Mobile), when, for example, your package is out for delivery or your flight is delayed.

Beneath the Settings option in Cortana's Notebook (see Figure 5-6) are the different categories of information Cortana can automatically provide via pop-up alerts on the Windows 10 taskbar (or again, by toasts in Windows 10 Mobile). These alert types are many and varied and can include watching the value of your stock shares, alerting you when your favorite band makes an announcement, providing traffic updates (voice only when you're driving, naturally), and making suggestions for meals and restaurants.

It can be worth spending a little time configuring these options because they can be extremely flexible (and will be expanded over time as Cortana is updated). If, like me, you don't like being bothered by pop-ups, you might want to just tell Cortana to alert you about reminders, packages, flights, weather, and nothing else. However, if you like being told about events in your area, being alerted about new artists based on the one you're currently listening to, or getting recommendations on a new Thai dish, Cortana's options are extremely flexible and powerful indeed.

Speaking of music artists... clicking the **Music search** option on Windows 10 Mobile smartphones has the phone listen to any music currently playing (perhaps on the TV or radio) and then uses Bing to identify the track and give you the name and the artist.

Lastly, in the menu options is a button that displays all of the reminders you have set with Cortana. Here you can edit them or delete them if they no longer apply. There is a multiple select button at the bottom of the window, including a (+) button for adding a new reminder.

File Explorer

Cortana isn't the only way to search your PC, however. Some people need much finer control over the searches they make. For anybody with more than a few photos and music tracks on their PCs, organizing them into an easily accessible and understandable hierarchy is extremely important. File Explorer is the place to start a discussion about organizing your files. You open File Explorer by clicking the yellow and blue folder icon on the taskbar, or by clicking the File Explorer link in the Start menu.

■ **Tip** The Ribbon interface is minimized by default in Windows 10, appearing only when you click a tab header. You can show or hide the ribbon at all times in File Explorer by clicking the small arrow on the right of the ribbon headers (see Figure 5-8) You can also double-click the ribbon to toggle the show/hide function.

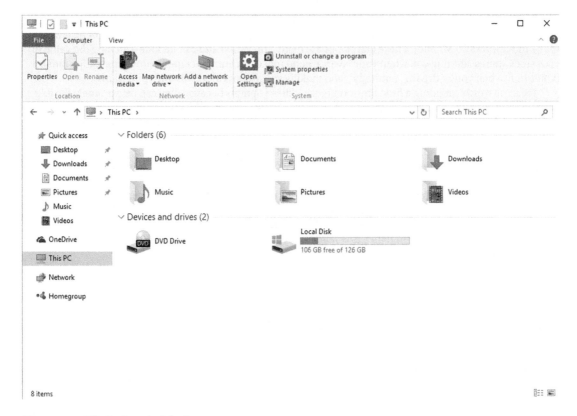

Figure 5-8. *File Explorer in Windows 10*

■ **Tip** Clicking a program icon in the very top left of its window first displays a menu of window controls; with a second click, the program closes.

Quick Access Toolbar

The Quick Access Toolbar remains next to the program button at the top of the window (see Figure 5-9). This area allows you to single-click access to commonly used commands. It is also customizable, with the down arrow to its right bringing up a list of additional buttons that you can add to the toolbar, including Undo, Delete, and Rename.

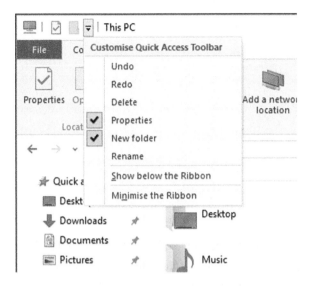

Figure 5-9. *The Quick Access Toolbar in File Explorer*

You can add and remove items from the Quick Access Toolbar by selecting and deselecting them in the toolbar options menu.

The Address Bar

Just below the ribbon, which I will talk about in depth shortly, is the address bar, sometimes known as the *breadcrumb bar*. On the left of it are buttons to move backward and forward in the current view. These buttons remember where you have been and allow you to return to locations, even if they are out of the current folder tree (see Figure 5-10).

Figure 5-10. *The address bar in File Explorer*

Next to these buttons is an up arrow that takes you one level up in the current folder hierarchy. To the right of the address bar is a search box that allows you to search for any type of file or text within a file. By default, the search prioritizes the contents of the current folder. For example, if you are looking at pictures, those pictures are prioritized in your search results over other types of documents.

The address bar is so called because it offers you ways back in the current folder tree that provide easy access to other parts of that tree (see Figure 5-11). Each of the two folder names has a small black arrow separating them.

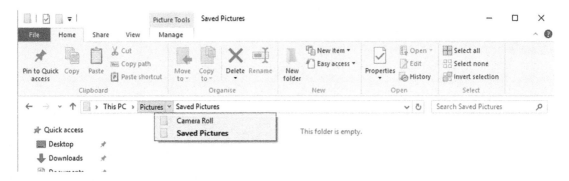

Figure 5-11. *Using the address bar in File Explorer*

■ **Tip** The address bar displays a list of recent places on your PC and your network that you have visited. You can clear this history from the File tab on the ribbon by clicking Delete History and then clicking Address Bar History. Similarly, deleting the Recent Places List clears the recent places history for the Recent Places link in the Favorites bar in the Navigation pane (see Figure 5-11).

If you click one of the arrows between folders, you are given quick links to jump to any other folder in that part of the tree. This can make it extremely quick and easy to navigate to different parts of your hard disk(s) and find what it is you are looking for.

■ **Tip** To find out the exact current folder location or to manually type a folder address into the address bar, click the icon located on the far left of the address bar. The exact current folder address is highlighted, so you can immediately start typing a new folder address; you can also press Ctrl+C to easily copy it while it's highlighted.

The Navigation Pane

To the left of the window is the Navigation pane, which is split into different categories. In the first, Quick Access, you can drag and drop folders (not files) that you want quick one-click access to, perhaps because you use them often. You can unpin a location from the Quick Access section by clicking the pin icon to its right.

File Explorer opens to the Quick Access view by default. The main view of File Explorer then shows you the folders and files that you have opened recently, making it easy for you to reopen documents that you might be working on.

When you visit folders, drives, and network locations, they automatically add themselves to the Quick Access area, although you can turn off this functionality. I show you how to do this later in the chapter.

■ **Tip** You can pin Favorite Links, folders, and files to the Start menu by right-clicking them and selecting Pin to Start.

Beneath the Quick Access links in the Navigation pane are quick, expandable groups for the following:

- **OneDrive** displays if you log in to your Windows 10 PC using a Microsoft account. It displays all the files and folders you have stored on OneDrive and gives you quick access to them.

- **This PC** displays all the hard disks and attached storage on your computer in addition to your user folders for your Desktop, Documents, Downloads, Music, Pictures, and Videos. External hard disks that you plug into your PC, such as USB flash drives, also appear in the Navigation pane.

- **Network** displays all available attached network locations, networked computers, and network storage.

- **HomeGroup**, which I discuss in detail in Chapter 4, provides access to documents, pictures, music, and video that is shared on your home network using the HomeGroup feature. HomeGroup does not appear if you are connected to a public network.

Customizing the Navigation Pane

You can customize the Navigation pane by clicking the **Navigation pane** button on the **View** tab in the ribbon (see Figure 5-12). The following describes the available options:

- Turn off the **Navigation pane**.

- Display a folder list underneath the clicked item in the Navigation pane to automatically **Expand to** [the currently] **open folder**.

- **Show all folders** on your PC in a traditional tree view. (Yes, this is where you can find it!)

- **Show libraries** that are hidden by default in Windows 10 but still exist. Libraries, which I show you how to use later in this chapter, can be extremely useful.

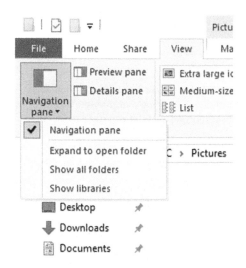

Figure 5-12. *You can customize the Navigation pane in File Explorer*

Status Bar and Folder Options

Running along the bottom of File Explorer is the status bar, which provides basic information about the current folder (such as the number of files in it) or the currently selected item. The status bar doesn't contain details about files; that can be found in the Details pane, which I will talk about shortly.

You can turn off the status bar in the Folder Options of File Explorer. It can be accessed by clicking the **Options** button under the **View** tab on the ribbon and then clicking **Change folder and search options**. In the options that appear, you find the **Folder views** under the View tab (see Figure 5-13).

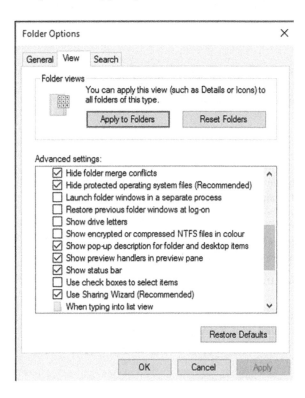

Figure 5-13. *The Folder Options for File Explorer*

In this list, you find a check box for **Show status bar**. Other controls are also very useful and include being able to uncheck the option to **Show drive letters** for your hard disks; showing compressed NTFS drives in color; or unhiding protected operating system files, which can prove useful if you need to troubleshoot and repair a problem with Windows.

Another useful feature in the Folder Options is the **Apply to folders** button that you can use to make all the folders on your PC (for general and mixed document types) look the same as the current folder. I will show you how to customize the views in File Explorer later in this chapter.

■ **Tip** At the far right of the status bar are buttons to quickly access two of the most common views in File Explorer: the Details view and the Thumbnail view. Clicking these buttons immediately changes the File Explorer view of the current folder.

Main Explorer View

In the main File Explorer pane, you see all of your files and folders, which can be arranged in a great many ways. You can also select files in the main view in several ways, including the following:

- **Right-click**: You can right-click a file or folder with your mouse to bring up a context menu of the actions you can perform on it.

- **Tap and hold**: You can tap and hold a folder or file to bring up the actions context menu.

- **Hover the mouse**: From the View tab you can select the **Item check boxes** option, which enables you to hover your mouse over a file or folder to bring up a check box to select an item. You can use this method to select multiple items if you want.

■ **Tip** To select multiple files and/or folders with your mouse and keyboard, you can use one of these options. To select everything between two items, click the first item, hold down the Shift key, and then click the item at the end of the list. To select multiple, randomly placed items, hold the Ctrl key while clicking the items you want to select.

Hiding Picture File Names

One very useful feature that has not made it into the ribbon is the ability to hide the file names of pictures in File Explorer. If you are looking at holiday photos or similar, why do you need to look at reams of DSCxxx file names anyway?

You can hide the file names for pictures by right-clicking in any blank space; then in the View menu, select **Hide file names** (see Figure 5-14).

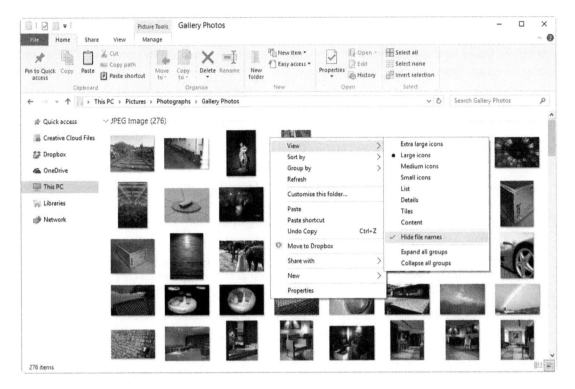

Figure 5-14. *Hiding file names in picture views*

File Explorer Ribbon

I have left the ribbon until last because I want to spend a little more time on it and talk about each tab.

By default, the ribbon in File Explorer is hidden; you display it by clicking one of the tabs at the top of the window: File, Home, Share, and View. Other tabs can appear, however, such as Computer, Library, or Picture. These extra tabs contain functions specific to those file types. When the ribbon is open, a **pin** icon appears on the right of the window. You can click this to lock the ribbon so that it is always displayed. Alternatively, double-clicking a tab on the ribbon pins it open, or unpins it.

I won't discuss every ribbon function in depth here, but I do want to concentrate on the ribbon functions that I think are most useful, most interesting, or most likely to give you a valuable productivity boost.

File

The main file tab, which is colored differently than the other tabs, is where you find options such as Open or **Open new window**. In addition to options for deleting your File Explorer history, there is a list of your frequently accessed folders. You can click the pin icon to the right to pin any of them to the **Frequent places** list (see Figure 5-15).

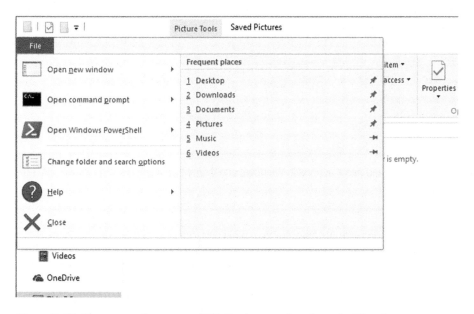

Figure 5-15. *You can perform general File Explorer options from the File tab*

Computer

The Computer tab is accessible from the This PC or network main drive (see Figure 5-16). The Computer tab provides context-sensitive options to perform actions such as adding a network location to File Explorer. You also get easy access to the Windows 10 Settings app and the Programs and Features panel, in which you can uninstall desktop programs.

Figure 5-16. *Computer tab*

Home

The Home tab (see Figure 5-17) is where you find all the common options associated with files and folders in Windows. These options include Cut, Copy, Paste, Move, and Delete. You can also create new folders and files in the New section of the ribbon. Of particular interest are the History button and the Selection buttons.

Figure 5-17. *The Home tab in File Explorer*

■ **Tip**   You can perform cut, copy, and paste actions in Windows and in any app using the Ctrl+X (Cut), Ctrl+C (Copy), and Ctrl+V (Paste) hot keys.

Windows 10 includes a better file versioning system than what was included in previous versions of the operating system. I discuss how to use the feature in depth in Chapter 12, but if you have a single file selected, the History button brings up the versioning for that file or folder, including any previous versions of the file, or the files in that folder, that Windows 10 has backed up.

Also, the Open section has a Properties button that you can click to quickly bring up the Properties dialog for any file, folder, or a selection of files and/or folders. In the Properties dialog for files, you can change or update information about a file, including artist and track information for music, as well as tags and ratings.

The Selection section includes very handy **Select all**, **Select none**, and **Invert selection** buttons. These can be very helpful when you want to work with a file, perhaps to change its properties, and then you need to perform another action on all the other files in the same folder.

Note that if you select a location such as a DVD or non-hard-disk location, the options on the Home tab change to better reflect the actions you can perform with that device.

Share

The Share tab (see Figure 5-18) contains the tools and utilities you need to share and back up your files and folders. These options include sending files via email, creating a zipped archive file, burning files to disc (CD/DVD/Blu-ray), and printing or faxing files. With a file, or files, selected, clicking the **Share** icon at the beginning of the Share tab opens a pop-out menu on the right of your screen, where you can choose a Store app with which to share the file.

Figure 5-18. *The Share tab in File Explorer*

If you are sharing files on your computer or across a network, or would like to, you can set who you want to share files with by using this tab.

View and Customizing File Explorer

In the View tab (see Figure 5-19), you can customize File Explorer to look and work the way you like.

***Figure 5-19.** The View tab in File Explorer*

There are different panes that can be switched on and off in File Explorer. The Navigation pane has a button to switch it off or to customize it. There is no way to turn on the traditional folder view, not that you were necessarily used to it in earlier versions of Windows anyway, but turning on Show All Folders in the Navigation pane displays the same result in the This PC section.

The Preview and Details panes are slightly different, although they can be confused with one another. Both of these panes appear on the right side of the Explorer window; they cannot be displayed simultaneously. If you turn on the Preview pane, a live image of the file appears, which you can review (this works for the most common file types, but won't work for custom or less common files). This includes being able to scroll through an entire Word, Excel, or Acrobat document.

■ **Tip**   Grouping, which is a great way to clearly organize your files and folders in File Explorer, can be activated for a folder by clicking the Group By option in the Current View section of the View tab. It separates the contents of a folder by a category that you specify, such as the size or file type. When you group items in File Explorer, each group is separated by a horizontal line. You can click this line to select all the items in the group, or you can right-click the line to display an option to hide the group (or all the groups). This makes folders that contain many files easier to navigate.

The Details pane in File Explorer gives you detailed information about a file that you select. The information presented in the Details pane is editable, meaning that you don't have to bring up the separate Properties dialog to edit information such as Author, Track Number, or Rating.

In the Layout section of the ribbon are some very useful tools for customizing the current view:

- The **Small**, **Medium**, **Large**, and **Extra Large buttons** change the default thumbnail size in the current view.

- **List** displays all items in view as a simple list, such as was the case in the very early versions of Windows.

- **Details** is a very common view. It can also be accessed from a button on the status bar at the bottom right of the window. This view displays extra information about files and folders that many people find useful, such as the file size and the date/time the file was created and last modified.

- **Tiles** and **Content** present files and folders in much friendlier ways than the default view, in my opinion. Tiles is an upgraded thumbnail view. Content presents more details about files in a way similar to the Details view.

In the Current View section are tools to help you sort and group content in different ways. You may want to sort items by Date Modified or Created By, for example. Grouping files and folders is an excellent way to keep yourself organized so that you know exactly what you have and where. Grouping files and folders by Type, for example, groups all the folders together, all the Word documents together, all the PNG images together, and so on.

■ **Tip**   At the bottom of the Sort By and Group By drop-down menus is a Choose Columns option. If you select this option, many other sort and group options appear, including album artist or rating for music, and EXIF data for digital photographs.

In the Show/Hide group are two functions previously hidden to many Windows users: the ability to show and hide file extensions. These are hidden by default for all known file types. The second option is to show and hide hidden files. This option is extremely useful if you need to drill down into the Windows system folder or your User folder to find specific information or a specific hidden file.

■ **Tip**   In the ribbon, you can set all folders to display in the same way as the current folder by clicking Options Folder and Search Options View Apply to Folders.

Copying and Moving Files in File Explorer

The feedback you get when you are copying and moving files in Windows 10 is excellent; you are provided with a great deal of information. There is more feedback and more control when duplicate copies of files are found. The copy file dialog is shown in Figure 5-20.

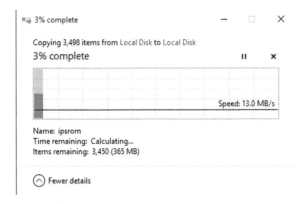

Figure 5-20. *The improved copy/move file dialog in Windows 10*

One of the best features of the copy-or-move-file process is that all operations appear in the same window. This means that if you have several copy or move operations running simultaneously, you only have one window on your screen that contains them all.

The other significant improvement is the addition of a Pause button to the dialog. You can now pause, copy, and move operations if you need to do something else or put your computer to sleep at the end of the day. When you return to Windows, you can continue with the operation by unpausing it.

When you click More Details on a copy or move file dialog, you are shown a graph of the copy or move operation. This graph gives you live feedback on the current speed of the copy, the number of megabits per second being copied, and a graph showing how the speed of the copy has changed. This is useful for diagnosing problems with copy or move operations when something else is happening in the background.

The Replace or Skip Files dialog is also easy to use and understand in Windows 10 (see Figure 5-21), as you will notice when you copy or move files into a folder or onto a drive where another copy already exists.

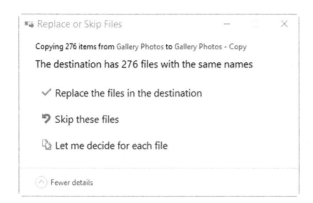

Figure 5-21. *The Replace or Skip Files dialog*

The Replace or Skip Files dialog is very simple to use, with choices to replace or skip all the files, or to choose which ones you want to keep in the destination folder.

If you want to choose which files you want to keep or overwrite, this dialog has improved as well. You still have a check box to select everything to keep or replace, but each individual file is more easily identifiable.

■ **Tip**   To keep all the source *and* destination files in a copy or move operation, check the **Files from** and **Files already in** check boxes at the top of both the left and the right columns (see Figure 5-22).

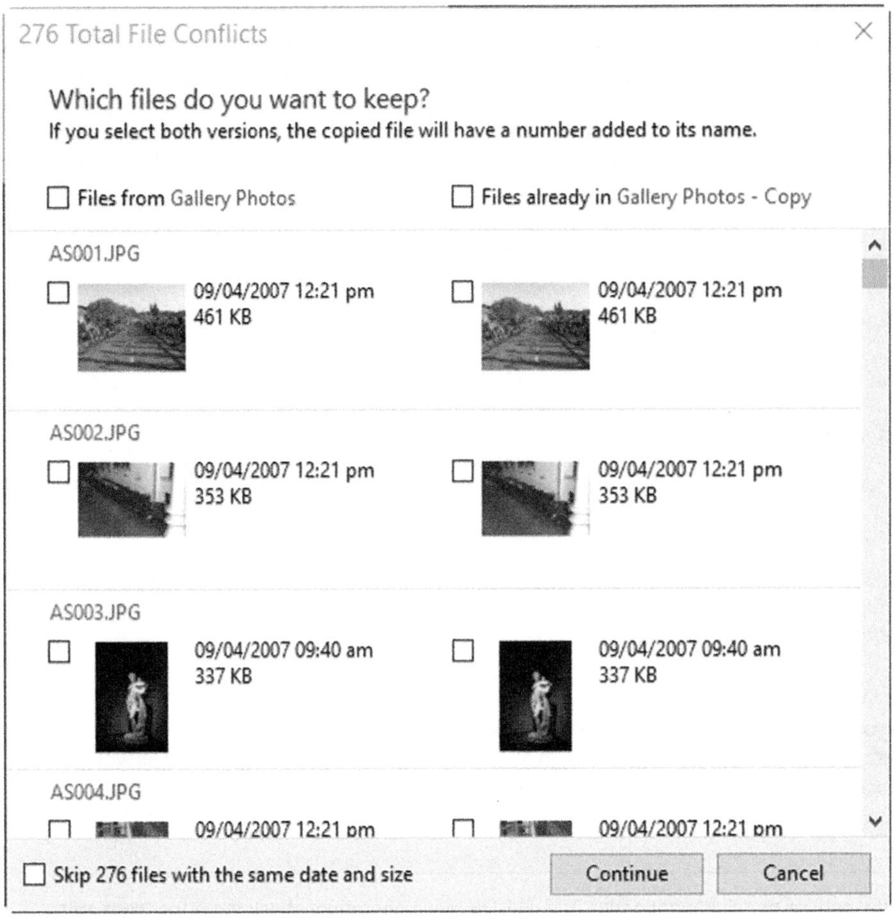

Figure 5-22. *You can easily select files to overwrite in Windows 10*

Pictures have a thumbnail image, but other file types just display the associated program's icon. This new dialog makes it much easier to decide which files to keep and which to replace than in Windows 7, in which you were given only limited information, such as the date and time stamps.

Using Libraries in Windows 10

Hidden from view by default in Windows 10, libraries are (in the opinion of this author anyway) one of the best ways to organize and manage files and folders on a PC that's ever been devised. Libraries actually are aggregated storage for many locations. They are customizable for specific types of content. They're actually very powerful with the way that content can be displayed (see Figure 5-23).

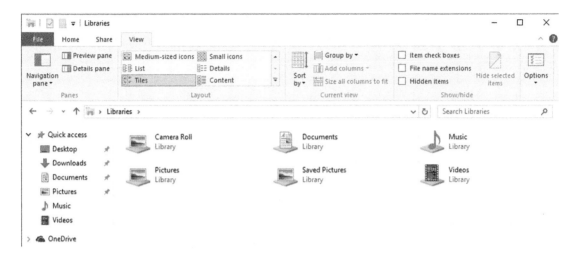

Figure 5-23. *Libraries in File Explorer*

You can turn Libraries on by clicking the **Navigation pane** button on the **View** tab in the ribbon and selecting **Show Libraries**. They then appear in the Navigation pane as an extra option. By default, there are libraries for your camera roll, documents, music, pictures, saved pictures, and videos; although if you install other software, others (such as Podcasts) may be added.

You can create your own libraries to view and arrange content in specific ways; for instance, you might want one for your work or school documents, and so on.

Creating a Library

You can add new folders to an existing library (I show you how to do this shortly), but you can also create your own custom libraries. I have one for Photos, in which all my pictures are arranged by their tags. You might want a separate library for your school, work, or household documents. You can have a library for anything, and it's a great way to organize files.

■ **Tip** You can add SD cards and other removable media to libraries in Windows 10. This is useful if your Ultrabook or tablet comes with a memory card slot for additional storage. To add these file locations, right-click them. From the context menu, click Include in Library. From the list, click the library in which you want to include the folder.

To create a new library, perform the following steps:

1. Open File Explorer on the desktop.

2. Click **Libraries** in the left pane.

3. Right-click (or tap and hold with your finger) any blank space in the main Explorer window (see Figure 5-24).

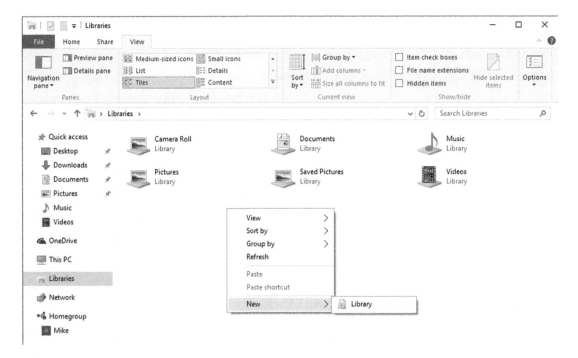

Figure 5-24. *Creating a new library*

4. From the context menu, select **New** and then **Library**. You are presented with a new empty library to which you need to give a name.

5. Once the library is created, double-click it to open it.

6. Click the **Include a folder** button and choose a folder to display in the library (see Figure 5-25). You can add additional folders later (I will show you how to do this shortly).

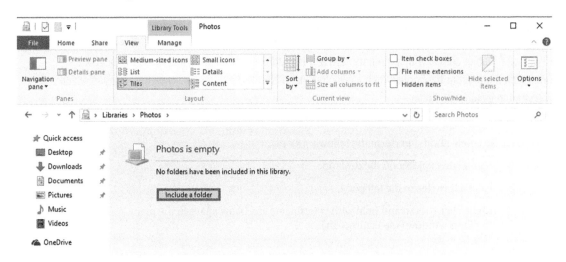

Figure 5-25. *Including a folder in a library*

Changing the Way a Library Displays Files

You now see your folder listed in the library, but it just looks like an ordinary Explorer window. It is now that the full flexibility of libraries can be used, because they can display content in ways that the normal Explorer folder view cannot.

1. To change the view, right-click (or tap and hold with your finger) in any blank space in the main window (see Figure 5-26).

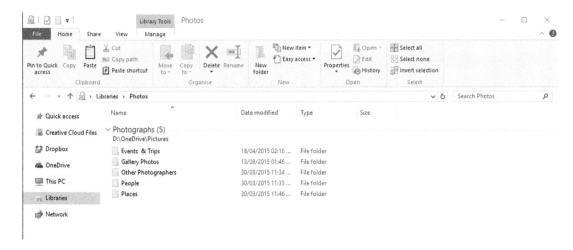

Figure 5-26. *Changing the way a library is displayed*

2. From the context menu, click **Arrange by**, and then choose how you want to arrange the contents of the library (see Figure 5-27). This action is performed only with a right-click, not from the ribbon. It is different from the ribbon's Sort By and Group By views.

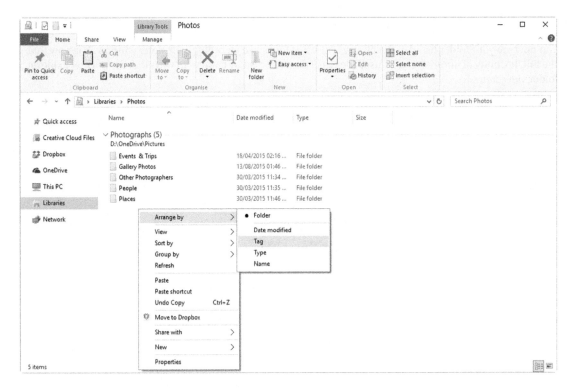

Figure 5-27. *Choosing how to arrange files in a library*

You see that the library is now arranged as you want it. In Figure 5-28, I have arranged a photo library by tag. Regardless of which folder the photographs are stored in, I can view all pictures of Brighton Pier (for example) just by opening the tagged group. A nice benefit.

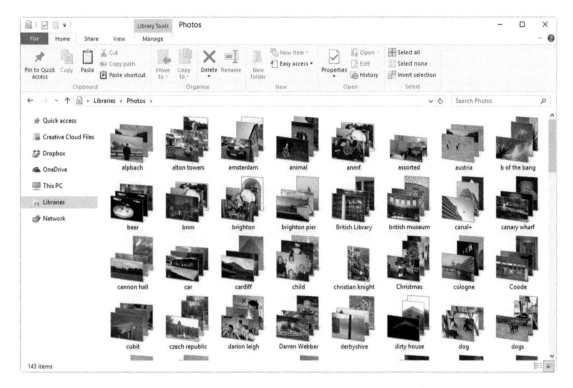

Figure 5-28. *Viewing photos by tag in Libraries*

These Brighton Pier photos may reside in a dozen or more different folders on my hard disk, but because they all have the same tag, they are all displayed together in the library when I arrange the files by tag.

■ **Note** Within Libraries, you can arrange files by type, which display the files as stacked groups for Word documents, PDFs, and so on. Sadly, you cannot specify just a single file type to be shown in a library, only complete folders.

Managing Libraries

When you are viewing a library, a **Manage** tab appears on the ribbon (see Figure 5-29). This library Tools tab contains tools for managing the library, including which folders are included within it, what type of content the library is optimized for (to aid in displaying that content correctly), and whether the library is displayed in the Navigation pane. Here you can also change the icon for the library to one of the standard Windows icons or to a custom .ico file of your choosing.

Figure 5-29. *You can manage a library from the ribbon in File Explorer*

The folders included by default in the standard Windows 10 libraries are the default folders found in C:\User\[Username]. In addition to the default folders, you can include other folders and remove folders in a library. To add or remove folders from a library, click **Manage library** on the Manage tab in the ribbon.

■ **Tip**   Although libraries don't allow you to add external hard disks and network locations, it can still be done through an easy cheat; see the "Adding Network Locations to Libraries" section later in this chapter.

The Documents Library Locations dialog has simple Add and Remove buttons for library locations. You must have at least one location for a library, but you can specify as many as you want (see Figure 5-30).

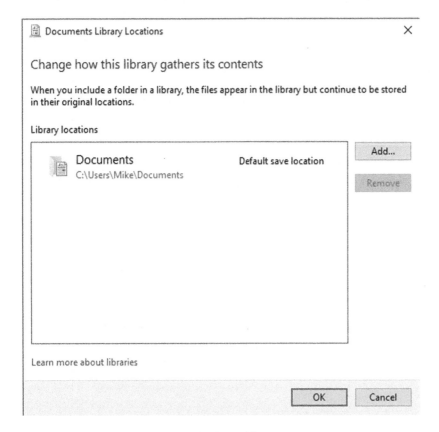

Figure 5-30. *Adding and removing folders to libraries*

■ **Tip** You can also add a local folder on your PC or SD card storage to libraries by right-clicking it and selecting Include in Library from the menu that appears.

Changing the Default Save Location

A question can be raised about where the default save locations for Documents, Music, Pictures, and Videos will be when you add new folders to a library. After all, when you save a file, where does it go? Into your Users folder on the C:\ drive? Into the library somewhere? Into a specific folder in the library?

In Chapter 12, I talk about how and why you should move your files away from Windows and onto a separate hard disk or partition to safeguard them, but one way to do it is to change the default save location for a library. You can do this from the Library Tools tab on the ribbon in File Explorer when a library is being viewed.

On the left of the ribbon, there is a **Set save location** button, which offers a drop-down menu of the folders contained within that library. To change the default save location, simply click the relevant folder that you want all new files saved to (see Figure 5-31).

Figure 5-31. *Setting the default save location for libraries*

Adding Network Locations to Libraries

It's fairly well known that you can't add network locations to libraries in Windows. Or can you? In fact, it's always been possible to add network locations to your Music, Pictures, and Videos libraries. You do it in two ways in Windows 10.

The first way is to create a symbolic link between the library and the folder on your network that contains the files you want to include.

1. Create a folder in your C:\Users\[Username] folder, named after the folder you want to include.

2. Add this new folder to your library.

3. Delete the folder from C:\Users\[Username], but do not delete it from the library.

4. Open the **Command Prompt** window from the Win+X menu.

5. Type **MKLINK /D C:\Users\Username\FolderName \\NetworkLocation**, substituting the correct paths to the folders.

This process adds the network location to the library, but does not add it to the index, which means that the library may be slow to refresh when you open it. (I will talk more about the Windows index later in this chapter.)

Using Tags and Ratings to Organize Files

Tags and ratings are two of the best ways to organize and categorize files. Tags are labels that help you find relevant documents. For example, you might have documents tagged as "work," "school," "household," or "auto." Thus, tags might help you locate documents related to your current college course quickly and easily.

If you have a lot of photos, you might label them "vacation," "children," or "Germany" to help you find them quickly for display to friends and family (this is, after all, why you took them in the first place).

You might already be familiar with tags called *metadata* for your music files, where the artist, album name, track number, track name, and more are all tags. They are labels used to help you identify the contents of a file.

You don't need to be limited to a single tag per file, either. You can stack multiple tags together so your recent vacation photos in Orlando might be tagged "vacation," "Orlando," "Disney," "Janell," and "Lidia."

Ratings are slightly different but easier to understand. Ratings in Windows 10 use one to five stars that indicate how significant the file is. In your music, you probably already use 4- and 5-star ratings to identify your favorite tracks; you may have been doing this for years. Many music playback apps automatically add star ratings to tracks you mark as the ones you like.

You can view the tags and ratings for any file or files in File Explorer by clicking the Details pane button on the ribbon under the View tab (see Figure 5-32). This opens a pane on the right side of the windows, showing all manner of information, which varies from one file type to another. Tags and Rating are always at the top of the list.

Figure 5-32. *The Details pane in File Explorer*

To add a tag or multiple tags to a file or a selection of files, click next to **Tags** in the **Details** pane and type as many tags as you like, each one separated by a semicolon (;). When you have finished adding tags, click the **Save** button. (Remember, you can press Ctrl+click to select multiple individual files; you can click and then Shift+click to mark a selected group.)

You can add a rating or change a rating by clicking the appropriate number of stars. Click Save when you are done.

■ **Tip**   You can remove all the metadata in a file by opening the file's properties (right-click and select Properties from the menu that appears). In the Details tab, click the Remove Properties and Personal Information link at the bottom of the properties panel.

Simplify Adding Tags and Ratings with Windows Photo Gallery

It can be a laborious process adding tags and ratings to files, but the important thing to remember is that *you need to do this only once.* There are tools that can make the process much easier for you as well. Windows Photo Gallery, part of the venerable Windows Essentials suite, can be downloaded for free from download. live.com. In the View tab on the ribbon in that app, you have the option to view files by tag (see Figure 5-33). Other apps, such as Google Picasa, can also help you with tagging photos.

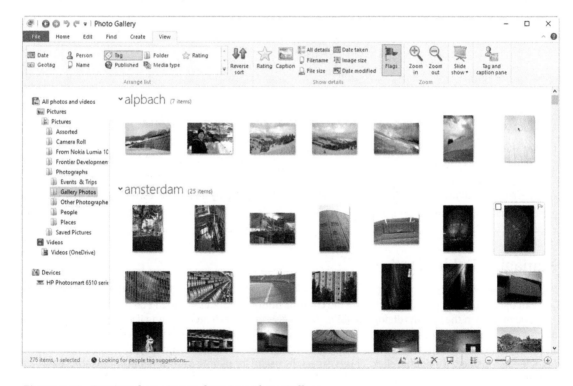

Figure 5-33. *Tagging photos in Windows Live Photo Gallery*

The View tab features a button to open the Tag and Caption pane (the button is on the far right of the ribbon). This pane offers a great way to simplify the addition of tags to photos and pictures because it lists all your photos by tag category, and shows all the photos that are *not tagged*. You can select these photos for tagging, making it much easier to know which pictures are already tagged.

When you import new photos to Windows 10 from your digital camera or memory card, the default import utility, the Photos app, doesn't permit adding tags. You can add tags automatically when you import photos to your PC, however, by doing so from within Photo Gallery. This is a good time to do it because all the photos are probably related, and having Windows automate the process of adding tags makes things much simpler.

You can also remove and amend tags and ratings later in Windows Live Photo Gallery using simple controls. The options for this appear in the right pane when a photo or photos are selected.

Windows 10 doesn't have its own photo importer, but other apps exist that fill the gap, such as Adobe Lightroom. If you are using Photo Gallery, you can import photos from your camera or digital memory card by clicking the **Import** button under the **Home** tab on the ribbon.

You are first asked to identify the media that you are importing your photos from. You can then click **Add tags** and type your tags (see Figure 5-34). This automatically adds the tags you enter to all of your imported photos. You may want to use general tags such as "vacation," "family," or "Munich." I talk more about importing photos and videos in Chapter 7.

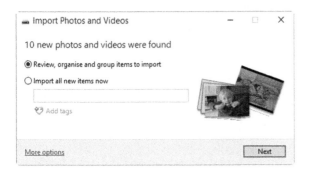

Figure 5-34. *Tagging photos on import from a camera*

■ **Tip** Most music players help automate adding tags to your music by finding the correct album from an extensive online database.

Managing Folder Options

Folder Options offers a huge amount of control over File Explorer and the way files and folders are viewed. You can open the folder options by clicking the **Options** button on the **View** tab in File Explorer.

The first tab in the options dialog, General, provides a drop-down menu asking if you want File Explorer to start with the Quick Access view or the This PC view. Next you're asked if you want folders to open in the same window or a different window. The third option gives you the choice of opening files and folders with a single-click instead of a double click. This is especially useful for people using a Windows 10 tablet (see Figure 5-35).

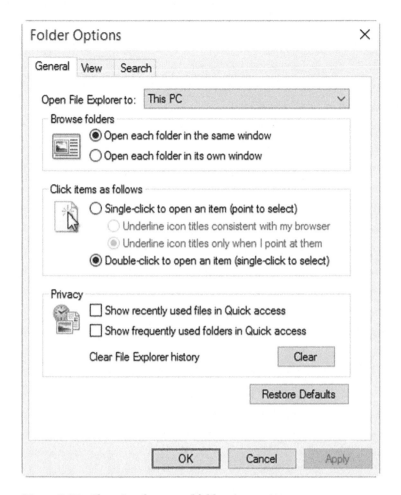

Figure 5-35. *Changing the general folder view options*

Next are the privacy options for the Quick Access view. After all, you may not want anyone looking over your shoulder to see the names of the files and folders you've recently accessed. Here you can disable recent files and folders individually, as well as clear the File Explorer history.

The View tab gives you extra control over the way files and folders are viewed and organized (see Figure 5-36). At the top of this window are buttons to **Apply [the current folder view] to [all] Folders** or to **Reset [all] Folders** to their default view. This enables you to decide the way you want your folders to look. If you want your folders tiled with items grouped by file type, for example, you can apply this quickly and easily to all the folder views on your computer.

Figure 5-36. *Changing advanced folder view options*

The following are brief descriptions of some of the more noteworthy options:

- **Display the full path in the title bar** forces the address bar to display the full drive and folder location at all times.

- **Hidden files and folders** allows you to show or hide all hidden folders on your computer.

- **Hide empty drives in the Computer folder** is checked by default. It hides empty USB flash drives or memory card drives that you might want to copy files onto. This won't hide optical drives, such as DVD/Blu-Ray drives, however.

- **Hide extensions for known file types** is checked by default, but some users want to know the file extensions for all their files.

- **Hide protected operating system files** can be unchecked to display hidden system files that you may need to work with.

- **Show drive letters** shows the legacy drive assignments (C:, D:, and so on) on File Explorer views. Uncheck to remove the ability to see the drive letters.

- **Show encrypted or compressed NTFS files in color** highlights files in blue when an encryption service such as EFS is turned on. Many people like to uncheck this option.

The last tab, Search, contains options for searching files and folders. For example, by default, Windows 10 doesn't search the content of compressed ZIP, CAB, or RAR files because they're commonly used for archiving. You might want to turn on this option if you work with compressed files often (see Figure 5-37).

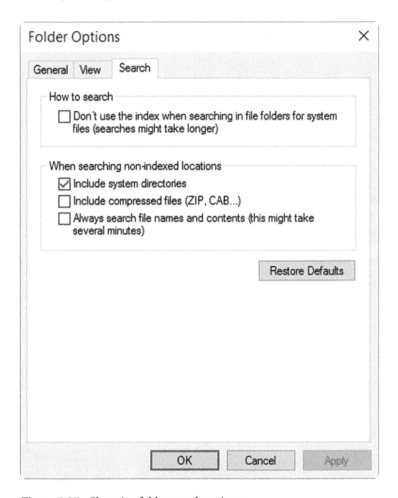

Figure 5-37. Changing folder search options

Searching in File Explorer

At the beginning of this chapter, I discussed how you can use Cortana to search your files, settings, and apps. For file search, however, using File Explorer offers significantly more power and flexibility. Windows 10 always contextualizes your searches, so a search in the Start menu always prioritizes apps and settings. Windows 10 searches by default for files, settings, and apps; and also searches online at the same time. Searching directly in File Explorer, however, still prioritizes the type of content displayed in that window (e.g., Photos).

File Explorer's search box can be found in the top right of the window, and offers a variety of ways to search. The search box prioritizes the content currently being displayed. It might be prioritized by documents, pictures, music, video, a specific disk drive (internal or external), a network location, or something else (see Figure 5-38). In this way, it is flexible and more dynamic than the Start screen search.

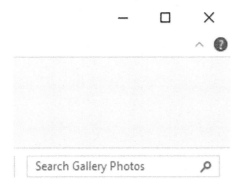

Figure 5-38. *File Explorer has its own search box*

When searching in File Explorer, a Search tab appears on the ribbon. It contains tools and buttons to make search even more powerful and useful, especially for people who are less familiar with search syntax. The Search tab on the ribbon (see Figure 5-39) allows you to filter your search by

- The current folder and all subfolders

- Libraries, email, notes, or the Internet

- When the file was last modified (opened)

- The type of file

- The file size

- File names

- Specific folders

- File tags

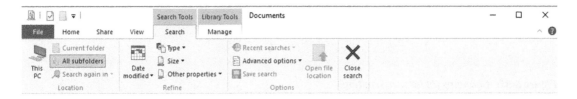

Figure 5-39. *The Search tab on the ribbon*

These options cover just about any search that you will undertake in Windows 10. You can choose multiple options in the Search tab as well (e.g., Size=large and Type=document). The Search tab on the ribbon appears automatically the moment you type anything in the search box in File Explorer.

■ **Note**   The Search tab on the File Explorer ribbon allows you quick access to recent searches that you have made, so that you can repeat them. You can also clear your search history here.

When you search from an Explorer window, you can also use Advanced Query Syntax (AQS) to narrow your searches (see Figure 5-40). I detail the full AQS in Appendix C, but some of the most useful search syntax options include Kind, Datemodified, Type, and Name, as shown in Tables 5-1 through 5-4.

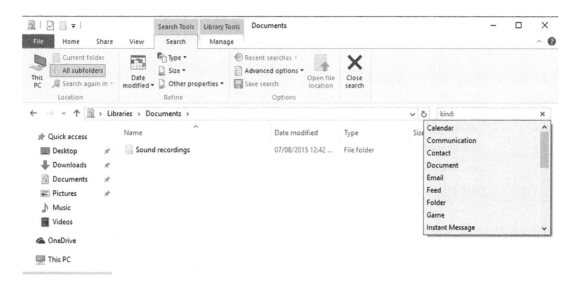

Figure 5-40. *Using AQS to search in an Explorer window*

Table 5-1. *Kind (to Search the Properties of a Document Type)*

Option	Example
Kind:=email	Rory Webster kind:=email
Kind:=task	Meeting kind:=task
Kind:=note	project kind:=note
Kind:=document	Apress kind:=document
Kind:=music	Metallica kind:=music
Kind:=song	Equinoxe kind:=song
Kind:=folder	Book kind:=folder
Kind:=program	paint kind:=program

Table 5-2. *Datemodified (to Search by the Date a File Was Modified)*

Option	Example
Datemodified:MM/DD/YYYY	Report datemodified:10/22/2012
Datemodified:MM/DD/YY	Report datemodified:7/4/12
Datemodified:MM/DD/YY..MM/DD/YY	Report datemodified:7/4/12..10/22/12
Datemodified:yesterday	Orders datemodified:yesterday
Datemodified:lastweek	Orders datemodified:lastweek
Datemodified:pastmonth	Orders datemodified:pastmonth

Table 5-3. *Type (to Search by File Type)*

Option	Example
Type:	Type:image
	Type:image jpeg
	Type:.doc
	Type:.pdf

Table 5-4. *Name (to Search by File Name or by a Property Name of a File)*

Option	Example
Name:	Name:vacation
	Name:wedding
	Name:budget

Typing **type:** initially displays a drop-down list of all the file types on your computer (for example, DOC or PDF), as shown in Table 5-3. If, for example, you continue by typing **type:image**, you can filter your search by various image types or search for all image types. You also can use other file types, such as type:document, type:audio, type:video, type:presentation, and so forth.

As you begin to type a search filter in File Explorer, a drop-down list (with all the supported filter options) is displayed. Clicking the appropriate one for your search helps you find what you are looking for more quickly. If you are searching for dates, a calendar assists you.

Expanding Libraries with Saved Searches

One of the criticisms of libraries is that you can add only folders to them; you cannot specify that a library should contain only one or two file types, let's say Word and Excel files; nor can you specify that libraries should contain only documents created by "Rory" or tagged as "college".

This is where the true power of search in Windows 10 comes into play, and it's such a cool feature that it will probably save you countless hours of lost productivity all on its own! I'm really not kidding.

After you complete a search, you can save it by clicking the **Save search** option in the Search tab on the File Explorer ribbon. Saving a search adds a quick link, named whatever you want, to the C:\Users\ [Username]\Searches folder (see Figure 5-41), which is also available by typing **%UserProfile%\Searches** into the File Explorer address bar. You can't pin this search to the Quick Access pane as you could in Windows 7 or Windows 8.1, but right-click it and you can send a shortcut to the desktop (or you can drag it to the desktop), and you can also pin it to the Start menu.

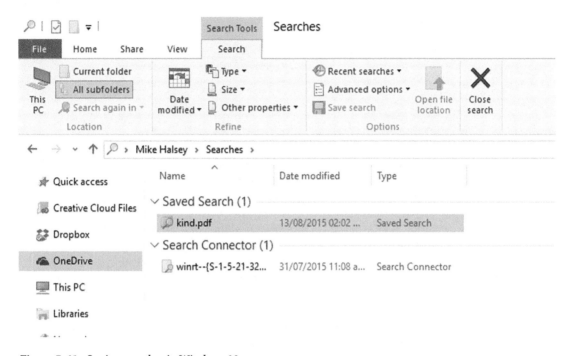

Figure 5-41. *Saving searches in Windows 10*

What is perhaps better, however, is that if you drag the Saved Search onto the Windows taskbar, it pins it to the Jump List for File Explorer, making it easy to find and open whenever you need it. The upshot of this is that you can effectively create those custom-aggregated libraries that aren't otherwise available, whenever you want, and each one is automatically and dynamically updated whenever you open it.

Let's say, for example, that you search for **type:.pdf** in the search box when looking in the **This PC** view. This brings up a list of all the Adobe Acrobat documents on your PC. Saving this search creates something that looks and behaves like a library consisting entirely of PDF files, which you can use whenever you need. Each time you open this saved search, the search is re-run (it literally takes a fraction of a second if the locations being searched are part of the Windows index), and the contents are updated automatically.

You can further sort, organize, and group the contents of this search however you want, perhaps by the dates that they were created or the tags associated with them.

I simply cannot overstate how powerful and useful this feature is, especially when used with properly tagged files. As a way of organizing home or work documents, it is a true time-saver! Let me give you an example of how powerful I believe saved searches really are. In Figure 5-42, I searched for ***.ppt? authors:mike halsey**, which displays all the PowerPoint files created by Mike (and optionally) Halsey.

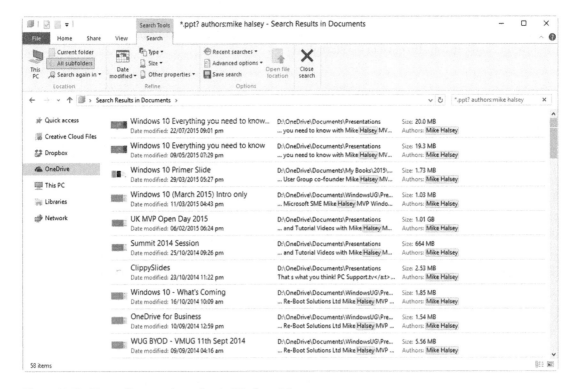

Figure 5-42. *Expanding saved searches in Windows 10*

Saving these search results creates dynamically updated folders in which you can quickly and easily find the information you need. Having a saved search for all documents relating to a project name, for example, enables you to keep track of all the documents related to the project in a single and always up-to-date location.

Saving and Sharing Your Saved Searches

Once you have created a saved search, you can create a copy of it to back it up or perhaps to share with a friend or colleague. You can do this by opening the %UserProfile%\Searches folder in File Explorer and selecting Open Folder Location from the context menu.

You now see the saved search(es) listed and you can create copies in the same way you would with any other file on your computer. They can be backed up or shared with other computers. Note, however, that if drive assignments are different on the other computers, the search may not function correctly because searches work with drive letters and folders that all have absolute references on your computer.

Tagging Files in Microsoft Office

I've talked about adding tags to documents as you create them to help find them later on. But how do you do this? Obviously, the method by which you can add tags to documents as you save them varies considerably from one software package to another, and it can be expected that many software packages won't support this feature at all.

Microsoft Office has supported tags for some time, however, and if you use Office 2007 or later, it is a simple matter to add tags to documents as you save them.

When you first save a document in Microsoft Office (or select Save As), you have the option to **Add a tag** (see Figure 5-43).

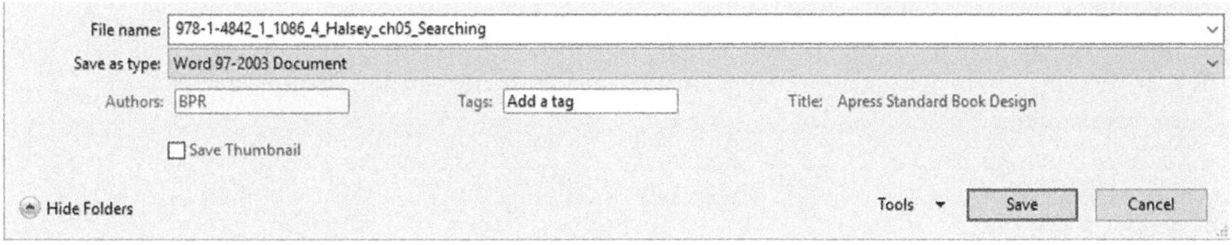

File name:	978-1-4842_1_1086_4_Halsey_ch05_Searching			∨
Save as type:	Word 97-2003 Document			∨
Authors:	BPR	Tags:	Add a tag	Title: Apress Standard Book Design
	☐ Save Thumbnail			

Figure 5-43. *Adding tags to documents in Microsoft Office*

You can add other details here, including authors and title, although the software will probably automatically add this information.

All Microsoft Office programs, and many programs from other software vendors, support adding tags to your files when you save them. In Microsoft Office, the Save dialogs for Word, Excel, PowerPoint, and so forth, allow you to add tags in the same way. You can also add information such as subjects and project managers to make files easier to find.

With other software, you need to check whether tags can be added when the file is saved. If not, you can always add tags afterward in the Details pane in File Explorer.

Managing the Search and File Index in Windows 10

The reason why search works very quickly in Windows 10, at least for internal storage on the computer, is that the details about the files are all stored in an index database. By default, this database stores information on anything in your user folders and default libraries. You can move, add, or remove folders (or even entire hard disks) to or from the index.

You can find the Indexing Options in the Search tab on the ribbon in File Explorer, but you need to perform a search for the tab to appear. A simpler approach is to type **Index** at the Start menu and run **Change how Windows searches** from the Settings search results.

In the main Indexing Options are all the indexed drive and folder locations and their current indexing status (see Figure 5-44).

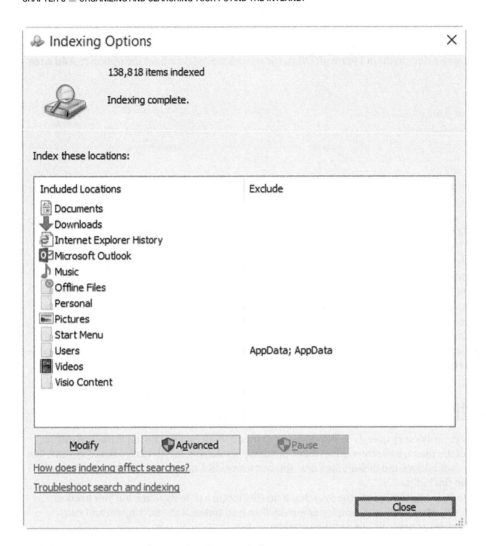

Figure 5-44. *Managing the search index in Windows 10*

You may find that not many files are indexed, perhaps because you have a relatively new Windows 10 installation and a great many files; initially, it can take time for Windows to build its index. In that case, the results you expect won't appear in the search results. You might see that some critical or important folders don't appear in the index.

Adding Folders to the Index

You can add (or remove) folders to the index by clicking the **Modify** button on the Indexing Options screen. It displays a folder list of all the drives on your computer. The current folder locations are checked (see Figure 5-45).

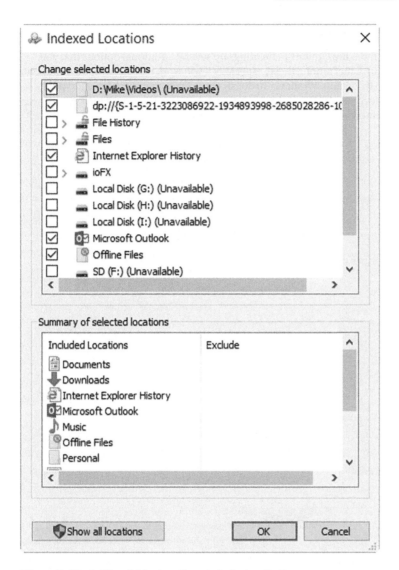

Figure 5-45. *Adding folder locations to Indexing Options*

To add or remove folders or entire drives to the index, simply check or uncheck their boxes. You can expand and collapse folders by clicking the chevrons next to folder names. When you press the OK button, the index is refreshed to include or exclude the folders you have updated.

■ **Note** It can take time for Windows 10 to index the contents of your hard drive, and the process slows when you are using the computer. If you need the index built quickly, leaving the computer switched on overnight can speed up the process significantly.

Changing the Advanced Indexing Options

Clicking the Advanced button in the Indexing Options pane brings up several additional options that you may want to consider (see Figure 5-46). Chief among these, especially if you work in a business environment, is the option to index encrypted files. By default, Windows 10 doesn't index files that you have encrypted with either Microsoft's Encrypting File System (EFS) or third-party software. This is because the key searchable contents of the files contained within the index aren't encrypted.

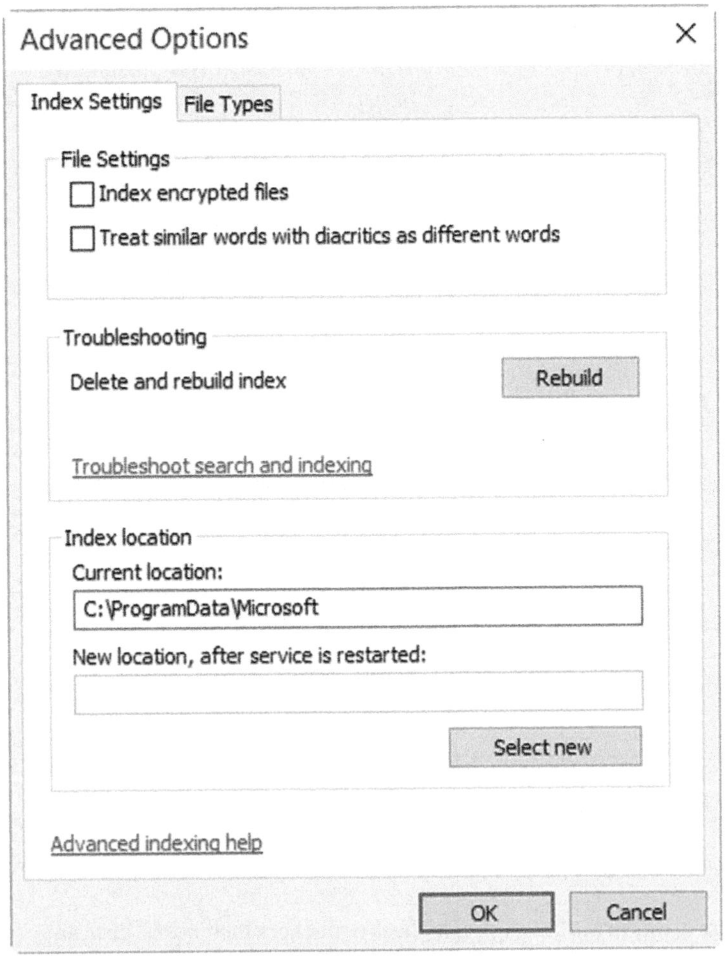

Figure 5-46. *Modifying the advanced index options*

For most scenarios, it is perfectly acceptable to tick this box. If you work in a governmental, financial, medical, or research and development organization, you should seek advice, although the choice will probably be made for you, and Indexing Options will not be available.

■ **Note** The Windows 10 automatic indexing of encrypted files includes the computer's hard disks that are encrypted with BitLocker (if you are a user who has access to those drives, because it is a full disk encryption system). It is assumed that if you are successfully logged into a BitLocker-encrypted PC, you have permission to access its files.

The next option in the File Settings section enables you to turn off Windows 10's automatic correction feature to accommodate the different (albeit correct) spellings of words and the oddly spelled word.

In the Index Location section is an option to change the default location of the index. I'd like to discuss why you might want to do this and what the benefits are. The most obvious reason is to increase the speed of your hard disk or to improve the resilience of an SSD. If you have a large number of files to index, this is the only circumstance when it's possibly worthwhile to move the index.

■ **Tip** If you are using a tablet or an Ultrabook on which you don't tend to keep files on the SSD, switching off indexing can dramatically increase your battery life (some people have reported an increase of up to 30%). You can do this by searching for **services** at the Start menu, and in the Services app, right-clicking Windows Search, choosing its properties and changing the start-up type to Disabled. Turning off indexing can impact other features within Windows 10, however, such as Cortana.

If you have an SSD in your computer (the number of maximum write operations is finite over the life of the disk), you may want to move the index. On modern SSDs, it shouldn't make a difference because the overall lifespan of the disk should be more than adequate. But you may have an older SSD or you perform duties that involve huge amounts of file work and modifications every day.

To change the location, type the *new* location of the index into the empty box with its full drive assignment (e.g., D:\Index\) and click the **Select New** button.

■ **Note** When you move the index, it is rebuilt from scratch when you restart your computer. Also, you cannot reuse an existing index when you reimage your computer; it rebuilds when you restart your computer.

Searching Network Locations in Windows 10

When you add extra folders and drives to the Windows 10 index, the system does not allow you to add network or other locations to the index. If you are a manager in a small office in which files are shared on a network-attached storage (NAS) drive, for example, and you want to create a saved search to monitor the progress of a project, you cannot add this location to the index. Although they won't be indexed, you can add network locations to libraries by creating a symbolic link between the two locations. I described how to do this in the "Adding Network Locations to Libraries" section earlier in this chapter.

However, you can open a network location in File Explorer from Network in the Navigation pane. When you are at the correct location, you can then perform a search and save that search.

Searches of network locations can take longer than searches of files on your own computer because the search system has to read each file every time instead of referring to its information in the index.

If you are logged in to a domain on a Windows Server system, the index usually allows you to add mapped server locations to the index.

Using Search Syntax in Edge and Internet Explorer

In the science fiction book *The Hitchhiker's Guide to the Galaxy* (Pan Books, 1985), author Douglas Adams wrote, "Space is big. You just won't believe how vastly, hugely, mind-bogglingly big it is. I mean, you may think it's a long way down the road to the shops, but that's just peanuts to space." As a quote, this is an excellent analogy for the Internet.

The problem is how to find what you are looking for online when there are usually millions and sometimes billions of search results. After all, the major search engines—Bing, Google, and so forth—do a reasonable job of filtering the results for you. Though how do you know that you're getting the *correct* results for what you type? Surely you're just getting the most popular generalized results.

This is where you can use search syntax options that are commonly supported by all the major search engines:

- **"Enclose a few words in double quotes"** to search for those words as a complete sentence. By default, typing the words without quotes returns search results that include one or more of all the words; it does not treat them as a full sentence.

- Use a plus (+) symbol at the front of a word (e.g., **+halsey**) to guarantee that this word *must* appear in the search results. You can also use a plus symbol in front of a string of words (see preceding bullet).

- Use a minus (-) symbol to exclude a particular word or string from the results. You may want to exclude the word **-buy** or **-shopping** if you are looking for technical information on a product and you want to exclude shopping and price comparison sites from the results.

- Search only a specific web site for a term by typing **site:*sitename*.com**. You may want to search for **"Windows 10" site:pcsupport.tv**, for example.

- Use * and **?** wildcard operators. The asterisk represents a selection of letters, and the question mark represents only a single letter; for example, you want to search for **"Mike H*"** or **Hals?y** if you are unsure of a spelling.

- Include Boolean operators **OR**, **AND**, and **NOT** in your search to narrow down the results. **Adobe software 2015 OR 2016**, for example.

There are other search operators that are specific to individual search engines. The ones I listed here are those that I find to be the most useful and the easiest to remember. I personally only ever use double quotes and the plus and minus signs, for example, and I get search results that I am happy with. Appendix D features a full list of the AQS options that you can use for Windows 10 searches.

Summary

Search in Windows 10 is incredibly powerful, but the full features can be hard to remember. I believe that by far the best feature for searching is the saved search, which allows you to search by subject, workflow, author, contributors, file type, location, and more. It also allows you to search for multiple parameters simultaneously. This truly powerful feature can help you get the best out of file management and organization in Windows 10.

Elsewhere, however, the ability to search from Cortana and from the Start menu by simply typing is very welcome. You can also expect both Microsoft and third-party providers to plug some extremely useful functionality into Cortana in the coming years. It's not quite as powerful and flexible for document search as the search options in File Explorer, however.

Libraries are also significantly more powerful than you might first believe; saved searches and symbolic links for network locations enable you to considerably extend their functionality. I have long argued that libraries should be more flexible by default, but the ability to create flexibility through simple workarounds greatly increases their usefulness.

■ ■ ■

CHAPTER 6

Printing and Managing Printers

In these days of external hard drives, flash drives, TV tuners, graphics tablets, HD webcams, cordless headphones, and more, it is always a printer that is commonly the first and most important peripheral that we purchase for our computers.

These days, wireless printers are becoming so common that you no longer need to have the machine physically connected to your computer. It can easily be shared between multiple computers and hidden out of sight where it isn't noticeable (or noisy) when you're relaxing.

Network printers in the workplace have been common for years now, and you'll be pleased to hear that setting up and managing printers in Windows 10 is as straightforward as ever.

Installing Printers

Windows 10 performs a very neat trick with printers (and other network devices). If these devices exist, and Windows 10 sees them on the network, it automatically installs them for you without you having to do anything at all.

This means that the first time you try to print a document, you'll probably find that your network printer is already listed. Windows 10 searches Windows Update for a driver and installs these devices quietly in the background. So ordinarily, you simply plug in your printer or connect it to your network, and Windows 10 takes care of the installation for you.

■ **Tip** Some printers allow you to connect to your Windows 10 laptop or tablet by NFC (near field communication) through a tap-to-pair system. All you need to do to pair your PC with these printers is to bring the two closely together. An authorization pop-up will appear on your PC that you can click to pair the PC and printer. NFC-connected printers only work at short range.

It is unlikely, however, that Windows 10 can install printers with drivers not included in Windows 10 or not available on Windows Update. If this is the case, you have to uninstall and reinstall the printer. There are two main ways to install printers and other devices in Windows 10, the simplest of which is using the Settings app. Open the Settings from the Start menu and navigate to **Devices**. A list of all the devices that are currently installed is displayed, but at the top of the screen is an **Add a printer or scanner** button. Clicking or tapping this button starts the Windows 10 autodetect for new hardware (see Figure 6-1).

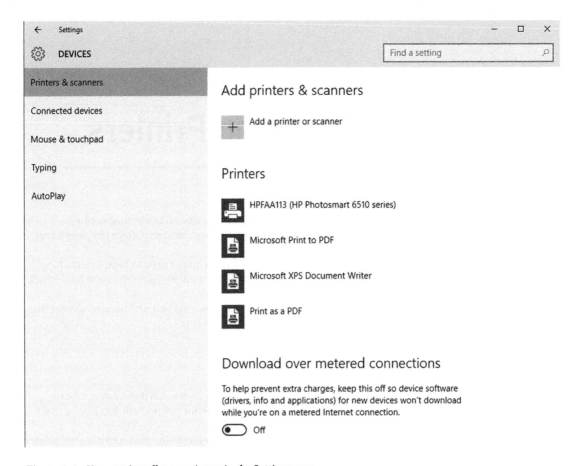

Figure 6-1. *You can install new printers in the Settings app*

If you want more control over your printer installation, or if a printer isn't being detected in PC Settings, you can open the **Devices and Printers** panel (see Figure 6-2). Type **printers** at the Start menu and you see Devices and Printers listed in the search results.

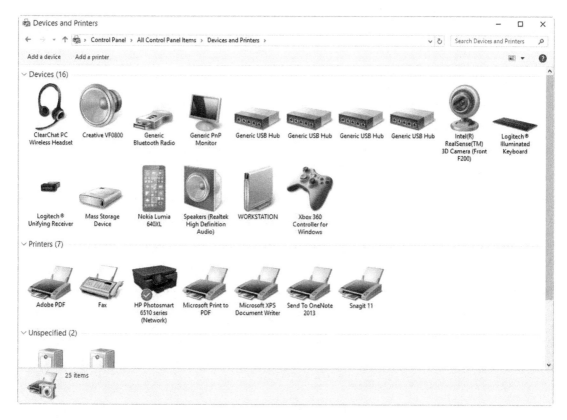

Figure 6-2. *Devices and Printers window*

■ **Tip** To uninstall a printer or another device in the Devices panel of the Settings app (perhaps because the driver is not properly installed), click the printer and then click the **Remove Device** button.

There are two main ways to add printers to Windows 10 using Devices and Printers. On the toolbar at the top of the window, you can select the link to **Add a device** or you can choose the **Add a printer**, both of which will work.

Initially, as you see in Figures 6-3 and 6-4, these options operate in exactly the same way, though they operate slightly differently. One searches for network printers and the other searches for other devices. They then display them for you. Where they differ most is in the driver installation for the hardware.

Figure 6-3. *Adding Devices and Printers to Windows 10 in the Add a Device dialog*

Figure 6-4. *Adding a printer to Windows 10 using Add Printer*

In the **Add a Device** dialog (see Figure 6-3), Windows 10 simply installs what it thinks is the best available driver for that piece of hardware. If Windows 10 has previously found your printer on its own and installed it with an incorrect driver, it will reinstall *the same* incorrect driver.

If the printer isn't found automatically, which is common in business environments, the **Not finding what you're looking for?** link simply opens a Help window with a note telling you how the problem may be fixed.

It is the **Add Printer** dialog (see Figure 6-4) that you will find helpful for all but the hardest to install printers.

If the printer is not automatically found, you can click **The printer that I want isn't listed** link to bring up additional installation options for the device (see Figure 6-5).

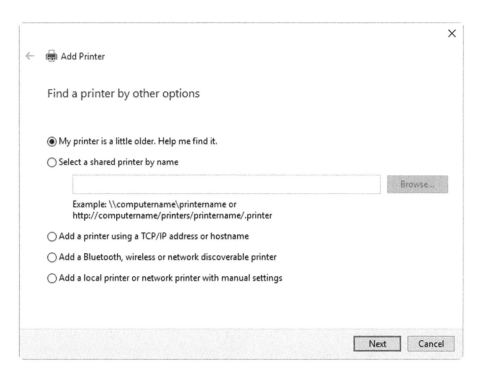

Figure 6-5. *Manually adding a printer*

In the Add Printer window, you have the following options:

- **My printer is a little older. Help me find it.** A function that searches for printers automatically, but also searches for printers that worked fine in Windows 7 or Windows 8.1, but may not be automatically detected by Windows 10.

- You can add a printer by its name on the network, which you type in the format **\\CompanyDomain\Printername** (if you know it; it is usually provided by your IT department).

- You can add a printer by its IP address (more on finding this in a minute).

- You can add a Bluetooth printer, if you have one.

- You can choose to manually configure the printer depending on the port in which it is located. This is useful for older printers that connect via serial and parallel connections, where you can specify the COM or LPT port you have connected the printer to.

■ **Tip** If you need to discover the IP address of a wireless or network printer, it is typically available within the printer settings in its own display. You should refer to your printer's owners' manual for the exact way to retrieve the IP address, because it differs from one printer to another.

All things being equal, you probably don't know the IP address or the network name of a printer. One quick way around this is to check how the printer is configured on another computer. You can do this in Devices and Printers (in Windows 7, Windows 8.1, and Windows 10). Right-click the printer and select **Printer Properties**. Under the **Ports** tab, you should see the IP address of the printer (see Figure 6-6).

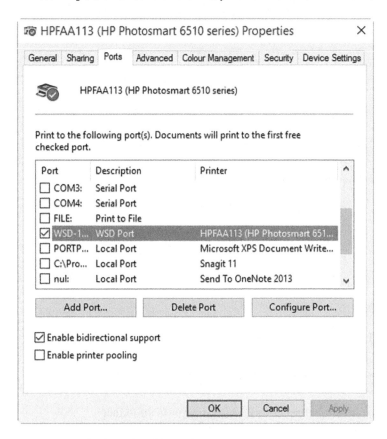

Figure 6-6. *Checking the address of a printer*

On a home or small business network, finding a printer's IP is relatively straightforward, though the actual method varies, depending on the make of your router. The following steps provide a general approach that you should be able to tweak for your own setup:

1. Open Internet Explorer.

2. Access your router login by typing **192.168.0.1** (sometimes 192.168.1.1 or 192.168.2.1) and pressing **Enter**.

3. Log in to your router with your username and password (if these are still *admin* and *password*, you should change them to prevent other people from signing in and compromising your network and PCs with malware and data theft attacks!).

4. Find the LAN settings.

5. Look for the Ethernet settings.

6. Look for the name of your network printer; its IP address is listed as shown in Figure 6-7.

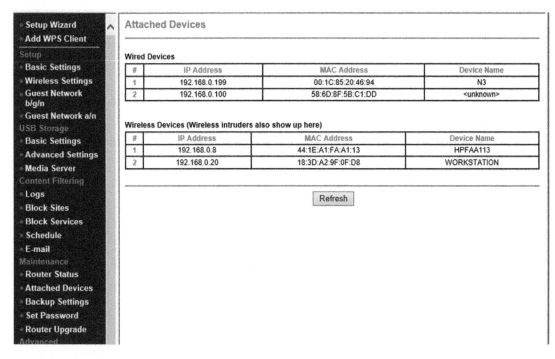

Figure 6-7. *Finding a printer's IP address on the network*

■ **Note** If you have to reset your router, perhaps because your Internet connection has gone down, the IP address of your printer might have changed. This requires that you uninstall and reinstall the printer on all of your computers because Windows locks the driver to a specific IP address. To get around this problem, you can set the printer to a static IP address in your router setup. Consult your manual or your ISP for details on how to do this.

Setting Default Printers

You can set the default printer—the one that will always be autoselected as the main one to use—in the Devices and Printers panel by right-clicking the printer and then clicking **Set as default printer** in the context menu. The default printer is displayed with a green circle and a check mark.

If you use the same computer in different places, perhaps at home and at work or in different office locations, you don't want to spend time setting and resetting the default printer whenever you want to print a document.

If you are using a laptop or tablet, Windows 10 allows you to set a different default printer for each network that you are connected to at the time. In Devices and Printers, select any printer by clicking to highlight it, and then click the **Manage Default Printers** link on the toolbar at the top of the window.

In the dialog (see Figure 6-8), you can set a different default printer for each network you connect to. The networks you have already connected to and previously-installed printers are all listed by name and are available from drop-down menus with the defaults showing in the main pane of the dialog.

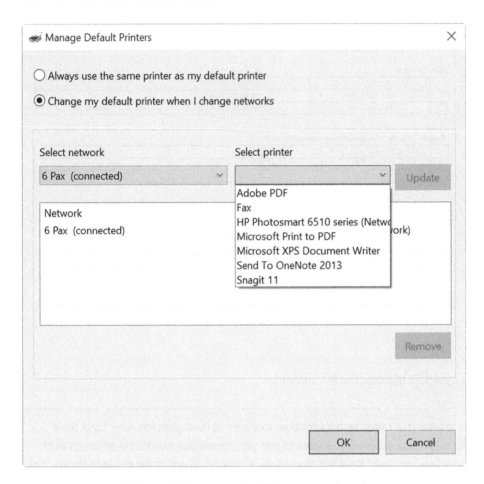

Figure 6-8. *Setting different default printers for different networks*

Using this feature, you can set Windows to automatically change the default printer on your computer the moment you connect to a different network. So you can be sure that wherever you are, whatever you print is always sent to the correct printer.

Managing Printer Properties

Long gone are the days when printers did only a single thing: accept an input and print it onto paper. Now printers come with a huge number of options for controlling every aspect of that output and the hardware. This, coupled with new eco-printing features intended to save both ink and paper, can make printers very complex to manage.

One Windows feature that can help manage printer properties is called **Device Stage**. Double-clicking a printer (this works for some printers, but not all) opens its Device Stage page (see Figure 6-9). The Device Stage page is created by the device manufacturer (the word *device* is used here because there are many different hardware devices in the Devices and Printers panel, from smartphones to network storage, which also have their own Device Stage pages).

Figure 6-9. *Device Stage in Windows 10*

On the Device Stage page are links to downloads for the printer (such as management apps), preferences quick links, and even quick links for buying cartridges and other consumables online. The links available vary from one device and printer to another, though they can be very useful.

Printers and their driver software differ by make and model, but most of the functionality across devices is the same. Thus, you may find that some of the following screenshots don't match up exactly with what you see on your own PC. Windows 10 does a good job of standardizing the settings for printers, however.

You can manage your printer in Devices and Printers by right-clicking the printer and selecting **Printer Properties** from the options.

In the main printer properties dialog, under the **General** tab (see Figure 6-10), you find the name of the printer (which you can change by simply typing a new name). You can also input comments about the machine's physical location, as well as other notes (perhaps about how to insert paper for double-sided printing if there is no duplex unit installed). These notes can be useful in the workplace, where many printers, often of the same make and model, are shared on the network.

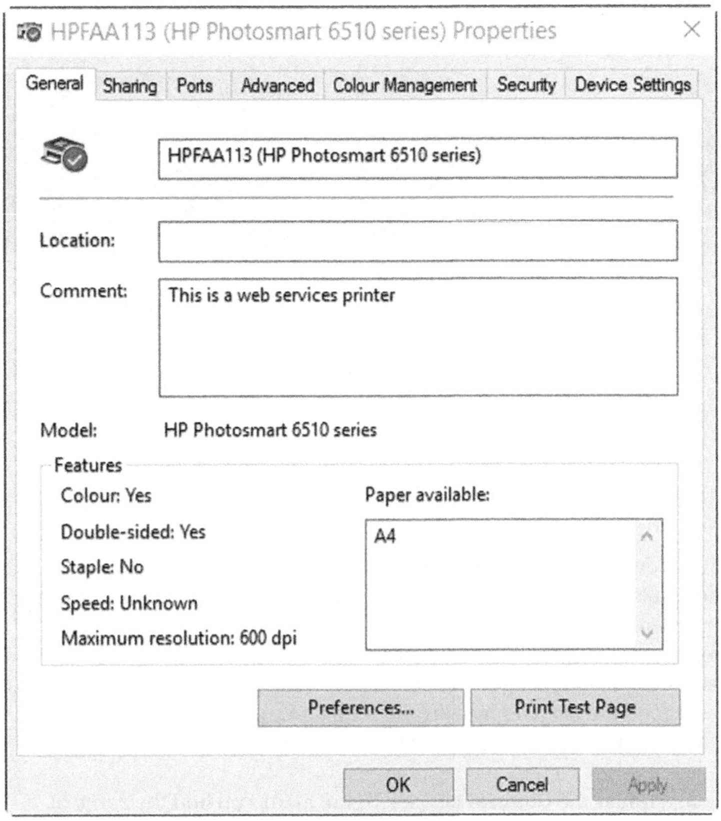

Figure 6-10. *Working with general printer properties*

The **Preferences** button opens the printing preferences, which is discussed in the "Managing Printing in Windows 10" section later in this chapter. You can also print a test page here to check that the printer is working.

■ **Note** The configuration and options in the printer dialogs vary according to the make and model of the printer.

On the **Sharing** tab, you can choose whether you want to share the printer over your network (the computer that is sharing the printer needs to be left on for the printer to be accessible) and you can give it a name (see Figure 6-11).

Figure 6-11. *Working with Sharing printer properties*

■ **Tip**   Earlier, I discussed finding a printer by its name. A printer with a simple name is easier for people to find and remember. Easy names may include a floor number, room number, and/or printer type.

Shared printers may be accessed by computers running other versions of Windows, such as Windows 8.1 or Windows 7. If this is likely, click the **Additional Drivers** button to choose drivers that automatically load from your computer as needed.

You probably shouldn't change anything in the **Ports** tab (see Figure 6-12), but if you have had to reset your router, the IP address of the printer may have automatically changed. Thus, after resetting a router, you may find that you can no longer print to a particular printer—and you have to reinstall it, though you often discover that Windows 10 can automatically rectify the problem on its own.

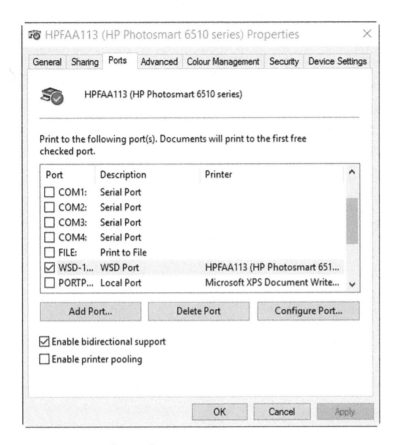

Figure 6-12. *Working with printer ports*

The **Ports** tab is also useful if you are using older parallel or serial printers, which are complicated to install and configure correctly, but are still in use in some business environments.

There are many useful options available in the **Advanced** tab (see Figure 6-13), including the following:

- The ability to specify that a printer is only accessible between certain hours. This option is useful if you are trying to cut down on paper and toner/ink usage.

- The ability to choose how the printer prioritizes print jobs that are sent to it. You might want to set this option on a shared printer to spool a job only after the previous one has finished (if the printer doesn't have much internal memory). Generally, you should not need to do this because Windows 10 is excellent at managing print jobs.

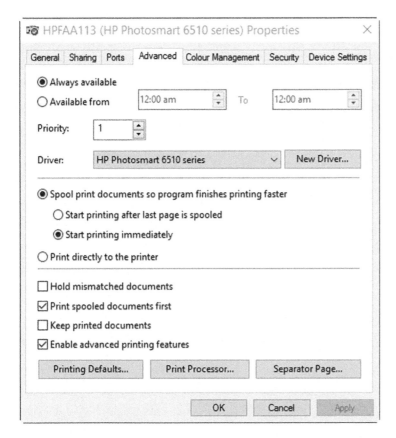

Figure 6-13. *Working with advanced printer properties*

■ **Tip**   Setting printers to be available only between certain hours of the day is not just a great way to cut down on printing waste but also a useful way to avoid causing inconvenience to others. My own printer is located in my home office, which is next to my guest bedroom. When in use, this printer can be heard through the wall and inadvertently wake up someone. Setting available *from* and *to* times can prevent accidental annoyance to other people.

The **Color Management** options (see Figure 6-14) allow you to set a color profile that matches your monitor. This is especially useful if you have a carefully calibrated screen for color accuracy and print photographs. (I will talk more about color management shortly.)

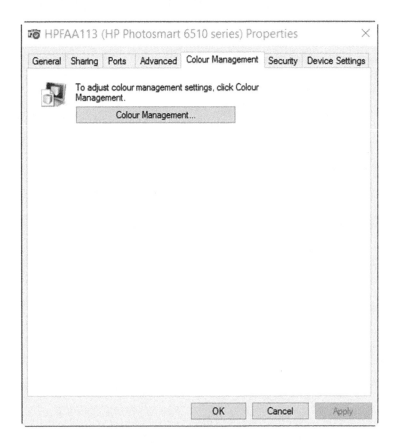

Figure 6-14. *Working with printer color management*

The options on the **Security** tab allow you to specify who can control what on the printer (see Figure 6-15). Here you may want to make changes, including giving users, or even groups of users on a company domain, permissions to manage print jobs (such as deleting stuck jobs). Not all users have permission to **Manage [this] printer** by default, as you may want a printer to only print using black ink to save money, but any user with management permissions could easily override this setting.

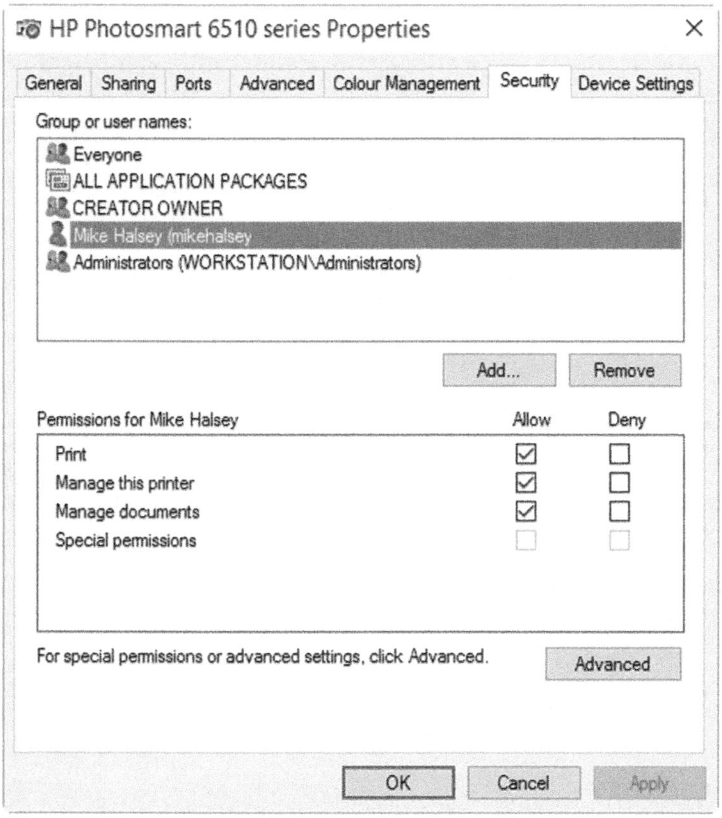

Figure 6-15. *Working with printer security*

To change permissions, select the appropriate users in the top pane. You can then change their options by checking the boxes in the bottom half of the tab. These basic controls are all you need to grant or deny user access to a printer. If you require more control over access to printers, such as printer availability time and which users can print and how often, click the **Advanced** button.

It is now common for printer manufacturers to add a custom tab that provides extra information, such as ink and toner status, and links to purchase official consumables and accessories online.

Managing Color Profiles for Printers and Displays

Sometimes you absolutely *must* have color accuracy, perhaps if you are a photographer or graphic artist. To help with this, you can load specific color profiles into Windows 10 for both printers and displays. Open the Color Management window by searching for the word **color** at the Start menu and running **Color Management** from the Settings results.

In Color Management (see Figure 6-16), you can load specific color profiles for both printers and displays if they have the correct manufacturer profile file. The file formats are Color Device Model Profile (*.cdmp), Color Appearance Model Profile (*.camp), Gamut Mapping Model Profile (*.gmmp), and ICC (*.icm).

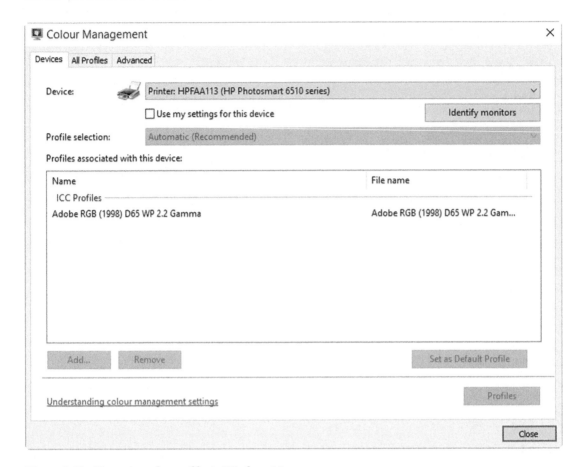

Figure 6-16. *Managing color profiles in Windows 10*

Choose the device in which you want to view the current color profile from the drop-down menu at the top of the window. To add a color profile to the currently selected device, check the **Use my settings for this device** box. You can then select an installed color profile.

You can add a profile from the **All Profiles** tab, in which you find the currently installed color profiles. Click the **Add** button at the bottom of the window to load a new color profile.

There are controls and options on the **Advanced** tab that enable you to further specify the way your color profiles are used for different types of images and art. You can also run a tool that helps calibrate the brightness, color, and contrast settings for your monitor so that what you see on screen are faithful representations of true color.

Managing Shared Printers in Windows 10

In the previous section, I talked a little bit about managing the security of a shared printer, which you can do directly from the Devices and Printers window. Click a printer to select it. You can open Print Server Properties from the toolbar.

You can also manage security properties for the printer in the **Print Server Properties** dialog (see Figure 6-17), which offers additional security options, such as whether users can edit the print queue or change the print settings.

Figure 6-17. *Managing print server properties*

If you share a printer between different Windows 7, Windows 8.1, and Windows 10 PCs, perhaps in a workplace, you want to make sure that anyone who connects to the printer is always able to get the correct drivers for it. These drivers are provided by the PC sharing the printer.

Under the **drivers** tab, you can see which drivers are installed for each printer. It may be that you have a 64-bit (x64) version of Windows 10 installed, and as a result, you don't have the 32-bit (x86) drivers on your PC for older PCs or smaller laptops and tablets that want to use the printer. To fix this, click the **Add** button. You will be presented with a checklist of drivers that you can add (see Figure 6-18).

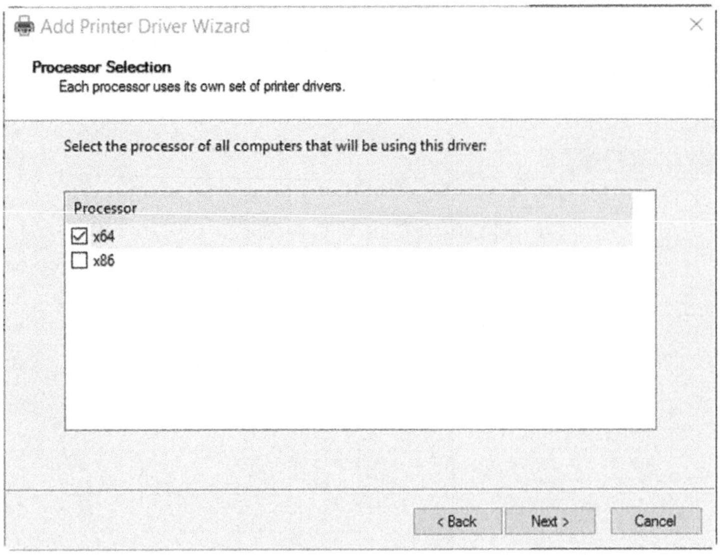

Figure 6-18. *You can add drivers for shared printers*

If Windows 10 doesn't have a copy of this driver in its store, you will be presented with a list of printer manufacturers and printers for which drivers are available. If your driver is not listed, click the **Have Disk** button and navigate to a downloaded copy of the printer driver.

Printing from Store and win32 Apps

Although there are many options for managing your printer(s), there are usually even more for managing printing. These features differ from one printer to another, but the general printing preferences are the same.

When you want to print from within a Windows Store app, you get a slightly different print dialog than if you are printing from a win32 desktop app. Your available printers are listed in the top left of the print dialog (see Figure 6-19). Below this are options for controlling the number of copies you wish to print, the orientation of the paper, and whether you wish to print in color or in monochrome. On the right is a preview of what the printout will look like.

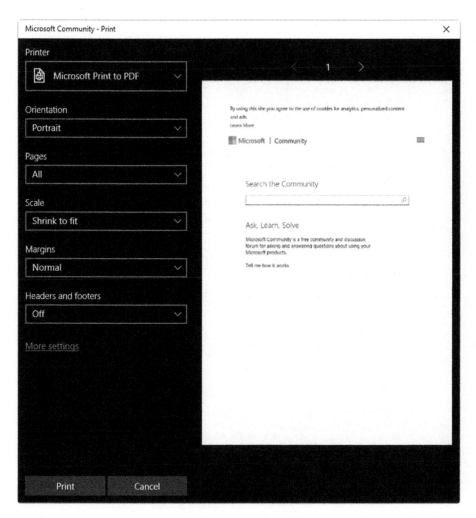

Figure 6-19. *You can control your printing from within apps*

If you want finer control over your print, click the **More settings** link to display further options (see Figure 6-20). These options may vary depending on the printer you have installed, but can include controls for duplex (double-sided) printing, paper size and tray choice, and print quality.

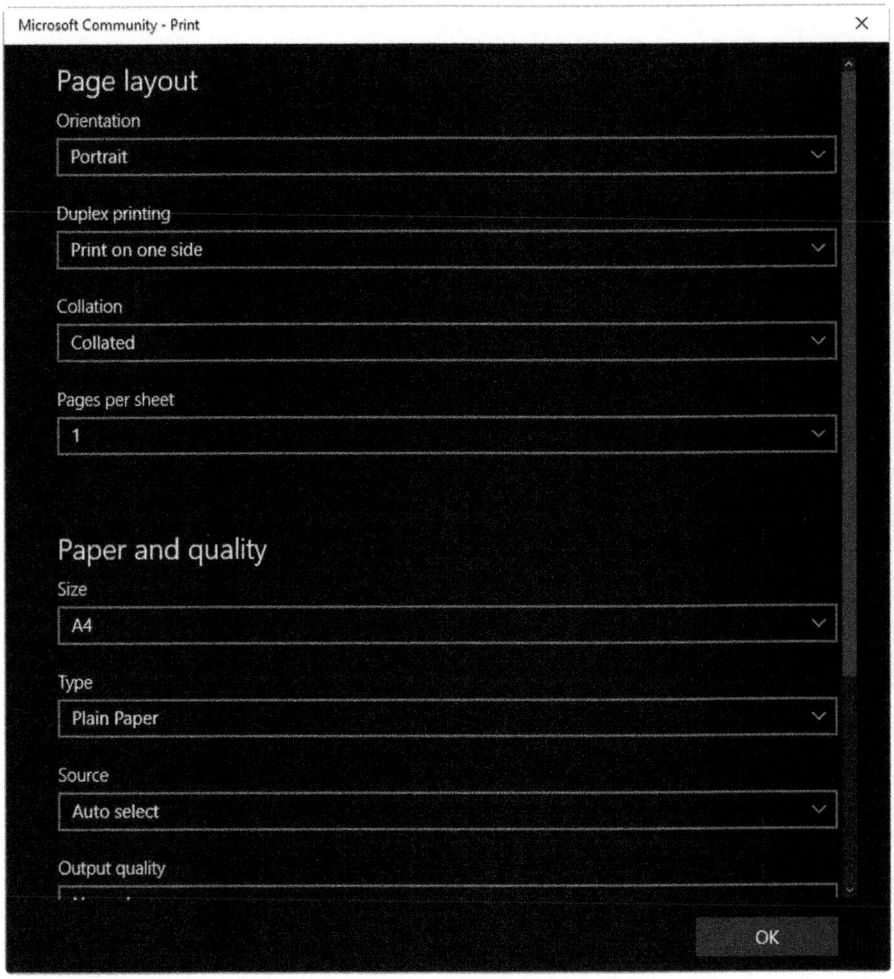

Figure 6-20. *Advanced print settings are available within apps*

When you print from a win32 desktop app, the print dialog is different and can sometimes vary from one app to another; for example, Microsoft Office has its own. The default print dialog, seen in Figure 6-21, presents a list of available printers along with options for the number of copies you want and the page range (see the following tip). You can access the advanced print options by clicking the **Preferences** button. I'll show you how to use these options in the "Managing Printers and Setting Default Options" section.

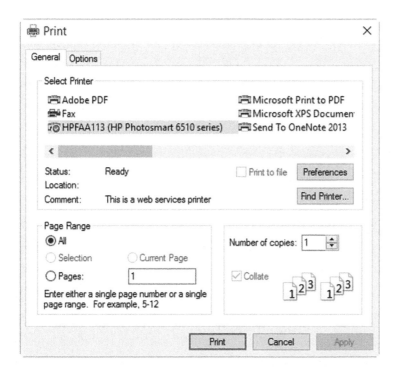

Figure 6-21. *The print dialog as seen in many win32 desktop apps*

■ **Tip**   To choose a page range use the **-** and **,** symbols in the formats **2-17** (for pages 2 to 17 inclusive) or **1, 3, 5-7** (for pages 1, 3, and 5 to 7).

Managing Printers and Setting Default Options

You can control many printing options when you send a document to print. You can also set default options for the PC so that, for example, the printer always prints using only black ink (to save money) unless specifically overridden. To access the print options for your printer for a single print-job, click the **Preferences** button in the desktop app print dialog. If you want to set global print preferences, however (for both local and shared use), you can access the printing preferences by right-clicking the printer in the **Devices and Printers** window and selecting **Printing Preferences** from the options.

On the first tab in this dialog, which may vary in name (see Figure 6-22), are the most common options, including the default page size, page orientation, and whether the printer uses single- or double-sided printing by default (you need an internal duplexing unit in your printer to take advantage of this).

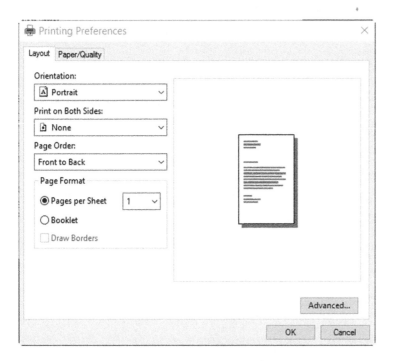

Figure 6-22. *Working with basic printing preferences*

■ **Tip** Once you know whether your printer's duplex unit flips the paper on its long or short edge, I recommend writing this information on a label and sticking it to the printer so that it is easy for others to use double-sided printing on their own computers without wasting paper on prints that end up upside down on the reverse side of the page.

The options on the **Paper** tab allow you to choose the default paper size, collation of multipage print jobs (a very useful option in an office), and the printer's default source tray.

■ **Tip** If you want to change the default printing options for the printer (perhaps to set it to print only in draft mode to save ink or toner), you can do it in the Advanced settings. Every time someone prints from that printer (and on that computer) afterward, these are the default print options (unless changed manually for just one job).

If you want finer control over the printer's settings, click the **Advanced** button (see Figure 6-23), which displays a list of all the controls.

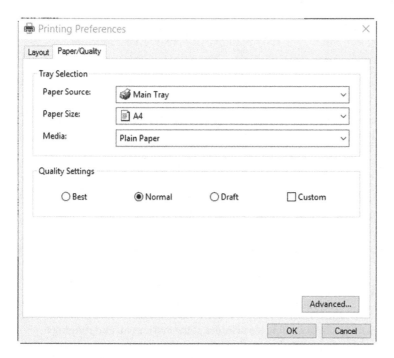

Figure 6-23. *Working with paper preferences*

■ **Tip** If you are printing photographs, you want to make sure that eco and draft features are switched off so that you get the best quality prints.

Once you have set the default print options in the Devices and Printers panel, such as only printing at draft quality and using only black ink (which is a great way to save money), all printing from that printer uses those options. For individual prints, however, the settings can be overridden in the print Properties dialog.

Working with Wireless Printers in Windows 10

I mentioned earlier in the chapter that resetting your router may also reset the IP address on your network wireless printer.

Windows 10 is really great at automatically reconnecting to the printer in a way that keeps it working happily. Sometimes, though, you'll be told the printer is *disconnected*. To rectify this, the best option is to uninstall and reinstall the printer. Although you can set the printer to have a static IP address in your router, not all routers support this functionality. Check the router's manual or consult your ISP's support department.

Sometimes it is difficult to figure out how to connect a wireless printer to your network. If you have a wired printer, it's easy enough to just plug the printer into the router via USB, as many routers support this, or by an RJ45 Ethernet cable, or plug it into your switch panel using an RJ45 Ethernet cable.

To connect a wireless printer to your network, you may need to find the WPS buttons on both the router and the printer. These buttons allow you to pair the two devices wirelessly without a password.

1. Press the **WPS** button on your router.

2. As soon as you can (within 30 seconds or so anyway), press the **WPS** button on the printer.

These two devices should now pair. Occasionally, however, a router refuses to see a printer, even when the WPS buttons have been pressed. In this event, you should contact your ISP's support department or consult the router manual to find the best way to pair the router with a wireless device.

▪ **Tip** You can also pair computers, printers, and other devices by pressing the WPS button on your router if the computer—normally tablets or laptops—or device also has a WPS or similarly labeled button. Check the documentation that came with the device to see if this function is supported.

Obtaining the IP Address of a Network Printer

The Devices and Printers page panel (see Figure 6-24) is a very useful way to manage network resources that your computer can see. You can best access it by searching for **printers** at the Start menu and running it from the search results. All printers and other network devices that Windows 10 can see are displayed here. You can use the information provided to find the IP address of a device.

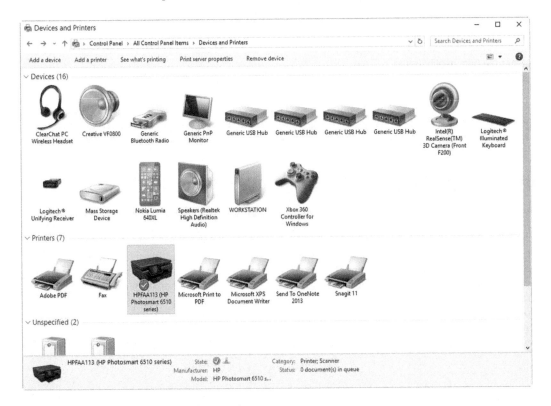

Figure 6-24. *The Devices and Printers panel*

Perform the following steps to find the IP address of a device in the Devices and Printers page:

1. Right-click the printer you want to find the IP address for.

2. Click **Printer properties** in the menu that appears.

3. Click the **Ports** tab in the dialog that appears. The port (with the IP address) that the printer is connected to will be checked.

The IP address is commonly listed in the location information at the bottom of the window. If you don't see the IP address listed here, check the onscreen display on the printer. The IP address is usually available through its settings menus, although the exact method of retrieving the IP address from the printer varies, depending on the manufacturer and model.

■ **Note**   Windows may display the IPv6 address for a device. If this happens, you can get the shorter, numeric IPv4 address from your router.

Top Printing Tips

There are some great ways to get a little more out of your printer's ink and toner. They begin with purchasing the right printer. When purchasing a printer, follow these tips:

- If you can afford it, buy a printer with in-built duplexing (double-sided printing). This saves paper.

- Check the cost of full-price consumables (ink cartridges and toner) and compare it against prices for similar printers by other manufacturers.

- Do some research online about the printer's TCO (total cost of ownership). This information may be provided in a magazine review or in a product group test.

- Find out if you can use cheaper compatible ink and toner cartridges. Some printers have "chipped" cartridges that require you to use official manufacturer ink.

To get more life out of your ink cartridges and toner, there are a few things you can do to prolong their life.

- If you are not going to use your printer for a while, keep the ink cartridges in a cool, dry place (you can even wrap them in plastic film and put them in the refrigerator). This prevents the ink from drying up. This *does not* apply to toner, which does not dry out.

- When your toner cartridge is low, you can shake the cartridge to loosen up more toner, which results in a longer lifespan. If you do this, you *must* read the following cautionary note!

- Think about if you *really* need to print something. Most of the people I know don't actually use most of the printed material they create.

- When printing, use the Print Preview mode (if available) to see if you really need to print every page, and then use the **Page Range** option so that you only print the pages you really need.

■ **Caution**   When shaking a toner cartridge, you should always make sure that your arms are fully covered, that you are wearing disposable gloves, and that you do not breathe in any waste toner. Some laser printer toners are carcinogenic. You should always wash your hands thoroughly after handling cartridges, especially refillable ones.

Summary

Working with and managing printers is always something people ask me about because these peripherals are generally used more than other devices. The one piece of eco advice I give on using printers is to first ask yourself the question, "Do I really need to print this document?" By far the best way to save paper, ink, and money is to not print a document or picture at all.

The controls for installing and managing printers in Windows 10 are excellent, although some of the most useful ones are hidden. These controls include the ability to autoset the default printer at different locations and for different networks; and the color management tools, which are essential to creative professionals and very useful to anybody printing high-quality photographs at home or at work.

CHAPTER 7

■ ■ ■

Having Fun with Games, Photos, Music, and Video

Despite the business origins of the PC, Windows is the biggest gaming platform in the world. Despite repeated predictions on the death of PC gaming in favor of consoles, Windows 10 brings some new features to the mix that put gaming front and center on the PC. There is new integration between Windows 10 and other Microsoft platforms, such as the Xbox, that will be built upon and expanded in the coming years.

Gaming on a PC comes with some responsibility, though, especially if you are a parent. Controlling the games that your children play is becoming increasingly difficult because the Internet provides access to games, entertainment, and content that may not be suitable for children.

When it comes to nongaming fun, Windows 10 is as good as any version before it—with excellent apps and services for music, video, and TV, and for enjoying and editing your photos.

Finally, there is what will probably become the perennial Windows 10 gaming platform in the coming years: tablets. With their sensors and accelerometers, these devices are perfect gaming platforms.

In this chapter, I'll talk you through how to have fun with your PC: integrating your PC with your Xbox One console, enjoying the latest gaming technologies (including 3D), and viewing your photos and videos.

Windows 10 and Xbox Integration

Windows 10 comes with an Xbox app (see Figure 7-1) that's capable of much more than just integration with your Xbox Live account. If you use a Microsoft account to sign in to your PC, and you have an Xbox Live account linked to it, you are automatically signed-in the first time you launch the app.

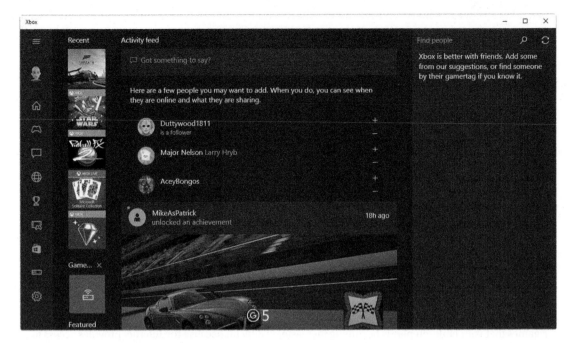

Figure 7-1. *The Xbox app for Windows 10*

■ **Note**   Because Windows Store apps are updated on a regular basis, your experience with the Xbox and other apps detailed in this chapter might be slightly different from what is discussed here. Overall, though, the core functionality won't change very much.

The app allows you to manage every aspect of your Xbox Live account, which can be considerably easier on a PC than through the Xbox itself. The main view shows a list of Xbox Live games you've recently played, and this is on any Windows 10 device from the Xbox console itself to your PC, tablet, and even your smartphone. Your activity feed alerts you to any messages from your friends, and you can respond and have conversations here too.

Where you have unlocked achievements in your games, these can be shared (as with many things in Windows 10) on your activity feed, through a compatible app or by email, with a single click of the Share button.

Adding Games to the Xbox App

You can launch any game that's installed on your PC by clicking the **My games** icon in the left panel of the app, and then clicking **Add a game from your PC** (see Figure 7-2). The app shows all the games installed on your Xbox console, but you can manually add any game that has a Start menu entry. You will also find that the Xbox app is extremely good at automatically adding games that you have installed in Services, such as Steam and Origin.

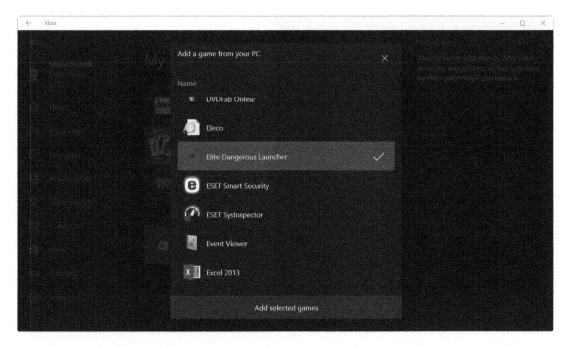

Figure 7-2. *You can add non-Xbox Live games to the app*

Any game you add to the Xbox app can be used to launch that game, so you can use the Xbox app as your central location for game management.

Recording and Sharing Your Gameplay with Game DVR

There are two incredibly cool features within the Xbox app for Windows 10 that I want to show you in detail. The first of these is Game DVR, which allows you to record any gameplay on your PC, just as you can on your Xbox console, and then share it with friends and web sites.

You start the Game DVR feature by pressing the Windows key + G; any footage that's recorded will be saved to your **Videos ➤ Captures** folder so it's easy to find. The main Game DVR interface includes five buttons (see Figure 7-3).

Figure 7-3. *Game DVR lets you record your gameplay in any device*

The first button launches the Xbox app if it's not already running on your desktop. Next, follow buttons for the **Record That** feature, which if enabled, records the last 30 seconds or so of gameplay so that you need never miss anything if something cool happened. I'll show you how to configure Record That shortly. Next are buttons for taking a screenshot and recording a video. The last button is for the Game DVR settings (see Figure 7-4).

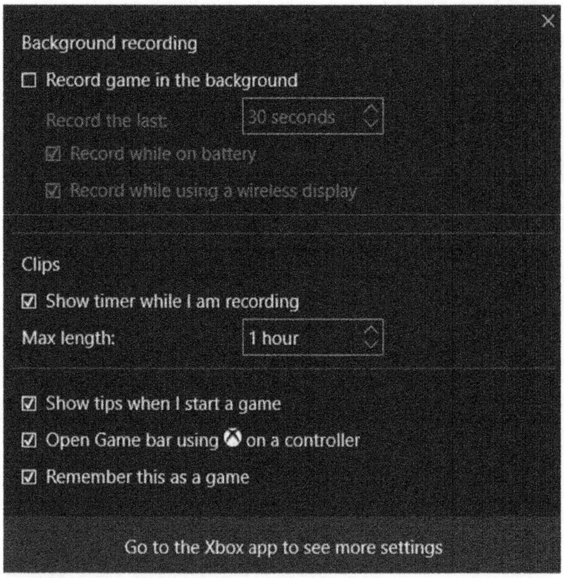

Figure 7-4. You can control features such as Record This from Game DVR

It is in the settings that you can activate and control the Game DVR feature, which records your gameplay in the background for anything from the last 15 seconds to the last 10 minutes. Once the feature is set up, click the **Record That** button on the Game DVR controls to start the background record.

You can control Game DVR on your PC with the following keyboard commands.

- **Win+G** to open the Game DVR bar

- **Win+Alt+G** to start and stop the Record That feature

- **Win+Alt+R** to start and stop recording manually

- **Win+Alt+PrtScn** to take a screenshot

- **Win+Alt+T** to show or hide the recording timer

Click **Settings** and then **Game DVR** in the Xbox app to control many aspects of the Game DVR feature, including the maximum allowed recording time for clips (if you don't have much storage space on your PC, you might want to keep this low), the recording quality and resolution, and the audio quality.

When you record your clips, they appear within the Xbox app in the Game DVR section. Here you can click any clip to reveal the Trim (edit) and Share controls (see Figure 7-5). You can only share recognized games through the app, but you can always share footage manually from its files in the Videos ➤ Captures folder on your PC.

Figure 7-5. *You can edit and share recorded game footage*

■ **Tip**   Game DVR can be used in Windows 10 to record *almost* any app; some video apps, like Netflix, aren't compatible, so you can't use it to record streamed movies. You can open Game DVR in any app by pressing Win+G; you are asked to confirm that the app is a game. Any video you record using the Game DVR feature is saved to your Videos ➤ Captures folder.

Streaming Games to Your PC from Your Xbox One Console

By far the coolest feature of the Xbox app, though, and quite possibly the coolest consumer feature in Windows 10, is the ability to stream games directly from your Xbox One console to any Windows 10 PC, and play the game on that PC using your Xbox controller. Why might you want to do this? It can be extremely useful if somebody wants to play an Xbox game while somebody else watches TV. The gamer can happily play on their PC, laptop, or tablet in the den or their bedroom, without the TV being monopolized.

■ **Note**   Because all the work of processing and displaying the game is done by the Xbox console, games can be streamed to any Windows PC—even low-power tablets.

You connect to your Xbox One console (this feature is not available for the Xbox 360) by clicking the **Connect** icon in the Xbox app. If your PC and the Xbox One are connected to the same network, either via Wi-Fi or a wired Ethernet connection, your PC sees the console and displays a **Connect** button (see Figure 7-6).

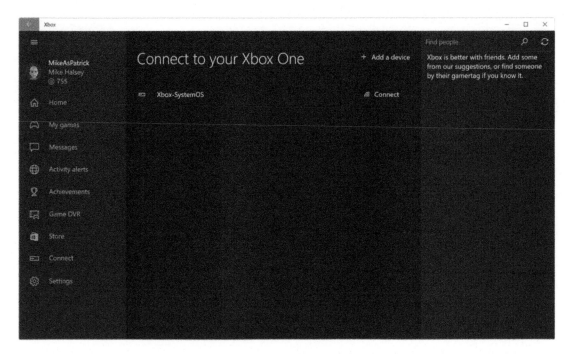

Figure 7-6. *You can connect to your Xbox One console through the Xbox app*

Once connected, the Xbox app shows you what is currently playing on the console (see Figure 7-7) and gives you various options.

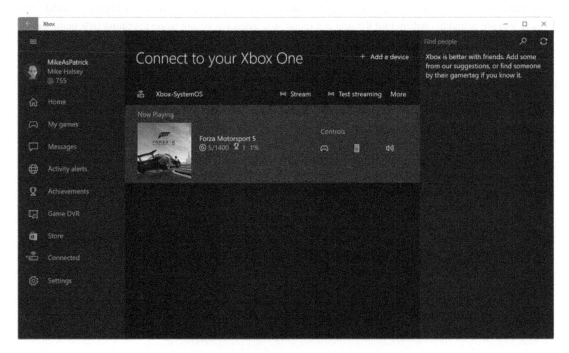

Figure 7-7. *The Xbox app shows you what's currently playing on the console*

Along the top of the Xbox One Connect display are buttons to **Stream** your Xbox One console to your PC, and also to **Test [the] Streaming** connection. Streaming a game to your PC allows you to play that game as if you were playing your Xbox, because there really isn't any lag at all.

■ **Note**   You can use your Xbox One controller with your PC to play streamed games. Just connect the controller to a USB port on the PC using a USB-to–micro USB cable, of the type that's commonly used to charge a smartphone.

To the right of the Now Playing display are three **Controls**. These can be used to control your Xbox without an Xbox controller, using touch controls instead. These allow you to play your Xbox on your TV by using as tablet as a controller.

The first of these enable you to emulate a standard Xbox One controller on a touchscreen, the second one allows you to control the Live TV features of the Xbox One (if you have a TV tuner installed), and the last one allows you to use your PC to talk to your Xbox One remotely.

To the right of the Stream controls is a **More** button, which you can click to present additional options on how your PC connects to your Xbox One console. These option include automatically connecting to the console every time you run the Xbox app, turning off the console remotely, disconnecting the PC from the console, or telling Windows 10 to forget the console altogether (see Figure 7-8).

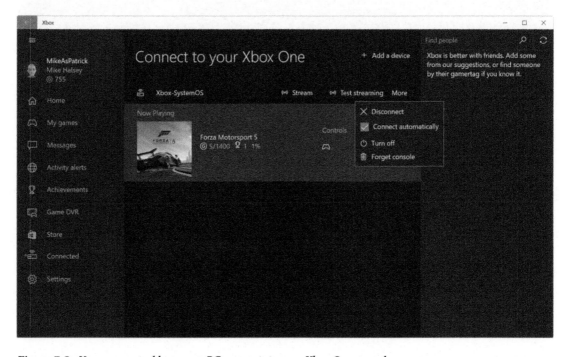

Figure 7-8. *You can control how your PC connects to your Xbox One console*

Other Xbox App Features

The Xbox app contains a series of control icons that run down its left side. From these you can control every aspect of your games and Xbox Live account.

- **Messages** is where you can send and receive messages and chat with your friends. Conversations appear threaded, as they do for SMS messaging on your smartphone.

- **Activity alerts** is where you see what your friends have shared from their own Xbox Live accounts, such as commenting on your achievements. New friend requests also appear here.

- **Achievements** is where you can monitor all of your achievements and progress in games (see Figure 7-9). You can click any listed game to get more detailed information about your achievements.

Figure 7-9. *You can view your achievements in the Xbox app*

- **Store** is a quick link through to the Windows Games Store, where you can buy games to play on your PC, tablet, laptop, or smartphone.

- **Settings** is where you can control the Xbox app and its integration with services such as Twitch.

Managing Game Ratings for Children

One of the biggest concerns for parents is the suitability of the games their children play in Windows. In Chapter 4 I showed you how to manage child accounts in Windows 10. Part of this feature includes managing acceptable game ratings for your children. Opening the Settings app and navigating to **Accounts**, and then **Family & other users** and clicking the **Manage family settings online** link takes you to a web site where you can manage the child safety features for your family.

Clicking a child's name reveals options to view their recent activity and to control their web browsing safety, allowed screen time, and which apps and games they can use. The apps and games section allows you to specify what age range of games is appropriate for that child from a drop-down menu (see Figure 7-10). These range from **Age 3** to **No restrictions**.

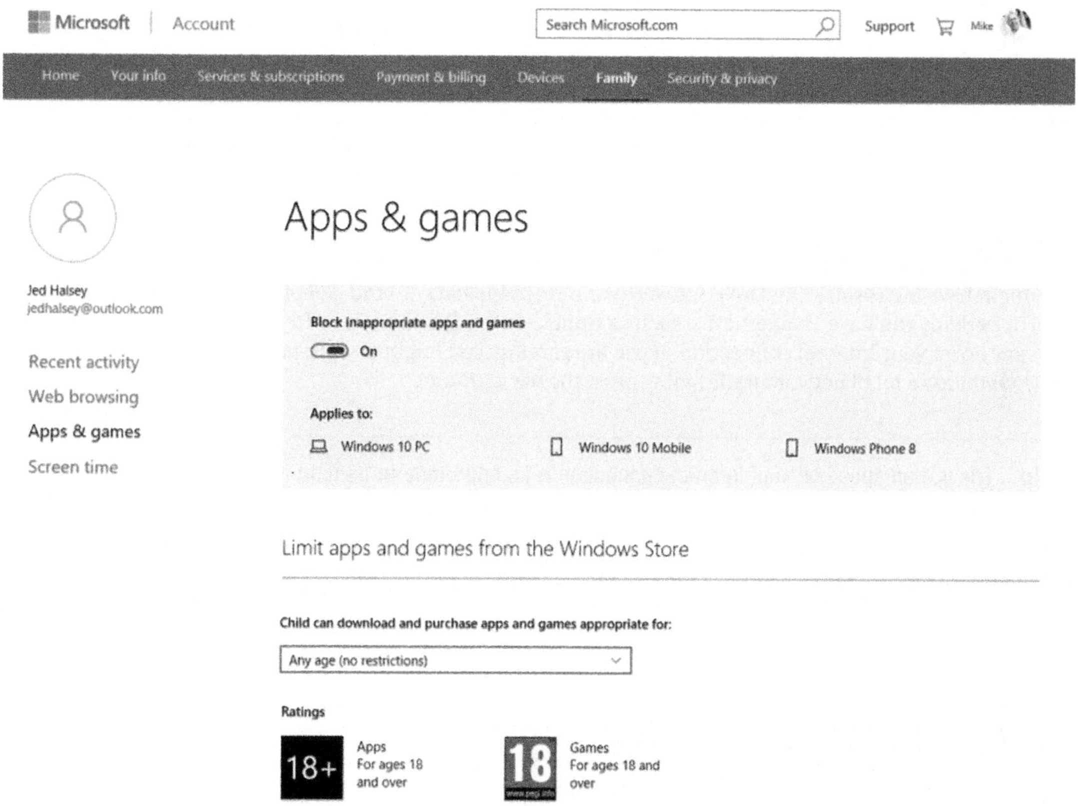

Figure 7-10. *Managing age ratings in Family Safety*

■ **Note**   Not every game complies with game age-restriction practices, so it is possible that your child may be able to play some age-inappropriate games regardless of these settings.

Configuring Windows 10 for the Latest Games

Casual gamers will have little trouble playing the latest games from the Windows Store or Games app on Windows 10 computers, tablets, and smartphones. Indeed, for some years now, games have been far more popular on tablets and smartphones than on desktop computers because of the new and fun ways in which we can interact with them and because the lower hardware specification of tablets means that game companies have had to create simpler games overall.

But what if you're an enthusiast? How can you configure your computer to run the latest first-person shooters?

I won't recommend specific graphics cards and other hardware, because they change so often that anything I write will quickly be out of date. There are some things you can look for when purchasing a new computer or computer parts, however, which I discuss in the next section. There are also things that you can do with Windows 10.

So how can you configure Windows 10 to run the best and newest games? One of the first considerations is your anti-malware software. Windows Defender, which is installed by default in Windows 10, is a good choice for gamers, primarily because it is lightweight but also because it doesn't do any major scanning when you use the PC for other things.

Many third-party anti-malware solutions, however, also detect when games are running—usually by detecting something running full screen—and hibernates their scanning engines. ESET, which is the anti-virus software that I use, is one example of an anti-malware app that includes a special gaming mode.

As a power user, I find Windows Defender perfectly adequate, so I don't use third-party anti-malware software. If you are a gamer, however, this is something you should think about if you are considering purchasing a third-party package.

The amount of software you have running in the background can also make a difference. For example, you might have Microsoft's OneDrive software running in the background, keeping a cloud backup of your files; or perhaps you have an alternative such as Google Drive, Dropbox, Livedrive, Mozy, and so on. They can slow down your Internet connection. If you are gaming, you might want to pause them or switch them off when there's a lot of network traffic going on in the background.

■ **Tip** The upload speed on your Internet connection is as important for gaming as your download speed. If you have an older broadband connection with a healthy download speed of 5 Mbps but only a 0.6 Mbps upload speed, for example, it can result in being kicked from servers. One player's slow connection adversely impacts the other players' experience (see Figure 7-11). The reason for this is that when you are gaming online, you are sending almost as much data as you are receiving.

Figure 7-11. *You can test your Internet connection speed using services like* www.speedtest.net

Do the following to close an app with touch or keyboard and mouse:

1. Swipe inward from the left edge of the screen, or press **Win+Tab** to display the running Task View.

2. Click the Close button in the top right of any app thumbnail to close the app.

Do the following to close a desktop task:

1. From the desktop, click the Show Hidden Icons arrow in the far right of the taskbar. This is the small up arrow next to the system tray. If you don't see this arrow, there are no minimized programs running in the system tray.

2. Right-click the program you want to terminate (hovering over an icon tells you what the program is).

3. Select Exit or Close from the options that appear.

You may also have software and driver updaters running in the background that are slowing down your computer. You may be able to shut these down from the desktop in the same way, but perhaps you don't need them running to begin with.

Some of these updates can be very useful and are very important indeed, including the updaters from Adobe, which are used to fix security flaws that are very commonly exploited by malware. There may be other programs that you don't need, however, including quick launchers for your scanner, printer, or Blu-ray software. Autorunning software also includes utilities that came preinstalled on your computer, such as a quick launcher for media files.

To shut down these programs so that they don't autostart with Windows, do the following:

1. Press **Win+X** on your keyboard.

2. From the options that appear, select **Task Manager** (it can also be launched by right-clicking the taskbar).

3. Click the **Start-up** tab in the Task Manager (see Figure 7-12).

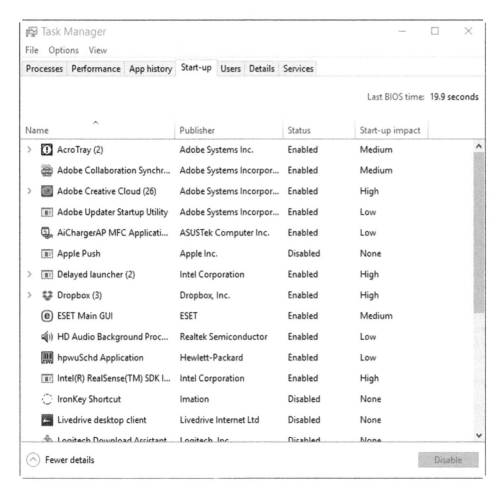

Figure 7-12. *Managing Start-up programs in the Task Manager*

4. Click the program you don't want to run at start-up.

5. Press the **Disable** button in the bottom right corner of the Task Manager window.

You should repeat steps 4 and 5 for all other software you want to disable at start-up.

■ **Note**   Once you configure your start-up programs, you should not need to switch off programs when you are gaming.

Choosing and Upgrading Your Gaming Hardware

Building a good gaming PC is a challenge, not least because the hardware can be extremely expensive for the best kit. But it is possible to choose or build a PC specifically for gaming while on a budget. I want to talk you through what to look for and what to purchase. This applies not only to traditional "tower" desktop PCs, but it's also very relevant when you're purchasing a desktop all-in-one or a laptop PC.

Motherboard

When choosing a motherboard, it is best to select one that can run the highest overall speeds (in GHz), even if it makes the board capable of running much faster than the hardware you plug into it. This is to ensure that the motherboard is upgradable in the future. It saves you money and gives you greater flexibility when it comes to upgrading.

Try to choose a board that offers the fast SATA 600 ports, and perhaps even an M.2 slot so that you can attach the newest generation of high-speed solid-state drives (SSD)—more on these shortly. Also, try to choose a board offering support for either Crossfire (AMD) or SLI (Nvidia). I talk more about this shortly too.

Processor

The processor is probably the least important consideration when it comes to choosing or building a gaming PC because most of the gaming processing is done by your graphics card. The important considerations here are the clock speed (again in GHz), and most importantly, having a processor with the same socket type as your motherboard.

■ **Tip**   Don't necessarily be tempted by an expensive Core i7 processor over a Core i5 for your PC. While a Core i5 is significantly preferable for gaming over the low-power Core i3 because of additional functions such as a dedicated graphics processor, the step up to the Core i7 guarantees hyper-threading support (which doesn't make much difference in games anyway) and builds in more onboard cache memory. This cache memory is only used for repetitive processor tasks, such as spreadsheets, computer-aided design (CAD), or video processing. It does not provide a boost to your games, and as such, a good Core i5 processor (perhaps one that can be overclocked) is often the best choice for a gaming PC.

A computer can run only as fast as its slowest component, so if you have chosen memory that runs faster than your processor, its overall speed throttles to match that of the processor. The same applies to the motherboard. If it has a slow clock speed, nothing can run faster than it can. Bear in mind, especially if you are buying a gaming laptop, that a more powerful processor negatively affects your overall battery life, sometimes dramatically.

Memory

It's long been established that if you don't have enough memory installed on your computer for Windows and your installed programs, the computer does not run as quickly as it otherwise could. This is certainly true of a low-end laptop or desktop PC upgraded from 1GB or 2GB of RAM to 4GB or more.

Above the 4GB level, the speed benefits begin to decrease, and above 8GB you won't really notice any difference unless you are performing tasks on huge files such as photographs, videos, or engineering designs. You can get the best performance on Windows 10 PCs by installing 6GB or preferably 8GB of RAM, but there is little need to install more than this unless you are also using your computer for very memory-intensive applications. When purchasing RAM, you need a type that's compatible with your motherboard and that will run at the fastest speed permissible by the motherboard and your processor.

■ **Note**   If you are using the 32-bit (x86) version of Windows 10 on your PC, your computer can "see" only a maximum of 4GB RAM, including any memory on your graphics card. If you have 2 × 2GB memory cards and 1GB graphics card memory, Windows 10 ignores one of the 2GB memory cards completely because it only sees complete cards.

Hard Disk

If you can afford it, put your money into an M.2 drive or a fast SSD if your motherboard supports the standards, preferably an SSD running on the SATA 600 socket type. However, purchasing SSDs is more complicated than traditional hard drives because manufacturers' memory chip speeds vary wildly. It is wise to seek up-to-date online reviews of SSDs before you buy. You can normally find them on computer magazine web sites.

Having an SSD as your main hard disk can significantly improve the speed of Windows 10 and your games. You need to make sure, however, that the main hard disk is of a suitable size. This is where the cost can rise sharply. In Appendix D, I show you how to best determine the size of the hard disk you need.

Graphics Card

Some motherboards come with onboard graphics that can handle full HD and even UHD (4K) video for nondemanding gaming. You might find that you want a separate graphics card, however, perhaps for online gaming or video editing. Earlier in this chapter, I spoke about SLI and Crossfire. These are technologies—by Nvidia and AMD, respectively—that allow you to connect two or more graphics cards so that they can be used in parallel. This doesn't *actually* double or triple the graphics processing power—each extra card adds about an extra 50% of the overall computing power of the first card. You need to choose your motherboard carefully, however, because you are locked into using cards from a specific company if you use the multicard feature.

■ **Tip**   If you want to display a UHD (4K) picture at a viewable 60Hz, you need a graphics card and monitor/TV that supports either the DisplayPort 1.2 or HDMI 2.0 or later technologies. DisplayPort is uncommon on TVs (I wanted DisplayPort on my own 4K TV and found that they were only really supported by Panasonic at that time). Before you buy, you should check if the graphics card supports UHD (4K) and if it is socket-compatible with your UHD monitor or TV.

Some laptops come with switchable graphics, effectively giving you two graphics cards: a low-end one that is part of the motherboard chipset and suitable for general work and watching movies, and a second one for gaming that either autoswitches when needed or that can be manually turned on. This is a great way to extend the battery life of a laptop; if you are buying a new gaming laptop, it's worth looking for.

If you want to use only a single graphics card on your computer, whether the motherboard supports SLI or Crossfire doesn't matter—you can use an Nvidia or AMD card as you desire.

Some people have strong preferences regarding AMD and Nvidia graphics cards. There is often tremendous brand loyalty from gamers toward one or the other. The overall quality and speed of the cards, especially in mid-range price/performance, does vary quite substantially—with different companies pulling ahead periodically with new, faster, and more powerful hardware, only to lose ground to a competitor's innovation.

Before you choose a graphics card, or even a motherboard in this respect, it is well worth checking out the online test reviews of hardware in PC magazines and at gaming web sites. Passmark (`www.passmark.com`) offers a service where you can benchmark your own PC hardware and compare it against other hardware on the market. To aid with your purchasing decisions, you can also view the benchmarks of the latest and previous generations of hardware.

Working with Gaming Peripherals

Sometimes you have USB gaming hardware attached to your PC, which could include a joystick or a paddle controller. To access the controls for managing them in Windows, search for **game** in Cortana and select **Set up USB game controllers** from the search results to run the Game Controllers dialog (see Figure 7-13).

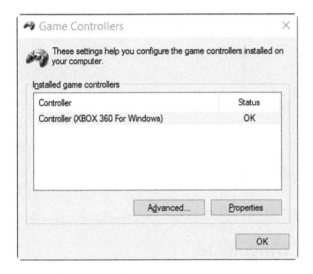

Figure 7-13. *Managing game controllers in Windows 10*

In this dialog, you can manage and change the properties of gaming controllers, such as inverting the horizontal and vertical axis of a joystick (see Figure 7-14).

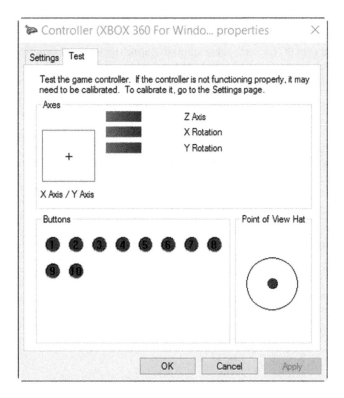

Figure 7-14. Managing gaming hardware such as joysticks

3D Gaming and Virtual Reality on Windows 10

Three-dimensional gaming and the use of virtual reality (VR) headsets such as Oculus Rift are still relatively new to PCs. Windows 10 requires third-party drivers and virtual reality requires specialized headsets to work, although some graphics cards are increasingly coming with their own 3D drivers and controls.

To take advantage of 3D gaming on your computer, you need a screen capable of displaying double the number of normal frame rates, upping the standard frequency from 60Hz to 120Hz. You also need a graphics card that supports 3D.

To use 3D gaming on your computer, you commonly launch your existing games through a 3D game management program or app, into which you probably have to download individual profiles for your games.

There are downsides to 3D gaming on PCs, however. First and most importantly, stable 3D profiles may not be released until well after the launch of the game. Also, 3D has a darkening effect on the image, especially in first-person shooters, which can make distances more difficult to see. Finally, the 3D effect can cause headaches when used for more than 30 minutes.

That said, I've used a 3D-equipped gaming laptop and have played several 3D games on it. The effect can be extremely immersive, which can add, if you'll excuse the pun, a whole new depth to your existing games titles.

Setup for dedicated VR headsets is normally straightforward and managed via USB plug-and-play interfaces and management software provided by the headset manufacturer.

Viewing and Editing Photos in Windows 10

The new Photos app is your default software for viewing photographs. It's preinstalled in Windows 10 and it has some extremely interesting and useful functionality. Photography is one of those areas where there is no shortage of apps in the Store; some even from big-name companies such as Adobe. You'll look at some of these later on.

The Windows 10 Photos app contains many useful features for organizing and working with your photos. One of which is that it's not only capable of compiling your photo library from multiple sources, including OneDrive cloud storage and your Windows smartphone, but it can auto-enhance the photos for you and even filter out duplicate copies.

The main interface for the Photos app is quite simple (see Figure 7-15); but don't let this fool you, as there's some very advanced functionality available.

Figure 7-15. *The Windows 10 Photos app*

There are two different ways to view your photos…

- **Collection** displays all of your photos aggregated by the date they were taken. You can scroll through the list of photos and also click the Dates links to quickly move to a different date range.

- **Albums** is all the more clever (see Figure 7-16). It automatically aggregates your photos into albums, depending on the date they were taken, where they were taken (if your camera supports geotagging), and who you were with. If you were on a holiday with a friend, for example, and you took photos with your smartphone or camera, and then got some photos from your friend, they'll all be intelligently grouped together. What's better is that if you have similar photos that were taken over several days, such as a vacation, they won't all be separated by day. Instead they'll all be presented together as a single trip.

235

Figure 7-16. *The Photos app intelligently organizes your photos into albums*

The main view of the Photos app comes with straightforward controls for importing photos from a memory card or digital camera (see Figure 7-17). Any photos that can be imported are intelligently found and placed in a folder in your Pictures library, named according to the current date. The Select option allows you to select multiple photos that can then be shared with other Store apps, copied to your PC's clipboard, or deleted.

Figure 7-17. *You can easily select, share, copy, delete, and import photos*

When you're viewing an album and choose to edit it, additional options are available. These include being able to rename the album and add or remove photos from the album (see Figure 7-18).

Figure 7-18. *You can edit photo albums*

Basic editing can be performed on a photo, including sharing the photo with another Store app, starting a slideshow of the current album, enhancing and editing the photo (more on this in a minute), rotating it, deleting it, setting it as a background image on your PC, and printing it (see Figure 7-19).

Figure 7-19. *You can perform basic editing on photos*

When you click **Enhance**, an automatic process takes place to straighten, brighten or darken, and fix contrast and color issues with the photo. This really is a one-click process; clicking Enhance again restores the photo to its previous state. **Edit** provides a series of basic controls (see Figure 7-20), which are good enough for many users, but falls way short of the power offered by a professional app such as Adobe Lightroom.

Figure 7-20. *You can perform basic photo editing in the Photos app*

The editing controls available to you include basic fixes (which is the same as the Enhance control I mentioned); adding preconfigured filters; adjusting light, color, and effects; rotating and straightening the photo; and applying crops and red-eye filters.

Third-Party Photo Editing Packages

There are many other photo management and editing apps, programs, and cloud services available. You may already have your favorite. I want to highlight three that I think are especially noteworthy.

Adobe Photoshop Express

Photoshop Express is available as an app in the Windows Store, and it's proven extremely popular since its launch. Offering more control than the Windows 10 photos app, and with some additional controls available through in-app purchases, it is a great tool for basic photograph editing on a tablet or other touchscreen PC.

Adobe Photoshop Elements

Adobe's Photoshop software has long been the king of desktop photo editing, but the full package is extremely expensive and very complex. It's really only for creative professionals. At the lower end of the price range, however, is Photoshop Elements, which you can download from www.adobe.com. It is an excellent desktop program that provides a significant amount of power and flexibility while still being very easy to use.

Pixlr

If you want something closer to the full version of Photoshop—but without its high price—I have never found a better app than Pixlr (www.pixlr.com). It is an extremely powerful, flexible, and (best of all) free photo-editing tool that offers many of the features you find in the full desktop version of Adobe Photoshop (see Figure 7-21).

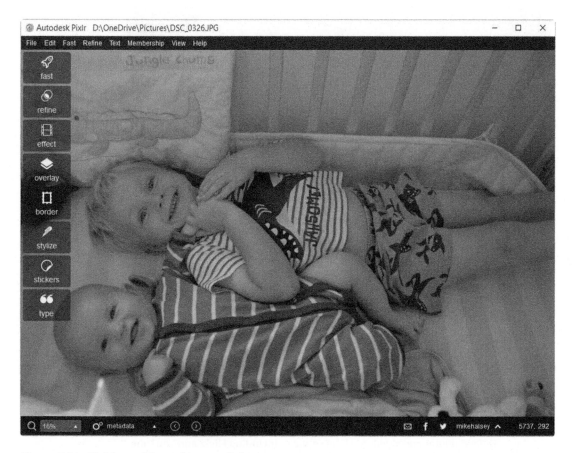

Figure 7-21. *Pixlr's graphics and image editing app*

Windows Photo Gallery

It's old now, and it hasn't been updated in several years, but Microsoft's free Windows Photo Gallery software is still a great photo viewing and editing tool, so it deserves an honorable mention here. It is part of the company's Windows Essentials suite, which you can download from download.live.com. It is based around the company's Ribbon interface, so it is instantly familiar to users of Microsoft Office (see Figure 7-22).

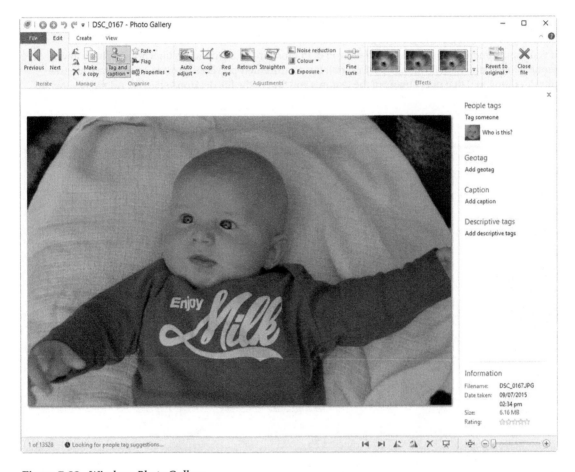

Figure 7-22. *Windows Photo Gallery*

The package allows you to perform many actions on your photos and pictures, such as the following:

- Manage your photo library with drag-and-drop actions between folders

- Upload photos and videos to cloud services, including Flickr and YouTube

- Basic editing (including automatic editing) of photographs

In Chapter 5 I discussed adding tags and ratings to your photo library to make individual images easier to find. I'll talk about this in more detail shortly when I show you how to import photos and video from a digital camera; but Windows Photo Gallery offers excellent, easy-to-use methods for adding tags and ratings to photos.

Windows Photo Gallery also includes excellent face recognition software that can help tag friends and family, making it much easier to find photographs of specific people.

Importing Digital Photographs and Videos from a Camera

When you insert a memory card from your digital camera or camcorder into your computer, you are asked if you want to import photos and video from the device (see Figure 7-23).

Figure 7-23. *The Windows 10 photo import wizard*

There are several advantages to allowing Windows 10 to import photos and video rather than manually copying the files using Windows Explorer. The first advantage is that the photos are automatically organized into a folder in your Pictures library, named after the current date. The second advantage is that Windows 10 is fantastic at determining the correct "up" position for photos and automatically rotates them for you.

To import photos or video, follow these instructions:

1. Insert your memory card, card reader, or connect your camera to your Windows PC.

2. If the autoplay options asking if you want to import your photos do not appear, open the Photos app and click the **Import** button. You may be asked to select the device or memory card that you want to import your photos from.

Sometimes you want more control over importing images. Let's say, for example, that you want to tag your photos with the place you took them or the people you were with. If you're using Libraries on your Windows 10 PC to organize your photos, then tagging can be a great asset. You can read how to use Libraries and tags in Chapter 5.

There are many advanced ways to import and tag your photos, such as with apps like Adobe Elements. I have always liked the simplicity and flexibility of Windows Photo Gallery to import photos from your digital camera or camcorder. To do this in Windows Photo Gallery, click the **Import** button on the far left of the **Home** tab.

If you have multiple devices attached to your PC, or more than one memory card inserted, you may be asked to choose which one contains your photos. Next, the Import Photos and Videos wizard (see Figure 7-24), lets you choose to import all the items on the memory card or to first review, organize, and group items to import. I'll show you how to do this in a moment, but if you want to import all items now, you can click **Add tags** to include descriptive tags with the images.

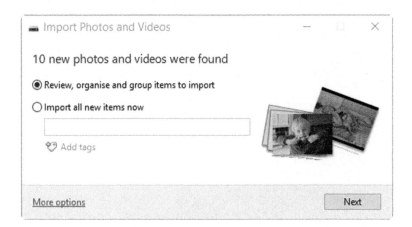

Figure 7-24. *The Windows 10 Import Photos and Videos wizard*

These descriptive tags which you separate with a semicolon (;), help you find and organize photos on your computer and enable you to search for files. For example, you can search for "Vancouver" or "Gilbert" to bring up all the related files and images in the Files search results after tags have been set (see Figure 7-25). For more information on using tags to organize files and photos, see Chapter 5.

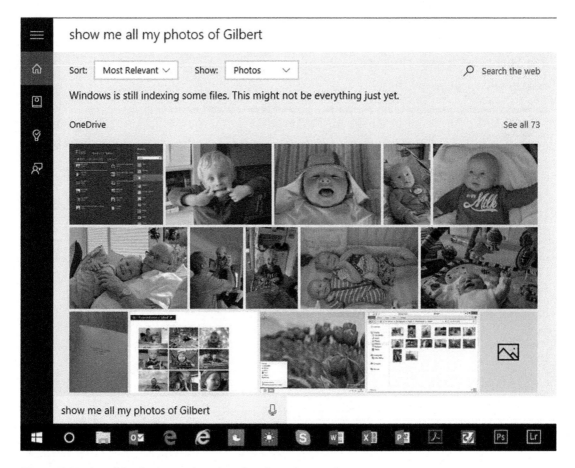

Figure 7-25. *Searching for images is easier when they are tagged*

The Import Photos and Videos wizard in Windows Photo Gallery also includes an option to **Review, organize and group items to import**. It brings up a page in which you can see photos and videos on the disk and select which ones you want to import (see Figure 7-26).

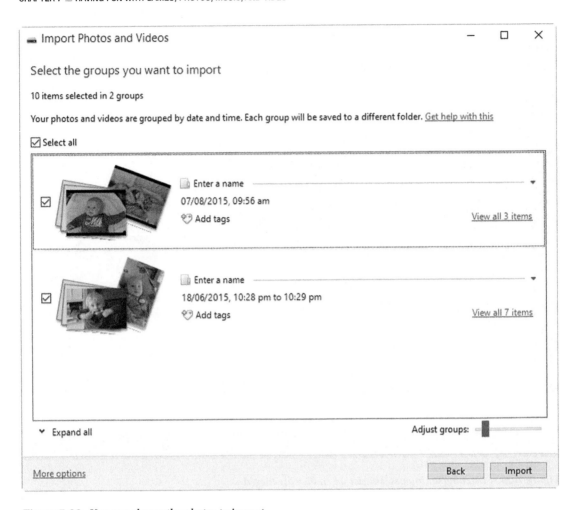

Figure 7-26. You can choose the photos to import

A slider near the bottom right of this window is particularly useful when it has been a while since you downloaded photos and videos from your camera. Let's say, for example, that you have been on vacation for two weeks, during which time you visited several European cities (Amsterdam, Dusseldorf, and Cologne).

Using this slider, you can separate the photos by the date they were taken. You can then tag photos as "Amsterdam; Netherlands", "Dusseldorf; Germany", and so on.

Clicking **More Options** on either of the import pages offers storage locations for the imported items, the ability to batch-rename imported items, and automatic rotation of photographs. If you want, Windows 10 can delete items from the device or memory card after they have been imported (see Figure 7-27).

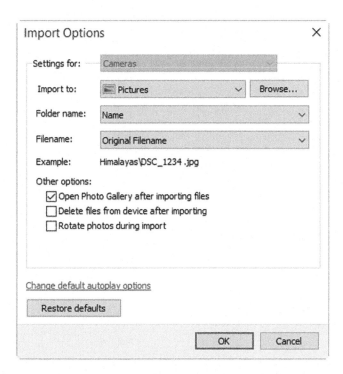

Figure 7-27. *There are additional import options available*

Manually Adding a Scanner to Windows 10

When you add a scanner to your PC, either one that's built into your printer or one that is separate, Windows 10 does a great job of automatically detecting and installing it. There might be some situations in which this doesn't happen, however, and you need to install the scanner manually. You can do this by searching for **scanner** in Cortana and clicking **View Scanners and Cameras** from the results.

This panel (see Figure 7-28) allows you to manually install a scanner using the driver software that was provided by the scanner's manufacturer.

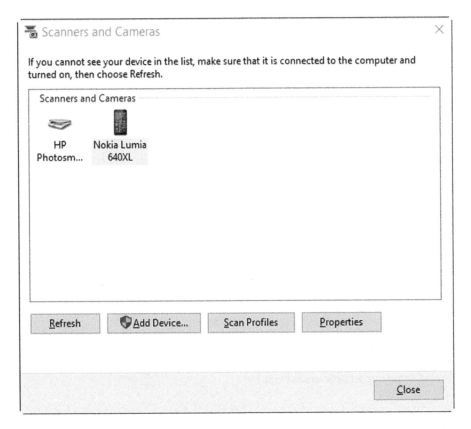

Figure 7-28. *You can install scanners manually using the Show Scanners and Cameras panel*

Once a scanner is installed, you can click the **Scan Profiles** button to manage the resolution at which it scans images and the file type used to save your scanned images.

Playing and Enjoying Music and Video in Windows 10

Windows 10 also ships with music (called Groove Music) and video (called Film & TV) apps and Windows Media Player. Unlike Windows Media Player, in which you play and manage your music and video libraries all in the same place, the music and video apps in Windows 10 are separate from one another, but both operate in the same way.

When you load the app, you have quick access to the music and video you have stored on your PC (see Figure 7-29), though it may take a few minutes on the first loading to index all of your files.

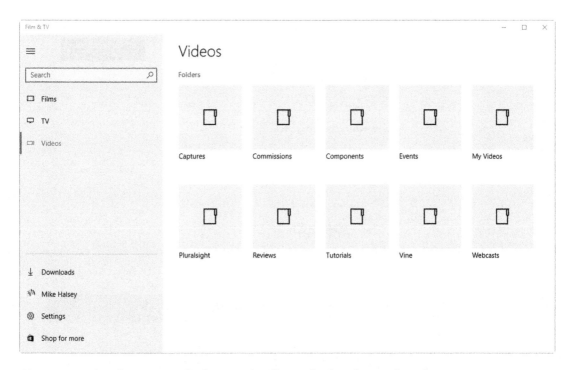

Figure 7-29. *The Film & TV app displays your locally stored video when you launch it*

On the left side of the apps are links to get music or video from the Windows Store or to view your own personal collection by different criteria, such as artist or album.

The music and video players in Windows 10 are rather good, having clearly evolved from the sadly defunct Windows Media Center. They feature large onscreen controls that are simple to use with both touch and mouse.

Creating and Managing Playlists with Groove Music

You can create music and video playlists in Music and Videos apps by selecting the artists, tracks, videos, or genres you want by clicking the **New Playlist** button on the left of the screen in the Groove Music app (see Figure 7-30). If you already have playlists created, they appear here as well, so you can add items to any of them with a single click.

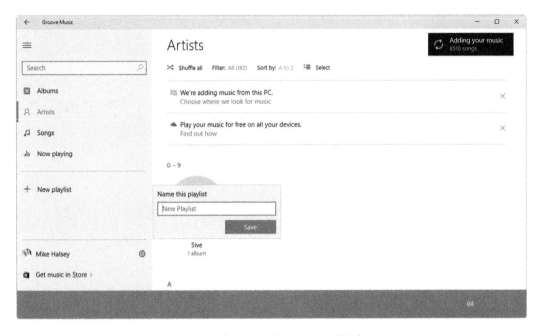

Figure 7-30. *Adding music and video to playlists in the Music and Video apps*

When you are viewing music in the Groove music app, you can right-click (or touch and hold) a track, album, or artist to select **Add to** from the options to add that music to a playlist (see Figure 7-31). Multiple tracks can be selected, as can multiple items on the desktop, by holding down the Ctrl button while clicking.

Figure 7-31. *Managing playlists in the music and video apps*

Audio and Video Codecs in Windows 10

Windows 10 comes with excellent audio and video support. Out of the box, it supports more music and video file types than any other version of Windows before it, including the popular HD format MKV. Support for DVD and Blu-ray playback is missing, however, though Microsoft has released a DVD player app in the Store (see Figure 7-32).

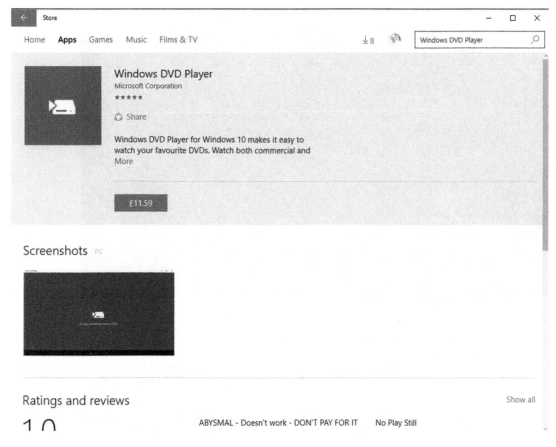

Figure 7-32. Microsoft has a DVD player app in the Store

■ **Note** If you were a Windows Insider during the development of Windows 10 and you upgraded to Windows 10 for free from Windows 7 or Windows 8.1, the DVD Player app is free to you and is autoinstalled through Windows Update.

If you find you are missing any audio or video codecs that you really need to play your music and video, I highly recommend the codec packs at shark007.net.

There are free third-party programs that can provide you with DVD and perhaps even Blu-ray playback codecs. Probably the best and most widely used is the VLC player, which you can download from www.videolan.org.

Alternatives to Windows Media Center

Windows Media Center (see Figure 7-33) was a hugely popular, if niche, app that first appeared in Windows XP for playing music and video, and for recording and watching live TV. Sadly the product was retired in Windows 10 (Yeah! Tell me about it.), but there are some alternatives if you wish to continue using software of this type; I thought I'd spend a little time discussing the best alternatives for you, all of which will work with existing Windows Media Center remote controls.

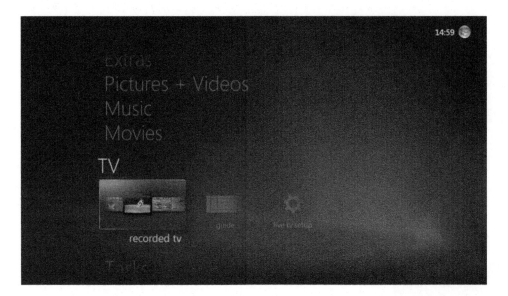

Figure 7-33. *Windows Media Center*

- **Kodi** is the new name for what used to be called XBMC (Xbox Media Center). It has a full PC version and offers playback of just about every music and video format, as well as viewing and recording of live TV. It is available at `http://kodi.tv`.

- **Plex** is a variant of XBMC that has both free and paid-for features. It can be used for viewing and listening to video and music, as well as recording and watching live TV. It has optional plug-ins for a wide variety of online content from the likes of TED and Cimeo, and can stream content from various cloud-storage platforms. It is available at `https://plex.tv`.

- **JRiver Media Center** can play and record a wide variety of audio and video formats, as well as live TV. JRiver has extensive tweaking potential for audio; it is highly respected by audiophiles for this. It is available at `www.jriver.com`.

Additionally, the Xbox One console has the ability to accept a variety of USB TV tuners from around the world, can play live TV and, perhaps even by the time you read this, will be able to record live and scheduled TV programs as well. It is a good alternative to Windows Media Center, especially if you already own a console.

Recording Audio Directly to Your PC

Sometimes you want to be able to record audio onto your PC. The good news is that Windows 10 includes a Voice Recorder app (see Figure 7-34) that can record through your PC's microphone and store audio files for playback later.

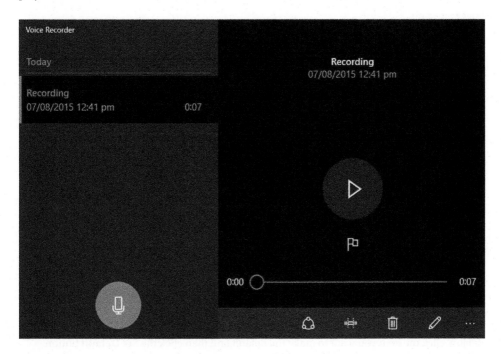

Figure 7-34. The Voice Recorder in Windows 10

■ **Tip**   If you're not a gamer, you might have missed where I discussed the Game DVR feature earlier in this chapter. It can be used to record video, not just from games, but from almost any app on your Windows 10 PC.

This little desktop app includes tools for sharing audio (only with other Store apps) and trimming audio. It can be useful for taking quick notes or for recording lectures at college. Recorded audio is saved in the **Documents ➤ Sound recordings** folder.

Changing the Default Audio Devices on Your PC

Sometimes you find that you have no sound or microphone on your PC. This commonly occurs when the wrong device is incorrectly assigned as the default because you might have several on your PC. You can access the Sound devices panel by searching for **Sound** in Cortana or right-clicking the Sound icon on the taskbar notification area and selecting **Playback** [or **Recording**] **Devices** from the options that appear. Both options open the same panel.

In the Sound panel (see Figure 7-35), you have tabs across the top for Playback, Recording, Sounds, and Communications. It is under the Playback and Recording tabs that you find the options for setting the default speakers and microphone.

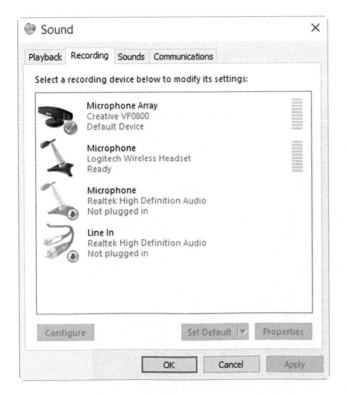

Figure 7-35. *Sound devices panel*

To set the default, click the item you want to make the default and then click the **Set Default** button. Sometimes, however, you might want different audio devices for music than for communications, such as Skype. You can set different systems, such as speakers and a headset, to be the default audio device for communications by clicking the chevron to the right of the Set Default button. From the options that appear, click **Default Communication Device**.

Burn CDs and DVDs Directly from the Desktop

Although USB flash drives are inexpensive and readily available, people still want to want to burn CDs and DVDs directly from their PC. In Windows 10, you can do this from the desktop, but only with data CDs and DVDs. The differences are that they are intended to be read by other PCs and that they don't play in a standard CD or DVD player.

To burn content to a disc, follow these instructions:

1. Put a blank disc in your computer's optical drive.

2. Select the file(s) or folder(s) in File Explorer that you want to burn to the disc (you don't need to select every file at once).

3. Right-click the file(s) and/or folder(s); and from the menu that appears, click **Send to** and then click the name of the optical drive.

4. A panel appears, asking whether you want to create a disc, like a USB flash drive (which you can add more files to after it's burned), or a standard CD/DVD that can't be edited later (see Figure 7-36). Make your choice and click **Next**.

Figure 7-36. *You can create fixed and multisession discs in Windows*

5. The files are copied to a temporary store, and a new File Explorer window opens, into which you can add additional files. Remember, however, that a CD has a maximum capacity of 650MB, and a DVD has a maximum capacity of either 4.7GB or 9.5GB, depending on whether it is single layered or double layered.

6. When you're ready to burn your disc, click the **Finish Burning** button under the Drive Tools tab on the ribbon (see Figure 7-37).

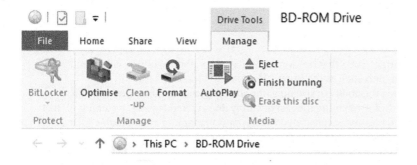

Figure 7-37. *Drive Tools tab on the File Explorer ribbon*

Burn Audio CDs in Windows Media Player

If you want to burn audio CDs, perhaps to play in the car, you can do this in Windows Media Player. In the top right of the Windows Media Player window are three tabs: Play (for creating custom playlists), Burn (for burning audio CDs), and Sync (for copying music to a compatible MP3 player), as shown in Figure 7-38.

Figure 7-38. *You can burn audio CDs in Windows Media Player*

You can burn music that is already in your music library to an audio CD by dragging it from the main music panel in the Windows Media Player window onto the Burn tab. You see how much time is left on the CD, enabling you to properly manage the amount of music that will fit on the disc.

When you have added all of your music to the Burn panel and are ready to burn the CD, click the **Start burn** button near the top right of the window.

Summary

Windows 10 is a very consumer-oriented OS that has some great apps for photos, music, video, and more. Finer control is still available from tools such as the Import Photos and Videos wizard.

If you're an enthusiastic gamer, the ability to stream games directly from an Xbox One console to any Windows 10 PC is incredibly useful, meaning the rest of family doesn't need to stop watching TV just because the last first-person shooter has been released. With support for gaming technologies such as 3D and virtual reality gaining ground, it will be interesting to see the innovative uses for this operating system.

The new Groove Music and Film & TV apps are excellent and can be easily docked to the side of the screen while you work. Although you now have to pay extra for DVD/Blu-ray playback, and Windows Media Center is gone, many alternatives exist to help keep you working the way you have always enjoyed best.

■ ■ ■

CHAPTER 8

Maximizing Your Productivity

Windows was born into the business space. It was the original IBM PC that was the powerhouse of the "modern" office in the 1980s, equipped with software such as Lotus 123 and WordPerfect. The introduction of the graphical user interface and the Microsoft Office suite solidified the PC's position as the productivity tool of choice. It was the flexibility of PCs that eventually brought them into homes, and now we take it for granted that we'll have access to our own PC at work. Many people expect to be provided a laptop—and a smartphone as well—and others have begun using their personal PCs, tablets, and smartphones at work.

Despite all of this, the computer is probably the biggest barrier to productivity in the workplace. Enormous barriers occur during a power outage or when the Internet connection goes down. There are ways to keep working in these circumstances, however; some of which are more clever than buying laptops.

When it comes to our communications, over half of all email is spam. There are alternatives to the spam mountain, though, and some people argue that the days of email are numbered and that instant messaging is the way forward.

As computers become more ubiquitous and we all get older, the ever-higher pixel densities on our screens can make text and other information difficult to read. Couple this problem with the barriers encountered by the disabled and people with motor skills disorders. Windows 10 includes some excellent tools to include everybody in a computing life. There is also excellent support to be found elsewhere.

These topics are just a few of the ones that I'll cover in this chapter, the aim of which is to help you maximize your productivity with the operating system.

Managing and Arranging Running Apps on a Tablet

Your experience of using and arranging apps on your screen will vary slightly depending on the type of device you are using. For almost all PCs, the usual way of having multiple windows open on your screen at one time is still the order of business in Windows 10. If you are using a small Windows tablet, however, with a screen less than 8 inches, then there is no desktop (as it's just impractical on a device that small). In Chapter 2 I discussed how these small tablets are limited to two apps running side by side.

For everybody else, though, you can have as many windows open as you like, and for the first time in Windows, on as many virtual desktops as you want. You can easily snap up to four apps side by side on your screen in Windows 10.

If you are using a tablet, then your apps run fullscreen. You can change this, however, and make them windowed any time you want. The easiest way to do this is to drag the app downward from the top center of your screen by using either a mouse or touch. You can also click the Maximize button in the top-right corner of the window to undock it and display it in its own separate window on the desktop.

If you want to dock your apps to the left or right of your screen you can drag the app to the far left or right side of the screen; a highlighted area indicates that the app will then be docked to that side of the screen. You can also dock your apps in the four corners of the screen. I'll show you how to do this later in the chapter.

Using Windows Task View to Switch Between Running Apps

You can switch between any of your running apps by using the Win+Tab keyboard shortcut. In Windows 10, however, there is a new Task View mode triggered by clicking the Task View button on the taskbar (it's next to the Cortana search box) or by pressing the Windows key + Tab. The Task view (see Figure 8-1) creates large thumbnail images of all of your running apps, allowing you to close one (or more) by clicking the close (X) icon at the top right, or to switch to a different app by clicking it.

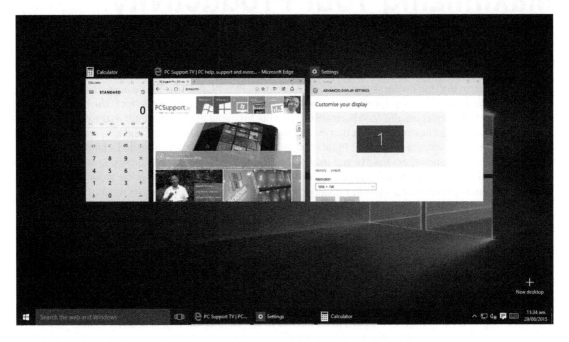

Figure 8-1. *The Windows 10 Task View makes it easy to switch between running apps*

■ **Tip** If you are using a tablet or touch screen, you can also invoke Task View by swiping inward from the left of your screen with your finger.

■ **Note** It is important to note that Win+Tab, which is used to invoke Task View, doesn't allow you to select a running desktop program itself. To do this, you should use the Alt+Tab keyboard shortcut.

Creating and Managing Virtual Desktops

Windows 10 is the first version of Microsoft's OS to include virtual desktops. Essentially, a virtual desktop is a second, third, or even eighth desktop, that looks just like the desktop you get when Windows starts up, on which can have different apps running. You might, for example, have Microsoft Word and your customer relations management software running on one desktop, while hiding an Edge browser on the Amazon web page, and a Minesweeper game on another (I call this the ol' switcheroo).

All jokes aside, I believe that virtual desktops can be useful for separating different aspects of your working and non-working life. If you like to keep one eye on your email or social networks, but need to concentrate on the main CAD (computer-aided design) software that you use, you can hide the email and social network apps off to their own desktop, only to be seen when you want them.

Virtual desktops are created in the Task View where you'll see a (+) **New desktop** button in the bottom-right corner of your screen (see Figure 8-2). Clicking this creates a new desktop and you'll see all of your virtual desktops as thumbnail images in the bottom center of your screen. You can create as many virtual desktops as you need.

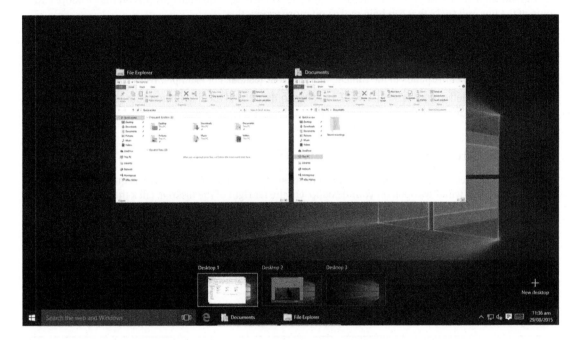

Figure 8-2. *You create and manage virtual desktops from the Task View*

■ **Tip** When you close a virtual desktop, any apps running on it are moved to the next desktop, so you won't lose them.

You can click a desktop thumbnail in the Task View to switch to a different desktop, or press Ctrl + Win + Left or Right Cursor on your keyboard to quickly switch to the next desktop. Apps can be moved from one desktop to another as well, because you may have opened your notes for your development software on the wrong one. To do this, open the Task View and drag and drop the app's large thumbnail image onto the thumbnail image of the correct desktop. This immediately moves the app to that desktop for you.

Working with Multiple Apps on the Desktop

Did you know that having lots of apps open in windows can run down the battery of a tablet or laptop more quickly than running one of those apps fullscreen (even if the others are open)? This is because your graphics processor has more work to do rendering multiple windows and your desktop wallpaper, rather than just one app, despite both having the same pixel count.

Store apps are also more power-efficient than more traditional win32 desktop apps, because their activity is suspended when they're not in focus and being used; so using Office Mobile apps instead of the full Office suite will also extend the battery life of a laptop or tablet.

These and other power-saving tips can be found later in this chapter when I discuss power management, but it's an interesting illustration of how the way we arrange and manage the open apps on our desktops can have a direct effect on things like battery life.

That being said, it's very common to want to have multiple apps open on your screen at one time; perhaps to compare two documents or web pages, or to copy or move files between two different places. Let's spend some time looking at the different ways you can arrange and manage apps on the desktop, and some of the tips and tricks that can help make you more productive.

■ **Tip**   A quick way to switch between running apps is to use the keyboard combination Win + 1 to 9, where the number you use corresponds to the running apps on your taskbar. For example, Win+1 switches to the first running app on the left of your taskbar, Win+2 switches to the second running app on your taskbar, and so forth.

Hiding and Restoring All Windows on the Desktop

If your desktop is getting *really* cluttered and you're struggling to concentrate, there is a quick and easy way to minimize all the windows open on your desktop. On the far right of the taskbar, click the blank space to the right of the clock (see Figure 8-3). There is a hidden button here that automatically minimizes all the Windows on your desktop.

Figure 8-3.   The minimize-all-apps button is on the far right of the taskbar

■ **Tip**   You can also minimize all of your open apps by pressing the Windows key + M or Windows key + D; the latter restores your windows on a second press.

Clicking this taskbar button again restores all the windows to their previous onscreen positions. This feature is sometimes referred to as *boss mode*, because if you're having a moment of downtime at work and the boss walks past, she doesn't have to see that you're playing a game on Facebook or shopping on eBay.

■ **Tip**   You can minimize all of your open apps on a laptop by swiping three fingers downward on the trackpad. Swipe three fingers back up again to restore the apps.

Minimizing and Restoring Windows Using Shake

You can minimize all but the app you want to work with, by grabbing its bar at the top of its window and shaking it. This minimizes everything except the app that you're shaking, which can be a useful way to quickly declutter your desktop so you can concentrate. Shaking the app again restores all the other apps that were previously minimized.

Snapping Two, Three, or Four Windows Side by Side

One of the most useful features in Windows, which I use all the time, is Snap. It allows you to view up to four side-by-side windows on the desktop, with each occupying exactly 50% or 25% of the screen. You can use it by dragging windows to the very left or very right of your screen to snap an app to the side, or into one of the four corners of your screen to snap an app to a corner. You can also snap an app to the side of your screen by pressing the Windows key + the left or right cursor keys.

As you drag a window to the left or right, or to a corner of your screen, a ghost outline of the program appears onscreen to show you that when you release the window, it will snap to one half or a quarter of the screen.

This feature is useful for many scenarios, including moving or copying files from one location to another, comparing two documents, side by side, or working with four windows simultaneously (see Figure 8-4).

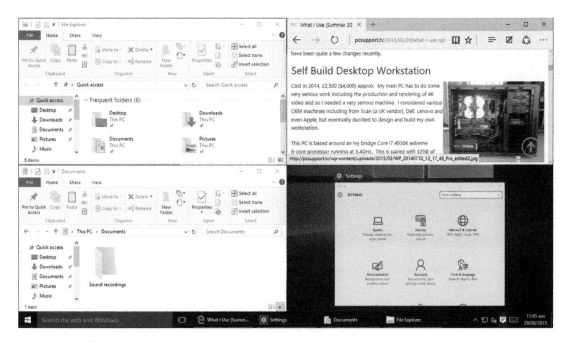

Figure 8-4. *Snap in Windows 10*

When you snap an app to the side of your screen, or snap three apps into the corners, a feature called **Snap Assist** displays thumbnail images of your other running apps in the remaining space. You can then automatically snap one of those apps to that space simply by clicking it.

You're not stuck with windows occupying exactly 50% or 25% of your screen either, as any app you snap can be resized in its snapped position. This won't affect the size of your windows when you unsnap them, because they always return to their original size.

Peeking at and Closing Windows from Thumbnails

Another extremely useful way to manage and work with apps on the desktop is through the use of taskbar thumbnails. When you move your mouse over the taskbar button of an open app, a thumbnail image of the app appears. There are several actions you can perform here.

- Hovering your mouse over a thumbnail displays that window in the main screen, even if the program is minimized. It shows only that program and temporarily hides all others that are open.

- You can select this window to bring it to the foreground by clicking the thumbnail.

- You can close a window by clicking the Close button in the top right of the thumbnail (see Figure 8-5).

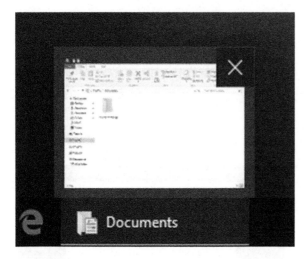

Figure 8-5. *You can view thumbnails of running desktop programs from the taskbar*

Pinning and Arranging Apps on the Taskbar

You can pin an app to the desktop taskbar in Windows 10 by right-clicking its tile or icon in either the Start menu or the All Apps list, and selecting Pin to Taskbar from the options that appear.

Once you have your programs pinned to the taskbar, you can rearrange them by dragging and dropping them so that they are in the order that best suits you. My advice is to use the taskbar to pin all the apps that you use on a regular basis, because it makes it much quicker and easier to launch them.

You can still access lesser-used apps when you need them because they are always available on the All Apps list, but the aim ought to be to keep the taskbar relatively uncluttered by showing only the program icons that you *genuinely* use on a regular basis.

Maximizing Productivity with Jump Lists

Jump Lists, first introduced in Windows 7, are a great way to organize the files you work with on a regular basis or for a current project. You can open a Jump List from the taskbar in one of two ways:

- Tap and push up on an icon with your mouse or finger.

- Right-click an icon with your mouse.

Jump Lists show the files or places that have been opened most recently in a program. By default, it's the 10 most recently opened documents.

You can pin documents, as many as you like, to Jump Lists by clicking the Pin button that appears next to the document name when you mouse over it. Pinning a document to a Jump List ensures that it always appears at the top of the list (see Figure 8-6). This makes access to commonly used files extremely quick and simple.

■ **Tip**   You can also pin a document to a Jump List by dragging its icon onto the associated app icon on the taskbar. The file will then be pinned to the Jump List for that app.

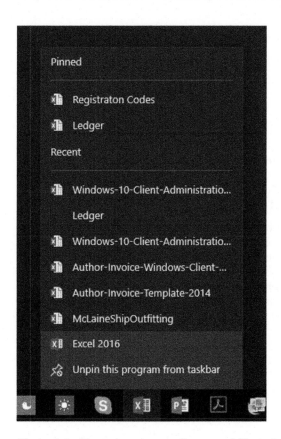

Figure 8-6. *Pin and unpin recently accessed files to Jump Lists*

Jump Lists also commonly provide quick access to certain features within programs; for example, links to the main user folders in File Explorer can be found in the program's Jump List (see Figure 8-7).

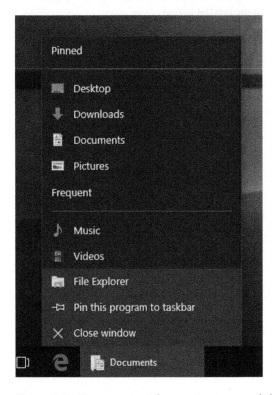

Figure 8-7. *You can get quick access to a program's features from Jump Lists*

Managing and Hiding Taskbar Features

Although Cortana places a search box next to the Windows button on the taskbar, it doesn't have to be this way; you might have a lot of apps pinned to the taskbar, for example, and be short on space. You might prefer to have a Cortana icon, or perhaps you want to remove the icon altogether. It's the same with the Task View, which you can access at any time by pressing the Windows key + Tab; this is also arguably quicker.

Windows 10 allows you to customize these options on the taskbar with a simple right-click in any blank taskbar space. The menu provides three options for Cortana (Hidden, Show icon, and Show search box) and offer controls for the Task View icon and the Touch keyboard (see Figure 8-8).

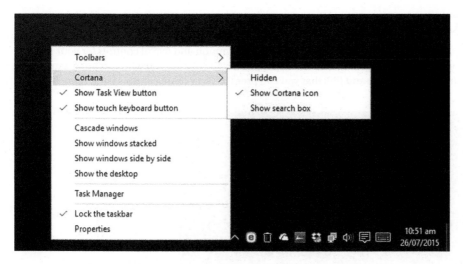

Figure 8-8. *There are different ways to display Cortana on the taskbar*

Maintain Your Concentration with Quiet Hours

If you need to get work done on your PC, it can be extremely distracting when a pop-up toast appears, informing you of newly arrived emails, forthcoming appointments and birthdays, app and Windows updates, and more. Just having a single small toast appear can really distract you and interrupt your train of thought.

Quiet Hours is a feature that's been available on Windows smartphones for a while; activating it silences all alerts and messages, allowing you to concentrate on the task at hand, have an uninterrupted meeting, and even get some much-needed sleep (though hopefully not during the meeting, even though we've *all* been to meetings like that!).

You can add a Quiet Hours button to the bottom of the Action Center; I'll show you how to do this shortly. A quick link exists, however, by right-clicking the Action Center icon, where an options menu appears with an on/off control for Quiet Hours (see Figure 8-9).

Figure 8-9. *You can easily activate Quiet Hours on your PC*

Managing Quick Actions Buttons and Notifications

At the bottom of the Action Center are four quick links to some common and useful controls for your PC. These links may vary depending on what type of Windows device you're using and who you purchased it from. Above the Quick Links is an **Expand** link that you can press to show more controls (see Figure 8-10).

Figure 8-10. *The Action Center contains quick links to useful controls*

■ **Note**   The Quick Links icons appear at the top of the Action Center in Windows 10 Mobile.

These first four control buttons are also configurable, so you can change them to provide a number of useful quick functions. To change the buttons, open the Settings app and navigate to **System** and then **Notifications & actions**. At the top of this screen are four quick actions buttons; you can click these to choose from a drop-down menu which action that button should perform (see Figure 8-11).

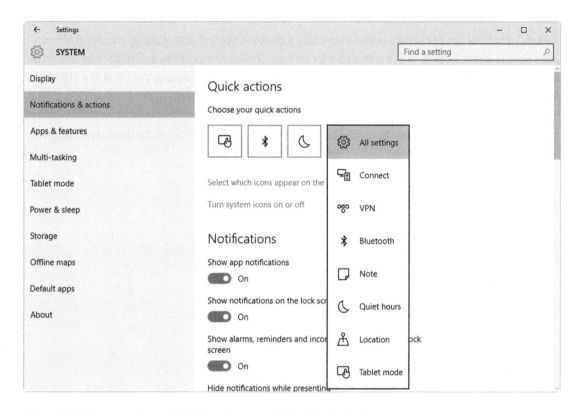

Figure 8-11. *You can change the Action Center quick links in the Settings app*

Below the action buttons are options to control notification toasts on your PC. You can turn off any of these, which include tips about how to use Windows 10 (you've got this great book after all!), alarms, reminders, and incoming calls. You can also turn off notifications for individual apps; all the installed apps that can present notifications are listed when you scroll down the page.

Using Microsoft OneDrive and OneDrive for Business

Microsoft's OneDrive and OneDrive for Business cloud storage services are built into Windows 10 in a significant way. In Chapter 12 I'll show you how to set up and configure the built-in OneDrive file backup and sync feature. Windows 10 provides easy access to the files that you have stored in OneDrive, when in any compatible app. It allows you to view and open any files that you have stored in Microsoft's cloud backup service. It can be very helpful on tablets and Ultrabooks, where local storage space is at a premium, or if you want to access the same file on multiple computers.

Additionally, any files you have stored in OneDrive are immediately available if you sign in to Windows 10 using the same Microsoft account, regardless of whether you want to sync files locally to the PC. This can be extremely useful for low-storage devices such as tablets and Ultrabooks, in which you want occasional access to files without the storage problems (and associated security concerns) of keeping a local copy all the time.

■ **Note**   OneDrive is a free service that everyone with a Microsoft account gets. It comes with 15GB of free cloud storage (expandable up to 1TB with a paid-for service). OneDrive for Business provides 1TB of storage for all users of Microsoft's Office 365 office and productivity service. In truth, the storage you get with a 1TB plan is actually unlimited, but most people are unlikely to ever have 1TB of files anyway.

To access files from OneDrive from the desktop on your Windows 10 PC, click the **OneDrive** link in File Explorer; you see all of your files and folders right away (see Figure 8-12).

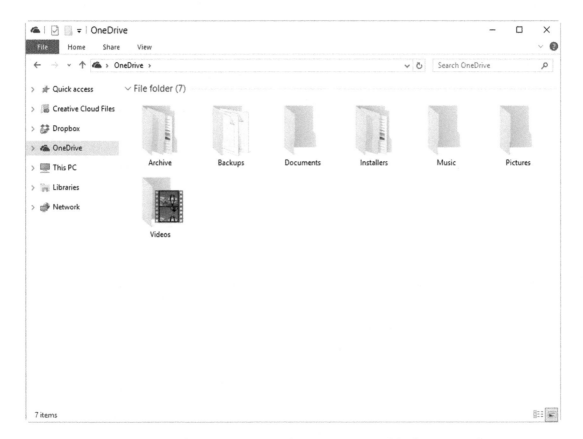

Figure 8-12. *You can access all the files you have stored in OneDrive, even if they're not synced to your own PC*

When you open a file that is stored in OneDrive, a local copy is downloaded and synced to your PC. This allows you to work on and make changes to the document or file locally on the PC; and you know that when you save it, the changes are automatically synchronized back to the cloud.

Sometimes, however, you want to force Windows 10 to keep (or not to keep) a local copy of OneDrive files or folders. You can do this by clicking **Choose OneDrive folders to sync** to open the OneDrive sync client (see Figure 8-13). This opens the OneDrive sync options, where you can select the individual folders and folder-trees that you want synced on the PC.

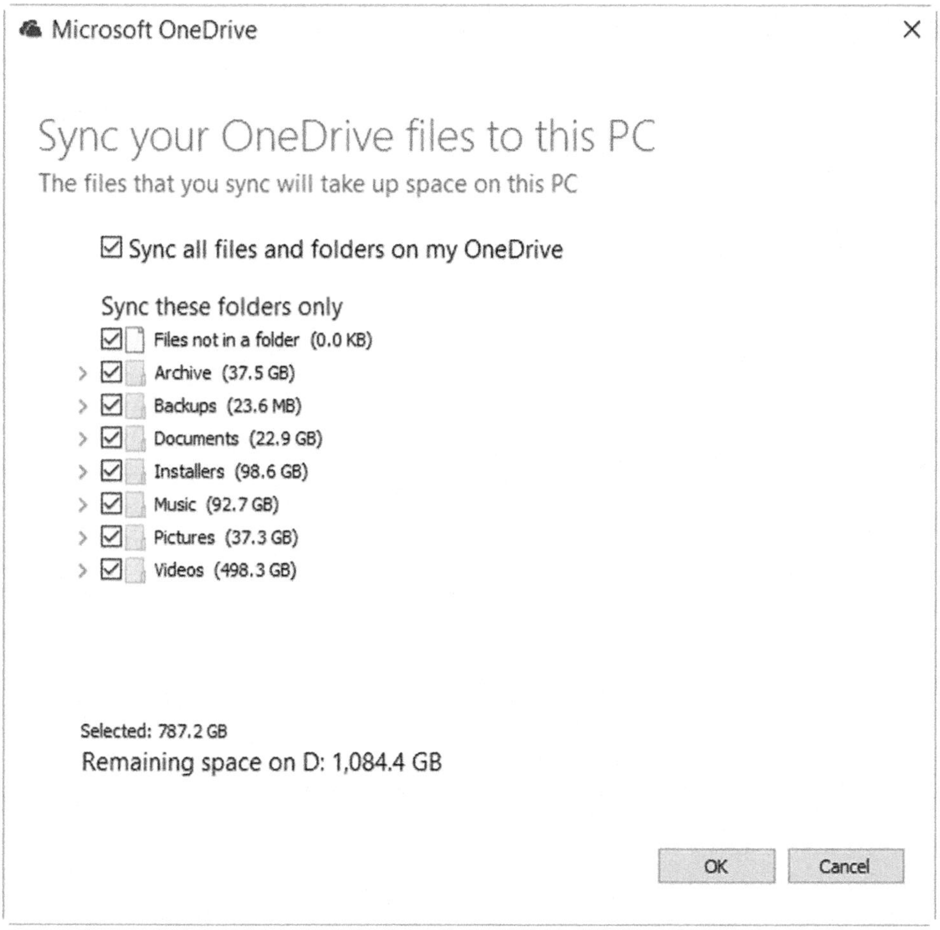

Figure 8-13. *You can force your PC to keep individual files and whole folders online or offline*

By default, a OneDrive account gives you 15GB of free storage, which is plenty for a lot of people. You can expand this amount, however, at the OneDrive web site by purchasing additional space (up to 1TB, or 1,024GB) for reasonable rates.

OneDrive is a great service to use with Windows 10, primarily because the amount of free storage that you get is quite generous, but also because it is easily accessible by other Microsoft products, such as Windows Phone.

Using the Windows 10 Spell-Checker

Windows 10 comes with a built-in spell-checker; this facility is available to you most of the time (the spell-checker doesn't work in every app), even when filling in web forms in Edge. When Windows 10 detects a word that is incorrectly spelled, it underlines it to highlight it. You can then click the word to either correct it from a list of options, ignore it, or add it to the dictionary (see Figure 8-14).

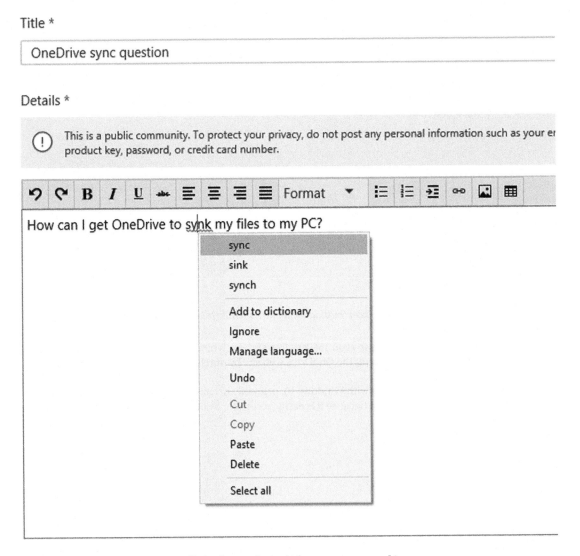

Figure 8-14. The Windows 10 spell-checker works in desktop programs and in apps

You can turn the spell-checker on and off in Windows 10 through the PC Settings panel. Navigate to **Devices** in the Settings app, and then click the **Typing** link in the left panel. Two options for controlling the spell-checker appear at the top of your screen. The first enables or disables the autocorrect, which is where Windows 10 automatically corrects a word for you if it believes you've misspelled a very common word; the second option turns the spell-checking on and off completely (see Figure 8-15).

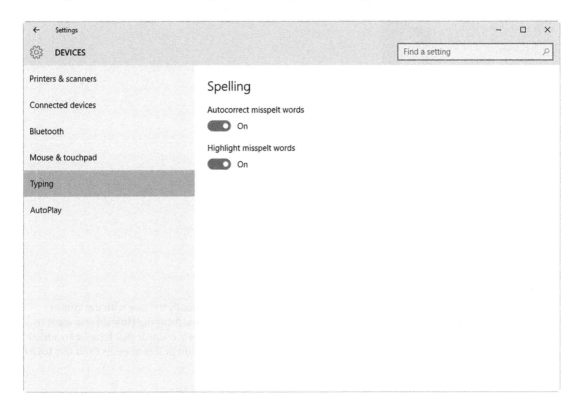

Figure 8-15. *Managing the spell-checker in Windows 10*

Sometimes, however, you might find ;that you added a word or words to the custom dictionary in Windows 10 that you didn't mean to, perhaps because they were misspelled. This isn't a problem, though. In a File Explorer window, click in the address bar, type **%AppData%\Microsoft\Spelling**, and press **Enter**. This process opens the file location for the custom dictionaries (see Figure 8-16).

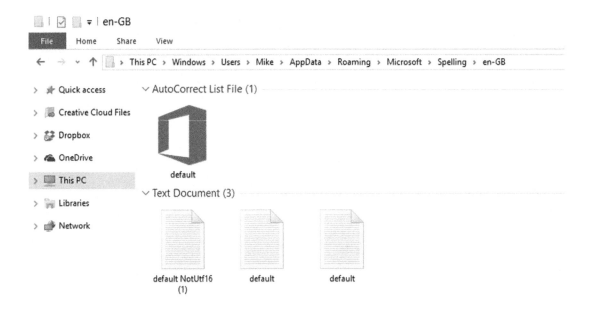

Figure 8-16. *The custom dictionary can be edited in Windows 10*

The file you want to ;edit is one of the `default.dic` document files (usually the one with the largest file size). You open this file by double-clicking it, and then selecting Notepad from the **How do you want to open this file** dialog. This opens the custom dictionary as a plain-text list of the words that have been added to the dictionary, listed in the order that they were added. You can simply edit or delete items from this list to change the custom dictionary.

■ **Tip**   If you work in an environment with many custom dictionary words, such as engineering or the legal profession, words can be added by system administrators by injecting a dictionary file into a custom Windows installation image.

Using Smart File Search in Cortana

I wrote about ;Cortana in Chapter 5, but there are some incredibly useful features in Cortana that can aid your productivity. For example, saying or typing the phrase "Show me all of my spreadsheets" into Cortana displays a list of all the spreadsheet files that you have, not just on your PC, but that you also have access to (see Figure 8-17).

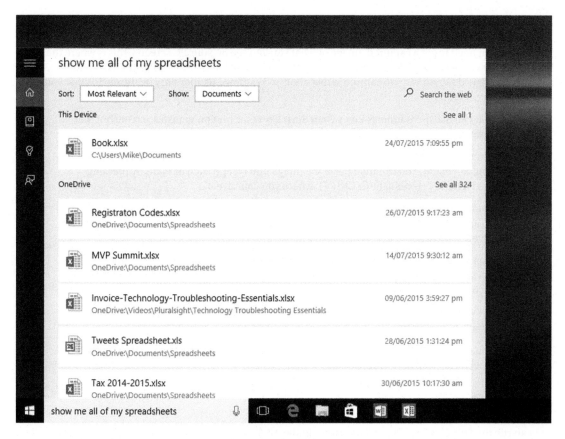

Figure 8-17. *Searching in Cortana can really aid productivity*

This means that Cortana can ;search across all of your hard disks and partitions, including OneDrive, OneDrive for Business, SharePoint, company or college file stores, and other available file storage locations. You can greatly improve the file search facility in Cortana by adding all of your file locations to the Windows Index, as I discussed in Chapter 5. Additionally, you can further refine this search by changing the **Most relevant** drop-down in the top left of the search results dialog to **Most recent**, which then prioritizes the files that you have been working on or that have been created recently.

■ **Tip**   Your productivity can be boosted further by searching for a program's real file name instead of its long name, when you want to run it. Here are some of the most common: `iexplore` (Internet Explorer), `explorer` (File Explorer), `calc` (Calculator), `wmplayer` (Windows Media Player), `control` (Control Panel), `regedit` (Registry editor), `msconfig` (System Configuration Panel), and `gpedit.msc` (Group Policy Editor).

Taking Screenshots in Windows 10

Sometimes you need to get a captured ;image of what you can see on your PC screen—this is where the Windows 10 useful screenshot features come in handy. You might be surprised to hear this, but there are actually many different ways to capture screenshots in Windows 10; they vary by the device that you are using.

- You can use the **Windows key + Prnt Scrn** key combination to take a screenshot that is saved to a Screenshots folder in your Pictures library.

- To capture a screenshot of a single app, select the app and press **Alt + Prnt Scrn** on your keyboard. You can then paste the image into an app such as Paint by pressing the **Paste** key combination (Ctrl+V), where you can save it.

- Some Pro tablets don't have a Print Screen button on their keyboard; the Microsoft Surface is one of these. In this case, you can press the **Windows key + Fn + Space** to save a screenshot to the Screenshots folder.

- On tablet devices, you can commonly press the **Windows button** on the bezel of the device while holding down the **Volume down** key. This saves a screenshot to your Pictures ➤ Screenshots folder. This does not apply on all tablets.

- On Windows 10 Mobile smartphones, you can touch the **Power button + Volume up** to take a screenshot.

- You can use the **Snipping Tool** to capture screenshots of specific windows or partial screens (see the following section).

Using the Snipping Tool

You can run the Snipping Tool by searching for it in the All Apps list or through Cortana. There are four different ways you can snip: a free form, in which you draw around an object, a rectangular snip, a window snip to capture a whole window, and a full-screen snip (see Figure 8-18). You can also use the delay feature to prevent the screen capture from taking place for up to 5 seconds, which can be useful for capturing an options menu or notification flyout.

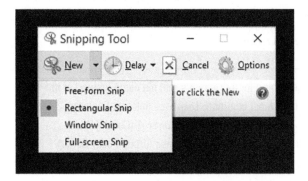

Figure 8-18. *The Snipping Tool is a flexible screen capture utility*

After creating a snip, an editing window appears, in which you can annotate, highlight, or erase parts of the snip. It is also in this editing window that you save the image; there are a wide variety of file formats that can be used.

Using Microsoft Office Mobile

Windows 10 introduces Microsoft Office Mobile touch apps for the first time. These apps, which are also available for Apple iOS and Google Android devices, offer much more power and flexibility than you might first think. There are some caveats with these apps, however, which we should first deal with.

1. If you are using a Windows 10 device with a screen size less than 10 inches, the Office Mobile apps are preinstalled on your device.

2. For any other device, you can get the Windows 10 Mobile apps from the Store.

3. The apps can be used to edit any existing document, but some functions, such as new document creation, require you to have an Office 365 account. You can sign up for a Personal (single user), Home (5 users), or Business account at www.Office365.com. Each subscription comes with extra features, such as 1TB of OneDrive storage, free Skype call minutes, and the full desktop apps as downloads, should you want them.

All the Office Mobile apps use the Ribbon interface, which is familiar to you if you've used Microsoft Office 2007 or newer (see Figure 8-19). These interfaces have tabs along the top row; under each are commands and functions relating to the tab name. Some ribbon functions are buttons that can be activated or toggled when clicked; others present flyout menu options. In Figure 8-19 you can see the ribbon tabs for Word, Excel, PowerPoint, and OneNote.

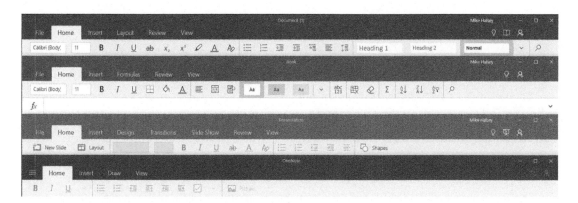

Figure 8-19. *Microsoft's Office Mobile apps use the familiar Ribbon interface*

■ **Tip** The Microsoft OneNote Mobile note-taking app is available for free on all Windows devices; it is also available on iOS and Android. It is unrestricted in all versions.

If you are using Microsoft Office Mobile on a Windows 10 Mobile smartphone, the interface is slightly different. All the functionality of the ribbon is present, but it is accessed by tapping the three-dots menu icon in the bottom-right corner of the screen. A pop-up scrollable menu then appears, with the tabs available on a drop-down menu (see Figure 8-20).

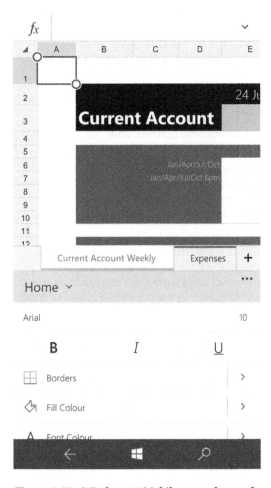

Figure 8-20. *Windows 10 Mobile smartphones also offer the same functionality*

These may be slimmed-down versions of the full Microsoft Office desktop apps, but they are also, as I mentioned previously, surprisingly powerful and well featured. Most people will likely find that these apps provide all the functionality they need, while avoiding all the extra confusion that can be caused by their feature-rich big brothers and sisters.

I also mentioned earlier that these are *touch* versions of the main Office apps. This doesn't mean that they won't work with a keyboard and mouse, and indeed all the functionality you might expect for things—like right-mouse clicks and Ctrl+ keyboard shortcuts—work fine. There are additional optimizations in these apps, however, that enable you to drag and swipe to manipulate, highlight, and edit documents when using a tablet or a smartphone.

There are two final points about Microsoft Office Mobile that are very important. The first point is that whereas these apps do not have editing support for all the advanced functionality, they do support and correctly display any document features that were created using those advanced tools—so your documents will always display correctly. The second point, and I'll talk about this more in the next section, is that on a laptop or tablet, these apps are significantly more power-efficient than their full desktop counterparts; they are worth considering if you spend a lot of time away from mains electricity.

Managing Battery Life in Windows 10

If you use a laptop, an Ultrabook, a tablet, or a smartphone, you're acutely aware that battery technology has not kept pace with the power and functionality of your devices over the last few years. Indeed, we're lucky these days to have a device that'll last more than a single day of average use. For this reason, effectively managing your battery life is crucial. Microsoft has built some excellent features into Windows 10 to help you achieve more with the battery that you have, but I'm going to start by discussing my top tips for maximizing the battery life of whatever device you're using.

Maximizing Your Battery Life: Top Tips

You can help maximize your battery life by following my top tips...

1. All versions of Windows 10 include a new Battery Saver mode that reduces background tasks when your battery level drops to 20%. I'll show you how to find and use this later in this chapter.

2. Change the Power Button control to shut down the PC rather than put it to sleep, or to shut down the PC when you close your laptop's lid. Windows 10 PCs start up very quickly anyway, so there won't be too much of a delay when you want to use the PC again. This feature is not available in Windows 10 Mobile.

3. Dimming your screen brightness down to around 50% improves your battery life considerably, as the screen lighting on any device is always the biggest power draw. Coincidentally, the Office Mobile apps are even easier on the eye when used at a lower screen brightness than at full brightness.

4. Using the automatic brightness control on a Windows 10 Mobile smartphone can save valuable power, brightening the screen only when you're in direct sunlight.

5. Turning off features such as backlit keyboards, Wi-Fi (if you can connect to the Internet via an Ethernet cable instead, or you don't need an Internet connection for a while), and Bluetooth can also save valuable power. Activating Flight mode is a quick and easy way to disable (and then reenable) all radio communications on your device.

6. Prevent any apps that you don't absolutely need from running at the PC's start-up. You can disable start-up apps by opening the Task Manager and navigating to the Start-up tab, where you can select and then disable apps. More information on how to do this is in Chapter 12.

7. Have only one app open at a time and run it fullscreen, not in a window. More power is used when the graphics processor has to draw more than one thing, including your desktop wallpaper, than just a single app running full screen.

8.   Use Windows Store apps instead of win32 desktop apps. Store apps are suspended by Windows 10 when they drop to the background, so as not to use any processor time. Win32 apps, however, keep operating as if they're currently being used.

9.   You can choose which Store apps are allowed to run in the background; reducing the number can increase your battery life. I'll show you how to do this shortly.

10. Reduce the amount of time before the screen turns off and the PC goes to sleep in the Power Options panel; more on how to do this shortly.

11. Don't use live tiles that auto-update with new information in your Start menu. While these only occasionally update in the background, they can also wake a PC from sleep temporarily to update themselves.

12. Reduce the number of web browser plug-ins you use. Use Microsoft Edge instead of other browsers; as a Store app, it auto-suspends when not in the foreground. Google's Chrome web browser is also a notorious power-hog.

13. Change some of the battery options in Group Policy. Disabling Search Indexing when running on battery power (Computer Configuration ➤ Administrative Templates ➤ Windows Components ➤ Search ➤ Prevent indexing when running on battery power to conserve energy) can sometimes boost your battery capacity by up to 30%. A document containing details of all the Group Policy power and battery options can be found online at `http://pcs.tv/1I4hfUs`. Note that Group Policy is not available in Windows 10 Home or Windows 10 Mobile.

14. Disable services that you don't need or won't use, such as the Windows HomeGroup Listener and Provider services, BitLocker Drive Encryption and Encrypting File System services, Bluetooth Hand-Free and Support services, File History service, GeoLocation service, assorted plug-in update and support services (from Steam, Google, Apple, and so forth), the Hyper-V services, Storage Spaces, the Remote Desktop services, Sensor services, and the Xbox services.

■ **Caution**   Be careful disabling Windows or third-party services, as you might prevent an essential service from running and cause your PC to become unresponsive, or even unable to start. Not all the services that I listed (such as BitLocker, Encrypting File System, and Bluetooth) apply to all PCs! To disable services, search for **services**, right-click the service that you want to disable, and select Properties from the context menu. Then change its **Start-up type** to **disabled**.

Monitoring Battery Usage in Windows 10

On laptops, Ultrabooks, and tablets, you can see a battery indicator in the system tray on the far right of the taskbar. Clicking the battery icon reveals the amount of battery power remaining, along with Quick Action buttons for Battery Saver, and if applicable to your device, screen brightness (see Figure 8-21). You can also use this as a quick link to access the **Power & sleep settings** for your PC.

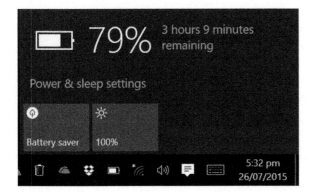

Figure 8-21. *You can monitor your battery life from the system tray*

■ **Caution**   On Windows 10 Mobile smartphones, the battery indicator is visible at the top of your screen. You can swipe downward to open the Action Center to reveal the percentage of battery life remaining.

Using the Windows Battery Saver Mode

All versions of Windows 10 (well the ones for devices running on batteries anyway) come with a special Battery Saver mode that helps converse power when the battery drops below 20%. The battery saver reduces power draw by suspending all back-end services, such as autochecking for new emails and social network notifications, and the updating of live tiles. You can access the Battery Saver options in the Settings by navigating to **System** and then **Battery saver** (see Figure 8-22).

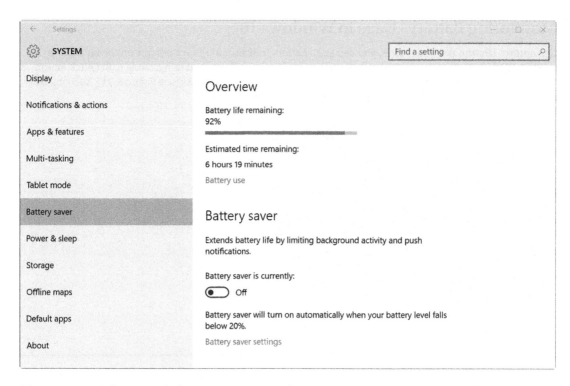

Figure 8-22. *Windows 10 includes a Battery Saver mode*

Clicking the **Battery saver settings** link allows you to change the percentage at which the battery saver mode starts, so you can set it higher (or even lower) should you wish. You can also disable the receipt of (push) notifications form services such as your email and social media accounts.

Monitoring Battery Usage and Managing Background Apps

Windows 10 on laptops, Ultrabooks, and tablets also includes a feature whereby you can monitor your battery usage and see which apps are using the most power. Clicking the **Battery use** link on the Battery Saver screen displays data on your battery use and which apps and services have consumed the most (see Figure 8-23).

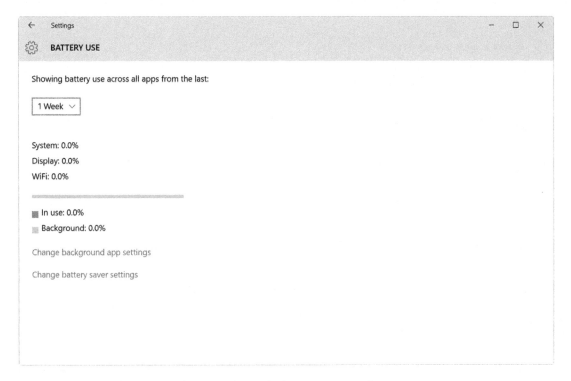

Figure 8-23. *Windows 10 can inform you about which apps are power-hungry*

If you see an app that is particularly resource-hungry, you are alerted that you may not want to use the app when on battery power, or perhaps you can find a suitable replacement for the app in the Windows store. It's important to note here that the figures for each app aren't representative of how power-hungry that app really is, but rather how it's fared compared to the other apps that you have installed and have used.

You can prevent apps from running in the background by clicking the **Change background app settings** link at the Battery Use screen. This presents a list of all the Store apps that you have installed on your PC (see Figure 8-24), with a switch control next to each one so that you can choose whether you want that app to run as a background task when you're not using it directly. As I mentioned earlier in this chapter, you cannot control win32 desktop apps in this way; they continue running as normal when not in focus or when minimized.

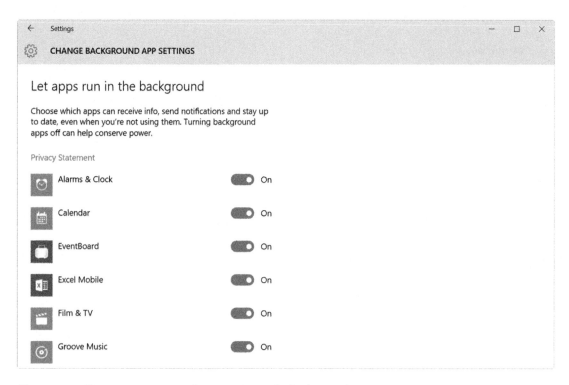

Figure 8-24. *You can prevent apps from running in the background*

Configuring Power and Sleep Settings

Whichever type of Windows 10 device you are using, power-saving options are always available to you in the Settings app. Navigate to **System** and then **Power & sleep** to find controls for putting the device's screen on standby or putting the PC to sleep. There are separate controls for devices using mains electricity, and if applicable to the device, battery power (see Figure 8-25).

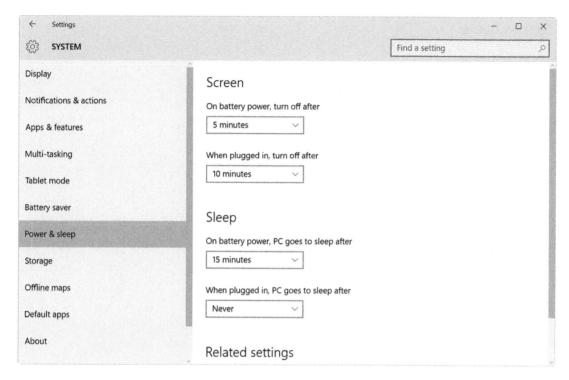

Figure 8-25. *You can change several battery-saving features in the Settings app*

Clicking the **Additional power settings** link opens a Control Panel applet in which you can choose from different power plans (including ones that may be have been provided by your laptop's or tablet's manufacturer); you can also edit these power plans. In this panel, you can **Choose what the power buttons do** and what happens when you close the lid on your PC.

If you click **Change plan settings** for a power plan, and then click the **Change advanced power settings** link, you get access to many additional power options (i.e., powering down the hard disk after inactivity, powering down USB devices during sleep mode, and automating screen brightness; note, however, that this last feature is dependent on your screen having a compatible light sensor), see Figure 8-26. I'll discuss these advanced settings more in Chapter 9.

Figure 8-26. *You can change advanced power settings in Windows 10*

Windows Mobility Center and Other Mobility Tools

The Windows Mobility Center (see Figure 8-27) is designed to help keep you productive on devices such as laptops, Ultrabooks, and tablets. The easiest way to find it is to search for **mobile** or **mobility**; you'll find it in the search results. I want to discuss the areas of the Mobility Center by the type of tasks you want to perform.

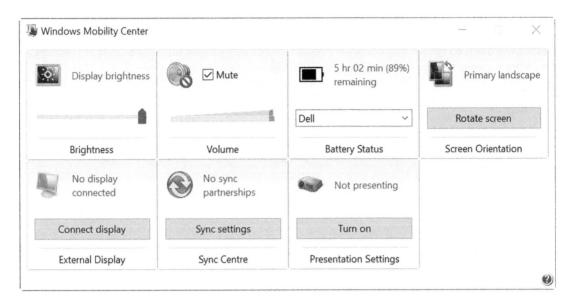

Figure 8-27. *Windows Mobility Center*

■ **Tip**   You can access the Windows Mobility Center by right-clicking the battery button on the taskbar or through the Win+X administration menu.

Managing Battery Life on Laptops, Ultrabooks, and Tablets

Battery life is critical on laptops, Ultrabooks, and tablets. Although many computer reviews and manufacturers now claim that some devices manage more than 10 hours of life on "light use," the definition of "light use" means you're probably not really using the machine the way you want to in an average day. There are several tools you can use in the mobility center to optimize your battery life:

- **Brightness** is a simple slider to adjust the brightness of your screen. Lower levels of brightness prolong battery life.

- **Battery Status** provides a quick indication of the amount of power your battery has remaining. It also provides a drop-down menu that includes a power-saving mode to prolong battery life.

For more information on advanced battery power management in Windows 10, see Chapter 9.

Maintaining Productivity Without Electricity/Internet Access

If you have ever been in a workplace during a power outage or when the Internet connection fails, you know that it commonly results in work stoppage and everybody resorting to playing games on their phones.

The absence of electricity or an Internet connection doesn't need to mean that you can't get any work done. There are ways around these problems. Most obviously, if you have a laptop, it can continue to run as long as its battery lasts, which is often long enough to wait out a power outage.

You can also install Uninterruptable Power Supplies (UPS) in your workplace, which keeps computers, and even the Internet connection, running smoothly. Remember that your broadband line comes through a phone cable that is on its own external power circuit. Having a UPS plugged into your router (and perhaps a switch box if required) keeps your Wi-Fi and network online.

PCs plugged into UPS boxes can keep running for an hour or more in the event of a power outage. This means that you should have plenty of power to continue working while you wait for the electricity to come back on.

■ **Tip**   Always make sure that your PC or laptop is plugged into a surge-protecting power supply when connected to mains electricity. This will filter out any sudden surges or spikes that can occur, not just during power cuts, but also at peak usage times, which can damage the components inside your PC.

Setting Up a Mobile Broadband Hotspot

When your Internet connection goes down, you don't have to do without Web access. If you have a laptop containing a mobile broadband (3G or 4G/LTE SIM card), you can share this connection through the laptop (or even an Intel-based tablet) and with other computers in the office.

If your PC or smartphone's data connection supports tethering, which is the sharing of your mobile data connection with other devices, you see a **Mobile hotpot** option in the **Network** panel of the Settings app. The options here allow you to set up a mobile broadband hotspot, where you can share your data connection with up to 10 other PCs and devices (this can include any device that can connect to Wi-Fi, including your iPad or Android tablet).

You can choose whether to share your connection over Wi-Fi or Bluetooth (in which case the other devices will need to pair over Bluetooth with your Windows 10 device). Connecting via Wi-Fi gives you a name for the network and a passphrase to enter on the other devices, so that they can share the connection (see Figure 8-28).

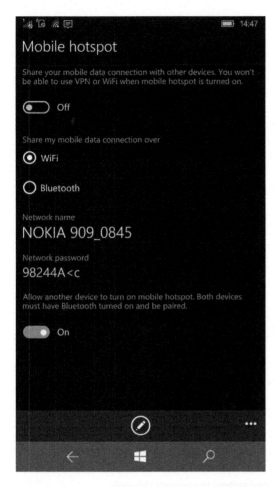

Figure 8-28. *You can share a mobile broadband data connection if your provider allows it*

Sharing an Internet Connection over a Wired Network

If your PC is connected to a network via Ethernet cable, you can also share a broadband from that PC connection in the Network and Sharing Center, which you can access from the desktop.

To share a mobile broadband connection from the desktop, perform the following steps:

1. In the Control Panel, open the **Network and Sharing Center**.

2. In the left pane, click **Change Adapter Settings**.

3. Right-click the **Mobile Broadband** connection and select **Properties** from the context menu.

4. Click the **Sharing** tab in the dialog (see Figure 8-29).

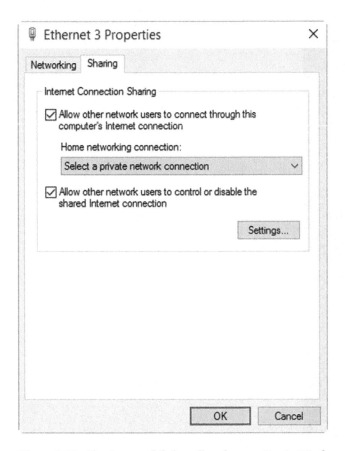

Figure 8-29. Sharing a mobile broadband connection in Windows 10

5. Select the check box to **Allow other network computers to connect through this computer's Internet connection**.

6. Click the **Settings** button and select the network services that other PCs can access through your PC, such as Web browsing (HTTP / HTTPS), and email (IMAP / SMTP / POP3).

Other computers in the vicinity can now get online using the mobile broadband connection of the host laptop.

■ **Note**   Be aware that mobile data can be costly, and you should not use metered mobile broadband connections for Internet activities that are bandwidth-intensive unless you are on an unmetered data plan. Even then you should check if a data usage cap applies to your account.

Mobile operators sell 3G and 4G/LTE Wi-Fi mini-routers that act in the same way as a standard DSL router in the home or workplace. Also, some standard DSK and cable routers include SIM card slots as a backup connection. They can usually be set to automatically switch the data connection if the main Internet connection stops working.

Working with Secondary Displays and Projectors

When you are a road warrior, you are often working with projectors or secondary displays. You can access them by clicking the **Connect** Quick Action button in the Action Center. In the Mobility Center, you have options to connect to and manage an external display, as well as to rotate the orientation of your screen (perhaps if you are working on a tablet or a vertically aligned screen).

■ **Note**   What is Presentation mode? This option, found in the Presentation settings, disables all Windows, email, and other notifications when you are using your computer for a presentation. It also disables Sleep mode during a presentation. This prevents the machine from switching itself off to save power (remember to have a main power adapter handy). It also prevents email pop-ups from appearing, so that your audience doesn't see that a friend just tagged you in a picture on Facebook.

Synchronizing Files with Other Computers and Devices

The Windows Mobility Center contains a quick link to the Windows Sync Center. It is here that you manage any ActiveSync devices that your computer or Windows Server domain account is linked to. These devices include smartphones and tablets. If you have a device managed through ActiveSync, it is commonly set up by your systems administrator through Microsoft Exchange.

The Sync Center allows you to manage your synced devices (see Figure 8-30). You may have a hardware device that you want to sync with your computer, but you can also use the Sync Center to keep an offline version of server files so that you can work on the move.

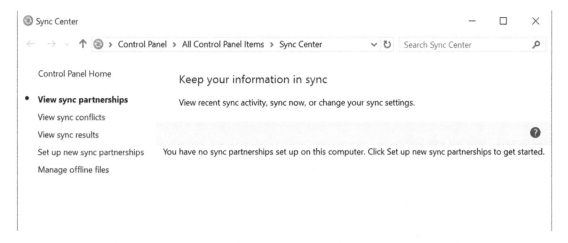

Figure 8-30. *Sync CenterOn the Sync Setup page, you can view your current sync partnerships and any conflicts that you might have. To check that everything is up-to-date, you can also get the current status of synchronization with devices*

Click **Set up new sync partnerships** to synchronize files with another device on Windows 10. Note that the other device needs to be connected to your computer to set up the partnership. When you select a sync partnership in the Sync Center, buttons to force a **Sync** and to set the sync **Schedule** appear across the top of the list of partnerships. You can click them to manage the partnership sync settings.

If you are using the Sync Center to keep offline copies of files from a Windows Server, click **Manage offline files** to control your settings for the sync partnership.

In the Offline Files dialog (see Figure 8-31), you can control the current state of the partnership, including the ability to specify the amount of hard disk space on your computer that is available for syncing. You do this on the Disk Usage tab. The more space you make available, the more files you can locally sync with your computer and store.

Figure 8-31. *Offline Files dialog*

This dialog also allows you to make sure that offline files are automatically encrypted. This option is very useful if you keep offline versions of files on a laptop that you travel with.

Setting Up and Using Work Folders

If your company uses the new Work Folders feature in the latest version of Windows Server, this is often a simpler and easier-to-manage system for the user to maintain offline versions of files. There are two ways to set up Work Folders on your PC. The easiest way—and this is on all Windows 10 devices, including smartphones—is through the Settings app. Navigate to **Accounts** and then **Work access** to connect your device to the company's network. You are asked for the email address associated with your work account (see Figure 8-32).

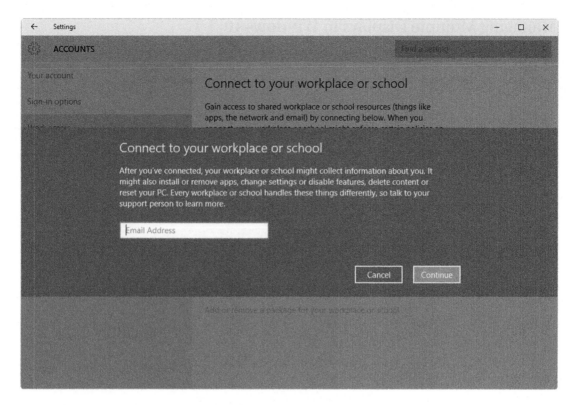

Figure 8-32. *You can access Work Folders from the Settings app*

You can also find Work Folders in the Control Panel. Click **Set up Work Folders** to get started; you are asked for your work email address or the URL of the work folder on the company server.

Once the first file sync has taken place, the Work Folders panel changes to display a status of the current file sync with the server. This panel can then be used to control how the file sync works, such as whether files should also sync over mobile broadband connections. You also turn off Work Folders here.

The synced work folders then appear in the This PC view of File Explorer and can easily be opened and accessed from there. In many ways, this makes Work Folders a significantly friendlier and powerful alternative to the older ActiveSync feature, although it does require a specially configured server that ActiveSync does not require.

Working with Multiple Screens and Desktops in Windows 10

Many people like to use multiple monitors with their computers. Laptops, especially, might have a secondary monitor, or you might work in a financial environment or a design environment, in which multiple displays are commonplace. In this section, I show you how to manage multiple displays in Windows 10, and how you can get the best from those displays through the use of multidesktop wallpapers and new taskbar options.

Managing Multiple Displays in Windows 10

You can manage multiple displays in Windows 10 from the Settings app. To get quick access to the multimonitor settings, right-click your desktop and select **Display Settings** from the options that appear. This displays a panel (see Figure 8-33) that is also available in the Settings app by navigating to **System ➤ Display**.

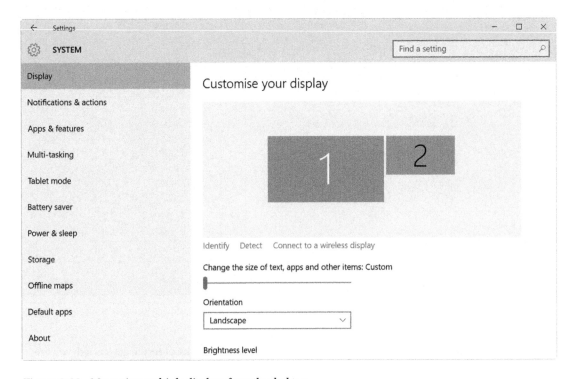

Figure 8-33. *Managing multiple displays from the desktop*

The **Customize your display** settings shows each monitor connected to your computer. Here you can drag and drop the monitor displays to the left and right, and even up and down to organize them. You also have several other options, including whether to duplicate or extend the main display onto the secondary screen.

You can also select to make a screen your **main display** (I'll explain why you might want to do this shortly). Simply select the display icon that represents the one that you want to be your primary display and then select **Make this my main display**.

▦ **Tip** Many laptops now come with a feature called Miracast, which allows you to project your screen to a compatible projector or screen that also supports the Miracast technology. If you use this feature, the wireless display may now appear on the Screen Resolution page. There are three ways to activate the wireless display: press Win+P (project to a second screen), click **Connect to a wireless display** in the Display Settings or click the **Connect** Quick Action button in the Action Center.

There are also some new tools for managing the taskbar in Windows 10. For example, on some screens there is no system tray shown; it is shown only on one screen. If you want to move the system tray to another screen, you can do this by right-clicking the taskbar on the target screen and from the context menu, click **Make this my main taskbar**.

You can also manage the taskbar in other ways when you have multiple monitors attached. By right-clicking the taskbar and selecting Properties, you see a dialog that shows additional multimonitor controls (see Figure 8-34).

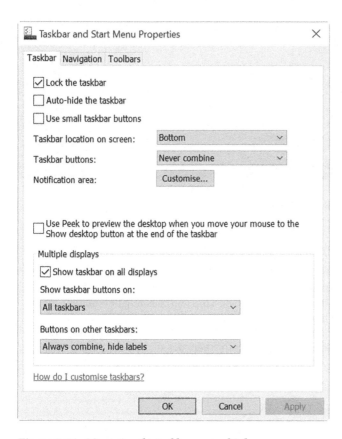

Figure 8-34. *Managing the taskbar on multiple screens*

In the taskbar properties, you can uncheck the box to automatically display the taskbar on all displays. If you do this, you see the taskbar only on your primary screen. Here are other options that you might find useful:

- Show taskbar buttons on **All taskbars** shows all of your pinned buttons for both open and inactive programs on every screen.

- Show taskbar buttons on the **Main taskbar and taskbar where window is open** shows all the pinned application buttons on your main display, but only the buttons for open programs residing on the secondary display(s).

- Show taskbar buttons on the **Taskbar where window is open** shows all of your pinned buttons, but open programs are indicated on the screen only where they are actually open.

You may want to show the taskbar only on a single display, however, because it enables you to use the whole of each secondary screen for programs without a (likely empty) taskbar getting in the way.

■ **Note** You can take screenshots of multiple monitor displays in Windows 10 by pressing Win + Prnt Scrn (see Figure 8-35), the screenshot is saved to your Pictures ➤ Screenshots folder.

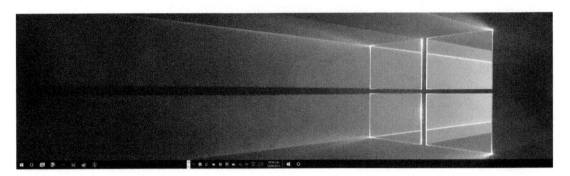

Figure 8-35. *Take multiple monitor screenshots in Windows 10*

Using Multimonitor Wallpapers in Windows 10

Windows 10 supports widescreen desktop wallpapers that can be spanned across multiple displays. Windows 10 also allows you to set different wallpapers on different screens. You select your multiscreen wallpaper in the usual way: by right-clicking a blank space on the desktop and selecting **Personalize**, or by right-clicking an image and then selecting **Set as desktop wallpaper**.

In the Personalization settings, you can choose the **Span** option. It sits in the **Choose a fit** drop-down box (see Figure 8-36). Windows 10 gives you the option to span your wallpaper across multiple screens.

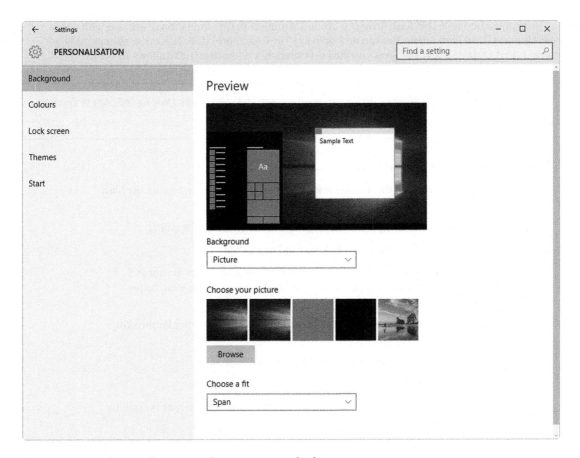

Figure 8-36. Desktop wallpapers can be set to span multiple screens

---

■ **Note**   Spanned wallpapers really work only when all the attached screens are running at the same resolution. If they are not, you may see areas of black.

Creating a Windows To Go Drive Without Windows To Go

Earlier in this chapter, I discussed the different ways you can conserve the battery life on your laptop, Ultrabook, or tablet. But surely the best way to conserve your battery life isn't to use the PC at all! It's actually possible to run a full copy of Windows 10, with all of your software from a USB flash drive on any other PC, and this is a feature called Windows To Go.

Windows To Go is a feature of Windows 10 Enterprise that allows system administrators to provide employees with USB flash drives containing Windows 10 and required software for work. You can start any USB-bootable PC from this drive to use your own copy of Windows 10 and your own software—anywhere, any time, and on any PC. I won't explain how to use Windows To Go here, because as an Enterprise feature, any Windows To Go drive that you use is most likely provided to you by your system administrator at work or college. However, it is still possible to create a Windows To Go drive yourself—after a fashion, anyway.

Creating a bootable USB flash drive gets around Windows To Go's limitation of working with only a few supported USB flash drives. You can do it with any 16GB (or more) USB flash drive, although a larger capacity and a fast USB 3.0 drive gives you the best experience. I like to call it Windows To Go-ish.

■ **Note**   Unlike when using Windows To Go, you need a spare and valid product key for the copy of Windows (as well as any software) that you want to install on the USB flash drive.

---

1. Plug your USB flash drive into the PC.

2. Press **Win+X** to open the Administration menu (you can also right-click the Start button on the desktop).

3. Open **Command Prompt (Admin)** and click through the UAC warning.

4. In the Command window, type **diskpart** and press Enter.

5. Type **list disk** and press Enter to display a list of available drives in your PC. Make a note of the number (0, 1, 2, etc.) for the USB flash drive, which is best identifiable through its capacity.

6. Type **select disk 2**, where the number represents the disk number for the USB flash drive, and press Enter.

7. Type **clean** and press Enter to prepare the drive for formatting.

8. Type **create partition primary** and press Enter.

9. Type **format fs=ntfs quick** to format the USB flash drive. This erases everything from it.

10. Type **active** and press Enter.

11. Type **assign letter=e** and press Enter. This assigns a drive letter to the USB flash drive. Make sure that the letter you want to use isn't already in use.

12. Type **exit** and press Enter.

13. Mount a Windows 10 ISO file on your computer by right-clicking it in File Explorer and clicking **Mount**, or by inserting a Windows 10 installation DVD on your computer. Make note of the drive letter; you will need it.

14. Back at the Command window, type **dism /apply-image /imagefile=f:\sources\ install.wim /index:1 /applydir:e:** , where **e** is the letter for your USB flash drive and **f** is the drive letter for your mounted ISO file or DVD. Press Enter. This copies the installation files from the Windows 10 installer to the USB flash drive.

15. Type **bcdboot.exe e:\windows /s e: /f ALL** and press Enter to set the USB flash drive as bootable.

You can now restart your PC; start it from the USB flash drive from the boot menu (usually F12 or Esc at start-up). The initial install can take some time, especially on slower USB 2.0 drives. To ensure hardware driver compatibility, it is also a good idea to run this installation process, if possible, on the PC you will most often be using the drive with. This is because there are differences in the Windows boot-loader between PCs running the older BIOS system on their motherboard, and those with the newer UEFI firmware. A Windows To Go-ish drive created in this way can only be used on a PC with the firmware type it was created on.

Once you have installed Windows (see Chapter 16 for full details on how to do this), you should then install all the software you want to use on the USB flash drive, because when you use it on other computers, it identifies as Windows To Go, and it doesn't allow you to install software. Any and all software should be installed when the USB flash drive is started on the same PC that it was installed with.

Summary

Windows 10 contains volumes of productivity tools and ways to make the operating system, your programs, and documents easier to use. The mobility features also help squeeze more life out of your laptop's battery. New productivity features such as the improved Snap feature can massively aid productivity, and the Quick Action buttons and Cortana can speed up your workflow considerably too.

There are other productivity tools that I discuss later in this book, including the new Hyper-V virtualization software. As a guide to help you maximize your time with Windows 10, this chapter has covered what most people need to know.

CHAPTER 9

Personalizing Your Windows Experience

Windows has always been one of the most customizable operating systems available, which is one of the things that has made it so popular over the years. Indeed, a whole industry of third-party products is well established with companies, providing ever-more imaginative ways for you to personalize your copy of Windows.

Windows has changed considerably over the last 20 years, although the main interface style of the Start menu, taskbar, and desktop has always remained in place (well, mostly anyway).

So how can you personalize your copy of Windows 10? What options exist to allow you to change the desktop in imaginative ways? What hacks and third-party software exist to change the look of Windows 10 by perhaps customizing the taskbar, or even restoring the Windows 7 Start menu?

You'll be pleased to hear that Windows 10 is just as customizable as its predecessors. In this chapter, I'll show you how to give it a look and feel that best suits you.

Personalizing Windows 10

In Windows 10, Microsoft has brought all of the main personalization options together for the first time, and created a Personalization category in the Settings app (see Figure 9-1). There are some additional options, such as managing and personalizing pop-up notification "toasts," which are still found elsewhere; I'll talk more about these later in this chapter. For the moment though, all of the main personalization options are handily available in one place. Let's begin by looking at these options one by one.

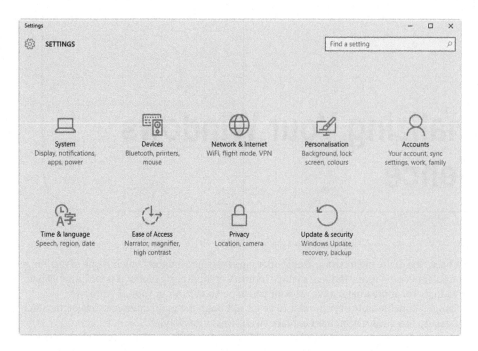

Figure 9-1. *Personalization options are available in the Settings app*

Personalizing the Desktop Wallpaper (Background)

PC users live on the desktop, and so the picture (or lack of picture) we choose for our desktop wallpaper and as the background to our PC experience is a highly person thing. Companies are fond of having a background that includes the corporate logo. Some people like to have a family photograph, or a memory from a vacation, or maybe even a slideshow of photos. Other people (and I include myself in this) want a plain and unfussy wallpaper that doesn't distract from the windows that are open on the desktop. A few people take this minimalism even further and just have a plainly colored background.

■ **Tip** It's possible to have animated and video wallpapers in Windows 10. Stardock's DeskScapes app, available at `www.stardock.com/products/deskscapes/`, enables this feature for you. If you are using a laptop or a tablet, be aware that animated wallpaper significantly reduces your battery life.

The first option in the Personalization settings is for your wallpaper (or *background* as it's called here), as shown in Figure 9-2. There are four options available from a drop-down menu...

- **Windows Spotlight** may not appear on every device. It uses Microsoft's Bing search engine to change the lock screen image on a rotating basis, and can also display handy hints and tips about how to get the best out of Windows 10 (as if you need that now).

- **Picture** allows you to have a single photograph or image as your wallpaper; by default, Windows 10 comes with this selected.

- **Solid color** lets you choose from a selection of 24 different colors for your desktop background (it's not really a wallpaper at this point); you should try orange—it's very nice!

- **Slideshow** presents a **Browse** button that you can use to add any of the pictures you have on your PC to an autorotating wallpaper slideshow. Below this is a drop-down menu asking how often you want the image to change. The options vary from every minute to every day. Above the drop-down menu is a display showing the Start menu and an open window, in which you can preview your chosen wallpaper or desktop color.

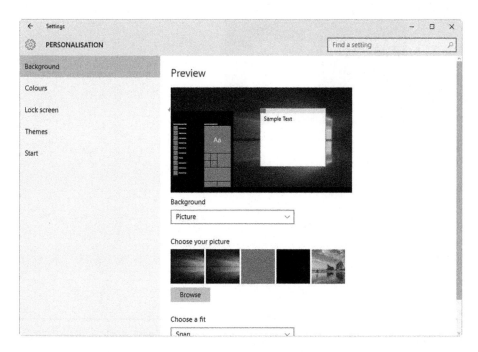

Figure 9-2. *You can choose any image to be a desktop wallpaper*

You might find (especially with photographs) that the picture you choose doesn't perfectly fit on your screen; it may leave black bars at the side or above and below the picture. You needn't worry, though, because Windows 10 has a feature to help with this. Below the picture choice option is a **Choose a fit** drop-down menu. Here there are options to auto **Fill** the picture on your screen, give it the best **Fit**, or perform other actions on the wallpaper, such as stretching, tiling, or centering it. If you are using more than one screen with your PC, there is an option here to **Span** the wallpaper across multiple screens, so that not every screen is showing the same image. There's more information about how to use multiple screens on your PC in Chapter 8.

■ **Tip**   On Windows 10 smartphones you may see a **Show more tiles** option (it doesn't appear on every device), which displays an extra column or tiles on the Start screen.

Choosing a Custom Color Scheme

When it's first installed, some areas of Windows 10 are black or battleship gray; but it doesn't always have to look like this, as you can choose a custom color scheme for your desktop. Clicking the **Colors** link in the Personalization options displays your various color options (see Figure 9-3).

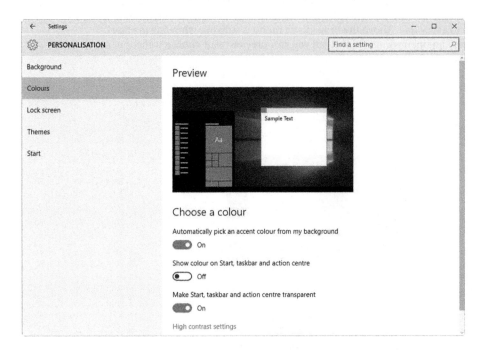

Figure 9-3. *You can choose a custom color scheme in Windows 10*

▪ **Note** Windows 10 smartphones have an additional option to change between a light and dark theme for the OS. This is a feature that's expected to be ported to all versions of Windows 10; it may already be available to you as you read this.

The first of these options, **Automatically pick an accent color from my background**, if turned on, chooses an accent color for the Start menu, icons, live tiles, and highlights in apps. You can select your own color by turning off this option, at which time you are presented with a panel of 49 different colors to choose from.

▪ **Tip** If 49 colors aren't enough, you can choose any other color you want. At the Start menu, search for **run** and click **Run desktop app** when it appears in the search results. Then in the box that appears, type **control color** and click the OK button. A panel with various color options and a **Color intensity** slider helps you modify the color. There is also a **Show color mixer** button. You can open the color mixer to get full control over the color hue, saturation, and brightness.

The next option is **Show color on Start [menu], taskbar and Action Center**, which allows you to switch between black and your chosen accent color. It can add more color and life to your desktop. This option is called **Apply color to navigation bar** on smartphones, which do not have physical back, Start, and search buttons.

Lastly, there's the **Make Start [menu], taskbar and Action Center transparent** option, which allows you to toggle between a semitransparent look and a solid look. You may find that you have a lovely accent color that just looks awful when made slightly transparent, for example. Alternatively, you might find that the Start menu, taskbar, and Action Center are easier to see and read when they're solid.

There is also an option to access the Windows 10 High Contrast Settings; I'll show you how to use this and other accessibility features in Chapter 10.

▓ **Note** Windows 10 smartphones have an additional Personalization option called Sounds, in which you can choose your ringtone and select options for the delivery of messages, emails, and alerts. You can also control the device vibration at this panel.

Personalizing the Lock Screen and Using a Tablet As a Digital Photo Frame

The lock screen, which is displayed before you sign in to your PC, has its own wallpaper in Windows 10, which can be chosen at the lock screen settings. Just as with the desktop background, you can choose a picture or a slideshow comprised of several pictures. The Picture option gives you a browse button so that you can choose any image on your PC, but the Slideshow option works slightly differently from the desktop wallpaper.

When you choose a slideshow for the lock screen, you are asked to add a folder of images, not just specific images. You might find this annoying, however, because some of the images in the folder may not fit the aspect ratio of your screen well. Don't worry, though, because below this is an **Advanced slideshow settings** link that you can click for more control.

The advanced slideshow settings (see Figure 9-4), allow you to include photos that you have taken with your cameras (on your Windows 10 smartphone as well as your PC and tablet), but also allows you to specify that only pictures that actually fit on your screen be used.

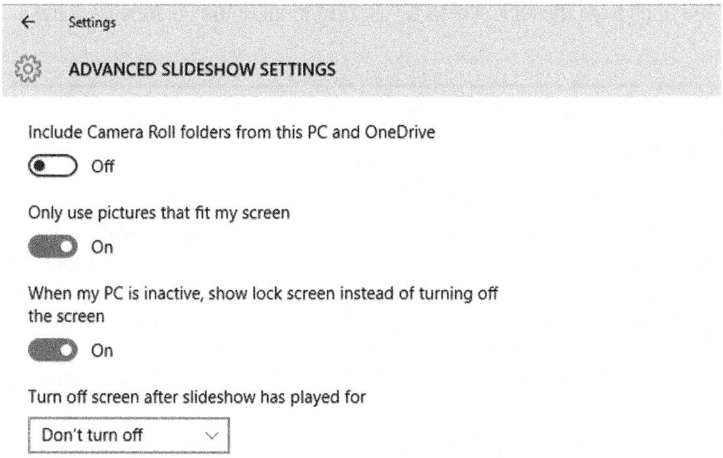

Figure 9-4. Personalizing the lock screen slideshow

Additionally, you can specify that instead of turning off your display, a slideshow of these pictures should be displayed, with an additional option to allow the slideshow to play for a period of time (between 30 minutes and forever) before the screen eventually turns itself off. Why would you want to do this? If you have a tablet (and a stand for it), you can use it as a digital photo frame. Bear in mind that it needs to be plugged into mains electricity for this to work effectively, or else your battery will be eaten very quickly. Still, it is a good way to display photos of friends, family, or that recent vacation to Austria.

Below the lock screen background options are controls for apps that can display information on the lock screen itself. You can choose from installed Store apps that are capable of displaying live information on the lock screen. Not every app is capable of this, but those that are greatly increase the functionality of the lock screen.

To examine just how useful this can be, let's have a look at earlier Windows versions and the way we use our computers. In Windows 7, for example, the lock screen didn't provide any information except which user was signed in.

In Windows 10, the lock screen always provides the time and date. It can also show additional information, such as the number of unread emails, the number of instant messages you have received, the current weather, and much more. You can also have an alarm app shown on the lock screen; Windows 10 ships with such an app. This makes low-power tablet devices suitable as alarm clocks because they wake from sleep to sound your morning alarm.

You can only use Store apps for the lock screen, but not all of them are compatible and some are capable of displaying only limited data. This includes the email app, because you don't necessarily want people who are walking past your computer to be able to read the names of the senders and the subjects of the emails you have waiting.

You can add up to seven apps, plus one app showing detailed information, to the Windows 10 lock screen. They always display in the bottom left of the screen under the date and time.

Some apps can provide much more information, including the calendar. It is very useful for providing details about your afternoon schedule (such as seeing what your friends are doing on social networks, or informing others that you'll be at the dentist for the next hour—so that they can mess around with your computer).

You can only have one of the seven apps display additional information (this is optional). If you want to turn off this feature so that you see only the basic apps, click the Detailed Status app and select **None**.

■ **Tip**   You can remove any or all of the apps from the lock screen by clicking them in the Personalize page and selecting **None** from the options.

Using Custom Desktop Themes

If you used custom desktop themes in Windows 7 or Windows 8.1, they're still present in Windows 10. The Themes options in the Settings app can act as a pointer to the Control Panel themes settings that you may be familiar with. Here you can choose from any installed themes, or click **Get more themes online** to personalize your PC more.

Alas, because the theme customization options have been removed in Windows 10, the **Save theme** option won't do much. However, you can use it with some of the options I've already described, such as changing the color scheme or changing the background wallpaper, to customize the theme to some extent.

It's not known what the future holds for themes. They may in a future Windows 10 update, be brought properly into the Settings app, or they may be quietly retired. If this has already happened by the time you read this, just forget that I told you this stuff.

Personalizing the Start Menu

Way back in Chapter 1, which seems like a long time ago now, I showed you how to use and get started with the Windows 10 Start menu. I promised you that I'd show you how to customize it beyond shuffling live tiles around.

The Personalize settings allow you to customize the Start menu (which is actually an app— I'll bet you didn't know that!). There are several options available to you.

- **Show most used apps** displays a list (much as existed in Windows XP, Vista, and Windows 7) of the apps you use the most, enabling you to launch them quickly with just two clicks. You can actually launch them with a single click by right-clicking them and pinning them to the taskbar.

- **Show recently added apps** is (I think, anyway) one of the most useful features ever added to Windows. EVER! Seriously, I'm not kidding. When you install an app, it displays on the Start menu in a **Recently installed** category, enabling you to find it quickly, and should you want, pin it to the taskbar or Start menu as a tile.

- **Use Start full screen**. Whatever people said about Windows 8, there were some who really liked the Start screen. It displayed all of your installed apps in a tiled way that made them quick and easy to find and launch. Normally, if you want to have a fullscreen Start menu in Windows 10, you have to invoke Tablet mode, but this also makes all of your apps run in fullscreen, which you might not want. To help out, Microsoft has included this option so that you can force the Start menu to always open in fullscreen, while also allowing your apps to run in windows on the desktop.

- **Show recently opened items in Jump Lists on Start or the taskbar**. Jump Lists are an incredibly useful feature that displays lists of your recently opened files for quick access on pop-up menus from icons on the taskbar. Jump Lists in Windows 10 also appear as flyouts from Start menu icons, via an > (arrow) to the right of the app name. You can enable these flyout Jump Lists to include your recently opened files.

- **Choose which folders appear on Start** displays a list of all the different folders that can appear as quick links in the Start menu (see Figure 9-5). You can turn these on and off to show and hide them, and to give you quick access to some of the file locations on your PC.

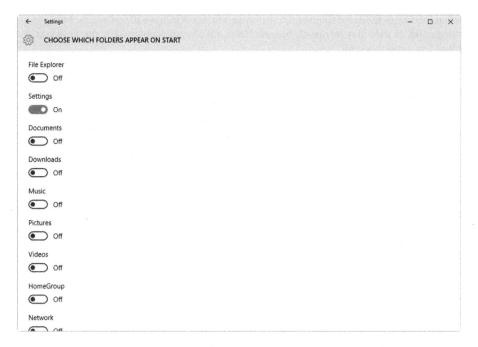

Figure 9-5. *You can choose which folders are displayed on the Start menu*

Managing Notification "Toasts"

Toasts in Windows 10 are the notifications that pop up in the bottom right of your screen. Depending on how many apps you have installed, they can become intrusive; they also appear in the Action Center anyway, so you can't easily miss them. You can silence, or at least tame, toast notifications in Windows 10 though.

You can manage your notifications in the Settings app by navigating to **System** and then **Notifications and actions**. Here you can choose which Quick Actions buttons appear at the bottom (or top on a smartphone) of the Action Center. I'll come back to this later in this chapter. In the Notifications section are controls for managing all notifications on your PC universally.

- **Show app notifications** allows you to turn toasts off universally. This can be extremely useful if you are using a PC at work and really don't want to be bothered every time there's something Windows 10 or an app wants to tell you.

- **Show notifications on the lock screen** also allows you to turn on and off all notifications for the Windows lock screen. You may want to do this for privacy reasons, so that anybody walking past your PC doesn't read a notification you'd rather keep private, such as an email from your therapist.

- **Show alarms, reminders and incoming VOIP [Skype] calls on the lock screen** is something you might want to turn off for privacy reasons. You may not want Skype calls appearing on your lock screen if you've not made it back in time for that all-important conference call, or you may not want a reminder to inform everybody in your office that you need to buy some hair removal cream on the way home.

- **Hide notifications while presenting** is an option every road warrior will want enabled. This automatically hides all toasts when you're playing a video or fullscreen presentation. If you've ever had an alert informing you that you've received a spam email about generic Viagra pop up during a presentation, you'll know just how useful this feature can be.

- **Show notifications from these apps** allows you to turn on and off notifications from all the apps installed on your PC that are likely to inform you about something. Perhaps you want email and calendar messages, but don't want to see ones about app update file sync operations.

That Syncing Feeling

Speaking of syncing, which is a useful segue, Windows 10 includes a facility that can synchronize many of your settings, configuration options, and more besides. You need to be logged in to the PC with a Microsoft account for this to happen. It's very controllable if you don't want settings to be synced (for example, to separate home and work PCs). You access your sync preferences (see Figure 9-6) in the Settings app by navigating to Accounts and then **Sync your settings**.

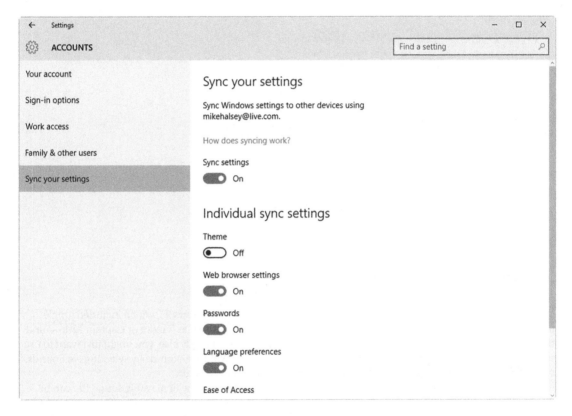

Figure 9-6. *You can choose what to sync using your Microsoft account*

These options allow you to synchronize different settings between all of your Windows 10 devices, including your smartphone. You can turn off the feature completely or choose what you want, or don't want to sync. This includes your desktop theme and wallpaper, web browser favorites, and web site passwords.

The sync settings also include the Ease of Access features, which I'll show you how to use in detail in Chapter 10. Should you use any of these features—perhaps because of a disability, or because you are near-sighted or you have a motor skills disorder—you can set up one of your PCs as you want it, and then have those settings automatically synchronized to all of your other Windows 10 PCs and devices.

Personalizing Sounds on the Desktop

Earlier in this chapter I discussed how you can change your sounds and ringtone on a Windows 10 smartphone. The sound options in Windows 10 on the desktop are quite different and they are found in a different place. You can most easily access the sounds in Windows 10 by right-clicking the volume icon on the far right of the desktop taskbar and selecting Sounds from the options. You can also search for **Sound** in Cortana to reveal the sound options (see Figure 9-7).

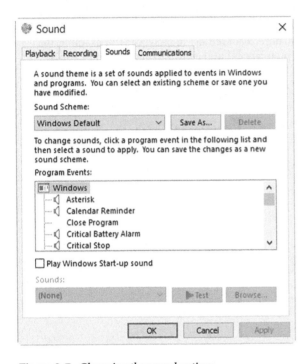

Figure 9-7. *Changing the sound options*

Sound schemes are audio collections that actually hark back to Windows 95, which included jungle and space themes with which to personalize your PC. If you fancy yourself as Tarzan or Captain Kirk, sound themes are still available online and you can search for them. For everybody else, you might just want to use the sound scheme drop-down list to easily and quickly turn off all Windows sounds by selecting No Sounds. Alternatively, you can modify any individual Windows sound in the list below.

You can use your own sounds in place of the standard sounds; any type of playable sound file can be used, including MP3s (which brings me back to Tarzan). After you choose your sounds and create your own customized sound scheme, click the Save As button. You can share your personalized sound scheme with friends and family, as well as keep a copy as a backup.

Managing Your PC's Volume When You Make a Call

The Communications tab in the Sound options (see Figure 9-8) allows you to choose what your audio does when you make or receive a Skype or other call on the device. This includes muting all other sounds completely, reducing them by 50% or 80%, or doing nothing. These settings are also useful for reducing the volume of toasts and other notifications when you're on an important call.

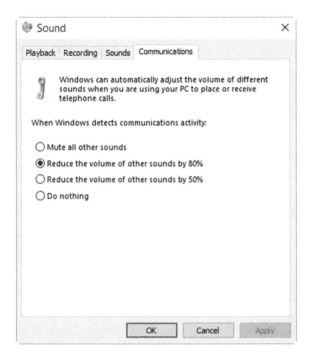

Figure 9-8. *You can choose to automute or reduce the sound of your PC when making a call*

Choosing a Screen Saver

The screen saver options have been all but removed in Windows 10, as it's a feature that's only really useful on older CRT monitors and OLED and plasma screens on which you can get screen burn-in when an image is left on the screen for too long. Unlike earlier versions of Windows, Windows 10 does not use a screen saver as the default setting, but instead turns off the display after 10 minutes. However, should you need them, the Screen Saver options (see Figure 9-9), are available by searching for **screen saver** in Cortana or through the Themes panel in Settings.

Figure 9-9. *Choosing a screen saver*

Some screen savers come with additional settings. You can preview the screen saver before turning it on by clicking the Preview button. There is also an option to control the amount of time the computer is inactive (i.e., not using the keyboard, mouse, or touchscreen) before the screen saver switches on. By default, Windows 10 returns you to the desktop when you return to the PC, but for extra security, you can check the option to instead return you to the logon screen.

■ **Note**   Do you need a screen saver? Screen savers are necessary for older cathode ray tube (CRT) monitors, in which a beam of electrons is fired at a phosphor layer inside the screen glass to display a picture. If a single electron beam fires for too long at the same patch of phosphor, the image could end up physically burned into the phosphor layer—an effect called *phosphor burn-in*. Most modern flat-panel monitors do not suffer from this because they use individual pixel lights instead of an electron gun, with the notable exception being OLED (organic light-emitting diode) screens, so Windows 10 is set by default to simply turn off the screen instead. This saves a considerable amount of power over the lifetime of your computer.

Changing the Desktop Icons

There is a well-hidden option (buried as a link in the Themes panel) that allows to change which icons appear on your desktop. To be honest, I love the argument about whether people have icons on their desktop or not. Many people like a desktop with icons and folders scattered over it, whereas other people, including myself, like a clean desktop.

So let me be fair here. The Desktop Icon Settings dialog is where you can turn on *or* off the desktop icons in Windows 10, including those for your computer, your files, the network, the recycle bin, and the Control Panel (see Figure 9-10).

Figure 9-10. *Changing the desktop icons*

You can also restore default icons or prevent desktop themes from automatically changing the icons to custom icons.

Changing the Mouse Settings

In the Settings app, under **Devices** and **Mouse & touchpad** are the controls for the mouse and/or trackpad on your PC. Here you can select the primary mouse button (left or right), how the scroll wheel works, and if inactive windows should also scroll when you move your mouse pointer over them.

Additional options can be found on the **Additional mouse options** link, which is also hidden as a link on the **Themes** options page. Here you have the ability to change your mouse pointers, which opens the Mouse Properties dialog. The mouse properties options, including those for mouse pointers (see Figure 9-11), are much more useful than you might think. I want to look at each tab in this window to explain what it does.

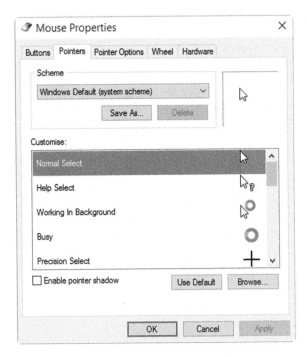

Figure 9-11. *Changing the mouse options*

- **Buttons tab**: Used for left-handed people to switch the left and right mouse buttons. It also swaps the buttons on a laptop trackpad. You can slow down or speed up the double-click speed, which is extremely useful for people who can't click as quickly. ClickLock allows you to avoid having to hold down the mouse button to drag items around the screen. These last two features are excellent for people with weaker motor skills.

- **Pointers tab**: Includes options to change the mouse pointer to a variety of high-visibility options, which is excellent for people who have difficulty seeing or reading the computer screen. There is more information about this in Chapter 10, in which I show you how to change the mouse and keyboard options in detail.

- **Pointer options**: Allows you to turn on useful features such as mouse trail so that you can see the mouse moving across the screen more easily. You can also display the position of the mouse by pressing the Ctrl key on your keyboard. You can slow down the mouse speed (or speed it up for gaming). You can also set the mouse to automatically snap to the closest button. This is a great feature for those with weaker motor skills.

- **Wheel tab**: Contains the vertical and (if your mouse supports it) horizontal scrolling options for Windows 10. If you do not have a wheel on your mouse, you might not see this tab.

- **Hardware tab**: Allows you to view information on the hardware driver and driver settings for your mouse.

■ **Tip**   If you find Windows 10 difficult to use because of challenges with eyesight or motor skills, changing your mouse settings can help make Windows 10 more accessible and usable.

Personalizing the Quick Task Buttons

I've previously mentioned that the Action Center contains some Quick Task buttons in the bottom-right of your screen (or at the top of your screen if you use a Windows 10 Mobile device). In the Settings app, in **System** and then **Notifications & actions** is the option to change the main row of these buttons (see Figure 9-12).

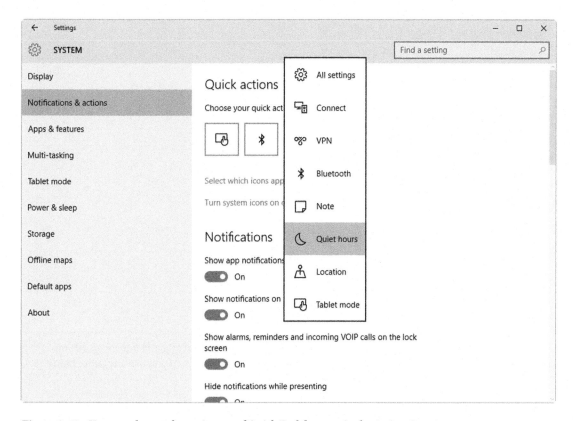

Figure 9-12.   *You can change the main row of Quick Task buttons in the Action Center*

You can click each of the icons (the number of icons will vary depending on what type of device you are using) to display a list of all the Quick Tasks available to you. These can include on/off switches for Bluetooth, Flight mode, Wi-Fi mode, and Tablet mode, as well as quick launch icons for VPN connections and note taking.

Personalizing the Taskbar

The taskbar is able to be personalized as well (I did mention that Windows 10 is the most customizable operating system currently available, didn't I?). Access the taskbar personalization options (see Figure 9-13) by right-clicking the taskbar and selecting Properties from the options that appear.

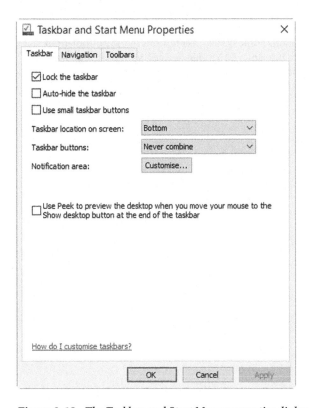

Figure 9-13. *The Taskbar and Start Menu properties dialog*

The options allow you to automatically hide the taskbar so that you can take full advantage of your screen when running apps. You can also lock the taskbar to prevent toolbars (if you use any) from being moved around, and you can change how icons appear on the taskbar.

■ **Tip** Aero Peek was a feature in Windows 7 that would hide all of your windows when you moved your mouse to the bottom right of your desktop. This feature is turned off by default in Windows 10, but you can turn it back on in the Taskbar and Start Menu properties dialog.

Personalizing the Notification Area

By default, Windows 10 hides all of your notification area (also known as the *system tray*) icons and their notifications behind a small white ^ (up arrow). Some people want to be able to see the tray icons, however; you can turn them on or further hide icons. To customize what appears in the system tray, in the Settings app, navigate to **System**, then **Notifications & actions**, and click the **Select which icons appear on the taskbar** link.

In the options that appear (see Figure 9-14), you can turn on and off the notification area icons for all the installed apps for which a system tray icon already appears.

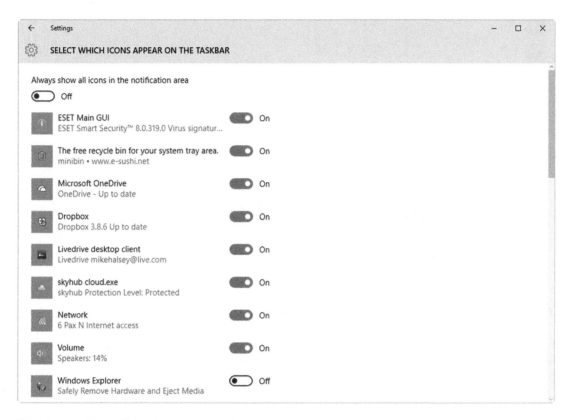

Figure 9-14. *Customizing the system tray*

Checking the **Always show all icons in the notification area** makes sure that all of your app icons are displayed at all times and makes the system tray more like the one in Windows XP (if you like that sort of thing). However, hiding icons and notifications is useful if you find a particular piece of software annoying.

Perhaps you really want to minimize things on the desktop and don't want to even see the standard notification icons or the clock. You can turn these icons off completely in the Settings app by clicking System, then **Notifications & actions** and clicking the **Turn system icons on or off** link. The System Icons screen shown in Figure 9-15 appears.

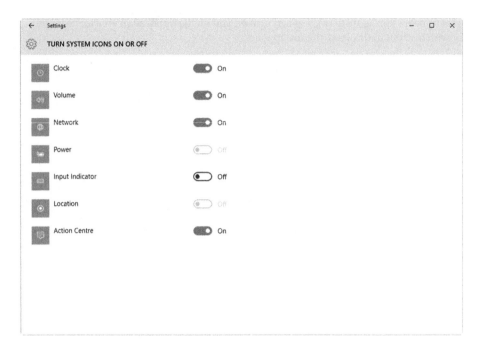

Figure 9-15. *Turning the system icons on or off*

Bear in mind, however, that if you turn off the icon for the Action Center, you won't be alerted when security issues arise unless you have toasts enabled. Also, turning off the laptop battery indicator could leave you running low and needing a recharge without realizing it.

■ **Tip**   You can rearrange the order icons appear in the notification area by simply dragging and dropping them. You can also click the ^ (up arrow) next to the notification area to reveal hidden icons and then drag them onto the taskbar to pin them.

Setting the Date and Time

In the Date and Time dialog, available by clicking the clock on the taskbar and then clicking the **Date & time settings** link when the clock and calendar appear, you can quickly change the time and date on your computer, use time-syncing services on the Internet to automatically keep your time and date correct, change your time zone, and control automatic adjustment for daylight saving time (see Figure 9-16). You can also get to the Date and Time dialog by right-clicking the clock on the taskbar and selecting **Adjust date/time** from the options that appear.

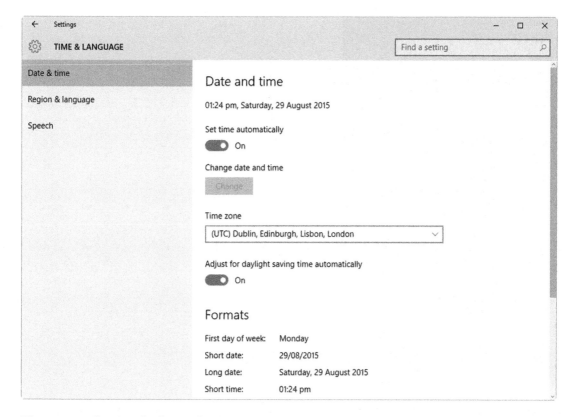

Figure 9-16. *Changing the date and time*

You also have the ability to add extra clocks to Windows. They appear when you click the date and time on the Windows taskbar. You can add up to two for different time zones, each with a custom name (see Figure 9-17). To enable this feature click the **Add clocks for different time zones** link at the bottom of the **Time & language** settings.

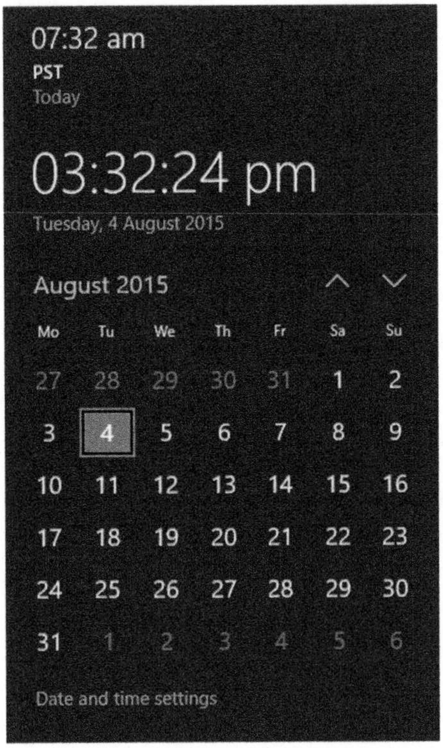

Figure 9-17. You can add clocks to Windows 10

Enabling Recycle Bin Warnings

When you delete a file in Windows 10, you don't get the "do you *really* want to delete this file" warning from Windows versions of old. This is because the recycle bin combined with the File History feature (which I show you how to use in Chapter 12) make it very easy to recover accidentally deleted files. You can turn this feature on if you want to, though, by *right-clicking* the recycle bin icon on your desktop and selecting Properties from the menu that appears.

The Recycle Bin Properties panel includes some simple controls, including one that allows you to bypass the recycle bin altogether and just permanently delete everything. At the bottom of this dialog (see Figure 9-18) is a check box for **Display delete confirmation dialog**; you can turn this back on if you want these warnings reenabled.

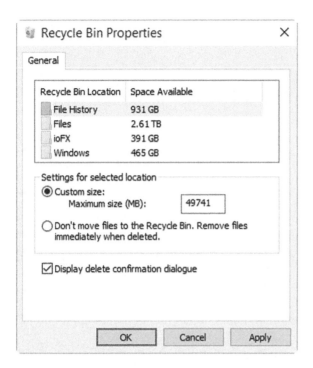

Figure 9-18. *You can reenable recycle bin warnings*

Changing the Default File Explorer View

When you open File Explorer for the first time, you're taken to the Quick Access view. This displays links to files and folders you have accessed recently. While this view can make it very quick to get access to anything you're currently working on, it can be untidy, and some people don't like to think that any file they have might appear in a view that colleagues can easily see.

You can change the default File Explorer view from the View tab on the ribbon, by clicking Options. This displays a panel of different display options for File Explorer, including a drop-down menu that can switch between the Quick Access and This PC views (see Figure 9-19).

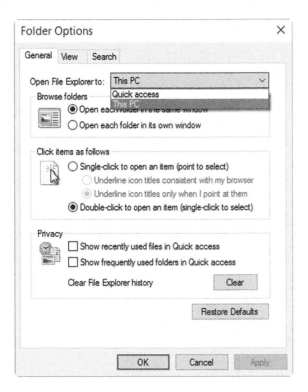

Figure 9-19. *You can change how File Explorer works in its options*

There are plenty of other options here, such as opening folders in the current or a new window, whether a single or a double click opens a file or folder (a single click can be a good option on a tablet) and turning off your frequently used files and folders in the Quick Access view completely.

Changing Your Region and Language Settings

The Region controls can be found in the **Time and Language** panel of the Settings app; they allow you to do much more than tell Windows the country in which you are located. You can customize the time, date, and numerical systems in Windows so that, for example, you can change the digit grouping symbol from a Western comma (,) to an Arabic point (.), or change the negative number format from a minus sign (-) to having the digit appearing in parentheses ( ).

The main options, as displayed, allow you to control the formats for your time and date (see Figure 9-20). This includes the first day of your work week, short or long display formats for the time and date, and showing the seconds or AM/PM indicators. Click the **Change date and time formats** link to customize these; each option is presented as a drop-down list.

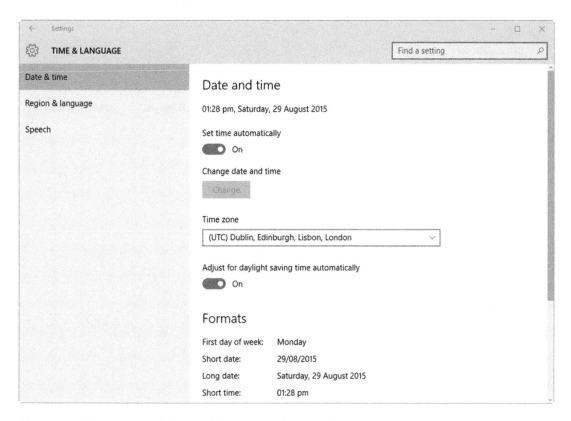

Figure 9-20. *You can control Time and Date settings for your PC*

There are additional options available by clicking the **Region & language** settings. Here you can select the main language for your PC (see Figure 9-21), as well as add new language packs, which are presented in a long scrollable list. Clicking a language presents several option buttons. If you have more than one language installed, **Set as default** and **Remove** buttons are available. An **Options** button allows you to choose handwriting and speech options for the language, as well as add specific keyboard layouts.

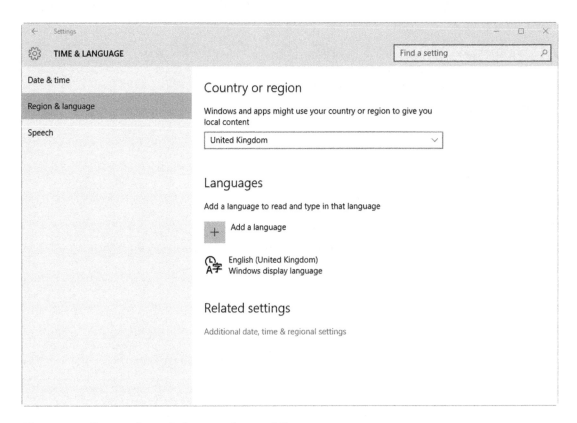

Figure 9-21. *You can choose the language for your PC*

From the both the Date & time and Region & language settings you see an **Additional date, time and regional settings** link. Clicking this opens the regional settings in the Control Panel, and these can give you much more control, such as allowing you to change your PC's geographical location. From this new window, clicking **Change date, time or number formats** displays a dialog with many of the same options seen in the Settings app. However, click the **Additional settings** button and considerably more options become available to you (see Figure 9-22).

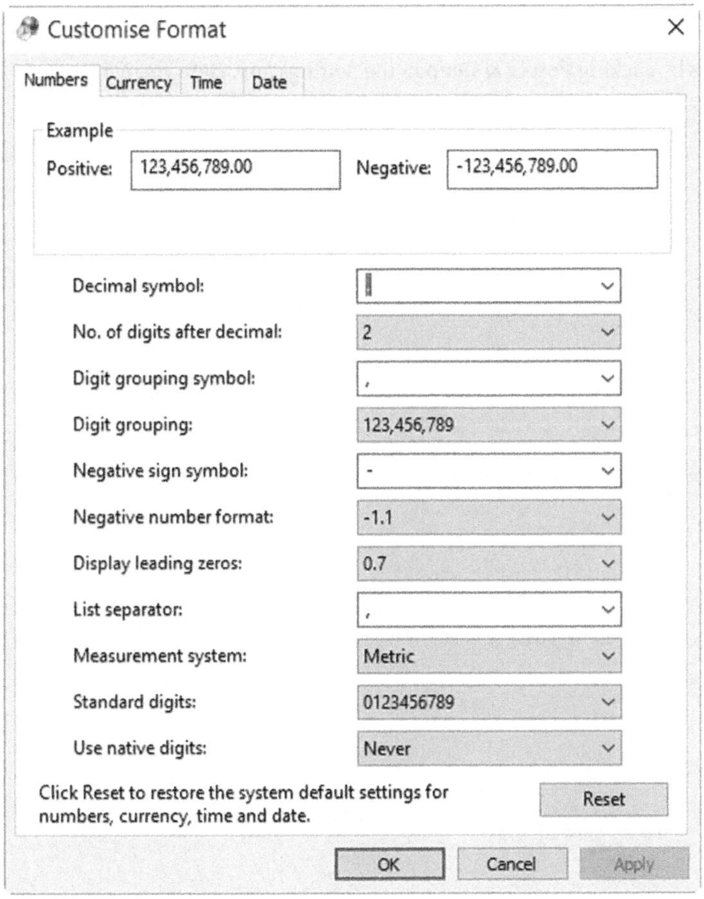

Figure 9-22. *Customizing region options*

Personalizing the Power Management Options

In Chapter 8 I talked you through my top tips for maximizing the battery life on your laptop, tablet, or smartphone to help keep you working throughout the day. No matter what type of device you're using, you still probably want to customize the power options for your Windows 10 computer. So why would desktop users want or need to change the default power settings? After all, the default settings of turning off the display after 10 minutes and putting the computer to sleep after 30 minutes must be pretty perfect, right?

Well, by default, when Windows 10 turns off the display, touching the keyboard or mouse returns you to the workspace you were at when you left the computer. Instead, you might want Windows 10 to return to the logon screen. This is especially useful if you are using your computer for work or perhaps don't want other people easily seeing your email correspondence or your social networking (especially if they're mischievous like *my* friends are).

When you put your computer to sleep, it also keeps drawing small amounts of power. Many people say that the average power draw for a Windows 10 PC in sleep is tiny. Multiply that by millions of machines, however, and you quickly see how this can balloon into a very considerable sum. When Windows 10 is capable of booting to the logon screen from a cold start in just 10 seconds, do we still need sleep at all?

In this section, I want to look at the power options thoroughly and holistically, so that you can select the best options for your needs.

Changing the Power Plan

You can access the main power settings by clicking **Power & sleep** in the Settings app. Here you can change when the screen turns off and when the PC goes to sleep. Much more control is available to you, though, by clicking the **Additional power settings** link (see Figure 9-23).

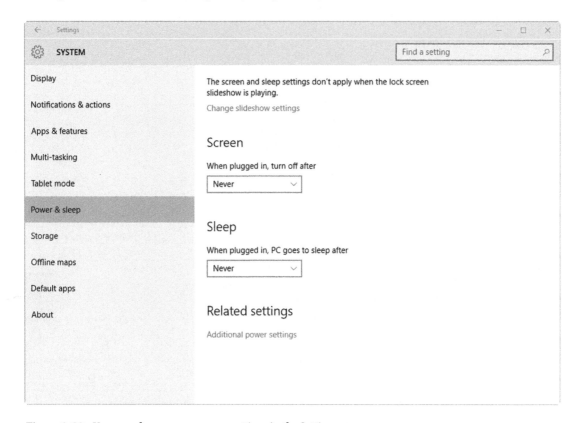

Figure 9-23. *You can change some power settings in the Settings app*

This opens a Control Panel window where you get quick and easy access to the power plans, which are preconfigured options for your screen (Shut Down, Sleep, and more), as well as the default plans added by PC manufacturers. Basic power plan options are available in PC Settings in the PC & Devices section and then by clicking Power & Sleep. Figure 9-24 shows a typical laptop, in this case a Dell, that has two default power plans, and a third that's hidden away, but that can be easily displayed. Your laptop or tablet may come with more, however, because hardware manufacturers may add their own power plans.

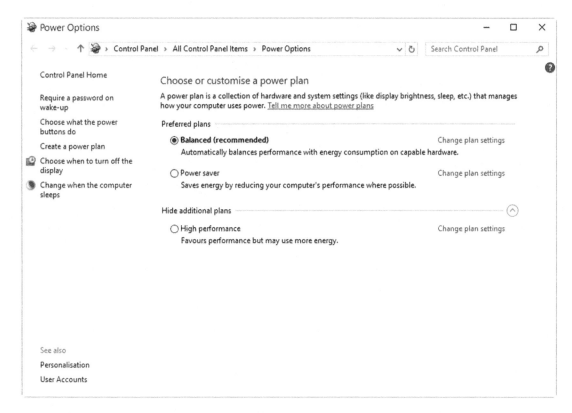

Figure 9-24. *The Power Options page*

The following are the default power plans:

- **Balanced**: The computer balances performance with energy consumption.

- **Power Saver**: Energy consumption is given top priority to extend battery life.

- **High Performance**: Battery life isn't an issue and you want the maximum performance from your PC (shown as an optional setting in Figure 9-24).

You may have additional power plans, such as Quiet or Cool. In the pane on the left of the page is the option to create your own power plan. It displays a wizard from which you can base your plan on one of the three default plans, but you can also choose from four more options: dimming or turning off the display, putting the computer to sleep, and the overall screen brightness.

You can choose a plan by clicking it. Each one can be modified by clicking **Change plan settings**.

Controlling the Power Button, Power Options, and Password Wakeup

You might want more control over the power options. Click **Require a password on wakeup** to take you to the System Settings screen (see Figure 9-25).

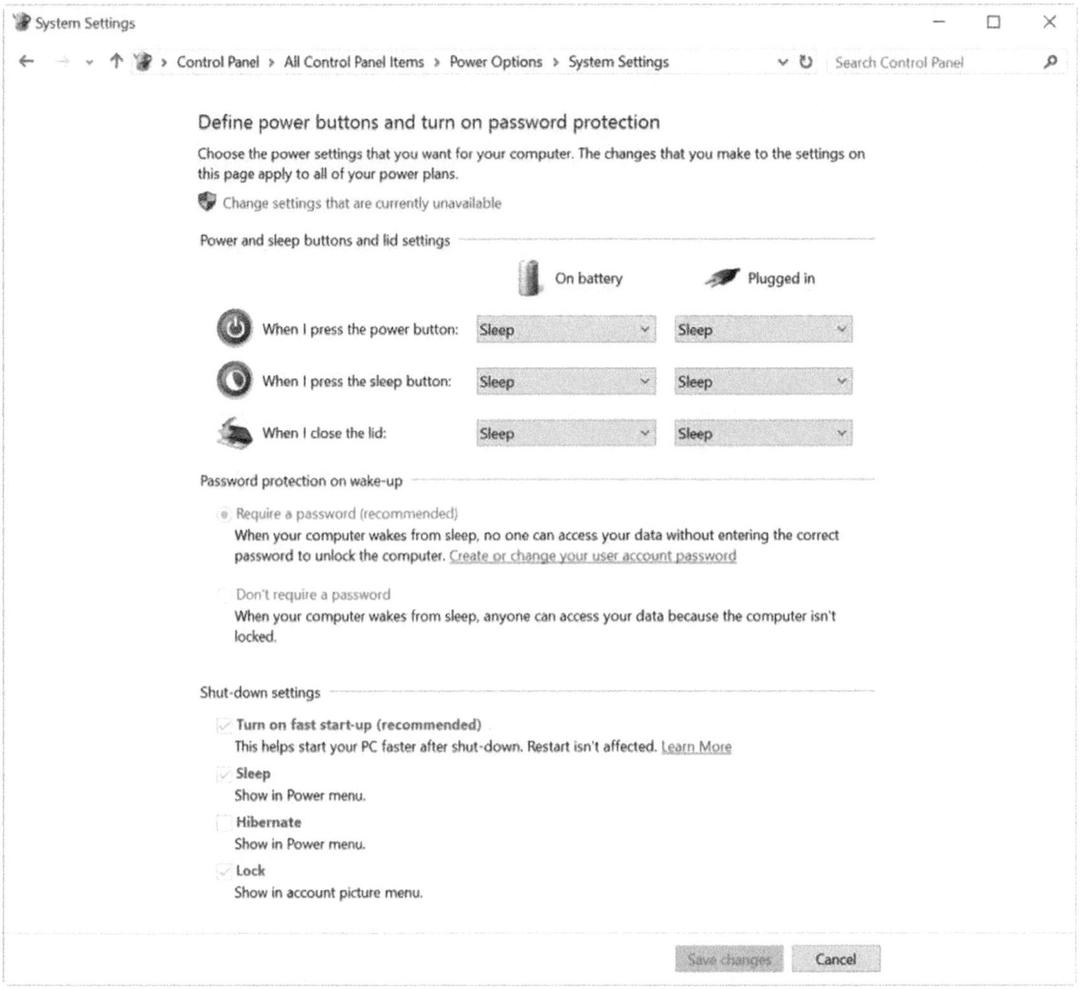

Figure 9-25. *Changing the power button options*

■ **Caution**   Remember that if you set a PC to shut down instead of sleep, you lose any work that hasn't been saved.

You can determine what the physical power and sleep (if you have one) buttons on your PC's case and keyboard do, as well as any actions that happen when you close the laptop lid. For example, if you set the close-the-lid action to Sleep, but the battery dies because you thought the computer was actually turned off, you will lose unsaved work.

The **Fast start-up** feature uses the sleep system to save the last-used state of the PC to the hard disk when you shut it down. On the next start-up, this saved state is restored as a memory image, saving the PC from having to load all of its Windows files again individually.

■ **Tip**   Clicking the **Change settings that are currently unavailable** link allows you to alter whether Windows requires you to enter a password when you start the PC. You can even disable settings such as Sleep on the Start menu power-button.

On the main Power Options page, clicking **Choose when to turn off the display** or **Choose when the computer sleeps** in the left pane shows the Edit Plan Settings options, which control the amount of time the computer remains idle before turning off the screen or putting the computer to sleep (see Figure 9-26). Note that if you have a desktop computer that does not have a battery, you see a slightly different screen.

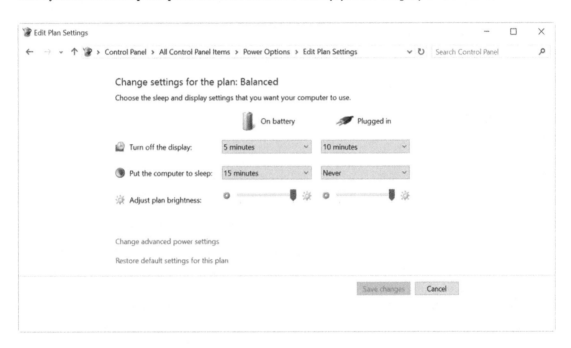

Figure 9-26. *Changing the display and sleep options*

If the computer is sleeping and Windows detects that the battery is very low, it changes to hibernate mode, in which the contents of memory are saved to the disc. This can prevent unsaved work from being lost, but it is always wise to check that your work is saved before you step away from your computer.

Alternatively, if you use your laptop with an external keyboard, mouse, and monitor, you may not want it to sleep when you close the lid. You can change this setting. I do not personally recommend that you use a laptop with the lid closed, however, because this can cause some models to overheat.

Controlling Sleep and Hibernation

While Sleep keeps the current contents of memory intact (including your running state of Windows 10 and your open apps), it requires a small and constant amount of power to keep the memory active. Hibernate (which is disabled by default) instead saves the contents of memory to a file on the hard disk, and restores it to memory when you next restart the PC. This can be useful for saving power, but it's obviously slower. The new Fast Start is a version of Hibernate that operates much more quickly; but you can turn Hibernate back on, which I discussed earlier.

You can choose the Sleep and Hibernation options for your computer by clicking either **Choose when to turn off the display** or **Change when the computer sleeps** on the Power Options page. You probably have seen these options available in other sections of Power Options; they remain the same.

Changing the Advanced Power Settings

When you are viewing the Sleep options, you see the option to **Change the advanced power settings**. Here you have many more options (click **Change settings that are currently unavailable** to edit them all). Figure 9-27 shows the advanced power settings.

Figure 9-27. *Changing the advanced power settings*

I want to talk about some of these settings and look at how they can be useful.

- **Hard disk**: Why might you want to turn off the hard disk? Hard disks unnecessarily consume a lot of energy when not in use. Perhaps you have multiple hard disks on your computer, and most of the time they are used only for file storage (perhaps files you don't often access) or for backups. Setting Windows 10 to turn off the hard disks on drives you are not using reduces overall power consumption on your computer. On any hard disk in use, the power remains. Remember that when you want to access a mechanical hard disk that is powered down, there is a slight delay as the disk spins up.

■ **Tip** If you want to set any timings in the advanced power settings to Never, change the default time to 0 (zero).

- **Wireless Adapter Settings**: Wi-Fi and mobile broadband are a huge power drain for a laptop, Ultrabook, or tablet because they turn your computer into a radio transmitter and receiver. If you change the default setting for locations in which you have a strong signal, you still get a good signal, which means that the computer uses less electricity to power the Wi-Fi system.

- **Sleep**: You can completely turn off Sleep and Hibernate if they cause problems on your computer.

- **USB Settings**: If your computer is connected to USB devices that draw power from the PC—perhaps an external hard disk or optical drive—you can enable a setting that cuts power to the devices when they are not in use. This can dramatically extend the life of a portable computer such as an Ultrabook.

- **Display**: While the main power options allow you to choose when to dim your computer's display to save power, these options give you finer control over exactly how much the display dims and how bright it is when plugged in. If your computer comes with a built-in light meter, you can turn on Adaptive Brightness, which automatically changes the brightness to match the available lighting.

- **Battery**: The battery options allow you to control what Windows 10 sees as low and critical battery levels. If you know that your battery is generally excellent and you don't want to be nagged, you could reduce the low-battery alert by 10 percent. If you often step away from your computer while it is running on battery, however, you might want to set Windows 10 to automatically hibernate when the battery runs low.

Summary

Windows 10, like all of its predecessors, is an extremely customizable operating system. Everything from the desktop and Start menu to the power systems can be customized in a variety of ways to suit many types of users.

Being able to personalize your computer is important to many computer users and it is a mainstay of the Windows operating system. Personalization options go far beyond what is included in this chapter. Chapter 10 shows how these options can be configured further to assist people who have difficulty using computers.

This all helps make Windows 10 the customizable operating system you want, while at the same time still affording you all the cool features it brings.

■ ■ ■

Making Windows 10 More Accessible and Easier to Use

User accessibility is one of the biggest challenges facing companies that make computers, operating systems, apps, and web sites. Accessibility is particularly important for touch-controlled systems, which improve computer use for people who have difficulty using a keyboard and mouse.

So who are the Windows' accessibility features for? People of all ages, from all walks of life, and of all abilities can benefit from them. Perhaps you need text to be larger, perhaps you've never used a computer, perhaps you're left-handed, or perhaps you find it difficult to stare at a screen for a long period of time.

In Windows 10, Microsoft has made the accessibility options easier to use than ever before; it begins when you sign in to your PC.

Accessibility Begins at Sign-In

Way back in Chapter 1, I described the various options and controls that can be found on the Windows 10 sign-in screen. One of these, next to the power button in the bottom right of the screen, is the Ease of Access (see Figure 10-1).

Figure 10-1. *You can access some accessibility options before signing in to your PC*

From here a pop-up dialog appears, containing on/off controls for the Narrator, Magnifier, permanent onscreen keyboard, high-contrast view, sticky keys, and filter keys (all of which I discuss throughout this chapter). Clicking or tapping any of these immediately turns on that feature for you on the PC.

Making Windows 10 Easier to Use

You can access the Windows 10 Ease of Access settings in the Settings app, found just above the power button in the bottom left corner of your screen when you open the Start menu; simply click Ease of Access (see Figure 10-2). Almost all the settings that make Windows easier to use are found here, certainly enough for general use, and most people find that there's no need to visit the full Ease of Access Center in the Control Panel (more on this in a moment).

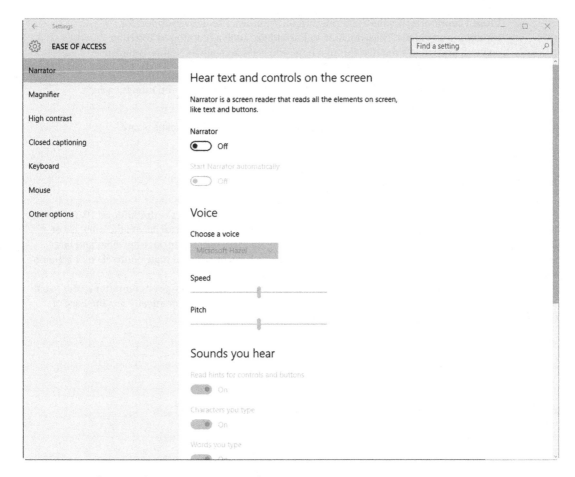

Figure 10-2. *The Ease of Access settings in Windows 10*

▪ **Note**   You can launch and switch to programs on the taskbar by pressing the Windows key + a number (1 to 0), where the number corresponds to the position of the icon on the taskbar.

The following lists the options listed in Ease of Access.

- **Narrator** turns on a facility whereby items onscreen are read to you by your PC.

- **Magnifier** makes the entire screen much larger and treats your monitor (and mouse) as a magnifying glass that moves across it.

- **High contrast** changes the default Windows color scheme to make the difference between background and foreground items much clearer and easier to see.

- **Closed captioning** is where you can turn on Windows 10's native support for captioning on videos. These include online videos, such as captioned YouTube content, and video streamed through apps and services such as Netflix, Amazon Prime, and Microsoft's own Film & TV app.

- **Keyboard** and **Mouse** feature controls for making your keyboard and mouse easier to use.

- **Other options** includes additional controls, such as the cursor thickness and whether the background wallpaper is displayed.

The Ease of Access Control Panel

So far, I've discussed how the Ease of Access options affect the way you interact with Windows 10. However, there are many more options available to you through the Control Panel. You can access the full Ease of Access Center through the Control Panel on the desktop. In the main part of the page are clear and large controls for turning on the Magnifier, the Narrator, the onscreen keyboard, and high-contrast color scheme (see Figure 10-3).

Below this, you see **Not sure where to start? Get recommendations to make your computer easier to use**. This option activates a wizard that asks you simple questions. The wizard automatically sets the Ease of Access Center settings according to the answers that you provide.

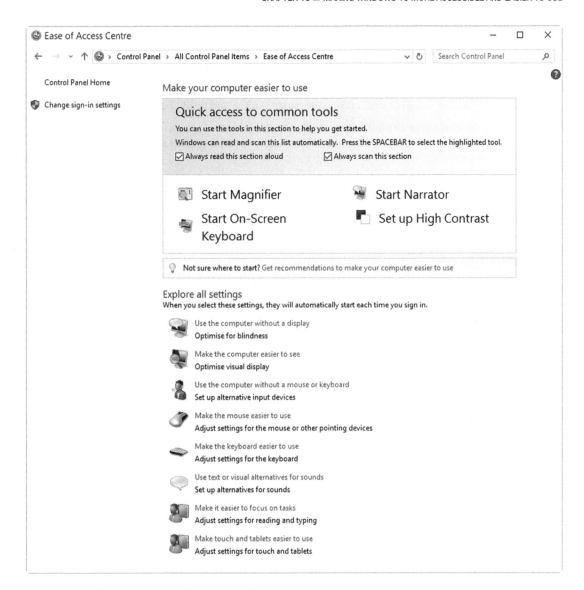

Figure 10-3. *The Ease of Access Control Panel*

■ **Tip**   If you have a motor skills disorder, you can turn off the snap and shake effects on the desktop (which snaps windows to the sides of your screen and minimizes all of your programs when you shake the mouse) by searching the Start screen for **shake** and clicking **Turn off automatic windows arrangement**. At the bottom of the window that appears, check **Prevent windows from being automatically arranged when moved to the edge of the screen**.

The following are the full Ease of Access Center options:

- **Use the computer without a display** optimizes the PC for use by the blind or partially sighted. It reads instructions aloud to help guide you through the settings.

- **Make the computer easier to see** contains many options, including turning on a high-contrast color scheme, making the cursor thicker, and turning on the Magnifier.

- **Use the computer without a mouse or keyboard** includes settings for permanently turning on the onscreen keyboard and for using speech recognition on your computer.

- **Make the mouse easier to use** switches the mouse buttons (if you are left-handed). It also offers other functions, including the ability to use the numeric pad on your keyboard as a mouse substitute.

■ **Tip**   As muscular problems such as repetitive stress syndrome (sometimes known as *repetitive strain injury* (RSI)) become more commonplace, it is becoming easier to find and purchase mice designed to help people continue to use their computer when a standard mouse and keyboard are uncomfortable to use. To find these devices, search online for **RSI** or **RSI mouse**.

- **Make the keyboard easier to use** turns on sticky keys so that you don't have to press two keys simultaneously when performing Ctrl + actions, among other functions.

- **Use text or visual alternatives for sounds** activates visual clues, such as flashing the desktop, on occasions when Windows 10 would ordinarily play a warning sound.

- **Make it easier to focus on tasks** turns off background images and animations. This option is useful for people who find background images distracting.

- **Make touch and tablets easier to use** offers the Windows key + Volume Up button options.

In the left navigation pane of the Ease of Access Center is an option to **Change sign-in settings**. It is here that you find additional options to automatically turn on Ease of Access features at Windows logon. This includes the onscreen keyboard, the Magnifier (so that you can see where to enter your password), and the Narrator (see Figure 10-4).

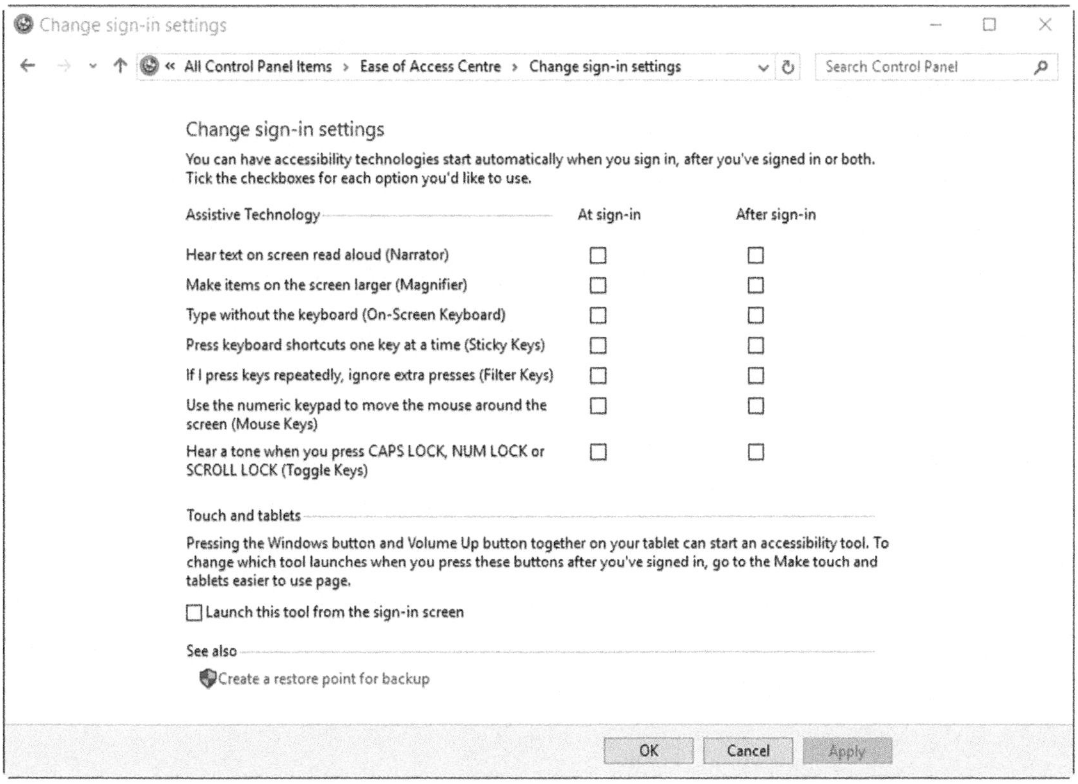

Figure 10-4. *Changing the Ease of Access sign-in settings*

Making Text and Windows Easier to Read

If you find the Windows desktop text and buttons difficult to see and read, there are several options that you can select and features that you can activate to help. These include the ability to scale up everything on the desktop to a maximum of 350% its normal size. Windows can do this without distorting anything on the screen.

To access this feature, right-click anywhere in a blank space on the desktop. From the context menu, select **Display settings**. You now see a **Change the size of text, apps and other items** slider control, which you can use to make everything larger or smaller on your screen (see Figure 10-5).

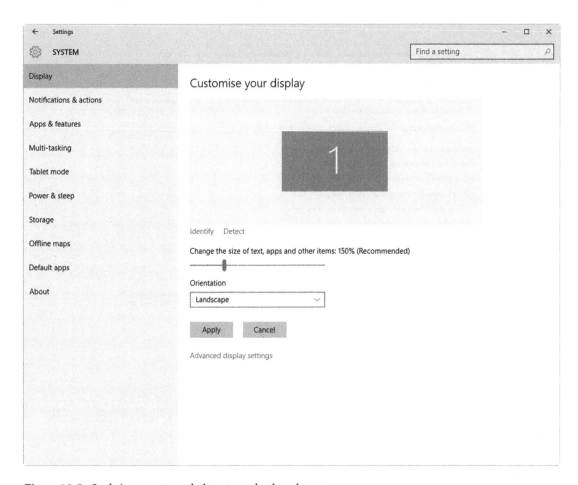

Figure 10-5. *Scale items on your desktop to make them larger*

This option makes everything on the screen proportionally larger without causing blurring, which is a common side effect of lowering the PC's screen resolution. You may want to scale up only certain types of text, however; perhaps even greater than the 150% offered. If you use multiple monitors, you can choose the scaling for your current screen by using the slider control, or you can set the scaling options for all of your screens by checking **Let me choose one scaling level for all my displays**.

You can alternatively scale only text on screen. To do this, click the **Advanced display settings** link, and then at the next panel, click **Advanced sizing of text and other items**. This displays additional scaling options (see Figure 10-6). Note that these text-scaling options tend to only be available on high-DPI (retina) displays and may not always be available to use.

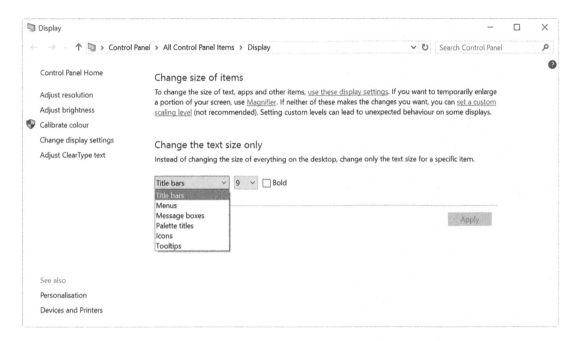

Figure 10-6. *You can just scale on screen text if you wish*

Below the main scaling options is an additional option to individually specify the size of a variety of text items on the screen. You can change the title bars on windows, menus, message boxes, palette titles, items, and tooltips. What this option doesn't allow you to do is further scale up the main text within windows and programs; but many software packages—including Edge and Microsoft Office—allow you to do this anyway, which I discuss shortly. Also with this option, you can specify that items always appear in bold to help them stand out.

In the left navigation pane, you see an option to **Adjust ClearType text**. ClearType is a system that Windows uses to make text more legible onscreen. There are many different types of screens, however, and people see in different ways, so the default settings may not be best suited for an individual user.

Clicking **Adjust ClearType text** displays a wizard in which Windows shows you different blocks of text. At each stage, you click the one that is most legible, and Windows automatically adjusts the ClearType settings accordingly, so that the text onscreen is at its most legible for you.

It is also possible to scale web pages and some document types. Not only does this make text easier to read, but it also makes some web sites easier to navigate because buttons and links become larger.

In both the Edge and Internet Explorer browsers (and in almost every other web browser too), you can zoom in and out of web sites by pressing the **Ctrl++** and **Ctrl+-** keys and also by holding down the Ctrl key and moving the mouse scroll wheel. These controls are also found in Edge options (see Figure 10-7). When you are using a touchscreen, most apps let you zoom in and out with two-finger pinch gestures.

Figure 10-7. *You can zoom in web pages*

Some document types allow zooming. For many years, the Microsoft Office desktop apps have offered a tool that is located on the bottom right of the Open window (see Figure 10-8). With this tool, you can zoom in and out of a document by using the slider or clicking the current percentage. If you are using Office Mobile apps, you can pinch-zoom with your fingers or use Ctrl + the mouse scroll wheel to zoom in and out of documents.

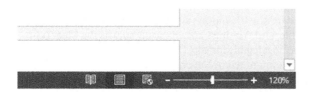

Figure 10-8. *Scaling documents*

■ **Tip**   You can zoom in and out of many apps and desktop programs in Windows 10 by pinch-zooming outward with a touch gesture. Some laptops come equipped with multitouch trackpads that support pinch-zoom gestures if you do not have a touchscreen.

Zooming in and out of documents on the desktop may not be sufficient enough to make text legible for some people; a high-contrast color scheme may be required if you are colorblind or visually impaired. To access the High Contrast options, open the Settings app, click **Ease of access**, and then **High contrast** (see Figure 10-9).

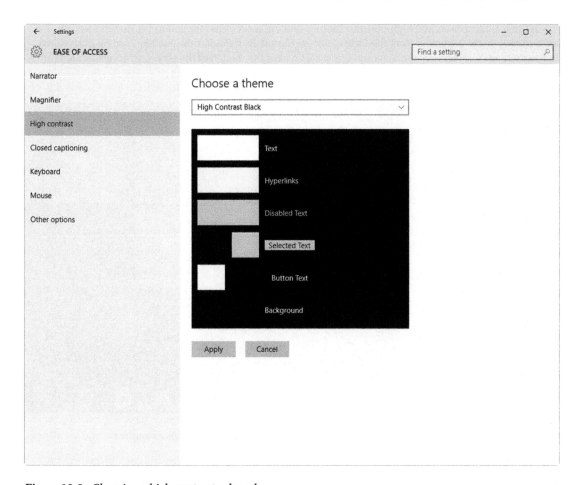

Figure 10-9. *Choosing a high-contrast color scheme*

There are also high-contrast desktop themes available from third-parties and charities to help with issues varying from poor eyesight to colorblindness and dyslexia. These are accessed from the Personalization options in the Control Panel. Your local charity or support organization can advise on the best combination of options for your specific circumstances.

If the scaling options and high-contrast themes don't make it easier for you to see in Windows 10, you can turn on the Magnifier from the Ease of Access Center. By default, this tool zooms in on everything on your screen. You can click the magnifying glass icon near the top left of the screen to access additional Magnifier controls (see Figure 10-10).

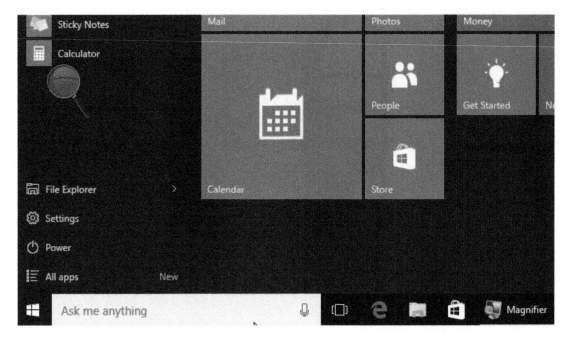

Figure 10-10. *The Magnifier displays a magnifying glass that you can click for more control*

The main controls for the Magnifier allow you to zoom in and out, as well as display the Magnifier in different ways:

- Your **Full screen** can be magnified, moving around under your cursor or finger as you navigate.

- A **Lens** can follow your cursor around the screen, zooming in on that portion of the screen.

- The Magnifier can be **Docked** to the top of the screen to display a larger version of the portion of the screen where your cursor is located.

All options are selected by clicking the magnifying glass icon to reveal the full Magnifier options (see Figure 10-11). Whatever view you choose, the Settings (cog) icon on the Magnifier options bar allow you to control how the magnifier works on your screen, helping you to find the settings that suit you best, including inverting screen colors to improve contrast and automatically jumping to text input boxes.

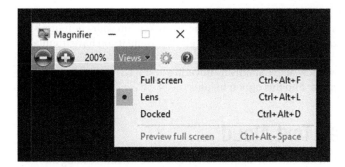

Figure 10-11. *Clicking in the magnifying glass reveals the full Magnifier controls*

■ **Tip**   If you are stuck in Magnifier view and are unsure how to disable it, look for the magnifying glass and click it (see Figure 10-10). It changes to the panel shown in Figure 10-11, in which you can click the Close button.

You can make the mouse cursor easier to see independently of the desktop theme as well. In the Ease of Access settings, click **Mouse**, which displays high-contrast options for the mouse, complete with images of what the cursor looks like for each option (see Figure 10-12).

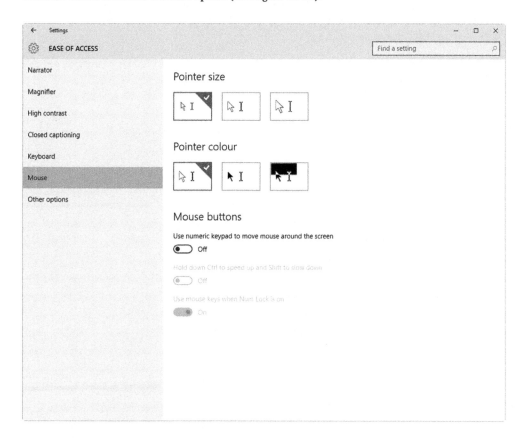

Figure 10-12. *Making the mouse easier to use*

By turning on Mouse Keys, you can also use the keyboard as a mouse, either as a replacement to or in conjunction with your regular mouse. This feature allows you to use the arrow keys on your computer's number pad (if your keyboard has one) to move the mouse cursor. It can also be useful if you have trouble using the mouse for long periods of time.

Other useful features include making a window active simply by hovering over it with your mouse. If you have difficulty with mouse buttons, you might find this option helpful.

Using the Narrator to Read Text Aloud

The Narrator tool assists those who are blind, or are partially sighted, or simply have trouble reading the computer screen. This feature reads out text and other items on your screen as you mouse over, touch, or click it. It also reads text in panels, such as web sites and Windows alert messages. As an onscreen item is read, it is highlighted in a blue box. This helps partially sighted people track what is being read. The Narrator is most easily switched on by pressing the Windows key to return to the Start screen, typing **narrator**, and then pressing the Enter key. You can start the Narrator from the Ease of Access Settings (see Figure 10-13).

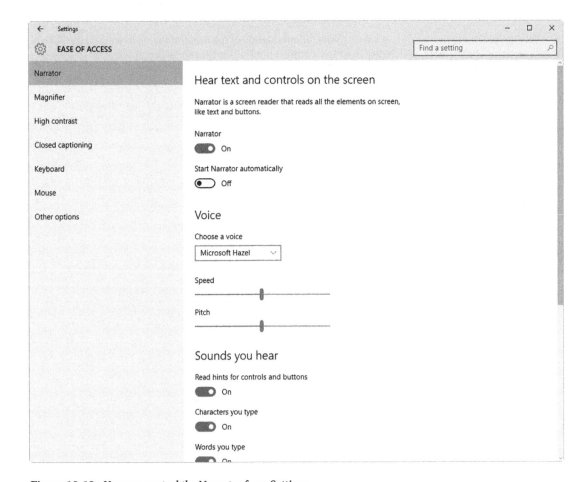

Figure 10-13. *You can control the Narrator from Settings*

Controls are available to make sure that the Narrator is automatically turned on when you sign in to your computer. Additional controls are found in the Narrator controls, including what the Narrator reads aloud (and if the volume of other things on your PC are lowered when the Narrator is on), if audio cues sound when an action is performed (such as successful button click), and how the mouse cursor and keyboard work with the Narrator.

There are also a significant number of keyboard shortcuts that you can use to control the Narrator. You can display a complete list of them at any time by pressing the **Caps Lock + F1** key combination. Most of the Narrator commands use the Caps Lock key because it isn't used for any other purpose. While the Narrator is on, you need to use the Shift key for capital letters.

The Narrator Settings (see Figure 10-14), which appear on your screen in a pop-up window when the Narrator starts, includes the welcome ability to speed up and slow down the narrator's voice. In the Voice section of the Narrator Settings window, there are slider controls that adjust the speed of the voice, which by default is set at 50%; the volume of the voice, which is set at maximum by default; and the pitch of the voice, which is set at 50%. There are also a variety of voices that you can select. The commands available for reading web sites have also been expanded to ensure that more items on a web page can be read aloud.

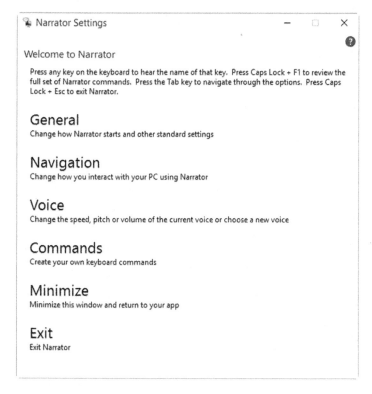

Figure 10-14. *The Narrator pop-out controls in Windows 10*

Windows 10 Narrator enhancements include ways to assist people with using touchscreen devices, including sounds to accompany actions that are performed with touch. These actions audibly confirm that your touch gesture was successful. The Narrator can also read text under your finger as you move it across the computer's screen.

It is important to note that if you want to use the Narrator with a touchscreen, the screen needs to support four or more touch points, because some of the Narrator touch gestures use three or four fingers. If you are buying a new touchscreen computer on which you want to use the Narrator, it is important to be aware of this.

Controlling the Narrator with Touch

When you use the narrator with a touchscreen, it reads aloud anything that you swipe your finger over, or you can tap an item to have it read individually. There are additional controls you can use, however, that directly control the Narrator (see Table 10-1).

Table 10-1. *Narrator Touch Gestures*

Effect	Action
Stop Narrator	Single, two-finger tap
Read all current window	Swipe up with three fingers
Click	Double-tap
Double-click	Triple-tap
Show or hide Narrator window	Tap with four fingers
Move to next or previous item	Flick left or right with one finger
Drag an item	Tap with three fingers
Scroll the window	Swipe up, down, left, or right with two fingers
Tab forward and backward	Swipe left or right with three fingers

When you are using the Narrator on a web site, additional controls are available, and as you flick up and down, you hear the PC read the following phrases. This is what they mean:

- **Heading view** speaks the headline and then highlights the previous/next one with a left/right swipe.

- **Item view** speaks and highlights the previous or next item on a page with a left/right swipe.

- **Paragraph view** speaks and highlights the previous or next paragraph with a left/right swipe.

- **Line view** speaks and highlights the previous or next line of text with a left/right swipe.

- **Word view** speaks and highlights the previous or next word with a left/right swipe.

- **Character view** speaks and highlights the previous or next character of text with a left/right swipe.

- **Table view** highlights and reads the previous or next table on the web site with a left/right swipe.

- **Link view** highlights and reads the previous or next link on the page with a left/right swipe. The link can then be activated with a double-tap.

Controlling the Narrator with the Keyboard

If you are using the Narrator with a keyboard, Table 10-2 describes the controls that you can use.

Table 10-2. *Narrator Keyboard Commands*

Effect	Action
Click the selected item	Spacebar or Enter
Move the cursor around the screen	Tab + cursor keys
Read item	Caps Lock + D
Read entire document	Caps Lock + H
Read last read item	Caps Lock + V
Read entire window	Caps Lock + W
Move to previous/next item	Caps Lock + left or right cursor
Adjust volume	Caps Lock + Page Up or Page Down
Adjust reading speed	Caps Lock + plus (+) or minus (-)
Turn Caps Lock on or off	Press Caps Lock twice quickly
Stop reading	Ctrl
Exit Narrator	Caps Lock + Esc

Making Your Keyboard and Mouse Easier to Use

It is common for people to have trouble using devices like the mouse. Windows features such as Shake, although perhaps very useful for some people, might prove to be hugely irritating for others. Shake is a desktop feature that minimizes all the windows on the screen when you shake the mouse; it is not very useful if you have difficulty in using a mouse.

To turn off Shake and Snap (they can only be switched off together), follow these instructions:

1. Search for **shake** in the Settings app search box (top right corner of the window) and open **Turn off automatic window arrangement**.

2. In the dialog that appears, check the box **Prevent windows from being automatically arranged when moved to the edge of the screen**.

Additional settings for the mouse, (see Figure 10-15), are located by opening **Devices** and then **Mouse & touchpad** in the Settings app, and then clicking the **Additional mouse options** link.

- The **Double-Click Speed** of the mouse can be modified to suit you. If you find that you can't double-click the mouse at the speed Windows wants, you can slow it down.

- **ClickLock** is a feature that makes it easier to drag items on the screen. With this feature activated, you don't need to hold down the mouse button to drag. Click the mouse button once to select an item and then click it again to drop it. This feature works with both the mouse and the trackpad.

- Windows 10 includes several different schemes to modify the mouse **Pointers**, including the option for large and high-visibility pointers.

- The **Pointer Speed** can be modified in Windows so that the mouse moves more slowly.

- **Snap To** is a useful feature that moves the mouse pointer automatically onto a button when you get close to it.

- **Pointer Trails** can be displayed so that you can more easily see where the mouse is on the screen.

- The ability to **highlight the location of your mouse pointer** on the screen is particularly useful. It is made available when you press the Ctrl key on your keyboard.

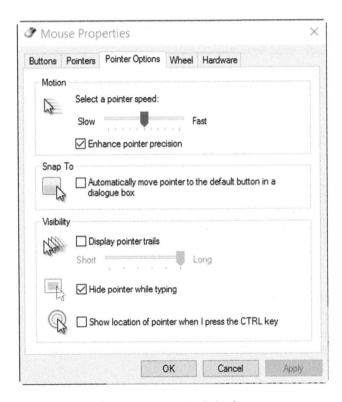

Figure 10-15. *The Mouse Properties dialog box*

■ **Tip** Left-handed computer users can switch the mouse buttons in the Mouse Properties settings.

In the Ease of Access settings, you can turn on various additional features for the computer's keyboard by clicking Make the keyboard easier to use, see Figure 10-16. A feature called Sticky Keys is particularly useful.

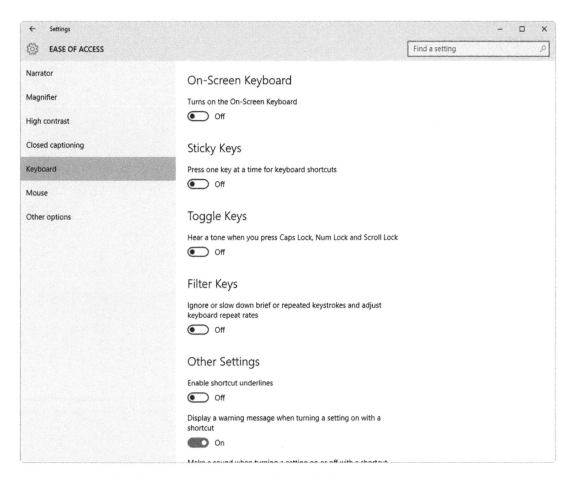

Figure 10-16. *Keyboard ease of access options are also available*

Sticky Keys allows you to use the keyboard one key at a time. If you need to press a keyboard combination involving the Shift, Ctrl, Alt, or even the Windows key (it is supported even though the Sticky Keys options don't specify it), just press one of these keys, wait to hear a tone while pressing the key, and then press the letter associated with that keystroke (for example Ctrl+C).

Filter Keys is a useful feature that prevents repeated instances of a letter, number, or other character when a particular key is pressed.

Making It Easier to Focus on Tasks

There may be times when you can't hear an alert or another sound on your computer; or to hear, you need the volume turned up to a level where other people complain about it. To help with these issues, Windows 10 offers visual cues to alert you when it would normally use a sound.

From the Ease of Access settings, click **Other options**. These include flashing the active window title bar to help you find it, playing or hiding window animation, and even hiding the desktop wallpaper altogether (see Figure 10-17). From this panel you can also choose how long pop-up toast notifications appear, from the default setting of 5 seconds or up to 5 minutes. Toasts can be dismissed by clicking the Close button in their top-right corner.

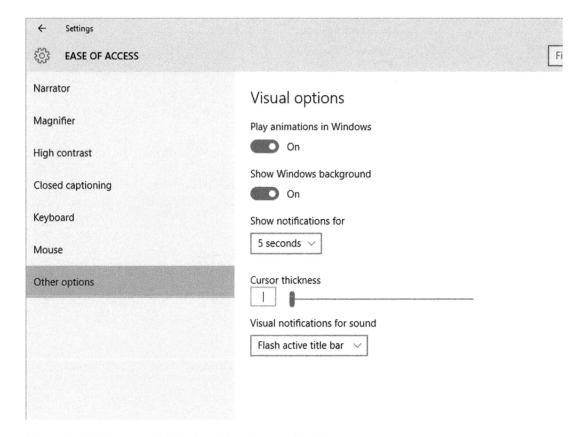

Figure 10-17. *You can make Windows 10 easier to work with*

You can find additional options by opening the Ease of Access Center in the Control Panel, which has an option to **Use text or visual alternatives for sounds** and **Make it easier to focus on tasks**. This page includes many of the common accessibility controls, such as Sticky Keys, the Narrator, and Filter Keys. You can also turn off the desktop background image in this option.

Training Windows 10's Handwriting Recognition

Windows 10's handwriting recognition is pretty good, but you might find that personally it could use some extra training. You can do this by opening the **Language options** from the Control Panel (available on the Win+X menu), highlighting the language you want to train, and clicking the **Options** link to its right. In the window that appears next, click the **Personalize handwriting recognition** link (see Figure 10-18).

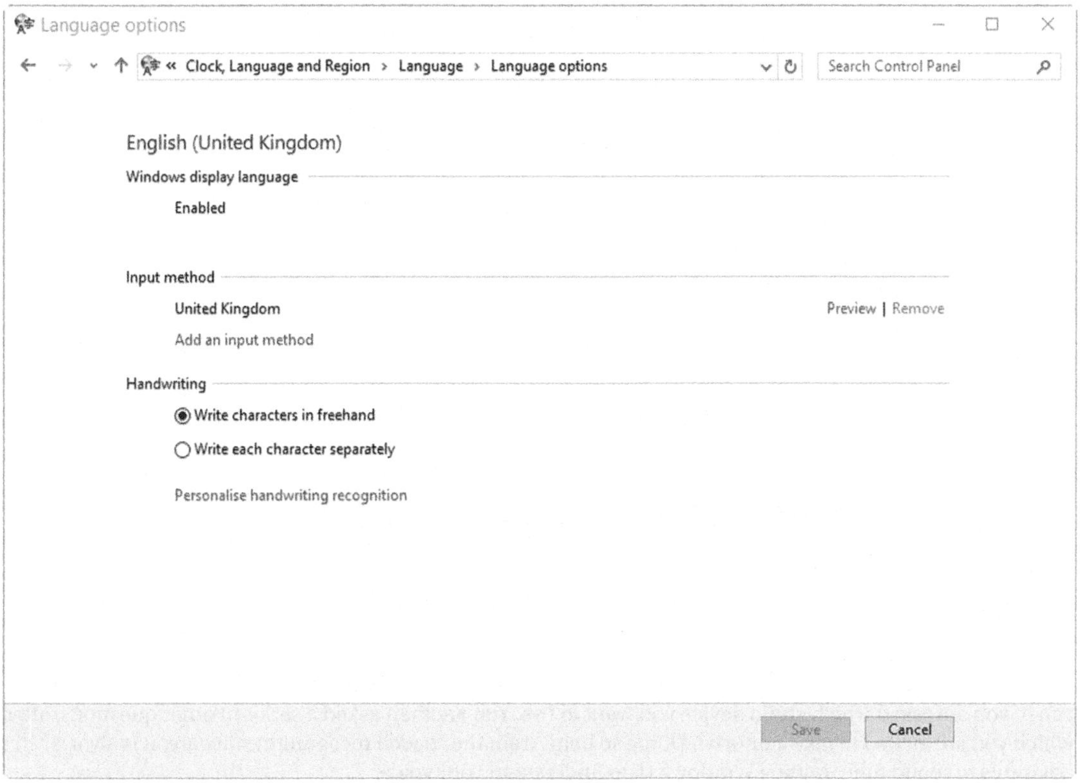

Figure 10-18. Accessing the handwriting recognition training

The training window now appears (see Figure 10-19). Here you can choose whether to retrain Windows where it makes specific errors with your handwriting or to train it more generally. Note that this second option can take time to complete.

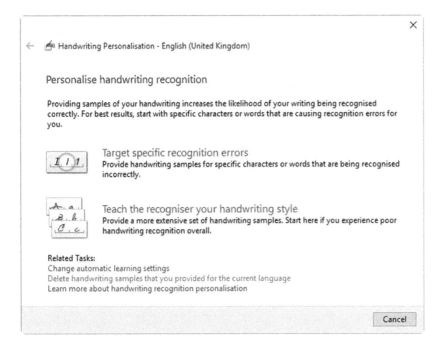

Figure 10-19. *You can train Windows 10's handwriting recognition*

Using Speech Recognition with Windows 10

Windows 10 allows you to control your PC using speech, either through a microphone built into a tablet, laptop, or Ultrabook, or through a headset. In the Settings app, under **Time & language** and then **Speech**, you can set up your microphone to work with your PC, which you may already have done if you're using Cortana.

You can access the speech recognition utility by searching for speech from the Start screen; when you run it, you are asked which audio device you want to use. You are then asked a series of other questions, after which you are invited to take a tutorial. Doing so helps train the speech recognition software; it is always advisable to spend time training Windows 10 to understand your voice.

There is a reference card that you are invited to view; printing this card can be extremely helpful in remembering the different voice commands for the speech recognition software. When it's running, the speech recognizer floats on your desktop and can be docked to the top or bottom of the screen (see Figure 10-20).

Figure 10-20. *The speech recognizer floats on your desktop*

Generally speaking, the speech recognition software in Windows 10 is excellent; indeed this section of the book was written by using it, which was rather handy because I had a fractured wrist at the time.

Full controls for the speech recognizer can be easily accessed by right-clicking the speech recognizer window. These controls include options to continue the speech recognition training and to configure both the speech recognizer and your microphone.

Common Speech Recognition Controls

Although it is a good idea to keep a copy of the reference card handy, there are some commands that you will often use:

- **Start** and the name of a program; for example, saying "Calculator," or "Word," or "Excel" starts these programs.

- **Switch to** and the name of a program switches to that program if it is already running.

- You can control programs that have drop-down menus by speaking the name of that menu and then speaking the name of the option you want to select from it. This also works for ribbon controls in Windows 10, Microsoft Office, and other programs that use it.

- **Show numbers** displays numbers overlaid on a program's controls; these numbers can then be spoken to activate the controls (see Figure 10-21).

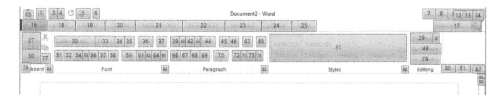

Figure 10-21. *You can activate a program's controls with the speech recognizer*

- On a web page, you can select a link by saying its name; for example, "Contact us."

- You can activate clicking an item by saying "double-click" or "right-click" for a specific item; for example, "Double-click Recycle bin."

- **Start Listening/Stop Listening** turns the speech recognition system on or off.

- **What can I say?** Will list the things you can say to your PC to activate commands and launch apps.

- **Show speech options** displays the list of options for the speech recognizer; it is also available via a right-click.

- **Show speech recognition/Hide speech recognition** minimizes the speech recognizer to the system tray or returns it to the desktop.

If at any time the speech recognizer does not recognize something you have said, it displays an Alternatives Panel that contains its best guesses at what you said (see Figure 10-22). You can make a choice from this panel by saying the number to the left of the correct item. This has the added benefit of helping train the Windows 10 speech recognition system. Alternatively, it might display a pop-up in the top-left corner of your screen, allowing you to type the command instead.

Figure 10-22. The speech recognition system lets you know if it is unsure of what you said

Where to Find Accessibility Help and Support

Many of the option pages in the Ease of Access Center from the Control Panel offer you the option to **Learn about additional assistive technologies online**. Clicking this link directs you to the Microsoft web site at www.microsoft.com/enable. Here you can read more about the accessibility features in Windows 10, as well as view videos and other tutorials on their use.

This web site also contains links to third-party help, support, and commercial web sites where you can find advice and products designed to help make your computer more accessible and easier to use.

Summary

The accessibility features in Windows 10 are extensive and make Windows 10 the most accessible operating system available today. I recommend starting at the desktop Ease of Access Center wizard. Run it by clicking **Get recommendations to make your computer easier to use**. The wizard asks you a series of questions about how you use your computer and where you find it difficult to use. It then makes recommendations for settings that you can select to make Windows 10 easier to use.

■ ■ ■

CHAPTER 11

Keeping You, Your Files, and Your Computer Safe

Back in the days of Windows 98 and Windows XP, Microsoft's desktop operating system had a reputation of being insecure and highly vulnerable to attack, and in fairness, this reputation was well deserved. Being designed in the days before pervasive Internet access, Microsoft didn't (or perhaps didn't have to) concentrate on much more than a PC being a stand-alone machine connected to nothing more than the office network.

This certainly isn't true anymore, however, as since the advent of Windows Vista, and a wholesale upgrading of the security systems in the OS, Windows is now one of the most secure operating systems on the planet. It's also not true that the security systems in Windows 10 are annoying, or lacking in flexibility, or difficult to use.

By default, Windows 10 is actually very good at taking care of itself. It needs to be. Most users don't want to worry about updates to Windows and anti-malware software. They certainly don't want to have to change firewall settings to allow a game through a port.

If anything, the default settings for security in Windows 10 really are perfectly all right for general computer usage. If anything will be exploited, it's the soft, squidgy thing sitting at the keyboard, vulnerable to criminals who get them to click something that allows malware through the already excellent security in Windows 10.

Windows 10 includes more than just anti-malware software and security features, though, because there are also government-level file and disk encryption technologies that can be as simple to set up and use as a fresh user account.

In this chapter, I'll talk you through all the security features in the operating system, explain what they do, and show you how you can customize them to meet your own individual needs.

How Secure Is Windows 10 Really?

Windows 10 is arguably the most secure version of Windows in the history of the operating system due to the inclusion of extensive new security features in the OS, for both Enterprise and home users. It builds on previous security features, including User Account Control (UAC), which was first introduced in Windows Vista and anti-malware in Windows 8.

You cannot rely on an operating system to be secure on its own, though. Every time you install a program or an app, you open the possibility of compromising your security. When you go online or check your email, you open the possibility that someone, somewhere, might attempt to trick you into installing malware.

It is important to look at Windows 10 security in a holistic way, not in isolation. In this chapter, I'll show you how to make sure that Windows 10 is completely secure. This chapter also sometimes refers to Chapter 3, in which I showed you how to stay safe when you are connected to the Internet.

Maintaining Security When Using Windows 10 with Other Windows Versions

Windows 10 is secure, and Windows 8.1 and Windows 7 are also secure, at least when all precautions and safeguards are put in place and when features such as UAC remain turned on at their default settings. The one caveat with this is the shelf life of each operating system, and this is why I've not included Windows Vista, which is also secure, in this list. All extended support (and by this I mean security, vulnerability, and stability patches and updates) for Windows Vista ends (or ended, depending on when you're reading this book) in April 2017. For Windows 7, it's in January 2020, and for Windows 8.1, it's in January 2023. Windows XP is already out of support.

After these dates, each of these operating systems should be considered unsafe to use, as there will inevitably be vulnerabilities—some of which criminals may already know about but have been quietly sitting on—that will *never* be patched by Microsoft.

Computers are commonly used in a networked environment with other Windows PCs, not all of which run the same version of Windows. It is possible that some of these PCs are running Windows 7, or perhaps even Windows XP for a mission-critical function. All security and update support ended for Windows XP in April 2014. This means that there are no longer updates or patches to fix security or other vulnerabilities. If you are using your Windows 10 computer in an environment in which there is an XP machine, that XP machine should be completely sandboxed and denied access to your network, and certainly the Internet.

The reason for this is that Windows XP is still used in the developing world and some countries in Asia. So the Windows XP operating system is a huge target for malware writers and hackers. After 12 years of patches and updates, there really shouldn't be any security flaws left, but you can be certain that some will still exist and be the targets of criminals.

You should also be wary of sharing files and folders with Windows 8.1, Windows 7, and Windows Vista, which is the main way that malware spreads on a home or work network. This is because you may not know how the other computers on that network are managed or what their security is like. You may be using your Windows 10 computer in a workplace in which all computers are managed the same way. Here you can be confident that the environment is enclosed with an SEP field[1] and is the responsibility of the IT department.

Maintaining Security When Using Windows 10 with Non-Windows Operating Systems

If you are using Windows 10 in an environment in which there are other operating systems, people's views might differ. If the other computers were Apple iMacs, for example, then some would argue that they're more secure than Windows. In fact, I would argue that the opposite is true because Apple doesn't adopt the same stringent policy for quickly issuing security updates and patches that Microsoft does. As a result, Apple can be slow to respond to threats such as the malware attack in early 2012 that infected some 600,000 Apple Mac computers.

---

[1]In the comedy science-fiction book, *Life, the Universe and Everything* by Douglas Adams (Pan Macmillan, 1982), an SEP field is described as "something we can't see, or don't see, or our brain doesn't let us see, because we think that it's somebody else's problem … The brain just edits it out, it's like a blind spot. If you look at it directly you won't see it unless you know precisely what it is. Your only hope is to catch it by surprise out of the corner of your eye."

The technology involved in making something properly invisible is so mind-bogglingly complex that 999,999,999 times out of a billion it's simpler just to take the thing away and do without it. The "Somebody Else's Problem field" is much simpler, more effective, and "can be run for over a hundred years on a single torch battery".

This is because it relies on people's natural predisposition not to see anything they don't want to, weren't expecting, or can't explain.

Computers running Linux are unlikely to pose a threat to your own computer security because the overall market share for this operating system isn't large enough to get the attention of malware writers.

This brings us to tablets, where Apple's iOS operating system and Windows 10 are perfectly secure—but Google's Android is anything but. This is because Google does not vet programs submitted to its app store in the same way that Apple and Microsoft do. As a result, any tablets or computers running Android should always be treated with caution.

The Myth of Mac and iOS Security   Although it's true that, historically, Apple's Mac computers have been *almost* invulnerable to malware attacks due to the way the security of the Unix-based operating system was designed, this is sadly no longer the case. In recent years, malware writers—primarily in response to improved security in Windows but also because of the popularity of the iPhone and iPad, which share the same core OS—have focused more on tricking the Mac user into installing and permitting malware. This—along with Apple's slow response to some malware threats, as well as the rapid market growth for Apple devices—has greatly increased the threat to the platform.

Managing Your Privacy

Our online privacy is extremely important in these days of ubiquitous Internet access. The firewalls I've described in this chapter are, pretty much, all that stands between us and every other PC, laptop, tablet, smartphone, and server on the planet. Okay, so that's an oversimplification, but it's an example of how our computers were designed to connect simply and straightforwardly to others, and how the Internet was designed to permit those connections over vast distances.

Almost every week there are new stories about hacking attacks on and privacy failures by companies, and even governments, where valuable data was stolen. Early 2015 saw a massive data breach on the US government, where the data of millions of government employees was compromised. This is just one example of why data security is crucial.

Managing Advertising and Handwriting

You can secure your own PC using the methods I've described in this chapter, but you can also minimize the surface for a breach of your own data by simply limiting the data that apps and companies are allowed to store about you in the first place. You'll be pleased to hear that Windows 10 makes this simpler than ever before.

The Settings app contains a whole section for Privacy (see Figure 11-1), so I thought I'd spend some time showing you how to leverage the settings here to your best advantage.

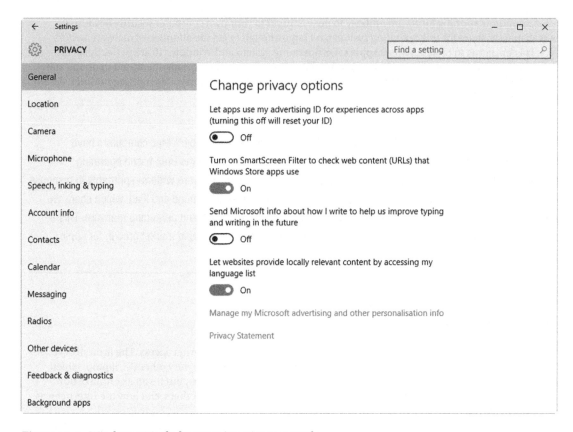

Figure 11-1. *Windows 10 includes extensive privacy controls*

Windows 10 and Microsoft's Bing search engine are heavily entwined, and have been since the days of Windows 8.1. Bing is used by features such as Windows 10 search and Cortana. Microsoft also uses information it knows about you to display new app suggestions in the Start menu.

Fortunately, Windows 10 makes it easy to control all of this, and the General tab of the Privacy options is where you start. The first option controls your Advertising ID, which is a unique ID assigned to you that permits advertisers to track what you do and look at online and in your apps, and which advertisements you click on.

■ **Note**   The option for the SmartScreen Filter should *not* be switched off. SmartScreen compliments Windows Defender and the Windows Firewall by intercepting malicious downloads and malicious software installs onto your computer.

Additionally, here you can control how you help Microsoft with its handwriting recognition. Occasionally, you might write something that Windows 10 doesn't recognize. This information can be sent to Microsoft to help them manually adjust the handwriting engine across all Windows 10 devices, although you would have no way of knowing what text is sent to Microsoft and you may wish to opt out.

Controlling Location Tracking

It might surprise you to learn that you don't need to have GPS hardware in your PC or smartphone for it to be trackable. For years we've watched spy thrillers where the protagonist was tracked across countries or even continents in real-time just though their phone or PC. Well, if you use a Windows 10 Mobile device and sign-into your account at `https://account.microsoft.com/devices/`, you can track your handset's location in near real-time by using the **Find My Phone** feature (see Figure 11-2).

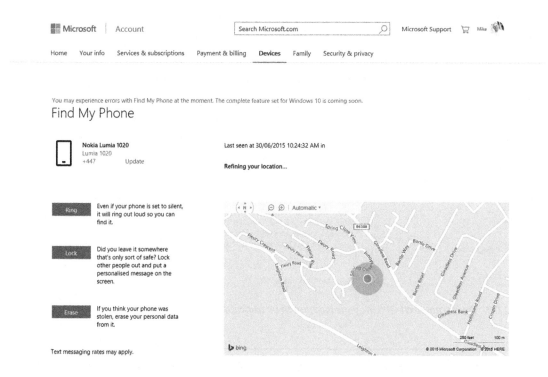

Figure 11-2. *You can track devices without GPS*

■ **Note**   To use the Find My Phone feature in Windows 10 Mobile it needs to be activated in Settings ➤ Update & security ➤ Find my phone.

Using the Find My Phone feature, you can also remotely ring, lock, and even completely erase your phone, should it be lost or stolen. While having this functionality on smartphones can be very useful, you might feel differently about your location being tracked on your PC, especially when it could pinpoint your home. If you're a business leader, the latest pop sensation, or even, heaven forbid, someone who just values your own privacy, you'll be pleased to hear that you can switch off this functionality.

The Location tab of the Settings app is where you will find the controls that you need (see Figure 11-3). You can also clear the location history for the PC with a single click to control which apps are allowed access to your location data (should you have it switched on). You might, for example, want the weather app to have access, but not social media apps. You can control each switch with a single click.

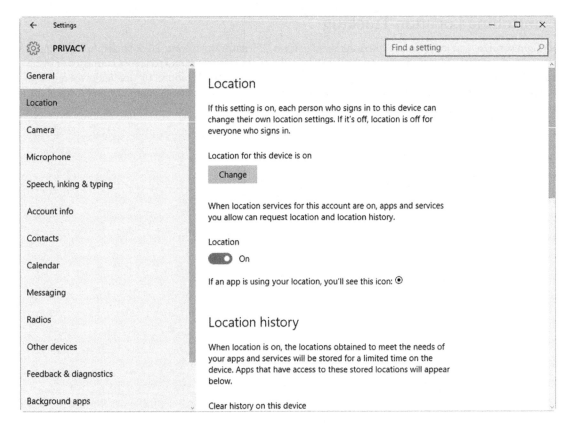

Figure 11-3. *You do not need GPS for your location to be trackable*

■ **Caution**   While you can control privacy settings for apps, this only applies to apps downloaded from the Windows Store. Classic win32 desktop apps will not be controllable in this manner.

Additional Privacy Controls

The Privacy settings for Windows 10 also include controls for your Microphone (see Figure 11-4), Camera (if your PC has one), Microsoft account information (such as your picture, email address, and name), Contacts, Calendar, and SMS and MMS messaging. For each of these, you can see which Store apps already have permission to access these devices or data, and you might not want to disable them completely. For example, you will still want an email app to access your contacts, calendar, and email address if you sign in to your PC using a Microsoft account.

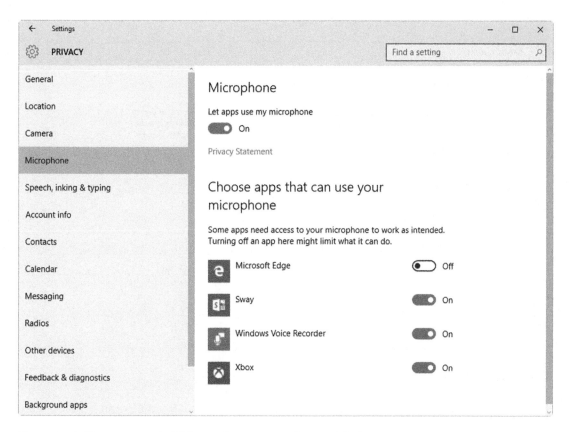

Figure 11-4. *You can control which apps have access to data and devices*

Speech and Writing

If you use speech recognition (to control your PC or to talk to Cortana) or write using a pen or stylus, your entries may not be easily understood by Windows 10, and thus could be sent to Microsoft to help improve the speech and handwriting recognition services. This happens automatically and transparently in the background and you won't be aware of it. However, this also means you have no control over what is sent, as there's no way for you to know what Windows 10 is likely to understand and what it isn't. Should you not wish to have this information tracked by Windows 10 and, if need be, sent to Microsoft, you can click the **Stop getting to know me** button on the **Speech, inking & typing** settings (see Figure 11-5).

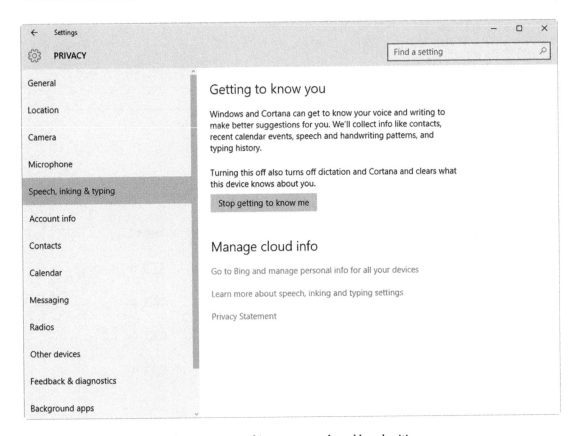

Figure 11-5. *You can tell Windows to stop tracking your speech and handwriting*

Radios and Other Devices

They might not appear to be, but modern PCs, laptops, tablets, and smartphones are constantly sending and receiving radio transmissions. It's not just Wi-Fi and your cellular signal either. Modern Bluetooth systems can transmit data up to 30—or even 100—feet from the device and can receive as well as send files and web links.

The **Radio** and **Other devices** privacy settings allow you to control all the wireless operations of your PC in relation to what apps are allowed to access them. For example, you'd want your fitness band app to have access to Bluetooth, but perhaps not the phone sync app you downloaded the other week.

Additionally, in the **Other devices** panel you can see a list of all the trusted devices your PC is connected to (see Figure 11-6). A trusted device is anything you have previously connected to, including an Xbox One console, a TV, a projector, a wireless display, a smartphone, network-attached storage (NAS), or Chromecast.

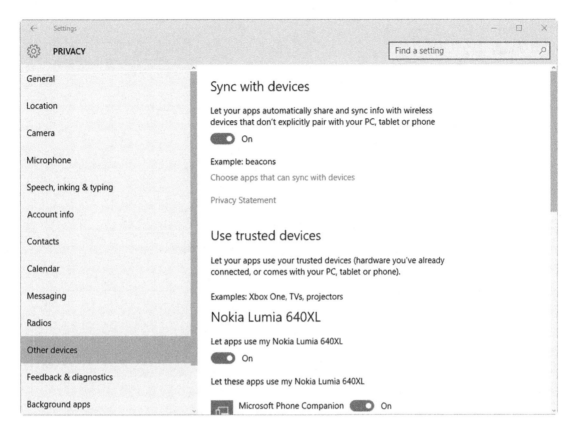

Figure 11-6. *Windows 10 allows you to control privacy for wireless and USB devices*

Trusted devices are ones that Windows 10 happily communicates and exchanges data with, because you've already approved it. If you later decide, however, that you no longer want to trust a particular device, or if you trusted a device that you hadn't intended to, you can disable it here.

Feedback and Background Apps

Much of what your apps and Windows 10 do goes on in the background, such as autochecking for new email, syncing with a fitness tracker, and so on. The **Background apps** settings allow you to choose which Store apps (this doesn't apply to win32 desktop apps) are allowed to run in the background. This is important for two reasons: first, you might not want a specific app running all the time, but perhaps more importantly, you can significantly extend the amount of run time for your laptop's, tablet's, or smartphone's battery by limiting the apps that can run on their own.

Additionally, Windows 10 will sometimes want to share information about your PC with Microsoft. This information is about how you use your PC(s) for their Customer Experience Improvement program. This data is analyzed by Microsoft and used to improve Windows and its other products and services. Should you not wish for your PC to share this data, perhaps even for a reason like reducing the amount of Internet data you use, you can disable it in the **Feedback and diagnostics** settings (see Figure 11-7).

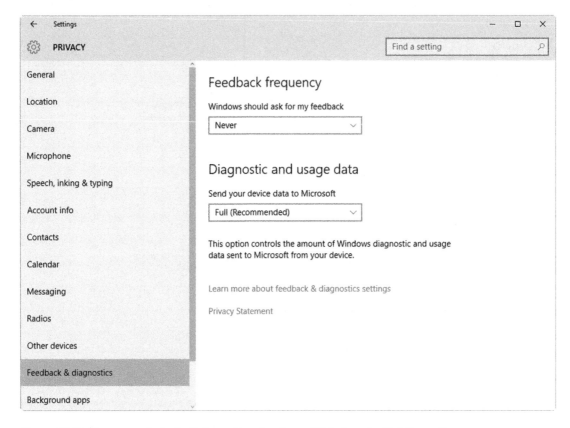

Figure 11-7. You can control what information about your PC is shared with Microsoft

Windows Defender

I started this chapter by saying that Windows 10 is the first version of Windows to come with built-in security software. Some of you may balk at the suggestion that Windows Defender—a rebadged version of Microsoft's free anti-malware solution, Security Essentials—is actually effective at defending against malware at all.

In truth, Windows Defender has often not stood up well against other anti-malware packages in tests. So unless you want a really resource-light PC and you are confident that you will never visit web sites where malware may be found, or are sent files that might contain viruses, you may want to consider an alternative. I talk through some of the alternative packages later in this chapter.

Windows Defender is based on Microsoft's System Center Endpoint Protection anti-malware package for Windows Server and it can be an effective package. When you look at the quarterly reports for the effectiveness of all the major anti-malware packages, there is always some fluctuation in the brand rankings, depending on the threats that have been found in the previous six months and how effectively the manufacturers dealt with them.

There is no really compelling reason not to use Windows Defender if you feel that you want to. I never recommend installing any software that duplicates functionality that's already in Windows because this adds layers of complexity that can lead to problems, although perhaps anti-malware is one area I'm prepared to allow some flexibility.

Configuring and Updating Windows Defender

Windows Defender can be found in the Settings app in the Update and Security section (see Figure 11-8). Here are the main controls you need to protect your PC with anti-malware. It's a straightforward affair with on/off switches that allow you control.

- **Real-time protection**: The main anti-malware scanning engine. **Do not** turn this off unless you are using a third-party anti-malware app.

- **Cloud-based protection**: Assists the Microsoft user community by automatically sending information about discovered threats to Microsoft.

- **Sample submission**: Sends samples of discovered or possible malware to Microsoft. This is a separate option, as it may involve sending copies of your infected or suspect files and documents to Microsoft.

- **Exclusions**: The area where you can specify the files that will not be scanned by Windows Defender, perhaps because they are special file types needed for work that are often misdiagnosed as being malicious.

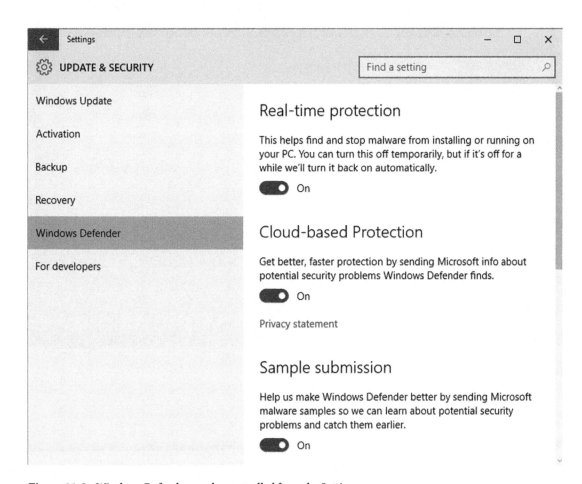

Figure 11-8. *Windows Defender can be controlled from the Settings app*

■ **Note**   Real-time protection should remain switched on. If you deactivate it, Windows Defender can't scan new files or web sites as you open them.

You might be used to being able to right-click any file or folder in File Explorer and perform an anti-malware scan from there. With Windows Defender in Windows 10, however, the entire process is automated, and as such, this option is not available to you.

It is possible to get much more control over Windows Defender in Windows 10, and to perform both full and custom scans. You can do this by opening the Control Panel in large or small icon view, and clicking the Windows Defender link. This opens the desktop control applet for the feature (see Figure 11-9).

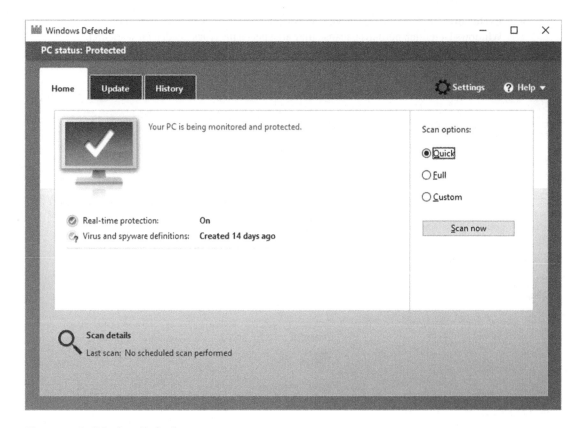

Figure 11-9. *Windows Defender*

Windows Defender has quite a simple interface with just three tabs: Home, Update, and History.

- The **Home tab** provides details about the current update and scanning status of the software. It allows access to perform quick, full, and custom scans. A custom scan includes scanning an external hard disk, for example.

- The **Update tab** provides information on when the software was last updated. The large Update button updates the software. It really is that simple.

- The **History tab** allows you to view reports of any suspicious or dangerous files. This does mean that Windows Defender isn't as configurable as some other packages, but why do we need anti-malware software to be configurable anyway? I would argue that the whole point of anti-malware software is to always provide complete protection while staying out of the way.

Staying out of the way is something that Windows Defender does extremely well, because it runs scans and downloads updates only when you're not using the computer. This means that if you're working, gaming, or doing some other intensive job on your PC, Windows Defender doesn't hog processor cycles or memory trying to update itself or run a full scan.

■ **Note**   Windows Defender is updated through Windows Update, so it is extremely important not to switch this service off.

Finding and Installing Third-Party Anti-Malware Software

So what other anti-malware packages are available? Which should you choose? I recommend six that I believe are worthy of consideration because they have consistently scored highly in anti-malware scanning tests over the last few years:

- **ESET Smart Security** (www.eset.com) is the anti-malware software that I use. It's powerful and flexible for those people who want a fine level of control, and straightforward enough for everyone else. This is a paid-for suite with no free version.

- **AVG Anti-Virus Free** (http://free.avg.com) has long been considered one of the best packages available. There is a free version, although in recent years it's become rather obtrusive with annoying ads encouraging you to upgrade to the full-paid suite.

- **Avast Anti-Virus** (www.avast.com) has free and paid-for versions that are highly effective and nonintrusive.

- **Norton 360** (www.symantec.com) isn't free, or even relatively cheap, but is well worth considering. It has a friendly, simple interface and is extremely effective at protecting your computer.

- **Trend Micro Titanium** (www.trendmicro.com) is another highly effective anti-malware package. It isn't free.

- **Kaspersky Anti-Virus** (http://usa.kaspersky.com) is an extremely configurable security package. For the power user who wants a very fine level of control, it is an extremely suitable option. This is not a free product.

It is not as easy to recommend McAfee's anti-malware products because they have been known to cause problems in recent years. Also, McAfee's scanning and protection capabilities are not as good as they used to be.

Online and Offline Anti-Malware Scanners

Most of the main anti-malware vendors have online scanning tools that can be run from within a web browser. You can search for these on the anti-malware vendor's web site. Additionally, there are some very effective offline malware scanners that start your computer from a USB flash drive or CD to scan for and remove malware.

Regardless of what I said earlier about McAfee, it is difficult to criticize the quality of its offline offerings (`www.mcafee.com/us/downloads/free-tools/index.aspx`), which include the malware removal tools GetSusp and Stinger.

Microsoft also has an offline anti-malware package called Microsoft Safety Scanner (`www.microsoft.com/security/scanner`), which scans your computer for malware and removes it.

AVG has a downloadable Rescue CD that you can get from (`www.avg.com/us-en/avg-rescue-cd`) that includes anti-malware scanning.

You should download these tools only as required. Do not use older versions. This ensures that the software version you use includes the most up-to-date malware data.

Using the Windows Firewall

Like Windows Defender, the Windows Firewall could be described as having a split personality, but in this case, there are no controls in the Windows 10 Settings app, because the firewall is intended to always be used as initially configured and not disabled. On initial examination, it's no more complicated to use than its anti-malware cousin, but the number of configuration options are huge under the surface.

Configuring and Maintaining the Windows Firewall

The basic Windows 10 Firewall window, which you can open by searching for **firewall** at the Start menu, doesn't offer many features and certainly doesn't offer a large Turn the Firewall Off button. It gives you information about the network you are currently connected to and shows you the current state of the firewall as it pertains to that network (see Figure 11-10).

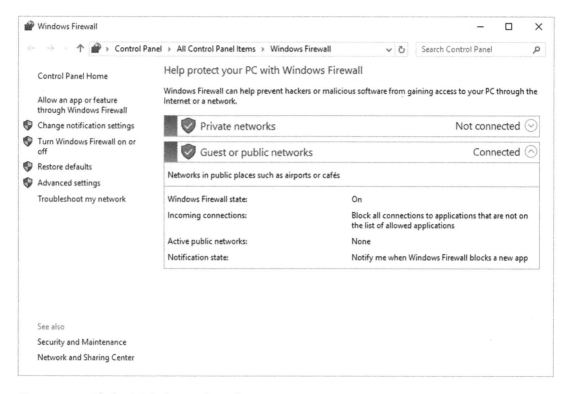

Figure 11-10. *The basic Windows 10 firewall*

There are many additional options, however, even for the basic firewall. You access these options through the left navigation. I want to talk you through each of them individually.

Allow an app or feature through Windows Firewall allows an app that has been blocked by Windows 10 because of suspicious activity (which is known to happen with older programs, especially) or because you accidentally denied it permission.

Changing this doesn't just do something as simple as allowing an app to install, however. You first have to click the **Change Settings** button to confirm to Windows that this is something you really want to do. This prevents malware from automatically coming through if you have inadvertently allowed it to install through UAC.

■ **Tip**   If you are having trouble with your firewall, you can click Restore Defaults in the Windows Firewall window to reset it to its default configuration.

Click the **Change settings** button in the top right of the window (see Figure 11-11) to allow or block an app through the firewall. Doing so allows you to check and uncheck the Private (such as home and work) and Public (such as cafes and libraries) network settings. You might want to set these individually if, for example, you have a file sync app such as LiveDrive or Dropbox that you want to block when connected to Public networks to minimize the risk of any transferred files being intercepted by hackers.

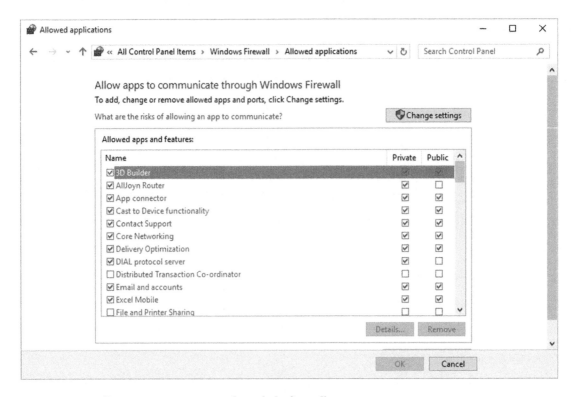

Figure 11-11. *Allowing a program or app through the firewall*

If you do not see the app that you want to let through the firewall listed, you can add it manually. Click the **Allow another app** button, and a new window appears again with a complete list of your apps and installed apps (see Figure 11-12). This shouldn't be any different from the main Allowed apps screen list, but there might be changes, depending on whether you have any custom software installed.

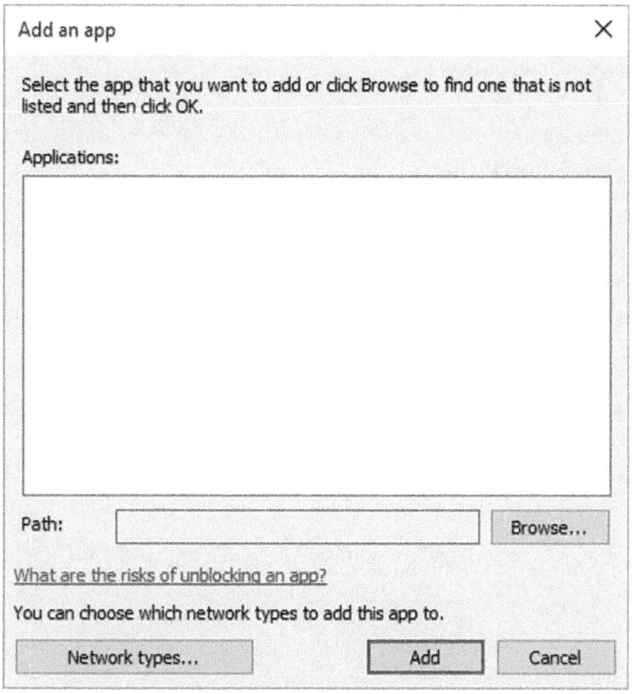

Figure 11-12. *You can manually allow a program through the firewall*

You can click the **Browse** button to add any win32 apps that aren't included in this list. You can't add Store apps this way because they are stored in a hidden and protected folder on the PC, to which even full Administrators can't get access.

When you select the app to add, click the **Network types** button to select which networks (Public and Private) you want to allow the program to connect to, and finish by clicking the **Add** button.

In the main Windows Firewall window, the **Change notification settings** and **Turn Windows Firewall on or off** links allow you to turn off the firewall if you *really* want to. Both links take you to the same place (see Figure 11-13). I recommend using these options only if you are using a third-party firewall that you're happy with.

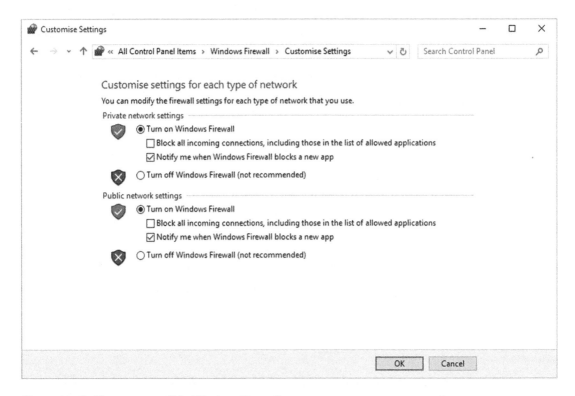

Figure 11-13. *You can turn off the Windows Firewall*

What's more, you can choose to have the firewall switched off in private networks, but remain on in public networks. But why would you want to do this? You might be a gamer and the firewall interferes with your online gaming at home, or you might be an office worker whose IT department asks you to switch off Windows Firewall because it conflicts with something on its system.

■ **Tip**   Many third-party anti-malware and security suites come with a Gaming Mode that will temporarily disable parts of the firewall that can interfere with gaming and anti-malware scans for a set period.

On a laptop or tablet, however, you still want to have the protection of the firewall when you're out and about. This is where you can leave the firewall turned on for public networks.

There is also a check box for blocking all incoming connections, which provides better security, especially on public networks, but you might find that some apps don't work because they require this feature to be switched off.

Restore defaults resets Windows Firewall to its default setting. This option is very useful if you made advanced changes and can't remember what they were to undo them.

Using the Advanced Firewall

From the main firewall window, clicking **Advanced Settings** takes you to a different management console (see Figure 11-14), in which you can set specific rules for both inbound and outbound traffic; and perform other operations, such as opening and blocking specific connection ports.

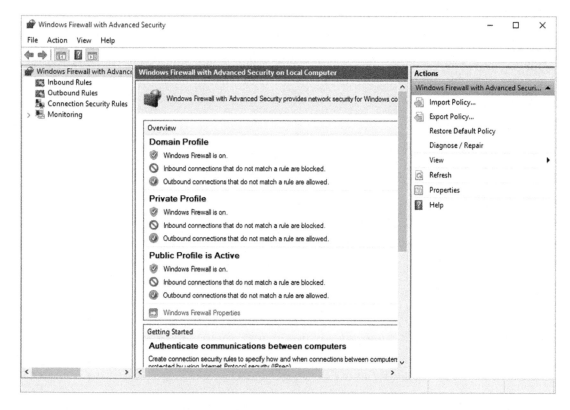

Figure 11-14. *The advanced firewall settings in Windows 10*

The main pane in the center displays the current firewall status, but there are two other panes here that you need to be familiar with. On the left side is a tree showing different options within the firewall: inbound and outbound rules, connection security rules, and firewall monitoring. (I will discuss each of these shortly.) On the right side are controls, including options to create and manage rules for the firewall.

To create a new firewall, first click Inbound Rules, Outbound Rules, or Connection Security Rules in the left pane; then click New Rule in the right pane to open the New Rule Wizard (see Figure 11-15).

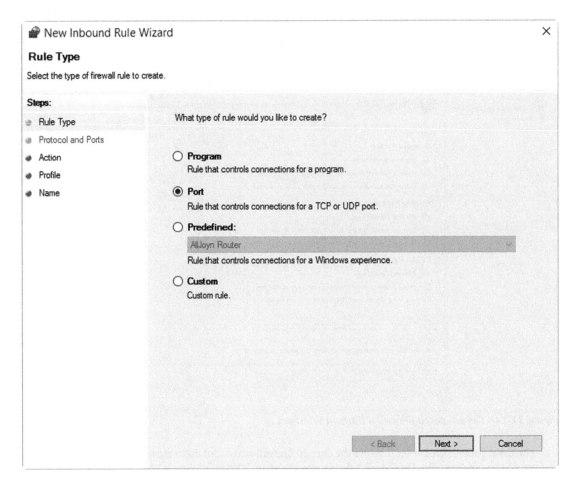

Figure 11-15. *All rules settings are done through helpful wizards*

Inbound Rules and **Outbound Rules** allow you to monitor and set rules for individual programs. You can click **New Rule** in the right pane to create a new rule for a program, or to allow or block a port on your computer. Table 11-1 shows a list of the common ports on your PC.

Table 11-1. *What Each Port Does on Your PC*

Port	Service
7	Echo
20 and 21	FTP
22	SSH
23	Telnet
25	SMTP
42	Name Servers/WINS
43	Who is/Nickname
53	DNS
79	Finger
80 (also 8080)	HTTP
81	Kerberos
101	Hostname
110	POP3 (email)
119	NNTP
143	IMAP (email)
161	SNMP
162	SNMP Trap
443	HTTPS
3389	Remote Desktop
5631	PCAnywhere
5632	PCAnywhere
5900 and above	VNC
6881 to 6990	Torrents

Port opening and blocking is common with applications such as gaming and file sharing, in which communications ports that are not normally used are blocked by firewalls by default.

Here you can set, for example, certain apps or ports to operate only if the data connection is secure. If you use your computer for work and perhaps work in an industry such as security, government, research, or pharmaceuticals, you might want your work applications to transmit and receive data only when you are connected to a secured and properly encrypted network. Here you can set specific apps to operate only under these circumstances (see Figure 11-16).

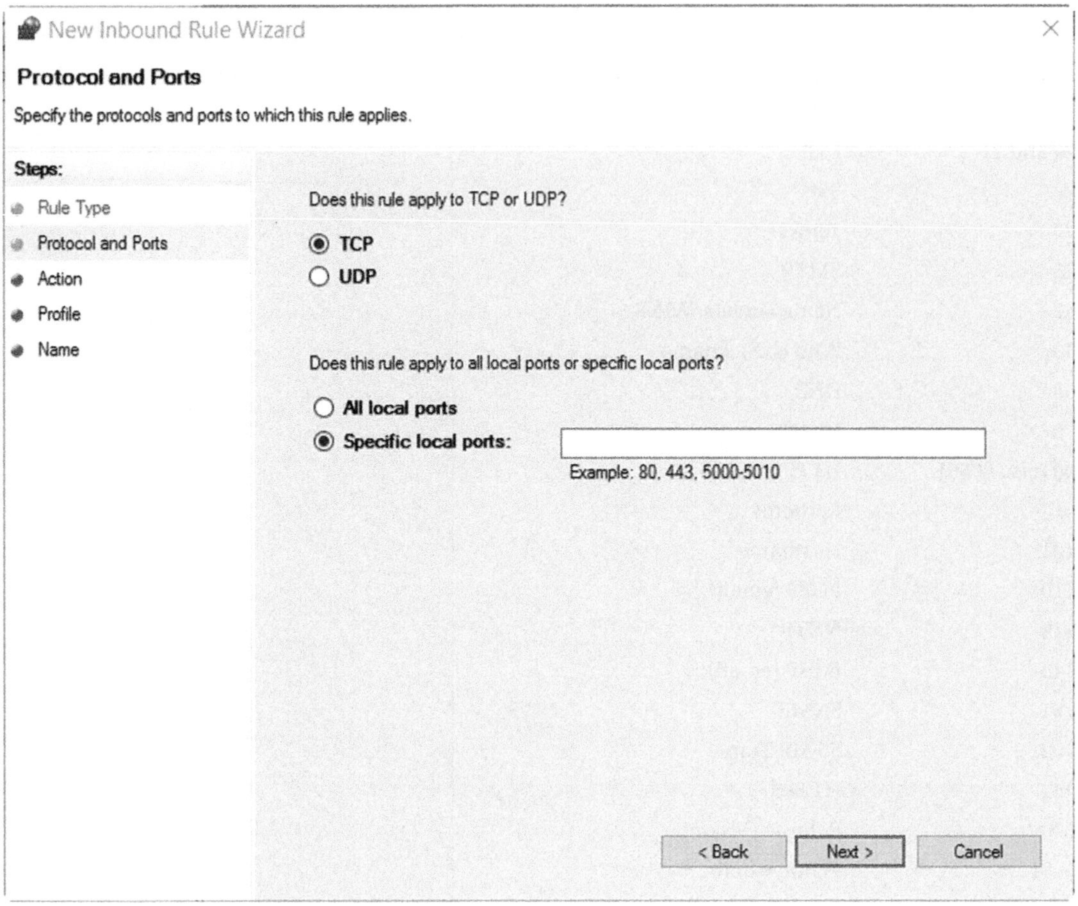

Figure 11-16. *Setting connection rules*

On the issue of secure connections, even if you only connect to your company through a virtual private network (VPN), you might be asked to set specific connection security rules so that your computer can be authenticated. You do this in the Connection Security Rules section, which specifies the type of connection you want (there are descriptions to assist you) and the type of authentication required by both computers before the connection is allowed.

When setting this up, you will likely have specific settings to input from your company or organization, and these will be specific to them alone.

One very useful feature is to create a custom connection rule whereby you can set—either with or without encryption or authentication—connections between two or more specific computers on specific IP addresses (see Figure 11-17).

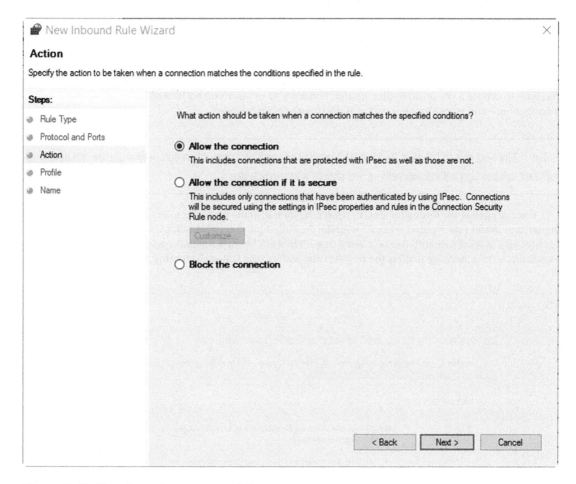

Figure 11-17. *The rules options are easy to follow*

If you have a closed connection in an office and only want computers in the payroll department (for example) to be able to see and connect to other payroll computers, you can set their IP addresses here. However, you need to set both inbound and outbound rules, as well as rules to clock all other IP address connections to the computer.

■ **Note**   If you are only allowing connections from your computer, you need to make sure that the permitted computers have static IP addresses set in your router.

User Account Control

User Account Control (UAC) is your main line of defense against unwanted software being installed on your computer, or unwanted changes being made to your copy of Windows or your computer's settings.

When a change is made to your computer that can affect other users or the PC's operation (for example, potentially allow the installation of malware, or cause the computer to become unstable), UAC changes the desktop to a secure mode (the same one used when you sign in to your computer) and displays only the UAC prompt on the screen.

In this mode, all other operations are suspended, so malware can't automatically click itself through. You have to choose a yes-or-no option, though Windows 10 can give you additional information about what is happening—and sometimes it is useful and written in plain language.

▪ **Tip**   The best rule to follow is that if a UAC prompt appears at a time when you personally are not installing software or changing a Windows setting, you should *always* click **No**.

You can change the setting for UAC by searching for **uac** at the Start menu, in which you will find it in the settings results (see Figure 11-18). As with the firewall, there is no control for User Account Control in the Settings app, as it's not intended to be altered or switched off. I always recommend that you leave UAC with its defaults setting, because it offers the best security without the feature becoming annoying.

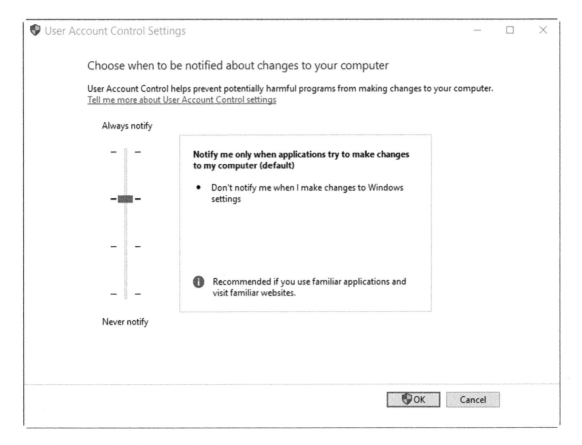

Figure 11-18. *Changing the UAC settings*

There are four UAC settings, which vary from off to annoying.

- **Never notify me** turns UAC off completely. I recommend never using this setting.

- **Notify me only when apps try to make changes to my computer (do not dim my desktop)** is another setting I don't recommend. Although this setting allows you to make whatever settings changes you want to Windows 10 without being bothered by UAC, it doesn't switch to the secure desktop mode when software is installed. This may permit malware to autoclick the UAC prompt for you.

- **Notify me only when apps try to make changes to my computer** is the default setting. I strongly recommend you leave it as is.

- **Always notify me** is otherwise known as "annoying mode."

So what is the difference between the default and the annoying modes? Some Windows 10 controls have a UAC shield icon next to them. This is to alert you that whatever you're doing here can affect other users or how the computer behaves.

In the default mode, Windows allows you to make changes that only affect your own user account, without popping up a UAC prompt. It is only when you're installing software or making changes that can affect other users (if you have only a single-user account, it assumes that more could be added later) that a UAC prompt appears.

Conversely, when in annoying mode, UAC gives you a security prompt for everything that can affect your own user account as well. This is much more secure but ... well, it is annoying.

Encrypting Files, Folders, and Drives

On your Windows 10 computer—be it a desktop, a laptop, or a tablet—you can encrypt your data and the entire hard disk. But should you—and how should you—do it? I want to carefully look at and consider the usefulness of each of the encryption technologies in Windows 10.

■ **Tip** Windows 10 Mobile devices and small Windows 10 tablets with screens less than 8 inches have a Device Encryption option that can be found in the System settings and activated via a simple on/off switch. These devices do not support EFS, BitLocker, or BitLocker To Go.

Encrypting Files and Folders Using the Encrypting File System

The question of whether to use a Windows encryption technology applies especially to the Encrypting File System (EFS). This system can be used to encrypt individual files or folders in Windows. It has been with us since Windows 2000. It uses 256-bit keys and a mix of several encryption systems based around Advanced Encryption Standard (AES) to provide overall security.

You can encrypt an individual file or folder (or a selected group) by following these instructions:

1. Right-click the item(s) to be encrypted. Select **Properties** from the options that appear.

2. Click the **Advanced** button in the Attributes section.

3. Check the **Encrypt contents to secure data** box (see Figure 11-19).

Figure 11-19. *Encrypting files and folders using EFS*

4. Click **OK** to begin the encryption.

The encryption process could take some time, depending on the number of files and folders that you are encrypting. You should not cancel the dialog box that appears onscreen because it cancels the encryption process.

You can *decrypt* files in the same way by following the same instructions and unchecking the **Encrypt contents** box.

How EFS Works

EFS is tied to your Windows user account (not your Microsoft account, but the account files on a specific PC). Whenever you sign in to Windows using this account, you can automatically read, write, and modify EFS-protected files. If you sign in to your computer using another account, or even if you have to reinstall Windows 10 and then log on using the same username and password you used before, you can't access these files until you import your EFS key. After you import the appropriate EFS key, you can read the files again.

Backing Up and Restoring Your EFS Key

When you have encrypted files or folders using EFS Windows, a desktop taskbar alert will prompt you to back up your EFS key. It is extremely important that you back up this key and keep it in a safe location *away* from the computer.

You are asked to set a password for your key, which prevents anyone from importing it onto their computer or user account and opening your files.

You can manually back up and restore EFS keys in Windows 10 by searching for **encrypt** at the Start menu and then clicking **Manage file encryption certificates** in the Encrypting File System window that starts the wizard (see Figure 11-20).

Figure 11-20. *Backing up and restoring an EFS key*

This is a wizard-based tool and it's extremely simple and easy to use. You can also set the EFS system to grant access to files only if used in conjunction with a smart card (assuming that your computer has a reader).

If you change your EFS key—let's say you've moved to a different computer—you can update the cipher used to encrypt the files to the new key on the new computer as well.

■ **Tip**   You can read about manually exporting, managing and working with EFS certificates in much more detail in my book *Windows File System Troubleshooting* (Apress, 2015).

Working with EFS-Encrypted Files

In practice, there are several reasons why I can't recommend using EFS. The first and probably the most important is that although it encrypts the contents of files, it still allows people to drill down into your files and folders and view all the file names, which can give away important information (e.g., M Halsey Disciplinary 2015-08-21.docx).

EFS also has what I personally consider a significant flaw. It lost a lot of files on both occasions that I've used it. Because it encrypts individual files and folders, not a whole disk, those files and folders are *still* encrypted when you copy them elsewhere.

If you have an automated backup solution that copies your files to an external hard disk or network-attached storage (NAS) drive, the backed-up files will also be encrypted. "Great!" you say. This is exactly what you want.

Unfortunately, EFS requires NTFS–formatted hard drives in order to work, but some external hard disks, especially NAS appliances, are often formatted using different methods. In such cases, you may find that your backups are completely scrambled and unreadable when you try to restore them.

Using EFS from the Command Line

If you're a command-line junkie, it's possible to manage the EFS there as well. This uses the `cipher` command in the format `cipher [/switch] [\folder-or-file-1] [\folder-or-file-2]`.

Table 11-2 lists the more common cipher switches, although more are available with the /? switch.

Table 11-2. *Switches for the cipher Command*

Switch	Action
/D	Decrypts the specified file or folder.
/E	Encrypts the specified file or folder.
/H	Displays a list of all files in a folder, including hidden and system files.
/K	Creates a new encryption certificate for the currently logged-in user. This switch must be used on its own.
/N	Can only be used with /U. Lists every encrypted file without updating the user's encryption key.
/R	Generates an EFS recovery key and certificate in the form of a .pfx file and a .cer file containing only the certificate.
/S	Performs the operation on all files and subfolders subordinate to the specified folder.
/U	Updates the currently logged-in user's encryption key on every encrypted file.
/W	Wipes any unused space on the drive.
/X *filename*	Backs up the currently logged-in users' certificate and encryption keys.
/ADDUSER *username*	Adds a specified user to an encrypted file.
/REMOVEUSER *username*	Removes a specified user from an encrypted file.
/REKEY	Updates files to use your current EFS key.

Encrypting Drives with BitLocker

A much better encryption solution is BitLocker, which is a full-drive encryption system that was first introduced with Windows Vista. It uses a 128-bit AES cipher and can combine a Trusted Platform Module (TPM) chip on your motherboard with a pin and/or a USB flash drive to enhance security.

The main advantage of this method is that the encryption is tied to a chip on your motherboard, which contains the decryption cipher; not even the removal of the hard disk allows people to read your encrypted files. The downside is that you need a TPM chip on your motherboard for BitLocker to work on your computer's hard drive(s), and it's uncommon for desktops to come with one fitted.

With Windows 10, however, Microsoft mandates that all laptops and tablets with screens larger than 10 inches should come with a TPM, and many desktop PCs also support TPMs either on board or as a plug-in module. If your PC doesn't have Windows 10 Pro or Enterprise installed, however, you will need to upgrade your copy of Windows to enable BitLocker, as it is not supported in Windows 10 Home.

Because BitLocker provides full disk encryption, any files that you copy from your computer are decrypted automatically. Although this might sound like a disaster, it does mean that backups are always readable (you do need to keep them safe, however) and that nobody can read any of the file names on your computer without unlocking the drive(s) with the appropriate key.

Preparing Your TPM Chip

Before you can use BitLocker on your computer with a TPM chip, you need to activate the chip. You can do this by clicking the **TPM Administration** link in the bottom left of the main BitLocker window. The main TPM administration page (see Figure 11-21) shows the status of your Trusted Platform Module chip. Before you can use BitLocker, however, you need to turn on the TPM chip on your motherboard.

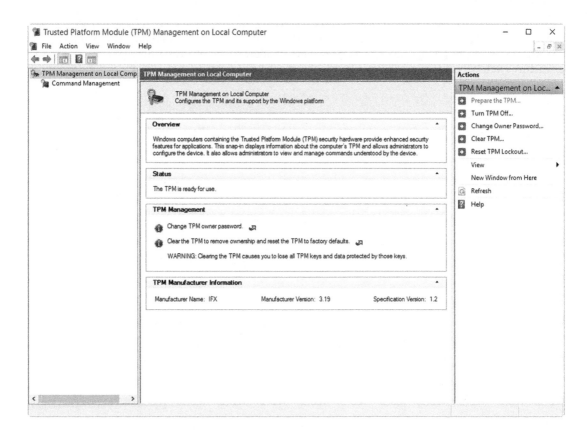

Figure 11-21. Managing your TPM chip in Windows 10

If you do not have a TPM-enabled computer, you can't encrypt your hard disk. If your computer is TPM-enabled, however, you will see options to prepare the TPM and more. For example, you can turn off TPM (be certain that you have no encrypted drives when you do this; see "When to Decrypt Your Hard Disks" later in the chapter) or completely clear the TPM of all its stored ciphers. If the TPM chip has locked you out of your computer (more on this later), you can reset a lockout after you gain access.

To use BitLocker, you need to prepare the TPM, which requires rebooting your computer, because settings are changed in the BIOS or UEFI firmware (you can also turn it on there). If you need to manage the TPM later on, this page provides all the controls to do so.

■ **Tip**   You can use BitLocker without a TPM in Windows 10 Pro and Enterprise by opening the Group Policy Editor (search at the Start menu for **gpedit**) and navigating to Computer Configuration ➤ Administrative Templates ➤ Windows Components ➤ BitLocker Drive Encryption ➤ Operating System Drives and enabling Require additional authentication at startup. With this done, you are able to use a USB flash drive to unlock your BitLocker-encrypted PC without using a TPM.

Activating BitLocker

Once your TPM chip is enabled, use the main BitLocker page to turn the feature on (see Figure 11-22), which you access from the Control Panel. You can encrypt all the hard drives on your computer, but you must complete the encryption of the drive on which you have Windows 10 installed first. In order to encrypt any extra drives with BitLocker, your Windows 10 drive *must also* be encrypted.

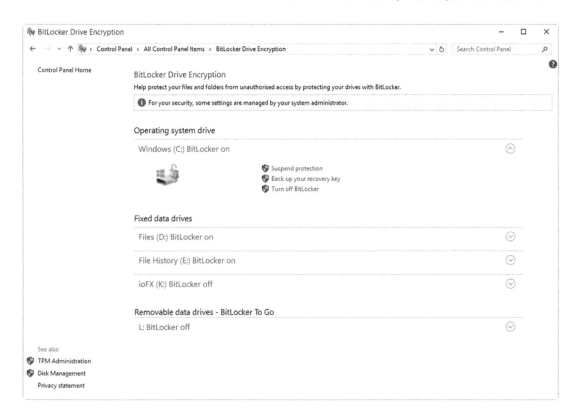

Figure 11-22. *Managing BitLocker in Windows 10*

■ **Note**   BitLocker does *not* work with dual-boot systems! If you have or are planning to have a dual-boot system on your computer, BitLocker locks you out of your computer each time you try to start it.

Unlike EFS, BitLocker encrypts your hard drive in the background, and it is perfectly fine for you to shut down your computer during the process because BitLocker simply continues when you next log on. This is useful because it can take many hours to encrypt a large hard disk that is already full of files and folders.

You can also turn off BitLocker on protected drives. This is where decrypting drives is slightly easier than encrypting them. If, for example, you have two or more physical hard disks or partitions on your computer and you want to encrypt several of them, you must first complete the encryption of your Windows 10 drive before you can manually start encryption of the others. When decrypting drives, however, you can start all the jobs at the same time—and Windows 10 happily continues if you shut down the PC occasionally.

Backing Up and Restoring Your BitLocker Keys

When BitLocker has encrypted your hard drive, you are automatically prompted to back up your BitLocker key. There are three locations where you can do this:

- **A file on your computer**: Do *not* save the key to a drive that has been encrypted with BitLocker or to a folder that has been encrypted with EFS, or else you might not be able to read it again.

- **A USB flash drive**: I always recommend you save your key to a USB flash drive and then store that drive in a safe place. I explain the reasons in the next section.

- **Microsoft OneDrive**: This cloud service is a secure location that can be found at https://onedrive.live.com/recoverykey. If you are using a Microsoft account with your PC, I strongly recommend that you store a copy of your key in OneDrive, and also keep a link to the recovery key on your "password-protected" smartphone.

Starting a BitLocker-Encrypted Computer

The reason I recommend that you keep a copy of your BitLocker encryption key on a USB flash drive is because if something happens to make BitLocker unhappy, such as a boot change, you will be completely locked out of your computer until you can input the key.

You can type the encryption key, but it is a very long and complex string of characters. You can insert a USB flash drive containing the key, however, and the Windows boot loader will recognize it and grant you access again.

Surely, you say, this defeats the purpose of having an encrypted computer. I argue that if you keep your computer *and* the USB drive containing the unlock key in the same place (there is a separate key for each encrypted hard disk or partition), then you run the risk that if your computer is stolen, the unlock key for your data will be stolen with it. If you are travelling, however, you don't need BitLocker locking you out. It might be some time before you can get to another Internet-connected computer to download the backup.

Therefore, I always recommend that you keep a copy of the backup key(s) on a USB flash drive in a safe location—because you never know when you might need it.

Using BitLocker after a Reinstall of Windows 10

If you are using BitLocker on a computer in which it has been used before—perhaps because you reinstalled Windows 10 or performed a clean install to upgrade from Windows 7 or Windows 8.1 (you should never upgrade an operating system encrypted with BitLocker), you will probably be asked to enter the owner password for your TPM chip (see Figure 11-23). This is set when you activate BitLocker. It is stored in the chip.

Figure 11-23. *Clearing the TPM*

You need to do this only if you still have BitLocker-protected drives on the computer, which I don't recommend because you never know what might go wrong, such as electricity surges or laptop drops that cause hard disk corruption. What you can do, however, is clear the TPM chip completely and start afresh, which is the best option if you have no BitLocker-encrypted drives in the computer.

You might be prompted to enter the owner password when restoring from a backup—if that backup was made before you encrypted your hard drives with BitLocker ... which brings me to the next section.

When to Decrypt Your Hard Disks

There are times when you should turn off BitLocker—purely to prevent disasters from occurring, as always happens with security technologies. These times include the following:

- When upgrading your copy of Windows or when installing a new operating system, such as migrating from Windows 7 or Windows 8.1 to Windows 10.

- When moving a hard disk from one computer to another.

- When sending a PC for repair. I always recommend wiping the data drive(s) in this case; and free software such as CCleaner (`www.piriform.com/ccleaner`) can perform a secure-erase of hard disks.

When you restore your computer from a backup, your drives won't be encrypted. You have to re-encrypt them.

Using BitLocker To Go

The BitLocker To Go feature doesn't require a TPM chip. This is a full-disk encryption system for USB and other attached flash drives and external hard disks. Unlike BitLocker, it is compatible with a variety of drive formats, including FAT32, exFAT, and NTFS—making it perfect for USB drives.

You encrypt an attached USB or other device with BitLocker To Go through the main BitLocker window. Again, there is the same on/off control as there is for your internal hard disks (see Figure 11-24). BitLocker To Go only requires that you set a password, which is entered when you want to read or access the disk on another computer.

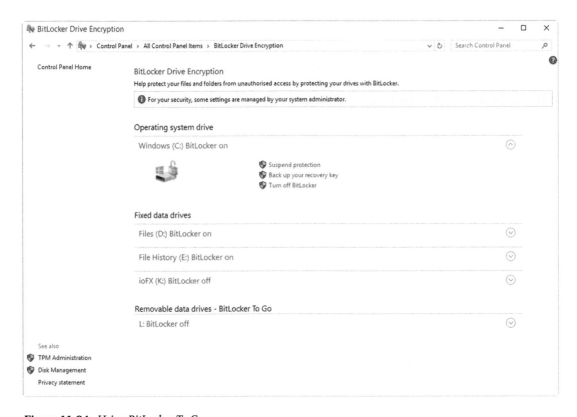

Figure 11-24. *Using BitLocker To Go*

■ **Note** You cannot create BitLocker To Go drives in Windows 10 Mobile or on PCs running Windows 10 Home.

When using a BitLocker To Go encrypted drive on another computer, there are limits to what you can do. For example, in Windows versions that support the same version of BitLocker, namely Windows 7 and Windows 8.1, you can get full access to the drive.

On Windows Vista and Windows XP, however, you have the BitLocker To Go Reader, which is software that, when you enter your password, allows you to read the contents of the protected drive, but doesn't allow you to write files back to it.

This is an important consideration when using BitLocker To Go. You should ask yourself, "Am I going to want to edit these files on another computer?" If the answer is yes, as long as the computer is running Windows 7 or Windows 10, you will be fine. If not, then you will have more difficulty.

■ **Caution**   Windows XP is completely out of all support. Windows Vista is out of support in April 2017. Using a BitLocker To Go drive with these operating systems can potentially present a risk of malware infection.

Because you can open and read files, however, there is nothing to stop you from saving a copy of a file locally and emailing the modified file to yourself once you have edited it. This is really the only way to edit files on a protected drive in Windows Vista or Windows XP.

Encryption Best Practice

BitLocker is an incredibly useful technology, and there are many situations in which you will want to use it. Having a password on your computer is not normally enough protection because a hard disk can be removed from a computer and read on another device.

If you are using a tablet or an Ultrabook, you have an advantage because the hard disk is a slim sliver of circuit board that sometimes requires highly specialized equipment to read it if it is removed. You can check the drive type on the manufacturer's web site. If it is an eMMC or M.2 drive, it can be read in many PCs, but anything else is only readable by using an identical laptop or tablet.

Even so, unless you store all of your documents and files on a cloud service such as OneDrive or Dropbox, and access them only over a live Internet connection, you probably have files on your computer that contain personally identifiable information about yourself or others.

Even the contacts database in your email account is valuable because it may contain not only names, addresses, and email addresses, but also dates of birth and other information that can be used to clone a person's identity.

If you are using an office laptop for work, you have tougher data protection rules governing how you use and protect the data of individuals. If you lose your laptop or it is stolen, you can face considerable fines or jail time if the laptop contains unencrypted data on individuals. This is on top of the damage done to your reputation or business, if it is discovered that you have lost sensitive and important information. If you travel abroad on business, you can also face penalties from data protection authorities in the country that you are in.

For these reasons, I recommend that you buy a laptop that comes equipped with a TPM chip (but all Windows 10 laptops and tablets with a screen over 10 inches should do so) and a copy of Windows 10 Pro or Enterprise, so that you can take advantage of BitLocker. It is no longer true that it is commonly just the high-end laptops that come with TPM chips, but consumer laptops do not often come with Windows 10 Pro. The cost of upgrading to the Pro edition of Windows 10 is small, and well worth the money. For businesses, a TPM chip is an essential business expense. For consumers, it can be a very worthwhile addition.

■ **Tip**   You can upgrade Windows 10 Home to Windows 10 Pro through the Control Panel, by opening the Settings app and navigating to Update & Security, and then to Activation.

If you are on the road, it is a good idea to carry—separate from your laptop—a USB flash drive containing the BitLocker keys for your computer. The system has been known to accidentally lock users out at the most inopportune moments.

Permitting and Blocking File and Folder Access with NTFS Permissions

Whenever you open a file or a folder on your PC, it is because you have permission to do so. These permissions are managed on a file level or a folder level, and can be controlled to allow (or prevent) specific users or groups of users from being able to open them.

To change the permissions on a file or a folder, right-click it; from the menu that appears, click **Properties** (see Figure 11-25).

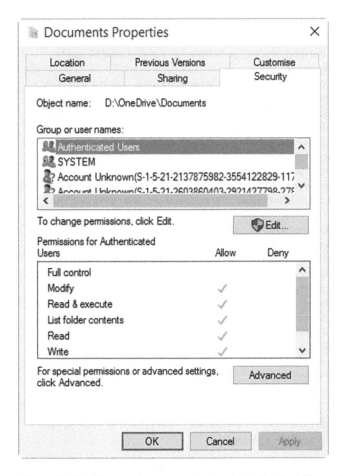

Figure 11-25. *You can change permissions for individual files and folders*

In the dialog that appears, click the **Security** tab. You see the users and user groups who currently have permission to use the file or folder, and in the bottom part of the dialog, the individual permissions they have. These permissions are easy to understand: Full Control, Modify, Read & Execute, List Folder Contents, Read, and Write.

You can edit the permissions for any of the users or groups listed by clicking that user or group, and then clicking the **Edit** button. The check boxes in the lower part of the window then become editable. If you do not see a user or group already listed, however, click **Edit**. In the next dialog, click the **Add** button.

A new dialog displays, in which you can type a username (or just a partial name), and click the **Check name** button to search for a specific user or group of users (see Figure 11-26).

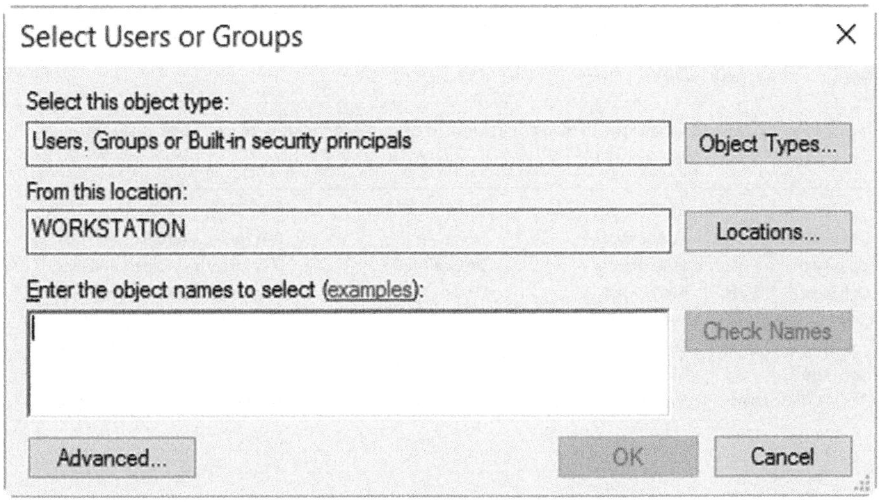

Figure 11-26. You can add user permissions to files and folders

After you add users or groups in this way, they are added to the main options.

Click the **Advanced** button in the security properties dialog for a file or folder that displays additional controls (see Figure 11-27). This includes the place from which permissions are inherited. Let's say, for example, that you give somebody access to your Documents folder. Every folder under this will also be open to them, and the permissions will have been inherited from the parent—the main Documents folder. At the bottom left of the dialog is a **Disable inheritance** button that is used to prevent the automatic inheritance of security and other sharing properties from the parent for the currently selected file or folder.

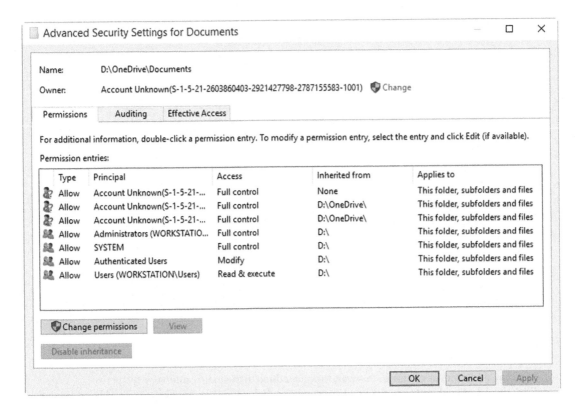

Figure 11-27. *Advanced permissions options are also available*

If you want to view the full permissions a user or a group has for a currently selected file or folder, click the **Effective Access** tab. It displays a clear list of all the permissions that the chosen user or group has for that item (see Figure 11-28).

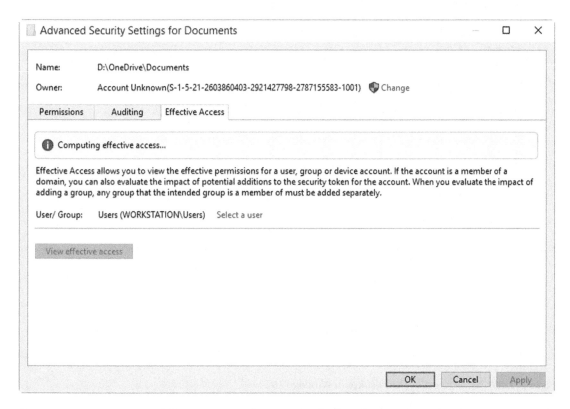

Figure 11-28. You can view full permissions information under the Effective Access tab

Using Biometric Devices with Windows 10

Encryption isn't the only way to secure your computer. There is a variety of biometric devices available for computers. They require third-party tools because they are not normally controlled by Windows, but Windows 10 does contain controls, which you access through the Windows Hello options in the Sign-in options of the Settings app (see Figure 11-29). This is a central location from which you can manage devices such as iris scanners, smart card readers and fingerprint scanners.

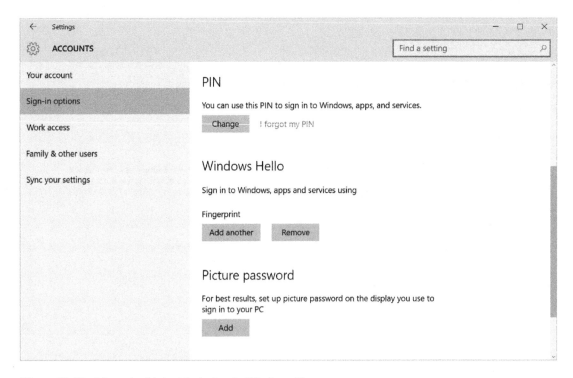

Figure 11-29. *Managing biometric devices in Windows 10*

You will sometimes find that when you open the management options for a particular biometric device in the Control Panel, it starts a third-party security utility rather than a Windows 10 wizard.

■ **Note**   Biometric devices use features unique to human physiology to identify a user. This commonly includes fingerprints, but can also include retinal scanners, voice and facial recognition, handwriting, and anything else that's noninvasive to the user.

It is possible to use Windows 10's Hello feature with a compatible webcam for facial recognition to unlock your PC.

Unless these security devices appear in the Device Manager, you should treat the actual security that they offer with caution. For example, third-party software that comes with a webcam is unlikely to prevent anyone who wants to hack into your computer from doing so (your photograph might be enough to fool it). If you are using Windows Hello with your PC, however, it relies on a 3D camera system that cannot be fooled by photographs.

If you have a fingerprint sensor in your PC, an easy way to use your fingerprint with Windows 10 is directly through Windows Hello, which allows you to use your fingerprint to log in to Windows. You can find this setting in Accounts and then **Sign-in options** under the Fingerprint section. Clicking the **Add [fingerprint]** button opens an easy-to-use wizard that scans your fingerprint (see Figure 11-30). A fingerprint option then appears on the Windows 10 login screen.

Figure 11-30. *Windows 10 allows you to use your fingerprint to log in*

Summary

When it comes to security, Windows 10 is very good at taking care of itself. With the default settings left unchanged for Windows Defender, User Account Control, and Windows Update, the operating system installs all the updates it requires as they become available.

Sometimes you may want to customize settings, perhaps to hide updates or to custom-configure the firewall. Some third-party anti-malware vendors will tell you that you need their software to get full and flexible control of anti-malware software and a firewall. This isn't always the case. Windows Defender is really quite flexible for a small and lightweight package. And Windows Firewall is very powerful and flexible, indeed. There are some excellent third-party packages available, however, some of which are free, which I detailed earlier in this chapter.

I never recommend changing the default settings in Windows. Making them tougher only makes life difficult for you, and turning them down takes away the protection that you need. These are parts of Windows 10 that you are wise to leave well enough alone.

When it comes to encryption, you have several options, and if you carry personal or sensitive files on your laptop or tablet, I strongly recommend that you purchase a device with a built-in TPM chip, and upgrade to Windows 10 Pro to allow you to use BitLocker. If you are using Windows 10 Mobile or a Windows 10 tablet with a screen smaller than 8 inches, device encryption technology is built into the operating system; you can find it in Settings under System ➤ Device Encryption. It works in the same way as BitLocker and it is just as secure.

CHAPTER 12

■ ■ ■

Maintaining and Backing Up Your Computer and Files

Nobody likes it when their PC begins to misbehave or when they lose files, work, or can't even use the PC at all, but creating a robust system with backups of both your files and the operating system can appear daunting. Sometimes, despite all your best efforts, problems arise—and for that my book *Windows 10 Troubleshooting* (Apress, forthcoming) has all the answers you need.

It is, however, not only possible but relatively easy to set up Windows 10 to be resilient and robust—and you might be surprised how much of this the operating system already does for you. So how can you set up Windows to maintain trouble-free use? And how can you set up file backups to help you return to work quickly and easily if something goes wrong?

Maintaining a Healthy Computer

Why is it important to maintain a healthy operating system and have backups in place? Surely, Windows 10 is the most reliable and robust version of the operating system that Microsoft has ever released. After all, it's the last major version of Windows, so why would Microsoft release a final desktop OS that's not completely perfect? Indeed Windows 10 comes with more tools for preventing, diagnosing, and mitigating problems than any version of Windows before it.

I have long found it ironic that as Windows becomes increasingly stable and reliable, the number of diagnostic and repair tools provided as part of the operating system also increases.

The simple fact remains, however, that your computer is still not a domestic appliance, and with the exception of Windows ARM–powered smartphones, which have the operating system embedded on a chip, every single file that makes up Windows can potentially be changed, deleted, or become corrupt quite easily.

What Causes Computers to Become Unstable

I want to talk about why computers become unstable, crash, and fail to boot. There are actually many causes for these problems, including the following:

- **Spikes, surges, and interruptions to the electricity supply** can cause Windows files to become corrupt. You should always have your computer plugged into a surge protector (as well as an uninterruptable power supply if you live in an area with an unreliable electrical supply). The power lead coming loose in the computer and the dog leaning against the power button are also causes. (I've suffered this many times, though it is very amusing when he switches on the Xbox console and then can't figure out why the laminate floor seems to make a noise when he lies down.)

Any interruption in the electrical supply can come at a time when a Windows file is being amended; it happens quite a bit. This problem can also cause the partition table—the database listing the physical location of each file on your hard disk—to become scrambled if the power is cut when it's being written to.

- **Poorly written software and drivers** are a very common cause of Windows failures. Don't assume for a moment that drivers delivered through Windows Update always gives you trouble-free operation; I've seen many a Blue Screen of Death happen this way. The problem here is that there is no way to predict or accommodate for the truly limitless variations in hardware and software on a specific machine. Also, graphics drivers and anti-malware software are both embedded deeply into the Windows OS, and as such they can cause utter havoc when their code includes an error or incompatibility.

  This is one of the reasons why Apple computers are reliable. As the manufacturer of both their operating system and all their hardware, they have complete and very tight control over the quality of drivers for the platform, and those drivers don't have to be compatible with practically every combination of hardware and software on the planet. It is the same with the App Store. Don't think that these app stores are just money-making schemes for Apple or Microsoft—they are, in fact, ways to ensure that the correct development tools are used and that apps are tested for stability, which encourages apps to be written in the right way.

  With the 64-bit (x64) versions of Windows 10, Microsoft has a strict signed-driver model in which all hardware drivers must be tested and signed off as stable using Microsoft certification tools. At the moment, it is recommended but isn't mandatory, and because it can be expensive, many hardware manufacturers choose not to pay for it. The 64-bit version of Windows 10 is installed by default on almost all new PCs with the almost sole exception of cheap, low-power tablets.

- **Malware and viruses** sneak onto the computer by taking advantage of the user. These malicious programs can cause all manner of havoc on a machine before you even know what's happened.

- **Installing too many programs and the creation of temporary files** causes a computer to fail over time. The more you try to do with your computer, the greater the risk that something will go wrong; and the more unnecessary files you have, the slower the computer will become over time. It used to be the case that Windows had a ceiling of about 30 installed programs it would happily accept. This hasn't been the case for some years, but the fact remains that you have no idea what effect the operating system, service and driver calls, and installed apps will have on your other installed apps or drivers.

How Is Windows 10 Mobile Different?

Windows smartphones run a modified version of the Windows 10 operating system—called Windows 10 Mobile—written onto a silicon chip instead of file-by-file onto a hard disk. This offers greater speed because operating system files can load as quickly as they can from the fastest solid-state drive (SSD) in a desktop or laptop PC, and it's far less likely that a sudden power surge will corrupt any files (and the fact that smartphones are much less likely to be in use when plugged into mains electricity).

You also cannot install win32 desktop software on Windows 10 Mobile handsets for use with Continuum (see Chapter 8). You can only download apps from the Windows Store. This reduces the chance of poorly written software causing problems. Also, desktop apps are incompatible with the different processor architecture of ARM chips.

Using the Windows 10 Security and Maintenance Center

Open the Control Panel (which is quickest from the Windows key+X menu) and in the **System and Security** category, you'll see a **Security and Maintenance** link. If you've used Windows 7 or Windows 8.1, you'll probably recognize what used to be called the Security and Maintenance Center that you would open by clicking the white flag icon on the taskbar; genuinely, the irony of finding out about Windows problems by clicking a white flag of surrender always made me chuckle.

You see that the Security and Maintenance Center is split into several collapsible panels (see Figure 12-1), with additional controls available beneath them. If there are any alerts for you, they are displayed with a traffic-light color to highlight their significance. Amber alerts inform you of things that could cause your computer to not perform optimally, such as a hardware driver or Windows Update being available but not yet installed. Red alerts inform you of critical problems, such as your anti-malware software being out of date, or the firewall being disabled.

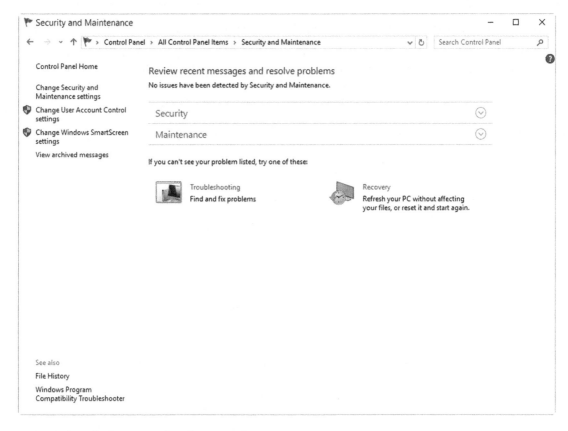

Figure 12-1. *The Security and Maintenance Center*

Each highlighted message includes a description and a link on how you can either fix the problem or get more information about it.

Next to each of the two main collapsible panels (Security and Maintenance) are expand icons you can click to see all the controls and get all the information available to you. The Security panel contains information on your firewall, anti-malware, spyware and unwanted software protection, user account control, SmartScreen web malware protection, and Microsoft account.

The Maintenance panel provides information on your PC's reliability history, its automatic maintenance schedule, HomeGroup settings (only in Home and Pro), and File History backup. Hard drive statuses and device driver updates. Here there are links to allow you to quickly open the settings for each item so that you can manage them, some of which we covered in Chapter 11, and others of which we'll look at in this chapter.

Beneath these sections are quick links for the Automated Troubleshooters, which can fix common problems across a wide-range of categories by resetting Windows components to their factory state, and a recovery **feature** to reinstall Windows without affecting your files or user account(s) should you encounter a more serious problem.

On the left side of the Security and Maintenance panel is a **View archived messages** link. If you believe you have missed an important notification or alert, or have dismissed something you perhaps shouldn't have, you can click this link to display a list of previously displayed security and maintenance messages and notifications.

Managing Security and Maintenance Center Messages

To customize the messages you receive in the Security and Maintenance Center, click **Change Security and Maintenance Settings** in the top of the left pane. This opens a settings window with check boxes that allow you to turn on or off messages for all the alerts in the Security and Maintenance Center (see Figure 12-2).

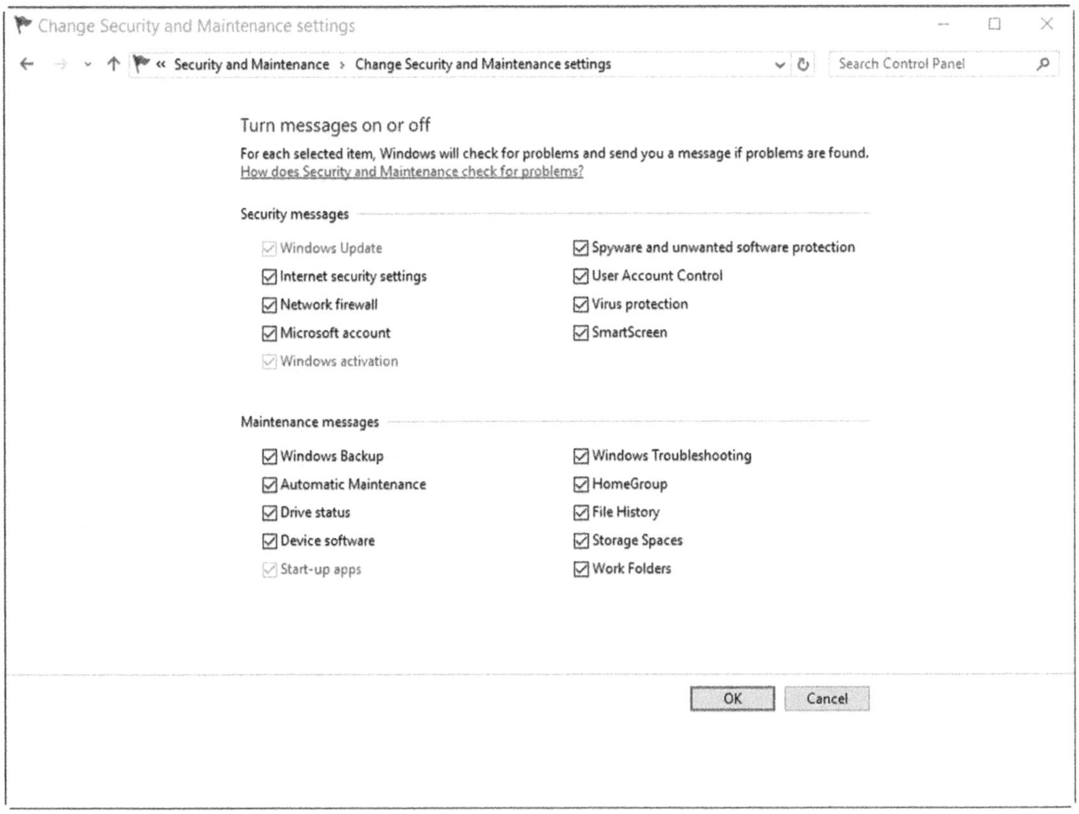

Figure 12-2. *Changing the Security and Maintenance Center settings*

■ **Tip**   I do not recommend turning off any of the alerts for Security Messages in the Security and
Maintenance Center.

Using the Automatic Maintenance System in Windows 10

Windows 10 includes an automatic maintenance system that helps keep your computer running happily
and healthily. These settings are in the Maintenance section of the Security and Maintenance Center. Click
Change maintenance settings, or search for **maintenance** in the Start menu.

The automatic maintenance includes deleting temporary and other unwanted files (such as those
used by Windows Update), defragmenting your hard disks, and checking for and installing updates for the
operating system.

You can configure how and when you want this tool to run (see Figure 12-3) by choosing the time of
day you want it to run. The time of day selection is important because if you are using a laptop or a tablet,
Windows 10 wakes from sleep to perform the maintenance. It doesn't wake the computer if it is switched off,
however. The Automatic Maintenance tool cannot be disabled from this panel, but it is an extremely useful
way to keep your PC running smoothly. Should you want to disable automatic maintenance, you can do so
from the Troubleshooters settings options (see Figure 12-3).

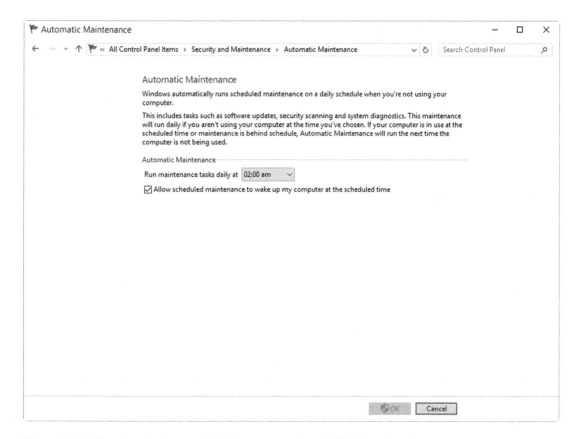

Figure 12-3. *Changing the Automatic Maintenance settings in Windows 10*

If you think your computer will be switched off at the time maintenance is due to be performed, you can choose the time that maintenance is performed.

You can run these tools independently as Disk Cleanup and Defragmenter, both of which are available by searching from the Start menu. I show you how to use these tools and the additional options they provide in Chapter 13 if you want finer control over the automatic and manual maintenance options in Windows 10.

Using the Automated Troubleshooters

In the Security and Maintenance Center, you can run Windows 10's automated troubleshooters by clicking **Troubleshooting**. There are many troubleshooters (see Figure 12-4) for almost every aspect of Windows, including networking and drivers.

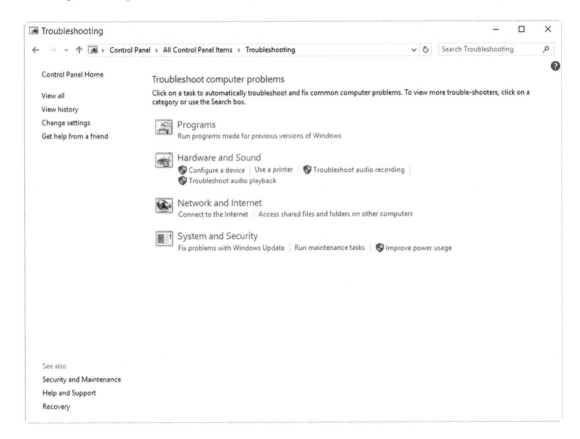

Figure 12-4. The automated troubleshooters

■ **Note**   The automated troubleshooters resets Windows components and drivers to their factory state. This is often enough to fix many problems, but if the issue is caused by a conflict with another driver or software package, the troubleshooters are unlikely to fix the problem. You can find much more detailed troubleshooting help in my *Windows 10 Troubleshooting* book.

The troubleshooters are wizard-based and give clear information. They can be run easily by users of any technical ability. They are split into handy categories covering Programs, Hardware and Sound, Network and Internet, and System and Security. Each troubleshooter is explained in plain language.

■ **Tip** You can also access the automated troubleshooters by clicking Troubleshooting in the Control Panel.

You can change settings for the troubleshooters by clicking **Change Settings** in the left pane (see Figure 12-5). I do not recommend changing any of these settings, however.

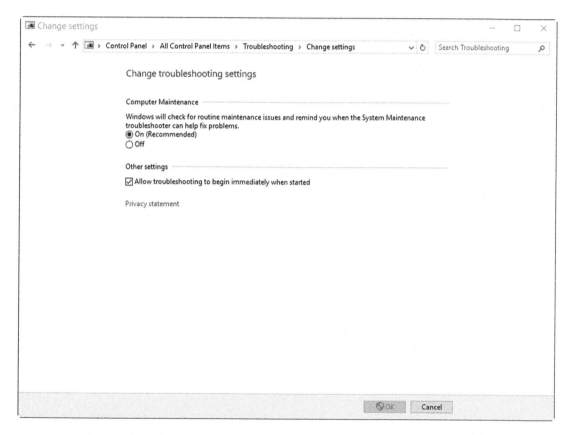

Figure 12-5. *Changing the troubleshooting settings*

The Windows 10 Task Manager

The Windows Task Manager is often seen as the place from which you can terminate hung up and offending apps, but it's actually a supremely powerful and useful tool. By default, you see a list of running programs with an **End Task** button in the bottom right of the window. It can be used to forcibly close troublesome apps, but clicking the **More Details** button expands the window (see Figure 12-6).

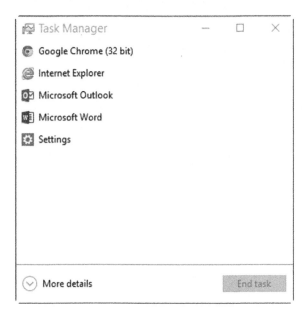

Figure 12-6. *The simplified Task Manager in Windows 10 with a More Details button*

When you click the More Details button, the Task Manager expands to display not just more information but also a wealth of data about your running programs, apps, services, processes, hardware, and connections. The first thing you see is the Processes tab, which provides a heat-mapped display of the current processor, memory, disk, and network usage for all your running apps and desktop programs. This means that if something is hogging huge amounts of memory, for example, you can see it straightaway (see Figure 12-7).

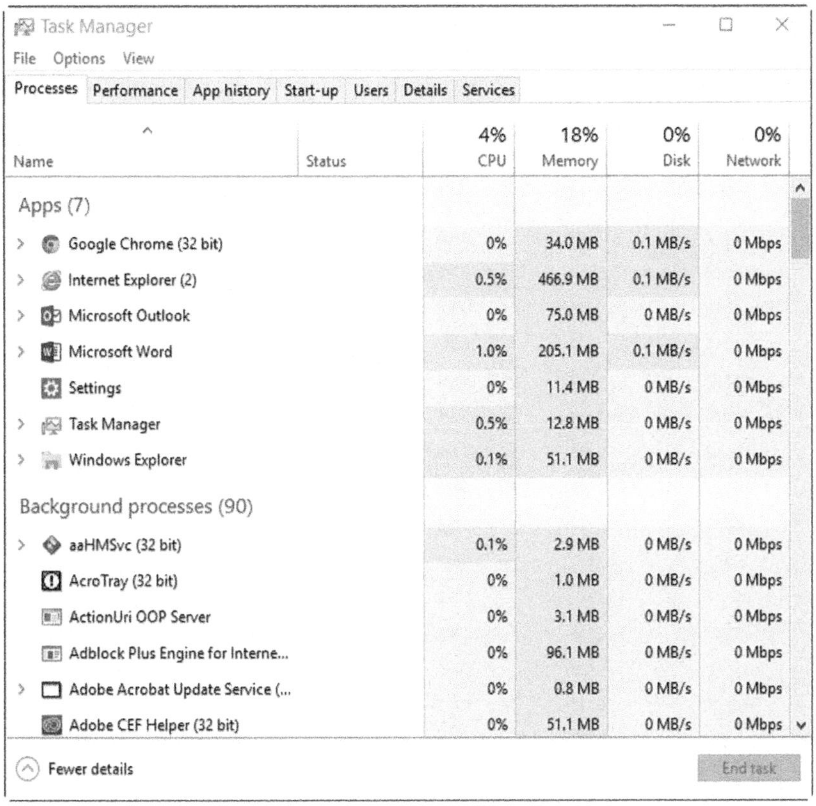

Figure 12-7. Monitoring software in the Task Manager

To close a program in the Task Manager, highlight the program and click the **End Task** button in the bottom right of the window.

■ **Tip** If you are unsure about which programs and processes you can shut down, the Task Manager offers several ways to find out. If you right-click a process, you can select options to view its Properties or open its File Location. Both reveal information about the process. You can also search online for this process from the context menu, which provides even more detailed information about the process.

There is a great deal you can now do with the Task Manager in Windows 10. The Performance tab now provides live graphs similar to the Performance Monitor, but with general overviews of performance information rather than the extremely detailed metrics offered by its big brother.

The App History tab is a great way to determine if the apps you are using in Windows 10 are well written and fit for purpose. Let's say, for example, that you are finding that something is chewing through your mobile broadband (metered network) allowance. On the App History tab, you can see the total amount of data that your apps have used, even when those apps are not running (see Figure 12-8).

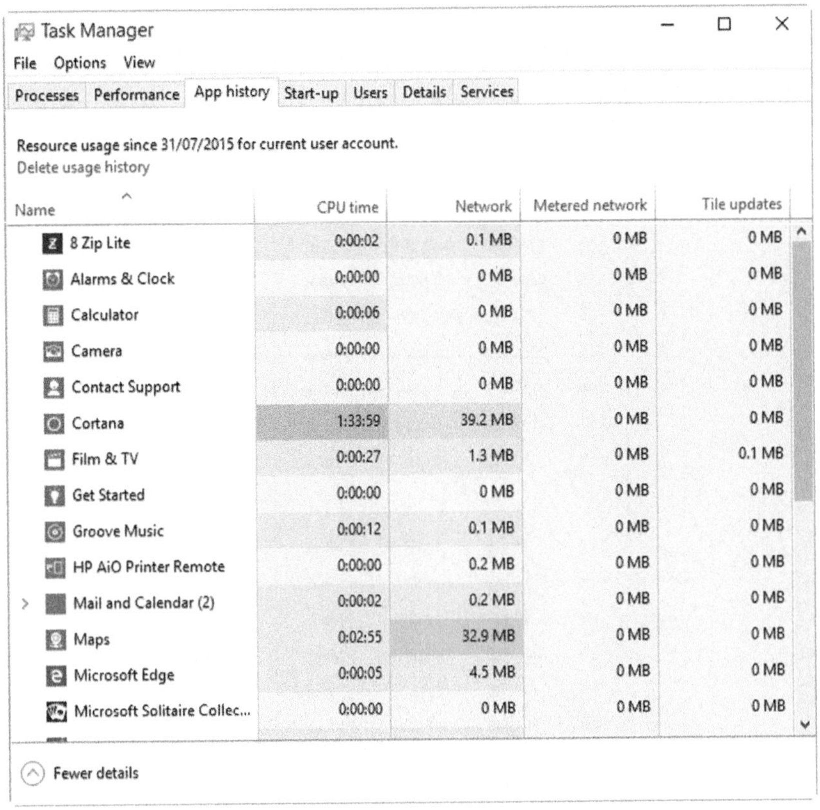

Figure 12-8. *The App History tab*

The Task Manager also allows you to see the amount of data consumed by the Live Tile for an app. Probably less useful is the processor time taken by an app. This chart doesn't take into account how much you use one app compared to another. Metrics that are more relevant are gained through the Processes tab when an app is running or through the Performance Information and Tools page.

■ **Tip** You can open the Task Manager by pressing Ctrl+Alt+Del on your keyboard and selecting Task Manager from the options, by right-clicking the taskbar, or from the Win+X administration menu.

The Details tab is more like the traditional Task Manager, if you prefer that look and usage (see Figure 12-9). Here you see a complete list of every app and process running in Windows 10. It works the same way as the old Task Manager in that you can right-click a program to shut it down.

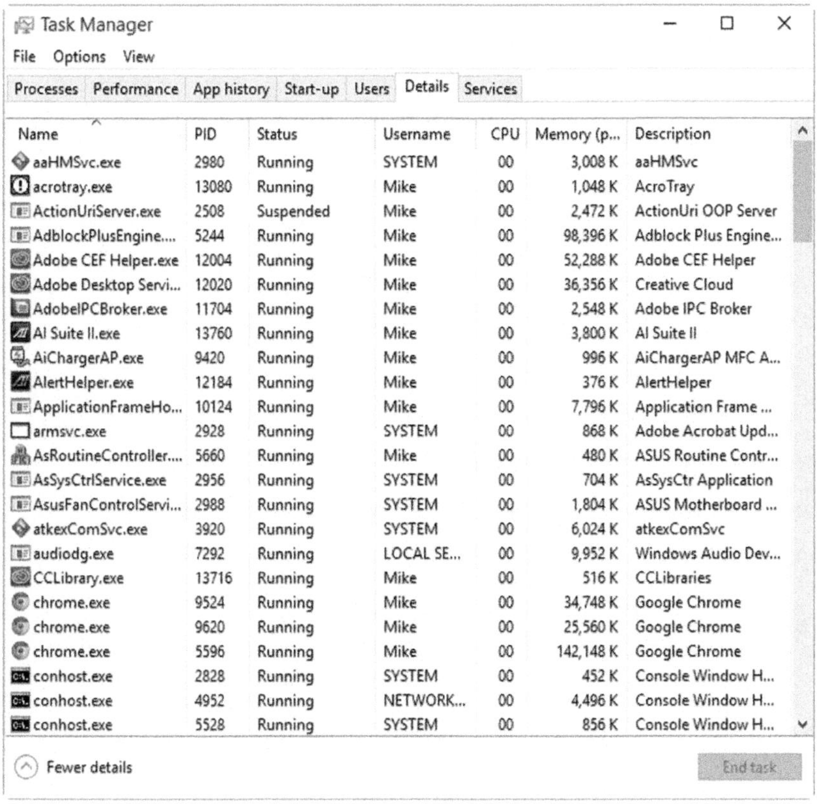

Figure 12-9. *The Details tab gives very detailed information*

It is interesting that only through the Details tab can you shut all the dependencies for a program. This means that when you shut down the app, all the processes and other programs that rely on it are also shut down automatically.

■ **Tip**   You can shut down all the dependencies for an app under the Details tab by right-clicking the app or process and selecting **End Process Tree** from the options.

Customizing the Task Manager

When you click the **Performance** tab in the Task Manager, you are presented with a series of live graphs displaying the current status of your PC's processor (CPU), memory, hard disk(s), networking (Ethernet), and Wi-Fi, and other network connections, if applicable. This view can be customized in a great many ways, just some of which can be seen in Figure 12-10.

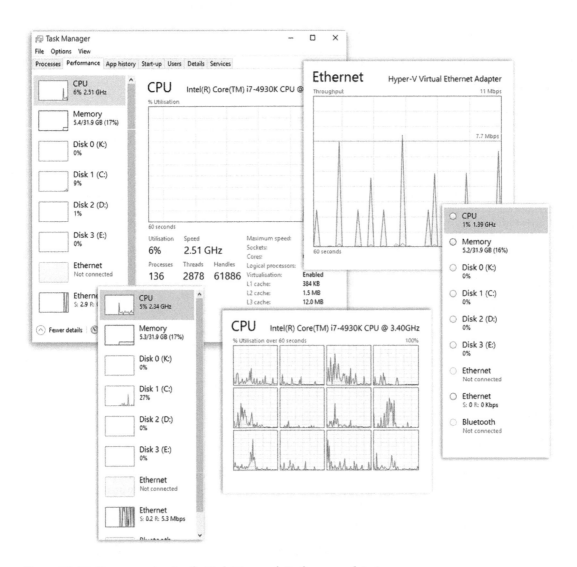

Figure 12-10. *You can customize the Task Manager's Performance data in many ways*

You customize these views by right-clicking any of the graphs, both in the left pane and in the main view, and it's worth spending a few minutes playing with these views because they not only provide a great deal of valuable (and additional) information, but they can also become useful widgets for leaving on your screen if you are troubleshooting a problem and want to keep an eye on something like your network connection. These mini windows can also be resized to make them smaller (or larger), making them even easier to leave running on your desktop, though you can only have only one open at a time.

Managing Startup Apps

The Task Manager is where you manage the apps that run at Windows startup. Not only does it make this feature simpler for nontechnical users, but it also adds a very helpful Startup Impact column, which tells you—in simple *low*, *medium*, and *high* terms—how long the app slows down your computer when you start up (see Figure 12-11).

Figure 12-11. *Managing startup apps*

You can disable apps by highlighting them and then clicking the **Disable** button in the bottom right of the window. You can also re-enable apps the same way because disabled programs are not removed from the list.

You only see win32 desktop software and not Store apps here because they can't be set to run at startup. Any Live Tiles are automatically enabled unless you disable them by right-clicking the tile and selecting **Disable Live Tile** from the context options that appear.

Using Windows Update

Windows Update in Windows 10 is managed through the Settings app, available from a quick link in the Start menu (or the All Apps view in Windows 10 Mobile) or the Notification Center. Windows Update keeps your PC up-to-date with the latest security and stability patches and updates, and also includes updates and improvements for both Windows and other Microsoft software that you have installed, such as the Windows Essentials Suite and Microsoft Office.

■ **Note** If you are using Windows 10 Home, you cannot choose to not download and install Windows Updates as you could in previous Windows versions.

Managing Windows Update Settings in Windows 10

When you have launched Settings, navigate to the **Update & Security** section to find Windows Update. It is a very simple affair. Windows Update automatically installs all critical, important, and recommended updates for a computer. There's very little the user has to do. In many ways, especially with regard to safeguarding people's personal privacy and security, it's exactly what the average nontechnical computer user needs (see Figure 12-12). More-technically savvy users, however, may prefer the added control that comes with the full Windows Update desktop settings, which are covered in the following section.

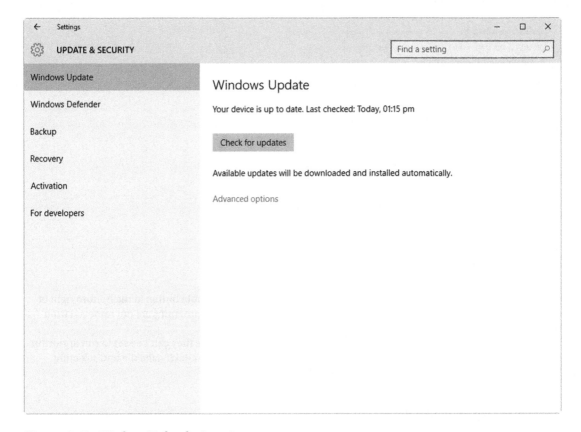

Figure 12-12. Windows Update basic settings

■ **Note** If you've been used to hiding updates you don't want installed in Windows 7 or Windows 8.1, such as language packs or regional antitrust updates, this option is no longer available in Windows 10. This is because of Microsoft's aim to ensure that all PCs are fully patched and up-to-date all of the time. Having a PC base that's up-to-date reduces support costs for Microsoft, and makes it easier for software, hardware, and particularly anti-malware vendors to make sure that their software is fully compatible with PCs.

The factory options for Windows Update are for all updates to be downloaded, and the PC user to be notified that they're ready to install when the user chooses, at the next shutdown, or automatically after a few days. To get more control, click the **Advanced Options** link and you'll see a drop-down box offering several choices of how and when updates are installed (see Figure 12-13). Additionally, a check box is available to install updates to other Microsoft products through Windows Update. This includes Microsoft Office, and it is recommended you check this option to maximize the security on your PCs.

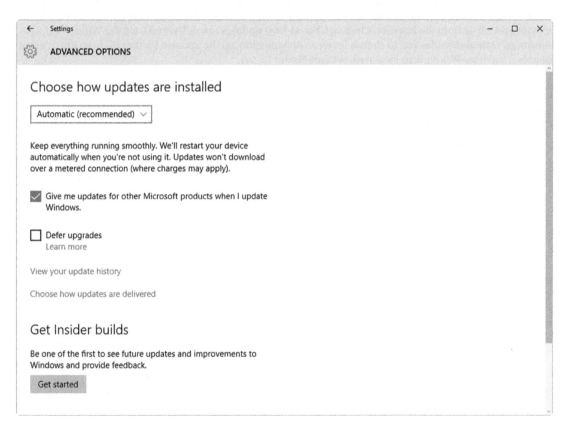

Figure 12-13. *You can configure Windows Update in a friendly way*

If you are using Windows 10 Pro, you also see an option to **Defer upgrades**. You should only check this option if your PC runs critical apps for your business and cannot face any down-time. This option allows you to delay the automatic installation Windows Updates for up to eight months.

> ■ **Note** Users of Windows 10 Enterprise running mission-critical PC system administrators have an additional option called Long Term Servicing, which only installs security and stability patches through Windows Update, and delays all feature updates for up to ten years.

Downloading Updates from Other PCs on Your Network

If you live in a rural area or somewhere else without a super-fast broadband connection, it can sometimes be difficult and frustrating to download large numbers of Windows Updates. The problem is compounded further when major updates to the operating system are released, and further still when you have multiple PCs in the home that are all trying to pull these updates down from the Internet. It's no easier in the workplace where even the fastest broadband connections can slow to a crawl with dozens, or even hundreds of PCs updating themselves simultaneously.

Fortunately, Windows 10 has a solution for this, and it's come from the most unlikely of places. You may be familiar with peer-to-peer networking, which is commonly associated with the illegal downloading of movies and music from the Internet. Clicking **Choose how updates are delivered** from the Windows Update Advanced Options enables you to choose between downloading all the updates for that PC from the Internet or only from other PCs on your local network (see Figure 12-14).

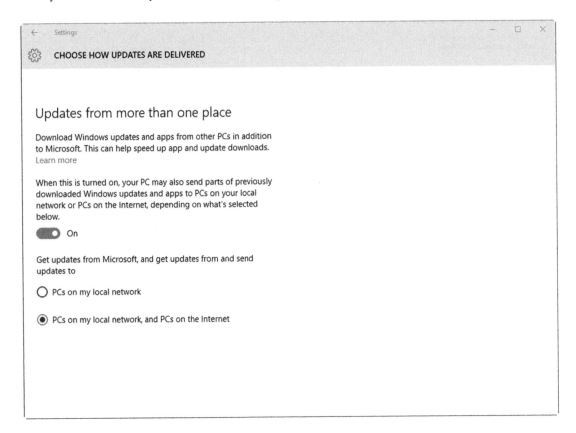

Figure 12-14. Windows Update on the desktop

Choosing the **PCs on my local network** option prevents that PC from downloading any updates from the Internet. Instead, it gets them from nearby PCs that have downloaded all, or even part of the updates. One of the best features of peer-to-peer networking is that a PC can share a file even it only has a part of it, with the remaining parts of the updates coming from other PCs.

In the workplace, there is a wired or a wireless network over which Windows 10 PCs can share updates. This ensures that every PC has all the updates it needs, without using unnecessary Internet bandwidth. In the home, if your PCs cannot see each other easily across the network (you can click Network in File Explorer to see if Network Discovery is turned off), you can set up a HomeGroup to share updates.

Viewing and Removing Installed Windows Updates

Sometimes you might want to uninstall a Windows Update, perhaps because it is known to cause problems, and installation has resulted in your PC or a device becoming unstable. In this case, you want to remove it and either install the correct driver manually, or wait for Microsoft to issue a fix before reinstalling it. You can see what updates have already been installed in the Windows Update Advanced Options by clicking the **View your update history** link. This shows you a list of all of your installed updates, what they were, when they were installed, and if they are still waiting for you to restart your PC to complete.

At the top of this page is an **Uninstall updates** link, which takes you to a Control Panel console (see Figure 12-15), where you can uninstall an update by right-clicking it and selecting **uninstall** from the context menu that appears.

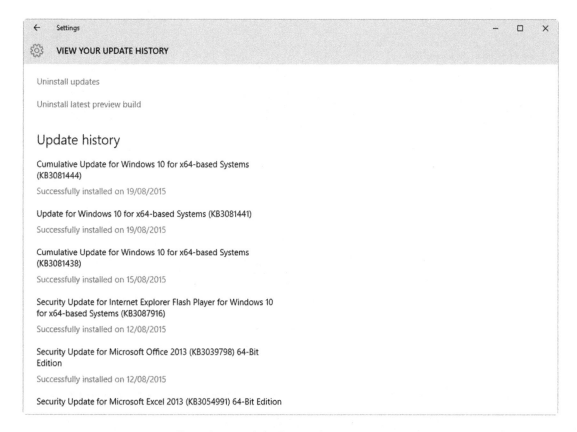

Figure 12-15. *You can uninstall Windows Updates, but not forever!*

It's important to note here that because you cannot hide updates in Windows 10, you also cannot prevent your PC from reinstalling an update. This option, therefore, is really only for businesses running Windows 10 Pro or Enterprise, where updates are delayed, or the PCs are on Microsoft's Long Term Servicing branch, where an update has been installed accidentally.

Managing Hardware Drivers and Rolling Back Windows Update

I mentioned that some updates, especially drivers, occasionally cause Windows to become unstable. If this happens to you, be aware that Windows 10 creates a System Restore Point on desktop and tablet PCs whenever it runs Windows Update, so you can roll back to the last restore point to undo the driver change.

To do this, open the Control Panel, which you can do from the desktop by pressing the Windows key+X and selecting it from the menu, or by searching for **Control Panel** in the Start menu. Next, change the **View by** option to large or small icons (either is good), and then click **Recovery**. In the Recovery panel, you have the option to **Open System Restore**.

You can now restore Windows to the way it was before the update was installed. When you run Windows Update again, you can hide the offending update so that it doesn't bother you (see Figure 12-16).

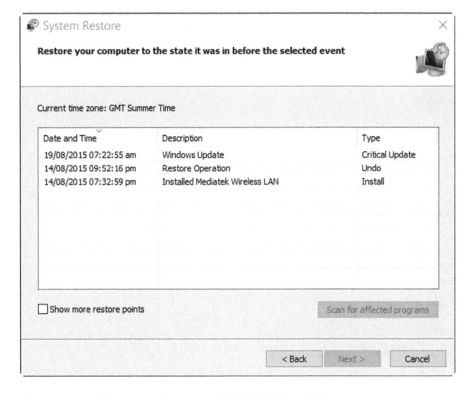

Figure 12-16. Using System Restore to roll back Windows Update

When you click an available restore point in the list, you also have the option to click the **Scan for affected programs** button. This presents details of any apps that might be uninstalled or changed, perhaps because they were installed or updated after this restore point was created.

You can also check the **Show more restore points** box to show the full list of available System Restore points on your PC, if any exist. The standard view only shows the two or three most recently created.

Getting App Updates from the Windows Store

Updates for your purchased and downloaded apps don't come through Windows Update, even if you have Microsoft Update turned on and the apps are written by Microsoft. All updates for anything downloaded from the Windows Store come *through* the Windows Store.

When you install Windows 10, all apps from then on are automatically updated when new versions become available. You won't be notified. You can control this, however, and turn it off by clicking your Account icon in the Windows Store app, and then clicking the **Settings** option in the menu that appears. This displays the updates panel (see Figure 12-17), which includes the update controls.

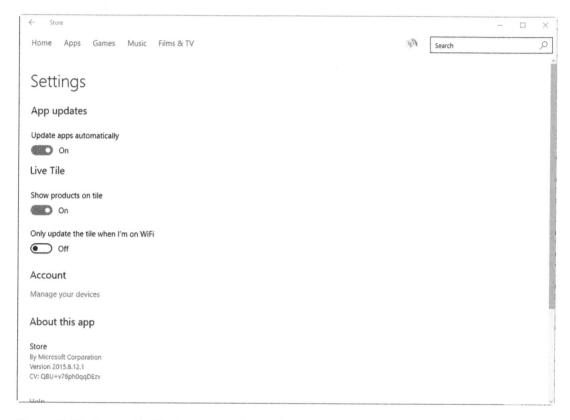

Figure 12-17. *You can disable automatic updating of apps*

Protecting and Repairing Windows

Although it is simple and straightforward to keep your copy of Windows 10 running smoothly and in a healthy state, it can also be simple and straightforward to rescue the OS in the event something goes wrong. In this section, I'll show you what the various options are and how they work.

Creating a Recovery Drive

A *recovery drive* is a USB flash drive containing the tools required to repair Windows and get to options such as Startup Repair, Refresh, Reset, and System Restore, if your copy of Windows 10 won't start. I'd like to begin this section by stressing just how important it is that you *do* create a recovery drive for your PC, laptop, or tablet. The worst thing that can happen to anyone's PC is that it fails to boot into Windows.

413

What do you do when this happens? You can't get into Windows 10 to recover things. You won't have been given installation media for the operating system with your PC. A laptop is unlikely to have a DVD drive anyway. A tablet certainly won't; it most likely only has a micro-USB port. And your USB flash drives (onto which you copied the ISO image file of Windows when you got your upgrade from Windows 7 or Windows 8.1) are all standard USB. (You *did* download this and kept a safe copy of the product key, right!?) And you don't know anybody with the tools to help you fix things.

So creating a USB recovery drive is pretty essential to help get you working again if it all goes horribly wrong. If applicable, you should invest in a USB flash drive for the job. One that has a micro-USB or USB Type-C plug for your Ultrabook or tablet. Or buy a USB converter cable, called a USB On the Go (USB OTG) cable, to use a standard flash drive.

Having said all that... You can create a recovery drive from the Control Panel. Click **Recovery** (in the large or small icons view; it doesn't appear in the Category view). Next, click the **Create a recovery drive** option. The Recovery Drive wizard will appear (see Figure 12-18).

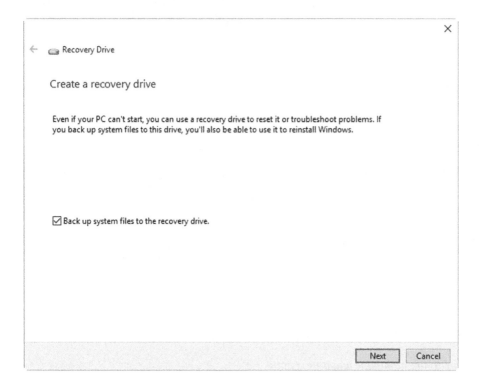

Figure 12-18. *Creating a recovery drive*

■ **Tip** Checking the **Backup system files to the recovery drive** option also saves the current Reset Image for your PC, making it easier and simpler to recover to a working copy of Windows in the event of a disaster.

Once the recovery drive is created, you can start your computer from it to access the recovery options. Note, however, that booting from a USB needs to be turned on in the BIOS or UEFI firmware on your motherboard.

Backing Up and Recovering Your Windows 10 Installation

In the IT industry, when a PC malfunctions, it is common practice that the operating system be wiped and reinstalled from a backup image that was created after all the apps were installed and the settings were configured. Windows 10 changes all of this for the first time with a new take on the backup image functionality.

The System Image Backup feature still exists, and you can use it if you like, but for many people, especially those who are less technically-minded, Refresh offers a compelling way forward for the future.

Resetting Windows 10

So let's have a look at the Windows 10 Reset feature, which is implemented so simply that users of any technical ability can use it. This feature reinstalls Windows, so that any corrupt files within the operating system are replaced with fully working and up-to-date versions while also keeping all of your files, settings, Store apps, and user accounts. This means that when the Reset operation is complete, you basically have nothing to configure or install, and you get back to working straightaway.

So how does it work? When Windows is installed, it automatically creates a backup image copy of itself that it can use to reinstall Windows. In Windows 8, which was the first version of Microsoft's OS to include the Reset feature, it essentially reinstalled Windows to the way it was when it was first installed. This meant you'd then have to spend time, and probably quite a lot of time, reinstalling a large number of Windows Updates. Improvements to this feature in Windows 10 means that it now uses the most recently downloaded Windows Updates when resetting the OS, so that the version you end up with is up-to-date, secure, and patched.

■ **Note** The Reset operation restores Windows system files from 30 days ago, so as to ensure that any recent Windows Update files that may have caused a problem are not automatically reinstalled.

One crucial consideration, however, is that Reset doesn't restore any of your installed win32 apps—that is, those desktop programs like Office 2016 or Adobe Creative Cloud that you haven't installed from the Windows Store. These apps need to be reinstalled after the Reset operation is complete. For this reason, heavy users of win32 apps might still find the System Image Backup option a more suitable alternative.

■ **Tip** If you are selling or giving away your PC, you can use the Reset feature to completely wipe the PC of all of your accounts, files, and apps. To do this, choose the **Remove everything** option when running Reset. Bear in mind, however, that all this does is delete the files; it is not a secure delete, so your files will still be recoverable using undelete software. For the average Joe selling his PC, this should not be a problem, but a business PC containing customer data should have its files securely deleted first; free software such as CCleaner (available from piriform.com) can do this for you.

There is one critical difference between Reset and the older System Image Backup that affects power users, IT pros, and system administrators. Although you can create a custom Reset image that restores all of your installed desktop software, it doesn't back up any of your settings for those programs. This means that software such as Microsoft Outlook is returned to its *installation* settings and you need to reconfigure email accounts in it, and the settings and preferences in all your other desktop software.

Many users won't be bothered by this, however, and indeed Windows 10 syncs a great many of its settings, including those for the desktop. App suites such as Office 365 and Adobe Creative Cloud can also synchronize many of their settings between different PCs.

Reset is also an excellent utility for anyone who supports friends or family and gets calls in the middle of the afternoon about a problem "that will only take a minute."

You can access the Reset from the Settings app by selecting **Update & recovery**, and then clicking the **Recovery** option in the left navigation pane (see Figure 12-19).

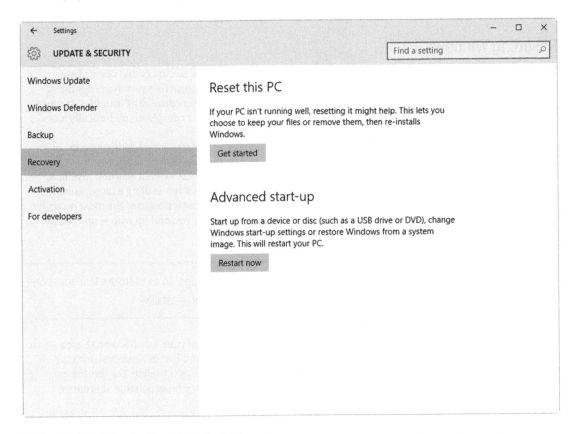

Figure 12-19. *Activating Reset from the Settings app*

Reset is the first option at the top of your screen; there is an explanation of what it does. When you are ready to reset your computer, click the **Get Started** button. The process is completely automated from that point. Your PC restarts several times during the reset operation.

When you want to reset your copy of Windows, Windows 10 explains what the Reset process does and asks you if you want to keep your files or to remove everything. If you want to get your copy of Windows to work again, click the **Keep your files** option. (The **Remove everything** option is useful when you are selling or giving away your PC.) If you have any win32 apps installed, you are presented with a list of them, and you are told that you need to reinstall them after the Reset has completed. A list of the software will be saved to your desktop for you to refer to at the time. You can click **Next** when you are ready to reset your PC.

You can also reset your PC from Windows 10 startup; the details on how this works can be found in the "Understanding Windows 10 Startup Menus" section a little later in this chapter. There are several ways to get to this:

- If your PC doesn't start after three attempts, Startup Repair runs. If it doesn't repair your computer, it offers you advanced repair options, which includes Reset. (For more on this, see "Using Startup Repair" later in this chapter.)

- You can start your PC using a recovery drive; note that you may need to access the boot device options on your PC (usually F12 or Del) to tell the PC to boot from a USB flash drive. Check the documentation that came with your PC to see which key (or which combination of buttons on a tablet) you press to "select the boot device."

- You can start your PC from a Windows 10 installation DVD. At the **Install** screen, click the **Repair your PC** link to take you to the repair options.

Creating a System Image Backup of Windows 10

Windows has included a system image backup facility for years; it's a great way—especially for tech enthusiasts, power users, and IT pros—to create a solid and robust backup of your installed copy of Windows 10, with all its win32 and store apps, accounts, and settings intact.

■ **Caution** You should not create a system image backup of any hard disk or partition on which you also store your files and documents, as restoring the image backup overwrites your current files with the older versions. You should move your files to a different hard disk or partition; I show you how to do this later in this chapter in the "Safeguarding Your Personal Files" section. If you use Microsoft OneDrive to access your files online, and they are not stored locally, you can safely create a system image without affecting those files.

I always recommend that the backup image be from a relatively clean installation, in which only essential changes were made and all temporary files were deleted. It's a good idea to run Windows utilities, such as the Disk Cleanup Wizard, which you can find by searching **clean** at the Start menu, and clicking **Disk Clean-up** in the search results. The image backup doesn't store temporary files, so you don't need to worry so much about those, but the cleaner the image of your PC, the less risk there is of any inherent problems also being backed up.

■ **Note** If you do not have a second partition or hard disk in your PC on which you can store a system image, it is straightforward to create one. You need enough free disk space, so it's a good idea to clear out any temporary files and defragment your disk first. On PCs with very small amounts of storage, such as low-end tablets with only a 32GB disk, performing a reset can clear many temporary and other files.

Press the Windows key+X to open the Administration menu, and then click the **Disk Management** option. In the Disk Management console, right-click your Windows drive (or the drive on which you want to make space) and select **Shrink volume** from the options that appear.

You need to reduce the partition in an amount roughly equal to your currently installed copy of Windows 10 with all its apps and settings. You can work this out by looking at the data in the top of the console, which tells you the capacity of the drive and the amount of free space that is left. Subtract the latter from the drive size to get your Windows installation size (e.g., 35GB).

When asked how much you want to shrink the drive by, enter this number (it only needs to be approximate) multiplied by 1000 (so 35GB would approximate to 35000MB, which, of course, it isn't; but like I said, you don't need to be exact).

In the "unallocated" space that's created, right-click and **Create [a] new simple volume** of the maximum size available. Give this a drive letter—any will do. You now have a partition on which you can save a system image.

Access the Windows Image Backup creation utility by clicking **File History** in the Control Panel, where you have the option to create a System Image Backup in the bottom-left corner of the window (see Figure 12-20).

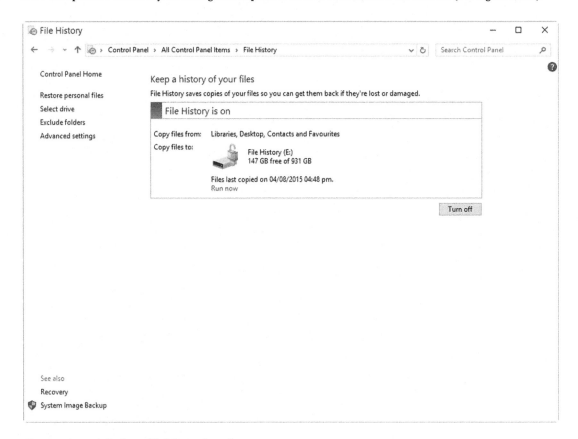

Figure 12-20. *Windows File History Panel*

Click **System Image Backup** to start the wizard, which guides you through creating a backup image of Windows 10. The backup image is a complete snapshot of your PC at that time, including all of your installed software, their configuration settings, and customized Windows settings, and all of your user accounts.

You are asked where you want to store the image backup (see Figure 12-21). You can choose another hard disk or partition in your computer, one or more DVDs (although bear in mind these can degrade over time), or a network location.

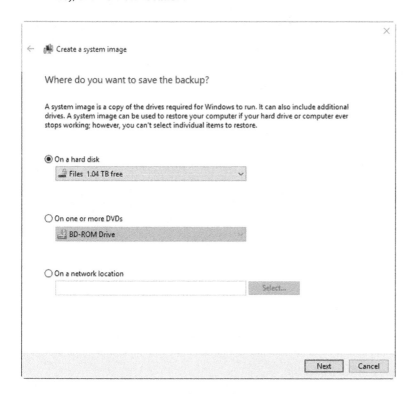

Figure 12-21. *You can save your backup in different locations*

■ **Note**   You cannot use removable media such as SD and MicroSD cards for a system image. These are common on Windows tablets, on which you probably won't have other backup options except Reset. In these cases, you need to rely on the Reset feature or any backup image provided by the tablet manufacturer.

If your computer always connects to your network via Wi-Fi, you should not choose a network location. This is because the image is restored from the Windows boot menu, where no Wi-Fi drivers are loaded. When restoring from a network location, the computer needs to be connected to the network via a physical cable.

■ **Note**   If you have several hard disks or partitions in your computer, you are asked if you want to add any of them to the image backup.

Before creating the backup, Windows 10 shows you what you're backing up and where the backup will be stored (see Figure 12-22). Click the **Start backup** button when you are ready to begin.

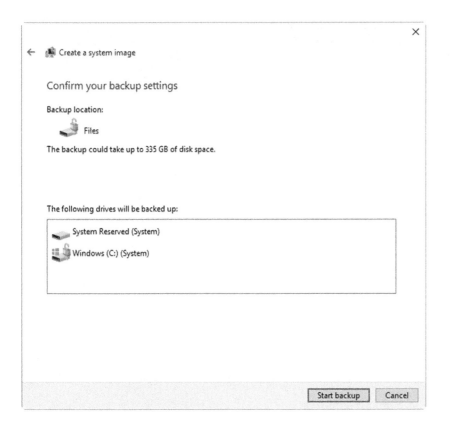

Figure 12-22. *Windows shows you the drives it back up*

You cannot restore a system image backup from within Windows 10 in the way you can with a reset image. You need to start your computer from the **Advanced startup** menu (available in the Settings app under Update & recovery ➤ Recovery), a USB recovery drive, or the Windows 10 installation DVD. When you do this, the System Image Recovery option can be found in the Advanced Options menu in Startup Repair. I show you how to access this shortly.

■ **Tip**   Whereas you can create a system image backup in File History, you can also create one from the command line using the Windows PowerShell Utility. Open a PowerShell (Admin) window and use the command `wbAdmin start backup -backupTarget:D: -include:C: -allCritical –quiet`, where `–backupTarget` is the hard disk (or network location) in which the image is to be stored, and `–include` is the drive letter of the disk on which Windows 10 is installed.

For network locations, you might need to insert the commands `-user:username -password:userPassword` just before the `–allCritical` switch. You can also specify more than one hard disk to be stored in the backup with the switch `–include:C:,D:,E:`.

This image backup can then be restored using a recovery drive or installation disc for Windows 10. You can find the System Image Recovery option in the Troubleshoot ➤ Advanced page.

Safe Mode and Diagnostic Startup Mode

With Safe Mode removed from the new boot menu, how do you get to it? You can see the older boot menu by pressing **Shift+F8** when starting Windows. Here you have the same familiar options, including **Safe Mode** and **Safe Mode with Networking** (see Figure 12-23). You can access these settings from the boot options by selecting **Troubleshoot ➤ Advanced Options ➤ Startup Settings**. You are prompted to restart your PC, after which the Safe Mode option will be available.

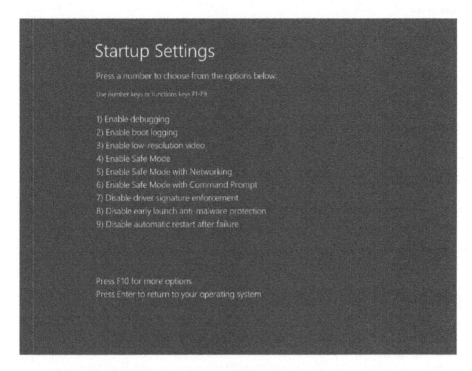

Figure 12-23. *Starting Windows 10 in Safe Mode*

Not all computers allow you to press F8 or Shift+F8, however, especially ones that start up really quickly. If you need to get into Safe Mode in this case, you can do so from the Windows System Configuration page, in which Safe Mode comes with a whole variety of additional and useful options.

You access the System Configuration dialog by searching for **msconfig** at the Start screen. Under the Boot tab, there is an option to turn invoke a **Safe boot** the next time it starts.

The most interesting option is under the General tab. Although Safe Mode is very useful, it is also extremely limiting and doesn't allow you to perform many actions.

Under the General tab, there is the option to turn on a diagnostic startup (see Figure 12-24). It is equivalent to Safe Mode+ in that, in addition to loading the bare operating system, it also loads some system drivers, such as for your graphics, and it allows you to perform the full range of Windows 10 configuration operations.

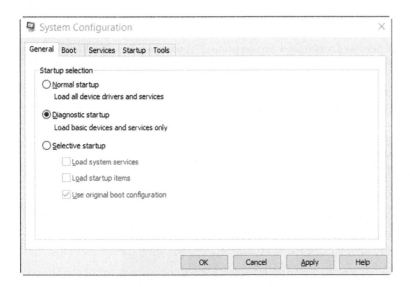

Figure 12-24. Turning on diagnostic startup mode

■ **Note**   When you switch on these options in the System Configuration dialog, they remain on until you run
`msconfig` again and switch them off.

Using Startup Repair

If Windows 10 fails to start three times, and the System Reserved partition isn't damaged, Windows launches
Startup Repair. This is an automated system that resets Windows components to their default settings in an
attempt to get things working again.

If Startup Repair can't repair Windows, it offers you advanced repair options, which are the menus
shown in Figures 12-25 through 12-28. A refresh might be the best option to get Windows 10 working again.

Figure 12-25. Windows 10 can self-repair when it can't start

Understanding the Windows 10 Startup Menus

The startup menus in Windows 10 have changed considerably to accommodate the mouse and graphical systems that were not supported on older computer systems.

This isn't to say that you can't access the previous DOS–type startup menu (it is still available with the Shift+F8 key press at startup), but the standard F8 key now takes you to the new graphical system if your hardware supports it.

At the first screen, you have three options: continue to start Windows 10, turn off your computer, or troubleshoot the machine (see Figure 12-26). Note that on some devices, you might also see a **Use device** option here that permits restoring from a system image stored on the drive.

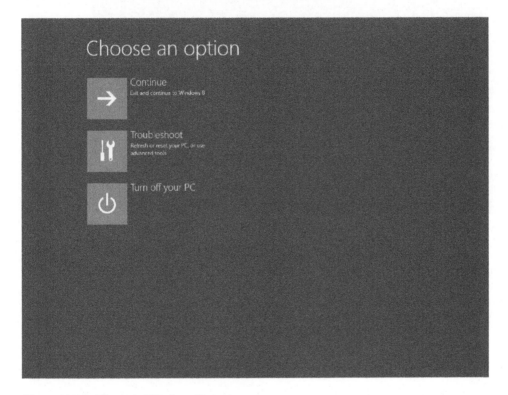

Figure 12-26. The main Windows 10 startup menu

The Troubleshooting options are straightforward and easy to understand, offering only the new option to reset your computer. You might expect to find the Startup Repair option here, for example, but it has been moved into the Advanced Options (see Figure 12-27).

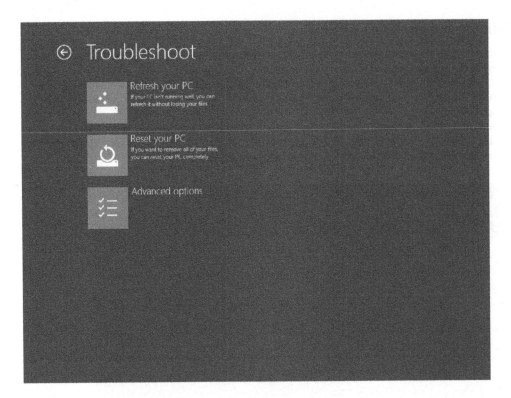

Figure 12-27. *The startup troubleshooting menu*

All the remaining options are found in the Advanced Options. Here you have access to the Command Prompt, in which you can perform actions such as manually repairing the boot options, performing a CHKDSK (check disk), and more. You can also change the Windows Startup Settings, which allows you to turn off the new graphical menu and have Windows 10 use the traditional DOS menu instead (see Figure 12-28).

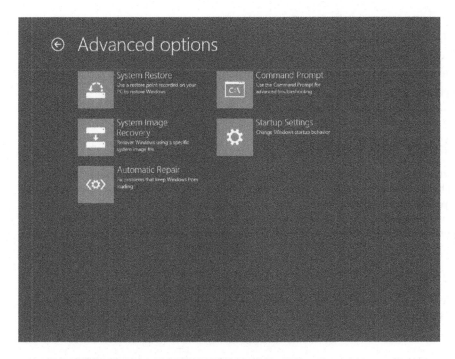

Figure 12-28. The advanced troubleshooting menu

Restoring Windows 10 to Factory Settings

If you are selling your computer or giving it away, you can use the Reset option with the optional switch to delete all of your files and accounts to restore Windows 10 to its factory settings. Doing this cleans the PC and returns it to a "factory state."

Reset this PC is in the Settings app under **Update & recovery ➤ Recovery** (see Figure 12-29). You are asked if you want to keep your files or **Remove everything**. If you have any files on the PC that you wish to save, you should make sure that you have backed them all up before performing a reset because they will be deleted from the PC.

Figure 12-29. You can restore your PC to factory settings using Reset

■ **Tip** Reset does not securely erase your files; they can be recovered later by using a file recovery program. If you want to securely erase deleted files and data on your hard disk, there are many third-party utilities that can do this, but the excellent—and free—CCleaner (`piriform.com/ccleaner`) does this job along, with providing other useful cleanup and maintenance tools for Windows.

Backing Up Files and Folders

Nothing is more important on your computer than your files and documents. Once you lose those precious family photographs of baby Gilbert's birth, or last year's vacation in the Maldives, they're gone forever—and you have nothing but your memories from then on.

It is critical that you safeguard your files on your computer. I'll show you how to do this later in this chapter. It is very important that you make backups and keep them in safe and sensible places.

Where to Store Backups

Choosing where to store backups of your files is critical because choosing to store your backups in the wrong location can often be as bad as having no backups at all. So where can you store your backups, and what are the pros and cons?

■ **Tip** Many Internet routers allow you to plug a USB hard disk into them to use the network as storage. This can be an excellent local backup location.

- **A second hard disk on your PC** is the fastest and least difficult way to store backups because an automated system can update the backup every time you change a file. However, an electrical spike through the PC could fry the original data and the backup. A theft or a fire destroys both copies.

- **Network-attached storage** (NAS) is a great way to store backups in your home or workplace. NAS drives can be hidden in inaccessible places. They are still vulnerable to fire, however.

- **CD/DVD/Blu-ray discs** aren't advisable for backups any more. Partly because, with the exception of Blu-ray, the discs don't have large enough capacities for our ever-growing collections of digital photographs and home videos. Also, these discs degrade—and there's little way to tell whether it will be 3 months or 30 years before they become unreadable.

- **USB hard disks** are one of the best options because they can be stored offsite in the home of a friend or family member, or at the home of the person responsible for backing up your vital business data.

- **USB flash drives** are of a size and price that you can consider storing backups on them. Bear in mind, however, that they are relatively easily broken (e.g., sat on, put in the washing machine, or chewed by the dog). If you store one on your key chain, it could very easily get wet when you're out in the rain.

- **Cloud storage** is becoming ever more popular and there are a lot of services to choose from, including Microsoft's OneDrive (which is built into Windows 10), LiveDrive, Google Drive, iCloud, Carbonite, Mozy, Amazon S3, and many more. The problem here is the initial upload can be tens if not hundreds of gigabytes, and unless you are on a super-fast broadband connection, it can take weeks or even months to upload.

■ **Tip** I always recommend using *at least* two backup solutions. I store backups locally on both a NAS drive and a second hard disk in my main PC for quick restoration, but I also use the OneDrive and LiveDrive services for cloud backup.

Remember to Encrypt Business Backups

You can normally consider your workplace relatively secure. You control who has keys and access to the building and the room(s) containing your computers. If you store business backups offsite, however, which is highly recommended, you should make sure that those backups are either encrypted or kept in a very safe location.

Sending unencrypted backups home with a senior staff member is one thing, but given that you have no control over this person's home security presents a data protection risk. The only safe strategy with business data—and the one the data protection regulators are most likely to endorse—is a virtual private network (VPN) or cloud-based encrypted solution designed specifically for business.

■ **Caution** Beware of synced network and cloud backups! If you use a service such as OneDrive that syncs the files on your computer with those in the cloud, or a backup solution that keeps files in sync by *deleting the file on the backup destination when that file is removed from the computer*, you could find that your backup is wiped completely if you accidentally delete the files from your computer. To avoid this problem, stop your backup software from running until you can restore the files or use a cloud provider that supports file archiving.

Backing Up and Syncing Your Files with OneDrive

There are two ways to back up your files in Windows 10. The first method is to use Microsoft's OneDrive cloud sync and backup service (see Figure 12-30). You can set this up by first searching for **OneDrive** in the Start menu. Then click the OneDrive "cloud" icon in the taskbar system tray.

Figure 12-30. Microsoft's OneDrive service is built into Windows 10

■ **Tip**   You don't need to be signed into your PC using your Microsoft account to access your OneDrive storage.

You set up the OneDrive file backup firstly by choosing the location of the OneDrive folder. The factory option is to store this in your C:\Users\[Username] folder on your hard disk. If you only have one hard disk or partition in your PC and you do not plan to create a system image backup, this will be fine. You can often find that you get better file security by storing your files in a location separate location from your copy of Windows. I show you how to do this later in this chapter in the "Safeguarding Your Personal Files" section.

■ **Tip**   The OneDrive app can also be used to back up and sync files from an Office 365, OneDrive for Business account.

A new OneDrive account offers only 15GB, but you can purchase more storage at www.onedrive.com. If you have an Office 365 account, Office 365 Home or Personal add 1TB (1 terabyte = 1,000 gigabytes) to your personal OneDrive account. OneDrive for Business comes with up to 1TB of storage for each account user.

The standard 15GB of free storage won't be enough for your files, photos, and video, but OneDrive remains one of the best and best-integrated cloud backup and sync solutions available. By choosing on each of your PCs which folder you want to sync, you always have the most up-to-date versions of those files on all of your PCs. Any files that are not synced are viewable in the OneDrive section of File Explorer, and when opened, are downloaded and stored locally on the PC.

Keeping Local File Backups with File History

If you want to keep a local backup copy of your files, Windows 10 comes with a file backup and versioning tool called File History, which keeps backup copies of files as you make changes to them so that if you accidentally make a change to a file that you didn't intend to make, the file can be restored.

File History also keeps copies of files that have been deleted and changed, helping you recover older copies of documents that were accidentally deleted or modified when they shouldn't have been. File History can be incredibly useful if you use your computer for work and change files (such as Office documents) frequently. It can roll back accidental or unapproved changes.

File History is accessed from both the Settings app and the Control Panel. You can use local internal hard disks, USB attached drives, and network-attached drives (though the latter two don't work if they're not plugged in or are inaccessible). Figure 12-31 shows the File History options in the Settings app.

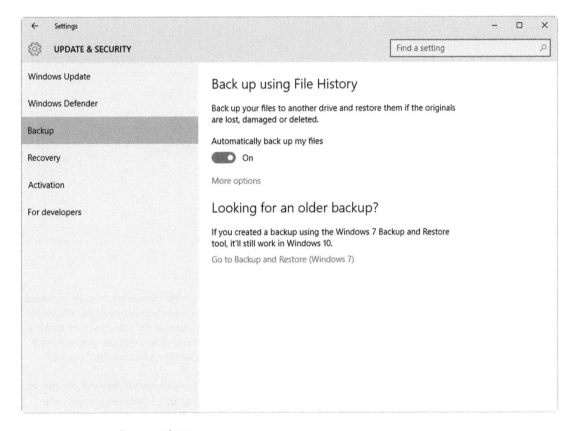

Figure 12-31. *Windows 10 File History*

The File History options in the Settings app automatically detects any USB-attached hard disks or additional internal hard disks on your PC, but (as I mentioned earlier in this section), you can use networked locations as well. They include NAS drives and USB hard disks that are plugged into your Internet router. If you want to select one of these locations as the storage for your backups, click the **Select a different drive** link.

To get more control over File History, click the **More options** link (see Figure 12-31). It provides much finer control over the feature (see Figure 12-32), such as choosing which folders on your PC to back up (the standard options are your Documents, Music, Pictures, Videos, and Internet Favorites folders).

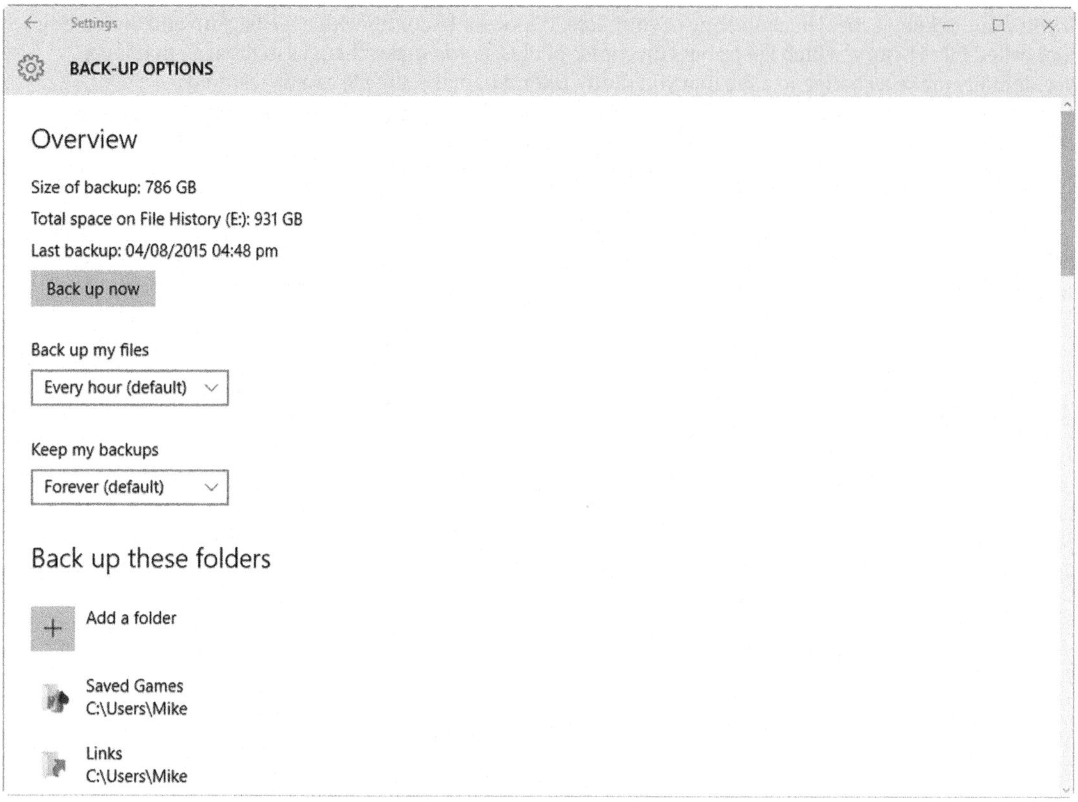

Figure 12-32. You can get finer File History options in the Control Panel

In the File History options panel, you can also choose to exclude folders that are automatically included in the backup. As an example, I exclude my Music folder. File History keeps a backup copy of a file whenever the file changes, and just playing a music track changes the "last accessed" time of the file, therefore making a change. As music tracks can be played often, and are quite large in size, excluding them can prevent your File History drive from running out of space too quickly. Remember that anything you exclude from File History should be backed up elsewhere.

You can also change the drive you use for File History here. You can do this without deleting any current backup files already created, although they won't be accessible to restore through File History unless you reconnect the drive to the service.

You can choose how often it saves copies of files. Remember that it doesn't do it automatically when a file is saved. You can also choose from periods as low as 10 minutes. If you use your Windows 10 computer for work, a shorter period may offer you more reassurance if you work on files that change regularly, such as Word documents.

430

You can also choose the amount of time that a version is kept. The Forever option is a little misleading because it is the same as the Until Space Is Needed option. Keeping files until space is needed is probably the best option, however.

The first time you run File History, it creates a full and complete backup of your Libraries (Document, Music, Pictures, and Video), and if you want to back up additional files, you should add them to your Libraries. This initial backup can also take some time, depending on the number of files you are backing up and your connection speed. You don't need to worry about leaving the PC on, however, because if you need to put the PC to sleep or shut it down, the backup pauses and resumes when you switch it on next.

You can click **See advanced settings** to open the Control Panel File History options. This provides a way to clean up your File History drive should it become full. In the Control Panel File History settings, click the **Advanced Settings** link in the left-side pane, and then click the **Clean up versions** link (see Figure 12-33).

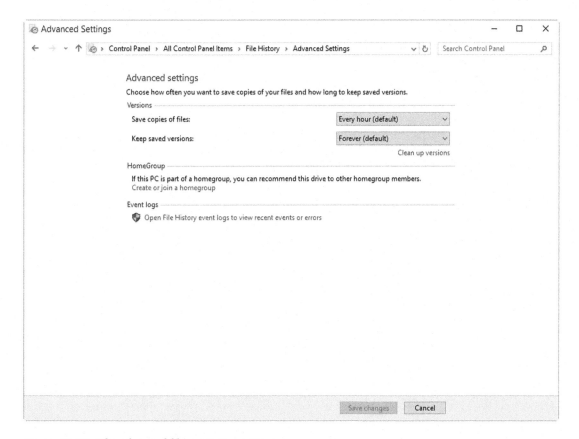

Figure 12-33. *The advanced file versioning options*

■ **Note**   If you are using a laptop or tablet that has only a single hard disk, you might not be able to keep File History versions locally on the computer because Windows 10 doesn't support keeping versions in the same location as the original files. Many Internet routers have USB ports so that you can plug in a hard disk to use as network storage. This is an excellent location for backups and File History versioning.

Restoring Backed up and Deleted Files with File History

File History is used to restore your files under four different circumstances: you had to reinstall Windows on your PC; you need to move your files to a new PC; you accidentally deleted a file or files and you need to recover them; or you accidentally made a change to a file that you didn't intend to make.

I want to show you these last two scenarios first. There are two ways to open the File History restore screen. In the Settings app, in the File History options, you can click the **Restore files from a current backup** link at the very bottom of the panel. Alternatively, when you are in File Explorer and are looking at a specific folder, or indeed have a file highlighted, you see a **History** button under the **Home** tab on the ribbon (see Figure 12-34). Click this to open the full File History restore window.

Figure 12-34. *You can restore files from File Explorer*

In the window that opens, you have several different sets of controls (see Figure 12-35). The Back button and the address bar at the top of the window operate in exactly the same way as they do in File Explorer. Typing a folder location in the address bar takes you to the corresponding backup.

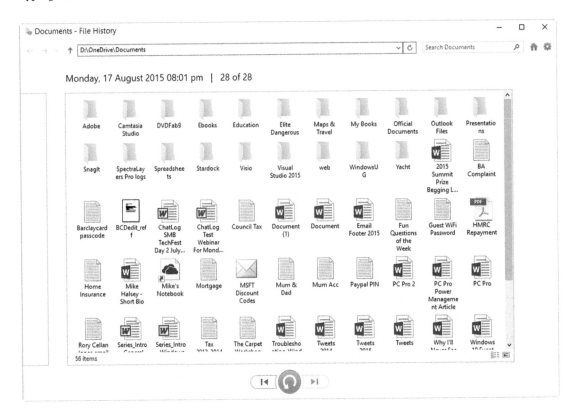

Figure 12-35. *The main File History restore window*

At the bottom of the window are back and forward (in time) buttons that move backward and forward through the different dates and times that changes were made to files. These buttons help you find the right version of a file to restore. Between these buttons is a large, green Restore button.

To restore files, select the file (or files) you want to restore and then click the green **Restore** button. It really couldn't be simpler to restore your files.

■ **Note** If you are restoring your files from File History after reinstalling Windows, you need to set up File History again. Point it at the same backup location you used before to reconnect the File History drive. You can then restore all of your files to your PC.

Safeguarding Your Personal Files

One of the problems with your PC's user folders that store your Documents, Music, Pictures, Video, Internet Favorites, and more, is the uncertainty of where files are stored. If your files and data are stored on the same partition as your Windows installation, and you are forced to reformat the hard disk and reinstall the operating system from scratch, you could lose everything, or at least any files that have been created or modified since your last backup.

Although turning on the Libraries feature and then changing the default save location for those Libraries is one way to do this, I prefer to move the user folders wholesale over to a new partition or hard disk in the computer.

A hard disk is a physical storage area in which everything is put in the same place, including your copy of Windows and all of your files (see the left image in Figure 12-36). This means that if something goes wrong with Windows, you can face the possibility of losing all of your files as well.

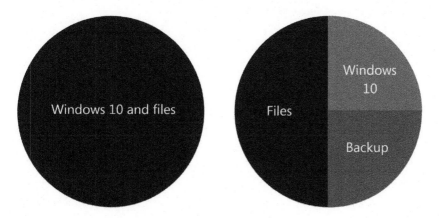

Figure 12-36. *An unpartitioned disk and a partitioned disk*

If you split your hard disk into several partitions, you are splitting that *physical* hard disk into several *logical* ones. File Explorer sees each partition as a different disk drive.

The image on the right in Figure 12-36 is my recommended setup. It has three partitions: one for Windows 10, a big one for files, and a third one for a backup copy of the operating system.

If you have a second hard disk in your computer, you might want to use it for files and backups. If something goes wrong with the hard disk on which Windows is installed, and this hard disk sees the most mechanical activity, your files and your backup copy of Windows will still be intact.

To create new partitions on your hard disk for files, perform the following steps. (You should always be extremely careful when managing partitions on your PC. If they are not managed correctly, all manner of things can go wrong, including wiping out your copy of Windows 10 and all your files).

1. Press **Win+X** to display the **Administration** menu.

2. Click **Disk Management**.

3. To create a new partition, you need to make space by shrinking an existing one. In the Disk Management window, right-click the hard disk partition you want to shrink (usually the C:\ drive containing your Windows 10 installation).

4. From the options, select **Shrink Volume** (see Figure 12-37). Note that "volume" is the terminology used here to describe both disks and partitions.

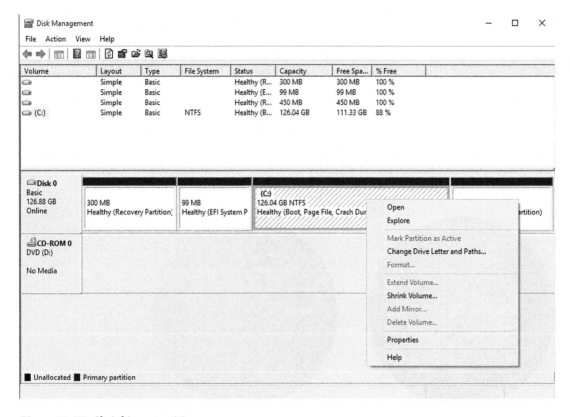

Figure 12-37. Shrinking a partition

■ **Note**   How big should you leave your Windows partition? For general light usage, 50GB is a good size (enter **51200** in the size box). An enthusiast might want 100GB to 200GB (**102400** or **204800**), but a gamer might want up to 300GB (**307200**).

---

5. Choose the amount by which you want to shrink the disk. You'll need to leave enough space for all of your files and an image backup. On a larger hard disk (1TB or more), I suggest shrinking the drive down to 25 percent of its current size (e.g., 250GB).

6. In the *unallocated space* remaining after shrinking the partition, right-click with your mouse (see Figure 12-38).

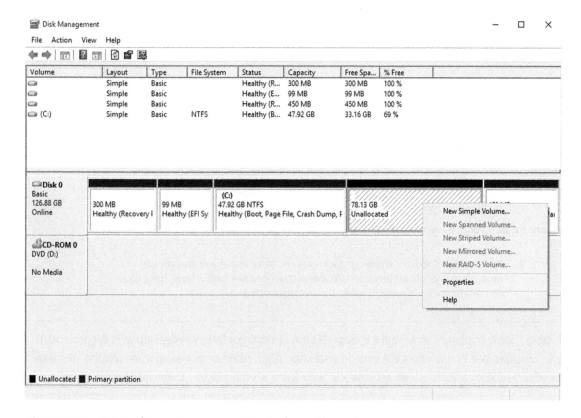

Figure 12-38. *You need to create a new partition in the unallocated space*

7. From the options, select **New Simple Volume**.

8. Create a partition of the appropriate size for files. I recommend 50 percent of the original volume size. Give it a name and a drive letter (see Figure 12-39).

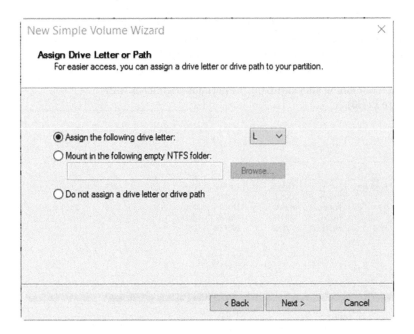

Figure 12-39. *Creating new partitions*

9. Repeat steps 6 to 8 for an image backup drive. Note that if you are using a professional-grade tablet or an Ultrabook that does not have a large hard disk, you might not have enough space for an image drive.

■ **Note** Many computers come with a backup partition containing a factory system image of Windows 10. If your computer didn't come with a Windows 10 installation disc, I recommend leaving it and creating your own secondary backup partition as well, because you never know when the factory image might come in useful.

Now you need to move the user folders and files to the new files partition.

1. Open **File Explorer**.

2. Click the small arrow in the File Explorer address bar at the far left of the current address location.

3. From the drop-down location options, click your username (see Figure 12-40).

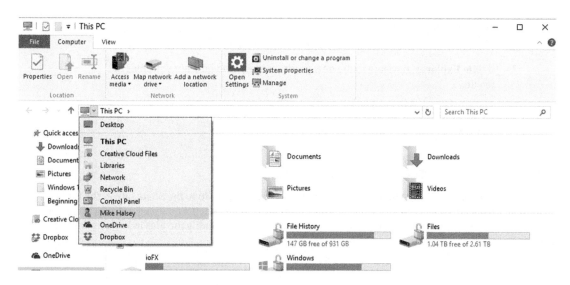

Figure 12-40. *Selecting your user folders*

4. Select the user folders you want to move, which are usually Downloads, Documents, Music, Pictures, and Videos (see Figure 12-41). Your Internet Favorites are automatically backed up and synced by default in Windows 10.

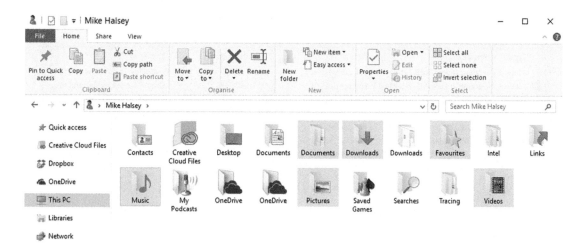

Figure 12-41. *Selecting your user folders to move*

5. Right-click the selected folders.

6. From the menu, click **Cut**. (It is *very* important that you *do not* click Copy!)

7. In **File Explorer**, navigate to the new partition in which you want your files to reside.

8. Right-click in a blank space.

9. Select **Paste** from the options that appear.

Taking Ownership of Files and Folders

You can change security options with any selected file(s) or folder(s). Go to the Share tab on the Ribbon to launch Advanced Security Settings (see Figure 12-42). By default, when a new user account is created in Windows 10, that user is given full permission to read, write, and modify the files in her user folders (Documents, Music, and so forth).

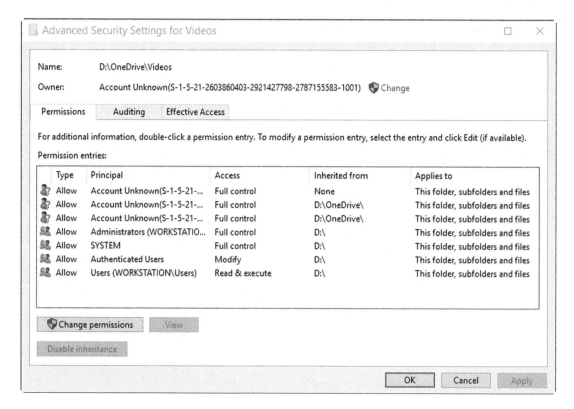

Figure 12-42. *Setting advanced file security in File Explorer*

At times, you might find that you have permissions set on files and folders from another user or another version of Windows. This is especially true if you have upgraded your system from an earlier version of Windows or if you store your files and folders on a separate partition or hard disk for added security and peace of mind.

■ **Caution**   You should always be very careful when changing permissions for files and folders on your PC, as you could find that you inadvertently lock yourself out!

When you try to access a folder for which you do not have permission, Windows 10 normally asks you if you want to take ownership of the folder; if you say yes, it automatically changes the permissions of its contents.

Sometimes, however, you need to do it manually by following these steps:

1. In the **Owner** section of the **Advanced Security Settings** dialog, click **Change**.

2. In the **Enter the Object Name to Select** section, type the username of the user you want to make the owner.

3. Click the **Check Names** button.

4. If the names are correct, they appear. Click the **OK** button to complete the ownership changes on the files/folders.

Summary

The tools available for you to back up not only your files and documents, but also Windows and your installed apps are both extensive, and for the most part, easy to use. There are certainly plenty of choices—whether you want to store your file backups locally on your PC, in your home or office, or in the cloud, and if you want to create your own backup of Windows 10, or have the operating system manage this itself.

Certainly if you're a non-technical user, or if you know people who are, there is a strong case for only using apps available in the Windows Store. In the event your PC needs to be reset, these apps can be downloaded and reinstalled automatically, which is more difficult for win32 apps, where you may not always have access to the original setup file.

Windows 10 certainly makes it easy to be protected, however, and it is useful to know the options that are available to you. Taking a little more time to safeguard your files by moving them away from your Windows 10 installation can only offer additional peace of mind.

CHAPTER 13

Configuring Your PC's Settings

Windows has always been renowned for being a very configurable operating system (OS). Despite the new look, Windows 10 offers an immense number of ways to customize the OS, tweaked from within the OS itself and with third-party software.

The ability to configure Windows extends to the computer's internal and external hardware as well. In this chapter, I will show you even more Windows 10 configuration and customization options. These options enable you to customize your Windows 10 installation in myriad ways, from simple changes to more complex customization that can help you build your computer skills.

The Settings App

When Windows 8 was first released, the new Control Panel replacement was a place for you to visit for a small number of user controls, such as changing your logon settings and adding a new user to the PC. In Windows 10, however, the Settings app has been significantly enhanced and now offers most of the traditional Control Panel features (which I discuss later in this chapter). It includes every feature a casual or nontechnical PC user will need. So let's take a look at the new the Settings app in detail, where there are a few new gems and treats in store.

■ **Tip**   You can move backward in the Settings app to the page you were at before by clicking the Back button that appears in the top-left corner of the window (desktop) or by tapping the Back button on your phone.

Front Screen

The new front screen of the Settings app contains easy-to-read icons for the different groups of settings (see Figure 13-1). Each can be clicked to display the settings available in that category, and in the top right of the window is a search box in which you can type the name of setting you're looking for.

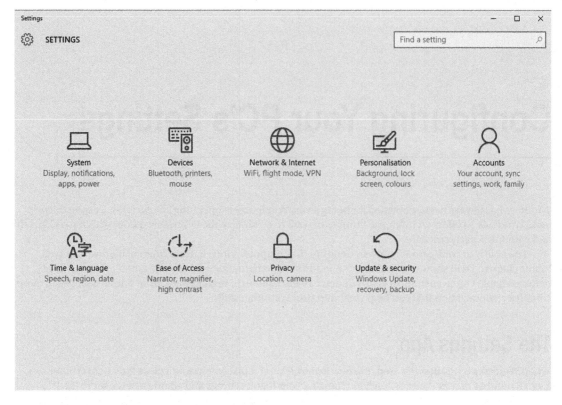

Figure 13-1. *The new front screen for the Settings app*

System

The System panel contains settings that pertain to the Windows operating system itself, such as managing notifications, apps, and power. This is also the place that you can get information about your PC and copy of Windows 10.

- **Display** is where you can change the resolution of your screen, change your screen rotation settings (for tablets and smartphones), and perform advanced functions such as calibrating the colors you see on screen and making text smaller or larger. These settings are covered in detail in Chapter 9.

- **Notifications and actions** is where you can select the quick action buttons in Windows 10 Mobile at the top of the notifications screen, and on the desktop at the bottom of the notifications fly-out panel. You can also select which icons appear in the taskbar system tray and which apps are allowed to display pop-up "toast" notifications. These settings are covered in detail in Chapter 9.

- **Phone** is the first of the Windows 10 Mobile exclusive settings. This is where you can control settings such as Caller ID, call forwarding, and voicemail. For those of you, like me, who can never remember your own phone number (well, I don't call *myself* do I!?), you can find it here.

  If you are busy on a call and receive a second call, you can set Windows 10 Mobile to provide auto-SMS messages that can be sent at the press of a single button, see Figure 13-2. To activate this feature, toggle the **Text reply** switch and then click the **Edit replies** link. You can set up to four custom relies; the standard options are "I'll call you back," and "Please text me." When a second call comes in, in addition to the option of switching calls and dismissing the second call, you are able to quickly send one of these text replies instead.

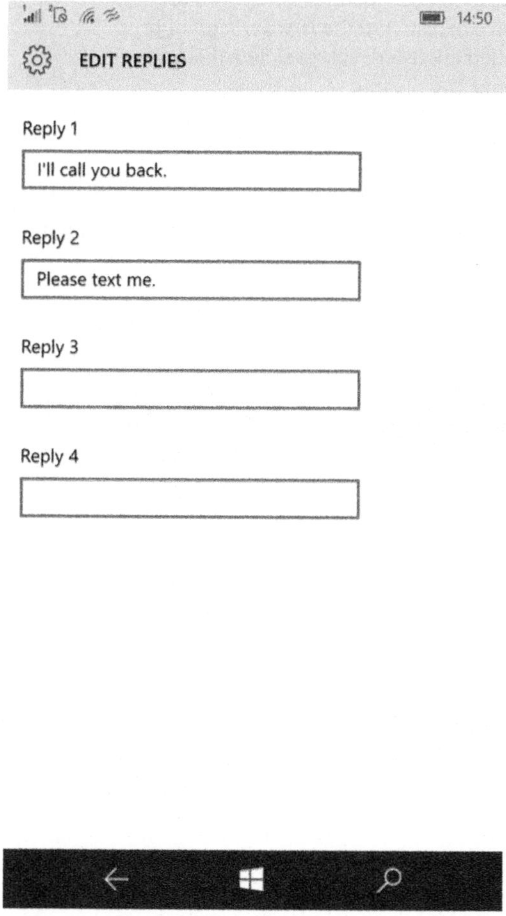

Figure 13-2. You can control automatic text-message replies in the Phone settings

The **Default apps** option allows you to choose which app you want to use for video calls, such as Skype, which comes as part of Windows 10 and Windows 10 Mobile.

- **Messaging** is the next Windows 10 Mobile–only setting. Options here include being able to backup and restore old text messages and request SMS and MMS delivery confirmations (your carrier charges for each one received). You can also disable the autodownloading of MMS messages, which is useful if you are on a low-data tariff.

- **Apps & features** does not appear in Windows 10 Mobile; it shows you how much space installed win32 and Store apps are taking up on your PC. You can search for an app and sort the list by app size, name, or installation date. If you have apps stored on several drives (such as your internal disk and on an SD card), you can view the apps on all drives or only on a single drive. If you click the **Manage optional features** link at the top of the window, you can install additional features for Windows 10, including language packs, handwriting and text-to-speech features, and if you are a member of the Windows Insider program, you can also find the **Insider Hub** app here. The option features that are already installed are listed; you can click the **Add a feature** button to add additional features to your PC.

■ **Note**   The Optional Features panel offers features available for your currently installed version of Windows. Should you want to upgrade Windows 10 Home to Windows 10 Pro, you should click **Activation** in the **Update & security** settings, and then click **Go to Store**.

- **Multi-tasking** is a feature for Windows 10 PCs only. Here you can control the Windows snap feature, which I covered in Chapter 8. You can turn various aspects of snap on and off, including the suggest companion apps feature and dynamic resizing of windows. You can also choose which open windows are shown on the taskbar, and how the Alt+Tab app switching function works when you are using virtual desktops.

- **Tablet mode** appears if you are using a tablet or convertible laptop. Here you can turn Tablet mode (also known as Continuum) on and off, and choose which mode your PC should be in (desktop or tablet) when you sign in. Additionally, you can tell Windows 10 to always or never prompt for confirmation to switch modes when you switch off your Bluetooth keyboard or detach your keyboard from your tablet.

■ **Tip**   Tablet mode settings offer a useful switch that you can use to hide, or not hide, all of your pinned app icons on the taskbar. If you have switched to Tablet mode and suddenly wondered where all of your taskbar icons have gone, you can reenable them here.

- **Battery Saver** is an option you see on Windows 10 Mobile and on laptops and tablets running Windows 10. Here you can view your remaining battery life and turn on the Battery Saver feature, which can restrict background app activity when the power level drops below 20%.

- **Power & sleep** appears on desktops, laptops, and tablets. This is where you can choose the length of time that your computer is inactive before the screen turns off, and when the PC goes to sleep.

- **Storage** is an interesting setting. Found in all Windows 10 devices, it shows you how full each of the drives (fixed and removable) in your PC are, and gives you the option to change the default storage locations for Store apps (not win32 apps), documents, music, pictures, and video (see Figure 13-3). On Windows 10 Mobile smartphones there is an option for downloads. Changing a setting here does not move any files or apps already on the PC or phone. You need to manually move files or uninstall and reinstall the app(s).

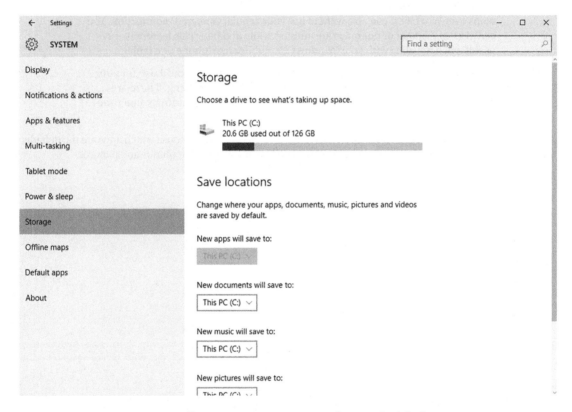

Figure 13-3. *You can automatically save new content to external storage by default*

■ **Tip** If you have a Windows tablet or Ultrabook and use a plug-in card (e.g., Micro SD) to store files, you can use the Save Locations setting under the Devices tab to automatically save new content types to this storage instead of the internal hard disk on your PC.

- **Device Encryption** is an option that is only seen on smartphones and small tablets with screens eight inches or less. Using Microsoft's BitLocker technology, Device Encryption allows you (with a single switch) to fully encrypt your device so that the data cannot be read if it is lost or stolen.

- **Driving mode** is a feature only in Windows 10 Mobile. It allows you to turn off all notifications except SMS text messages and phone calls (you can also set the phone to ignore these) when you are driving. Driving mode can be set to automatically activate when you are in the proximity of a specific Bluetooth device, such as your in-car hands-free kit.

- **Offline maps** allows you to download maps for anywhere in the world. It is available on any Windows 10 device. You can decide if you want to only download and update maps over Wi-Fi, or if you also want to use your cellular (metered) connection. You can also set whether or not maps are automatically updated. This feature is very useful when traveling with your Windows 10 Mobile smartphone or a tablet.

- **Default apps** is where you can choose the apps Windows should use for your calendar, email, maps, music, video, photos, and web browsing. There are several different options available to you, and it's worth spending some time examining them.

The main page of the Default apps view (see Figure 13-4) allows you to choose which apps are the defaults for the main file types on your PC; for example, which apps open your email or photos and pictures.

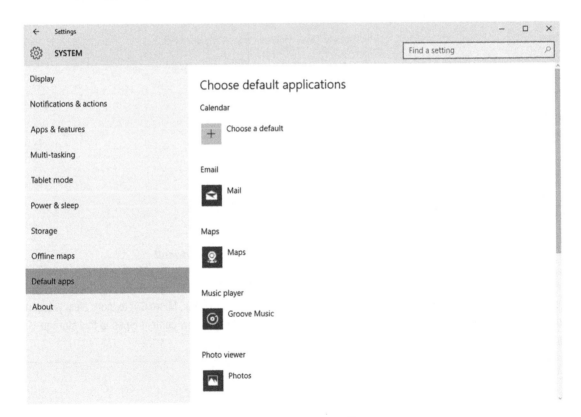

Figure 13-4. *You can choose the default apps to use for common file types*

If a default is not set for the file type, click the **Choose a default** button. You can select from a list of installed compatible apps. At the bottom of this list is a **Look for an app in the Store** link, which opens the Windows Store app so that you can search for an app to use.

It's worth noting that if you already have an appropriate app installed, but it doesn't appear in this list, there isn't a browse button to help you find it. You can set defaults for those apps through a Control Panel applet that I'll show you shortly.

At the bottom of the list of app types are some links. The first of these, **Choose default applications by file type** displays a full list of all the file types known to both Windows and your PC (see Figure 13-5). Next to each file type is the app that the file type opens in, or if no app is set, the **Choose a default** button.

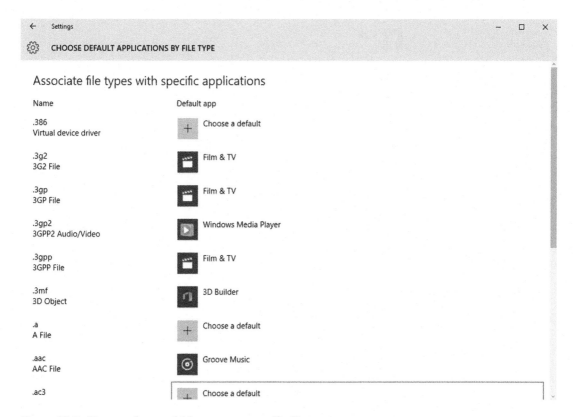

Figure 13-5. *You can choose which apps open specific file types*

This panel is useful if you have a custom app, perhaps in your business, or an older app for which the file link is broken. Windows 10 is very good at setting the default apps for all the file types that it knows, but if it is a less well-known file type, you can set the app link manually here.

Next, the **Choose default applications by protocol** (see Figure 13-6) presents a list of known web app types (preceded by URL:) and Windows functions; you can set the default apps for the protocols.

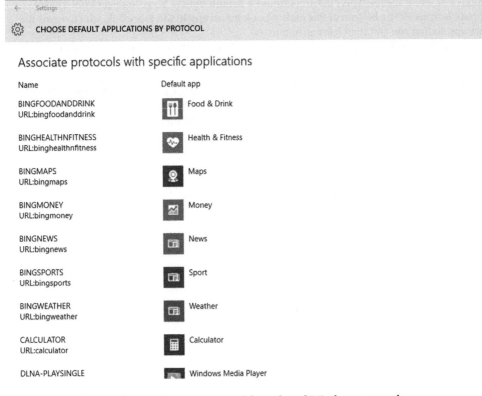

Figure 13-6. *You can choose what apps are used for web and Windows protocols*

The last option, **Set defaults by app** opens the full app defaults controls in the main Windows 10 Control Panel. I show you how to use this later in this chapter.

- **About** is a panel with several different uses. Here you can learn useful information about your PC, such as its processor, the amount of memory, and the installed Windows 10 edition (see Figure 13-7).

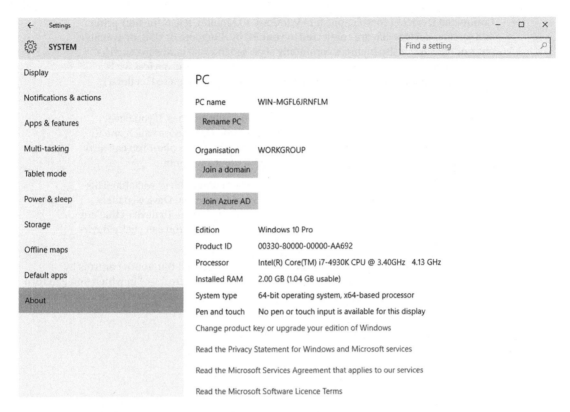

Figure 13-7. *The About panel provides useful information about your PC*

There are also buttons to rename the PC and join a work network *Domain* or *Azure AD* (Active Directory) service. If you are using your PC at work, you might be asked to sign in to one of these using your work email address.

There are also links to the Administrative tools, BitLocker, Device Manager, and System Information, all of which I cover later in this book.

Devices

For advanced control of hardware device drivers in Windows 10, the full Device Manager still exists, and I will show you how to use it later in this chapter. Most users will find the Control Panel confusing to use, however, and despite the presence of the Devices and Printers panel (more on this later), Microsoft has implemented a simpler way for users to manage devices on their PCs.

- **Printers and Scanners** (does not appear in Windows 10 Mobile) is where you can install and manage locally connected (USB), and wired and wireless (Wi-Fi) printers and scanners. An **Add a printer or scanner** button at the top of the screen autodetects the printer or scanner attached to your PC or on your network. If a device can't be found, **The printer that I want isn't listed** link appears. I showed you how to manually add printers and scanners in Chapter 6. At the bottom of this page is a switch to permit the downloading of device updates over metered (cellular) connections.

- **Connected Devices** (doesn't appear in Windows 10 Mobile). It lists the non-printer and scanner devices that are connected to your PC by Bluetooth or USB, or available on your network; it also includes commonly accessed internal hardware, such as your sound card. You can click any device to remove it. Below the devices list is a switch to permit downloading and updating of drivers over a metered (cellular) connection.

- **Default Camera** is an option on Windows 10 Mobile smartphones. If you have more than one camera app installed on your phone, you can choose which one to use when you press the phone's shutter button (if the phone has one). You can also chose to activate the camera without having to first unlock the phone.

- **Bluetooth** appears in all versions of Windows 10 where Bluetooth is available. This panel is very similar to the Printers and Scanners and Connected Devices panels. It presents an on/off switch for Bluetooth and a list of any Bluetooth devices that are discoverable or that are already connected to the PC or phone. You can click a device to pair it or remove it.

In Windows 10 Home, Pro, and Enterprise, you can access additional Bluetooth controls by clicking the **More Bluetooth options** link. This opens an applet (see Figure 13-8) in which you can turn Bluetooth discovery on or off, and control other features, such one that alerts you when a new Bluetooth device is in range.

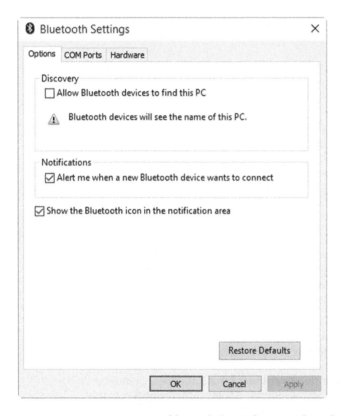

Figure 13-8. *You can access additional Bluetooth settings from the Settings app*

- **NFC** appears if you have the technology installed in your Windows 10 laptop, tablet, or smartphone. There is an on/off switch for NFC on your device, as well as a list of installed apps that you have given permission (at install time or later) to use NFC. Below this, and if you have an app installed that supports it, is a **Tap to pay** option, where you can choose a payment method—a debit card or PayPal account, for example—that can be used to pay for items when you tap your device to an NFC payment device.

- **Mouse/Mouse & touchpad** (the name of this setting varies, depending whether you are using a Windows 10 PC or a smartphone). Why would you want to use a mouse with a smartphone? This feature is tied to the Continuum feature in Windows 10, which I discussed in Chapter 8. It is not available on all Windows 10 Mobile smartphones, and it may not appear on your device. You can select options such as your primary mouse button, scroll speed, and the ability to scroll within inactive windows. The link to **Additional mouse options** provides some useful accessibility features; I discussed these in Chapter 10.

- **Typing**. This option is only in Windows 10 Home, Pro, and Enterprise. The controls the settings for the autocorrect feature within Windows 10. Did you know that the OS has a built-in spell-checker and can autocorrect words? Well, if you'd rather it didn't, you can turn off these features here.

- **AutoPlay** (this option is only in Windows 10 Home, Pro, and Enterprise) is where you can choose what happens when memory cards, CDs, and DVDs are inserted into the PC, or when USB devices such as smartphones and USB flash drives are connected (see Figure 13-9). For each device type, there is a menu of options that include **Ask me every time** and **Take no action**. If you do not want Windows or your apps to do anything at all when you insert removable media or a device, you can completely turn off AutoPlay using the switch at the top of the page.

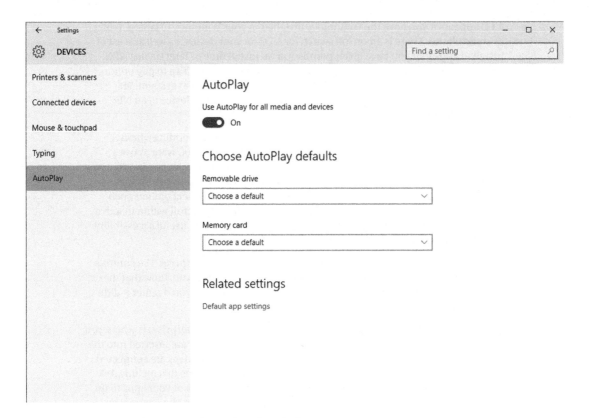

Figure 13-9. *You can choose autoplay settings for Windows 10*

Network and Internet

A PC that is not connected to the Internet might as well just be left switched off and unused these days. Fortunately, Windows 10 provides a great many ways to get online and connect to networks of many types. To summarize:

- **Cellular & SIM** is the first of three settings that only appear in Windows 10 Mobile and on laptops and tablets that have a SIM card slot. Any SIM cards you have inserted in your phone display here with the name of the cellular operator that each is connected to. Beneath each is a switch to turn the data connection off for that network.

- **WiFi**. I showed you how to connect to Wi-Fi networks in Chapter 3, but the experience is very different on phones. It is here that a list of available networks appears, so that you can choose one to connect to. At the top of the page is a Wi-Fi on/off switch and at the bottom are buttons for WiFi Sense and Manage.

- **WiFi Sense** allows you to share Wi-Fi passwords with the people in your contacts list and on networks such as Skype and Facebook. The feature can also automatically connect to networks that your contacts have shared with you. The **Manage** button is where you can get more information about a Wi-Fi network by tapping it. You can also delete one or more of your stored Wi-Fi network settings in this panel; this is useful if the connection settings for a network became corrupt.

- **Flight mode** appears on smartphones but also Windows 10 laptops and tablets. Here you can turn off all radio network activity. On laptops and tablets, you can turn off Wi-Fi and Bluetooth independently of one another, which is useful if your flight supports in-flight Wi-Fi.

- **Data usage** is where you can monitor the amount of data your Windows 10 device is using over Ethernet, Wi-Fi, and cellular over the last 30 days. Clicking the **Usage details** link shows you exactly how much data each of your apps used in that time. This is useful for identifying traffic hogs.

- **Mobile hotspot** is a setting available on all smartphones, laptops, and tablets that are equipped with a SIM card slot. Here you can create a mobile tethering hotspot that can be shared with up to ten other devices; these can be any devices that can connect to Wi-Fi. Optionally, you can choose to share the data connection over Bluetooth. You are given a network access name and password to use on the other device. You should only use this feature if your cellular carrier supports tethering.

■ **Tip**   When setting up a mobile hotspot, you can set the ability for other devices (that have already connected to the hotspot before) to turn it on automatically. This is handy when using your laptop or tablet away from Wi-Fi, as you don't have to first turn the hotpot on in your smartphone.

- **VPN** is for people who need to use a virtual private network (VPN) connection to access files or email on a workplace network. This feature is in Windows 10 Pro and Enterprise and Windows 10 Mobile, but *not* in the Home edition.

- **Dial-up** one that's just for desktop PCs and laptops (it'll appear in tablets but it isn't much use there). If you have a dial-up Internet modem attached to your computer, it appears here with any settings, such as baud rate, that can be configured. These settings vary from one modem to another. You are also able to define dial-up connections here, including the access phone number.

- **Ethernet** is for desktop PCs and laptops that are connected to a network by a physical Ethernet cable. The settings here are pretty basic, with a list of available Ethernet connections. If you click one of the connections, you are taken to a page showing any potentially available properties for that adapter.

- **Proxy** is for anybody who needs to connect to the Internet via Ethernet or Wi-Fi using a proxy server. Settings are available here for setting a proxy using a script for manually setting a proxy server's settings.

Personalization

In Chapter 9 I showed you around the personalization features in Windows 10, so I won't repeat myself here. Here are brief overviews of the settings available in the Personalization panel.

- **Start (Windows 10 Mobile)** allows you to modify the Start screen in several ways; for example, placing a background image on either the screen or just the live tiles, and displaying more live tiles columns.

- **Start (Windows 10 Home, Pro, and Enterprise)** contains switches that allow you to control the desktop Start menu. These include being able to show and hide app content suggestions (otherwise known as *adverts*), recently opened files and apps, recently installed apps, and whether the Start menu should appear in full screen.

- **Background** is the settings for the desktop. Here you can choose your background wallpaper and how it fits on your screen.

- **Colors** is where you can ask Windows 10 to automatically choose a color scheme for your windows to compliment the color of your wallpaper, or you can specify a custom color. You can also choose whether that color is to be shown on the taskbar and Start menu.

- **Sounds** is available in Windows 10 Mobile; here you can choose your ringtone and other system sounds.

- **Themes** is available on the desktop and merely serves as a front end to the main themes settings in the Control Panel.

- **Lock Screen** is where you choose your background image for your lock screen and the apps that display detailed or quick status information.

Accounts

Two of the biggest advantages that Windows tablets have over other tablet operating systems are support for multiple users on a single-device and advanced parental controls. In Windows 10, these features have been extended further with support for families and new child-friendly options. I'm not going to detail these features in full here, as I talked about setting up and managing user accounts in Chapter 4.

- **Your account** is where you can switch your own account between a Microsoft account and a local account. It's also where you can change your avatar (photo) and where you can see any other accounts you may use with the PC, including Azure Active Directory.

- **Sign-in options** is where you can change your password, create a pin or picture password, and manage the Windows Hello biometric login feature.

- **Work access** allows you to connect your PC to your workplace, school, or college if the establishment supports Bring Your Own Device (BYOD) PCs.

- **Sync your settings** is where you can choose which settings are synched between all of your Windows 10 devices, including PCs, laptops, tablets, and smartphones. This includes your theme (color scheme) and passwords on a phone, and ease of access and language settings on all other devices. The sync feature requires you to be signed-in to your PC using a Microsoft account.

- **Family & other users** is only found on PCs, laptops, and tablets. This is where you can create and manage additional users on the device, including children and other family members. This is also where you can manage the Windows 10 family safety features.

- **Kid's Corner** is a feature of Windows 10 Mobile. When activated, it allows children to open their own custom Start screen containing only the apps that you have approved for their use by swiping left on your smartphone's lock screen.

- **Apps Corner** is like Kid's Corner, but for adults. If you need to demo an app on your phone, but don't want people to have access to your personal apps and information, you can set up Apps corner to give them access to only what you have approved. There is a version of this feature on PCs, laptops, and tablets called **Assigned Access**, which you can activate in the **Family** & **other users** panel.

Time & language

Do you remember getting off a flight and having to wind a wheel control on the side of your watch to set it to the local time? Well some of you, like me, still prefer the craftsmanship and precision of a quality Swiss watch, but for everybody else, this can be a chore. It's not just about changing the date and time on your PC either, as depending on where you are in the world, you'll use either a comma (,) or period (.) as a thousandths delimiter in math. You'll also have a different keyboard layout too. All of these controls are managed in the Time & language panel.

- **Date & time** is where you set not just the time and date on your PC, but also the number formats (see Figure 13-10). Windows 10 offers the option to automatically set the date and time (note that it needs an Internet connection to do this). I won't go into too much detail here because I discussed how to change these settings in Chapter 9.

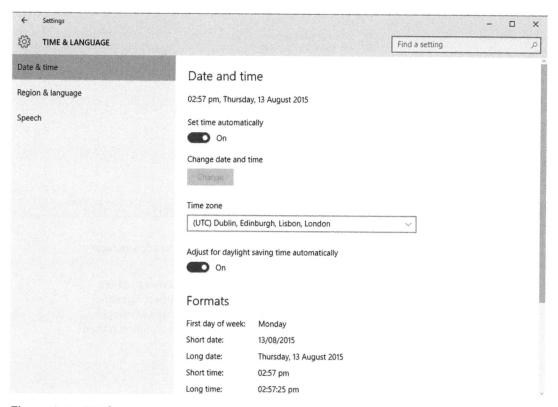

Figure 13-10. *Windows 10 can autoset the date and time on your PC*

- **Language/Region/Region & language** (depending on whether you are using a PC or a smartphone). This setting might be named differently or even be two different panels. On a PC, laptop, and tablet you can choose the region you are in and add language packs to the PC (see Figure 13-11). Again, I covered how to change these settings in Chapter 9.

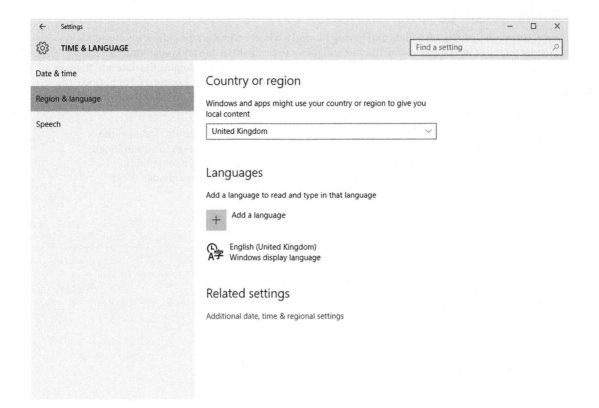

Figure 13-11. *You can set your country and install multiple languages on your PC*

- **Keyboard** is a feature only on Windows 10 Mobile; it allows you to add language packs to your smartphone.

- **Speech**. In Chapter 10 I discussed all the options that make Windows 10 easier to use. Here is where you can choose the text-to-speech and speech recognition settings for your particular language (see Figure 13-12). Why are these settings separate from the Ease of Access features? It is because speech recognition is used extensively by Cortana.

456

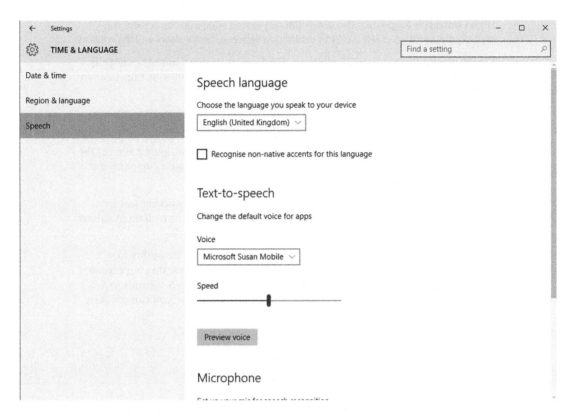

Figure 13-12. *You can control both text-to-speech and speech recognition for multiple languages*

Useful features include being able to **Recognize non-native accents for [your] language**, which permits the speech recognition system to use heuristics to recognize particularly thick regional accents, though the speech recognition feature may be slightly slowed as a result, and that's your fault, not Windows :P.

The voices—both male and female—that Windows uses for text-to-speech vary by country. It's worth noting here that Cortana uses her own voice and cannot be configured here. For more information on how to configure Cortana, see Chapter 5.

Ease of Access

In Windows 10, the Ease of Access features are front and center. This is a marvelous thing because it's not just people with disabilities who can benefit from these features. If you have a motor skills disorder, such as a slight shake, the mouse can be difficult to use, and keyboard combinations like Ctrl+C (Copy) or Ctrl+Alt+Del (invoke Admin panel) can be difficult if not impossible to use. Color-blind people might have difficulty with the Windows color schemes, and if you are farsighted, you might have difficulty reading what's on your PC screen. If you find Windows 10 in any way difficult to use, then it's worth spending some time looking through the Ease of Access features, which I detail in full in Chapter 10.

- **Narrator** is a text-to-speech option that can read aloud the text in your documents and web pages, but also controls, links, and buttons as you move your mouse or hover your finger over them.

- **Magnifier** is where you can create a magnifying glass for your desktop, making everything on your screen much larger and easier to read.

- **High Contrast** is for people who have difficulty seeing what's on the screen; the high-contrast settings create a clearer distinction between the windows and the content.

- **Closed captioning** is new to Windows on Windows 10; it allows some (but not all) videos to automatically display subtitles. Here you can choose the font, transparency, and size of the text.

- **Keyboard** is not available on smartphones, but here you can choose if you always want to use the onscreen keyboard, sticky keys, and other features.

- **Mouse** is not available on smartphones, but here you can choose options such as the pointer size and color, and whether you want to use your keyboard's cursor keys to move the mouse pointer.

- **More options*/Other options** (a different name depending on whether you are using a PC or smartphone). These options include the ability to turn off the Windows desktop background and window animations.

- **Other options**. A feature that's well worth mentioning offers the ability to choose how long pop-up notifications (known as *toasts*) appear on your screen before disappearing (see Figure 13-13). The options vary from 5 seconds to 5 minutes. It is useful if you find that the toasts disappear before you can properly read them.

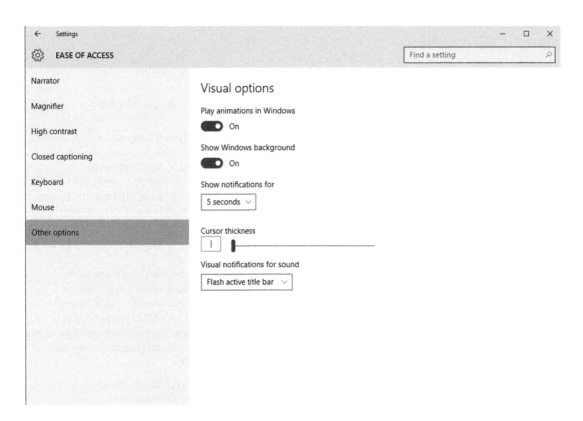

Figure 13-13. *You can choose how long toasts are displayed in Windows 10*

Privacy

Privacy is the buzzword of the early part of the twenty-first century. It's been entirely brought to the forefront of political and commercial discussions because of the Internet. Our PCs are now connected, theoretically anyway, to every other PC, laptop, tablet, smartphone, and server on the planet. It's mostly only software features such as firewalls and network access rights that keep them separated. It's for this reason that action and spy movies regularly show hackers gaining access to remote systems, but also people breaking into firewalled premises to gain physical access to a computer network.

While we may enjoy the drama of a good hacker movie (and if I've just made you paranoid, you can skip back to Chapter 11 for information on how to keep your own PC safe), the simple fact remains that every day we surrender large volumes of personal information to companies and individuals across the planet; but Windows 10 has some advanced features to help you manage this. In Chapter 11 I go into detail about the privacy features in the Settings app, but here's an overview:

- **General** is where you can manage the privacy settings for advertising, and where you can control the SmartScreen feature that helps protect your PC from malicious downloads. This section is not available in Windows 10 Mobile.

- **Location** is where you can change your tracking options for the PC. On a modern PC, you don't need GPS to use tracking, as this can also be done from your cellular signal or IP address. You can control tracking for the PC generally and also for individual apps that request it.

- **Camera**. Did you know your PC is watching you? In fairness, unless you are using Windows Hello to log in to your PC, then it likely isn't watching you, but some apps request access to your camera—and here you can choose which ones.

- **Microphone.** A similar story for your PC's microphone; you can choose which apps are allowed to listen for the sound of your voice.

- **Motion** is a Windows 10 Mobile feature, though also appears in some tablets. Here you can control which apps are allowed to collect information from motion sensors in your smartphone.

- **Speech, inking, and typing** is where you can control the way Windows 10 and Cortana get to know your handwriting when you write on a touchscreen with your finger or a stylus.

- **Account info** is where you can deny apps any access to your local or Microsoft account, including your name, avatar, and personal information.

- **Contacts** is where you can control which apps have access to your contacts. By default, your email app(s) and other apps, such as the Windows 10 People app, require this information.

- **Calendar** works in the same way as Contacts, allowing you to decide which apps can have access to your calendar.

- **Messaging** is where you can control which apps can read or send SMS and MMS text messages. It appears on Windows 10 Mobile smartphones, and laptops and tablets that have a SIM card slot.

- **Radios** are features (such as Wi-Fi and Bluetooth) that are used to send and receive data and files on your PC. Here you can choose to let apps that require access to manage this on their own (most do) or you can choose which apps have radio access. Denying certain apps access can increase the battery life of laptops, tablets, and smartphones.

- **Background apps** is a feature in Windows 10 Mobile that allows you to choose which apps can run in the background on your smartphone. Minimizing the number of apps that run in the background can extend your battery life.

- **Accessory apps** are tied to a specific hardware accessory, such as a Bluetooth headset, a smart watch, or a health band. Here you can control the notifications you receive from these apps, as well as the data that the apps can have access to.

- **Other devices** include those that are not covered in other categories. Here you also see controls for devices that you have paired with Windows 10, known as your Trusted Devices. This can include your smartphone.

- **Feedback & diagnostics** is where you decide if and how diagnostic data is sent to Microsoft when an app or Windows encounters a problem. Sending this information may help Microsoft fix problems more quickly, but it also may send a copy of one of your files to Microsoft. Should a file be requested, perhaps because a problem caused an app to crash, you are *always* explicitly asked for permission.

Update & security

It's always essential to keep your PC patched and up-to-date. In our always-on, connected society, malware, hacking, and other attacks are everywhere. Additionally, the personal data and information we keep on our PCs, not just about ourselves but others too, makes our PCs a valuable target no matter who you are. Needless to say, Microsoft takes security very seriously, and in Windows 10 there are some significant policy changes.

- **Windows Update/Phone Update** is your sole location for security and stability updates for Windows 10, as the Control Panel applet in previous Windows versions has been removed. This isn't the only change Microsoft has made to Windows Update either.

In Windows 10 you can no longer ignore updates the way you could with previous Windows versions. All updates are downloaded and installed automatically as they arrive; the only choice that you have is to install them automatically or for Windows 10 to notify you that updates are ready to be installed on the next restart (you have three days before your PC automatically restarts, although even then it does it at a time you're not likely to be using it, the default being 3 a.m.).

The reason for this policy change is to improve the security of Windows 10 overall (and to reduce support costs) by making sure that all Windows 10 PCs are patched and up-to-date. It also helps improve the security of your own PC. In fairness, Windows 10 is now such a modular and componentized OS that only a small few updates will ever require a restart. Most updates are installed silently in the background without you ever knowing.

If you have Windows 10 Pro, you have an additional option available to you. The **Defer Upgrades** switch (see Figure 13-14) allows you to defer all but critical security and stability Windows Updates for a maximum of 90 days. This feature, called the Current Branch for Business (CBB), exists because a rare few Windows and hardware driver updates can be unstable and cause problems. The 90-day period gives Microsoft (or the relevant third-party vendor) time to fix any problems and provide a replacement update. It also gives businesses time to evaluate the new updates and set in place any plans or training that might be required. The updates still show as available to you during this time, however, and they can be installed manually if you desire.

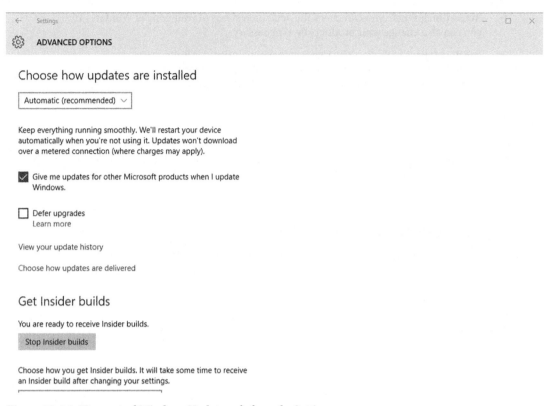

Figure 13-14. You control Windows Update only from the Settings app

If you are using Windows 10 Enterprise in an environment managed using Windows Server or System Center Configuration Manager, an additional option is available through your system administrator. Called Long Term Servicing Branch (LTSB), it installs only security and stability patches and drivers through Windows Update. All Windows feature updates, however, remain optional for up to ten years (five years of mainstream support plus five years of extended support). This is so that businesses with mission-critical PCs can keep them patched and secure, while avoiding the headaches caused by training staff in feature and OS changes. It's worth noting that choosing LTSB for your business removes the Edge web browser because it is a Store app that is intended to be updated regularly.

■ **Note**   Windows 10 Mobile updates are now delivered directly by Microsoft, and no longer by cellular carriers. This means all Windows 10 Mobile handsets get the latest updates as soon as they are available.

- **Windows Defender** is a feature I wrote about in Chapter 11. It is Windows 10's built-in anti-malware engine; it can be managed here.

- **Backup** is where you can access the File History backup feature that I covered in Chapter 12.

- **Find My Phone** is a useful feature if your Windows 10 Mobile device is lost or stolen. I discussed how to manage it in the "Privacy" section in Chapter 11.

- **Recovery** was detailed in Chapter 12. There are options to reset your PC should Windows 10 become unstable and to access the Advanced start-up options.

- **Activation** is where you can check the activation status of your copy of Windows 10; you can also change your product key, if necessary.

- **For developers** tools won't be relevant to the majority of Windows 10 users. However, if you write apps for Windows 10, there are options here to allow you to load non-Store apps onto your PC or smartphone for testing.

Extras

Some Windows 10 Mobile smartphones come packaged with additional controls and settings outside of the main Settings. These appear in a group called **Extras** and include model or range-specific features such as the Glance screen on Microsoft Lumia phones, touchscreen controls for when you wear gloves, and graphic equalizers for audio.

Defragment and Optimize Drives

The Disk Defragmenter helps keep file access on your computer quick by making sure that all parts of files are stored together on your hard disk. This also helps maintain file integrity and prevents files from becoming corrupt.

By default, it's set to automatically defragment all of your hard disks once a week. It automatically adds new hard disks to the defragmentation schedule as well (see Figure 13-15).

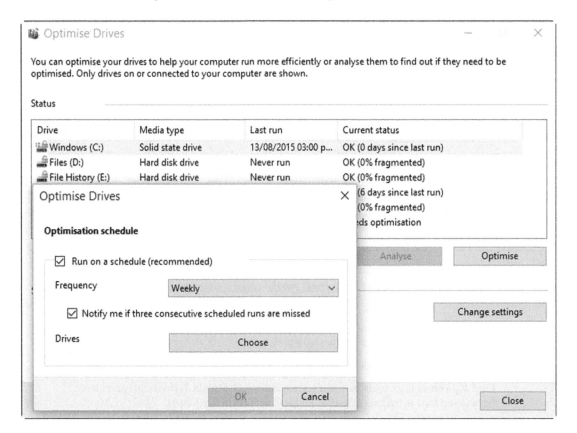

Figure 13-15. *Using the Disk Defragmenter*

There are some hard disks that you might want to exclude from the automatic defragmentation process, however. These disks include SSDs, in which there is no speed advantage to be gained from keeping files together because the drives are random access, anyway.

Defragmentation also puts a significant strain on mechanical hard disks, so if you have a disk in which the contents do not tend to change, such as for installers or for an image backup, it is worth excluding it from the defragmentation cycle.

Disk Clean-up

The Disk Clean-up tool, which you can also find by searching for **clean** at the Start menu, removes temporary files from your computer. These files fill up space on a small SSD, or generally slow programs down, including Internet Explorer. It's a very simple tool to use, and as a basic alternative to more advanced freeware like CCleaner (`www.piriform.com/ccleaner`), it is worth running once in a while.

In the bottom-left corner of the Disk Clean-up window is a **Clean up system files** button. Clicking this provides more options that can help reduce the amount of space used on a PC. It's especially useful on devices such as tablets and Ultrabooks, which only have a small amount of storage available.

These tools include being able to remove all but the most recent system restore points and shadow copies; useful if your PC is running smoothly anyway. Additionally though, when you upgrade your PC to Windows 10, your old Windows 7 or Windows 8.1 installation remains in place for a period of one month in a `Windows.old` folder. This folder can take up many gigabytes of space on your PC, but you can delete it in the Disk Clean-up tool by checking the **Previous Windows installation(s)** option (see Figure 13-16).

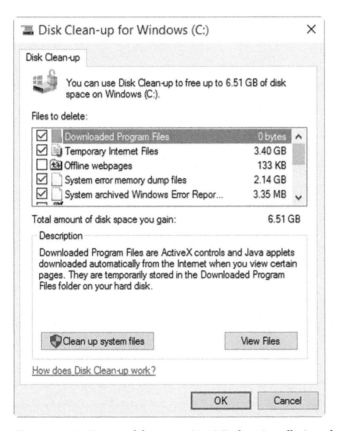

Figure 13-16. *You can delete a previous Windows installation after an upgrade in the Disk Clean-up tool*

Other options that are good to check and that can free up a lot of space on your PC are **Windows upgrade log files**, **system error memory dump files**, and **Temporary Windows installation files**.

Summary

Windows has traditionally been highly configurable, and Windows 10 is no exception with its sheer volume of settings. With Windows 10, Microsoft has done an excellent job of organizing the Settings app with all the configuration options that PC users will need, while not confusing them with the more advanced options that can be found in the Classic Control Panel and Administrative tools.

The advanced options still offer a lot of power and flexibility for PC users, however, and so in the next chapter you'll look at them in depth.

CHAPTER 14

Advanced Configuration and Customization

The new Settings app contains just about every configuration option that PC users will need, but sometimes you want more control. For this the Windows classic Control Panel and Administrative tools still exist. Some of these functions are designed purely for IT system administrators in businesses, but there are many others that can give you much more flexibility over your Windows setup.

Control Panel

The Control Panel still exists in Windows 10, although it's been on a significant diet, as many of its controls have been subsumed into the new Settings app. If you want administrative control of your PC, however, or if you want to use more advanced (non-consumer-focused) features, this is where you find them.

The Control Panel is most easily accessed in Windows 10 by pressing the Windows key + X to display the administration menu, which reveals a Control Panel link, or by searching for **control** at the Start menu. If you have used Windows 8.1, you will already be familiar with the layout of the Windows 10 Control Panel; but there have been a few changes since Windows 7, and some Control Panel options aren't where you might expect to find them.

■ **Tip** You can find any Control Panel item by using natural language search in the search box at the top right of the Control Panel window (and from the Search charm). This means you don't need to know the exact name of a control, but you can instead search for words such as *password* or *files* to display a list of all the controls that are relevant to that word.

Customizing the Control Panel

By default, the Control Panel appears in the Category view, in which all the Control Panel items are organized into groups, such as network and Internet controls (see Figure 14-1).

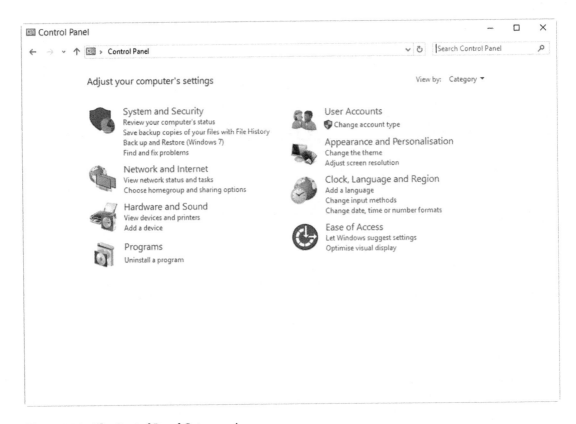

Figure 14-1. *The Control Panel Category view*

In the top right of the Control Panel window is a **View by** drop-down menu, in which you can choose to display the Control Panel items as either large or small icons. The icon views simply list all the options available to you in the Control Panel (see Figure 14-2).

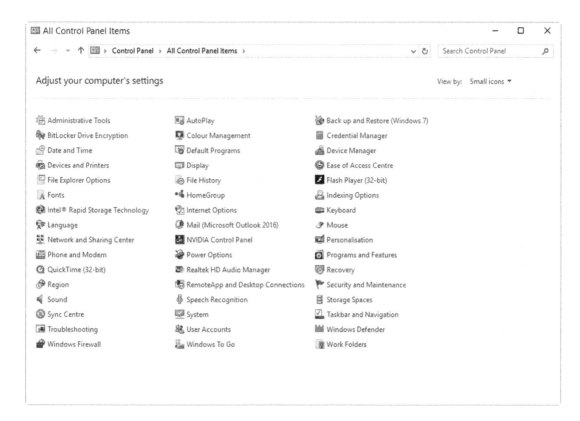

Figure 14-2. *The full Control Panel items list*

Your list of Control Panel items might differ from those seen in Figure 14-2 in that they might show fewer or slightly different controls. If you don't have biometric devices on your computer, for example, you don't see the Biometric controls, and if you don't have a touchscreen, you probably don't see the Tablet PC or the Pen and Touch settings.

The Control Panel shows only the controls that relate to your specific computer, and no more. This ensures that you're not distracted by controls that won't do anything.

I won't discuss every Control Panel item, but I do want to talk about the most important ones and show you how you can use them to configure your copy of Windows 10.

■ **Tip**   You can create a folder on your desktop that contains a link to every individual Control Panel item. This folder, which many people call "God Mode," can be created by right-clicking in any blank space on your desktop and creating a New ➤ Folder that you rename as **GodMode.{ED7BA470-8E54-465E-825C-99712043E01C}**.

Choosing AutoPlay Options

The main AutoPlay options have been moved into the Settings app. Should you want finer control over these options, however, the Control Panel applet is certainly where you can find it.

The AutoPlay options to select which program or app opens for a particular media or device are sensibly laid out (see Figure 14-3). (It's also very easy to stop Windows from asking you what you want to do with a device every time you insert it.) It includes all removable drives for all types of media—including pictures, music, and video; storage cards for a camera (you might want to choose between the custom software that came with your camera or Windows importing the images); and DVDs, CDs, Blu-ray disks, and software.

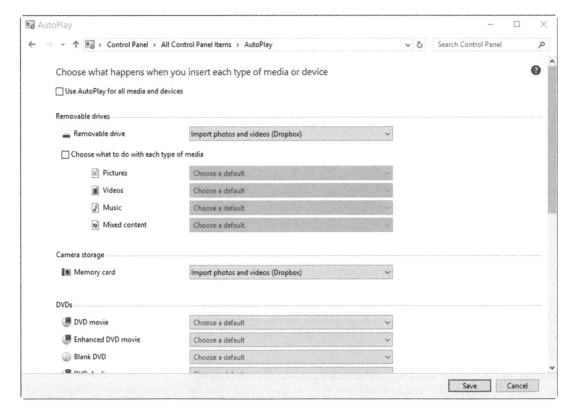

Figure 14-3. *Choosing the AutoPlay options*

At the bottom of this page is a **Reset all defaults** button to return all the settings to their default, in case you make changes that you later decide you want to reverse.

■ **Note** When you insert a USB flash drive, you may be asked if you want to use it to speed up your system using a Windows feature called ReadyBoost, a useful feature primarily for older computers with slower hard disks and small amounts of physical memory. It uses the flash drive as cache memory to speed up access to commonly opened Windows files. The speed improvements come with flash memory being much faster than a mechanical hard disk drive. Only faster USB flash drives are compatible with ReadyBoost.

Setting Default Programs

You can set your default programs in the Settings app, but as with AutoPlay, the options in the Control Panel provide much finer control. There are four options in Default Programs:

- Set your default programs

- Associate a file type or protocol with a program

- Change AutoPlay settings (discussed in the "Choosing AutoPlay Options" section)

- Set program access and computer defaults

Set Default Programs lists all the software installed on your computer. Clicking a program in the left pane will show the number of its file defaults (see Figure 14-4). This means that the program will open a certain number of file types. The Windows Disc Image Burner, for example, just opens ISO files, but Microsoft Word opens many more files, including RTF, DOC, and DOCX. Windows Media Player opens even more file types.

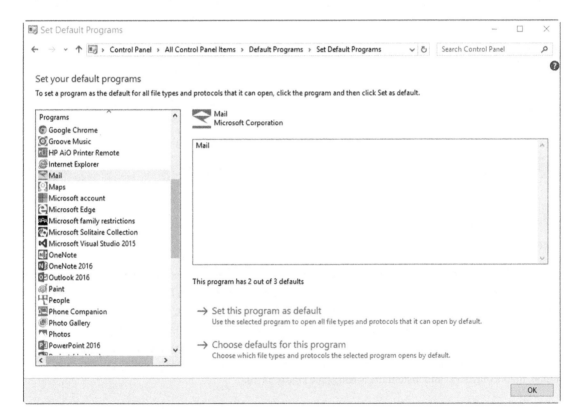

Figure 14-4. *Choosing default programs in Windows 10*

Here you have two options. You can **Set this program as default**, which sets the program as the default for *all* the file types it can open. Otherwise, you can **Choose defaults for this program**, which takes you to the **Associate a file type or protocol with a program** options.

Associate a file type or protocol with a program offers finer control over the program or app by displaying a list of every file type Windows can open. You have the option to associate a single or multiple file types with a certain program or app (see Figure 14-5).

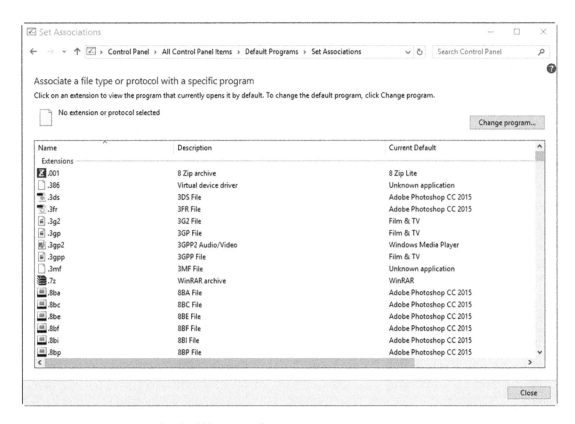

Figure 14-5. *Associating individual file types with programs or apps*

■ **Tip** File types can only be set one at a time. However, if you enter this page from Set Default Programs, you have check boxes that make it simpler to associate file types with programs.

Another way to control the default programs in Windows is through **Set Program Access and Computer Defaults**, which allows you to easily change the default programs for browsing the Internet, email, media playback, and instant messaging (see Figure 14-6).

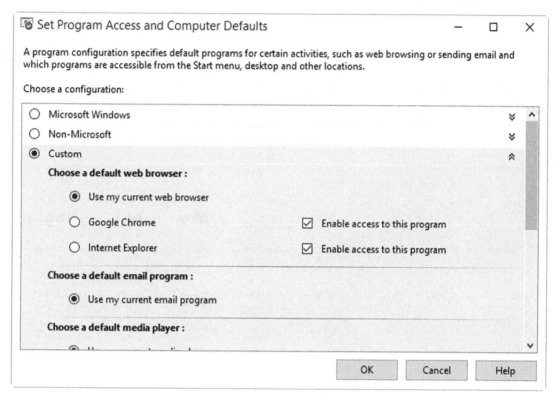

Figure 14-6. *Choosing the default web browser, email client, and media player*

Managing Fonts in Windows 10

Windows 10 doesn't have an advanced font manager, but the Fonts page is generally an excellent alternative. It shows thumbnail previews of letters and characters in the installed fonts (see Figure 14-7).

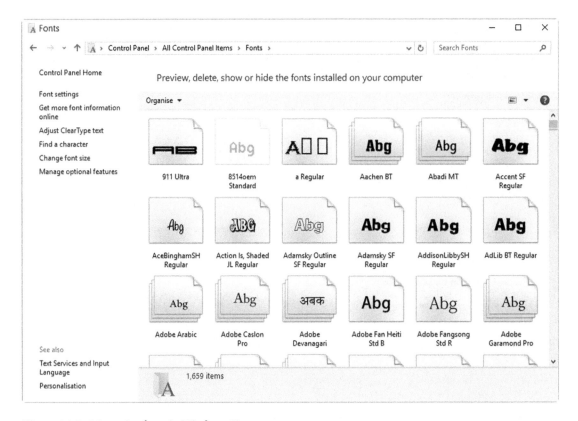

Figure 14-7. *Managing fonts in Windows 10*

■ **Tip** You do not need to be in the Fonts page to install a font. You can install a font from any location by right-clicking it and selecting Install.

If you want to view more of a font's characters, you can double-click it to open it. Some fonts first open into a font group, but each font shows you more characters, although not the complete character set (see Figure 14-8).

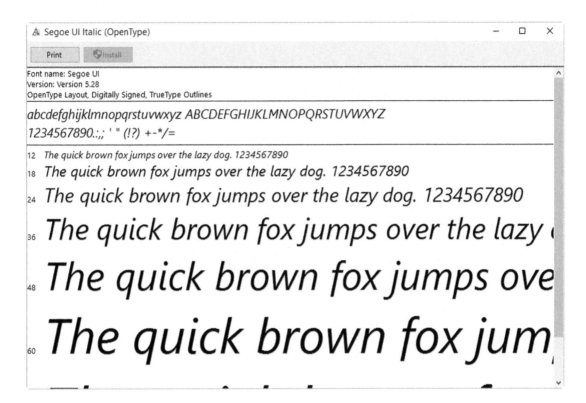

Figure 14-8. *Viewing fonts in Windows 10*

Configuring the Windows 10 Advanced System Settings

When you click **System** in the Control Panel, you are shown information about your computer. The System Properties page is where you find the type of processor and the amount of memory you have, as well as which edition of Windows 10 you are using. This information is useful when you need to describe your PC to a support professional.

Clicking **Advanced System Settings** in the left navigation pane brings up the System Properties dialog, which has settings that you may want to change (see Figure 14-9).

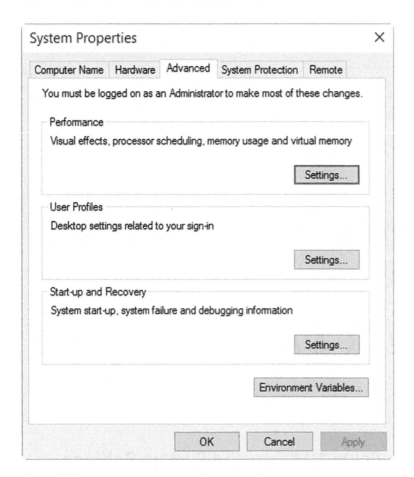

Figure 14-9. *Changing the advanced system settings*

In the Advanced tab of this dialog, there is a page with three sections: Performance, User Profiles, and Startup and Recovery.

To open Performance, click the **Settings** button. In the Performance Options dialog, the first tab is Visual Effects, which allows you to control some of the ways the Windows 10 desktop is displayed (see Figure 14-10). Some of the changes you can make here are purely cosmetic. For example, some people believe that removing shadows under windows makes the desktop look cleaner.

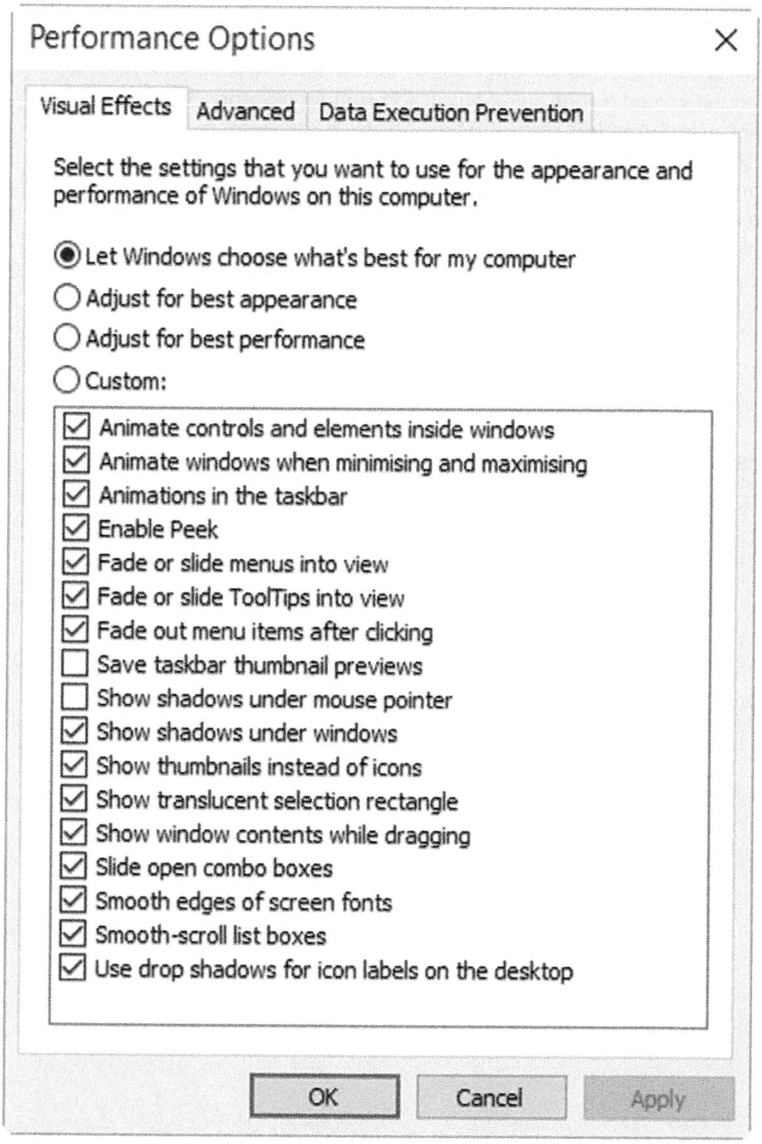

Figure 14-10. *Adjusting the visual effects*

If you have an older computer, you can adjust the look of the Windows desktop to get the best possible performance. Stripping the visual look of the desktop back to basics can improve the overall responsiveness of the computer.

Managing Virtual Memory Settings

The Virtual Memory settings are under the Performance Options' Advanced tab. Virtual memory is a file on the hard disk that your computer uses when it runs out of physical computer memory. This is much less of an issue than it used to be because computers ship with increasingly more memory, but you still may want to manage your Virtual Memory settings manually. The reason for this is that the virtual memory (sometimes known as the *swap file* or *paging file*) default settings have this file automatically increase and decrease in size. This can lead to disk defragmentation, which ultimately may cause the mechanical hard disk to slow down in accessing your files. If you use a solid-state disk in which hard disk space is at a premium, you may want to reduce the overall size of the paging file. To do this, click the **Change** button on the Advanced tab. The Virtual Memory dialog appears, as shown in Figure 14-11.

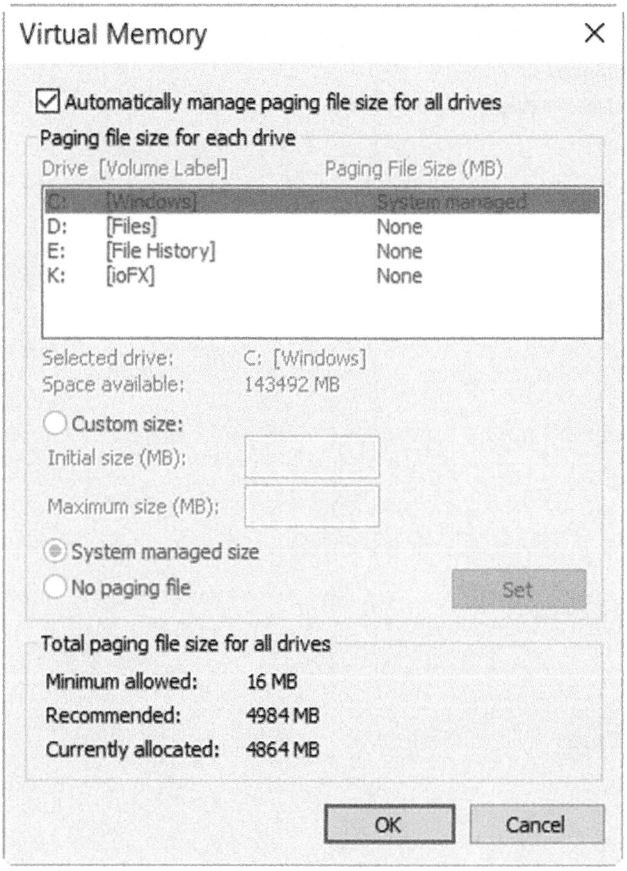

Figure 14-11. *Changing virtual memory*

To manage virtual memory manually, uncheck the box at the top of the Virtual Memory dialog and instead select the Custom Size option. At the bottom of the dialog, Windows 10 suggests minimum and recommended sizes for virtual memory. If you have large amounts of physical memory, however, such as 8GB or more, and you run Windows from a solid-state drive (SSD), you may want to set virtual memory to the minimum settings. Otherwise, Windows 10 suggests a recommended amount for the virtual memory. Setting both values in the Custom Size fields to the same amount prevents the virtual memory file from shrinking, expanding, and ultimately fragmenting your hard disk.

In the drives view on the dialog, you can also move the paging file to a different physical hard disk or partition if you want.

Managing Data Execution Prevention

Data Execution Prevention (DEP), accessed from the Performance Options dialog, is a feature that prevents certain viruses and malware from damaging your Windows installation. On occasion, it can also prevent particular games or other software from running.

If you find that a program isn't running properly, try allowing it through DEP. To do this, first select **Turn on DEP for all programs and services except those I select** and click the **Add** button (see Figure 14-12).

Figure 14-12. *Managing DEP settings*

Now you can navigate to the folder on your hard disk in which the program is located and select it to allow it through DEP. It is possible that this will rectify the problem. You can't turn off DEP completely.

Configuring and Managing System Protection

System Restore allows you to roll back changes to Windows settings if something goes wrong on your computer.

In System Properties, you can turn on System Protection for other drives and add them to the System Restore feature. You can also specify how much space on the disk is allocated to System Restore so that you can increase space if you have plenty available, or reduce it if you are using a small SSD (see Figure 14-13).

Figure 14-13. *Managing system protection*

Let's have a look at these two options to see what they do:

- **System Restore** keeps copies of critical operating system files when a major change, such as software installation or an update, takes place. This information is kept in the System Volume Information folders on your hard disk (if you ever wondered what they were for). You can run System Restore to restore system files to an earlier point in time if a recent change has made your computer unstable.

- **System Protection** keeps version-controlled copies of the operating system and other files so that they can be reinstated if an unwanted change is made to a file. This system works closely with System Restore.

Using and Configuring Storage Spaces

Storage Spaces is a feature new to Windows that allows you to aggregate, or pool, several hard disks onto a single large storage drive. This pooled storage then appears on your computer as a single drive that you can expand by adding extra hard disks, as you require.

The advantages that Storage Spaces bring include ensuring that Windows automatically keeps a backup (mirrored) copy of your files in case a hard disk fails. This should not be considered an alternative to a good backup policy, however.

Hard disks that are connected to your computer by SATA, SAS, and USB links can be joined to the Storage Spaces (note that if you remove a USB drive at any time, you lose temporary access to the files stored on it). This means that you can use external hard disks to expand the storage of an all-in-one PC.

■ **Note**   Hard disks that are added to Storage Spaces need to be formatted by Windows. They will be wiped of all data. You will then need to copy files back to them.

When you first set up Storage Spaces on your computer, you are shown a list of compatible hard disks. Windows tells you which hard disks are suitable for use with Storage Spaces, and you can choose which drives to add (see Figure 14-14).

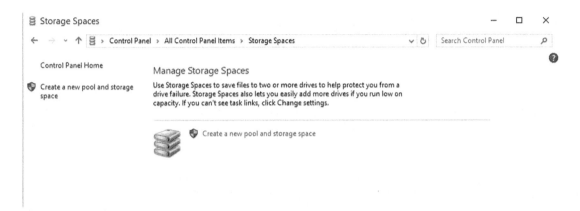

Figure 14-14. *Using Storage Spaces*

There are three different types of storage layout from which you can choose for storage spaces (see Figure 14-15):

- **Basic space**: The assembled hard disks are aggregated into a single hard disk.

- **Mirror space**: At least two copies of your files and data are kept on separate physical disks.

- **Parity spaces**: Saves parity information about the data stored. This information can be used to reconstruct data in the event of a disk failure.

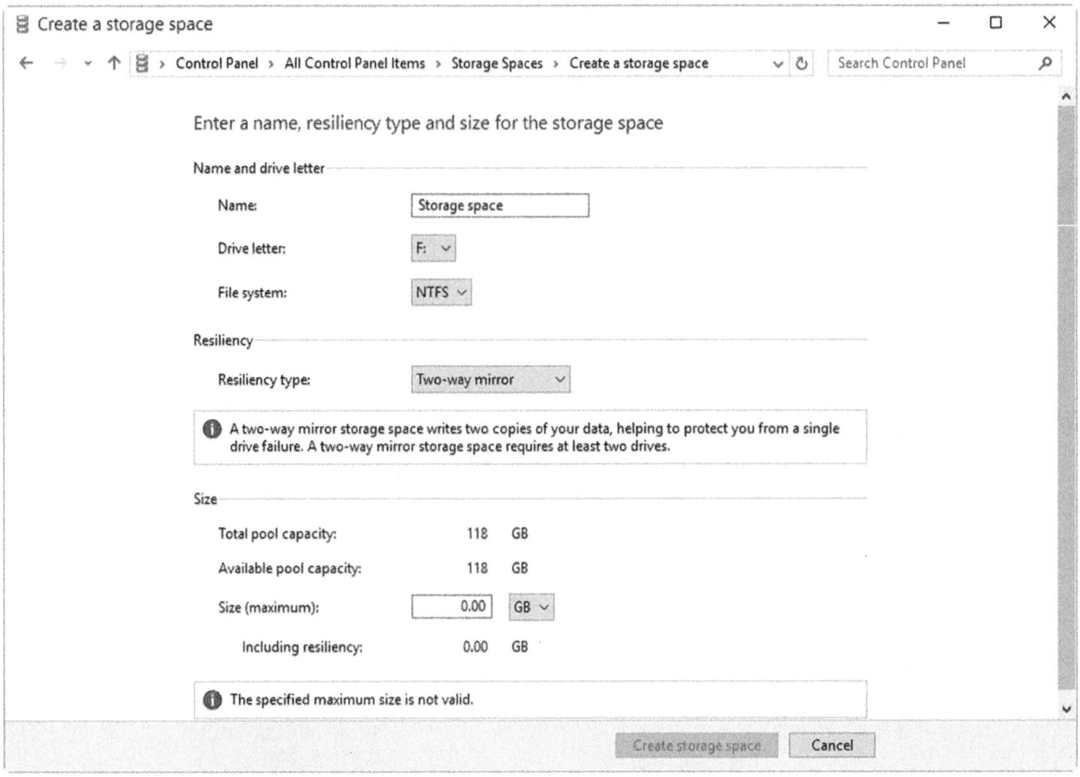

Figure 14-15. *Configuring storage spaces*

Storage spaces are configured via a helpful wizard that allows you to choose the storage layout that best suits you. Windows 10 explains what a particular layout does and how it can help protect your data. You can also choose a name for the new pooled drive and assign a drive letter to it.

Consider Storage Spaces to be a software equivalent of a redundant array of independent disks (RAID), which is a collection of physical hard disks in a computer that are configured so the user sees them as a single large drive. Storage Spaces is very useful in computers that have no RAID system or where storage can be added only via USB-attached hard disks.

■ **Tip** Unlike many RAID systems, you can add hard disks of any size to Storage Spaces.

Working with Hardware Devices

Whatever you do with your copy of Windows 10, there is no escaping hardware drivers. These pieces of code interpret the signals between your computer and both internal and external hardware, and enable everything to communicate.

Earlier in this chapter, I spoke about how some hardware can be added through the Settings app. Indeed, Windows 10 is excellent at recognizing and installing hardware with network-attached hardware such as Wi-Fi printers.

Drivers can cause problems, however, so I want to talk you through the process of installing, managing, and repairing troublesome drivers.

Device Manager

The Windows 10 Device Manager (see Figure 14-16) hasn't changed since earlier versions of the operating system. It contains some extremely useful tools that are commonly hidden.

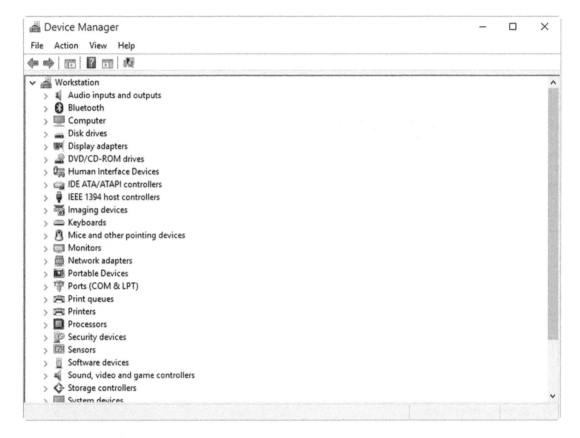

Figure 14-16. *Device Manager*

By default, it shows the hierarchical view of all the computer's attached and installed hardware devices, grouped into collapsible sections. If there are any devices that are not properly installed, or have not been correctly configured, or have been disabled, they are highlighted in the list with a small yellow warning triangle. If a device is not working properly, it may have a warning icon superimposed on it.

There are other useful views in the Device Manager that can give you all sorts of additional information about your computer. From the View menu, you have several options. Looking at the resources on your computer provides information such as I/O ports and interrupt requests (IRQs). These are the cycles on which information is exchanged with the processor. If you are experiencing problems, it is useful for determining whether too many devices are set to communicate with the processor at any one time (see Figure 14-17).

Figure 14-17. *Viewing resources in the Device Manager*

What types of problems might you have with your hardware that you can use the Device Manager to help resolve? The most common are faulty or incompatible drivers, which can come from any source directly downloaded from the Internet or provided through Windows Update. (I will show you how to resolve problems with faulty drivers in a short while.) You can use the custom views to see whether conflicting drivers are trying to use the same Windows Resources simultaneously. This problem is very uncommon and always caused by sloppily written drivers. Another rare problem is a driver inadvertently loaded twice by Windows. By looking at the way drivers are interactive with Windows, such as viewing IRQ requests, you can see whether multiple instances of a driver have been loaded. A restart normally rectifies this problem.

You can also view hidden devices on your computer. These are commonly Windows system drivers that don't relate specifically to a piece of hardware. However, some hardware can also install hidden devices, and you will want to check whether this hardware is causing a problem (see Figure 14-18).

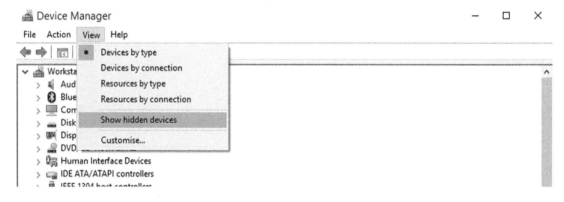

Figure 14-18. *Viewing hidden devices*

When you want to install a driver for a piece of hardware that isn't visible, select **Scan for hardware changes** from the Action menu in the Device Manager.

You will need to perform actions on hardware drivers when using Windows 10, including installing, removing, and updating them. The following sections describe how to perform these actions.

Installing Device Drivers

Windows 10 commonly detects hardware and tries to install a driver for it. If the hardware came out after the release of the operating system, it may be unable to find a driver using Windows Update. If this happens, right-click the driver and click **Update Driver Software** (see Figure 14-19).

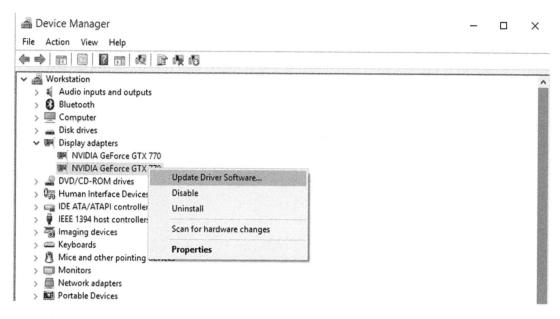

Figure 14-19. *Manually installing or updating a driver*

You will be asked if you want Windows to search for drivers or if you want to install the driver manually. If it is hardware that Windows 10 has already failed to correctly install, you should choose the **Browser my computer for driver software** option (see Figure 14-20).

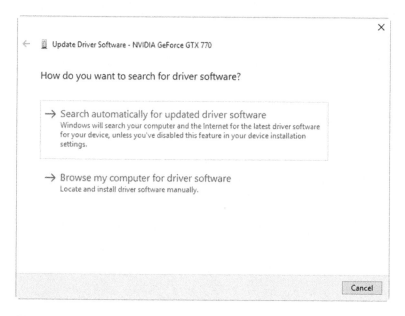

Figure 14-20. *The device driver wizard*

Here you have two options.

- **Search automatically for updated driver software** searches the preconfigured driver folders that come with Windows 10. If you have an active Internet connection, it also searches Windows Update. It also looks for drivers on any optical disc or USB-attached drive on your computer.

- **Browse my computer for driver software** gives you additional control. It allows you to manually specify the location(s) on your hard disk(s) or optical drives where the driver might be found. You can browse to a location on your computer, on an attached hard disk or flash drive, or on a network location. You can also choose from a very long list of drivers that Windows 10 comes equipped with (see Figure 14-21).

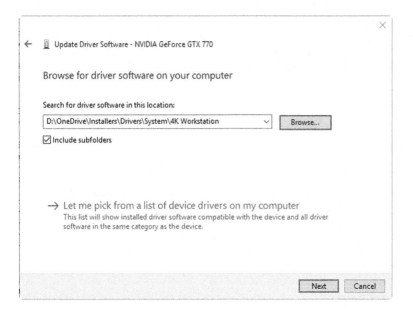

Figure 14-21. *Manually choosing a driver*

When might you want to choose which hardware driver to install? It might be useful if you are using older "legacy" hardware for which you know drivers exist, because it's been out for years, but that perhaps Windows 10 doesn't recognize.

If you choose the **Browse my computer for driver software** option, Windows will try to identify the hardware for you. It may not get it right, but if it does, select the correct option from the list and then click the **Have Disk** button to point Windows 10 at the correct driver (see Figure 14-22).

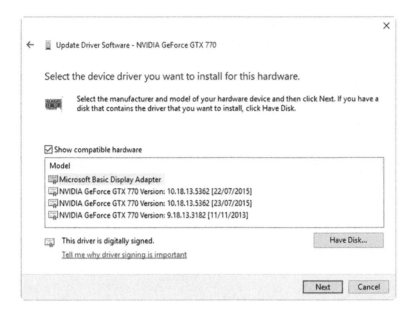

Figure 14-22. *Finding compatible hardware*

If you don't see your hardware in the list, uncheck the **Show compatible hardware** box. You are presented with a long list of hardware by various manufacturers. These are drivers that Windows 10 ships with, and if you find your hardware in the list, choose the manufacturer and product name that correctly matches the hardware that you are trying to install (see Figure 14-23).

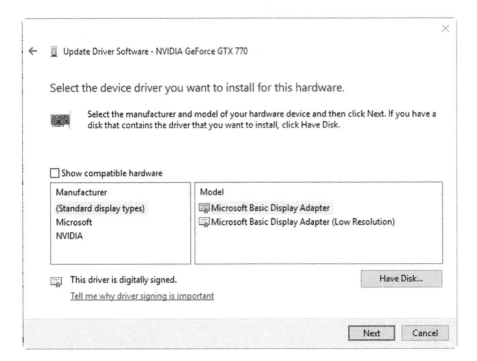

Figure 14-23. Selecting hardware from Windows 10 default drivers

---

■ **Tip**   If a driver is showing in Device Manager as Unknown, right-click it to open its properties. In the dialog that appears, click the Details tab and select Hardware IDs in the drop-down menu. You can search online for the **&VEN_** (vendor) and **&DEV_** (device) codes to identify the hardware device (see Figure 14-24) so that you can install or download the correct driver.

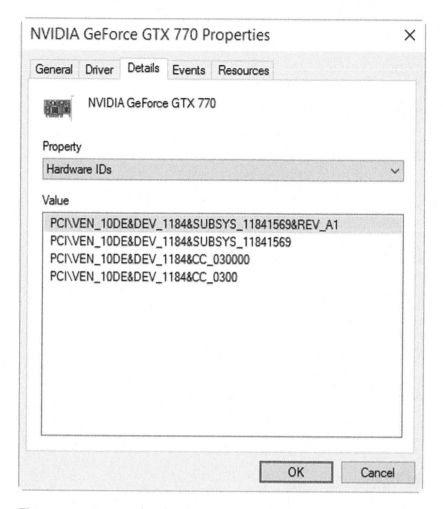

Figure 14-24. *You can identify unknown drivers by their &VEN_ and &DEV_ codes*

Uninstalling and Repairing Device Drivers

Sometimes a device driver can cause problems and it needs to be uninstalled or reinstalled. When you uninstall most (but not all) of the hardware on your computer, you are given the option to also completely **Delete the driver software for this device** (see Figure 14-25).

Figure 14-25. *Uninstalling device drivers*

Checking this option completely removes the driver software from your PC. This prevents a faulty driver from being automatically reinstalled by Windows. If you need to repair a driver, you can reinstall it from Windows Update or another source, such as the original driver disc that came with your hardware.

Also, if an updated device driver is misbehaving, you can roll it back to the previous version of the driver software. You do this in the device driver properties window, as described next.

■ **Tip**   You can disable hardware you don't need to use or that causes problems by right-clicking it and selecting Disable.

Working with Device Drivers

In addition to uninstalling drivers, you can roll back a driver to a previously installed version (if it has been updated through a service such as Windows Update) by right-clicking the driver and selecting its Properties.

If an earlier version of the driver is available, the **Roll Back Driver** button is highlighted (see Figure 14-26).

Figure 14-26. *Rolling back device drivers*

A driver's Properties dialog provides a lot of information about it, but there's nothing here you can change or modify. The General tab is where Windows tells you whether the driver is working correctly.

Manually Connecting to Networks

Clicking **Set up a new connection or network** in the main pane of the Network and Sharing Center, which I showed you how to use in Chapter 3, allows you to manually connect to a network. You might want to do this if you need to connect to a hidden Wi-Fi network, a virtual private network (VPN), or a dial-up Internet connection (see Figure 14-27).

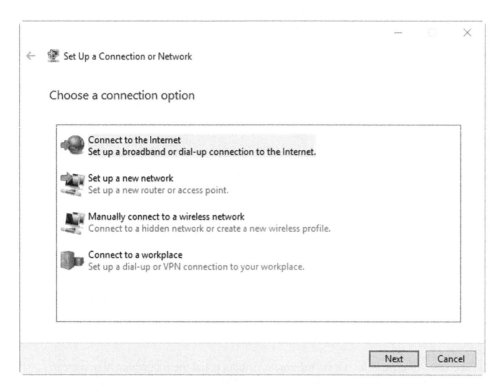

Figure 14-27. Connecting to networks manually

Whichever option you choose, Windows opens a wizard to guide you through the process, which includes manually entering the SSID of a hidden Wi-Fi network and setting the type of encryption.

■ **Note**   You may not see the dial-up Internet connection, even if you have a modem installed on your PC. If this is the case, click the **Show connection options that this computer is not set up to use** check box.

Choosing the **Connect to the Internet** option might be required for some broadband ISPs that require you to log on from your computer to gain access. If you must enter a username and password before getting online, click through **Set up a new connection anyway**, and at the next screen select **Broadband (PPPoE)**, as shown in Figure 14-28.

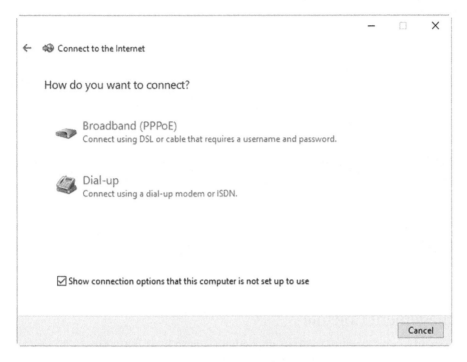

Figure 14-28. *Manually connecting to dial-up or cable Internet*

You are prompted to enter the username and password that your broadband provider has assigned to you. This is required only if you must log on from your computer, not from your router, to get a connection. This probably applies only if you have an ISDN connection.

Windows 10 Administrative Tools

So what are the Windows Administrative Tools (see Figure 14-29) and how do you get the best out of them? In this section, I'll focus on the tools that allow you to get the maximum benefit and performance out of your Windows 10 PC.

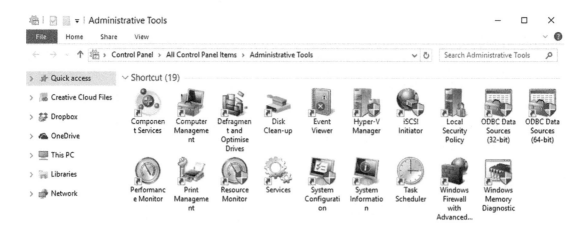

Figure 14-29. *Windows 10 Administrative Tools*

Computer Management Console

The Computer Management console provides access to other Administrative Tools, but it is probably most commonly used to access the Disk Management tools. Here you can partition drives; grow and shrink partitions; and change, assign, and remove drive letters.

■ **Tip**   You can also open a dedicated Computer Management window from the Win+X Administration menu.

The main Computer Management window is split into a text details pane at the top, and a graphical representation of your hard disks and partitions at the bottom (see Figure 14-30).

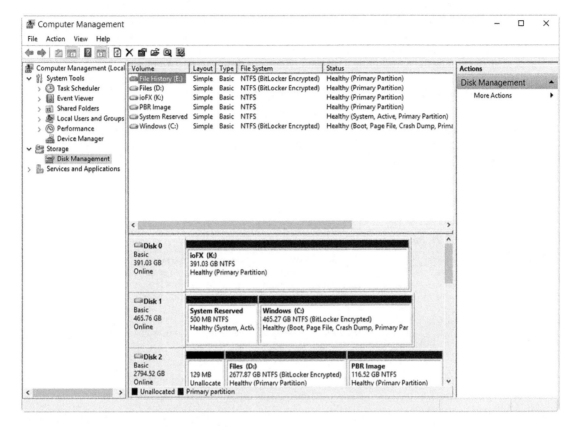

Figure 14-30. *The Disk Management console*

You can right-click any hard drive or partition to perform a series of actions on it. These actions include the following:

- **Change drive letter and paths**: If you have two disks that have the same drive letter assignment (perhaps one is an external drive), or if a disk does not appear to have a drive letter, you can change or assign it here. Another task you can perform is to turn the disk or partition into a folder within another disk.

■ **Tip**   Some third-party software is available to help fix a USB–attached hard disk to a specific drive letter. This can be especially useful if you use a USB hard disk for backups and your backup software is set to work only with a specific drive letter. In my opinion, one of the best is the USB Drive Letter Manager, which can be downloaded from www.uwe-sieber.de.

- **Extend Volume** and **Shrink Volume:** These are used to resize the partition. Windows 10 has a fairly basic partitioning tool that may not be prepared to shrink a partition as much as you want. If this happens, try using the Defragmenter and then running the partitioning tool again. There is a simple wizard for partitioning; I've never known any reports of Windows corrupting partitions. That said, it is always a good idea to keep an up-to-date backup of all of your files.

- Create a **New Volume** and **Delete Volume:** These are tasks that you can perform in blank space on disks or on existing partitions. You can use this to create RAID arrays, as well as simple partitions, with Windows 10 supporting spanned, striped, mirrored, and RAID-5 arrays (see Figure 14-31).

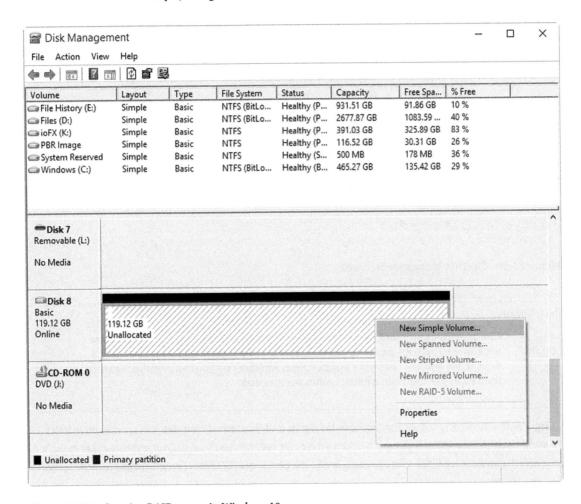

Figure 14-31. *Creating RAID arrays in Windows 10*

Event Viewer

No major event happens on your computer without its being logged. These events include warnings and critical errors, including Blue Screen of Death errors.

You can view errors by type in the Log Summary to get additional information for clues as to what caused the error—so that you can rectify it. This can include error codes, descriptions, and information about the driver, program, or service that failed (see Figure 14-32).

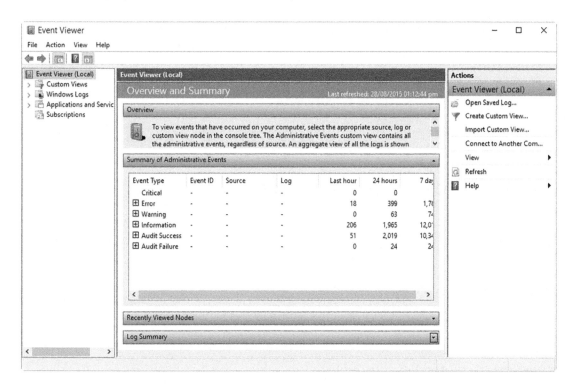

Figure 14-32. *Event Viewer*

Errors are grouped by importance. For example, each event type can be opened with a double-click to display more information, such as the error code, description, and any associated system file. You can look up these details online to get more specific information about what it means and help you to diagnose and repair the problem. You can find more information about Windows 10 troubleshooting in my book *Windows 10 Troubleshooting* (Apress, forthcoming 2016).

Local Security Policy

You probably won't need to worry about local security policies unless you are a systems administrator, in which case you administer group and security policies over a domain. There are a few settings here, however, that small business owners might be interested in.

You can set password expirations and rules for governing the strength and length of passwords chosen by users. If needed for additional security, you can also lock out users after a specified number of failed logon attempts.

If you choose to turn on this feature, however, there must be several administrator accounts on the computer; otherwise, Windows 10 might be completely locked out to you (see Figure 14-33).

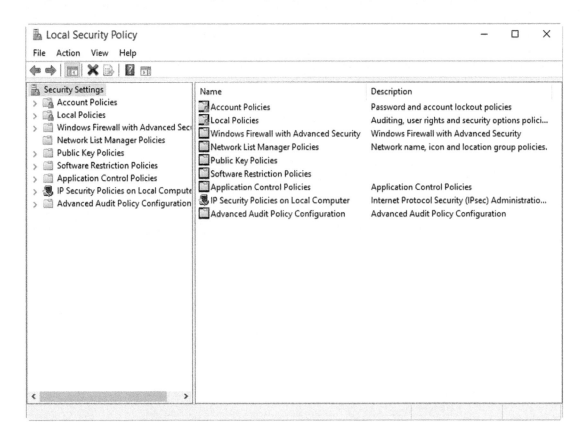

Figure 14-33. *Setting the Local Security Policy*

Performance Monitor

The Performance Monitor provides live graphs that show literally hundreds of metrics about Windows and your hardware. Are you concerned about your Wi-Fi traffic or your hard disk's write capability? To add data to the live graph, click the green + icon on the toolbar and choose the metrics to add from a Category view (see Figure 14-34).

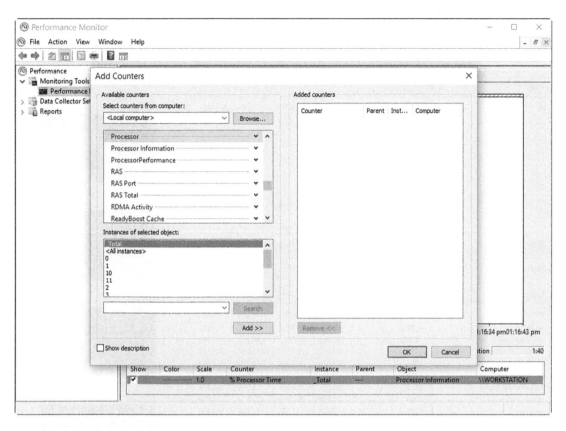

Figure 14-34. *Performance Monitor*

These additional metrics provide valuable real-time information on the processes happening both inside and external to your computer. For example, you can see whether all of your processor cores are indeed working or whether there are any bottlenecks with your networking.

Each counter is sensibly labeled, and if you're not sure which counter to add, you can add a whole stack of related counters with a single click of the Add button.

When you are viewing the live data in the Performance Monitor, the graph can be confusing. You can turn a specific graph on and off in real time by checking or unchecking the box next to its label at the bottom of the page.

Resource Monitor

The Windows 10 Resource Monitor provides even more detailed information about processes running on your computer, including the drivers, programs, apps, and Windows services.

It works with tabs across the top of the page that give quick access to a general overview of your computer and more specific information about your CPU, memory, disk, and network.

Each of these sections contains collapsible panes with large amounts of real-time information about your computer (see Figure 14-35).

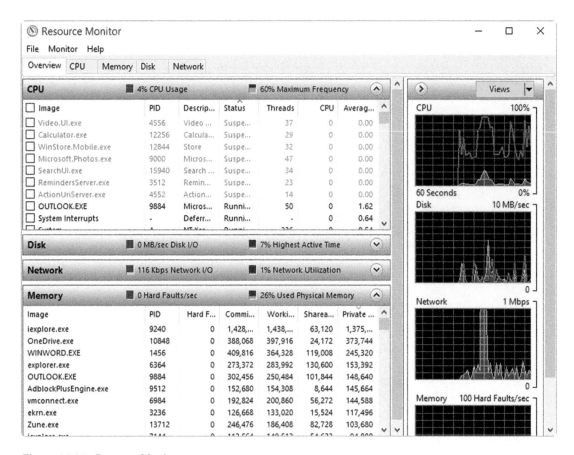

Figure 14-35. *Resource Monitor*

In the top pane of each tab, each item has a check box next to it. Checking one or more of these boxes filters the graph information on the right of the pane to show information only about those particular processes. For example, to diagnose whether it is connecting correctly to the Internet, you might be interested in the amount of data that your SkyDrive app is sending and receiving.

Services

Services are programs that perform specific functions in Windows, such as running the print spooler or the firewall. Occasionally, you will want to disable a Windows or third-party service that you either don't need or that misbehaves.

You can do this in the Services page by right-clicking a service. From there, you can start, stop, pause, resume, or restart the service (see Figure 14-36).

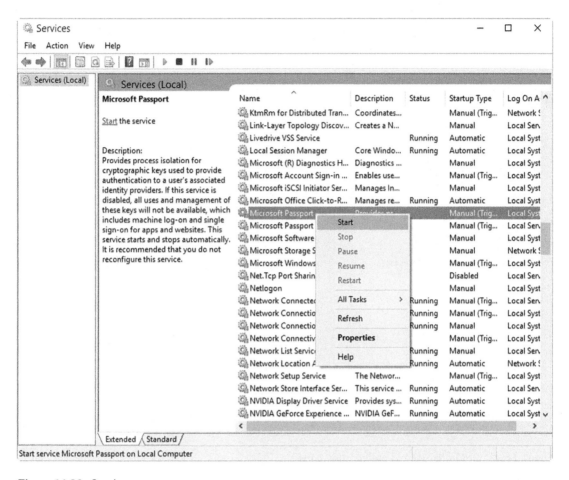

Figure 14-36. *Services page*

In Windows XP and Windows Vista, it was common to completely disable services that you didn't need that were running in the background. In Windows 7, this was sorted so that only the services that you actually needed were running at any one time.

Sometimes a service fails, especially if it is part of poorly written third-party software or a hardware driver. You can disable a service by selecting its Properties and setting its Startup Type to **Disabled**. From this context menu, you can stop and restart services. This is useful if you find that a service is hung up and doesn't respond.

System Configuration

The System Configuration page is most commonly known to Windows users as MSConfig. It was used in previous versions of Windows to disable unwanted startup programs. This is now managed through the Task Manager, but MSConfig is not without its uses.

The Boot tab allows you to manually set the computer to start in Safe mode. This is useful if you have a UEFI firmware system that doesn't allow access to the F8 and Shift+F8 boot menu.

On the General tab are options that allow you to start the computer in a special Diagnostic Startup mode. This offers more functionality than Safe mode in that it gives you more access to Windows features and controls, and it loads a few more hardware drivers. Diagnostic Startup is a great way to diagnose and repair problems with Windows 10 (see Figure 14-37). When you check this option, however, Windows continues to boot into this new mode until you return to the System Configuration panel and change the option back to **Normal startup**.

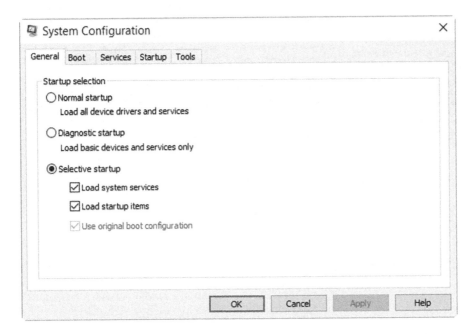

Figure 14-37. *MSConfig System Configuration panel*

I do not recommend that you change the options under the Boot tab, especially not the advanced boot options. On the face of things, controlling the number of processor cores, which is an option here, might look like a tempting way to save electricity when using a high-power computer for lightweight tasks. In reality, though, these features are strictly for IT pros, because changing something here can render your copy of Windows 10 unbootable.

System Information

The System Information page provides extremely detailed information about your hardware, your installed software and devices, the running processes, and more. This information can be exported to a file through the File menu if you need to send comprehensive information about your computer to a support person.

Task Scheduler

The Task Scheduler can be used in several ways. First, you can use it to launch programs such as the Disk Cleaner on a set schedule, such as once a month.

You can also set custom tasks that can be triggered in specific events, such as a driver failure. The Task Scheduler can then perform a series of tasks, such as popping an alert window onscreen to inform the user that a problem has occurred, and automatically running a Command Line or PowerShell script.

The controls for setting up tasks are found in the right pane, in which you can either create tasks or import them from another computer (see Figure 14-38).

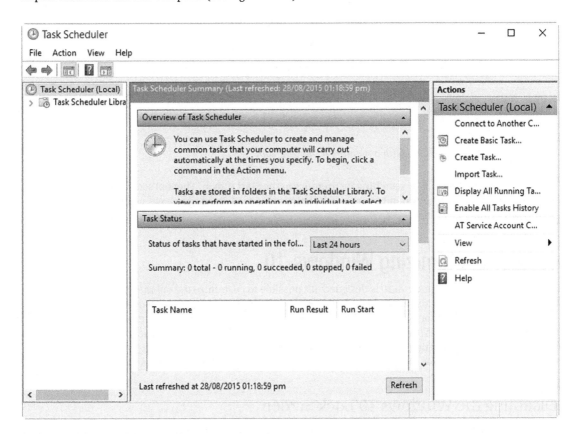

Figure 14-38. *Task Scheduler*

Windows Memory Diagnostic

For many years, Windows has included a very useful and well-hidden Memory Diagnostic tool (see Figure 14-39) that you can use if you suspect that your computer's physical memory has developed a fault.

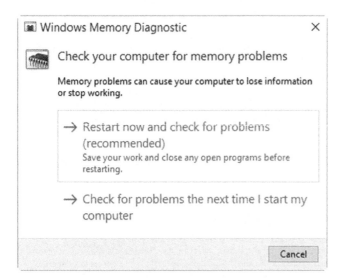

Figure 14-39. *Windows comes with a memory diagnostic tool*

You can access the tool by searching for **memory** at the Start screen. The tool scans your computer's memory, which can take considerable time, so be prepared to walk the dog or have a coffee break. The tool reports any errors that it finds.

Further Customizing Windows 10

Because of the way that Windows 10 is designed, it's possible to customize the operating system in an almost limitless number of ways. My mailbag regularly swells with questions about this. I'll discuss some of the more popular customizations. I should point out, however, that you should always be very careful making these kinds of changes to Windows. You should create a restore point, make sure that you have an up-to-date image backup of the operating system, and follow instructions very carefully, because you could be making changes to the core OS. (See Chapter 12 for information on creating backup images and restore points.)

Disabling the Windows 10 Lock Screen

The new Windows 10 lock screen provides valuable information over and above what is available in previous versions of Windows, including the number of emails and messages received and appointment information.

Opening the lock screen is another step you need to go through to log on to Windows 10. You may want to disable it completely and have Windows 10 start directly at the logon screen.

The lock screen can be disabled if you are using Windows 10 Pro or Enterprise; they have the Group Policy Editor. To open it, search for **gpedit** in the Start menu.

Once in the Group Policy Editor, navigate to Computer Configuration ➤ Administrative Templates ➤ Control Panel ➤ Personalization (see Figure 14-40).

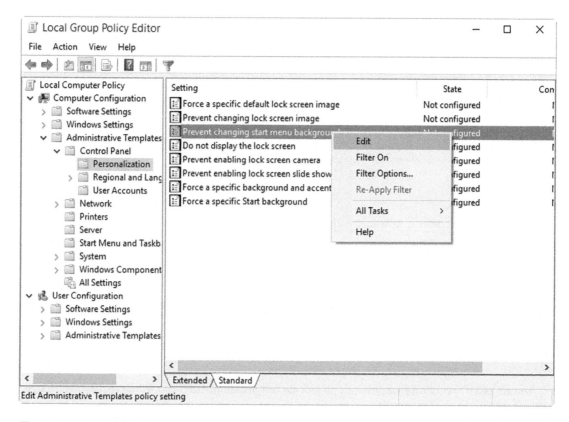

Figure 14-40. *Disabling the lock screen in Group Policy*

Here you see an option labeled **Do not display the lock screen**. You should right-click it, select **Edit**, and change the setting to **Enabled**. The lock screen will no longer appear on the computer.

Automatically Signing in to Windows 10

You may want to have Windows 10 automatically sign in every time you start the computer. After all, if you are the only person using the computer and you sign in with your Microsoft account—bringing the benefits of automatically syncing your email and calendar, and allowing you to buy apps, music, and video from the Windows Store—why would you need to type your password every time you start your computer?

Automatic sign-in is very simple to do and requires unchecking only a single box. Search for **netplwiz** at the Start menu. In the User Accounts dialog, click your main user account (it is the one labeled Administrator), and then uncheck **Users must enter a user name and password to use this computer** (see Figure 14-41).

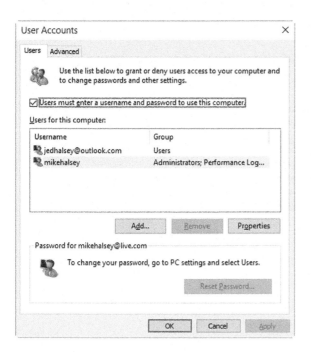

Figure 14-41. *Automatically logging on users to Windows 10*

You are asked to confirm your password to provide authorization. Afterward, Windows 10 will no longer ask you for your password at sign in.

Useful Windows Registry Hacks

One of the best things about the Windows registry is how easy it is to edit, and how much control you can get over Windows by doing so. I'd like to share some of my favorite registry hacks. As with any work in the Windows registry, be very careful adding, deleting, or changing settings; and always make sure that you have both a backup copy of the registry and a backup image of your copy of Windows. Each registry change for a feature within Windows requires you to restart the computer; for registry changes involving programs, restarting the program is normally enough.

Backing Up the Windows Registry

The registry is a database of all the settings and configuration options for Windows, your hardware, and all of your installed software. It's the main file (actually a series of files) that tells the operating system what's what and what's where. If you're making changes to the registry, you should make a backup copy of the files.

You can do this from within the Registry Editor. Search for **regedit** at the Start menu to find it. Then from the File menu, click **Export** and save your backup of the registry file in a safe place (see Figure 14-42).

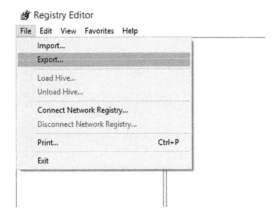

Figure 14-42. *Backing up the Windows registry*

If you need to restore your backed-up registry keys, open the Registry Editor and from its File menu, click **Import**. You are asked which file you want to import and then to confirm that you *do* want to add this key to the registry. Adding a backed-up key overwrites any changes made to that key.

■ **Tip** My book *Windows Registry Troubleshooting* (Apress, 2015) contains more than 60 registry tips, tweaks, and hacks for Windows 7, Windows 8.1, and Windows 10.

Add Copy To/Move To Options to the File Explorer Context Menu

Although it's useful for the File Explorer context menu to include Cut and Copy commands when you right-click a file or folder, it's also possible to add **Copy to folder** and **Move to folder** options to this context list (see Figure 14-43).

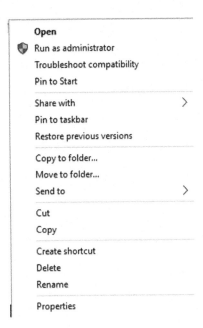

Figure 14-43. Adding Copy To Folder and Move To Folder options to File Explorer

Here's how to add the **Copy to folder** command:

1. Open the Registry Editor by searching for **regedit** at the Start menu.

2. Navigate to the HKEY_CLASSES_ROOT\AllFilesystemObjects\shellex\ContextMenuHandlers key.

3. Right-click the ContextMenuHandlers key and add a New Key with the name **Copy to folder**.

4. Double-click this new key's default value and change the value to **{C2FBB630-2971-11D1-A18C-00C04FD75D13}**.

To also add a **Move to folder** item to the context menu, repeat these steps, but create a new **Move to folder** key with the default value **{C2FBB631-2971-11D1-A18C-00C04FD75D13}**.

Add/Remove Options to the Send-To File Explorer Menu

When you right-click a file or folder in File Explorer, one of the options that appears is Send To, which allows you to send that item to a particular program, piece of hardware, or location. You can add and remove items from this menu by navigating to C:\Users\[Username]\AppData\Roaming\Microsoft\Windows\SendTo in File Explorer, in which you can paste or delete shortcuts to devices, network locations, and more.

Add Defragment to the File Explorer Context Menu

You can add a Defragment option to the context menu in File Explorer when you right-click a hard disk (see Figure 14-44). This starts a command-line version of the Defragment tool.

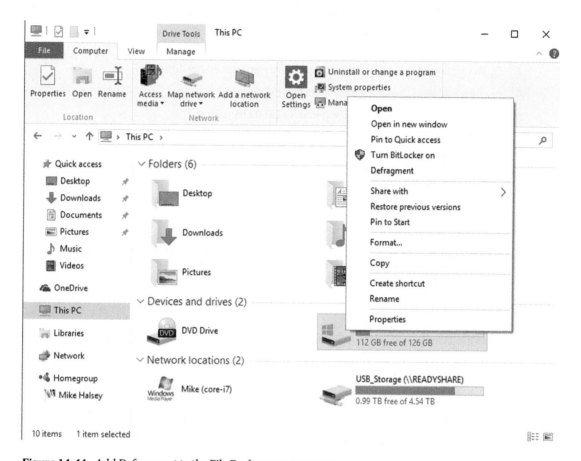

Figure 14-44. *Add Defragment to the File Explorer context menu*

Follow these steps to add Defragment:

1. Open the Registry Editor by searching for **regedit** at the Start menu.

2. Navigate to the HKEY_CLASSES_ROOT\Drive\shell key.

3. Create a new key under this called **runas**.

4. Double-click **Default Value** to open it and set its default value to **Defragment**.

5. Create a subkey under runas called **command**.

6. Double-click the Command subkey. Change its default value to **defrag %1 -v**.

Add Command Prompt to the File Explorer Context Menu

You can also easily add the command prompt to the right-click menu in File Explorer.

1. Navigate to the HKEY_LOCAL_MACHINE\Software\Classes\Folder\Shell registry key.

2. Create a new key called **Command Prompt**.

3. Double-click the **Default** setting for this key and change its value to **Open Command Prompt**, or similar text if you want something different.

4. Create a subkey of Command Prompt called **Command**.

5. Double-click the **Default** value for Command and change it to **Cmd.exe /k pushd %L**.

Here the /k switch leaves the Command window open on your screen, rather than executing this one command and closing it. The pushd control contains the name of the current folder, and the %L switch opens the Command window in that folder.

Show Drive Letter Before Volume Name in File Explorer

You might want to turn off the display of driver letters in File Explorer, which you can do by selecting Options and then opening the View tab. Select **Change folder and search options** and then uncheck **Show drive letters**.

You can also have File Explorer display the drive letter before the drive volume name:

1. Open the Registry Editor by searching for **regedit** at the Start menu.

2. Navigate to the following key: HKEY_LOCAL_MACHINE\SOFTWARE\ Microsoft\Windows\CurrentVersion\Explorer.

3. Right-click and create a new DWORD (32-bit) Value called **ShowDriveLettersFirst**.

4. Double-click the new addition to open it and change its value from 0 to **4**.

Add an FTP Location to File Explorer

If you maintain a web server, you can add a direct link to your FTP service from File Explorer. Doing this enables you to manage files on the server as though they were on your own PC; you are able to drag and drop files into the FTP site, as well as delete them, without the need for separate FTP software.

1. In a File Explorer window, click the **Computer** tab on the ribbon.

2. Click the **Add a Network Location** button.

3. Click **Next** in the window that appears.

4. Click **Choose a custom network location** and then click the **Next** button.

5. Enter the name of your FTP site in the format `ftp://ftp.contoso.com` and click **Next**.

6. If you log in to your FTP site with a username and password, uncheck the **Log on anonymously** box and enter your username; then click **Next**.

7. Give your FTP site a name and click **Next**.

8. Leave the **Open this network location** box checked and click **Finish**.

9. In the window that appears, enter your password for the FTP site. You can optionally check the **Remember my password** box.

You now have direct access to your FTP site from within File Explorer every time you log in to your PC.

Modifying the Taskbar Using Group Policy

Although there are many controls available for modifying the taskbar, such as a simple right-click and opening the taskbar's properties, additional controls are available to users of Windows 10 Pro, Enterprise, and Windows RT. These exist in Group Policy, which can be opened by searching for **gpedit** at the Start menu.

Once in the Group Policy Editor, navigate to **User Configuration ➤ Administrative Templates ➤ Start Menu and Taskbar**, in which you see a menu with additional options, such as turning off balloon notifications and completely hiding the notification area.

Unlock the Hidden Super-Administrator Account

Although the main user of a PC is always set up as Administrator, which enables this user to make whatever changes they need to the computer, there is also a hidden super-administrator account available. This super account isn't hamstrung by such things as the User Account Control (UAC); it has permissions to do things to files in Windows that you may need, but that are normally denied to you for reasons of stability and safety in the operating system.

You can unlock the super-administrator account from an existing Administrator account. Open **Command Prompt (Admin)** from the Win+X menu and type the following command: **net user administrator /active:yes**. When you log out, the new Administrator account is available to you. You can disable it with the **/active:no** switch.

Hiding Unused Items from the Control Panel

The Control Panel in Windows 10 can get very messy with controls that you may never want to use or that you do not want other people to see. Fortunately, it is possible to remove some of these controls.

1. Search for **regedit** at the Start menu and open the Registry Editor.

2. Navigate in the Registry Editor to HKEY_LOCAL_MACHINE\SOFTWARE\ Microsoft\Windows\CurrentVersion\Control Panel\don't load.

3. Here you see a list of Control Panel items that are already hidden (see Figure 14-45). To hide an additional item, create a new String value with the .cpl name for the control that corresponds to Table 14-1.

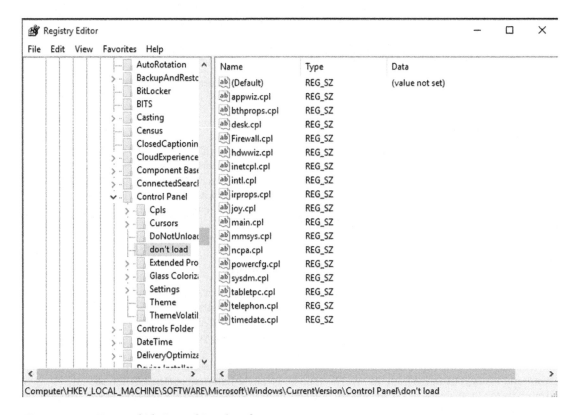

Figure 14-45. *You can hide Control Panel applets*

Table 14-1. *Control Panel Applet Names*

Control Panel Applet	Name
Accessibility Options	access.cpl
Add New Hardware Wizard	hdwwiz.cpl
Display Properties	desk.cpl
Game Controllers	joy.cpl
Internet Options	inetcpl.cpl
Mouse Properties	main.cpl
Network Connections	ncpa.cpl
ODBC Data Sources	odbccp32.cpl
Phone and Modem Options	telephon.cpl
Power Options	powercfg.cpl

(*continued*)

Table 14-1. (*continued*)

Control Panel Applet	Name
Programs and Features	appwiz.cpl
Region	intl.cpl
Sound	mmsys.cpl
Speech	sapi.cpl
System	sysdm.cpl
Time and Date	timedate.cpl
User Accounts	nusrmgr.cpl

Summary

The advanced Control Panel and Administrative Tools in Windows 10 are powerful indeed; there's very little that you can't do when configuring your copy of Windows to behave the way you want and meet all of your requirements.

Getting to know how these tools and utilities work can help with managing PCs at home or in the workplace; they can also help considerably when troubleshooting problems and repairing issues with your software, hardware, and Windows itself.

CHAPTER 15

■ ■ ■

Getting Started with Virtualization

Each new release of Windows, whether major or minor, brings not just new features and new ways of working, but also fresh challenges. One of those challenges is maintaining compatibility with the older app packages that we've used for years and that are as comfortable as an old shoe.

I am not excluded from this scenario. I have used the same graphics package—Microsoft PhotoDraw v2—for more than a decade. I love it. It does everything I want and it's extremely easy to use. Why should I change?

Sadly, with upgrades to Windows come software incompatibilities. The biggest change came with the move from Windows XP to Windows Vista. The whole core of the operating system was rewritten from scratch. It included some major restructuring, such as removing, replacing, or rewriting features. With PhotoDraw, I found that although most of the package still worked, some features treated me to only an annoying *"donk!"* noise when I tried to use them.

There are also times when you want to be able to use or try a different operating system on your computer, such as Linux or even another copy of Windows 10, for testing an app or other purposes. Setting up a dual-boot system can be extremely complex, especially because Windows 10 usually needs to be installed last (see Chapter 15 for notes on this). A good option is to install the second operating system in a virtual machine (VM).

When Windows 7 was launched with the accompanying Windows XP Mode virtualization client, I was delighted. At long last I could use PhotoDraw again on the desktop without worry or problems. When all support for Windows XP ended in 2014, so did support for XP Mode, which had never been included in Windows 8.1 for this very reason.

It's not all bad news, though. Windows 8.1 Pro and Enterprise editions contained a feature called Hyper-V, which is carried over into Windows 10. It is Microsoft's virtualization client, originally ported from Windows Server. It's more than powerful enough to get your legacy software working again.

Virtualization isn't just about maintaining compatibility with older software, however, because it also has important roles to play in testing stability in software and updates for deployment, and also for providing customizable working environments for users. For example, I use virtual machines to demonstrate Windows services and features for the tutorial and education videos I make. In this chapter, I'll show you how to set up and maintain Hyper-V for all of these roles.

Note that using virtualization is an advanced feature and something that less-technical Windows users will likely avoid. You can't do anything to harm or damage your current Windows installation, but if you want to use Hyper-V and you're not completely comfortable with computers, you should follow the instructions in this chapter very carefully to ensure the best results.

■ **Note**   Hyper-V is available only in the 64-bit versions of Windows 10 Pro and Enterprise, if running on compatible hardware. You should check the specifications for your PC's processor to see if virtualization is supported.

What Is Virtualization?

Virtualization allows any operating system to run inside another in a specially configured environment that simulates the hardware of a full PC. Think of it a bit like the "virtual world" as it appeared to people trapped in *The Matrix* in the popular film trilogy. Virtualization effectively tricks the virtualized operating system into thinking that it's running on its own hardware.

Older VMs that simulated hardware were very slow because every hardware action had to be re-created in software. This is called *emulation*, where every action of the PC's hardware has to be simulated by the host operating system, because the virtualized PC cannot see the actual hardware.

Newer VMs, including Hyper-V, enable the virtualized operating system to access your computer's own hardware. They manage the sharing of that hardware between the host OS and the virtualized OS on the machine to make sure that conflicts don't occur. This means that Hyper-V acts on your computer and your network as if it's just another computer attached to that network.

The main benefit of virtualization is that the hardware management allows VMs to harness the full power of modern computers with multiple processor cores and large volumes of memory. For example, if you have a quad-core (or even a six- or eight-core) processor, and 8GB, 16GB, 32GB, or even 64GB of memory in your computer, a good VM can assign each of three operating systems a single processor core and up to or even more than 4GB of memory without breaking a sweat or slowing anything down, depending on how much memory you have in your PC. The host OS uses the remaining cores and memory—thus maximizing the computer's potential and reducing overall costs.

When Should You Use a Virtual Machine?

There are several scenarios in which the use of a VM is helpful, including keeping your older legacy software working. If you really must use software that worked fine in Windows XP but doesn't work in Windows 10, installing a copy of Windows XP into a VM is a way to continue using that software.

■ **Caution**   All support for Windows XP ended in 2014, so if you really *must* install XP in a virtual machine, it is crucial you sandbox it completely, and deny it any access to the Internet (see the "Setting Up Networking with Hyper-V" section later in this chapter). There are no longer any security patches available for Windows XP, so if you give it Internet access, and therefore also network access, it becomes a weak point of attack for all of the PCs and devices on your network.

VMs are also commonly used for testing scenarios. Let's say you want to roll out a patch or software upgrade across your computers, but you're unsure of how it will interact with the existing software that you use. You can test it first in a VM so that you are certain that everything works fine beforehand and avoid the risk of any downtime.

■ **Tip**   Always make sure that Windows Updates is turned on and that anti-malware software is installed on any operating system in a VM with Internet access.

You might also use virtualization to provide custom working environments. On one machine you could set up VMs for development, accounting, or other purposes that provide workers with the tools and environment they need to be productive, while also making those environments easy to transport between computers in different locations.

I used Hyper-V while writing this book so that I could install a clean copy of Windows 10. There are all manner of scenarios in which it is useful to have a VM running.

■ **Note**   You need a valid license (product key) for each operating system you install in a VM using Hyper-V.

Can't Find Hyper-V on Your PC?

Hyper-V exists in the Pro and Enterprise versions of Windows 10, but it is commonly hidden in Windows 10 Pro. You can activate it, however, by selecting **Programs and features** from the Win+X menu, which is the Control Panel applet you use for uninstalling desktop programs. This panel contains a link on the left of its window called **Turn Windows features on or off**.

The new window that appears when you click this link (see Figure 15-1) contains a full list of all the Windows 10 features that can be either enabled or disabled. Hyper-V appears in this list. To activate it, check the box to its left, click OK, and then restart your PC. Hyper-V now appears in your Start menu.

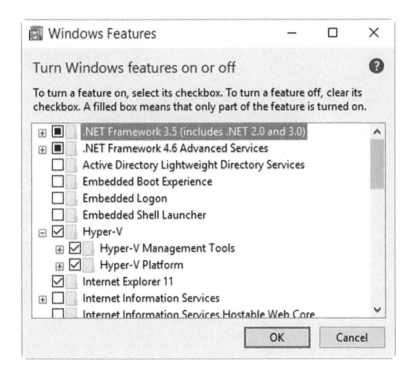

Figure 15-1. *Enabling Hyper-V in Windows 10 Pro*

Installing an Operating System in Hyper-V

How do you install an operating system in Hyper-V and what types of operating systems does it support? You can install any version of Windows or other Intel (x86 and x64)–based operating systems in Hyper-V, including GNU/Linux, by following these steps:

1. Find the Hyper-V Manager in Windows by searching for **Hyper** at the Start menu, and open it.

2. The Hyper-V Manager (see Figure 15-2) looks and operates much like the other management consoles in Windows 10. The left panel contains a navigation tree, the central panels contain the main information and status windows, and your main and other contextual controls are in the right pane.

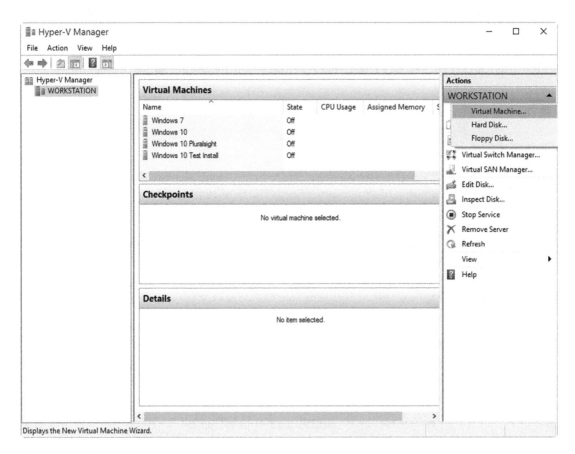

Figure 15-2. Hyper-V Manager

3. Click **New** and then **Virtual Machine** to create a new VM.

■ **Tip**   When you set up your first VM in Hyper-V, it has no networking available to it, either local or Internet. You might want to jump ahead in this chapter to the "Setting Up Networking in Hyper-V" section to configure it before creating the VM.

4. Click the **Next** button at the bottom of the New Virtual Machine Wizard (see Figure 15-3) to set up your own VM.

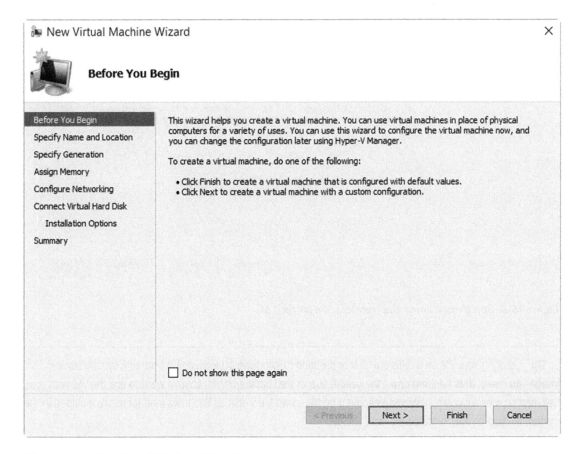

Figure 15-3. *New Virtual Machine Wizard*

5. Give your VM a name and a store location (see Figure 15-4). By default, Windows 10 suggests storing it on the same hard disk on which Windows is installed. You may want to specify a different hard disk, however. Click Next.

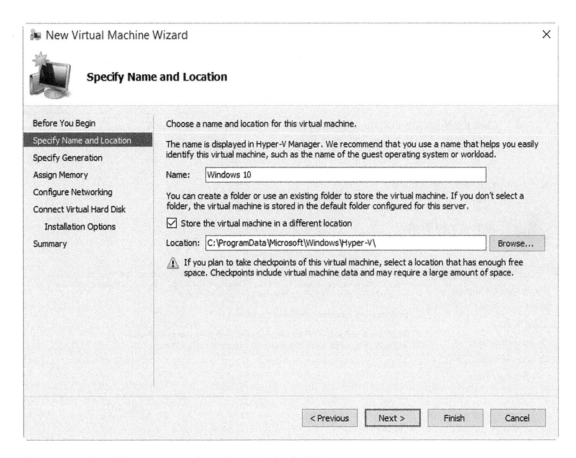

Figure 15-4. *Specifying a name and store location for the VM*

■ **Tip** Storing your VM on a different disk or partition to Windows 10 excludes it from any system backup image you make, thus bringing down the overall size of that backup. If you always want to use the VM *with* your installed copy of Windows, however, keeping it on the same hard disk as Windows (and therefore included in the system backup image) might be the best choice.

---

6. You are next asked which "generation" of VM you want to create (see Figure 15-5). The Generation 2 VM type is fully compatible with Windows 10 and Windows Server 2016 (as well as Windows Server 2012 R2 and Windows 8.1). It includes support for features such as UEFI and Secure Boot, but it doesn't work on Hyper-V installations on earlier operating systems, such as Windows 7 and Windows Server 2008. If you think you will want to use your VM on computers running these older operating systems, you should choose the Generation 1 option to maintain full compatibility. You can read more about Generation 2 VMs and their advantages at http://pcs.tv/1Lxmsun.

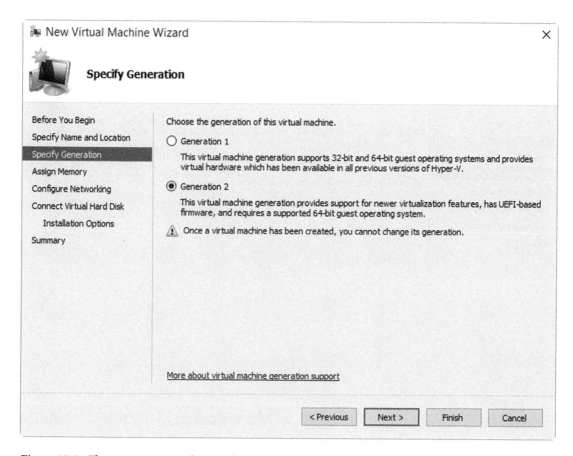

Figure 15-5. *There are now several types of VM you can create*

7. Assign the amount of memory you want to dedicate to the VM (see Figure 15-6). The amount depends on the type of operating system that is running in the VM and how much physical memory your PC has.

For example, you might be installing Windows 7 into the VM, which means you would need around 1024MB of RAM for a 32-bit installation and 2048MB for the 64-bit. If you plan to do graphics work in the VM, however, more memory would be required. If your PC has only 4GB of memory, you should probably not specify more than 1GB for the VM; if you have 16 GB, you could dedicate a much healthier 4GB of memory to the VM. There is usually little point in assigning more than 4GB of memory to a VM unless it will be running hugely analytical or mathematical tasks.

There is also the option to use Dynamic Memory. This feature allows the VM to automatically assign additional memory through the Hyper-V Manager, if it is required and if there is available memory on your PC. You may find this option useful because it is used only when required. Click Next.

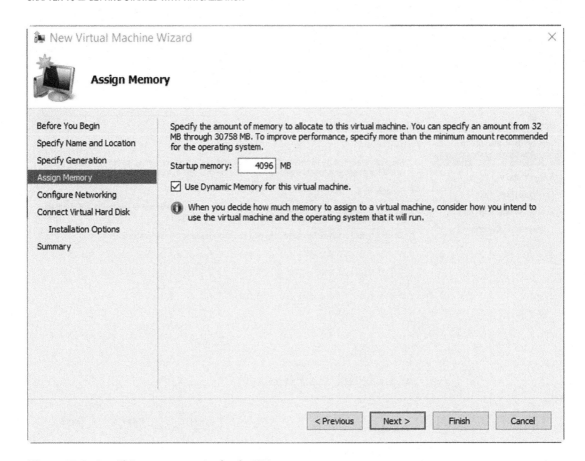

Figure 15-6. *Specifying a memory size for the VM*

8. Configure the networking options for the VM by choosing from a drop-down
    list of the preconfigured networks you have set up for Hyper-V (see Figure 15-7).
    Click Next.

    If you want a completely sandboxed operating system with no local computer,
    network, or Internet access, there is no need to configure a network adaptor to
    work with the VM. This isolates the VM completely from the outside world, but it
    also means that you can't access the files and documents on the host computer
    and that you don't have access to the VM using Remote Desktop.

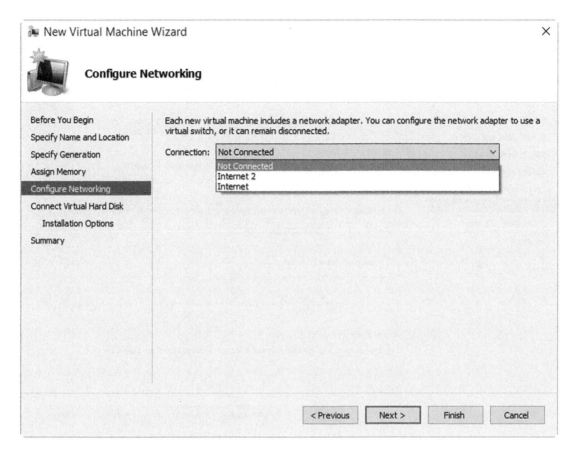

Figure 15-7. *Configuring networking for the VM*

■ **Note**   You may not be able to add networking options at this time because networking in Hyper-V must be configured independently of any individual VM. VMs can share individually configured networks to give them Internet access, access to the local computer, or access only to other VMs. If this is the case, you may need to install Integration Services in the VM when it is installed (depending on what operating system is running in the VM), and set up a virtual switch. I show you how to do this later in the chapter.

---

9.   Connect the virtual hard disk (VHD). This wizard page lets you specify the size of the VM's hard disk (see Figure 15-8). It suggests a size, although you can change this if you require the VM to be larger or smaller. An alternate option is to reattach an existing VHD. Click Next.

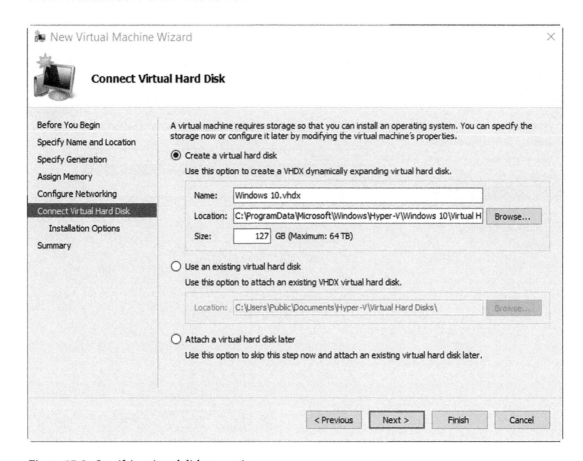

Figure 15-8. Specifying virtual disk properties

10. Install an operating system (see Figure 15-9). You can do this from a virtual floppy disk, CD, DVD, USB flash drive, or ISO file.

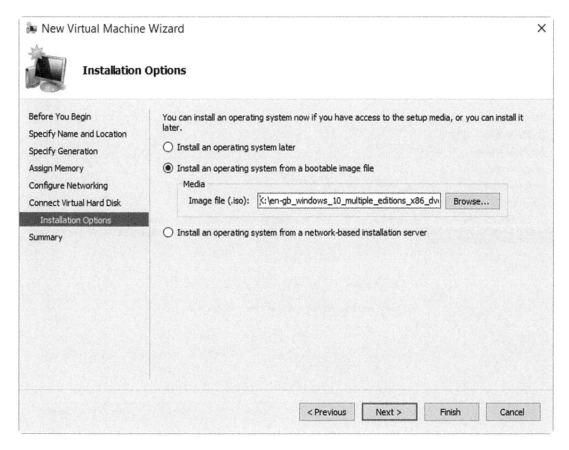

Figure 15-9. *Installing the OS into the VM*

■ **Note**   If you choose not to install an operating system at this time, you will later need to add a new SCSI hardware device in the VM settings to create a virtual DVD drive, and then change the boot order to prioritize this new drive over network boot. If you are installing Windows 7 or earlier, or an OS that does not support Secure Boot, make sure that you uncheck this option, or else the boot from a DVD will not work.

---

11.   Confirm all the details that you have entered (see Figure 15-10). Click **Finish** when you are done.

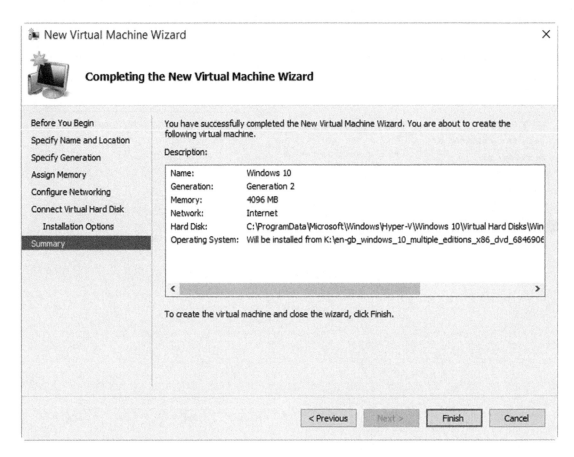

Figure 15-10. *Confirming the VM details*

12. Start the VM. In the Hyper-V Manager, you now see your VM listed in the top-center pane (see Figure 15-11). Click it. In the bottom half of the right pane, click **Connect** to connect to the VM.

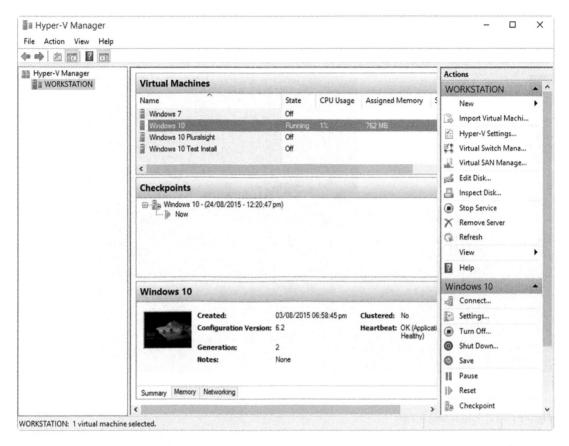

Figure 15-11. *Running a VM*

13. Open the **Action** menu and select **Start** to launch the VM (see Figure 15-12).

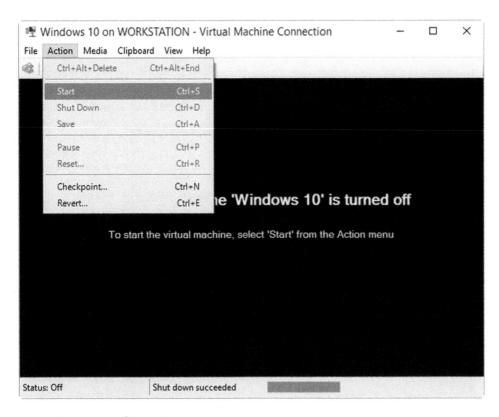

Figure 15-12. *Launching a VM*

After you start the VM, you see a window with the virtualized OS running inside it.

When you start a VM, you see a connection options dialog (see Figure 15-13) that asks at which screen resolution you want to run the VM; the slider goes all the way up to your full-screen resolution. This makes it simple to run the VM at different resolutions, depending on what you're doing with it, without always having to change the resolution within the display properties of the VM. At the bottom of this dialog is a **Show options** button that includes more settings, including audio for the VM.

Figure 15-13. *You are presented with additional options when launching a VM*

■ **Note**   Not all screen resolutions are supported for virtual machines in Hyper-V. For example, you might find that only 4:3 ratio resolutions can be used when you want widescreen. To use a virtual machine with other resolutions, you can connect to it using Remote Desktop; see the "Connecting to a Virtual Machine Using Remote Desktop" section later in this chapter.

Setting Up Networking with Hyper-V

By default, all Hyper-V VMs are sandboxed and completely isolated from the computers and networks around them. When you want a VM to interact with other VMs, your physical computers, the network, and the Internet, you need to create a virtual switch. You can do this from the main Hyper-V Manager, in which you click Virtual Switch Manager in the right pane.

You need to decide the type of virtual switch that you want to create. The Virtual Switch Manager gives you a text description of each type of switch (see Figure 15-14).

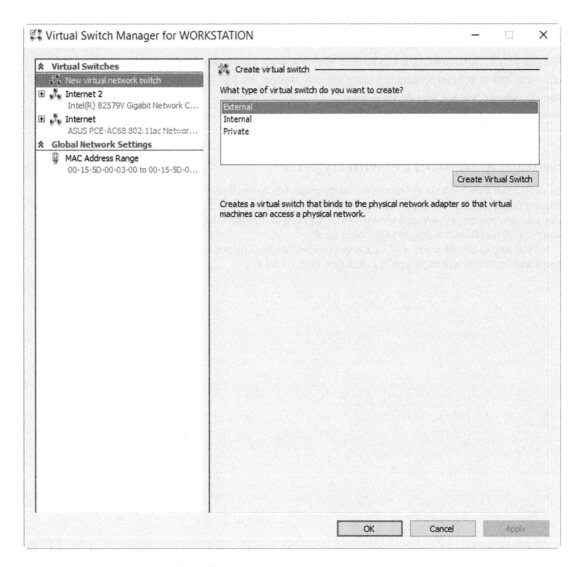

Figure 15-14. *Creating a virtual switch*

If you want your VM to see and access files on the host PC and on your network, you need to select External, which is also the option that gives the VM access to the Internet (so be careful with it if using Windows XP or another operating system that is out of support). The Internal option allows Hyper-V VMs to communicate only with each other, which is best for an OS that must be completely sandboxed.

After you highlight the option you want, click the Create Virtual Switch button. You now need to configure the options for your virtual switch (see Figure 15-15). It is important to determine which network adapter in your computer you attach it to. You may have both wired and wireless network adapters in your computer; you need to choose the right one.

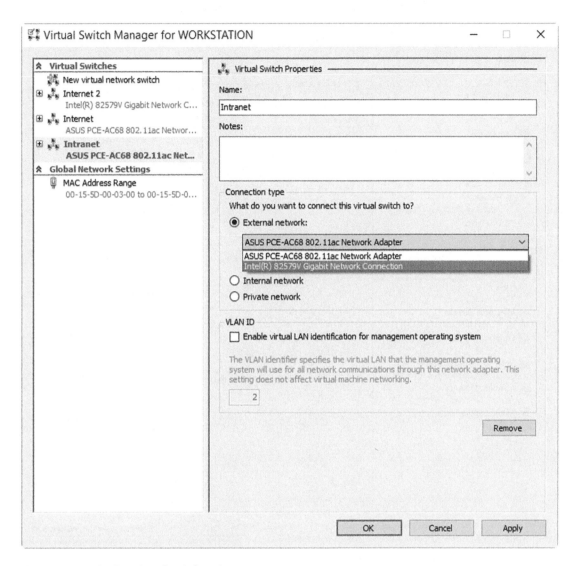

Figure 15-15. *Setting virtual switch options*

■ **Tip**   Let's say that you want a VM to access files on the host PC, but you do *not* want it to have access to the network or the Internet. If your PC has wired and wireless connections, connect the switch to the one that you *don't* use to get online. If you don't have a physical network cable plugged into the PC, choose the Ethernet (non-Wi-Fi) connection. This gives the VM access to the host PC *only* and helps isolate it from malware and attack.

After you create your virtual switch, you need to attach it to your VM. Click the appropriate VM in the top-center pane in the Hyper-V Manager. Then in the bottom-right pane, click Settings, which brings up the settings for the VM (see Figure 15-16).

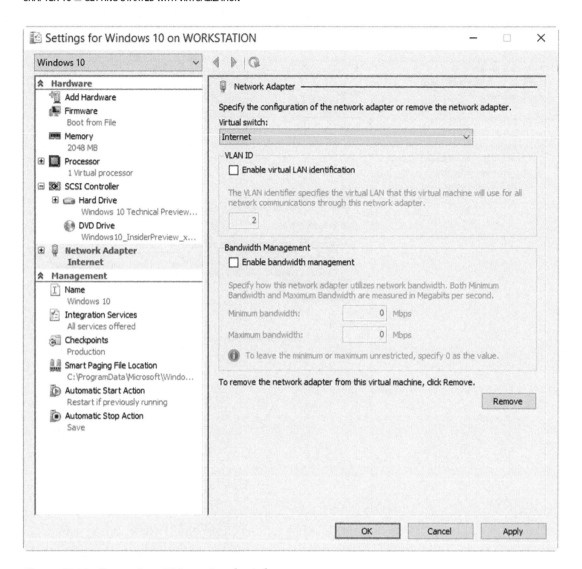

Figure 15-16. *Connecting a VM to a virtual switch*

Click Network Adapter option in the left pane. If you do not see this option, click Add Hardware to add a network adapter. A useful feature is Bandwidth Management, which ensures that whatever the VM does, it can't use more than a specified amount of your network bandwidth. This throttling control is a useful way to ensure that the VM has the network connection it requires without becoming a bandwidth hog.

Where you choose the virtual switch at the top of the Network Adapter settings, select the switch you created and press OK. No further configuration should be necessary. Your VM now has network access.

Although other options can be changed in the VM Settings, some settings that are set when you first create the VM can't be changed. To change these settings, the VM needs to be switched off.

Saving VM Checkpoints

When a major change is made to Windows 10, such as the installation of a desktop program or a Windows Update, a System Restore point is kept. It keeps copies of critical operating system files, such as the Windows registry, from just before the change was made. Thus if something then goes wrong, this change can be rolled back to revert your copy of Windows to its earlier state. In Hyper-V, this procedure can be a pain, however, because you first have to start the VM and then run System Restore from within it. This process can be annoying and time-consuming.

Hyper-V gets around this annoyance by having a feature called a *checkpoint*, each of which is a snapshot of the VM taken at a specific time. You can create a checkpoint at any time by selecting the VM that you want to create one for in the top center of the Virtual Machines panel of the Hyper-V Manager, and then clicking the **Checkpoint** link in the bottom right of the management window.

Created checkpoints are then listed in the center of the Hyper-V Manager (see Figure 15-17). You can click one to either apply it (to roll the VM back to that point), export it (more on exporting VMs in the next section), or delete it.

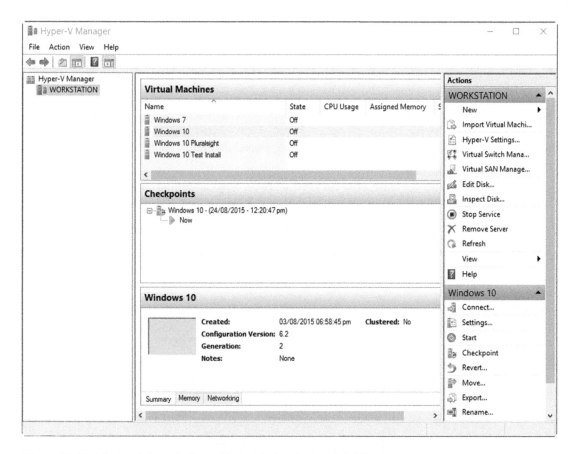

Figure 15-17. *Checkpoints are to Hyper-V what System Restore is to Windows*

Importing and Exporting Virtual Machines in Hyper-V

You may want to create VMs that are to be used on other PCs or that you want to keep copies of. Just creating a VM and then opening that VM file after copying it to another computer doesn't work for importing VMs in Hyper-V, which is why a special import and export option is available. To export a VM, select it in the Hyper-V Manager. In the bottom right of the Hyper-V Manager window, the Export option displays (see Figure 15-18). Click it and you are asked which folder you want to store your exported VM in. The export process is invisible and fairly quick.

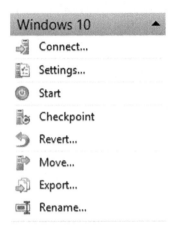

Figure 15-18. *You can export VMs from the Hyper-V Management console*

1. You can import previously exported VMs into Hyper-V by clicking the **Import virtual machine** link in the top right of the Hyper-V Manager window (see Figure 15-19) when no VM is currently selected.

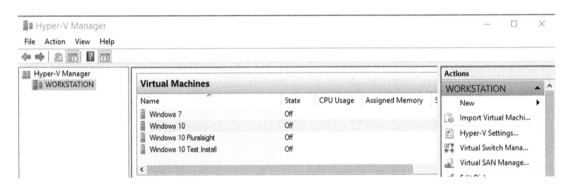

Figure 15-19. *VMs are also imported using the Hyper-V Management console*

2. The Import Virtual Machine Wizard opens. It first asks you to specify which folder (not which file) has the stored VM (see Figure 15-20).

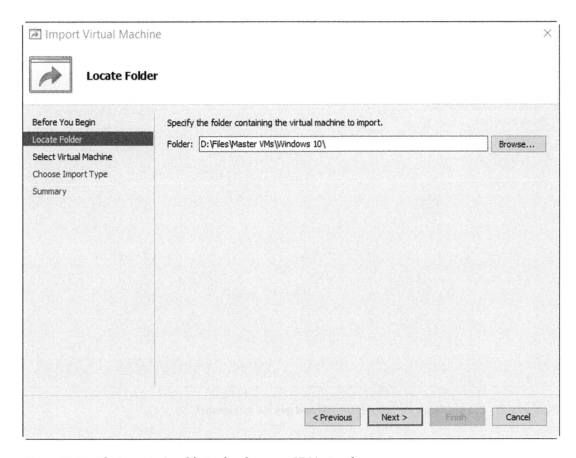

Figure 15-20. *The import wizard first asks where your VM is stored*

3. Next you are shown the name of the VM along with information on when it was created (see Figure 15-21). If this is the correct VM, click **Next**.

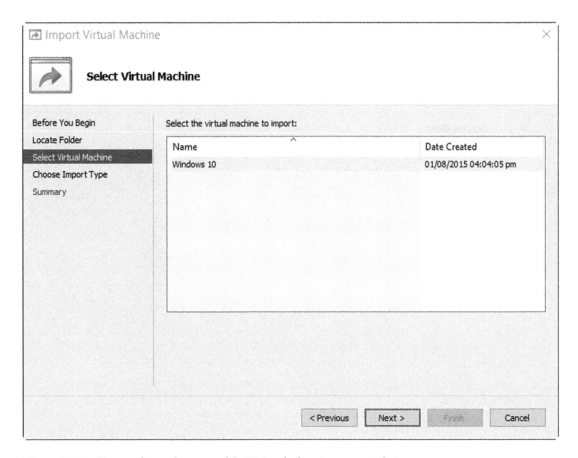

Figure 15-21. *You are shown the name of the VM and when it was created*

4. You are now asked how you want to import the VM (see Figure 15-22). The three options are as follows:

- **Register the virtual machine** is used when you are performing a straight import; the VM is still in the same folder location it was exported to and you want to leave it there. Any changes you make to the virtual machine, either in its settings or when you are using it, will be permanently made to this "master" VM, however.

- **Restore the virtual machine** is used when the VM is not in the same folder location it was exported to; for example, if it is a copy taken from a master image on a server.

- **Copy the virtual machine** is used when you want to create a local copy of an existing VM, leaving the "master" VM intact for importing onto the PC later, or onto another PC if required. This option is also used if you want to create a copy of an already imported VM and leave the original as a "master" copy.

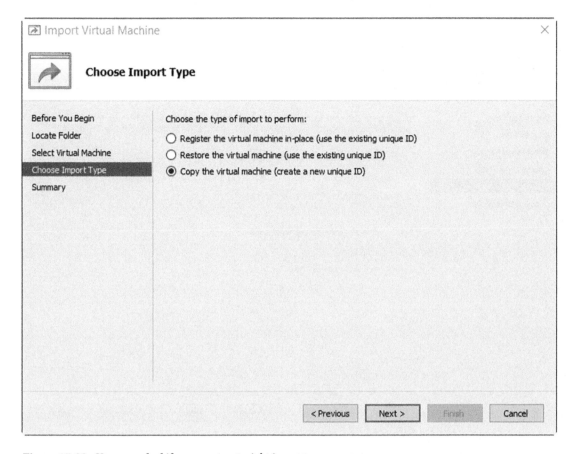

Figure 15-22. *You are asked if you want a straight import or a copy*

■ **Note** If you import a VM without making a copy of it, any changes you make to the VM and any problems that occur become part of it, which means that you effectively lose your clean *master* copy.

---

5. If you choose to create a copy of the VM, you are asked where you want to store it in your PC (see Figure 15-23).

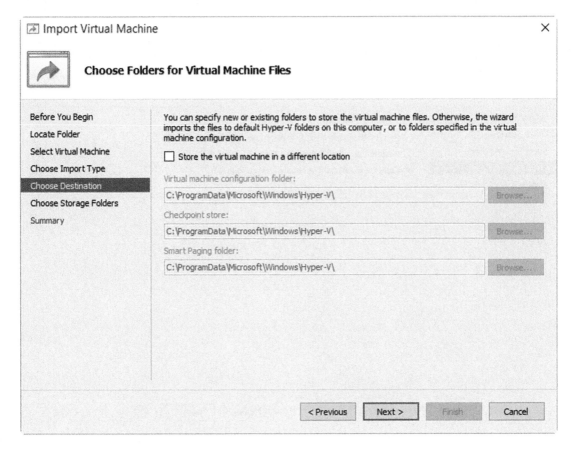

Figure 15-23. *You can choose where to store the VM copy*

6.   The last step is for Hyper-V to confirm all of your chosen settings (see Figure 15-24) before it completes the VM import process.

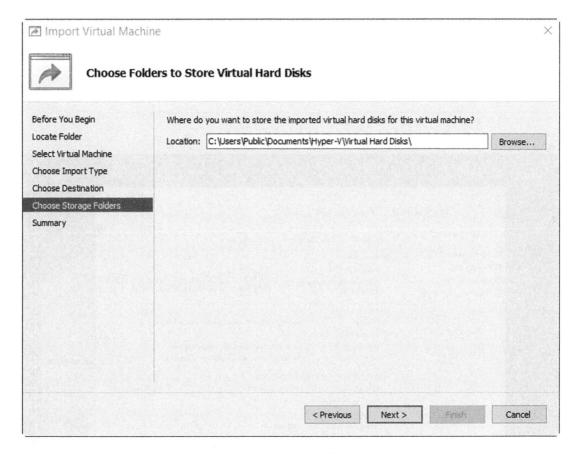

Figure 15-24. *Hyper-V asks where you want to store the Virtual Hard Disk*

Integrating Additional Services into a VM

Some operating systems, especially earlier versions of Windows, won't give you network access or other features at this point. This is where you need to plug extra features into the VM. You must do this with the VM running.

These additional features, which are required for some operating systems (but not Windows 8.1 or Windows 10, in which they're already installed) include the ability to move your mouse cursor freely between your main desktop and open VMs without having to first unlock it from the VM window. They also include networking and USB support for some operating systems.

From the Action menu, click **Insert Integration Service Setup Disk**. This loads an ISO file containing software that enhances the functionality of the VM.

Connecting to a Virtual Machine Using Remote Desktop

I mentioned earlier that sometimes not all screen resolutions are available to you when using a virtual machine in Hyper-V. Under this circumstance, you can connect to the VM using Remote Desktop so that you can use the VM at any resolution up to the maximum supported by your monitor.

There are other reasons why you might want to connect to a VM using Remote Desktop, not the least of which is a cleaner experience that also makes is quicker to launch the VM.

You first need the name of the Hyper-V PC, which you can get (if it is a Windows operating system), from the System screen in Control Panel (see Figure 15-25). With this information and your user name, you are ready to connect to the VM.

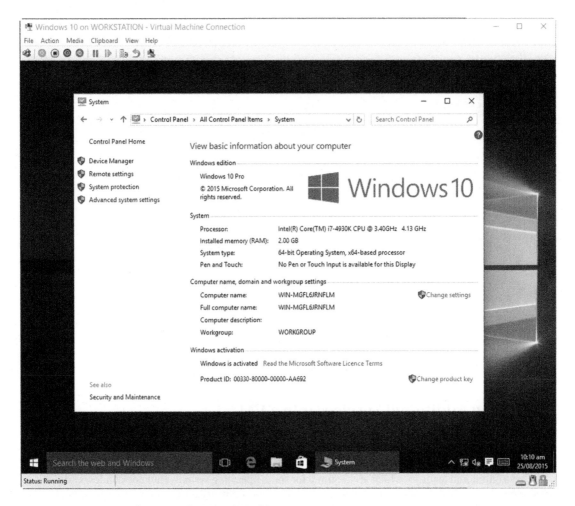

Figure 15-25. *Getting the name of a Virtual Machine*

1. Start the VM in Hyper-V and open its **System** panel in the Control Panel. Make a note of the name of the PC (you will also need your username and password, and you *must* have a password on the account in the VM or you will not be able to connect to it).

2. Make a note of the Computer Name of the VM, you'll need it, and then click the **Remote Settings** link in the left panel.

3. In the panel that appears, click the **Remote** tab. Make sure that in the Remote
    Desktop section, the option to **Allow remote connections to this computer** is
    selected (see Figure 15-26). For security reasons, it is a good idea to also check
    the box to **Only allow connections from computers running Remote Desktop
    with Network Level Authentication (recommended)**, which includes all
    modern versions of Windows.

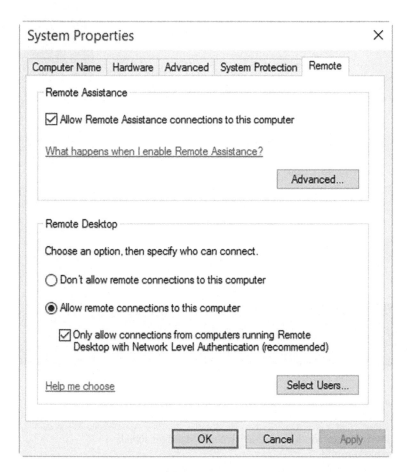

Figure 15-26. You allow Remote Desktop connections in the Control Panel

4. Click the **Select Users** button. Add a user account to the approved users list by
    entering the name and then clicking the **Check Names** button to authenticate it
    (see Figure 15-27).

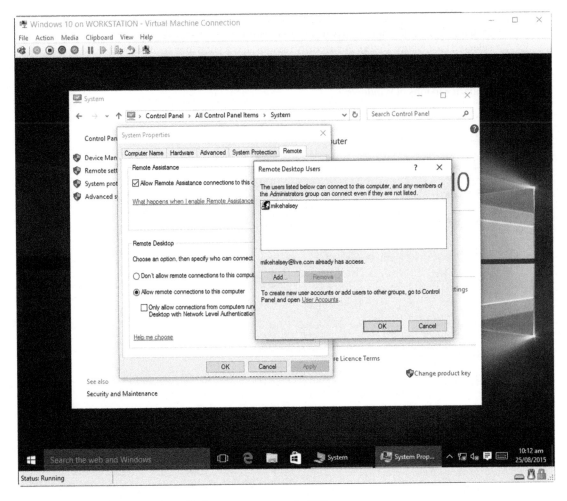

Figure 15-27. *You need to select which users can access the VM*

5. Leave the VM running but close its window and the Hyper-V Manager, which remains running in the background.

6. Open the Control Panel and in the Large or Small Icons view, click **System**.

7. In the System panel in your main copy of Windows 10, click the **Advanced System Settings** link in the left panel.

8. In the panel that appears, click the **Remote** tab. Make sure that in the Remote Desktop section, the option to **Allow remote connections to this computer** is selected, just as you did in the VM.

9. Search for **remote desktop** in the Start menu and launch **Remote Desktop Connection**.

10. With the VM running in Hyper-V, enter the computer name in the Remote Desktop Connection dialog (see Figure 15-28).

Figure 15-28. *You type the VMs name to access it*

11. When the connection is made, enter your username (in the format **Hyper-V\Username**) and password (see Figure 15-29). You can optionally tell Remote Desktop to remember these so that you don't need to enter them again in the future.

Figure 15-29. *You need to sign-in as an approved user*

12. You are presented with a security dialog asking if you trust the PC you are connecting to (see Figure 15-30). You can check the **Don't ask me again for connections to this computer** check box if you trust the VM.

Figure 15-30. You are presented with a security dialog before connecting for the first time

    13.   Click **Yes** to connect to the virtual machine.

The default connection always runs the VM full screen. There is a toolbar across the top of your window (see Figure 15-31). The icons you see on this toolbar may vary depending on your particular setup, but the standard icons are a pin icon (to always show the toolbar or to only show it when you move your mouse cursor to the top center of the screen), a quality of connection icon, and Minimize, Window, and Close buttons.

Figure 15-31. The Remote Desktop Control Toolbar

If you want to use a different screen resolution when connecting to the VM, then when you first open the Remote Desktop connection dialog, and at the point where you enter the name of the VM, click the **Show options** button. The dialog expands to present additional controls, including a Display tab where you can set the resolution you want to use (see Figure 15-32).

Figure 15-32. *You can select the screen resolution you wish to use for the VM*

Additional controls here include the ability to save the connection settings for this VM, to choose the connection quality, and to allow Internet connection to the VM, so that you can access it remotely without having to be on the same network.

Perhaps most useful, however, is the Local Resources tab. Here you can specify local printers for the VM to access, and on the **More** button you can specify local hard disks and even USB resources (see Figure 15-33). VMs running in Hyper-V cannot get access to devices such as USB flash drives; if you wish to use these devices with the VM, a Remote Desktop connection is a great way to do it.

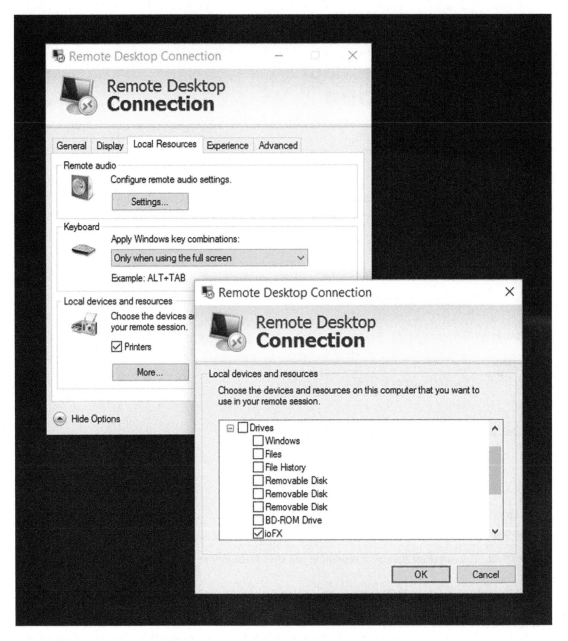

Figure 15-33. *You can use Remote Desktop to give the VM access to USB drives*

Using Virtual Hard Disks

You can also use virtual hard disks (VHDs) within Windows, both as file containers and as boot drives for the operating system. You can create a VHD within Hyper-V, but also from the Windows 10 Disk Management console (available by using the Win+X keyboard shortcut).

On their own, VHDs are of limited use because you need to manually reattach them to Windows 10 when the computer is restarted. It is in booting from a VHD that they become useful. Let's say you have a project that requires that everybody have their own copy of certain resources. You can create a VHD containing these resources that people can mount on their own PCs.

Also, you might have a laptop that you regularly and quickly repurpose for different roles within a company, such as sales, accounting, or production, for example. Rather than having a complicated multiboot system that is difficult to maintain, you can create a series of VHDs and copy the correct one to the laptop when you need to assign the laptop a different departmental role.

Creating a VHD in Windows 10

Create a VHD from the Disk Management console (press Win+X to open options). From the Action menu, click **Create VHD** (see Figure 15-34).

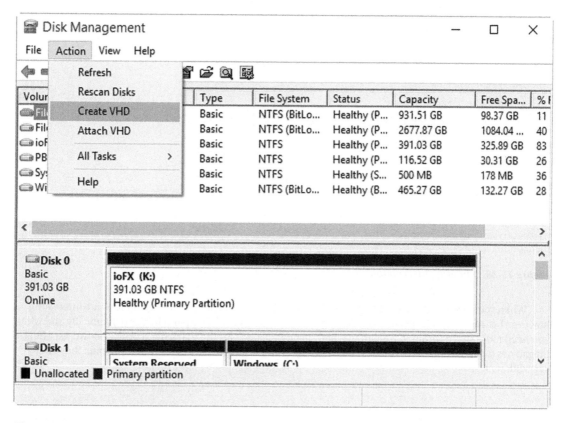

Figure 15-34. *Creating a VHD*

A dialog allows you to specify the VHD size and the hard disk location for VHD storage (see Figure 15-35).

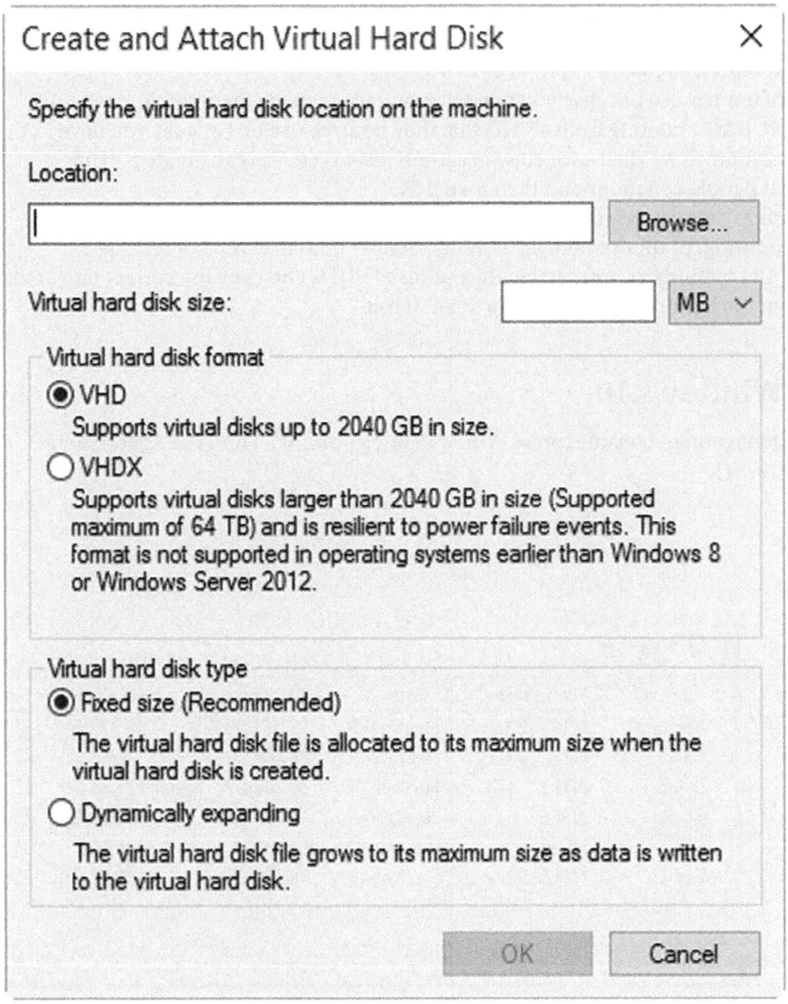

Create and Attach Virtual Hard Disk   ✕

Specify the virtual hard disk location on the machine.

Location:

[   ]   Browse...

Virtual hard disk size: [   ]   MB ⌄

Virtual hard disk format
  ⦿ VHD
    Supports virtual disks up to 2040 GB in size.
  ○ VHDX
    Supports virtual disks larger than 2040 GB in size (Supported
    maximum of 64 TB) and is resilient to power failure events. This
    format is not supported in operating systems earlier than Windows 8
    or Windows Server 2012.

Virtual hard disk type
  ⦿ Fixed size (Recommended)
    The virtual hard disk file is allocated to its maximum size when the
    virtual hard disk is created.
  ○ Dynamically expanding
    The virtual hard disk file grows to its maximum size as data is written
    to the virtual hard disk.

                                              OK   Cancel

Figure 15-35. *Choosing VHD options*

When you choose the location for the VHD, you also specify its name. The size options are interesting, however, because you can specify a fixed size or you can have the VHD expand in size dynamically and when you need more space within it. Note than when specifying a size for the VHD, the size drop-down list offers megabytes (MB), gigabytes (GB), and terabytes (TB). Don't accidentally choose the wrong one; they're all very different.

■ **Tip**   You can also create VHDs in the Hyper-V Manager using a wizard process, like when you create a VM. VHDs created and managed by Hyper-V include additional functionalities, such as dynamically expanding when needed and being able to automatically import the contents of other drives.

When the VHD is created, you can attach it to Windows 10 in the Disk Management console by selecting Attach VHD from the Actions menu.

Booting Windows from a VHD

Creating a VHD doesn't let you install an operating system in it or boot from it. To do this, you need to start your computer from your original Windows 10 installation media. After you select your installation language, perform the following steps:

1. Press **Shift+F10** at the installation screen to open a Command window.

2. Type **diskpart** and press Enter.

3. To use an existing VHD, type **Select vdisk file=C:\Path1\Path2\disk.vhd**, substituting the path and disk names for the location on the disk of the VHD and its name.

4. If you don't have an existing VHD and need to create one, type **Create vdisk file=C:\Path1\Path2\disk.vhd maximum=20000 type=dynamic**, again substituting the path and disk names with where you want the VHD to be created and what you want it to be called (the path folders must already exist). Also, substitute the number of megabytes and create either a fixed or dynamic disk.

5. If you have just created a new VHD, type **Select vdisk file=C:\Path1\Path2\disk. vhd** and press Enter to attach the VHD if you have just created one, as per step 2.

6. Type **attach vdisk** and press Enter.

7. Type **exit** and press Enter.

8. Type **exit** again and press Enter.

9. Click **Install Custom: Install Windows Only (Advanced)**.

10. Locate the newly attached VHD in the hard disk pane in which you want to install Windows. This is Disk 1 if you have only one hard disk in your computer. You can identify it by its size. Click **Next** when you are ready to install Windows onto the VHD.

You can install Windows 7 Enterprise and Ultimate, Windows 8.1 Pro and Enterprise, Windows 10 Pro and Enterprise, and Windows Server 2008, 2012, and 2016 onto a VHD.

■ **Note**   Each operating system and software package you install into a VM needs to have its own license, and if necessary for that product, its own product key. Some versions of Windows are not licensed for use inside a VM. You can find out more about licensing for your particular copies of Windows and other Microsoft software at www.microsoft.com/About/Legal/EN/US/IntellectualProperty/UseTerms.

You now need to add the VHD to the Windows boot menu so that you can boot your PC from it.

1. Press **Win+X** to open the Administration menu.

2. Click **Command Prompt (Admin)**.

3. Type **bcdedit /v** in the Command window. Press Enter.

4. Locate the VHD you installed and make a note of its globally unique identifier (GUID) code. It is a long string of numbers and letters in the Identifier section for the OS (see Figure 15-36).

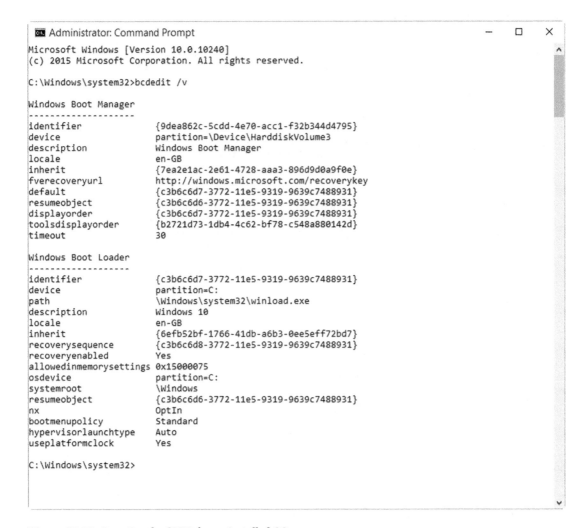

Figure 15-36. *Locating the GUID for an installed OS*

5. Type **bcdedit /set {GUID} description "OS Name"**, substituting the actual GUID for the OS for the letters *GUID* and assigning the OS its proper name. Press Enter.

6. Optionally, you might want this VHD to be the OS that loads by default. Set this by typing **bcdedit / default {GUID}**. Press Enter.

You can now boot your computer from the VM in the same way that you boot into your normally installed copy of Windows. In fact, you won't even be able to notice the difference. Most people booting into a VM have no idea that they're not using an operating system that's installed on the computer's hard disk.

■ **Note**   The Secure Boot feature in Windows 10 on UEFI-equipped motherboards might prevent some VHDs from booting. You should check in the UEFI firmware settings to see if this feature can be turned off on your computer.

Summary

The virtualization options in Windows 10 are powerful, but remember that they are available in only the Pro and Enterprise editions.

I have shown you how it is also possible—as long as you have two network adapters in your PC—to isolate a VM from the Internet while still giving it access to your own PC. It can really be done only if you connect to the Internet via Wi-Fi and *do not* have a physical network cable plugged into your computer. Doing so helps to protect older Windows installations, especially those that are out of support, from viruses and other malware infections that can then spread to and attack the Windows 10 PCs on your network.

■ ■ ■

CHAPTER 16

Installing Windows 10 on Your Computer

Whether you get your copy of Windows 10 with a shiny new PC, off the shelf from your local store, or on a software subscription package from Microsoft, you have to install it at some point—either to replace an earlier version of Windows on your computer or when something goes wrong.

Installing Windows 10 is something that can be done fairly simply and without fuss. In fact, it's the least fussy version of Windows ever. It allows you to upgrade from an earlier version of the operating system or wipe out an existing one, while keeping all of your files intact.

Back Up Your Files and Documents First!

When you install Windows 10 onto an existing computer, make sure that you keep all of your files and documents intact. To guarantee this, you should *always* make an up-to-date backup of all of your files and documents beforehand.

Although the Windows installation process is very robust, there's no knowing when and how something might go wrong. Problems could be due to a power outage, a driver failure, or simply forgetting that you had some important files in a different folder that Windows 10 doesn't save because it doesn't know it needs to do so.

The best place to keep a files backup is on an external USB hard disk, but if you have a second physical hard disk or a hard disk that's split into several different partitions on your computer, you can keep your files there. Bear in mind, though, that a *proper* backup should be one that's external to the computer, which covers you in case of fire, theft, or hard-disk failure. (See Chapter 12 for information on performing backups.)

Windows 10 Edition Differences

There the several editions—sometimes known as *flavors* or *stock-keeping units* (SKUs)—of Windows 10. Be aware that some are available only to certain customers and in certain ways:

- **Windows 10 Home** is the general consumer version and comes preinstalled on most new PCs. It is also available through retail purchase.

- **Windows 10 Pro** is the version aimed at IT professionals and enthusiasts. It comes preinstalled on some PCs and is available for purchase.

- **Windows 10 Mobile** is the version for smartphones and cannot be purchased as a retail edition. It comes preinstalled on your Windows phone.

- **Windows 10 Enterprise** is available only to business volume-licensing customers or through an MSDN (Microsoft Developer Network) subscription.

There are other specific editions that are only available through Microsoft's volume licensing services, such as Windows 10 for Education and Windows 10 Mobile Enterprise. These editions are not relevant to this book because they can only be purchased by large organizations.

Windows 10 Differences by Screen Size

There are also a few differences in versions of Windows 10 that vary by the size of your screen:

- **Screens smaller than 8 inches** do not have a desktop on which apps can be run in separate windows. For devices with screens less than 8 inches, all apps can only be run fullscreen or in a side-by-side two-app view.

- **Screens smaller than 10 inches** have the full versions of Microsoft's Office Mobile apps preinstalled (or available to download later from the Store). This includes the ability to create new documents. For devices with screens larger than 10 inches, the full functionality of the Office Mobile apps (such as document creation) requires that you have an Office 365 subscription. You can purchase one at www.Office365.com.

Deciding How to Install Windows 10 on an Existing Computer

One of the perennial questions asked in computing circles when migrating from one version of Windows to another is whether to perform an upgrade over an existing copy or completely wipe the old installation and start from scratch. So what are the pros and cons of both?

Upgrade pros:

- Upgrading is much faster and easier overall, especially if you have a lot of software on your computer, because it saves reinstalling everything afterward. With Windows 10 it's possible to argue that upgrading the operating system in-place is actually faster than cleanly installing it.

- Performing an upgrade leaves your files intact if your files and documents are on the same hard-disk partition as your old copy of Windows and you don't have an external backup (more on this shortly because it's very important).

Upgrade cons:

- Any problems associated with your software or Windows installation might be carried forward into Windows 10.

- Upgrading does not guarantee that your software will work properly afterward, and some software programs might need to be uninstalled and reinstalled.

Clean install pros:

- Your new installation is fresh and clean with no problems associated with it.

- There are no bugs and incompatible software.

Clean install cons:

- Installation and configuration can be time-consuming, especially if you have a lot of software.

- You need to have an up-to-date external backup of your files and documents kept separately from the installation.

In truth, you might not have a choice but to perform a clean installation, at least as far as the Windows 10 upgrade options go, because Windows 10 will not be able to migrate your software from Windows XP or Windows Vista.

Now let's look at the process of actually upgrading to Windows 10. Once you have physical media for installing Windows 10, be it a DVD or a USB flash drive, you can set about the process of installing the operating system (OS) on your computer. If you want to upgrade from a version of Windows other than Windows 7, you have to reinstall your software, as I will explain shortly.

Windows 10 Product Keys and Activation

I want to make an important note here about product keys and activation, as Microsoft has changed the process significantly from previous versions of the OS. When you installed a copy of Windows previously, you were required to enter your product key, which is a series of 25 letters and numbers in the format XXX1X-XXXX1-X111X-XXXXX-111XX.

If Windows 10 has already been installed on a PC (i.e., it was supplied with the PC when you purchased it, or you upgraded from Windows 7 or Windows 8.1 during the new operating system's first year when it was offered for free), the product key is tied to your hardware and it does not need to be entered. In fact, if you are asked for a product key at installation, you can skip it.

When Windows 10 activates (in this case, it would be activating for the second or perhaps third time), Microsoft's servers recognize the hardware ID (which is tied to your computer's motherboard) and activate without the need for entering your product key.

Are there limits on the number of times Windows 10 will autoactivate in this way? There certainly are. And if for any reason you have to change the motherboard in your PC, perhaps because it fails, then you need to call Microsoft to activate your copy of Windows 10 over the phone. It's worth noting, however, that Microsoft almost never argues over activation, so this is not something you should worry about unless you are deliberately trying to install your copy of Windows 10 on another machine.

One last point to note here is that because the copy of Windows 10 is tied to the hardware, and not the product key, you cannot keep it should you sell or give away your PC. The activation always follows that PC. This also means that if you purchase a new PC, you also need to purchase a new copy of Windows 10.

When Is an Upgrade *Also* a Clean Install?

Each and every upgrade path to Windows 10 allows you to move **Just [the] personal files** for each user on the computer. Is this a clean install? Is it a clean installation alternative? The answer to these questions depends on the version that you're upgrading from and the setup that you have in place.

When Windows performs an upgrade, it copies your old Windows installation, complete with programs, into a `Windows.old` folder. You can then recover any files from the installation that you need to—such as Internet Favorites from Windows XP, which weren't stored in a separate user folder and weren't considered part of the user's files.

All new folders are thus created for the new operating system containing all new files. You essentially have a clean installation because there's nothing left over from your old Windows installation that can cause problems, malware infection, or incompatibilities.

When You Should Perform a Clean Install

So when might you want to choose to perform a clean installation instead of upgrading? There are a few scenarios in which you should just choose to perform a completely clean installation, formatting your hard disk and starting from scratch:

- **If you already have Windows 10 installed on the PC**, as here you can use the Reset feature in the Settings app to effectively perform a wipe and clean install. This removes your installed apps, and optionally all of your files and user accounts; but because of the way the Reset feature works in Windows 10, all the latest Windows Updates (up to 30 days ago) and your hardware drivers are installed.

- **You already store your files and documents on a different physical hard disk or partition to your copy of Windows**. I always recommend storing your files on a separate partition of Windows for data security, and there is nothing really to be gained from creating the Windows.old folder. In this circumstance, it's best to reformat the Windows drive, which removes any trace of doubt that the former installation might cause problems.

- **Your Windows disk isn't large enough to store both Windows 10 and your old Windows installation in a Windows.old folder**. If there isn't enough space on your hard disk to upgrade Windows, the installer informs you before the upgrade process begins.

- **You are upgrading from Windows XP or Windows Vista**. You should always reformat your hard disk because Windows 10 (as with Windows 7) wants to create a System Reserved partition at the beginning of your primary hard disk (Disc 0), in which it places its start-up and system repair files. This partition contains the boot information for Windows, and crucially, all the rescue tools and utilities for when the operating system doesn't start. If the Windows installer can't create this partition, you lose valuable Windows 10 features.

- **You have UEFI firmware on your computer**. Windows 10 might create support and rescue partitions, in addition to the System Reserved partition. If you have a Windows 7 computer that you are upgrading to Windows 10, performing a format and clean installation is the only way to create these additional troubleshooting and rescue partitions.

Acquiring a Windows 10 Installer

Windows 10 is the first version of the operating system that you can purchase online directly from Microsoft. You have the choice of downloading the operating system or ordering it on a DVD. You can purchase the operating system as a download on an existing computer that is running another version of Windows. There is no requirement, however, to install the downloaded copy of Windows 10 on the computer you download it to; you can install it on another computer if you want.

You can purchase Windows 10 at www.microsoftstore.com or through the Windows Store on another Windows 10 PC. Purchasing Windows 10 through one of these stores helps you through the process of downloading and paying for your new copy of Windows 10. At the end of the process, the Windows 10 setup and media creation tool that the Store loads for you presents you with several options (see Figure 16-1). If you choose to purchase a packaged DVD or a USB flash product, you can skip ahead to the "Preparing to Install Windows 10" section in this chapter.

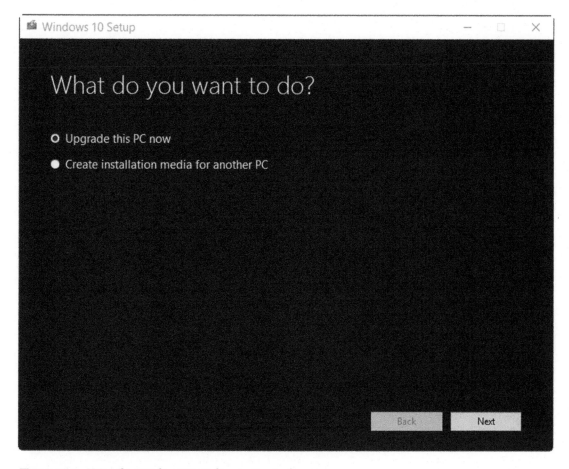

Figure 16-1. *Using the Windows 10 media creation tool*

If you already have Windows 10 installed and you need to reinstall it, you can download the Windows 10 media creation tool from `http://pcs.tv/win10dwnld`. You are asked if you want to use the tool to do an in-place upgrade on the current PC or create installation media for another PC (see Figure 16-1). The second option allows you to create a Windows installer that can be used to reinstall Windows 10 on your current PC too, which is useful should something go horribly wrong and Windows becomes unbootable.

You are asked which language you want, which edition of Windows (Home or Pro), and if you want the 32-bit or 64-bit edition of the operating system (see Figure 16-2). If you are not sure which edition and architecture you currently have on your PC do the following: in Windows 10, open the Settings app and then click **System** ➤ **About**; in Windows 7 or Windows 8.1, open the Control Panel and click **System**.

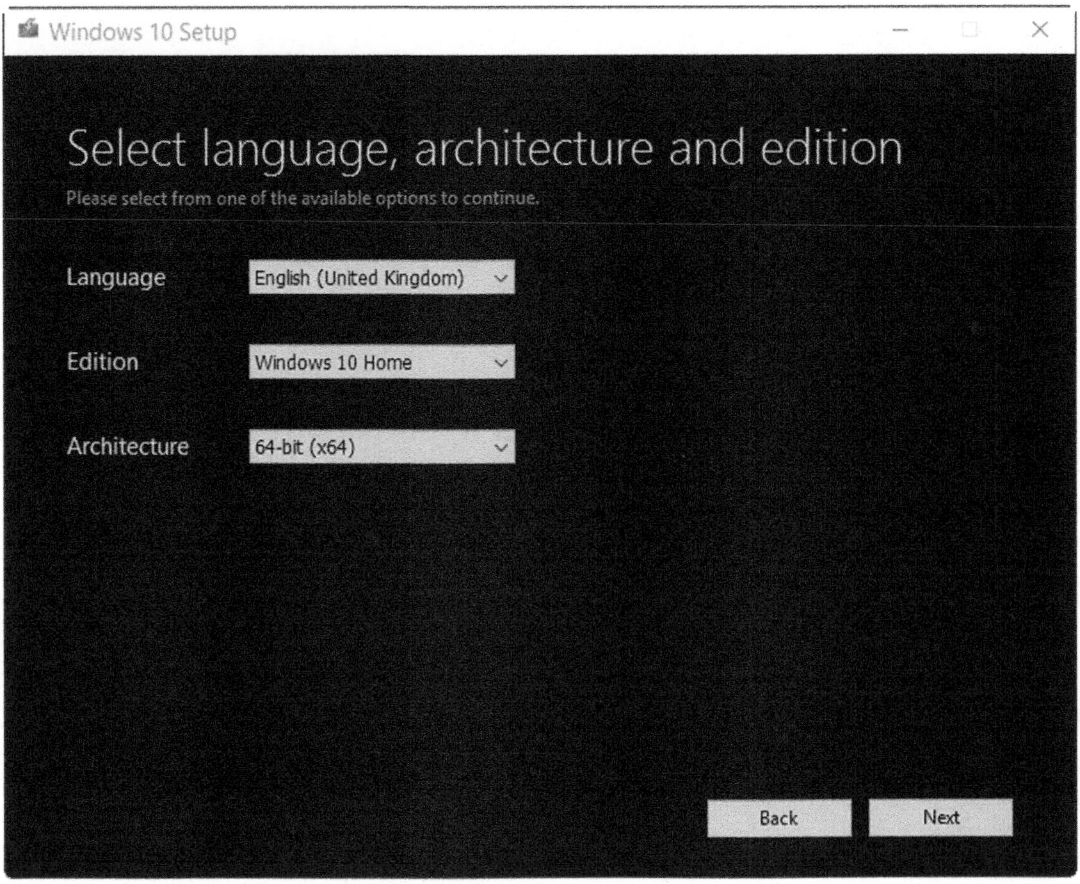

Figure 16-2. You have a choice of languages and Windows editions to download

The next question is which type of media you want to create. You can create a USB flash drive (you need one at least 3GB), or if you want to download the ISO file to burn to DVD later (see Figure 16-3). An ISO file is a DVD disc image that contains the Windows 10 installer. You can download this and keep it safe to burn to a DVD should you need it. If you think you might not have a DVD disc burner available when you need to install (or reinstall) Windows 10, it's probably best to create a USB flash drive, label it, and keep it somewhere safe.

■ **Tip**   You can burn an ISO file to a DVD by right-clicking it in File Explorer (in Windows 8.1 and Windows 10) and choosing **Burn disc image** from the options that appear. In Windows 7, double-click the ISO file to start the disc image burner utility.

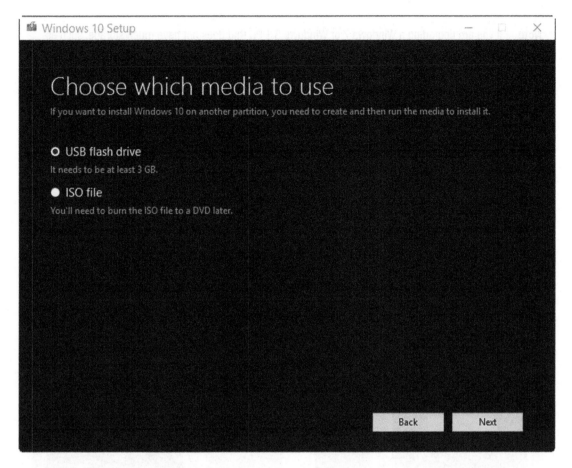

Figure 16-3. You are asked if you want to create a bootable USB flash drive or download an ISO file

Preparing to Install Windows 10

After you download or buy a retail copy of Windows 10, or if you need to reinstall it, the process varies, depending on whether you are upgrading an existing Windows installation or performing a clean installation. If you are upgrading, the process depends on the version of Windows from which you are upgrading.

Therefore, the options that present themselves to you can vary considerably, so in this section, I'll show you what those options are and how the installation can vary depending on how you choose to perform it. I'll also help you make sure that the installation you perform is stable and reliable.

▓ **Note** If you are upgrading a Windows 7 or Windows 8.1 PC that does not have much storage, such as a low-cost tablet or a laptop with just 16GB of internal storage, you are asked for a USB flash drive to assist with installation. There are three important considerations here. First, if you have to plug it into the socket you normally use to charge your device, make sure that the device is fully charged before installing Windows 10. Second, if the socket is a micro or Type-C USB, then you might need a USB OTG (On-The-Go) adapter cable to use your flash drive. Third, if you want to roll back to Windows 7 or Windows 8.1 (more on this shortly), you need to keep this USB flash drive safe, as it will be needed.

Migrating to Windows 10 Using Zinstall WinWin

When upgrading from an older installation or PC, you used to be able to use a Windows feature called Easy Transfer, with which you could move your user account(s), Internet Favorites, Documents, Music, Photos, and Videos from the old to the new. In Windows 8.1, Easy Transfer was retired and not replaced by anything.

Several third-party companies have stepped up to the mark, however, to make easy-to-use PC migration tools for home users and comprehensive tools for businesses. Some of the best I've ever found, and that I can recommend completely, are the tools from Zinstall. WinWin is their home-use package. It can migrate an older Windows installation like XP or Vista, or an older PC, to Windows 10 in easy steps (see Figure 16-4). You can purchase and download WinWin from `www.zinstall.com`.

Press Go on New PC to start migration

WinWin transfers everything from Old to New PC

Applications, settings, files have been copied to new PC

Figure 16-4. *Zinstall WinWin can be used to migrate from an old PC or OS to Windows 10*

Upgrading from Windows XP and Windows Vista

Windows 10 *does not* support a direct upgrade path for users of Windows XP or Windows Vista (see Figure 16-5). If you currently have Windows XP installed on your PC and you want to install Windows 10, you need to perform a format and a clean install of the new OS.

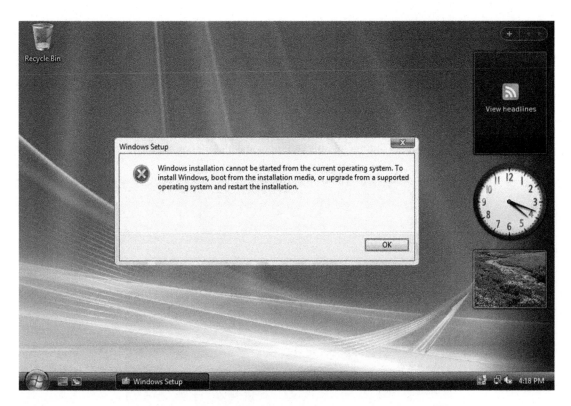

Figure 16-5. *You cannot do an in-place upgrade from XP or Vista*

The reason you can't upgrade your full Windows XP or Vista installation to Windows 10 is because these operating systems and Windows 10 are based on completely different core code (the OS kernel) and are incompatible with one another. If you want to upgrade from Windows XP or Windows Vista to Windows 10, you have to format your disk and clean install, and then set up your accounts and reinstall all of your apps afterward.

■ **Note** Some older and custom apps designed for Windows XP will never run happily in Windows 10, not even in compatibility mode. To use older software in Windows 10, you may need to install it in a virtual machine (VM). I showed you how to do this in Chapter 15.

Upgrading from Windows 7

It is only when upgrading from Windows 7 that you can actually migrate all of your software to the new OS. Windows 7 and Windows 10 are similar in many ways, but this doesn't mean that software incompatibilities don't appear.

■ **Tip**   If you need assistance in maintaining compatibility with your software and hardware in an upgrade from Windows XP, Vista, Windows 7, or Windows 8.1 to Windows 10 my book *Windows Software and Hardware Compatibility Troubleshooting* (Apress, 2015) is available to purchase from Apress at `http://pcs.tv/1KVJ7QK` and all good book retailers.

When upgrading from Windows 7, the Windows 10 installer gives you the options to migrate all of your personal files, apps, and Windows settings, or only your personal files, or nothing (see Figure 16-6).

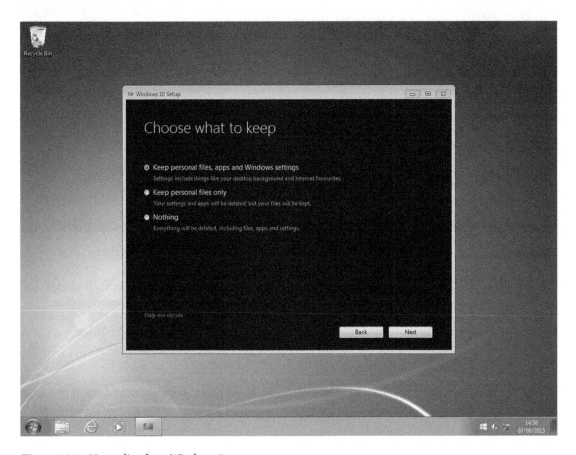

Figure 16-6. Upgrading from Windows 7

Because the editions of Windows 10 are slightly different from those of Windows 7, you may get a slightly different version than the one you currently have installed on your PC. If you are currently using Windows 7 Starter, Home Basic, or Home Premium, you will be upgraded to Windows 10 Home. If you are using Windows 7 Pro or Ultimate, you will be upgraded to Windows 10 Pro.

■ **Tip** When you upgrade from Windows 7 or Windows 8.1, the installer lets you know if any hardware or apps on your PC are incompatible and might need updating, or if any features in your current version of Windows, such as Media Center, will be removed.

Upgrading from Windows 8.1

The upgrade process from Windows 8.1 to Windows 10 is identical to that of Windows 7, enabling you to keep your personal files, apps, and Windows settings, or just a subset of those. The upgrade process from both Windows 7 and Windows 8.1 is extremely quick, even if you have a lot of software installed, and can take anywhere from 20 minutes to around an hour.

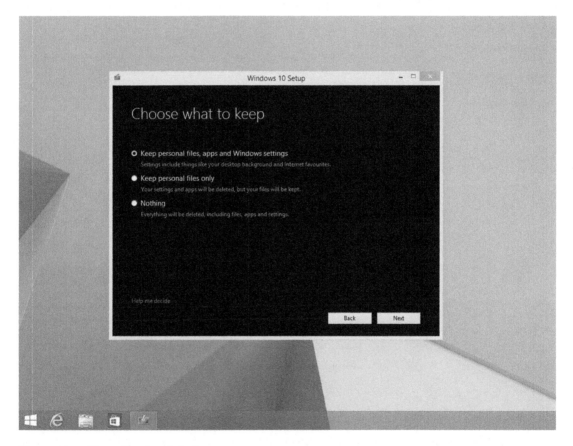

Figure 16-7. *Upgrading from Windows 8.1*

Because the editions of Windows 8.1 are slightly different from those of Windows 10, you may get upgraded to a slightly different version to the one you are currently using. Windows 8.1 and Windows 8.1 with Bing upgrade to Windows 10 Home, and Windows 8.1 Pro does a straight upgrade to Windows 10 Pro.

Rolling Back Windows and Deleting the Windows.old Folder

When you upgrade from Windows 7 to Windows 8.1, your previous installation is moved to a Windows.old folder on your hard disk. This cannot be deleted the way you would normally delete files, but it can be removed.

The reason this Windows.old folder exists is twofold. First, so that you can extract from it any files or documents that may still be lurking in its Users folder. And second, so you can roll your installation back to it, and effectively reinstall it, should something go horribly wrong with your Windows 10 installation, perhaps because you have major app or driver incompatibilities and would prefer to wait for updates.

To roll back to your previous version of Windows, open the Settings app, navigate to **Update & recovery** and then **Recovery**, where you see a **Go back to an earlier build** (see Figure 16-8). Clicking this removes Windows 10 and reinstalls your older operating system. Note that this option is only available for a month after upgrading to Windows 10, after which time the Windows.old folder is automatically deleted.

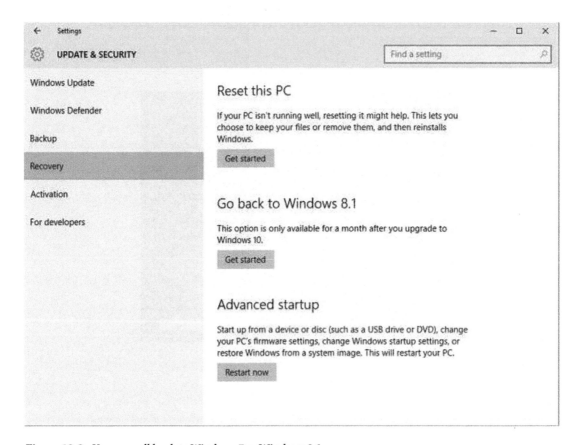

Figure 16-8. *You can roll back to Windows 7 or Windows 8.1*

If you're happy with your Windows 10 installation and don't want to wait a month for the `Windows.old` folder to be automatically deleted, you can search Cortana for **disk clean-up** and run the Disk Clean-up tool. Click the **Clean up system files** button. In the list, your **Previous Windows installation(s)** appears as a checkable option that can be cleaned.

Figure 16-9. *You can delete the Windows.old folder in the Disk Clean-up tool*

Moving from 32-bit (x86) to 64-bit (x64) Windows

If you are currently running a 32-bit (x86) version of Windows—perhaps because you are using a Windows 7 netbook, or a low-cost tablet or laptop that came with Windows 8.1 with Bing—there are some things you should know. First and most importantly, you can't upgrade any 32-bit version of Windows to the 64-bit version, for Windows 7 or Windows 8.1; the installer simply doesn't support it (see Figure 16-10).

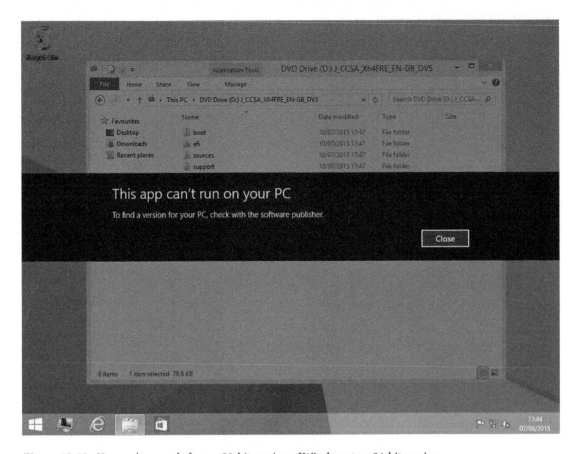

Figure 16-10. *You can't upgrade from a 32-bit version of Windows to a 64-bit version*

You can't upgrade because the differences between the 32-bit and 64-bit versions of Windows are very pronounced, not the least of which are with the hardware driver support, for which the x86 and x64 drivers are very different from one another and that the BIOS boot loaders are often extremely different.

This means that if you want to move to a 64-bit version of Windows 10, perhaps because you have already upgraded the memory in your computer to more than 4GB (including your graphics memory), you have to reformat your hard disk and perform a clean installation of Windows 10.

This 4GB memory limit is important because it *does* include your graphics memory. Let's look at an example. Your computer has three 1GB memory cards installed, and your graphics card has a memory standing at just 512MB (0.5GB). In this situation, the 32-bit version of Windows happily sees *all* 3.5GB of your memory.

If you upgrade the graphics card to one with 2GB of installed memory, however, you have a total of 5GB. Windows discards your memory in chunks of entire memory cards, so the total amount of memory your PC sees is only two of the three 1GB memory cards on your motherboard (in some configurations, it might see only one of them!) and the graphics card.

In this circumstance, the only way to see above the 4GB memory ceiling is to install the 64-bit version of Windows 10, which can see all of your installed memory.

Windows 10 Minimum Hardware Requirements

If you have an older computer, you might wonder whether Windows 10 will run on your computer. The good news is that the minimum hardware requirements for Windows 10 are very low, meaning that it runs on most computers:

- **Processor:** 1GHz or faster

- **Memory (RAM):** 1 gigabyte (1GB) for the 32-bit version and 2GB for the 64-bit version

- **Hard disk space:** 16GB for the 32-bit OS and 20GB for the 64-bit OS

- **Graphics card:** DirectX9 or later with WDDM 1.0 driver

- **Display:** 1024 × 600 pixels or greater

Bear in mind that these are the *minimum* requirements. You should not expect the full Windows 10 experience to run on older hardware as well as it does on a newer computer.

Installing Windows 10 on Small Tablets and Low Storage Laptops

I have already mentioned that there are special circumstances surrounding the installation of Windows 10 on small, low-cost tablets and laptops. This is because these devices have smaller screens and generally come with small amounts of storage, from as little as 16GB. This is what you need to know when installing Windows 10 on one of these devices.

- **Before you upgrade**, see if you can perform a Refresh or Reset operation (Windows 8.1) or a Disk Cleanup (Windows 7 and 8.1) to free up valuable disk space that the installer will need.

- **If there is less than 9GB space available**, you are asked to plug in a USB flash drive that will be used to cache setup files during the install. This flash drive is essential if you later need to roll back to Windows 7 or 8.1, so don't delete its contents until you're sure you don't need it.

Performing a Clean Install of Windows 10

To perform a clean installation of Windows 10, you need to start your computer from the boot media that you created (either a DVD or USB flash drive) or from your retail copy of Windows 10 (if you do not have installation media, you can create some; see the "Acquiring a Windows 10 Installer" section from earlier in this chapter). You may need to enter the boot menu of your computer (normally the F12 key when you start the PC, although this may differ on your computer or tablet; check the documentation that came with the PC) to tell the PC to start from the media that you have inserted.

1. When the Windows installer starts, you are asked to enter the country and language that you want to install (see Figure 16-11). Click **Next** when you have selected the appropriate options.

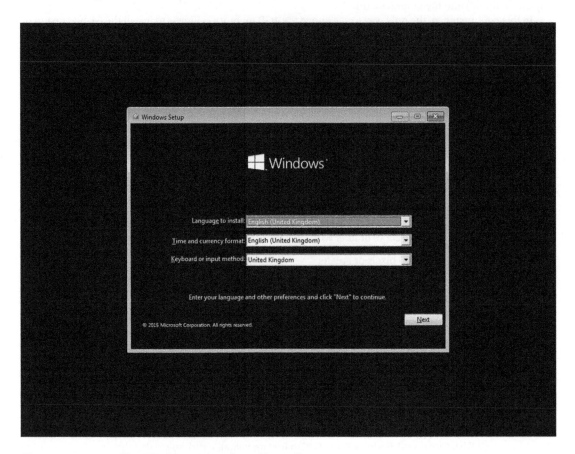

Figure 16-11. *Installing Windows 10 from bootable media*

■ **Note** The Windows 10 installer fully supports touch interfaces to make it easy to install on *most* tablet computers. Some tablets do not support touch during setup, but you can use a USB keyboard and mouse.

---

2.   The next screen is important. Because you are installing Windows 10, click the
     Install now button in the center of the screen (see Figure 16-12). In the bottom
     right of the screen, notice Repair Your Computer, which can be useful if you later
     need to rescue and repair a faulty Windows 10 installation.

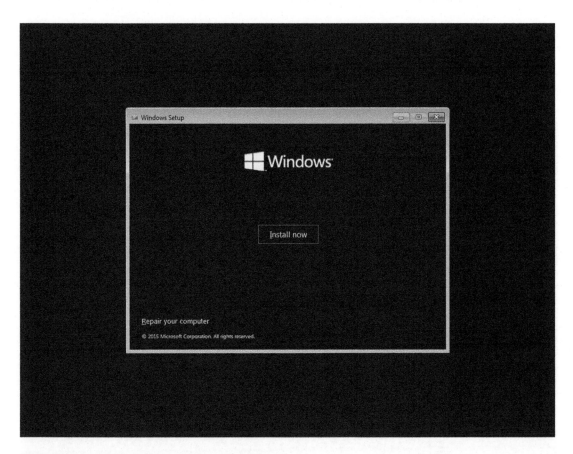

Figure 16-12. *Click Install Now to install Windows 10*

3. At the next screen you are asked for your Windows product key. At the beginning of this chapter, I mentioned the changes Windows 10 has brought to Windows activation. If you are reinstalling Windows 10 on the PC it was on before, and you are installing the *same* version (Home or Pro) that you had before, you can click **Skip** at this step.

■ **Tip**   You can also skip the product key if you had the 32-bit (x86) version of Windows 10 installed but you are now clean installing the 64-bit (x64) version after a memory upgrade.

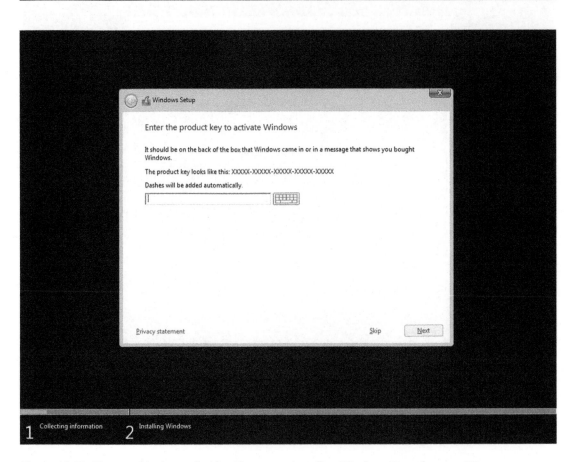

Figure 16-13. *You can skip the product key if you are reinstalling Windows 10 on the same PC*

4. You *may* be asked which edition of Windows 10 you are installing, Home or Pro. Be certain to check the version you have purchased or that you had installed on the PC previously.

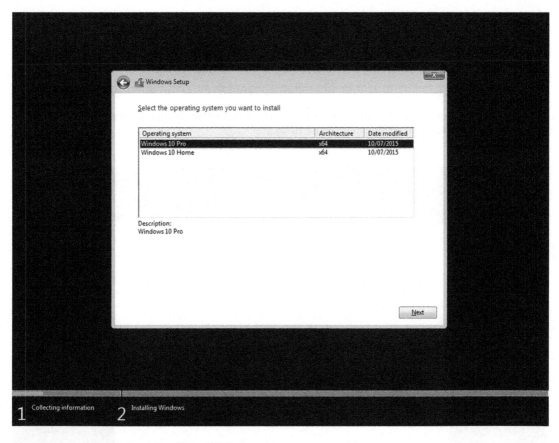

Figure 16-14. *Choose the right edition of Windows 10*

5. After accepting the install Terms and Conditions, you can upgrade your
   current copy of Windows to Windows 10 through the bootable installer. This
   feature is most useful when rescuing a faultily installed copy of Windows 10,
   because it creates a completely new and fresh (i.e., without your software and
   apps installed) installation of Windows 10. It also places your old installation,
   complete with all of your files, in a Windows.old folder so that you can recover
   them afterward (see Figure 16-15).

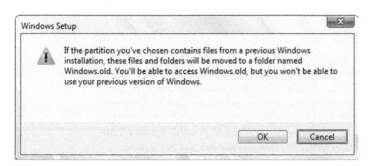

Figure 16-15. *You can rescue files in a non-functioning Windows installation*

■ **Tip**   When you start the PC from the Windows install media, the Upgrade option is grayed-out and unavailable. Also, if you want to rescue a faulty Windows 10 installation and you haven't been able to upgrade from the desktop, click Custom at this point, to save the current installation to a `Windows.old` folder.

6. To perform a clean installation of Windows 10, click **Custom: Install Windows only (advanced)**, as shown in Figure 16-16.

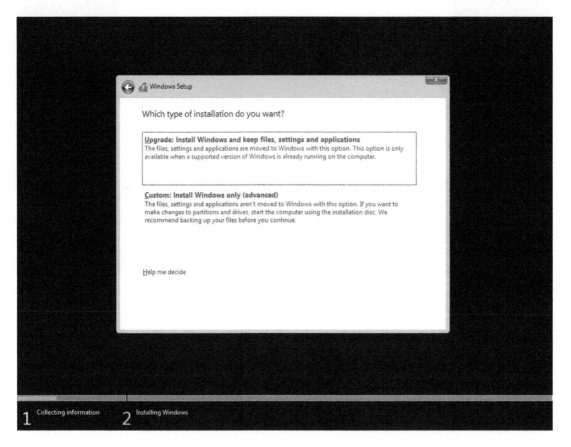

Figure 16-16. *You can also upgrade to Windows 10*

7. You are presented with a list of hard disks and partitions in your computer, on which you can install Windows 10 (see Figure 16-17). On most computers, you likely see only a single disk listed, which is where you install Windows 10. You should choose to install Windows 10 on Disc 0 (zero) because this is where the System Reserved partition with the OS boot files will be placed. If you have UEFI firmware in your computer, the Windows 10 installer will possibly create other start-up and rescue partitions as well). The installer *always* places them on Drive 0 (zero).

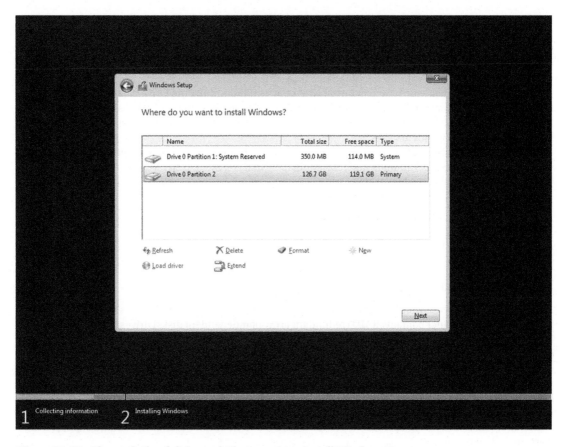

Figure 16-17. *Choose the hard disk on which you want to install Windows 10*

8. The installation process is completely automated from here. You aren't required to do anything with your computer until Windows 10 is completely installed. When this happens, you are asked to choose the color scheme for Windows and to either log in to the computer with a Microsoft account or to create an account.

Best Practices for Installing Windows 10

Installing your copy of Windows on Drive 0 is important because in computers with more than one physical hard disk, you might find that your *second* hard disk, which contains your files, might read as Drive 0 in the drives list (because of the motherboard socket you plugged it in to), and your Windows drive might read as Drive 1.

■ **Tip** In a tower PC with more than one physical hard disk, unplugging all but the Windows disk drive before installing Windows 10 mitigates any problems associated with the Windows, and System Reserved, and UEFI System partitions ending up on different disks. It ensures that these critical start-up partitions are on the correct disk.

The problem arises when you come to create a system backup of your computer. With the System Reserved partition *always* residing as the first partition on Drive 0, if that hard disk already has files on it, Windows will insist that you back up the entire files disk as part of your Windows image backup.

The upshot is that your image backup file can be huge, and when you restore it, it is an older copy of your files, wiping out all of your new and updated files.

You should also make sure that you install your copy of Windows 10 onto Drive 0. With the System Reserved partition always on Drive 0, if your Windows installation is on another hard disk—let's say Drive 1—removal or failure of Drive 0 (where the boot menu resides) results in a Windows installation that won't start and that is very difficult to repair.

In the bottom half of the **Where do you want to install Windows?** page is **Drive options (advanced)**, which provides the basic partitioning and formatting tools that you need to create a clean installation of Windows 10 successfully (see Figure 16-17).

Using these tools, you can perform the following actions:

- **Delete** an existing partition on a hard disk

- **Format** a partition or disk

- Create a **New** partition on a physical hard disk

- Join partitions to create an **Extend**ed partition

Sometimes, however, your hard disks don't appear in the drives list in the Windows installer. This happens if your computer contains RAID (redundant array of independent disks) drives, but by clicking Load Driver, you can specifically load the driver required for the Windows 10 installer to work with those disks if they don't appear in the drives list. You need a copy of the driver on CD, DVD, or a USB flash drive.

My best recommendation is to *always* delete your existing Windows partition and create a new one where one already exists (i.e., if you used another version of Windows on the computer). You should do this because the boot and system partitions that Windows 10 creates are different if your computer contains UEFI firmware on the motherboard and you are installing from a USB flash drive created using the Windows 10 media creation tool, but you previously installed from a USB flash drive or DVD that didn't support UEFI start-up.

On some computers, the Windows 10 installer might create four of these partitions, and you need to make sure that there is space for them. The reason you want these partitions is because they contain all the tools that you need to troubleshoot and repair Windows 10 when it doesn't start. If you don't allow the installer to create them, the troubleshooting and repair tools might not work when you need them.

If you have enough hard disk space, I also recommend that you create two (preferably three) partitions so that you can keep your Windows installation and your files (and optionally a backup copy of Windows) separate. Moving your files away from Windows 10 in this way helps make sure that if something goes wrong with Windows 10 and you need to reinstall it, there is no question about the integrity of your files.

The size of your main Windows partition might vary, depending on how you use your PC. The following are some recommended Windows 10 partition sizes for different types of users:

- **General business user:** 50GB (enter **51200** in the partition size box)

- **General home user:** 50GB to 100GB (51200 to 102400)

- **Power user:** 100GB to 200GB (102400 to 204800)

- **Developer:** 100GB to 300GB (102400 to 307200)

- **Gamer:** 200GB to 400GB (204800 to 409600)

If you create a separate backup partition for a Windows image backup, it should be the same size as your Windows 10 partition, otherwise the backup won't start. You should also add any additional space you need for a backup copy of the hardware drivers and desktop app installers for your computer, perhaps an extra 5GB.

Finally, the files drive should occupy all the remaining space. Obviously, this setup is suitable only for computers with very large hard disks of at least 1TB, and preferably 1.5TB or more. You might be installing Windows 10 on a tablet or Ultrabook with precious little storage space, perhaps just a 64GB or 128GB solid-state drive (SSD). If this is the case, you can install Windows 10 into a 30GB partition and save the rest for files, or you can simply create one big partition that occupies the entire hard disk. If you do this, however, you should make sure that you keep regular up-to-date backups of all of your files and documents.

■ **Note**   Many enthusiasts and power users keep a copy of their hardware drivers handy on a hard disk, either internal or USB-attached. You can install all the hardware drivers in this folder at one time, as long as all the files are in the same folder and not located in subfolders, through a Command Prompt (Admin) control. Type **pnputil –a <DriversFolder>/*.inf** in the command window.

Summary

Migrating from an earlier version of Windows, even Windows 7, is simple and straightforward. Migrating your user account, user files, and documents is equally straightforward. If you are moving to another PC, however, or upgrading from XP or Vista, you need a third-party tool like WinWin, which I mentioned at the beginning of this chapter.

Microsoft worked hard to make the Windows 10 installation and upgrade experience as quick and easy as possible; it has succeeded in ways that make moving to this OS a joy.

Then there are the advanced administrator tools, such as Unattended Setup and SysPrep. These tools, especially when coupled with the Windows Assessment and Deployment Toolkit (ADK), can make the automated deployment of Windows 10 on PCs a simple procedure, though they can be complicated to set up.

As for this book, I have covered all that you need to really get to grips with the power that lies under the surface of Windows 10, from customizing the look and feel of the OS to knowing the hidden tools and utilities that can make you more productive.

I hope that you have found this book useful and informative. Should it all go horribly wrong, however, I've also written *Windows 10 Troubleshooting*, forthcoming from Apress, Amazon, and all good book stores.

—Mike Halsey

APPENDIX A

■ ■ ■

Windows 10 Touch and Trackpad Gestures

For many people, touch is new to their Windows experience. In many ways, such as with tapping and double-tapping, touch operates in the same way you expect a mouse click to work. Table A-1 contains a complete list of the touch gestures that you can use with Windows 10. Those people who have already used touch will be pleased to hear that the gestures haven't changed.

Table A-1. *Windows 10 Touch Gestures*

Touch Gesture	Command	Action
Tap	Click	Tap the screen with your finger.
Double tap	Double-click	Tap the screen twice in the same place with your finger.
Drag vertically	Scroll	Touch the screen and vertically drag your finger upward or downward.
Drag horizontally	Drag selection	Touch the screen and horizontally drag your finger left or right.
Press and hold	Right-click	Touch and hold the screen with one finger while tapping it briefly with another finger.
Zoom	Zoom	Move two fingers apart (zoom in) or toward each other (zoom out).
Rotate	Rotate	Move two fingers in a circular motion.
Two-finger tap	Programmable in some apps	Tap the screen with two fingers.
Flick	Pan up, down, back, forward	Flick your finger up, down, left, or right on the screen.
Swipe from left of screen	Open Task View	Swipe inward from the left side of your screen.
Swipe from right of screen	Open Action Center	Swipe inward from the right bezel of your screen.

Narrator Touch Gestures

The Accessibility features in Windows have long been a strength of the operating system, but with Windows 10, they have been extended to add support for touch gestures that work with the Narrator. In Table A-2, the touch gesture listed in the left column executes the corresponding command in the right column.

Table A-2. *Narrator Touch Gestures*

Touch Gesture	Command
Tap or drag	Read aloud the item under your finger.
Double tap **or** **Hold with one finger and tap with a second finger**	Activate an item (equivalent to a single mouse click).
Triple tap **or** **Hold with one finger and** **double-tap with a second finger**	Select an item.
Flick left or right	Move to the next or previous item.
Hold with one finger and **two-finger-tap with additional fingers**	Drag an item.
Two-finger tap	Stop the Narrator from speaking.
Two-finger swipe	Scroll.
Three-finger tap	Show or hide the Narrator settings window.
Three-finger swipe up	Read the current window.
Three-finger swipe down	Read from the current text location.
Three-finger swipe left or right	Tab forward and backward.
Four-finger tap	Show all commands for the current item.
Four-finger triple tap	Show the Narrator commands list.
Four-finger swipe up or down	Enable/disable semantic zoom (semantic zoom provides a view of large blocks of content; on a web site, for example).

Trackpad Gestures

Windows 10 includes gestures that can be used from the trackpad on a laptop or Ultrabook, as shown in Table A-3. These are performed by using multiple fingers simultaneously on the trackpad.

Table A-3. *Windows 10 Trackpad Gestures*

Touch Gesture	Command
Swipe downward with three fingers	Show desktop
Swipe upward with three fingers	Undo show desktop Open Task View
Swipe three fingers left or right	Switch between open apps

APPENDIX B

■ ■ ■

Windows 10 Shortcut Keys

Table B-1. *Keys with No Modifier*

Key	Function
Space	Select or clear the active check box.
Tab	Move forward through the options.
Esc	Cancel.
NumLock	Hold for 5 seconds to get ToggleKeys.
Del	Delete file (File Explorer).
Left arrow	Open the previous menu or close the submenu.
Right arrow	Open the next menu of the open submenu.
F1	Display help (if available).
F2	Rename item.
F3	Search for the next instance in a search.
F4	Display items in active list.
F5	Refresh.

Table B-2. *Windows Logo Key Combinations*

Windows Logo Key+	Function
No other key	Toggle the Start menu.
PrtScr	Capture a screenshot (saved in Pictures as `screenshot.png`, `screenshot(1).png`, `screenshot(2).png`, etc.).
A	Open the Action Center.
C	Open the Cortana Voice Input.
D	Show the desktop.
E	Open File Explorer.
H	Open the Share fly-out.
I	Open the Settings app.

(*continued*)

Table B-2. (*continued*)

Windows Logo Key+	Function
K	Open the Connect to devices flyout.
L	Switch users (lock computer if on a domain).
M	Minimize all windows (desktop).
O	Change lock-screen orientation.
P	Open the second screen and projection options.
Q	Open the Full Cortana dialog.
R	Open the Run dialog box.
T	Set focus on the taskbar and cycle through the running desktop programs.
U	Open the Ease of Access Center.
V	Cycle through notifications (+Shift to go backward).
X	Opens the Administration Commands menu.
1-9	Go to the app at the position on the taskbar.
+	Zoom in (Magnifier).
-	Zoom out (Magnifier).
, (comma)	Peek at the desktop.
Enter	Narrator (+Alt to open Windows Media Center, if installed).
Spacebar	Switch the input language and keyboard layout.
Tab	Open Task View
Esc	Exit the Magnifier.
Home	Minimize nonactive desktop windows.
Left arrow	Snap window to the left (+Shift to move to left monitor).
Left arrow, plus hold Win + Up Arrow	Snap window to the top-left corner of screen.
Left arrow, plus hold Win + Down Arrow	Snap window to the bottom-left corner of screen.
Right arrow	Snap windows to the right (+Shift to move to right monitor).
Right arrow, plus hold Win + Up arrow	Snap the window to top-right corner of screen.
Right arrow, plus hold Win + Down arrow	Snap the window to bottom-right corner of screen.
Shift + Left	Move an app to the monitor on the left.
Shift + Right	Move an app to the monitor on the right.
Ctrl + Left	Switch to the virtual desktop on the left.
Ctrl + Right	Switch to the virtual desktop on the right.

(*continued*)

Table B-2. (*continued*)

Windows Logo Key+	Function
Ctrl + F4	Close the current virtual desktop.
Up arrow	Maximize desktop window (+Shift to keep width).
Down arrow	Restore/Minimize desktop window (+Shift to keep width).
F1	Open Windows Help and Support in a browser.

Table B-3. *Ctrl Key Combinations*

Ctrl+	Function
Mouse wheel	Desktop: Change icon size. / Start screen: Zoom in/out
A	Select All
C	Copy
E	Select search box (Explorer)
N	New window (Explorer)
R	Refresh
V	Paste
W	Close current window (Explorer)
X	Cut
Y	Redo
Z	Undo
Esc	Start screen
NumLock	Copy
Left arrow	Previous word
Right arrow	Next word
Up arrow	Previous paragraph
Down arrow	Next paragraph
F4	Close the active document

Table B-4. *Alt Key Combinations*

Alt+	Function
D	Select the address bar (Explorer)
Enter	Open the Properties dialog box
Spacebar	Open the Shortcut menu
Tab	Switch between apps
Left arrow	Move to the previous folder (Explorer)
Up arrow	Go up one level (Explorer)
F4	Close the active item or app

Table B-5. *Shift Key Combinations*

Shift+	Function
No other key	Five times: Sticky keys
Tab	Move backward through options
Esc	Open the Task Manager
NumLock	Paste
Left arrow	Select a block of text
Right arrow	Select a block of text
Up arrow	Select a block of text
Down arrow	Select a block of text

Table B-6. *Ctrl + Alt Key Combinations*

Ctrl + Alt+	Function
D	Toggle Docked mode (Magnifier)
I	Invert colors (Magnifier)
L	Toggle Lens mode (Magnifier)
Tab	Switch between apps using arrow keys

Table B-7. *Alt + Shift Key Combinations*

Alt + Shift+	Function
PrtScr	Left Alt + Left Shift + PrtScr: High contrast
NumLock	Left Alt + Left Shift + NumLock: Mouse keys

APPENDIX C

■ ■ ■

Advanced Query Syntax for Search

In addition to the search methods that I discussed in Chapter 5, there is a large volume of Advanced Query Syntax options that you can use when searching (especially for files) in Windows 10. These options are available both at the Start screen and in File Explorer.

Data Store Location

Table C-1. *Data Store Location*

Restrict Search by Data Store	Use	Example
Desktop	desktop	Gilbert store:desktop
Files	files	Mike store:files
Outlook	outlook	Jed store:outlook
A specific folder	foldername or in	foldername:MyDocuments or in:MyVideos

Common File Kinds

Table C-2. *Common File Types*

Restrict Search by File Type	Use	Example
Calendar	calendar	kind:=calendar
Communication	communication	kind:=communication
Contact	contact	kind:=contact
Document	document	kind:=document
Email	Email	kind:=email
RSS feed	feed	kind:=feed
Folder	folder	kind:=folder

(continued)

Table C-2. (*continued*)

Restrict Search by File Type	Use	Example
Game	game	kind:=game
Instant Messenger conversations	instant message	kind:=instant message
Journal	journal	kind:=journal
Link	link	kind:=link
Movie	movie	kind:=movie
Music	music	kind:=music
Notes	note	kind:=note
Picture	picture	kind:=picture
Playlist	playlist	kind:=playlist
Program	program	kind:=program
Recorded TV	tv	kind:=tv
Saved search	saved search	kind:=saved search
Task	task	kind:=task
Video	video	kind:=video
Web history	web history	kind:=web history

Properties by File Type

Table C-3. *Properties by File Type*

Property	Use	Example
Title	title, subject or about	title:"Windows 10"
Status	status	status:pending
Date	date	date:last week
Date modified	datemodified or modified	modified:last week
Importance	importance or priority	importance:high
Deleted	deleted or isdeleted	isdeleted:yes (no)
Is attachment	isattachment	isattachment:yes (no)
To	to or toname	to:mike
Cc	cc or ccname	cc:chris
Company	company	company:Microsoft
Location	location	location:"office"

(*continued*)

Table C-3. (*continued*)

Property	Use	Example
Category	category	category:pilot
Keywords	keywords	keywords:"pending"
Album	album	album:"equinoxe"
File name	filename or file	filename:Report
Genre	genre	genre:metal
Author	author or by	author:"Mike Halsey"
People	people or with	with:(jed or gilbert)
Folder	folder, under or path	folder:downloads
File extension	ext or fileext	ext:.txt

Filter by Size

Table C-4. *Filter by Size (Note that the NOT and OR operators here must be in uppercase.)*

Size	Use	Example
0KB	empty	size:empty
0 > 10KB	tiny	size:tiny
10KB > 100KB	small	size:small
100KB > 1MB	medium	size:medium
1MB > 16MB	large	size:large
16MB > 128MB	huge	size:huge
> 128MB	gigantic	size:gigantic

Boolean Operators

Table C-5. *Boolean Operators (Note that the NOT and OR operators here must be in uppercase.)*

Keyword/Symbol	Use	Function
NOT	draft NOT edition	Finds items that contain *draft*, but not *edition*.
–	draft –edition	Finds items that contain *draft*, but not *edition*.
OR	draft OR edition	Finds items that contain *draft* or *edition*.
Quotation marks	"draft edition"	Finds items that contain the exact phrase *draft edition*.

(*continued*)

Table C-5. (*continued*)

Keyword/Symbol	Use	Function
Parentheses	(draft edition)	Finds items that contain *draft* and *edition* in any order.
>	date:>10/23/12	Finds items with a date after October 23, 2012.
	size:>500	Finds items with a size greater than 500 bytes.
<	date:<10/23/12	Finds items with a date before October 23, 2012.
	size:<500	Finds items with a size less than 500 bytes.
..	date:10/23/12..10/11/12	Finds items with a date beginning on 10/23/12 and ending on 10/11/12.

Boolean Properties

Table C-6. *Boolean Properties*

Property	Use	Function
is:attachment	draft is:attachment	Finds items that have attachments that contain *draft*. Same as isattachment:no (yes).
isonline:	draft isonline:yes (no)	Finds items that are online and that contain *draft*.
isrecurring:	draft isrecurring:yes (no)	Finds items that are recurring and that contain *draft*.
isflagged:	draft isflagged:yes (no)	Finds items that are flagged (Review or Follow up, for example) and that contain *draft*.
isdeleted:	draft isdeleted:yes (no)	Finds items that are flagged as deleted (Recycle Bin or Deleted Items, for example) and that contain *draft*.
iscompleted:	draft iscompleted:yes (no)	Finds items that are not flagged as complete and that contain *draft*.
hasattachment:	draft hasattachment:yes (no)	Finds items containing *draft* and having attachments.
hasflag:	draft hasflag:yes (no)	Finds items containing *draft* and having flags.

Dates

Table C-7. *Dates*

Relative to	Use	Function
Day	date:today	Finds items with today's date.
	date:tomorrow	Finds items with tomorrow's date.
	date:yesterday	Finds items with yesterday's date.
Week/Month/Year	date:this week	Finds items with a date falling within the current week.
	date:last week	Finds items with a date falling within the previous week.
	date:next month	Finds items with a date falling within the upcoming week.
	date:last month	Finds items with a date falling within the previous month.
	date:this year	Finds items with a date falling within the current year.
	date:last year	Finds items with a date falling within the next year.

Attachments

Table C-8. *Attachments*

Property	Use	Example
People	people	people:gilbert

Contacts

Table C-9. *Contacts*

Property	Use	Example
Job title	jobtitle	jobtitle:author
Instant messaging address	imaddress	imaddress:mike@MVPs.org
Assistant's phone	assistantsphone	assistantsphone:555-1234
Assistant's name	assistantname	assistantname:Darren
Profession	profession	profession:designer
Nickname	nickname	nickname:Gilby
Spouse	spouse	spouse:Victoria
Business city	businesscity	businesscity:Seattle
Business postal code	businesspostalcode	businesspostalcode:96487
Business home page	businesshomepage	businesshomepage: www.thelongclimb.com

(continued)

Table C-9. (*continued*)

Property	Use	Example
Callback phone number	callbackphonenumber	callbackphonenumber:555-555-2345
Mobile phone	mobilephone	mobilephone:555-555-2345
Children	children	children:Gilbert
First name	firstname	firstname:Jed
Last name	lastname	lastname:Halsey
Home fax	homefax	homefax:555-555-1234
Manager's name	managersname	managersname:Tom
Business phone	businessphone	businessphone:555-555-1234
Home phone	homephone	homephone:555-555-1234
Mobile phone	mobilephone	mobilephone:555-555-1234
Office	office	office:sample
Anniversary	anniversary	anniversary:1/8/94
Birthday	birthday	birthday:1/8/81
Web page	webpage	webpage: `www.thelongclimb.com`

Communications

Table C-10. *Communications*

Property	Use	Example
From	from or organizer	from:Jed
Received	received or sent	sent:yesterday
Subject	subject or title	subject:"Editing Report"
Has attachment	hasattachments, hasattachment	hasattachment:true
Attachments	attachments or attachment	attachment:presentation.ppt
Bcc	bcc, bccname or bccaddress	bcc:Gilbert
Cc address	ccaddress or cc	ccaddress:mike@MVPs.org
Follow-up flag	followupflag	followupflag:2
Due date	duedate or due	due:last week
Read	read or isread	is:read
Is completed	iscompleted	is:completed
Incomplete	incomplete or isincomplete	is:incomplete
Has flag	hasflag or isflagged	has:flag
Duration	duration	duration:> 50

Calendar

Table C-11. *Calendar*

Property	Use	Example
Recurring	recurring	recurring:yes (no)
Organizer	organizer, by or from	organizer:Rory

wDocuments

Table C-12. *Documents*

Property	Use	Example
Comments	comments	comments:"needs final review"
Last saved by	lastsavedby	lastsavedby:mike
Document manager	documentmanager	documentmanager:mike
Revision number	revisionnumber	revisionnumber:1.0.3
Document format	documentformat	documentformat:MIMETYPE
Date last printed	datelastprinted	datelastprinted:last week

Presentations

Table C-13. *Presentations*

Property	Use	Example
Slide count	slidecount	slidecount:>20

Music

Table C-14. *Music*

Property	Use	Example
Bit rate	bitrate, rate	bitrate:192
Artist	artist, by or from	artist:Lacuna Coil
Duration	duration	duration:3
Album	album	album:"shallow life"
Genre	genre	genre:metal
Track	track	track:12
Year	year	year:> 2006 < 2016

Pictures

Table C-15. *Pictures*

Property	Use	Example
Camera make	cameramake	cameramake:sample
Camera model	cameramodel	cameramodel:sample
Dimensions	dimensions	dimensions:8×10
Orientation	orientation	orientation:landscape
Date taken	datetaken	datetaken:yesterday
Width	width	width:1600
Height	height	height:1200

Video

Table C-16. *Video*

Property	Use	Example
Name	name, subject	name:"Family holiday in Germany"
Ext	ext, fileext	ext:.avi

APPENDIX D

■ ■ ■

Windows 10 Features by Edition

Windows 10 includes many new features, as well as those carried forward from Windows 7 and Windows 8.1. Not every feature is available in every edition of Windows, however, so I have listed each feature in Table D-1. I have excluded some editions, such as the IoT (Internet of Things) edition and the Xbox One edition, from this table because they contain only a subset of the full feature list. Also, please note that the Education edition contains the same feature set as Enterprise.

Table D-1. *Windows 10 Features by Edition*

Feature	Home	Pro	Mobile	Enterprise	Notes
Action Center	X	X	X	X	
Administration Menu	X	X		X	On Win+X
Administrative Tools	X	X	X	X	
AppLocker				X	
Assigned Access		X		X	
Autoplay	X	X		X	
Azure Active Directory	X	X	X	X	
Battery Saver	X	X	X	X	
BitLocker Encryption		X		X	Requires TPM
BranchCache				X	
Business App Store		X	X	X	
Character Map	X	X		X	
Command Prompt	X	X		X	
Compressed Installation	X	X		X	On low-storage devices
Connected Standby	X	X	X	X	
Continuum	X	X	X	X	Operates differently on Mobile
Control Panel	X	X	X	X	
Cortana	X	X	X	X	
Credential Guard				X	

(continued)

Table D-1. (*continued*)

Feature	Home	Pro	Mobile	Enterprise	Notes
Credential Manager	X	X		X	
Default Apps Choice	X	X	X	X	
Defer Windows Updates		X		X	Defer for 10 years with Enterprise LTS
Defragmenter and Disk Cleanup	X	X		X	
Developer Mode	X	X	X	X	
Device Encryption	X	X	X	X	
Device Guard				X	
DirectAccess				X	
DirectX 12	X	X	X	X	
Domain Join		X	X	X	
Ease of Access	X	X	X	X	
Edge Browser	X	X	X	X	Not in Enterprise LTS edition
Encrypting File System		X		X	
Enterprise Data Protection		X		X	
Event Viewer	X	X		X	
Family Safety	X	X		X	
File Explorer	X	X		X	
File History	X	X		X	
Flight Mode	X	X	X	X	Not on desktops
Game DVR	X	X		X	Not in Enterprise LTS edition
Group Policy		X		X	
HomeGroup	X	X		X	
Hyper-V		X		X	Requires Processor Support
Internet Explorer		X		X	
Local Security Policy		X		X	
Math Input Panel	X	X		X	
Microsoft Office Mobile Apps	X		X		Not on 10-inch or larger screens
Microsoft Passport	X	X	X	X	
Miracast	X	X	X	X	
Mobile Tethering	X	X	X	X	
Mobility Center	X	X		X	
Multiple Monitor Support	X	X	X	X	Requires Continuum hardware in Mobile

(*continued*)

Table D-1. (*continued*)

Feature	Home	Pro	Mobile	Enterprise	Notes
NFC Printing	X	X		X	
Notepad	X	X		X	
OneDrive Sync/Backup	X	X		X	
Paint	X	X		X	
Performance Monitor	X	X		X	
Phone Companion	X	X		X	
Powershell	X	X		X	
Print to PDF	X	X		X	
Privacy Controls	X	X	X	X	
Problem Steps Recorder	X	X		X	
Recovery Media Creator	X	X		X	
Remote Desktop	X	X		X	Home can't be a host but can connect to other RD machines
Reset	X	X	X	X	
Resource Monitor	X	X		X	
Secure Boot	X	X	X	X	Requires UEFI firmware
Services Panel	X	X		X	
Settings App	X	X	X	X	
Settings Sync	X	X	X	X	
Snap	X	X		X	Limited to two apps on screens smaller than 8 inches
Snap Assist	X	X		X	
Snipping Tool	X	X		X	
Start Menu	X	X	X	X	
Sticky Notes	X	X		X	
Storage Sense	X	X	X	X	
Storage Spaces	X	X	X	X	
Stream from Xbox	X	X		X	
Tablet Mode	X	X		X	
Task Manager	X	X		X	
Task Scheduler	X	X		X	
Task View	X	X	X	X	
Touch Support	X	X	X	X	
Virtual Desktops	X	X		X	Not on 8-inch or smaller screens

(*continued*)

Table D-1. (*continued*)

Feature	Home	Pro	Mobile	Enterprise	Notes
VPN Connect	X	X	X	X	
Wi-Fi Direct Printing	X	X		X	
Wi-Fi Sense	X	X	X	X	
Windows Advanced Firewall	X	X		X	
Windows Defender	X	X	X	X	No interface in Mobile
Windows Fax and Scan	X	X		X	
Windows Firewall	X	X	X	X	No interface in Mobile
Windows Hello	X	X	X	X	Requires compatible hardware
Windows Journal	X	X		X	
Windows Media Player	X	X		X	Not in N and KN editions
Windows Memory Diagnostic	X	X		X	
Windows Store	X	X	X	X	Not in Enterprise LTS edition
Windows To Go				X	
WordPad	X	X		X	
Work Access		X	X	X	
Work Folders		X	X	X	
XPS Viewer	X	X		X	

Features Removed from Windows 10

Windows 10 brings many new features to PCs and smartphones, but some features that were present in Windows 7 or Windows 8.1 are not included in the new operating system (as listed in Table D-2).

Table D-2. *Features Removed from Windows 10*

Feature	Notes
Desktop Gadgets	Not available in Windows 8.1
DVD Playback	Now available via Store app
Solitaire, Minesweeper, Hearts	Now available via Store apps
Start Screen and Charms	Not available in Windows 7
Windows Media Center	
XP Mode	Not available in Windows 8.1

APPENDIX E

■ ■ ■

Upgrading Your Computer

A PC isn't just for Christmas, it's for life. You'll want to make sure that your computer lasts for as long as possible because, let's be honest, these things are expensive and you can't afford to buy a new one before the current machine is out of its warranty period.

In this appendix, I'll talk you through not only the options for upgrading your copy of Windows 10 and its features, but also the options for upgrading your entire PC—and even buying a new one. Most likely you'll get Windows 10 with a new computer because it is the cheapest way to buy a copy of the operating system.

Choosing a New Windows 10 Computer

I went through the specific hardware requirements for Windows 10 in Chapter 15, but most computers you buy today can run Windows 10 with no problems whatsoever. This makes it more important to know what you need to buy, so that you don't get ripped off by unscrupulous salespeople when choosing and paying for a new computer.

I've split this section into three categories: desktop PCs (including all-in-ones), laptops, and Ultrabooks and tablets.

Do You Need a New Computer?

So do you really need a new computer? Well, if you are using a computer that's running a copy of Windows Vista or Windows 7, then you probably do not need a new one because the hardware requirements for Windows 10 are the same and it'll run fine.

The only considerations you need to think about here are these:

- Do you want to take advantage of the new multitouch technology in Windows 10?

- Is your current computer more than four years old?

If the answer to either one of these is yes, then it could be the right time to buy a new computer. Any computer more than four years old is more prone to failure than you might like, and the new touch technology in Windows 10 enhances usability considerably. Also, if you have a laptop more than three years old, I recommend replacing it.

Remember that if you buy a new PC, your copy of Windows 10 is effectively free. That $500 budget computer the salesman tried to steer you away from will probably be perfectly good for years to come.

Choosing the Right Desktop PC

When it comes to buying either a desktop PC, by which I mean a separate tower and monitor, purchasers have traditionally had the hardest time avoiding over-zealous salespeople. "You want to edit photographs? Then you'll benefit from having the fastest processor. . ." commonly goes the line.

The first decision is whether you want a desktop PC or an all-in-one. Both have their advantages and disadvantages.

Desktop PC pros

- More easily upgradable by the user

- If one part fails, the entire PC doesn't need to be repaired

- As you upgrade the PC, old parts can be sold secondhand

- More powerful than all-in-ones, making them more suitable for some tasks

Desktop PC cons

- Can look big and unsightly in the home

- Can be noisy

All-in-One pros

- Stylish and won't look unsightly in the home

- Commonly very quiet computers

- Only one power lead is required, reducing overall power consumption

All-in-One cons

- If one part fails, the entire PC needs to be repaired

With computer parts changing so rapidly these days, you'll commonly find that all you can ever do with a tower is add more memory, add a second hard disk, and change the graphics card. You might be surprised how big a difference these changes can make, so if you want a tower case, even a small one, ask to see how easy it is to work with the components inside.

Does it have any spare memory sockets? Does it have a spare hard disk bay? If/when the internal power supply fails, how easy is it to replace? Is it a custom-made unit (common in small towers) or a standard, big-box PC PSU (power supply unit)? Does the PC have any expansion ports, and can these take a graphics card?

Never let the salesperson dictate to you what type of processor you *must* have to get the maximum benefit. These things change often, but Intel's Core series (which should be around for a few years yet) provide a good guide.

If you only want a PC for light email, web browsing, and basic photo editing, then an inexpensive Core i3 is a great option. If you want to watch HD video but don't need a separate graphics card, you'll want a Core i5 with integrated graphics. That leaves the faster Core i7 processors for enthusiasts and those doing design, animation, HD video editing, and gaming.

You'd be hard-pressed to find a modern PC with less than 4GB of RAM, but do you need any more than this? For very light duties, such as email and Internet browsing, this amount of memory is fine. Hard-core gamers and people using their computers for the other intensive tasks I mentioned need more RAM. You might need more if you want to edit your digital photos and videos. Go for the fastest speed memory you can get, such as 2 GHz instead of 1,333 MHz, because this is where the benefits are.

Next, do you need a solid-state (SSD) hard disk? These are expensive and do not yet come in big capacities at an affordable price. If you are a gamer, then you'll certainly benefit from the extra speed; but with modern games occupying 24GB or more or space, and Windows itself requiring up to 40GB with software and temporary files taking up room, you won't get more than two games on an average SSD before filling it up. This doesn't give you space for any of your files and documents.

If you use a mechanical hard disk, try to get a 7,200 rpm (revolutions per minute) drive, which operates faster than the 5,400 rpm hard disks.

You should only buy a dedicated graphics card if you have to do thoroughly intensive work such as HD video editing, gaming, or graphic design. For general use, including watching Blu-ray discs, the onboard graphics of a modern PC are perfectly adequate.

When it comes to choosing between a tower and an all-in-one, it's worth considering where the computer will live. If it's in a home office or a work office, then a tower is fine; but in your living room, you may want something less intrusive and with a smaller overall profile.

Finally, does the monitor have a touchscreen or a built-in Kinect sensor? With Windows 10, these are two options well worth having.

Choosing the Right Laptop or Ultrabook

Many of the considerations for choosing a desktop or an all-in-one PC are the same for laptops and Ultrabooks. One of the main differences is that whereas you can upgrade the memory and the hard disk in a laptop, you can never upgrade an Ultrabook. What you get is what you're stuck with!

There is the consideration of how you will use a mobile computer. If you want to do serious work, storage is probably important and thus you should choose a laptop. Ultrabooks are perfect for light use if you enjoy working at the local coffee shop or if you want something that you can put in a bag and easily carry.

Get a touchscreen if you can, although it can make some smaller and lighter laptops topple over backward. A big factor is in the build quality. Poke the back of the screen to see if you can distort the picture).

Test the keyboard too. Is it genuinely comfortable to type on? Are all the keys a sensible size and in a sensible place? Is the touchpad usable? Does the touchpad have additional functions, such as multitouch? A keyboard with a backlight is a welcome addition.

More important with laptops and Ultrabooks is the length of the battery life, and whether the battery can be changed by the user.

Choosing the Right Tablet

With Windows 10 tablets, there is a fairly straightforward choice: budget or expensive. Pro Windows tablets can be very expensive, but with a Bluetooth keyboard (those like the Microsoft Surface come with a detachable keyboard) can serve as a credible laptop replacement. They also come with good amounts of internal storage for your files, music, and videos. Cheaper tablets need to be tested before you purchase them, because some come with very poor-quality screens. That's not to say you can't get a great, budget tablet. Although these devices come with limited storage and processing power, they are extremely affordable and useful for lounging in front of the TV to do some light browsing.

There's also an argument on what size screen to get with a tablet. With a professional-grade tablet, a screen around 12 inches should be the maximum, otherwise it's far too big to hold and your arm will tire quickly. With a tablet, I personally find 10-inch tablets (original iPad size) to be too bulky to carry around and even use casually on the sofa. Personally, I prefer smaller 7-inch screens.

Microsoft's Surface tablets provide a great deal of flexibility. They come with lower-power processors that offer long battery life and provide the full Windows 10 desktop experience. The integration of a keyboard in the cover is a bonus that may make a Surface tablet a suitable alternative to an Ultrabook.

Windows 10 and OEM Installation Discs

I want to tackle one of the biggest problems facing people buying new computers. This is the omission of a Windows 10 installation DVD.

Original equipment manufacturers (OEMs) have worked with Microsoft for years now to reduce the number of pirated copies of Windows. Most OEMs no longer ship new computers with a copy of the Windows installation DVD; instead, they provide recovery partitions with a copy of the installed factory image that can be restored if need be.

The downside is that if you need to restore the operating system and you haven't backed up your files and documents (which you have, right!?), then you will almost certainly lose them all because restoring the rescue image that came with your computer always destroys any files you have stored on the same partition as your Windows 10 installation. You will also take the machine back to its default state, reinstall all your software, and reconfigure the computer from scratch.

Sure, you can create your own custom disc image, even wiping out the factory one to save disc space, but haven't you paid for a copy of Windows, which includes the installation disc?

My best advice here is to always check the manufacturer's policy regarding installation discs before you buy. High-end and business computers commonly come with an option to get the disc, or they provide it automatically, but budget computers don't.

Many OEMs allow you to get a copy of the disc separately for a small shipping fee (usually $10), which many people think is reasonable. If an OEM flatly refuses to provide a disc under any circumstances, however, I recommend that you spend your money elsewhere.

It is important to note that OEM discs are commonly tied to the computer's BIOS or UEFI firmware purchased with a new PC. This means that if you try to install them on another computer, they will not work.

It's not all bad news, though, because you can create backup media and also a fresh installation USB flash drive. When you create a Recovery Drive for your PC (see Chapter 12 for details of how to do this), you can include a copy of your Windows 10 Reset image, so you can restore even if the PC fails to start. Also, you can create a USB flash drive installer for Windows 10 with Microsoft's Media Recovery Tool (`www.microsoft.com/software-download/windows10`). Both of these methods require a blank USB flash drive with at least 8GB storage.

SHOULD YOU BUY EXTRA SOFTWARE?

The subject of discs brings me to the age-old question of should you buy all the extra software that salespeople want you to buy because they make more money on that than on the PC itself. Most often, they try to sell you an antivirus suite and a full copy of Microsoft Office, saying you need both because what comes with Windows 10 is just not good enough.

What comes with Windows 10, both in terms of anti-malware tools and the availability of the Office Mobile apps in the Store, is good enough for most people. The advice I've included throughout this book helps you get the most out of them. Perhaps you'd find a copy of Adobe Photoshop Elements very useful. Windows 10 doesn't come with DVD or Blu-ray players, so you might like one of these. But anti-malware tools and general Office apps—forget buying anything extra!

Adding More Memory to a PC or Laptop

It is widely known and accepted that the quickest, cheapest, and fastest way to get a performance increase out of an older computer is to add more memory to it. You always need to make sure that you add the correct type of memory, however.

When you open the computer's case or the panel where the memory is located (see Figures E-1 and E-2), you see that the memory sticks have labels on them. The information you need from the labels are memory type (DDR, DDR2, DDR3, etc.) and speed in MHz.

Figure E-1. *Adding memory to a desktop PC*

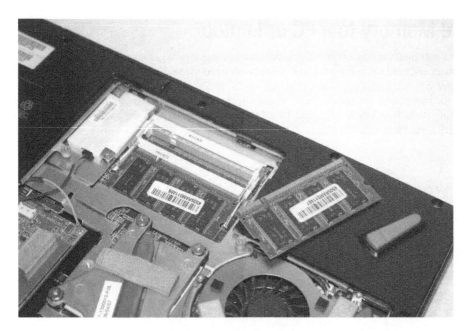

Figure E-2. *Adding memory to a laptop or all-in-one PC*

These are the two things you need to match when buying additional memory. You also need to check if there are any free memory slots. The documentation that came with your motherboard can tell you what types of memory are compatible.

There is a clip at each end of the memory slots on a desktop PC. When you insert the memory, you need to make certain that these are clipped into place firmly.

When adding memory to a laptop, you also find small clips that need to be firmly fixed in place on either side.

■ **Note**   If you are using the 32-bit (x86) version of Windows, adding more than 3GB of memory won't result in greater speed because Windows won't see it. A 32-bit operating system can only see a maximum of 4GB of memory, including what's on the graphics card. You can determine which version of Windows you are using in the System section of the Control Panel.

Changing or Adding a Hard Disk

In Figure E-3, you see two SATA hard disks and an SSD. The power and data plugs that attach to the back of these drives only go in one way. You shouldn't force them because the plastic on the connectors could snap.

Figure E-3. *Adding hard drives to a desktop PC. The drive on the far left is the SSD*

You should always make sure that hard disks are properly screwed into the computer's case.

When it comes to laptops and all-in-one PCs, hard disks commonly come in a slide-out caddy (see Figure E-4). They are less accessible than the memory in some laptops. You should check your computer's manual to determine whether the hard disk is a user-serviceable component.

Figure E-4. *Changing the hard disk in a laptop or all-in-one*

Changing or Adding a Graphics Card

At times, people want to change the graphics card on their computers. Doing it is usually a simple matter of pulling out the old card and slotting in the new one. Each type of card only fits in the correct slot (see Figure E-5). You should check the documentation that came with your motherboard to determine the type of slot it has before buying a graphics card.

Figure E-5. *Changing the graphics card in a PC*

You should always check if your graphics card requires additional power, usually provided by a six- or eight-pin plug, because not all power supplies come equipped with these.

If your power supply does not have the relevant plugs (apart from the question of whether you need a new power supply to supply the additional current the graphics card requires), you can buy a power lead adapter cable to give you the plug that you need.

Changing the Power Supply in Your PC

The power supply is commonly the first thing in a PC to fail. The power supply is the big box in the back of the computer into which you connect the mains electricity cable. In the desktop PC, a power supply is simple to change. The leads coming from it need to be unplugged (make a note of what it's plugged into so that you can easily reconnect everything again). There is a power lead for each drive, perhaps one for the graphics card and two for the motherboard.

There are four screws on the back of the case, at the top and bottom corners of the power supply (not the ones on the fan) that, when undone, allow the old power supply to pop out (see Figure E-6). Screw the new one in place and reconnect the wires, and all is done.

Figure E-6. *A power supply*

If you have an all-in-one or a small form-factor PC with an internal power supply, you probably need to take the computer to an authorized service center to have it replaced.

Safely Working with Your PC, Laptop, or Tablet

To work safely with your computer when you are adding or changing hardware, you should always follow these instructions:

- Place the computer on a firm, flat surface.

- Make sure that the computer is switched off and unplugged from the main electricity.

- Touch unpainted metal inside the computer's case to ground yourself and release any static electricity discharge from your body.

- Avoid working on nylon carpet or other locations where static electricity build-up is common.

Upgrading Windows 10

Throughout this book, I have made reference to features that are only available in the Pro edition of the operating system, such as Group Policy, or that need to be bought separately.

You can add these features to Windows 10 by upgrading it. In the Settings app, click **Update & Security** and then **Activation**. You see buttons to **Change [your] product key** if you already have a key for a different edition of Windows 10, or **Go to Store** if you need to purchase one (see Figure E-7).

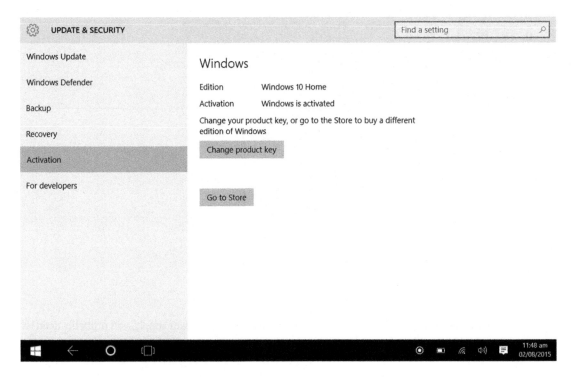

Figure E-7. *Upgrading Windows 10 from the Control Panel*

Summary

The instructions on how to upgrade and change the parts inside your computer are fairly short. This is because it is actually much simpler and easier to perform these actions than you might think.

On a computer, every cable only plugs into the right thing, so you never need to worry about incorrectly plugging in something somewhere it will cause harm or damage. Laptop and all-in-one PC sockets and plugs are all hard-wired and fixed in place, so you can only slot in components.

The short instructions prove just how easy it is to upgrade a PC and breathe new life into it.

Index

■ X, Y

■ Z

Get the eBook for only $5!

Why limit yourself?

Now you can take the weightless companion with you wherever you go and access your content on your PC, phone, tablet, or reader.

Since you've purchased this print book, we're happy to offer you the eBook in all 3 formats for just $5.

Convenient and fully searchable, the PDF version enables you to easily find and copy code—or perform examples by quickly toggling between instructions and applications. The MOBI format is ideal for your Kindle, while the ePUB can be utilized on a variety of mobile devices.

To learn more, go to www.apress.com/companion or contact support@apress.com.

Printed by Printforce, the Netherlands